The Deliberations
of the Council of Four
(March 24–June 28, 1919)

VOLUME I

The Council of Four in their usual meeting place, the library in Wilson's house at 11 Place des États-Unis. (Princeton University Library)
From left to right: Orlando, Lloyd George, Clemenceau, Wilson.

The Deliberations of the Council of Four (March 24–June 28, 1919)

NOTES OF THE OFFICIAL INTERPRETER

PAUL MANTOUX

I

To the Delivery to the German Delegation of the Preliminaries of Peace

SUPPLEMENTARY VOLUME TO THE PAPERS OF WOODROW WILSON

Translated and Edited by

ARTHUR S. LINK

With the Assistance of MANFRED F. BOEMEKE

PRINCETON UNIVERSITY PRESS
PRINCETON, NEW JERSEY

Barnard
D
642
.P3
1920
v.1

This is Volume I of two volumes

Copyright © 1992 by Princeton University Press
Published by Princeton University Press, 41 William Street,
Princeton, New Jersey 08540
In the United Kingdom: Princeton University Press, Oxford

All Rights Reserved

Library of Congress Cataloging-in-Publication Data

Paris Peace Conference (1919–1920)
   [Délibérations du Conseil des Quatre, 24 mars–28 juin 1919. English]
   The deliberations of the Council of Four (March 24–June 28, 1919) / notes of the official interpreter, Paul Mantoux; translated and edited by Arthur S. Link with the assistance of Manfred F. Boemeke.
   p.   cm.
   Translation of: Les délibérations du Conseil des Quatre, 24 mars–28 juin 1919.
   Includes bibliographical references and index.
   Contents: v. 1. To the delivery to the German Delegation of the preliminaries of peace — v. 2. From the delivery of the peace terms to the German Delegation to the signing of the Treaty of Versailles.
   ISBN 0-691-04793-6 (set : alk. paper)
   1. World War, 1914–1918—Peace—Sources. 2. World War, 1914–1918—Diplomatic history—Sources. I. Mantoux, Paul, 1877–1956.
II. Link, Arthur Stanley. III. Boemeke, Manfred F. (Manfred Franz) IV. Title.
D642.P3 1920
940.3'141—dc20   90-28089 CIP

Publication of this book has been aided by a grant from the Woodrow Wilson Foundation

This book has been composed in Melior Typefaces

Princeton University Press books are printed on acid-free paper, and meet the guidelines for permanence and durability of the Committee on Production Guidelines for Book Longevity of the Council on Library Resources

Printed in the United States of America by Princeton University Press, Princeton, New Jersey

10 9 8 7 6 5 4 3 2 1

Contents

VOLUME I

Paul-Joseph Mantoux (1877–1956)	vii
Mantoux and His Notes	xiii
Editor's Introduction	xix
Acknowledgments	xxxi
Author's Preface	xxxiii
Abbreviations	xli
Maps	xliii

THE MEETINGS OF THE COUNCIL OF FOUR

I. March 24, 1919, 3 P.M.	3
II. March 25, 1919, 11 A.M.	4
III. March 25, 1919, 3:30 P.M.	9
IV. March 26, 1919, 11 A.M.	16
V. March 26, 1919, 3:30 P.M.	23
VI. March 27, 1919, 11 A.M.	31
VII. March 27, 1919, 3:30 P.M.	39
VIII. March 28, 1919, 11 A.M.	49
IX. March 28, 1919, 4 P.M.	55
X. March 29, 1919, 4 P.M.	68
XI. March 31, 1919, 11 A.M.	80
XII. March 31, 1919, 3 P.M.	86
XIII. April 1, 1919, 11 A.M.	100
XIV. April 1, 1919, 4 P.M.	105
XV. April 2, 1919, 11 A.M.	113
XVI. April 2, 1919, 4 P.M.	118
XVII. April 3, 1919, 11 A.M.	123
XVIII. April 3, 1919, 4 P.M.	129
XIX. April 4, 1919, 11 A.M.	135
XX. April 4, 1919, 4 P.M.	144
XXI. April 5, 1919, 11 A.M.	146
XXII. April 5, 1919, 4 P.M.	154
XXIII. April 7, 1919, 3:30 P.M.	165
XXIV. April 8, 1919, 11 A.M.	181
XXV. April 8, 1919, 3 P.M.	187
XXVI. April 9, 1919, 11 A.M.	197

XXVII. April 9, 1919, 3:30 P.M.	204
XXVIII. April 10, 1919, 11 A.M.	210
XXIX. April 10, 1919, 4 P.M.	218
XXX. April 11, 1919, 11 A.M.	226
XXXI. April 12, 1919, 11 A.M.	232
XXXII. April 12, 1919, 5 P.M.	236
XXXIII. April 13, 1919, 6 P.M.	238
XXXIV. April 15, 1919, 11 A.M.	247
XXXV. April 15, 1919, 4 P.M.	252
XXXVI. April 16, 1919, 11 A.M.	257
XXXVII. April 16, 1919, 4 P.M.	265
XXXVIII. April 18, 1919, 11 A.M.	269
XXXIX. April 19, 1919, 11 A.M.	276
XL. April 20, 1919, 10 A.M.	290
XLI. April 21, 1919, 10 A.M.	297
XLII. April 21, 1919, 4 P.M.	304
XLIII. April 22, 1919, 11 A.M.	317
XLIV. April 22, 1919, 4 P.M.	328
XLV. April 23, 1919, 11 A.M.	339
XLVI. April 24, 1919, 11 A.M.	350
XLVII. April 24, 1919, 4 P.M.	358
XLVIII. April 25, 1919, 4 P.M.	370
XLIX. April 26, 1919, 11 A.M.	381
L. April 26, 1919, 3 P.M.	388
LI. April 28, 1919, 11 A.M.	392
LII. April 29, 1919, 11 A.M.	401
LIII. April 29, 1919, 4 P.M.	408
LIV. April 30, 1919, 10:30 A.M.	419
LV. April 30, 1919, 4 P.M.	427
LVI. May 1, 1919, 11 A.M.	435
LVII. May 1, 1919, 5:45 P.M.	443
LVIII. May 2, 1919, 11 A.M.	448
LIX. May 2, 1919, 4 P.M.	456
LX. May 3, 1919, 10 A.M.	465
LXI. May 3, 1919, 4 P.M.	473
LXII. May 5, 1919, 11 A.M.	481
LXIII. May 6, 1919, 11 A.M.	488
LXIV. May 6, 1919, 5 P.M.	496
LXV. May 7, 1919, 11 A.M.	500
LXVI. May 7, 1919, NOON	505
LXVII. May 7, 1919, 4:20 P.M.	507

Paul-Joseph Mantoux (1877–1956)

Paul-Joseph Mantoux was born in Paris on April 14, 1877, the son of Adrien Mantoux (1839-1921) and Esther Berthe Mantoux (1847-1937). Adrien Mantoux spent his childhood in Nancy, in Lorraine, and moved at the age of fourteen to Paris to work in the cotton-goods wholesale firm of his two older brothers; he later became a partner in a firm of goldsmiths in Paris. Largely self-educated, Adrien Mantoux at an early age developed a passion for English literary classics. From his father, Paul Mantoux imbibed a love of English literature, along with a devotion to republicanism and the ideals of the French Revolution.

Paul Mantoux's academic career gave early evidence of intellectual genius. He won the baccalaureate from the Lycée Condorcet at the age of sixteen and, after only a year of preparation, admission to the École Normale Supérieure, from which he was graduated in 1897 as *agrégé* in history. He was graduated the same year from the Sorbonne as *Agrégé de l'Université de Paris* in history and geography. Like so many young French intellectuals and liberals of the time, he was an ardent Dreyfusard and a follower of Jean Jaurès, father of liberal French Socialism.

Mantoux was also a disciple of Auguste Comte and shared his belief that objective scientific knowledge provided the key to the solution of contemporary problems and the means to the progressive betterment of humanity. A year's residence at the Passmore Edwards Settlement in London in 1899 brought him into contact with leading English Fabians and fostered an intense interest in English working-class history and the English labor movement. The stay at this settlement house was also the impetus for his first book (edited with Maurice Alfassa), *La Crise du Trade-Unionisme* (Paris: A. Rousseau, 1903).[1]

Looking toward an academic career, Mantoux conceived the idea of a *thèse d'État* on the origins of the industrial revolution in England and its impact on the social fabric of that country. He began extensive research on the subject while in London in 1899. He continued his work while secretary of the École des Hautes

---

[1] Reprinted by B. Franklin of New York in 1971.

Études Sociales in Paris from 1900 to 1902 and while he taught history and geography at the Collège Chaptal, beginning in 1903.

Mantoux's dissertation, for which he was awarded the degree of Docteur ès Lettres by the Sorbonne, was published in 1905 as *La Révolution Industrielle au Siècle XVIIIe: Essai sur les Commencements de la Grande Industrie Moderne en Angleterre* (Paris: Cornély and Co., Volume IX of the Library of the Thiers Foundation). It was reprinted in a regular library edition in 1906 by G. Bellais of Paris.

La Révolution Industrielle was warmly commended by scholarly reviewers for its depth of research, lucidity, and above all its comingling of economic and social history.[2] Henri Hauser's review in *Revue Historique* was full of praise and also prophetic. "We do not hesitate to say again," he wrote in conclusion, "that, at a time when good works of economic history are still so rare, this one must be placed in the rank of the best."[3] It was not long before scholars and publicists recognized that, in T. S. Ashton's words, Mantoux was "one of a long line of French men of letters—the names of Voltaire, Taine and Halévy spring to one's mind—who, in interpreting England to their own countrymen, have also made her more understandable to Englishmen." To quote Ashton again, Mantoux's "book is one of a few works in economic history that can justly be spoken of as classics."[4]

Mantoux continued to teach at the Collège Chaptal until 1910, when he joined the faculty of the École des Hautes Études Commerciales. He published an article on Socialism in a book edited by Georges François Bernard in 1907[5] and *À Travers l'Angleterre*

---

[2] E.g., *The American Historical Review*, XII (July 1907), 884-86; *The English Historical Review*, XXI (July 1906), 594-96; and *Political Science Quarterly*, XXIII (March 1908), 187-88.

[3] *Revue Historique*, XCII (Sept.-Dec. 1906), 395-99; the quotation from p. 399.

[4] Foreword to *The Industrial Revolution . . .* (London: Jonathan Cape, Ltd., 1961), pp. 19, 22; printed as a Harper Torchbook in 1962; reprints by Methuen of London, 1964 and 1966.

With the translation of a revised version of *La Révolution Industrielle* into English by Marjorie Vernon and its publication in the United States in 1927 and Great Britain in 1928, Mantoux reached a worldwide audience. His book was also brought out in Russian, Italian, Spanish, Polish, and Japanese translations from the 1920s through the 1970s, and there was a new French edition—the first since 1906—in 1959. *The Industrial Revolution* remains the standard work on its subject. The University of Chicago Press brought out the last edition, with a new Foreword by John Kenneth Galbraith, in 1983. We found a copy of this edition on reserve in the Princeton University Library for a course in economic history.

[5] *Le Socialisme à l'Oeuvre*, G. Renard, ed. (Paris: E. Cornély and Co.).

Contemporaine (on English public opinion and the Boer War, the organization of the Labour Party, etc.) in 1909.

When the University of London established a chair of modern French history and institutions in 1912, Mantoux was appointed its first incumbent upon the recommendation of Ernest Lavisse, *doyen* of French historians. In the congenial Fabian environment of Russell Square and Gower Street, he lectured at University College, London, the London School of Economics, and Bedford College during the academic year 1913-1914.

Upon the outbreak of war in the latter year, Mantoux was mobilized as a second-class private and sent to the front with a knapsack and shovel to help dig graves for the dead of the First Battle of the Marne. In January 1915, he was detailed as interpreter to the headquarters of the British Twenty-Fourth Division, operating in the area of Saint-Omer and Ypres. A few months later, he went to London as representative of his former schoolmate, Albert Thomas, the Socialist French Minister of Munitions, to the office of David Lloyd George, who had just assumed the newly created Ministership of Munitions in the Asquith Cabinet. Hand in hand with Lloyd George, Mantoux was soon in the thick of Anglo-French collaboration on problems involving recruitment of labor, the procurement of raw materials and the production of munitions, even questions of military strategy. He was also present at almost every high-level Anglo-French meeting in 1917 and early 1918.

Mantoux's venue and duties changed radically in May 1918, when the French Premier, Clemenceau, called him back to France to serve as interpreter to the Supreme War Council at Versailles. He was afterward interpreter to the Council of Ten, January 12-March 24, 1919; the Council of Four, March 24-June 28, 1919; and the Council of the Heads of Delegations, July 1, 1919-c. January 10, 1920.

Just a few weeks before the latter date, Mantoux accepted appointment as Director of the Political Section of the League of Nations, the third highest position in that organization, and took up the duties of his new post in January 1920 in London and, soon afterward, in Geneva. He began his work with much hopefulness, but there are reasons to surmise that he was soon disillusioned and disappointed by the failure of the League to develop into a truly effective supranational organization.[6] In any

---

[6] For retrospective evidence that this was true, see his "A Contribution to the History of the Lost Opportunities of the League of Nations," in Professors of the

event, he did not seek reappointment when his term expired in 1927. But the main reason for his decision not to stay on in the League Secretariat was a turn of fortune that offered him an unrivaled opportunity for service to the cause of international cooperation in scholarship and world peace.

The opportunity grew out of the desire of the Rockefeller family to make some kind of contribution to the League of Nations. The family and their advisers, Dr. Abraham Flexner and Raymond B. Fosdick, first decided to build and equip a library in Geneva for the use of the League staff and visitors.[7] At the suggestion of William Emmanuel Rappard, Vice-Rector of the University of Geneva, the Rockefellers agreed in 1926 to establish and support a Graduate Institute of International Studies (Institut Universitaire des Hautes Études Internationales Genève). Mantoux accepted at once when Rappard asked him to become director.

The Graduate Institute opened with a small permanent faculty and visiting lecturers on November 3, 1927.[8] Mantoux and Rappard were the guiding spirits and energizing force of the institute until Mantoux's retirement in 1951 and Rappard's four years later. Mantoux moved back to Paris with his family in 1928,[9] but he maintained a close connection with Geneva by frequent residences and by correspondence with Rappard. He and Rappard were in fact co-directors, and they worked in perfect harmony.[10] The Graduate Institute, to quote from Mantoux's obituary in The Times, "was designed to bring together in special courses of study advanced students of politics, economics, and the social sciences generally from all parts of the world, and thus to foster the temper and methods of world cooperation. In seeking in this way to create an international centre of objective research and

---

Graduate Institute of International Studies, The World Crisis (London, New York, Toronto, 1938), pp. 3-35. Also, from the obituary in the London Times, Dec. 18, 1956: "Mantoux himself was one of the first at Geneva to entertain serious doubts of the league and to question the capacity of the member-States for rising above purely national and sectional interests."

[7] Abraham Flexner, An Autobiography (New York, 1960), p. 220.

[8] The professors: Paul Mantoux, Mark Eastman, Eugène Borel, and William E. Rappard; the visiting lecturers: Alfred Zimmern, Henri Hauser, Gaston Jèze, Georges Scelle, Louis Locheur, Nicolas Politis, Ernst Jäckh, Walter Schücking, and A. J. Toynbee. Institut Universitaire des Hautes Études Internationales Genève, Quarantième Anniversaire 1927-1967 (Geneva [1967]), p. 5.

[9] Mantoux was also professor of economic geography at the Conservatoire des Arts et Métiers, 1934-1940.

[10] Quarantième Anniversaire 1927-1967, pp. 5-18.

teaching, from which national schools and universities might take their inspiration and line of conduct, Mantoux anticipated many of the specific ideals of Unesco."[11]

Upon the outbreak of war in September 1939, Mantoux became head of the British Section of the French Ministry of Information. After the French defeat in June 1940, he spent a year in Lyons. He then returned to Geneva, where he resumed his position as director of and professor at the Graduate Institute. Old friendships had never faded, and he was able to resume personal contact with a host of friends once the war ended. When he retired in 1951, there was an outpouring of tributes of affection and esteem from around the world.

Mantoux's years were productive to the very end. From 1945 to 1952, he and Mme. Mantoux prepared for publication the major work of their eldest son, Étienne-Gabriel, a Doctor of Law and Economics (Lyons, 1941), who was killed in action near Dillingen, Bavaria, on April 29, 1945. Étienne Mantoux wrote his book, *The Carthaginian Peace or the Economic Consequences of Mr. Keynes*,[12] the classic refutation of Keynes' *Economic Consequences of the Peace*, in English while on a Rockefeller Fellowship at the Institute for Advanced Study in Princeton from 1941 to 1943. Then Paul Mantoux set himself to the task of preparing for publication his notes of the discussions of the Council of Four with the assistance of his wife and the National Center for Scientific Research. He remained active in several associations, among them Les Amis de Georges Clemenceau and Le Souvenir d'Albert Thomas, and he and Mme. Mantoux traveled widely during these years. Mantoux's last public lecture was a moving tribute to Woodrow Wilson, delivered in June 1956 at a symposium celebrating Wilson's centennial sponsored by the University of Geneva, the Graduate Institute, and the Carnegie Endowment for International Peace.[13] He had long suffered from heart disease and died in Paris from a heart attack on December 13, 1956.

Numerous honors came to this distinguished scholar and man of affairs: the honorary degree of Doctor of Political Science, University of Geneva, 1951; Chevalier, *à titre militaire* (later *Offi-*

---

[11] The ideals of UNESCO, at least as originally conceived.

[12] With a Preface by R. C. K. Ensor, Oxford University Press, 1946; Charles Scribner's Sons, 1952; University of Pittsburgh Press, 1965; Arno Press, New York, 1979; in French translation by Professor Mantoux, Gallimard, Paris, 1947.

[13] "Le Président Wilson au Conseil des Quatre," *Centenaire Woodrow Wilson* (Geneva [1956]), pp. 17-28.

cier), of the Légion d'Honneur; Companion of the Order of the Bath (civil); Italy: Knight of the Royal Order of Saint Lazarus and Mauritius; Japan: Knight Commander of the Imperial Order of the Rising Sun; Poland: Knight Commander of the National Order of the Polish White Eagle; Rumania: Knight Commander of the National Royal Order of Rumania.

Mantoux and his wife, Mathilde Babette Mantoux (1889-1986) were married in Paris on October 10, 1911, and from this union issued Étienne-Gabriel (1913-1945), Philippe-Roger (1918-), and Jacques-Adrien (1921-).

Mantoux and His Notes

It was obvious by late March 1919 to nearly everyone that the Paris Peace Conference was in trouble. The supreme decision-making body, the Council of Ten,[1] composed of the heads of government and their Foreign Ministers, had convened on January 12. But its accomplishments were few by February 14, when Wilson left Paris to return to the United States to attend to business necessitated by the end of the sixty-fifth session of Congress. By this date, the Council of Ten had substantially agreed upon the military, naval, and aerial terms of the preliminary treaty with Germany; had taken an initiative, which failed, to arrange for the appointment of delegates to the conference by the warring factions in Russia; had approved a draft of a Covenant of the League of Nations; and had agreed that former German colonies should be given over to various countries and dominions for administration under mandate of the League of Nations.

The near impossibility of rapid progress in the Council of Ten was evidenced by the state of affairs upon Wilson's return to Paris. For one thing, decisions upon French demands for security against future German aggression were at hand. For another thing, Colonel House had muddied the waters (from Wilson's point of view) by tentatively agreeing to acquiesce in these French demands and to defer postponement of consideration of the League Covenant to a second conference. Thirdly, to cite only one other example, discussions of a reparation settlement were in complete disarray. The hard decisions lay immediately ahead, and the setting of the Council of Ten seemed to preclude its making them. The council met in the great conference room of the Foreign Ministry at the Quai d'Orsay, which was usually crowded with aides and rang with the cacophony of voices. Confidentiality, and the opportunity for serious and undistracted discussion by the men who had to make the final decisions, was impossible. Wilson saw that there was only one *modus operandi*

---

[1] Theoretically, the Plenary Session, consisting of all the plenipotentiary delegates, which met from time to time, was the supreme authority. However, the Plenary Session at no time did otherwise than ratify the work and decisions of the representatives of the Principal Allied and Associated Powers—France, Great Britain, Italy, Japan, and the United States.

which promised any success—private meetings of himself, Clemenceau, Lloyd George, Orlando (and Sonnino), and the Japanese delegates when questions involving the Far East were involved. In a meeting with Clemenceau, Lloyd George, and Orlando on March 24, Wilson suggested this method of proceeding, and his colleagues at once accepted his invitation to meet thereafter at his residence at 11 Place des États-Unis.

The council, known informally as the Council of Four and officially as the Supreme Council of the Principal Allied and Associated Powers, met for its first session on March 25 and thereafter usually at Wilson's house. Mantoux describes the setting well in his Preface, printed below. Although there is no record of the fact, there must have been ready agreement that Paul Mantoux, the interpreter of the Council of Ten, should continue as interpreter for the Four.

Clemenceau was fluent in English, and much of the discussion among himself, Wilson, Lloyd George, and other English-speaking people who came in from time to time was in English. Nonetheless, since Orlando and other occasional participants in the discussion neither spoke English nor understood it but were fluent in French, Mantoux translated everything said into French or English, as the circumstance required, from notes, written both in English and French. Each morning, he went to the Foreign Ministry and dictated transcripts of his notes of the previous day to a secretary. One copy was laid on Clemenceau's desk; one was left for the archives of the Foreign Ministry, and he kept two for himself. As Wilson was insistent upon maintaining the absolute confidentiality of their discussions, the Four did not have a secretary of any kind between March 24 and April 20,[2] even though they were taking decisions, some of them of great significance, during this period. It was at this point, just when they were beginning to discuss Italy's claims, that the Four apparently decided that they could no longer do complicated business by memory and, undoubtedly at Lloyd George's suggestion, brought in Sir Maurice Hankey (later Lord Hankey) to keep an official record, the *procès-verbaux*, of discussions and actions.[3] Still unbe-

---

[2] There were meetings on March 29 and April 5, 7, 8, 10, and 19, 1919, with military, economic, and other advisers, at which an official secretary was present and formal minutes were kept.

[3] There was probably another reason why Wilson consented to having an official record kept. Orlando brought Count Luigi Aldrovandi Marescotti, Secretary General of the Italian delegation, with him to the meeting on April 19 to take notes for reports to the Italian delegation. Wilson probably agreed that it

knownst to Wilson, Lloyd George, and Orlando, Mantoux continued to keep his own record, and did so until the final meeting of the Four on June 28, 1919.

Mantoux was present at every meeting of the Council of Four (except for a brief meeting on April 26) and at several informal meetings, and his record provides complete coverage of all the discussions from March 24 through June 28. Hankey was not present at thirty-seven sessions; moreover, toward the end of the conference, Hankey was too busy recording official decisions and attending to a large volume of papers to keep a sustained record of discussions. Moreover, Hankey was sometimes out of the council room on errands for the Four or Three. Thus it can be said that Mantoux's record is the only complete one that we have of the *délibérations*. This is not to make an invidious comparison between Mantoux and Hankey's achievements. They had different tasks, and they performed them superbly.

Mantoux did not use a shorthand system and had to rely upon abbreviated notes and his memory in reconstructing the conversations of the Four while dictating them. The reader of these transcripts must wonder, in the light of these facts, how full and accurate Mantoux's transcripts are. We can render a judgment on this question by (1) comparing Mantoux's texts with Hankey's notes when both were reporting the same conversations; (2) by comparing Mantoux's text with the only transcript made by a shorthand reporter: the transcript of Charles Lee Swem, Wilson's confidential secretary, of the meeting of the council on June 5, 11 a.m.; and (3) by textual analysis of comments and long discourses by Wilson to determine, as best we can, whether Mantoux's renditions conform to what we know to have been Wilson's conversational and rhetorical styles.

Any judgment based upon a comparison of Hankey's and Mantoux's texts is bound to be somewhat inconclusive. Hankey, too, did not practice a shorthand system and, like Mantoux, dictated his notes to a secretary. Since he cast the conversations in the form of indirect discourse, his versions are usually necessarily longer than Mantoux's, who cast his versions in the form of direct discourse. Both were skilled and excellent recorders; nei-

---

was necessary to have an official secretary present now that an Italian secretary was present and discussions of Italian claims were beginning in earnest. Aldrovandi published his notes relating to discussions of the Italian question in the Council of Four in *Guerra Diplomatica, Ricordi e Frammenti di Diario (1914-1919)* (Milan, 1936) and *Ricordi e Frammenti di Diario* (Milan, 1938).

ther's version contradicts nor impugns the other's. And both men worked closely together. As Hankey's biographer has written: "Paul Mantoux, his old friend and colleague of many wartime Inter-Allied meetings, acted as interpreter, and he and Hankey between them produced the French and English procès-verbaux and 'Secretary's Notes' in intimate cordiality.' "[4]

A comparison of Mantoux's notes for the meeting of June 5, 1919, 11 a.m. with Swem's transcript of the conversation of that same meeting[5] yields more interesting evidence on the question of the completeness of Mantoux's record of what was said in the Council of Four. The Swem and Mantoux transcripts of the meeting of June 5 parallel each other perfectly. The shorter sentences are almost exactly the same in both versions; Swem's transcripts of the more extensive comments are, roughly speaking, about 25 per cent longer than Mantoux's. Yet no shorthand reporter ever produces a perfect transcript. Swem was presumably at the meeting when it began, yet he failed to record the first remarks by Clemenceau, Orlando, and Wilson, about the fighting between the Rumanians and Hungarians. In addition, Swem missed some sentences that Mantoux heard and recorded.

From what we know about the spoken language of Lloyd George, Clemenceau, Orlando, and others (most particularly Balfour and Foch), we conclude that Mantoux succeeded extremely well in reproducing their individual rhetorical styles. About Mantoux's reproduction of Wilson's language, we can speak more confidently: Mantoux reproduced Wilsonian language with consummate skill. This judgment applies as much to Wilson's brief comments, often sprinkled with colloquialisms familiar to us, as to Wilson's long discourses.

Our conclusions regarding the verisimilitude of Mantoux's transcripts can be stated briefly. Many of them repeat discourses virtually *verbatim*; others are compacted in varying degrees. If Mantoux omitted or compacted certain sentences, he did not manufacture any, and his record of the discussions seems to us utterly trustworthy. He accomplished what he calls in his Preface his "more modest task," as compared to Hankey's: "It consisted of reproducing as faithfully as possible what I had just heard, and in such a way as to communicate the same impression I had received. I set myself to retaining, not only all that the person who

---

[4] Stephen Roskill, *Hankey: Man of Secrets*, 3 vols. (London, 1970-1974), II, 50-51.

[5] Printed in *PPC*, VI, 191-201.

had just spoken meant (while preserving to each idea and fact enunciated its relative place and value), but also the expression and the significant or simply characteristic words."

Mantoux was learned in modern history and geography; trained in scholarly skills; a master of the French and English languages; blessed with a nearly photographic memory; and was a person incapable of misrepresentation. To our everlasting benefit, he brought all these talents and personal qualities to the task set before him in 1919.

Mantoux's transcripts had a perilous history after 1919. At some time between 1930 and 1935, Mantoux gave one of his copies to his lifelong friend, André Tardieu, who was then writing his memoirs in retirement on the French Riviera. Tardieu never completed his memoirs or returned Mantoux's manuscript to him.[6] The two copies in the Foreign Ministry Archives were burned along with tons of documents in the courtyard of the Quai d'Orsay by ministry officials just before the Germans entered Paris in June 1940. Fleeing to southern France with French officialdom, Mantoux left the sole surviving copy of his transcripts behind in his Paris apartment. However, he was soon able to get in touch with his friend, Georges Scelle, Professor of Law at the Sorbonne, and Scelle retrieved the transcripts and hid them in the cellar of the Faculty of Law building. When Mantoux recovered them at the end of the war, they were complete and in perfect condition.

Aware of the hazards to material things and the limitations of life, Mantoux wanted to publish his transcripts as soon as possible,[7] but each time he approached the Foreign Ministry for permission to do so, he was told that they were official documents, and that the fifty-year rule[8] stood athwart his plans. However, publication by the State Department from 1944 to 1946 of Hankey's minutes of the Council of Four in the Peace Conference volumes of *Papers Relating to the Foreign Relations of the United*

---

[6] Perhaps they will be found in the Tardieu Papers in the French Foreign Ministry Archives when the papers in that collection relating to the Paris Peace Conference are opened to scholarly investigation.

[7] For example, in 1946 he suggested to Hankey that the two of them get out editions of their minutes. P. Mantoux to Lord Hankey, Oct. 30, 1946, copy of letter in the possession of J.-A. Mantoux.

[8] That no confidential governmental documents could be seen by scholars or published until fifty years had elapsed since their creation. Both the British and French governments enforced this rule until 1972, when they put a thirty-year rule into effect. Meanwhile, numerous persons like Lloyd George, Clemenceau, etc., had blithely ignored the fifty-year rule.

States caused the Foreign Ministry to give the green light for publication to Mantoux under the sponsorship of the National Center for Scientific Research. With Mme. Mantoux's assistance, he prepared the manuscript for publication without making any changes, proofread the galley and page proofs, and compiled the Index. The two-volume edition, entitled *Les Délibérations du Conseil des Quatre* (24 mars-28 juin 1919), was published by the National Center in 1955, just a year before Mantoux's death.

Editor's Introduction

No OTHER international conference in history, except the Congress of Vienna (1814-1815), compares to the Paris Peace Conference as a high stage upon which dramatic events were played out, or in the complexity of problems discussed and the decisive impact of the decisions taken upon the future of the world. Indeed, the Paris conference was the only meeting in history that ever attempted to effect a worldwide settlement. It also created a new concert of power to succeed the Concert of European Powers that held tenuous sway from 1815 to 1914.

Almost two centuries have passed since the Congress of Vienna, and its work in rearranging the map of Europe and creating a new European balance of power is sufficiently remote, and enough knowledge about it has accumulated, to make it possible for historians to view it as part of an antique past and to write narratives of its deliberations and decisions in single volumes.

Such cannot be said about the Paris Peace Conference. We now have a number of fine monographs on various issues and problems of that congress of the nations. Kay Lundgreen-Nielsen's *The Polish Problem at the Paris Peace Conference* tells us all we will ever need to know about this subject. Philip M. Burnett, *Reparation at the Paris Peace Conference*, Étienne Mantoux, *The Carthaginian Peace*, and Marc Trachtenberg, *Reparation in World Politics*, cover this subject through its ironical dénouement. Harold I. Nelson, *Land and Power: British and Allied Policy on Germany's Frontiers, 1916-19*, is another exemplary monograph. We mention these books only as examples of the large extant body of good monographic literature on the Paris Peace Conference. There is also a large mixed bag of memoirs and some semihistorical accounts on the conference by its participants. The knowledge derived from the growing scholarly literature is just beginning to have an impact on general historians; it has had hardly any at all on the great majority of popular historians, commentators, and public perceptions.

To this point, no single historian has succeeded in writing the great general work on the Paris Peace Conference. Such a study might well be a life-time work, but it can now be written. The best starting point, in our opinion, is Mantoux's record of the deliberations of the Council of Four, which is surely the single most important source for the work of that body. Mantoux's record, presented below in its entirety in English for the first time, affords a focused view of all the major issues and decisions taken at Paris before the end of the first major phase of the peace conference on June 28, 1919. More important, that record provides that view as seen through the prism of the discussions of the men who made all important decisions.

Since Mantoux's notes were not, and were not meant to be, a formal record, we have provided readers with guides to printed sources for the reports, position papers, telegrams, and other communications laid before the council. When the council discussed important papers of this kind with specific reference to them, we print them as appendixes to their discussions for ready reference by the reader. Finally, we have provided annotation intended to give the general historical and contemporary context of the council's deliberations. Our objective has been to produce a work that provides all readers, except specialists, with a self-contained record as complete as we could make it within the limits set by the nature of Mantoux's work.

We respectfully urge readers of these volumes to read these volumes with minds wiped clean of the stereotypes and preconceptions produced by the conventional wisdom about the Paris Peace Conference and the men who dominated it. It is salutary and rewarding to take a seat alongside the members of the Council of Four and to look at events through their eyes, and we think that old stereotypes will vanish once the reader does this.

We have given the background of the conference, which opened on January 12, 1919, in the preceding essay, "Mantoux and His Notes," and in some detail in the annotation accompanying the discussions of the early meetings of the Four. Mantoux's record opens during the first great crisis of the conference—what some writers have called the "dark period"—occasioned by French demands for the creation of a Rhenish republic under French influence on the left bank of the Rhine and French annexation of the coal-rich Saar Basin. At the same time, the French and British are demanding that the former German Emperor and other German civilian leaders and military and naval persons be brought to summary trial for alleged war crimes. The Four's earlier invitation to the warring Russian factions to meet on Prinkipo Island and select delegates to the conference in Paris having been rejected by Lenin and Trotsky, the Four are challenged by Marshal Foch to create a *cordon sanitaire* to hold

EDITOR'S INTRODUCTION

back a phantasmagorical Bolshevik tide rolling against the West. Discussions over reparation by Germany are in a morass of disputes among the English, French, and American representatives on the Reparation Commission and the principals for whom they speak.

At this point, Wilson intervenes by implicitly threatening to go home and then by taking command of the Council of Four. He breaks the log jam in the council by forcing adoption of a compromise agreement on the trial of the former German Emperor. He persuades Clemenceau definitively to abandon demands for the detachment of the left bank from Germany; he offers in return French occupation of that area for a certain period and his promise to join the British in signing with France treaties of guarantee against future German aggression. Wilson also persuades the French to reduce their claims to the Saar to ownership of the coal mines of the basin and a fifteen-year administration of the area, in compensation for wanton German destruction of French mines in northern France.

During this period of Wilsonian supremacy in the council, the major agreements on those portions of the German treaty involving French territorial claims are hammered out. In addition, Wilson wins the approval of the conference of the inclusion as Article 1 in the preliminary German treaty of the Covenant establishing the League of Nations. During these weeks of sometimes bitter acrimony and sharp debate in the council, Wilson has Lloyd George's consistent support; at the same time, the Prime Minister is content to let Wilson take the lead in, and accept the onus of, forcing the French to yield to what the British and American spokesmen think are reasonable territorial compromises and acceptance of an Anglo-American constitution for the League of Nations. But the question of reparation continues unresolved. Wilson, following the advice of his experts, continues to demand a fixed sum, based upon Germany's capacity to pay, and a stipulated time period for reparation payments. The French remain intractable in their insistence upon all compensation due them; and the British continue to demand the last farthing that can possibly be exacted from Germany.

Just when it seems that the council's ship has passed safely through heavy waters and commissions are working harmoniously on the sections of the German treaty to create the new state of Poland and draw its boundaries, a second crisis erupts in late April. It is set off by the demand of Orlando and his Foreign Minister, Sonnino, for the award to Italy of Fiume, along with the

Dalmatian littoral, Albania, and the islands off the Dalmatian coast. These questions involving an Adriatic settlement, which will presumably be incorporated in the Austrian treaty, come to the fore, ironically, because the council is making such good progress on the German treaty. As Orlando points out, the time is now not only right, from the point of view of Italian public opinion, but also available to the council to address itself to Italy's claims.

Clemenceau and Lloyd George let Wilson shoulder the burdens of what at once becomes a bruising battle. The British and French Premiers are, to be sure, in an impossible moral and political situation. The British and French governments, in signing the Treaty of London with the Italians on April 26, 1915, had bought Italy's entry into the war on their side in return for the concession to Italy of the Austrian Tyrol, Istria, and the Dalmatian littoral and islands, but not Fiume, which was to go to Croatia, now a part of the new Kingdom of the Serbs, Croats and Slovenes. Clemenceau and Lloyd George feel morally bound by the Treaty of London. Yet they will cause catastrophe whatever they do. If they stand firm against Italian claims, they risk Italian withdrawal from the conference and rupture of the alliance. If they stand by their commitments in the Treaty of London, Wilson will not sign the Austrian treaty and might even refuse to sign the German treaty and leave the conference.

Orlando resolves the dilemma for the British and French Prime Ministers by going back to Rome on April 24, when Wilson issues an appeal to the Italian people to repudiate the policies of their leaders.

At this moment of despair and confusion, the Japanese delegates come into the council and lay down their terms for those articles of the German treaty relating to the Far East. They demand award to Japan of all Pacific islands north of the equator that formerly belonged to Germany. More important, they demand the cession to Japan of former German rights in the Chinese province of Shantung. They have an airtight legal case because the British, French, and Chinese governments have already confirmed these concessions in treaties. Moreover, the Japanese delegates make it clear that they will not sign the German treaty unless the council consents to their demands. Wilson once again takes leadership in finding a compromise. By exquisitely courteous diplomacy, he persuades the Japanese to agree to say that they will withdraw their armed forces from Shantung Province, restore full political sovereignty over it to China, and retain in it only such economic privileges as Germany had enjoyed before the war.

This agreed to, Clemenceau presents the now completed preliminary treaty to a German delegation at the Trianon Palace on May 7. Orlando has just returned to Paris and signs the treaty.

Now begins what become more than seven weeks of meetings and discussions about revision of the preliminary German treaty, the preparation of the Austrian treaty, the Turkish treaty, and special treaties with Poland, Czechoslovakia, and Rumania for the protection of ethnic and religious minorities, principally Jews. The Four are also engrossed in discussions about the determination of Poland's eastern borders, Rumanian aggression against Hungary, and a separate convention with Germany for inter-Allied occupation of the Rhineland. And always in the background is the question of whether the Allies can affect the course of the civil war between the Bolsheviks and the anti-Bolshevik forces under Kolchak and Denikin.

Through an exchange of published notes, the Four spend much of their time between May 7 and June 2 in dialogue with the German delegation headed by Count Brockdorff-Rantzau. The preliminary treaty, as the Four make clear, is not an ultimatum, and they not only invite the Germans to comment on the treaty, but also instruct them to do so on all its major provisions.

The Germans begin their attack against the preliminary treaty on May 9. It is the beginning of what is known in the historical literature as revisionism—that long and sustained attack against the alleged injustices of the Versailles Treaty, which was carried on by German historians and publicists, ably assisted by sympathizers with the German case in the United States and Great Britain, in the 1920s and 1930s and which provided the rationale for appeasement in the latter decade. After accusing the Four of intending to dismember the German nation and enslave the German people for generations to come—all in flagrant violation of Allied promises and, most particularly, of Wilson's Fourteen Points—the Germans come back again and again with cleverly conceived proposals that would make possible the restoration of German power. They challenge the Four to prove that Germany had been responsible for the war; they say that they like the idea of a league of nations but propose a plan of their own for such an organization. They demand immediate admission into a league in any event. They accept the very substantial disarmament of Germany, but only on the assumption that the Allies will disarm also. They admit liability for reparation and offer to pay reparation in the sum of $25 billion dollars, to assist in the reconstruction of Belgium and northern France, and to supply coal and other raw materials to France for a certain period—but on their own terms. They complain bitterly of the nonreparation economic clauses of the preliminary treaty. They accept the principle of and agree to the creation of a Polish state but protest against the alleged violation of the principle of self-determination by the dismemberment of East Prussia and the award of Upper Silesia to Poland. They ask for Germany's immediate admission to the International Labour Organization, the charter of which is being drafted by a special commission. Implied in these protests and counterproposals is the clear warning that Germany will never sign the preliminary treaty.

Clemenceau is not disposed to make any concessions. Wilson takes the German protests to heart. He is willing to respond to all just German complaints, but he is unwilling to pay blackmail in order to obtain German signature of the treaty. However, the German notes (put together in a long communication to the Council of Four on May 29) have a tremendous impact, particularly upon Lloyd George because of the implied German threat not to sign.

During this interlude of Allied-German dialogue, May 7-June 2, the Four also begin serious work on the Austrian treaty, and this sets off constant negotiations with Orlando and Sonnino over an Adriatic settlement. Allied proposals draw either Italian rejection or counterproposals unacceptable to Wilson. Tempers rise and provoke bitter exchanges. Further exacerbating this situation is Italian occupation of the Dodecanese Islands and ports in Asia Minor, which causes Wilson, Lloyd George, and Clemenceau to come together in a solid bloc to prevent Italian expansion into Asia Minor. Perhaps even more discouraging at this time is the obvious helplessness of the Four to force the Poles to cease their aggression against the people of the western Ukraine and the Rumanians their aggressions against Hungarians in Transylvania.

This is the parlous state of affairs when Lloyd George comes to the council meeting in the afternoon of June 2 and announces that he and the British plenipotentiary delegates cannot and will not sign the German treaty in its present form. The well-designed German protests have precipitated a wave of sentiment in the British Isles among church groups and leaders, liberals, Labour party leaders, and academic people in favor of softening the terms of the preliminary treaty. Moreover, Lloyd George and his colleagues are now convinced that no government can be found in Germany that will sign the treaty in its present form, and that the only alternative to substantial appeasement of Germany is an Allied invasion and occupation of Germany at immense cost, without any end or productive results in sight. Lloyd George demands a plebiscite in Upper Silesia to determine the fate of that province; rectification in Germany's favor of the Polish-German borders; a drastic shortening of the period of Allied occupation of the Rhineland; virtually immediate admission of Germany to the League of Nations; and downward revision of Germany's reparation obligations. If these changes are not made, the Prime Minister says, he will withdraw from the conference, go home, and lay the entire matter before Parliament. There is not much that Wilson and Clemenceau can say except that they will consult their colleagues and advisers.

Lloyd George's pronouncement marks the beginning of the period of his supremacy in the Council of Four, which lasts until the end of the conference on June 28. He behaves like a bully at times and nearly breaks up the conference in pique on two occasions, and the strain on Wilson and Clemenceau is great, particularly on Wilson, who is just recovering from what was almost certainly a small stroke in late April. The weeks between June 2 and June 28 see shifting alliances among Clemenceau, Wilson, and Lloyd George. (Orlando, facing a parliamentary crisis at home, leaves Paris on June 12; his government falls a week later.) But for the most part Wilson stands with Clemenceau against Lloyd George, and for the most part the latter prevails.

Wilson has always favored Germany's immediate or very early admission to the League of Nations and supports Lloyd George on this point. Clemenceau will not give in, and the three agree on a compromise statement. The Allies, it says, never had any intention of indefinitely excluding Germany from the League. If the Germans only show good faith in carrying out the peace treaty, the Three see no reason why Germany should not become a member of the League in the near future. The Three agree without much controversy to make numerous changes in Germany's favor in the provisions defining the Polish-German border in Pomerania and East Prussia. They also approve, again without disagreement, a convention that assures control of domestic affairs to the Germans in the Rhineland during the period of the Allied occupation. Clemenceau, himself, drafts a special protocol promising early evacuation of the area under certain conditions and greatly reducing Germany's share of the costs of the occupation.

However, the discussions over revision of the final reparation provisions and the issue of a plebiscite for Upper Silesia are prolonged and bitter. Wilson has never been a softliner on Germany's duty to make reparation for its wanton aggression and destruction in Belgium and France. He has simply insisted on setting a definite sum and period of payment, and he stands by the sum that his advisers have recommended—$30 billion. But Lloyd George says that the only sensible solution is to instruct the Reparation Commission in the near future to work out the total sum and the method and schedule of payments in collaboration with German experts on a basis of Germany's capacity to pay. Clemenceau agrees, and, when Lloyd George rides roughshod over him, Wilson demurs, saying that the reparation settlement is a shambles. As it turns out, his statement is more accurate than he realizes. Lloyd George also has his way on Upper Silesia.

Events of the last two weeks of the conference bring into sharp relief the variousness of and limitations on the power of the Four. In dealing with Poland, which is utterly dependent upon their support, they can and do impose a minorities treaty and territorial changes favorable to Germany, but they cannot stop Polish aggression in the western Ukraine. They send threatening notes to Bucharest, and the Rumanians ignore them. They abandon as futile Lloyd George's plans for squeezing contributions to the reparation fund from Poland, Czechoslovakia, Yugoslavia, and Rumania. They are helpless to restrain Italian initiatives in the Adriatic region and Asia Minor.

The limitations of the power of the Four are revealed again, on June 20, when the Scheidemann government of Germany resigns rather than sign the revised treaty and the admiral of the interned German fleet scuttles the High Seas Fleet at Scapa Flow. Even though all Allied leaders in Paris, since the presentation of the preliminary treaty on May 7, have feared that Germany would refuse to sign any peace treaty at all, the Four have made no plans to meet this dire contingency. All they can do is to prepare for a sudden drive toward Berlin, but they do not have the military force to guarantee the success of this operation, much less to occupy and administer all of Germany. In sum, they cannot impose their will upon the defeated foe. The war has to be resumed, with no political settlement in sight.

Resolution of this, the worst crisis of the conference, comes on June 23, when the German National Assembly votes to accept the revised treaty, and a government of nondescripts is formed to carry out the final formalities. A new German delegation goes to Paris and signs the treaty in the Hall of Mirrors of the Versailles Palace—the room in which the German Empire had been proclaimed in 1871—in the afternoon of June 28.

The superficial grandeur of the event and of the celebrations afterward masked the reality of the misery of victory. The Four experienced that misery personally within a short time. Orlando was the first to feel the wrath of his countrymen; his government fell on June 19, 1919. He lived long in retirement and recovered a little stature as President of the Italian Constituent Assembly in 1946. But his last bid for vindication—his campaign for the presidency of the Republic of Italy—failed. Clemenceau's unstable coalition fell apart not long after the Versailles Treaty was ratified by the French Parliament. After an unsuccessful bid for the presidency of France in January 1920, he lost the premiership when his enemies combined against him. Wilson, crippled by strokes after his return to the United States, failed to win the Senate's consent to ratification of the treaty. He was repudiated by the voters in the election of 1920 after he forced his party to run on a platform of no important reservations to the League Covenant. Lloyd George stayed on in power the longest of the Four, but he, too, fell from power in 1922.

Even so, the Four were the great leaders of the world during the heyday of their power, and their conversations in the library of Wilson's house in Paris provide a window into their minds and souls. They were the four great liberal statesmen of the first third of the twentieth century, and they shared, variously, a common vision for the world. But the strain of trying to reconcile that vision with the conflicting demands of their public opinions and national interests was severe, at times too severe to be endured.

About Wilson, it can be said that he served as the conscience of the council in recalling the ideals for which the war had been fought, and that he set the tone of many of the discussions. He also took the lead in arranging the compromises that were necessary to win French acquiescence in the treaty. At the end, he was instrumental in keeping peace between Lloyd George and Clemenceau. His intractability regarding Italian claims is understandable, but that intractability turned into unyielding hostility. What became a near paranoia about Italian intentions blocked his usual ability to find expedient compromise, contributed to the downfall of democracy in Italy, and prevented him from playing a significant role in the final Adriatic settlement in 1920. This failure aside, and it might have been induced by his small stroke in late April, Wilson's accomplishments in the Council of Four constitute, altogether, the single greatest achievement of his career, and no one who reads the records of his conversations in these volumes will ever again think of him other than as a practical idealist, deft and agile in negotiation, a realist of the highest type, who achieved many of his objectives, the greatest of which was the establishment of the League of Nations.

Given the course of future events, Clemenceau emerges from the pages that follow as the wisest and most far-sighted of the Four. Among all significant French leaders of the time, he was the most moderate in his attitudes toward Germany. He was not revengeful toward Germany. He asked only for justice for France. Above all, he wanted for his country a reasonable chance to survive against a new surge of *furor Teutonicus*. He failed to achieve what might have been the most effective instrumentality to protect the security of France and the peace of Europe—a NATO-like continuation of the wartime coalition. But such an arrangement was impossible in 1919, and Clemenceau took what he could get and made the compromises that in turn made the German treaty acceptable to his American and English colleagues. He obviously failed to achieve lasting security for France, but that was not his fault. The peace-keeping machinery of the Versailles Treaty broke down, not because it was structurally weak, but because British and French leaders did not have the courage and will to use it effectively in the 1930s.

Orlando leaves the impression from these discussions of both an attractive and a pathetic figure. He was a liberal and an idealist, whose good intentions are evident in all discussions that did not involve Italian interests. In defending them, he was obviously intellectually and emotionally torn by what he thought was right and by what he knew he had to say and do. He was the last hope for Italian democracy for a long time to come, and it would have been better for his reputation if history had spared him the duty of championing so compromised a cause.

Lloyd George emerges from this record as a person whose character is revealed in an unflattering light. He was capable of noble thoughts, high motives, and of altruism, particularly when altruism demanded no sacrifice of British interests. His best achievements came about as the result of the work of his wisest advisers, persons like Cecil and Headlam-Morley, and he must be credited for following their lead in supporting the Covenant and matters such as the minorities treaties. However, Lloyd George had the spirit of a petty English shopkeeper when it came to money. He caved in on reparation at the end, but only in order to win German acquiescence in the treaty. He was rude and overbearing in dealing with the representatives of the small powers, for whom he had open contempt, and he ended the conference as the bully of the Four. He was inconstant, but inconstancy was probably part of his method. On the other hand, he was the most successful member of the Four. Whether by using Wilson as a foil against the French and Italians, or by largely dictating the terms of the Versailles Treaty himself, he achieved all the major objectives of the British Empire at the peace conference—all objectives except the long-term peace of Europe.

A FEW WORDS OF ADVICE AND EXPLANATION TO OUR READERS

In translating Mantoux's text, our task has consisted in large part of putting it back into the language in which it was originally spoken. Thus we have used the English form of certain words—"whilst," "amongst," "towards," "amidst," etc., and usages such as "take a decision," because these were the words and phrases that Lloyd George, Clemenceau, and Wilson used. Also, we have tried to reproduce idioms and colloquial language according to English and American usage of 1919. The contractions are of course our own. We have followed Mantoux's punctuation as closely as possible. We can only hope that our translation does justice to Mantoux's elegant and precise French.

The names of speakers whose direct discourse follows are printed in bold-face type. A dash before a sentence signifies indirect discourse, paraphrase, or the summary of a document. Sentences in italics indicate actions taken and the direction of the conversation, e.g., *"to M. Clemenceau."*

For the convenience of the reader, we have identified all persons, except for well-known historical personages, whose names appear in the text in a *Dramatis Personae* section at the back of these volumes. Except for leading figures, the identifications describe persons only as of their position in 1919.

All place names that have changed since 1919 are listed in the Index under the place names as they appear in the text; their present names are given in parentheses.

We call the attention of readers to the maps on pages xliii-liii.

The section, "Sources and Works Cited," includes many of the important writings on the Paris Peace Conference. For nearly complete bibliographies of sources and works, see Max Guzenhäuser, *Die Pariser Friedenskonferenz 1919 und die Friedensverträge 1919-1920: Literaturbericht und Bibliographie* (Frankfurt am Main, 1970), and the bibliography in Arthur Walworth, *Wilson and His Peacemakers: American Diplomacy at the Paris Peace Conference, 1919* (New York and London, 1986).

Finally, the reader should be reminded that two separate armistices concluded the war in Europe in 1918. One was the well-known Armistice of the Forest of Compiègne, signed by representatives of the Allied and Associated Powers and of Germany on November 11, 1918. Whenever this agreement is mentioned, we capitalize the word "armistice." The second was the Armistice of Villa Giusti (near Padua, Italy), signed by representatives of the Allied and Associated Powers and of Austria-Hungary on November 3, 1918. When this agreement is mentioned in the text, the word "armistice" is not capitalized.

ACKNOWLEDGMENTS

We are grateful to the late Mme. Mantoux for suggesting that we translate and edit her husband's work and for her confidence in us. Virginia Reinburg and Alice L. Conklin made a preliminary draft translation of *Les Délibérations*. August Heckscher read the entire draft of our translation and made many fine suggestions for stylistic changes. For assistance in the translation, we are most indebted to Philippe-Roger Mantoux. Bilingual and a professional translator himself, he reviewed every line and made numerous suggestions which corrected and improved the translation. Any misreadings or stylistic infelicities that remain are our own. Jacques-Adrien Mantoux has been an ardent supporter of this undertaking from the beginning; he also supplied us with most of the materials upon which the sketch of his father is based and documents relating to *Les Délibérations* from his father's papers. L. Kathleen Amon prepared the *Dramatis Personae* and helped in many other ways. Susannah Jones Link edited the manuscript with her usual careful eye and flair. David W. Hirst read the galley and page proofs with his eagle eye. We are indebted to him and to Anne Cipriano Venzon for her masterful index. Finally, we are grateful to the Woodrow Wilson Foundation for underwriting the work on and publication of these volumes, and to Princeton University Press for producing them so handsomely.

We dedicate this work to the memory of Paul-Joseph Mantoux, historian in the service of history.

                                              Arthur S. Link
                                              Manfred F. Boemeke

Princeton, New Jersey
February 1, 1991

AUTHOR'S PREFACE

WHEN the Supreme Council, having conducted the war, took responsibility for the direction of the peace conference in January 1919, it included the heads of governments of the five Principal Allied and Associated Powers, with their Foreign Ministers; hence the commonly used name, the Council of Ten. On March 24, 1919, President Wilson invited his partners, the Prime Ministers of France, Great Britain, and Italy, to form a smaller council with him: it was a matter of speeding up the work of the conference by direct conversations among those to whom, in the final analysis, the power of decision making belonged.[1]

From March 24, until the signing of the Treaty of Versailles, the supreme authority resided in this council. Japan had her place there, so that her representative came every time a question touching Japanese interests came up. For more than three months, the council met every day, with very few exceptions, and usually twice a day. It had to take the most important decisions, not only in deciding the provisions of the treaty of peace with Germany and in preparing treaties with the other enemy states, but also in confronting urgent questions which continually arose from incidents which swept over a Europe profoundly convulsed by the war and the Russian Revolution. To its diplomatic functions were added those of an actual international Directory.

The Council of Four usually met at President Wilson's private residence on the Place des États-Unis.[2] Its last session was held between the signing of the treaty and the departure of the President—who had to leave France the same day—in the foyer of the Court Opera, adjacent to the Château of Versailles. It was in that place, decorated with sculptured panels of the most exquisite art,

---

[1] Moreover, it was, above all, in conversations of two or three that the great problems of the left bank of the Rhine and the guarantee pledged to France against unprovoked aggression had already been discussed. [All footnotes in Preface by Mantoux.]

[2] A dozen times at Mr. Lloyd George's place, 23 rue Nitot, and, on very rare occasions, in the office of M. Clemenceau on the rue Saint-Dominique, or in one of those of the Minister of Foreign Affairs at the Quai d'Orsay.

that the Four had their last meeting[3] and settled some unresolved questions and took note of a letter from Bethmann Hollweg, who had asked, in his capacity as Chancellor of the German Empire in 1914, to be tried in place of his sovereign. Lt. Col. Sir Maurice Hankey—today Lord Hankey—who had been serving since April 19 as Secretary General of the Four and had drafted the reports being distributed daily at Lloyd George's orders to each member of the council, then put the following question: "After the departure of President Wilson and Mr. Lloyd George, are the minutes of the Council of Four to be sent to Mr. Balfour and Mr. Lansing?"

The exchange of remarks which followed is related at the end of our second volume, but it is necessary to give the gist here in a few lines. President Wilson's reply was categorical: in inviting his colleagues to come to his house in order to tackle the most pressing problems, he had insisted on the confidential and, so to speak, private character that their conversations had to assume. This character had to be preserved: he added that, if he had thought the question might even be raised, he would have been opposed to anyone taking notes. "Our decisions have been recorded; they are what our successors have the right to know. What I don't want to be divulged is our conversations." M. Clemenceau supported him, indicating the danger of breaking the secrecy of deliberations in which, thanks precisely to this privacy, it had been possible to move things along without occasionally fearing to change one's mind, while using direct language without worrying about diplomatic niceties: "No one must be able to quote the remarks we have made in conversations as free as ours have been, or be able to say: 'On such a day, this one spoke against France; on such and such a day, that one spoke against England.'" However, he made the reservation that, having sat on the council only in the capacity of head of the French government, it would be impossible for him not to transmit the reports to his successor. Messrs. Lloyd George and Sonnino being of the same mind on this point, it was finally agreed that, under this express reservation, these documents could neither be circulated nor published. No time limit was stipulated. It is rather ironical to point out that the first infraction of this rule was committed by one of President Wilson's secretaries at the peace conference, who, in a work written three years later to justify the

---

[3] The Orlando government having fallen, Italy was represented by Baron Sonnino.

policy of his chief,[4] reproduced in its entirety one of the reports drafted by Sir Maurice Hankey.

These were published only after a very long delay. It was the British government which for the longest time opposed that publication: its successive heads thought it was not desirable to do it so long as Mr. Lloyd George was alive. Indeed, it was the American Department of State which had to undertake it. A first volume appeared in 1944, the second in 1946; they are part of the collection, *Papers Relating to the Foreign Relations of the United States*.[5]

The documents presented here for the first time are not, any more than those which have just been mentioned, official minutes in the proper meaning of the word, whose text could have been established only after the approval of those who had participated in the debates. For the historian, it is a great advantage, for he will have at his disposal two parallel sets of evidence, completely independent from each other, which have never been submitted to any revision or change.[6] Moreover, mine are not minutes like those in the Hankey series, drafted in the form of official documents, of which the Four, if they did not countersign the text, received copies as soon as they were produced. They are simply the notes that I had to take in order to be able to carry out my duties as interpreter. Each morning, I dictated their contents on the basis of my manuscript, written in haste the day before and rapidly becoming illegible, to an excellent supervisory stenographer of the Chamber of Deputies put at my disposal for that purpose. The next day, I would turn over the typewritten sheets to the office of the French Prime Minister.

One will find few discrepancies between these notes and Colonel Hankey's minutes. However, there are notable differences between the two series. My notes cover a more extended period; their contents, like their object, are, on the contrary, more lim-

---

[4] Ray Stannard Baker, *Woodrow Wilson and World Settlement*, 3 vols. (New York, 1922-1923). [Actually, André Tardieu, in articles in *L'Illustration* in 1920 and in *La Paix* (Paris, 1921), quoted occasionally from Mantoux's transcripts.—Ed.'s note.]

[5] *Papers Relating to the Foreign Relations of the United States: The Paris Peace Conference*, Vols. 5 and 6 (Washington, 1944-46).

[6] There can be added here, for the sessions where questions of interest to Italy were discussed, the notes of Count Aldrovandi Marescotti, then Secretary-General of the Italian delegation: *Guerra Diplomatica, Ricordi e Frammenti di Diario (1914-1919)* (Milan, 1936), and *Nuovi Ricordi e Frammenti di Diario* (Milan, 1938).

ited; and, moreover, their style and, if I may say so, their color, are quite different.

Of 148 reports of meetings,[7] the series of my notes contains thirty-seven which are lacking in Sir Maurice Hankey's. The latter attended the deliberations of the Four regularly only from April 19 onwards. Until then, because of their desire to preserve the most confidential character of their meetings, the Four had not wanted to use regular services other than those of an interpreter. Many of the meetings in question are of great importance: for example, in the first days, those in which the evacuation of Odessa was decided upon, and the idea of a *cordon sanitaire* to oppose Bolshevism was discussed; in which Clemenceau voiced his objections to the proposals presented by Lloyd George in his "Fontainebleau Memorandum," asking for a softening of the terms of the treaty; in which Marshal Foch explained to the Four his views on the Rhine, conceived as a permanent strategic frontier of the West; those in which the question of reparation began to emerge from the quicksand of the commissions of experts. I shall not attempt to give a list of them here. A note at the beginning of each report indicates if its equivalent is or is not found in the parallel series.

Sir Maurice Hankey—I come to the second point to which I must draw attention—was a high civil servant of exceptional merit and experience. During the war, he had served as Secretary of the Committee of Imperial Defence. He became the head of the secretariat of the [War] Cabinet from its creation at the beginning of 1916. And, at the peace conference, he was Secretary-General of the British delegation. When Mr. Lloyd George proposed to his three colleagues that he make available to them Colonel Hankey's services, it was to provide the Council of Four with a much-needed secretary: a secretary entrusted with multiple executive tasks, whose notes of meetings had to serve as a basis of action. That is why those notes contain a large number of references corresponding so closely, step by step, to the agenda of the meetings, the form to be given to decisions taken, and the instructions to be transmitted to the commissions. And to these are added a mass of documents, some of them very voluminous: drafts, reports with their annexes, pieces of correspondence. One will find there, at the end of the second volume [Volume VI], all the notes

---

[7] My numbering is different from that of Hankey, who counts as one meeting each change of the principal subject of discussion or of the people called in by the Four.

exchanged with the German delegation about the terms of peace. Of all these documents, some had been read in the meetings of the council and translated by me—but they only passed through my hands. Others had been presented to the council only in order to be sent to the appropriate commissions. All these pieces of information and documents (whose immediate importance was considerable, to say nothing of the interest that they present for a complete study of the work of the conference) fill hundreds of pages. If one adds them to those which contain the records of the meetings, they have enormously enlarged and enriched the two volumes issued under the auspices of the State Department.

My task was more modest and of another kind. It consisted of reproducing as faithfully as possible what I had just heard, and in such a way as to communicate the same impression I had received. I set myself to retaining, not only the meaning of what each speaker had just said (while preserving to each idea and fact enunciated its relative place and value), but also the expression and the significant or simply characteristic words.[8] The duties of Sir Maurice Hankey, on account of his assignment, were above all of an administrative order. Mine were, so to speak, of a psychological kind. Concerning form, I made use of the style of direct discourse—that of the same discourse I had to repeat in another language. According to English usage, it is the style of indirect discourse, comparable to that of Latin, which is always used in official records. That is why the two accounts give appreciably different impressions, even when they agree in detail.

The secrecy which has for so long surrounded the deliberations of the Four, and which the present publication helps to dispel, has encouraged, as always happens in such cases, the birth of legends and the persistence of distorted impressions. The pages which follow show the Council of Four and its members just as they were in their sometimes difficult discussions and afterwards, in their efforts to arrive at common solutions which were often imperfect and demanded sacrifices. Have they not too often been judged as if each of them had to decide alone? The brilliant and cruel picture, painted by the author of a celebrated work, has greatly contributed to the increase of the number of his readers and to the subversion of their judgments. What he de-

---

[8] I did not always have to translate: since M. Clemenceau spoke very good English, certain meetings took place in that language. But I had to be alert at every moment. Moreover, I had to translate, without writing them down, some bits of conversation, for example, when the Four had already adjourned.

picts for us is one of the meetings in which the Four heard the often contradictory arguments of a number of more or less eminent experts on economic and financial matters. These meetings took place on the first floor of the private mansion where President Wilson resided, in a large drawing room adorned by two magnificent portraits by Goya. It is there that Keynes represents to us "the President and Prime Minister in the midst of a milling crowd and a tumult of voices . . . and Clemenceau, taciturn and detached, seated on his brocaded sofa as on a throne, his soul disillusioned and withered up, very old and very weary, casting on that scene a look of almost diabolical skepticism."[9]

In the little library on the ground floor, where, day after day, the work of the Four took place, things went on completely otherwise. There was not room for many persons, to begin with, and Clemenceau, as will be seen, had nothing of a royal and malevolent mummy about him. If, moreover, the Council of Four took the place of the Council of Ten (in which the heads of governments and the Foreign Ministers were often surrounded by delegates, members of commissions, and assisted by a full secretariat) it was precisely in order to reduce to a minimum—along with the risk of indiscretions—the delays which accompanied important decisions.

A faithful account of the meetings of the Council of Four shows their true atmosphere: the respective positions and the reciprocal attitudes of its members and the tone of their meetings which, contrary to certain ill-natured gossip, remained always courteous, even when the opposition of views and of interests was most serious. Concerning the character and role of each of the speakers, knowledge of their conversations makes it possible to complete or correct what one already knows about them. President Wilson has been represented by some as an imperious idealist, incapable of compromise; by others as an idealist without consistency, easily turned from his path by the Machiavellis of the Old World. We will see with what impolitic obstinacy he launched, against the advice of his French and English colleagues, his appeal to the Italian people on the Adriatic question. But one will also find him concerned to inform himself and to understand, taking great account of what he had learned, and showing—for example, in his negotiations with the Japanese on

---

[9] John M. Keynes, *The Economic Consequences of the Peace* [London, 1919], p. 28. [The Editors have been unable to find this exact quotation. However, see the portrait of Clemenceau in Keynes, pp. 29-31.]

the Shantung question—a tenacity intermixed with a sense of the possible, the merit of which has not been acknowledged. The liveliness of perception, the ingenuity derived from the unexpected resources of a Lloyd George, his supple maneuvering, will reveal themselves in the service of his unremitting designs. From my notes, we will learn perhaps nothing new about M. Orlando, pathetic defender of a compromised cause, or about the concentrated obsession of M. Sonnino, going so far as remorse, openly expressed, for having involved his country in a murderous war without power to assure all the benefits promised it. But they will allow us to read for the first time certain powerful speeches for the defense by Clemenceau, to hear, so to speak, his incisive observations, to measure the strength of his staying power and the realism of his concessions.

It goes without saying that, in documents like these, the heart of the questions counts more than the behavior of the men. In this report, the records that one is about to read add certain important points to Sir Maurice Hankey's. I will give two examples. No article of the Treaty of Versailles engendered more passion and criticism between the two wars than the famous Article 231, placed at the head of Section VIII (Reparation). It is the one in which Germany acknowledged that she and her allies "are responsible for having caused all the losses and damages suffered by the Allied and Associated Governments and their nationals as a consequence of the war which has been imposed upon them by the aggression of Germany and her allies." This dangerous text grew out of the search for a compromise formula between the total claims, more theoretical than real, inspired by the preoccupation of domestic politics at least as much in England as in France, and the categorical objections of President Wilson, who pointed to the commitments taken before the conclusion of the Armistice.

The discussion had been exhausting. I have noted, at the date of April 5 (Colonel Hankey was not present at the meeting), the following suggestion of Mr. Norman Davis, one of the principal American experts: "We can write that Germany is morally responsible for the war and all its consequences and that, legally, she is responsible for damages to property and persons, according to the formula adopted"—which meant a formula conforming to the terms of the note in which President Wilson had, on November 5, 1918, conveyed to the Germans the interpretation of the Fourteen Points accepted by the Allied governments. To which Clemenceau replied: "It is a matter of wording; I believe we can find a way out." Hence Article 231, immediately followed by the one which, acknowledging the impossibility of total reparation, limited it to the damages caused to the civilian populations and their property. But what was only a "question of wording" was bound to have considerable psychological and political consequences.

Another example relates to the erratic attitude of the Allied and Associated Governments towards Bolshevism, as it was then called. The conversations of the Four make it possible to observe that position at close range during a period when the situation in Russia appeared very uncertain. From its first meetings, the council had to decide on the questions of Odessa and the defense of Rumania. It was unanimous in rejecting the plan of a military barrier extending from the Baltic to the Black Sea, an undertaking that President Wilson compared to trying to use a broom to sweep back a spring tide. One will see in other meetings how inadequate the Big Four's information was, and how their conclusions could be affected by this fact.

I have wished, in this brief preface, only to explain the nature of the documents which follow and to give a few indications of what makes them interesting. The Ministry of Foreign Affairs and the National Center of Scientific Research have recognized the usefulness of their publication, which they made possible by their support. I here express to them my indebtedness.

Paul Mantoux.

N.B. The letter H in the notes designates the series of the reports drafted by Sir Maurice Hankey.

Abbreviations

EMH	Edward Mandell House
FR 1919, Russia	Papers Relating to the Foreign Relations of the United States, 1919, Russia
PPC	Papers Relating to the Foreign Relations of the United States, The Paris Peace Conference, 1919
PWW	Arthur S. Link et al., eds., The Papers of Woodrow Wilson, 65 vols. to date (Princeton, N. J., 1966-)
WW	Woodrow Wilson

Maps

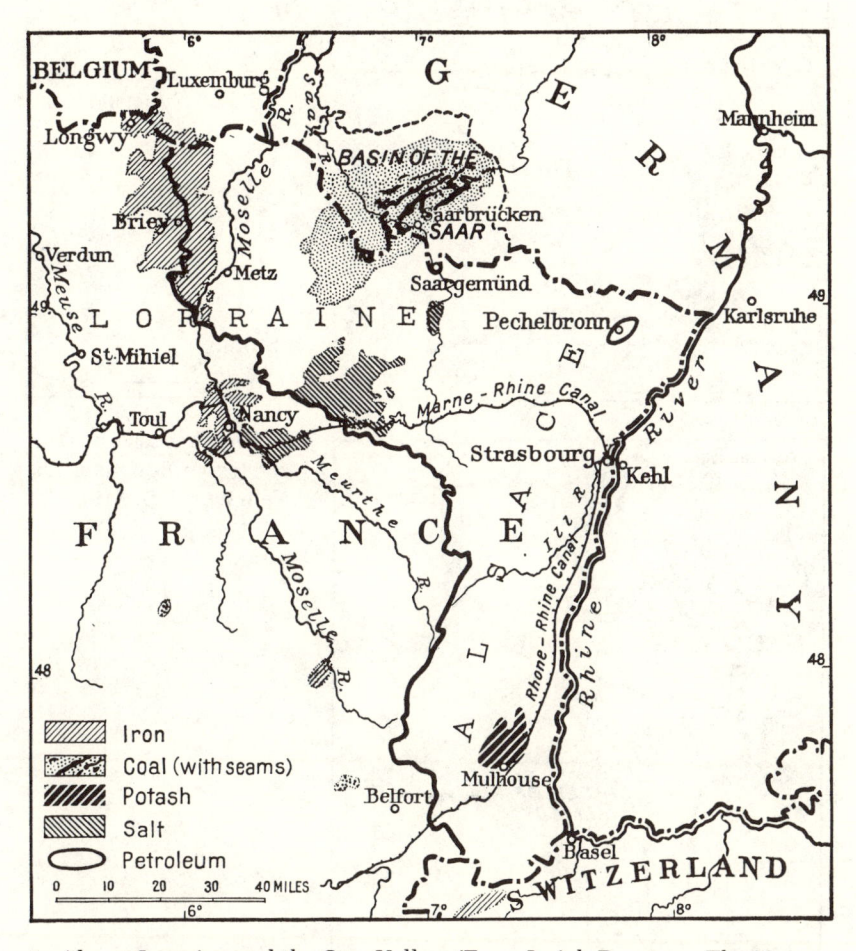

1. Alsace-Lorraine and the Saar Valley. (From Isaiah Bowman, *The New World: Problems in Political Geography*, 4th ed. [Yonkers-on-Hudson, N. Y., and Chicago: World Book Co., 1928], p. 155)

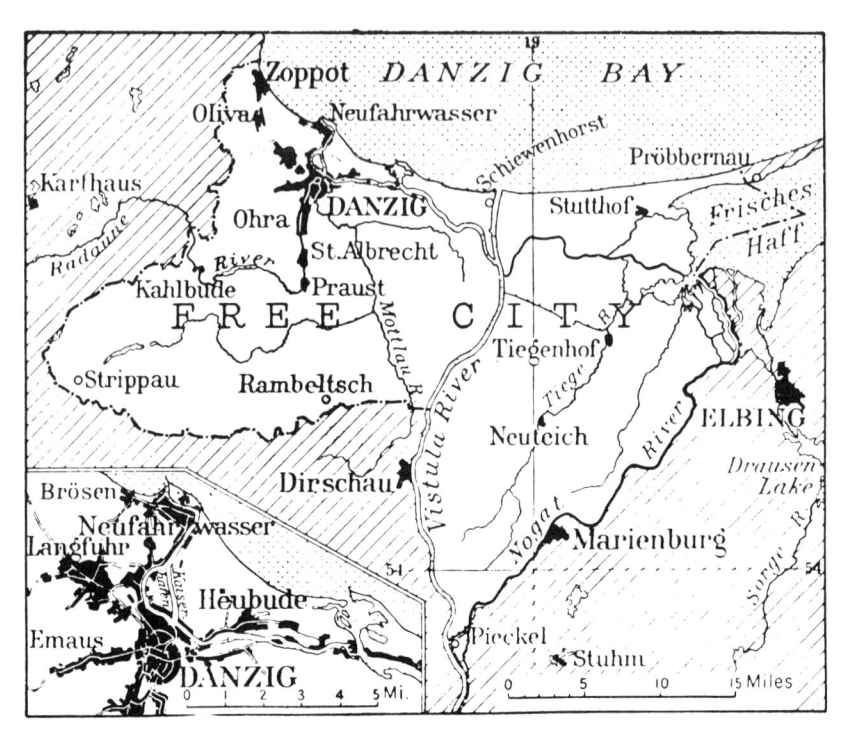

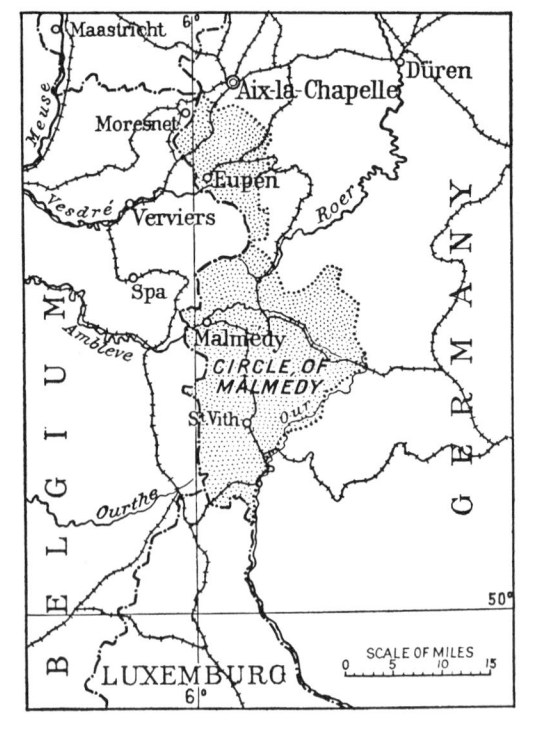

2. The Free City of Danzig. (From Bowman, *The New World*, p. 419)

3. Eupen and Malmédy. (From Bowman, *The New World*, p. 201)

4. Disputed Areas of the Adriatic Region. (From Charles H. Haskins and Robert H. Lord, *Some Problems of the Peace Conference* [Cambridge, Mass.: Harvard University Press, 1920], facing p. 262)

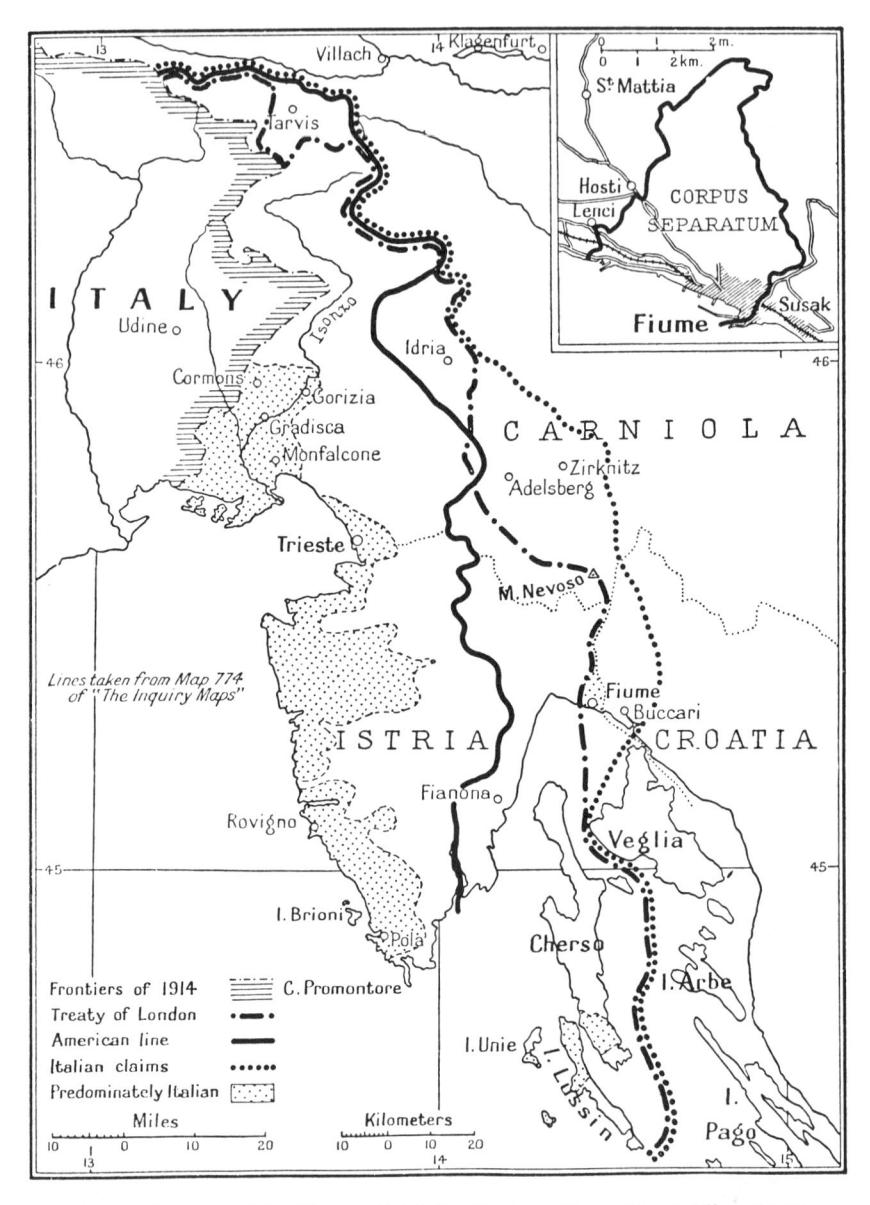

5. Disputed Areas of the Upper Adriatic Region. (From René Albrecht-Carrié, *Italy at the Paris Conference* [New York: Columbia University Press, 1938], p. 93; used by permission of Columbia University Press)

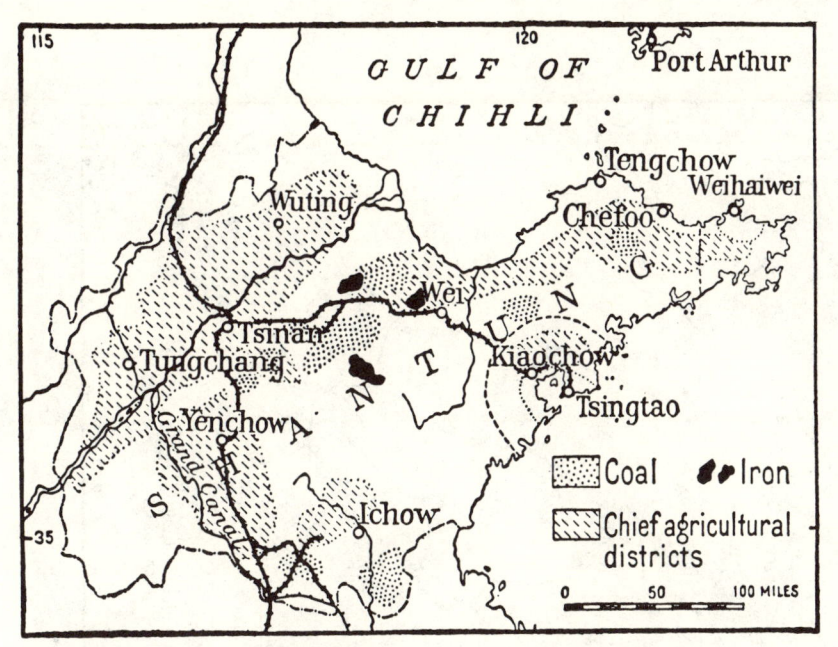

6. The Shantung Peninsula. (From Bowman, *The New World*, p. 575)

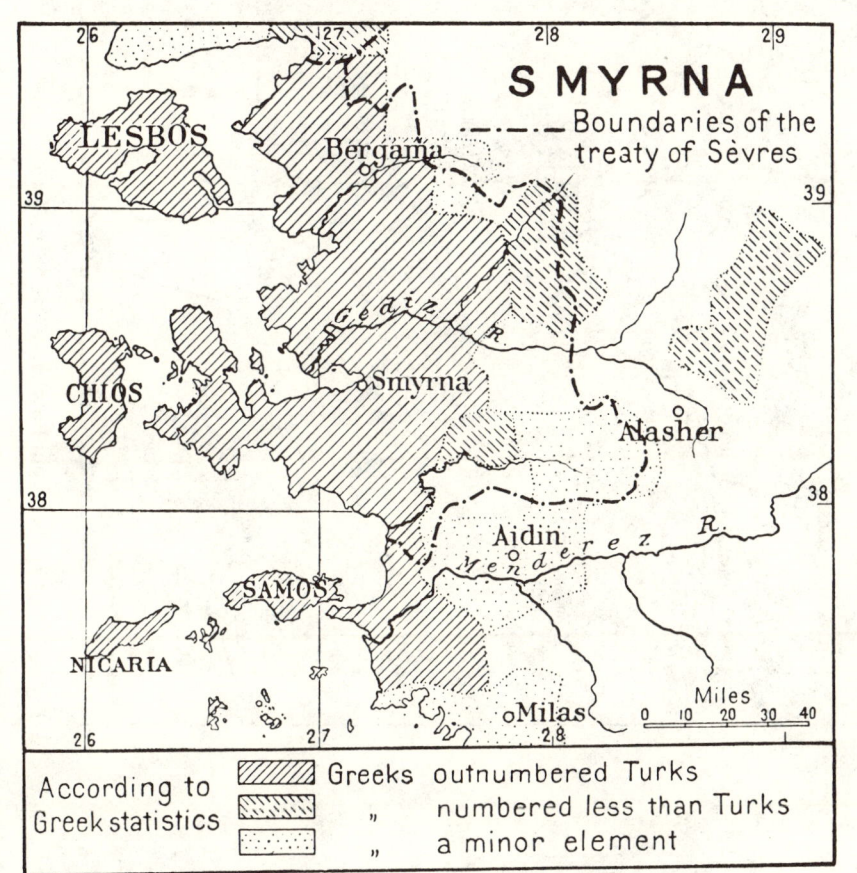

7. Smyrna and Its Environs. (From Bowman, *The New World*, p. 403)

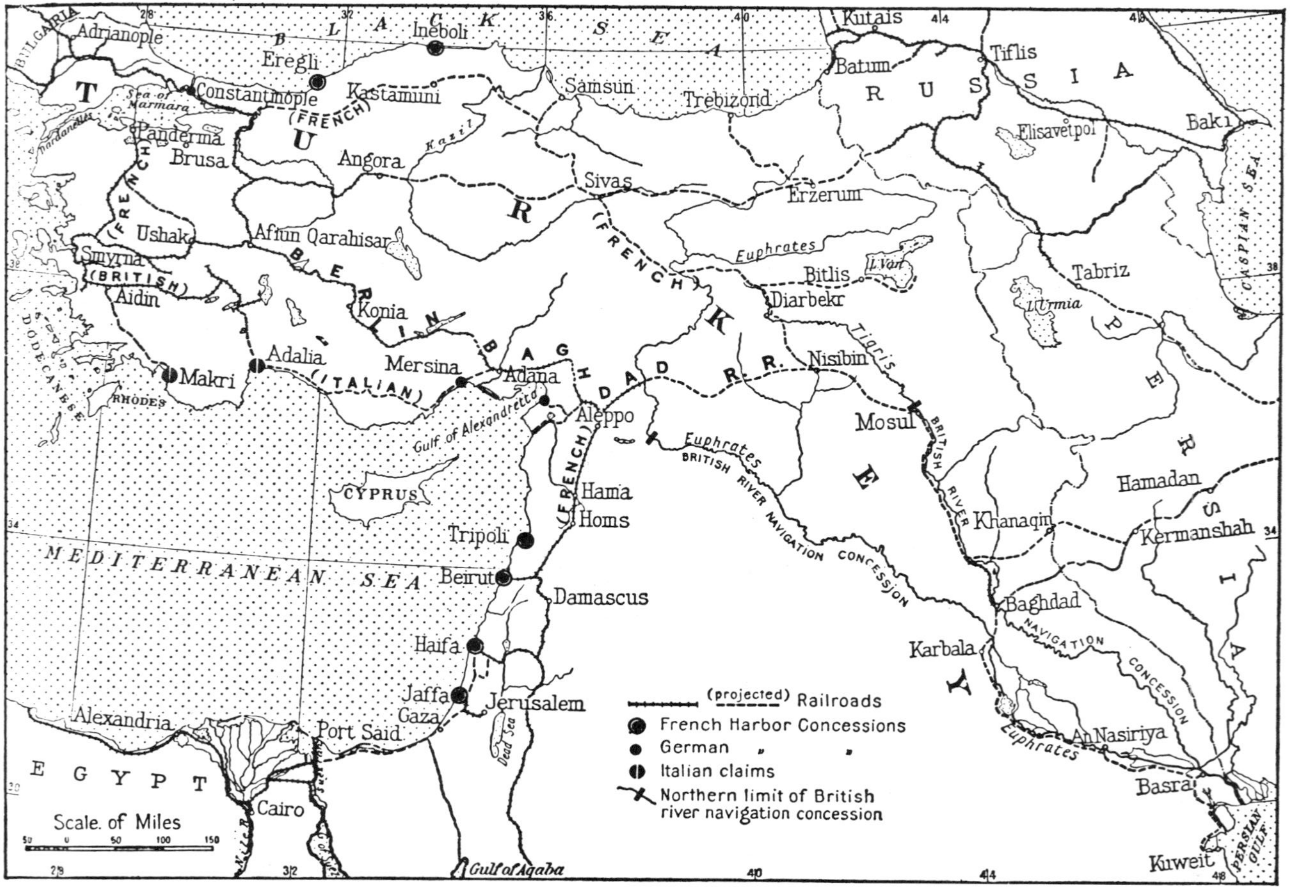

8. Turkey in 1919. (From Bowman, The New World, p. 489)

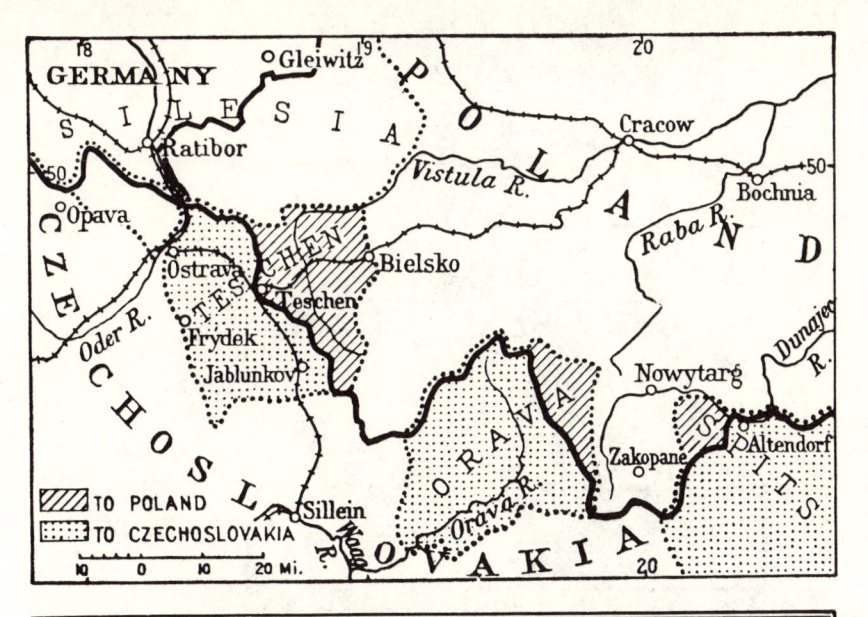

9. The Duchy of Teschen. (From Bowman, *The New World*, p. 415)

10. The Klagenfurt Basin, Tarvis, and the Assling Triangle. (From René Albrecht-Carrié, *Italy at the Paris Peace Conference*, p. 165; used by permission of Columbia University Press)

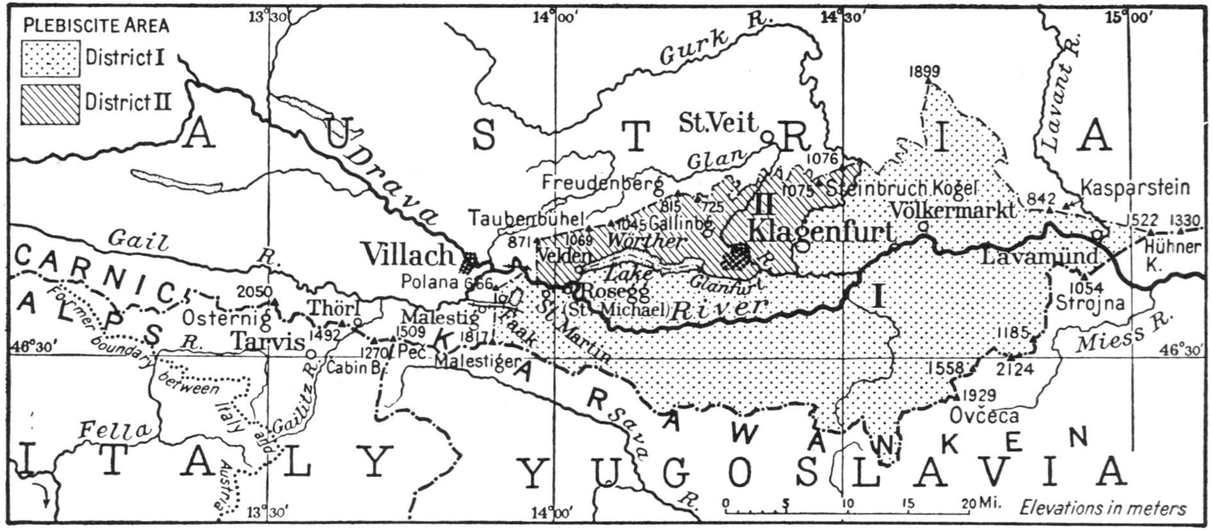

11. The Klagenfurt Basin. (From Bowman, The New World, p. 313)

12. Hungary's Shifting Borders. (From Harold W. V. Temperley, A History of the Peace Conference of Paris, 6 vols. [London: Oxford University Press and Hodder & Stoughton, 1920–1924], Vol. I, facing p. 352)

REFERENCE
1. Hungarian Armistice line. 13th November 1918
2. Extension of Rumanian line, February 1919
3. Rumanian Treaty line of 17th August 1916
4. Permanent boundary of Czecho-Slovakia as announced by the Supreme Council, 13th June 1919
5. Approximate line of greatest Rumanian advance

NOTE On the 19th March 1919 Col Vix in the name of the Allies summoned the Hungarian Government to withdraw its forces to line ③. The area between ② and ③ was to be treated as a neutral zone. On the 13th June 1919 the Conference ordered the Soviet Government at Budapest to withdraw its forces behind the lines of permanent frontiers accorded to Czecho Slovakia ④ and to Rumania approximately that of ②.

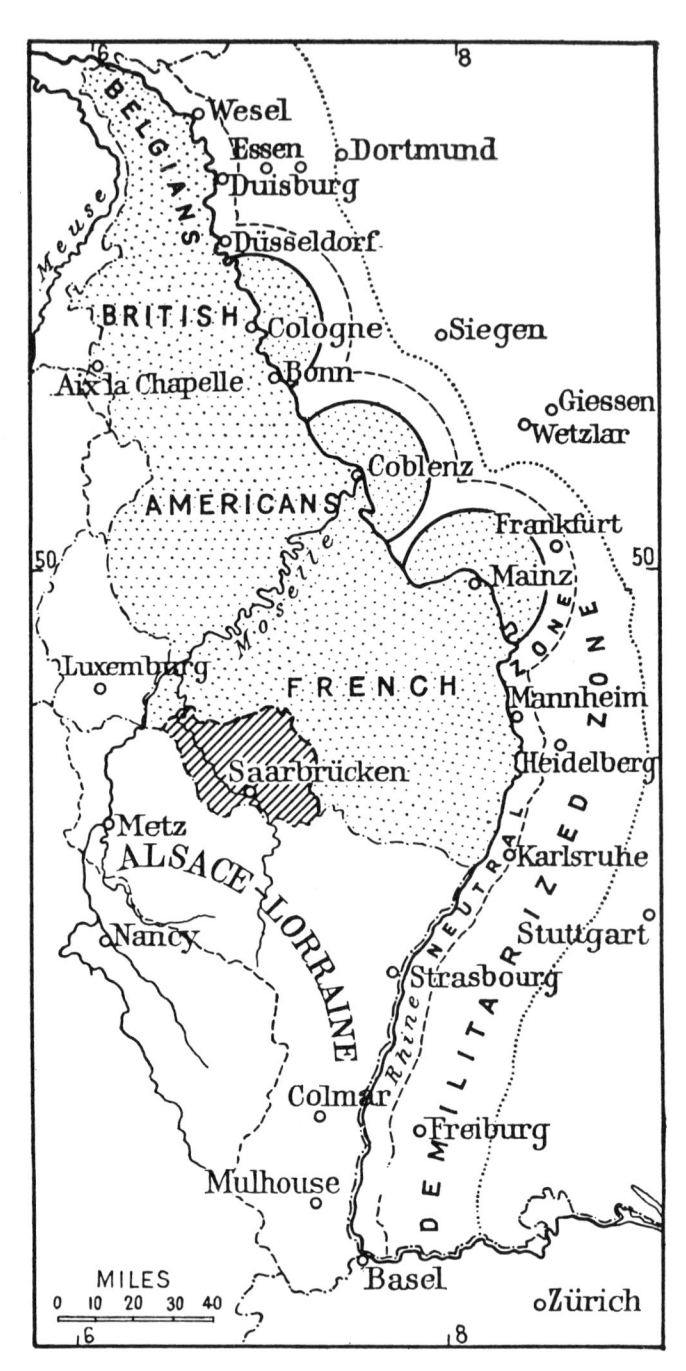

13. The Left Bank of the Rhine and Occupation Zones.
(From Bowman, *The New World*, p. 156)

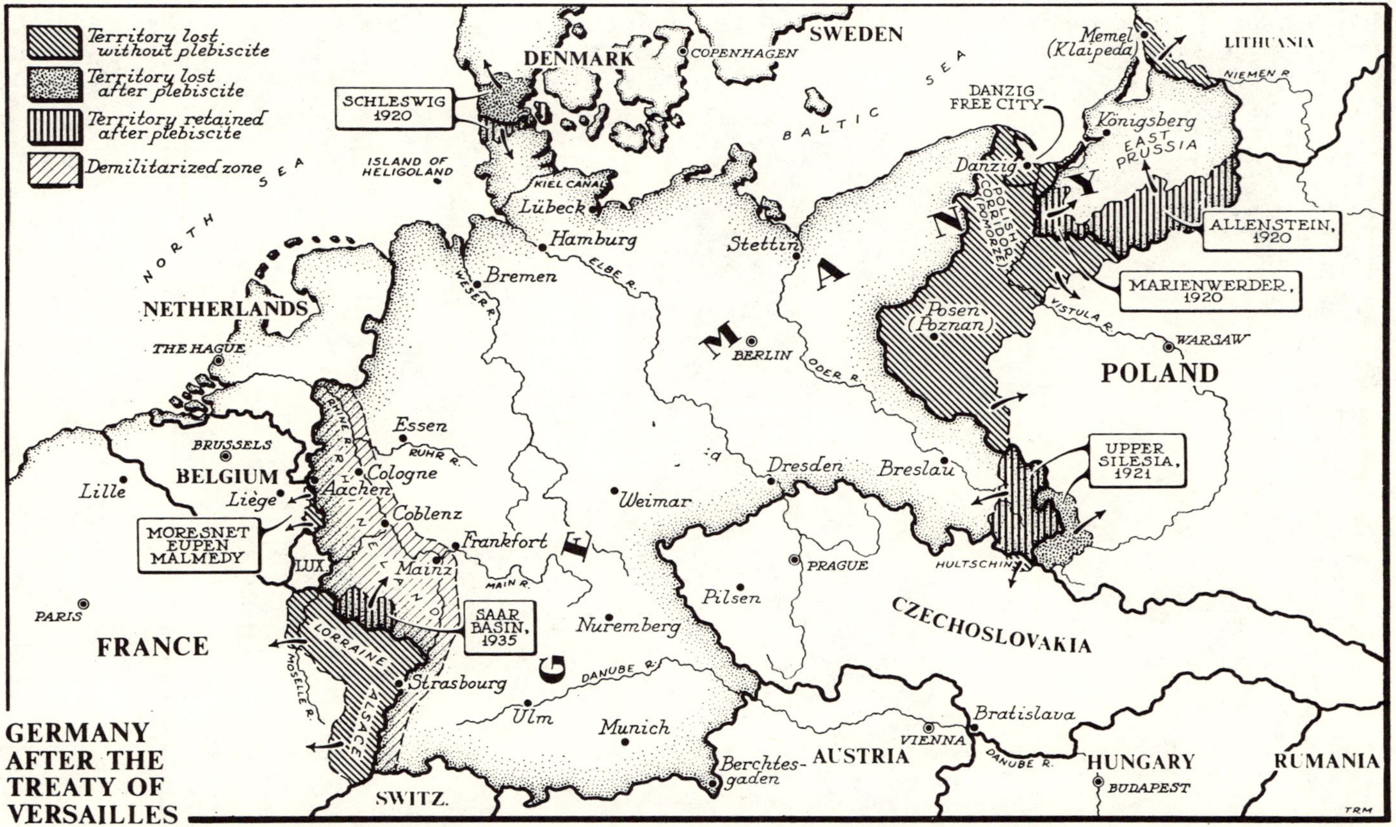

14. Germany after the Treaty of Versailles. (From Arthur S. Link, *American Epoch: A History of the United States Since the 1890's* [New York: Alfred A. Knopf, Inc., 1963], p. 221)

The Deliberations
of the Council of Four
(March 24–June 28, 1919)

VOLUME I

I

Conversation between President Wilson and MM. Clemenceau, Lloyd George, and Orlando*

MARCH 24, 1919, 3 P.M.

President Wilson. At this moment, there is a real race between peace and anarchy, and the public is beginning to show its impatience. Yesterday, amidst the ruins of Soissons,[1] a woman, speaking to me, said: "When will you give us peace?"

I believe we should take the most difficult and urgent questions in hand amongst the four of us—questions such as reparations, the protection of France against aggression, and the Italian frontier along the Adriatic coast. Once the most important and difficult questions have been settled, the road will be cleared, and the rest will go quickly.

M. Clemenceau. I would add to your list the fate of German Austria.

Mr. Lloyd George. I support President Wilson's suggestion, especially regarding the question of reparations, which is the most difficult of all. This is the only method that can extricate us from our difficulties. Our experts will never come to an agreement. The problem is twofold: we must know what the Germans will be able to pay, and how we will distribute it amongst ourselves. The experts will never extricate themselves unless we agree on a common policy and assume the risks of our decision. I propose then, along with President Wilson, that we have a meeting of the heads of governments, twice a day if necessary, in order to move more quickly, and that we begin tomorrow.

M. Clemenceau. I join in this proposal, and I think as you do that it will allow us to speed up the course of business.

*Not represented in H. [hereinafter H., also *PPC*, V and VI].

[1] Wilson had spent the previous day, a Sunday, visiting the battlefields in northern France. For a detailed account of this trip, see the extract from the Diary of Dr. Grayson, March 23, 1919, printed in *PWW*, Vol. 56, pp. 194-200.

II

Conversation between President Wilson and MM. Clemenceau, Lloyd George, and Orlando*

MARCH 25, 1919, 11 A.M.

—President Wilson explains the reasons for including the document relating to the League of Nations in the peace preliminaries.[1] It would be no trouble to get this text approved along with that of the treaty if the two were part of a whole. Otherwise, the discussion on the League of Nations in the American Senate will cause prolonged debates and perhaps some difficulties.

M. Clemenceau. If the Germans are not admitted to the League of Nations—and this is out of the question—how can the clauses relating to the Covenant of the League be included in the peace preliminaries which the Germans will have to sign?

—President Wilson observes that, even if the Germans are not admitted to the League of Nations at the beginning, the fact that this League has to be mentioned in more than one article of the treaty, and that it will be used to enforce a number of measures which the Germans must accept, is enough to justify joining the two documents.

M. Clemenceau. I accept, if it is well understood that this can be done without the Germans being admitted to the League of Nations at the start.

Mr. Lloyd George. For my part, I would rather see the Germans in the League of Nations than outside it. That would give us a stronger hold over them. But I understand M. Clemenceau's objection and the public feeling behind it.

M. Orlando. It seems to me necessary to join the two documents, given the fact that the administration of colonies under the mandate system, the mutual territorial guarantee against all aggression belonging to members of the League and, finally, disarmament rest on the existence and functioning of the League of

---

*Not represented in H.

[1] That is, the Covenant of the League of Nations. For the draft that was at this time still under discussion by the Commission on the League of Nations, see Wilson's address to the Third Plenary Session of the peace conference on February 14, 1919, printed in *PWW*, Vol. 55, pp. 164-78.

Nations. On the last point, Germany, being compelled to disarm, might hesitate to sign without a guarantee of the League of Nations against unjustifed aggression.

—*President Wilson's proposal is accepted.*

—M. Clemenceau draws attention to the fact that he maintains his objection to the proposed text creating the League of Nations, as it has been drafted. He would like to see it made complete by clauses establishing (1) control of German armaments and (2) a military sanction. If this sanction does not exist, there will have to be other guarantees for us.

REPARATION AND GERMANY'S CAPACITY TO PAY[2]

President Wilson. In determining Germany's capacity to pay, we must avoid pushing our demands to a point which would allow

---

[2] Almost from the outset of the conference, the question of the kind and amount of reparation to be demanded from Germany had been one of the most contentious issues in the negotiations among the British, French, and American delegations. During the pre-Armistice talks in Paris on November 4, 1918, both Lloyd George and Clemenceau had agreed with the American position that demands for compensation by Germany should be strictly limited to all civilian damages caused by German aggression. However, at the same time, the two Prime Ministers had also repeatedly assured their people that they would insist on exacting the highest possible amount from Germany and would, in fact, try to make Germany pay for the total cost of the war to England and France.

Thus, when the Council of Ten, on January 22, 1919, appointed the Commission on Reparation of Damage (the Reparation Commission) to evaluate the losses suffered by the Allies and to assess Germany's capacity to pay, this commission soon reached a deadlock, with the British and French experts arguing for the inclusion of war costs in the total reparation bill and the American members determined to adhere to the terms of the Pre-Armistice Agreement. Even after Lloyd George and Clemenceau finally abandoned their insistence on reimbursement for total war costs, the Reparation Commission still failed to come to an agreement. While avoiding the term "war costs," the British and French members continued to ask for reparations large enough to fulfill the promises of their Prime Ministers, and their figures ran as high as $120 billion (£24 billion) and $200 billion (£40 billion), respectively. The American experts, on the other hand, consistently maintained that Germany's capacity to pay could not exceed $30 billion (£6 billion).

In an effort to break this impasse, a special committee composed of Norman H. Davis, Edwin S. Montagu, and Louis Loucheur met on March 10, 1919, and agreed to adopt the American figure. However, although the Big Three endorsed the committee's recommendations on March 15, three days later, Lloyd George, surrendering to the demands of his hard-line financial advisers, Lords Sumner and Cunliffe, repudiated the understanding and called for an amount almost double what had been agreed upon. As a result, the special committee, on which no German government to sign the peace treaty. We must also take into account the fact that Germany's capacity to pay is reduced, due to her loss of important and economically very valuable territories, such as Lorraine with its mines.

Sumner and Cunliffe had replaced Montagu, abandoned its attempts to arrive at a mutually agreeable figure and, on March 25, presented a set of widely divergent calculations to the Big Three.

The draft of the reparation terms, the so-called Third Revise, submitted by the committee on March 25, thus avoided mentioning any specific figures and merely contained general statements about the total war losses for which the Central Powers were responsible, the portion of this total amount which would be demanded in reparation, and a schedule of payments of whatever sum would eventually be specified. The committee also recommended that the Allied and Associated Powers establish a permanent commission to oversee the payment of reparations and, if necessary, to postpone or modify those payments. In an amendment to its report, the committee listed the American, French, and British proposals for the total amount of reparations to be demanded from Germany. The American proposal suggested a minimum of $25 billion (£5 billion) and a maximum of $35 billion (£7 billion); the French, a minimum of $31 billion (£6.2 billion) and a maximum of $47 billion (£9.4 billion); and the British, a single figure of $55 billion (£11 billion).

It was these recommendations and figures that the Big Four had before them in the present meeting and that formed the basis for future discussions on the reparation question. The draft provisions and proposals, together with explanatory memoranda prepared for Wilson by his financial advisers, are printed in Philip M. Burnett, ed., *Reparation at the Paris Peace Conference: From the Standpoint of the American Delegation*, 2 vols. (New York, 1940), I, 704-706, 711-19. See also the memorandum by Norman H. Davis, March 25, 1919, printed in *PWW*, Vol. 56, pp. 270-72.

Burnett's lengthy introduction provides a good overview of the discussions over reparation. David Hunter Miller, *My Diary at the Conference of Paris, with Documents*, 21 vols. (New York, 1924), includes many drafts and position papers, as do Volumes 55 to 61 of *PWW*. For succinct discussions of the reparation settlement, see Paul M. Birdsall, *Versailles Twenty Years After* (New York, 1941), pp. 238-63, and Seth P. Tillman, *Anglo-American Relations at the Paris Peace Conference of 1919* (Princeton, N. J., 1961), pp. 229-59; A[ntony]. Lentin, *Lloyd George, Woodrow Wilson and the Guilt of Germany* (Baton Rouge, La., 1985), is an insightful retrospective view. Marc Trachtenberg, *Reparation in World Politics: France and European Economic Diplomacy, 1916-1923* (New York, 1980), and Étienne Mantoux, *The Carthaginian Peace or the Economic Consequences of Mr. Keynes* (London, New York, and Toronto, 1946), put the reparation settlement in historical perspective and address the arguments in John Maynard Keynes' scathing attack, *The Economic Consequences of the Peace*. For accounts by participants, see Thomas W. Lamont's chapter in Edward M. House and Charles Seymour, eds., *What Really Happened at Paris: The Story of the Peace Conference, 1918-1919* (New York, 1921), pp. 259-90; Bernard M. Baruch, *The Making of the Reparation and Economic Sections of the Treaty* (New York and London, 1920), pp. 15-75; André Tardieu, *The Truth about the Treaty* (London, 1921), pp. 280-352; and David Lloyd George, *The Truth about the Peace Treaties*, 2 vols. (London, 1938), I, 435-513.

Our financial advisers have been unable to agree on the figures up to now, and there are great divergences among the estimates.

—Mr. Lloyd George believes that M. Loucheur agrees with Mr. Norman Davis on the sum of seven billion pounds as representing the present sum of what Germany would be able to pay.

—M. Clemenceau declares that M. Loucheur said nothing of the kind to him. Confusion must be avoided. What M. Loucheur accepted was an arrangement that would reduce the annual payments for a certain number of years.

—President Wilson examines the figures submitted to him. The minimum estimate gives 8.7 billion pounds sterling as the total sum of annual payments, which corresponds to an actual present value of five billion pounds sterling, if interest and amortization are taken into account. The maximum corresponding estimates are thirteen billion pounds and seven billion pounds.

President Wilson. The report I have before me expresses doubts as to the duration of payments; it may not be in the interest of the Allies to prolong it. It indicates the present value of what Germany can pay to be a maximum figure of thirty-five billion dollars and a minimum figure of twenty-five billion. Each year a commission would determine the sum to be paid—between the maximum and the minimum—and would also decide the proportion payable in marks. A great degree of uncertainty remains in all these figures.

Mr. Lloyd George. On the subject of distribution—a much more difficult question, because here there is no longer agreement but competition amongst our interests, and because we have to consider our public opinions—I refer to the letter we jointly addressed to President Wilson before the signing of the Armistice.[3] We declared that we would demand reparation for property and damages suffered by persons in the civilian populations.

On this last point, we can take as a base figure each state's costs for pensions granted to families of men killed or disabled by the war. Under this procedure, we must be careful not to allow the figures to rise beyond what is strictly justifiable. Belgium, for example—where, even though the enemy deprived the country of much of its industrial equipment, direct devastation was lim-

---

[3] Actually, the memorandum of observations by the Allied governments on the correspondence between Wilson and the German government. It affirmed, among other things, the understanding of the Allies that compensation would be made by Germany "for all damage done to the civilian population of the Allies and their property . . . by the aggression of Germany by land, by sea, and from the air." See EMH to WW, Nov. 4, 1918, *PWW*, Vol. 51, pp. 580-82.

ited—presents very exaggerated claims to us. She puts in the debit column, amongst others, losses sustained by commercial establishments. We cannot allow claims of this type, since it would raise all our figures to unbelievable proportions.

As for France, no one doubts that in strict justice the most complete possible reparation is due her; but it seems to us that the figures presented in her name are excessive. After all, the area of land devastated is very limited in relation to the whole of her territory, and it includes no very large cities. Lille, Valenciennes, etc., were occupied and more or less pillaged, but not destroyed. The figure the French financiers have arrived at is so high that it approaches the value of the total national wealth in 1908, which cannot be admitted.

I propose to settle the question on a simple basis of distribution between us and France. What Germany can pay being represented by 100, I propose that France receive 50, and Great Britain 30, 20 being reserved for the other powers. This proportion would give France a very marked advantage; but I could not, in the face of British public opinion, go below the proportion I propose to reserve for Great Britain.

M. Clemenceau. I enter my strong reservations on the observations just presented, and I ask that the figures be compared and submitted to a new study, if that is necessary.

President Wilson. Another important question is the interdependence of claims. Do Italy and Serbia have a claim against Germany? Certainly Austria-Hungary, having been dissolved, cannot indemnify them.

—M. Orlando observes that, without abandoning the principle of the liability of the successor states of the Austro-Hungarian Empire, he sees no solution to the problem unless there is an interdependence amongst all who are to pay and all who are to receive. The principle of interdependence cannot be rejected, both for a factual and a moral reason. In fact, German artillery bombarded Italian cities, and submarines in the Mediterranean were more often German than Austrian. From a moral point of view, it is impossible to admit that Italy should be without remedy because her debtor has disappeared.

—M. Orlando concludes by pointing out that Italy is the nation which bears the highest war costs in proportion to its total prewar wealth.

—Mr. Lloyd George asks for information about the Italian war debt and the cost of pensions.

M. Orlando. The debt is eighty billion lire, and national wealth before the war was 140 billion, and the annual amount of pensions will be 560 million lire.

—Mr. Lloyd George returns to the proposal to assign 50 per cent of the payments to France, 30 per cent to Great Britain, and 20 per cent to Italy, Serbia, and Belgium.

M. Orlando. There must be a clear definition of what will be allowed as reparation.

Mr. Lloyd George. I believe we are agreed on this point: reparation should be understood to mean compensation for property destroyed and losses caused to civilians through the death or mutilation of their next of kin.

III

Conversation between President Wilson and MM. Clemenceau, Lloyd George, and Orlando*

MARCH 25, 1919, 3:30 P.M.

THE SITUATION AT ODESSA[1] AND IN RUMANIA

M. Clemenceau. We have three questions for immediate consideration: (1) victualing Odessa; (2) aid to be given to the Poles by way of Danzig—but this might be considered settled; (3) help to be given the Rumanians who, threatened by the appearance of Bolshevism in Hungary,[2] ask us to provide them with outfits for

---

*Not represented in H.

[1] A contingent of French troops landed at Odessa on December 18, 1918, at the request of various anti-Bolshevik Ukrainian and Russian groups for an Allied intervention in the Ukraine to help stop the southwestern advance of Bolshevik forces. In the following months, two French and two Greek divisions, part of a Rumanian division, and a Polish brigade, amounting to about 65,000 men, occupied a sizable area along the northern shores of the Black Sea from Tiraspol to the Crimea, with main concentrations at Odessa and Sevastopol. For a detailed discussion, see Arthur E. Adams, *Bolsheviks in the Ukraine: The Second Campaign, 1918-1919* (New Haven and London, 1963), pp. 94-105, 186-214; John S. Reshetar, Jr., *The Ukrainian Revolution, 1917-1920: A Study in Nationalism* (Princeton, N. J., 1952), pp. 234-49; Dimitry V. Lehovich, *White against Red: The Life of General Anton Denikin* (New York, 1974), pp. 252-65; and Arno J. Mayer, *Politics and Diplomacy of Peacemaking: Containment and Counterrevolution at Versailles, 1918-1919* (New York, 1967), pp. 294-303.

[2] Although the provisional Hungarian government of President Mihály Károlyi had suffered from mounting economic chaos and social unrest, the catalyst for its fall had been the apparent Allied support of Serbian, Czech, and, partic-

their troops. On the Odessa question, I suggest we hear General Alby.

—General Alby is introduced.

General Alby. A series of telegrams from Generals Berthelot and Franchet d'Esperey raise the issue of the victualing of Odessa.

In his telegram of March 12, General Berthelot reveals that the loss of the resources of the southern Ukraine compels us to find

---

ularly, Rumanian military aggression. By the terms of the Armistice of Belgrade of November 13, 1918, Rumanian troops had occupied a large part of Hungarian territory in eastern Transylvania. However, by mid-December, Rumanian forces had begun to advance beyond the armistice line and had pushed ever deeper into Transylvania in an effort to seize all the territory which the Allies had promised Rumania in the Treaty of Bucharest of August 17, 1916, and which Rumanian representatives had claimed at the peace conference. In late February 1919, the Council of Four had finally decided to halt a further Rumanian penetration by establishing a neutral zone between Hungarian and Rumanian forces in Transylvania. Although short of the frontier promised the Rumanians in 1916, the eastern boundary of this neutral zone actually allowed the Rumanian troops to move even deeper into Hungarian territory than they had already advanced, while its western boundary compelled the Hungarians to withdraw their forces beyond the line of the Treaty of Bucharest.

When the Hungarian government was informed of the decision of the peace conference in a note presented on March 20 by Lt. Col. Ferdinand Vix, the French representative on the Allied Military Mission in Budapest, Károlyi concluded that the Allies intended to dismember Hungary, and he declared that no Hungarian government could accept such an ultimatum and survive. Károlyi's own party and the other moderate parties immediately withdrew from the governing coalition, leaving the field to the Social Democratic party. The Social Democrats in turn immediately began negotiations with Béla Kun and other leaders of the Communist party. The outcome of these talks was a fusion of the Social Democrats and Communists on March 21 and the proclamation, on March 22, of the Hungarian Soviet Republic. Kun, a former Socialist party functionary and political journalist who had only recently returned from Soviet Russia, became People's Commissar for Foreign Affairs and the real leader of the new soviet government.

For the various aspects of Allied policy toward Hungary and the rise of the Hungarian Soviet Republic, see Peter Pastor, *Hungary Between Wilson and Lenin: The Hungarian Revolution of 1918-1919 and the Big Three* (Boulder, Colo., 1976); Francis Deák, *Hungary at the Paris Peace Conference: The Diplomatic History of the Treaty of Trianon* (New York, 1942), pp. 3-58, 355-410; Sherman D. Spector, *Rumania at the Paris Peace Conference: A Study of the Diplomacy of Ioan I. C. Brătianu* (New York, 1962), pp. 67-123; Mayer, *Politics and Diplomacy of Peacemaking*, pp. 521-55; Rudolf L. Tökés, *Béla Kun and the Hungarian Soviet Republic: The Origins and Role of the Communist Party of Hungary in the Revolutions of 1918-1919* (New York, 1967), pp. 1-136; and Iván Völgyes, ed., *Hungary in Revolution, 1918-19: Nine Essays* (Lincoln, Neb., 1971) pp. 31-60.

another way to feed a million people in Odessa and the surrounding area. If we are unable to do this, it is useless to dream of holding Odessa.

—In answer to a question by Mr. Lloyd George about total Allied strength at Odessa, General Alby answers that there are approximately 25,000 men.

M. Clemenceau. This very morning General d'Esperey asked that Polish troops be sent him from Italy for Odessa.
General Alby. Italy is prepared to send 7,000 Poles; there are approximately 25,000 in Italy.

A second telegram from General Berthelot, dated March 17, reveals that the Russian authorities in Odessa are asking for 1,000 tons of bread a week. Another telegram of the same day warns us that the city of Odessa has only fifteen days of flour, five days of meat, etc. Fifteen thousand tons of coal per month are absolutely necessary; without it, the danger of a popular revolt would be very great.

A telegram from General d'Esperey, dated March 22, asks that the Allies send fifteen thousand tons of wheat a month to Odessa and at least ten thousand tons of coal, as well as manufactured goods which could be used, at the end of two months, to obtain, by way of exchange, wheat from the Kuban to replace the wheat sent by the Allies.

M. Clemenceau. This question is in the hands of the Food Commission.

—M. Clemenceau asks General Alby to discuss the situation in Rumania.

General Alby. Regarding the aid to be provided Rumania, we have a telegram from General Berthelot of March 12, which asks for 300,000 clothing kits and 400,000 pairs of shoes, harnesses, etc., for the Rumanians. If the Rumanian army was sufficiently outfitted, it could put ten divisions on the Dniester, for whose support two Allied divisions would suffice.

General Franchet d'Esperey telegraphed on March 19 that the Army of the East cannot provide the articles requested for the Rumanian army, and that, consequently, they must be sent from France. On March 14, a *note verbale* presented by the Rumanian Minister in Paris[3] asked the Allies to provide the means to combat the Russian and Ukrainian Bolshevik offensive and warned

---
[3] Victor Antonescu.

of a possible agreement between the Bolsheviks and the Hungarians.

—General Alby shows a map indicating the disposition of troops in Rumania.

General Alby. Without the outfits the Rumanians request, they cannot effectively use their own manpower, which is adequate.

President Wilson. Our situation is difficult to define. Nominally, we are friends of the Hungarians and even better friends of the Rumanians. What exactly is our position with regard to the Bolsheviks? No one can say. We have tried to prevent conflict between the Rumanians and the Hungarians by drawing a line and declaring that whoever crosses it would prejudice his own claims; it doesn't seem this method has produced the desired result.

M. Clemenceau. The Hungarians are not our friends but our enemies. Whilst other peoples of the Austro-Hungarian Empire have fought us despite themselves and, whenever they could, fought on our side, the Hungarians have been our resolute enemies and their leaders, like Tisza, are amongst those responsible for the war.

The boundary drawn in Transylvania is short of the border promised the Rumanians in 1916, and the imposition of this line was enough to induce the Károlyi government to give way to the Bolsheviks.

President Wilson. I am struck to see Rumania asking for the same material means which she has always complained of lacking in earlier circumstances.

Mr. Lloyd George. Since it is France which has taken particular responsibility for this region, I propose that she let us know the limit of what she can provide and what she will ask us to provide additionally. For our part, we take the same responsibility for that part of Russia occupied by Denikin's troops.

President Wilson. In the dispatches which have been read to us, I am struck by these words: "The population of Odessa is hostile to us." If this is the case, we might wonder about the wisdom of preserving this encircled island nearly submerged by Bolshevism. This confirms me in my policy, which is to leave Russia to the Bolsheviks—they will stew in their own juice until circumstances have made the Russians wiser—and to confine our efforts to preventing Bolshevism from invading other parts of Europe.

Mr. Lloyd George. Recently I heard M. Brătianu state what he considers to be the most important order of business in Rumania: (1)

to feed the population; (2) to outfit the army; (3) to give land to the peasants. These are intelligent and effective means of protecting Rumania from Bolshevism. But should we persist in defending Odessa, when its population will rise as soon as the Bolsheviks make their appearance? It would be better to concentrate on the defense of Rumania and establish our barrier against Bolshevism there.

—General Thwaites is introduced at Mr. Lloyd George's request and gives details about what England can send to General Denikin. It is proposed to divert 100,000 clothing kits to Rumania.
—Questioned about Denikin's situation and that of the other anti-Bolshevik chieftains, the General replies that Denikin is holding his own, despite the loss of the Tsaritsyn salient. Kolchak's troops have recaptured Ufa.

Mr. Lloyd George. It then seems that the Bolsheviks are weak in eastern Russia.
Colonel Kisch. They have concentrated on the Ukraine, where they have around 180,000 men.
Mr. Lloyd George. Are the Siberian populations favorable to Kolchak or not?
General Thwaites. Kolchak seems to be supported by the population; but an opposition movement and a tendency towards Bolshevism are developing in the region occupied by the Japanese.
Mr. Lloyd George. If Odessa falls, what will happen?
General Thwaites. The Bolsheviks will immediately attack Rumania.
Mr. Lloyd George. What would it be better to do? Defend Odessa or concentrate our forces in Rumania?
Colonel Kisch. According to a witness who has lived in Russia for a long time, the occupation of Odessa by the Bolsheviks will give Russia the impression of a great victory by them over the Allies. Thus the event would be important from the point of view of morale. But that is the only serious reason we have for defending Odessa.
Mr. Lloyd George. If it was necessary to choose between Odessa and Rumania in shipments of food and clothing, which they ask of us, which would you choose?
General Thwaites. Of the two, Rumania is the more important, if a choice must be made.

—Marsh Foch, summoned by the heads of government, is introduced.
—M. Clemenceau informs him of the subject under discussion and asks

him the following question: do you believe the danger is very pressing for Rumania? If we possess only limited means, would it be better to use them to support Odessa or to send them to Rumania?

Marshal Foch. Everything depends upon the intentions of the governments: what do they want to do?

M. Clemenceau. It is rather a question of knowing what we can do.

—Marshal Foch shows a map indicating the situation between the Black Sea and the Baltic.

Marshal Foch. The Bolshevik peril now extends towards the south and towards Hungary; it will continue to expand as long as it is not stopped; we must stop it at Odessa and at Lemberg. From the latter point, the Bolsheviks plan to break through towards Hungary. We have to close the door at Lemberg and hold on to the area of Odessa. Are the governments considering the necessity of linking these operations, and in what measure can they participate in them? The Allied forces in this region are rather small; it will be easiest to use the Rumanian army, but only if it is outfitted.

Do we want a comprehensive solution? Without it, we will be attacked on one side just when we succeed in stopping danger at another point.

M. Clemenceau. How would you plan to build a continuous barrier?

Marshal Foch. It should be done by reorganizing the Polish and Rumanian armies, whilst holding on to Odessa.

M. Clemenceau. What is the importance of Odessa itself?

Marshal Foch. Odessa has no importance, except from the point of view of morale.

Mr. Lloyd George. What would you do, as far as supplies are concerned, if you had to choose between Odessa and Rumania?

Marshal Foch. I would try to keep both as long as possible. I would not cut off my left arm because I value my right arm more. But we need to send a general to Rumania to take command of the Rumanian army, whose mission would be to defend the entire Rumanian front and to look for a way to effect a junction with the Poles.

Mr. Lloyd George. Are there enough Rumanians to defend their front?

Marshal Foch. They have twelve divisions which, admittedly, lack outfits and shoes. If they were outfitted, they could organize up to sixteen or eighteen divisions.

President Wilson. Is it essential to send thirty thousand tons of coal and wheat a month to Odessa if Rumania needs them at the same time?

Marshal Foch. No, Odessa is not a starting point.

Mr. Lloyd George. The French, because it is they who are responsible for Rumania, will see what they can supply to this country and what they must ask us to provide ourselves. I am convinced we must not waste our resources in maintaining a precarious and hopeless position at Odessa. We should recall to Rumania the twenty-five thousand men now surrounding this city and also send to Rumania the thirty thousand tons Odessa would require.

Marshal Foch. To abandon Odessa is to abandon southern Russia; but, to tell the truth, it is already lost, and we can't lose it a second time.

M. Clemenceau. We take it that the 100,000 clothing kits originally intended for General Denikin will be rerouted to Rumania.

Marshal Foch. Whatever is sent to Denikin is lost. I attach no great importance to Denikin's army, because armies do not exist by themselves. There must be a government, laws, an organized country behind them. It would even be better to have a government without an army than an army without a government. This is why I tell you: build upon Rumania, because there you have not only an army, but also a government and a people. An army should not be spontaneous vegetation from artificial soil.

M. Clemenceau. If we have to evacuate Odessa, may I emphasize that it is important that nothing be said about this in advance. Any indiscretion could endanger this delicate operation. I would ask Marshal Foch if he can give us the name of the general to assume command of the Rumanian army.

Marshal Foch. I would have several names: Mangin, Guillaumat, Degoutte. But whatever man is chosen, we must not clip his wings by placing him under the command of Franchet d'Esperey; he must have complete freedom of action.

Mr. Lloyd George. I propose that Marshal Foch prepare a plan for us which we will read carefully before deciding. We can immediately order the 100,000 clothing packages destined for General Denikin to Constanta.

IV

Conversation between President Wilson and MM. Clemenceau, Lloyd George, Orlando, and Loucheur*

MARCH 26, 1919, 11 A.M.

President Wilson. We want to question M. Loucheur about Germany's capacity to pay. I thought I understood, at a meeting which took place at my residence,[1] that Mr. Davis and M. Loucheur had reached an agreement.

M. Loucheur. On the principle, but not on the figures. At our meeting yesterday,[2] Lord Sumner, Mr. Davis, and I agreed on the principle of a maximum and a minimum annual payment. As for the figures, Mr. Norman Davis arrives at twenty-five billion dollars as a minimum—total present value—and at thirty-five billion dollars as a maximum. But these figures were not accepted by the French and English delegates. The French figures are thirty billion dollars minimum and fifty billions maximum. Our minimum figure is based on what I sincerely believe is Germany's capacity to pay, and it corresponds approximately to reparation for material damages. The figure of fifty billion dollars would cover, not only material damages, but also pensions, calculated at a uniform rate for all countries. It is not preposterous to think that Germany can manage to pay this maximum figure.

Concerning the fixing of annual payments, we agree on the establishment of a commission which will determine annually a figure between the maximum and the minimum and which will also fix the proportion to be paid in exportable securities.

—President Wilson observes that the national wealth of France in 1908 was estimated at fifty billion dollars.

M. Loucheur. Sixty billion dollars would be closer to the truth. But we must allow for the change in prices since the war. The prices upon which we have to base our estimates for reconstruction are two and a half or three times higher than those of 1914.

President Wilson. Agreed. But how can one believe that Germany can pay such amounts?

*Not represented in H.

[1] On March 14. About this meeting, see the extract from the Diary of Colonel House printed at March 14, 1919, PWW, Vol. 55, p. 499.

[2] Of the special committee on the reparation issue.

M. Loucheur. Before the war, according to Helfferich, Germany put aside between eight and ten billion marks each year. Now, the average annual installment corresponding to the figures I have given would vary between ten and fifteen billion francs, that is eight and twelve billion marks. It is true that Germany will have lost the production capacity of Lorraine and Silesia. But the depreciation of the currency reduces appreciably the sum of what we are asking. Besides, we are ready to grant Germany a few years of respite for recovery. From 1921 to 1926, we envisage only substantially reduced payments.

Mr. Lloyd George. If, during this transitional period, you require less of Germany, will you carry forward the unpaid balance to the following years, which could make the burden too heavy?

M. Loucheur. What we propose is to make Germany pay 200 million pounds sterling in 1921, this sum gradually increasing to 400 million pounds in 1926. We have provided that, if Germany cannot pay the total required during these six years, the deficit would be distributed over the total thirty-five-year payment period, without interest. The British, American, and French delegates agree entirely that Germany's recovery should be facilitated during this transitional period.

Mr. Lloyd George. What is the normal figure envisaged?

M. Loucheur. Six hundred million pounds maximum and 400 million pounds minimum. Also, the commission could grant Germany the option of paying up to 50 per cent of the sum due in paper marks at an agreed rate.

Mr. Lloyd George. Suppose France had to find 150 million pounds sterling each year in gold, foreign assets, or exports. Could you come up with this sum? We certainly couldn't do it if we had to pay 150 million pounds a year to America.

M. Loucheur. We have been much concerned about the question of how Germany can pay. Indeed, unless we know that, everything else is useless speculation. I estimate that, since the price of the materials Germany can export has risen permanently—more than the price of her imports—it will be possible for her to improve her commercial balance in the future. For example, instead of exporting forty million tons of coal worth 500 million francs, she can receive 2.5 billion francs for fifty million tons exported after the war. I don't think the price of coal will fall.

President Wilson. There is a variable factor here. In the United States, it is the price of coal that will fall and the price of wheat that has a good prospect of remaining steady. But don't you find it unduly optimistic to think that Germany, considering all we will take from her, will find herself in a more favorable position regarding exports?

Mr. Lloyd George. We are taking from her six or seven million inhabitants, three quarters of her iron, one third of her coal, and 20 per cent of her potash. France has grounds for hoping to take her place in the metallurgical industries. Add to this the probability of reduced work hours in Germany, as elsewhere. Can it be imagined that, in these circumstances, Germany could increase her production enough to raise the surplus of her balance of payments from the prewar figure of fifty million pounds to 200 million pounds?

M. Loucheur. Taking lignite into account, we are taking only one seventh of Germany's exportable coal, and we must also take price inflation into account. Moreover, we must recognize that it is difficult to know how much Germany can pay; that is why we must allow considerable latitude to the commission responsible for determining the annual payments.

Mr. Lloyd George. Prices will not remain at triple the former prices.

M. Loucheur. Yes they will, at least for coal. For the other items, they will remain at least double.

Mr. Lloyd George. I ask M. Loucheur to reply to me as a statesman as well as a great businessman. Suppose the Germans share the point of view of the American experts and refuse to accept responsibility for paying beyond a certain maximum amount. Has M. Loucheur considered the consequences of a refusal to sign the treaty?

President Wilson. And what we would have to do in such a case?

M. Loucheur. Without our concern to repair damages, according to the solemn obligation we have undertaken towards our peoples, I would have accepted the American minimum. But I must repeat that it does not allow us to repair all damage to persons and to property; what will our people say if this is confessed to them? As for knowing what must be done if they refuse to sign, this is not a question peculiar to the financial problem.

Mr. Lloyd George. We must face the possibility of a refusal to sign. According to my latest information, what the Germans are most concerned about, in addition to the left bank of the Rhine, are the questions of Danzig, Silesia, and the payment of reparations. If the German leaders conclude that it is best for them to imitate Hungary and ally themselves with the Bolsheviks, if they prefer the risk of several years of anarchy to thirty-five years of servitude, what will we do? Areas such as Danzig and Silesia can be occupied militarily; but as for money, how will we make them pay?

M. Loucheur. In that case I would occupy the Ruhr Basin. This region and the left bank of the Rhine could yield four to five billion marks per year. This involves risks, and I do not offer it as a firm solution. Like you, I am convinced we must be moderate in order to avoid, as far as possible, the danger of a refusal.

Mr. Lloyd George. I am surprised at the figure which M. Loucheur has just given. The total annual profit of Great Britain's coal mines is twenty million pounds sterling. I fear, moreover, that the German miners will not work much if they know they are only working for their enemies.

M. Loucheur. I didn't mean that mining profits would be four or five billions per year, but that, in the part of Germany we would occupy, it would be possible to obtain an annual sum of four or five billions, which could be added to the German payments. A domestic debt of 100 billion marks at the end of thirty-five years would constitute for Germany a budget that her people could bear perfectly well.

Mr. Lloyd George. This leads us beyond the limits of common sense. At this time, we are holding only bridgeheads on the Rhine, Germany is putting up no resistance, and this occupation costs 350 million pounds sterling a year. If we had to occupy a very populous region, like Westphalia, whilst Germany, all around us, is in revolt or agitated by contagious Bolshevism, what then would be our outlays and our risks? And do you believe we could maintain that situation until we received 100 billion marks?

It will be as difficult for me as for M. Clemenceau to dispel the illusions which surround the subject of reparation. Four hundred members of the British Parliament have sworn to extract from Germany the very last penny to which we are entitled; I will have to face them. But our duty is to serve our country in the best possible way. If I am defeated because I did not do the impossible, my successor, whoever he may be, won't be able to do better; one year later, if he has made extravagant promises without keeping them, everyone will say he was foolish and we were right.

I am convinced the Germans won't sign the proposals we envisage. In their place, I wouldn't sign them. Germany will go over to Bolshevism. Europe will remain mobilized, our industries will be halted, our states will go bankrupt; it will be said rightly that we are to blame because we were unable to make peace. We must decide to act wisely, whatever your opposition and ours will think.

President Wilson. I can only express my admiration for the spirit shown in the words of Mr. Lloyd George. There is nothing more honorable than to be turned out of power because one was right.

We must look at this financial problem from a political point of view. Those who have studied the question have too often based their calculations on prewar Germany. That Germany rested upon a powerful organization, that is, a rich, enterprising government determined to lead the country to economic mastery of the world. That Germany no longer exists. We are reducing its territory. The Weimar government[3] has no credit. If it cannot remain in office, it will be replaced by a government we will be unable to deal with.

We can only hope that a disorganized and demoralized Germany will do as much as prewar Germany, which might have taken pride in satisfying our demands. We owe it to the peace of the world not to tempt Germany to plunge into Bolshevism; we know only too well the relations of the Bolshevik leaders with Germany.

I believe that, if we offer reasonable proposals and take pains to explain them, not a parliament in the world would dare blame us. We mustn't ask ourselves too often what we have the right to demand because of our losses, but rather what it is possible and wise to demand. We can receive what we demand only if we can do it without crushing Germany for thirty-five years.

This question is more difficult to solve than that of Danzig.[4] We can say: we will occupy Danzig. But we can't militarily occupy fifty billion dollars. Besides, Germany could pay very large sums only by taking an even larger share of world markets than before the war. Is that in our interest? Wouldn't it be better to try to earn this money ourselves in the markets, instead of encouraging Germany to take them from us?

M. Clemenceau. I basically agree with Mr. Lloyd George and Mr. Wilson, but I don't believe they disagree with M. Loucheur, who, as an experienced businessman, would carefully avoid killing the goose that lays the golden egg.

I have no fear of affronting Parliament; but I cannot forget the document which we signed and sent to President Wilson about reparation for war damages. If we admit that such reparation is

---

[3] That is, the government elected by the German Constituent National Assembly at Weimar on February 13, 1919, headed by Philipp Scheidemann.

[4] That is, the question of how to turn the German port of Danzig into an outlet to the Baltic Sea for the new Polish state.

impossible, we must frankly say so, but we should only say it if we are certain it is impossible.

I propose that we submit figures for damages suffered by each of our nations to a small arbitration commission; in cases where its members could not agree, President Wilson could decide. Fortunately, we don't have to discuss the question of distribution today. What we have to do is to notify Germany what she will have to pay. I'm impressed by the ingenuity of the system of a permanent commission proposed by our financial delegates. It enables us to deal with the circumstances. The commission will act freely within certain limits; but the governments will be able to reserve the right to reduce or even to abolish the minimum. I don't believe we could find anything more flexible.

What impresses me in M. Loucheur's lucid report is how close we are to an understanding. The only possible difficulty lies in the distribution. Hence my suggestion of an arbitration commission; any one of us who presents exaggerated figures would dishonor himself. To tell the truth, I would agree to discuss the amount to be paid with the Germans themselves. If they can show me good reasons why we should lower our figures, I am ready to listen to them.

What we must avoid is going to the other extreme and, because we fear demanding too much, not demanding enough. Can we proclaim the principle of payment of war damages and establish a minimum and maximum rate of annual payment without indicating a total amount due? At the same time, we would create the commission I referred to. I believe public opinion would support us.

I would ask our experts to try harder to come to an agreement whilst taking our political point of view into account. We might ask them to give us their solution within forty-eight hours. When we have adopted it, the hardest question will be settled, and we'll be able to resolve many other questions during the following week.

This solution is necessary. It is necessary because of the condition in which Europe, which the war has left in pieces, finds itself; it is made necessary by the universal desire to demobilize the armies and resume normal life. From all sides come complaints about the slow pace of the work of the conference. I don't pretend that we have done our job very rapidly; but, if we consider the crushing weight of its task and the complexity of the problems to be solved, our conference will bear comparison with any other human assembly.

We know that public opinion demands an early peace. President Wilson has repeated to us the words of the woman from Soissons asking him to "make peace very quickly." I am ready to hasten a conclusion by asking, from the financial point of view, what is just and possible, and nothing more. We can ask our financial advisers to help us to conclude within forty-eight hours.

President Wilson. I believe our experts have already done what they can to come to an agreement, and some of them have reached a position from which they do not budge. I agree with everything M. Clemenceau has said, but we haven't yet found a way to avoid specifying in the treaty the total amount of payment we will demand. If we confine ourselves to demanding annual payments, they will ask us this question: "For how long?" If we confine ourselves to saying that a commission will be able to regulate the payment according to the situation in Germany, I fear this won't satisfy public opinion, which has no confidence in the good faith of the Germans. I agree with you that we should allow them to discuss it, but we can't avoid saying what they will have to pay.

M. Loucheur. We still have the option of not fixing the final figure before discussing it with the Germans at Versailles.

Mr. Lloyd George. It seems useless to have our specialists meet yet again. My own are competent but obstinate people. When I spoke to Lord Sumner, who is an eminent judge and a man of great character, about the Bolshevik danger in Germany if we go too far in our demands, Lord Sumner answered me: "In that case, the Germans will be cutting their own throats, and I would like nothing better." It is a waste of time to argue with a man in that state of mind. Lord Cunliffe is more tractable, despite much innate stubbornness; but he is under the influence of Lord Sumner, who never leaves his side.

Our experts have taken their stand and won't change. Wouldn't it be better to ask them to provide us with figures representing the damages caused to the civilian populations, both to property and to persons? We must limit the definition so as to exclude failure to earn by business firms, etc. We must also consider price inflation. I think, with M. Loucheur, that prices should be calculated at a rate at least double the prewar rate.

There is a difficulty with regard to persons. Pension payments are different for us and for France, for ourselves and for our dominions. I propose to ask our specialists to give us only the figures such as they are, and to leave the responsibility of determining the principle of division to us.

V

Conversation between President Wilson and MM. Clemenceau, Orlando, Loucheur, Keynes, Norman Davis, Lamont, D'Amelio, and Lord Sumner*

MARCH 26, 1919, 3:30 P.M.

Mr. Lloyd George. The subject of our conversation is not Germany's capacity to pay, but compensation owed for damages to persons and property. Concerning property, what is due for reparation is equivalent to the cost of replacement. We agree to assume that prices have doubled, at least if one considers a period of several years; for if everything had to be replaced on this very day, the difference would be greater. We also agree to leave aside all indirect losses, such as failure to earn by business firms. Great Britain, moreover, has never included these indirect losses in its accounting.

As for persons, there are two ways of treating this question. We can take the figures covering war pensions to be paid by each state. The objections, presented by France especially, is that pensions are calculated at different rates in different countries, and that, by purely and simply registering each state's budget figures, injuries would be done to those that give the lowest pensions. But it may be said in reply that any intermediate figure between these two rates would give an advantage to states which have fixed pensions at the lowest level.

Let us begin the discussion by examining property damages.

M. Loucheur. I have a preliminary remark to make. Mr. Lloyd George said that it was necessary to calculate repairs to double the prewar price; that is true for the reconstruction of houses, but not for the replacement of raw materials stolen or destroyed. Wool requisitioned by the Germans at Roubaix can be replaced only at five times the price of 1914. I would accept the ratio of 1 to 2 as a basis, but with this reservation.

I reviewed carefully the statistics prepared by the different French ministries, and I have eliminated all indirect damages. We arrived at the following figures [in French francs]:

---

*Not represented in H.

Buildings and furnishings	35,000,000,000.
Agricultural damage	16,000,000,000.
Industrial damage	19,300,000,000.
Public works	5,150,000,000.
Post offices and telegraphs	135,000,000.
Merchant marine (at forty pounds sterling per ton)	1,610,000,000.
Value of cargoes	500,000,000.
State schools and fine arts	1,000,000,000.
War levies paid to the Germans	1,414,000,000.
Total	80,109,000,000.

Mr. Lloyd George. If this figure represents damages done to such a limited part of French territory, France must be far richer than we imagined.

M. Loucheur. France does not want to receive one dollar more than what is due her. She is ready to accept any audit of the figures she presents. But you would be greatly mistaken if you thought such a study would yield a noticeable reduction. I made a study of what would be necessary merely to restore the mines of northern France: it couldn't be done for less than two billion francs.

Mr. Lloyd George. The value of all the coal mines of Great Britain before the war was estimated at 130 million pounds sterling, and, according to you, these mines, inferior by comparison, would require eighty million pounds sterling for their repair? How can we justify that? The distribution of reparations must be made equitably; and, also, in presenting our bill to Germany, we shouldn't give the impression that we demand from her a payment double or triple what it ought to be. I say to M. Loucheur that, if he was entrusted with spending the money he claims for the reconstruction of the devastated lands of northern France, he wouldn't be able to spend it. The national wealth of France in 1908 was estimated at 250 billion francs, and you are asking one third of that for your reconstruction, when such a small part of France was devastated.

M. Loucheur. The figure you cite comes from a book by M. Edmond Théry,[1] and I attach no value whatever to it. The true figure, if it was possible to calculate it, would be much higher. Consider the value of the buildings in Paris alone and everything they contain. I cannot accept the observation just stated, and I simply repeat that what France asks is the cost of the reconstruc-

---

[1] Edmond Amédée Théry, *La fortune publique de la France* (Paris, 1911).

tion of her pillaged or devastated regions. She doesn't want one sou more.

President Wilson. Don't you have official statistics on the total wealth of France?

M. Loucheur. I have only one reliable figure, which is that of the negotiable securities belonging to France before the war: they amounted to 120 billion francs.

President Wilson. The United States and, I believe, England have official estimates of national wealth.

M. Loucheur. I don't believe we have calculated it and, in any case, I was unable to procure it. As for the estimates I present, I ask only that you have them examined by whomever you wish; but I repeat that it would be erroneous to believe they could be reduced seriously.

Mr. Lloyd George. In England we have the income tax, which allows us to know fairly exactly the national wealth, and the total at which we have arrived allows me to judge that the present figure I have quoted for France—given the relative position of the two countries—must not be far from the mark. If this is so, then, what France is asking for the reconstruction of a limited region is necessarily very exaggerated. France wouldn't be able to spend all she claims on reconstruction.

M. Loucheur. We think reconstruction will require ten years and one million men. In the urban area of Lens alone, which includes Courrières, there are 12,000 houses to be rebuilt, each costing 5,000 francs before the war and worth 15,000 today.

Mr. Lloyd George. These high prices won't continue.

M. Loucheur. Let's say they will cost an average of 10,000 francs, which makes 120,000,000 merely for this very limited reconstruction.

Mr. Lloyd George. When we calculate the total wealth of a country like France, we include the value of the land. Now, the land did not disappear in the invaded regions, however much it was damaged in certain spots. But even if you sold the Chemin des Dames[2] you would find a buyer.

President Wilson. In order to consider figures such as those presented to us, we must be able to make comparisons.

Mr. Lloyd George. As for what concerns us, it is very simple: we demand compensation for our sunken ships, so much per ton; we have to pay pensions, and we know the exact amount. It's this

---

[2] A ridge in northern France extending twelve miles west from Craonne to Fort Malmaison parallel to the Aisne River. It had been the scene of desperate fighting during the war and was at this time totally devastated.

figure that we claim. The rate of our pensions is in between that of France and the United States.

M. Loucheur. What we are asking is that pensions be calculated on a common basis, corresponding to the rate of pensions in the country paying the lowest scale. Otherwise, it would be too easy to double the rate of our pensions in order to claim this amongst war damages.

Mr. Lloyd George. To fix a uniform scale at the lowest rate would not be fair to England. The English public wouldn't understand why the entire cost of every destroyed chimney in France should be reimbursed, but not that of lives lost by England.

M. Loucheur. We can't admit that the price of a human life is different in different countries, unless it is based on the price of consumer goods.

Mr. Davis. To avoid some of these arguments and unfortunate comparisons, couldn't we agree purely and simply on the proportion of the payment to which each country has a right?

Mr. Lloyd George. That would be much better. I proposed an arrangement according to which, out of 100 pounds sterling received from Germany, fifty would be given to France and thirty to Great Britain; France hasn't accepted.

The great advantage of this system is that we could avoid going into these unpleasant details. What France claims is not fair to her allies. If M. Loucheur wants to accept this proportion, which I consider a very generous offer, it will become pointless to study the figures. This study is not without danger. If we don't agree amongst ourselves here, it will lead to a public scrutiny, and, if the figures we have just heard are published and compared to what we know about the total wealth of France, it will produce a very unfortunate impression.

M. Loucheur. I'm distressed to seem to be demanding more for France than she deserves. France has the most solemnly recognized right to reparation after her sufferings and sacrifices. What she demands is reparation for damages conforming to the principles accepted by the American delegation. If I acted otherwise, I would be acting against the interest and rights of my country.

Mr. Lloyd George speaks of the drawbacks of a public debate; we don't fear it at all, and we fear even less a comparison of our figures with those which result from the arbitrary studies of more or less qualified economists. No one today can make an absolutely certain estimate of the total reparations due. It is easy when it is a question of sunken ships; we know these ships are worth so much per ton. It is more difficult, if not impossible, when it is a question of an entire region devastated and ruined.

France asks only what it will cost to repair the damages suffered. I regret to seem to be defending a cause which is not absolutely just, and I believe it is this impression that wrongs my country.

Mr. Lloyd George. Doesn't M. Loucheur agree to discuss the principle of proportional distribution?

Mr. Davis. M. Loucheur seemed so disposed in our conversations.

Mr. Lloyd George. In that case, it would be better for our specialists to meet again and resume this discussion.

President Wilson. The maximum figure must be not only moderate, but reasonable; that is to say, it must take political necessities into account. That is why it seems to me that we should inform our specialists of our desire to do nothing which would have the consequence of completely destroying Germany and of preventing her from accepting our terms.

Mr. Lloyd George. My impression is that the figures which have been presented are beyond what Germany can pay. I am much less interested in these figures than in the proportion according to which the distribution is to be made.

—The heads of governments withdraw and leave M. Loucheur and the financial experts to confer.

Mr. Davis. What is M. Loucheur's idea about a fair percentage to be established amongst the different governments?

M. Loucheur. I would like to establish a proportion between France and England; we can then see what we have to reserve for the others. France had always understood that she had an absolute priority for damages proper. To accept the idea of proportional division is contrary to this principle; it is a great concession on our part. At first I said that, in my opinion, the fair proportion was 72 for France and 18 for England, while the English proposed 50 and 33. In a conversation with Mr. Montagu, I came down to 58 and 25. Mr. Montagu suggested 56 and 28, which would have given England 50 per cent of what France would receive. I did not accept that suggestion, which, moreover, was not a firm proposal. Mr. Montagu concluded from this that no agreement was possible.

Mr. Keynes. Do you still propose 58/25?

M. Loucheur. I am not authorized to do so by M. Clemenceau. But I am quite ready to recommend that proportion to him. I had occasion to mention it to M. Lebrun, who raised his arms to the heavens. I must add, to be complete, that in a conversation with Lord Sumner, I said I could, as a last resort, envisage the proportion of 56/25.

Lord Sumner. Would you recommend that proposition today?

M. Loucheur. Yes, in order to give proof of good will.

Lord Sumner. What will the situation of the other countries be? If a proportion is fixed only between France and England, the distribution amongst other rightful claimants will be prorated, I suppose?

M. Loucheur. That is what I suggest. We would have to determine what is due the other nations in such a way that the proportion between England and France remains unchanged. We don't yet know what might be due the other powers.

M. D'Amelio. It seems to me that the plan must be made amongst the three of us, with Italy being party to it.

M. Loucheur. It is first necessary that we see your figures and, above all, that the governments be agreed on the principle of the interdependence of the claims.

Lord Sumner. Are M. Loucheur's proportions based on calculations of the relative value of claims presented by Great Britain and France, or are they simply a means of arriving at a compromise?

M. Loucheur. If I relied on the figures while respecting the spirit of President Wilson's Fourteen Points, the proportion would be 70 for France and 25 for England. I wanted to give proof of a spirit of conciliation.

Lord Sumner. Here is what I mean: how shall we reply to the questions we will certainly be asked about figures as specific as 56 and 25? Another question: the value of the Saar Basin could count in the reparations,[3] but I understand that nothing in Alsace-Lorraine will be entered in the account line.

M. Loucheur. One of the Fourteen Points promises France reparation for the wrong done in 1871 in Alsace-Lorraine, and we are not claiming the 5 billion [francs] of indemnity we had to pay with compound interest. We could not agree that anything in Alsace-Lorraine should be credited under the heading of reparation. I remind you of the two principles that were accepted: (1) the restitution, pure and simple, of stolen objects must not be counted in reparation, and (2) one must not include the manpower we intend to demand of Germany in order to clean up the battlefields.

Lord Sumner. I am not discussing that right now; I would only like to explain our position to you. It will be difficult for us to justify

---

[3] For the French claim to the Saar Basin, see the notes of meeting IX printed below.

a complicated proportion such as 56/25, 100 representing all that is due all the Allied nations. Our proposal is 50 for France, 30 for Great Britain, and 20 for the other powers. If this last figure proved inadequate, the difference would be taken from the portions of France and Great Britain in the proportion of 5 to 3.

M. Loucheur. I could not recommend these figures to my government.

M. D'Amelio. That procedure would not be acceptable to Italy. We would like a definite proportion to be established for each of the three powers.

Mr. Davis. We must come to some solution; otherwise, we will be compelled to examine the demands of each in detail. Could we accept 55 for France, 30 for Great Britain, and 15 for the others?

M. Loucheur. I don't accept that. Mr. Montagu went as far as a ratio of 1 to 2. Lord Sumner proposes 3 to 5 to us.

—The meeting is adjourned to permit individual discussions.

M. Loucheur. It is impossible for me to go beyond what I have agreed to.

Mr. Davis. I don't have to emphasize the danger of delay in our decisions and in the signing of the peace treaty.

M. Loucheur. I agree with you on that. But if one takes the word "reparation" in a literal sense—according to the promise made in the beginning to France and Belgium—these two powers would divide between them 80 per cent of the payments, and England would have 20 per cent. We made a concession to England in taking account of her political situation; but no French government could go further than that without being repudiated.

Mr. Davis. Each country thinks above all of its own sufferings. In England, a sunken ship is considered a very serious loss. If we Americans were to follow our own instincts, we would have to confine ourselves to a strict interpretation of the Fourteen Points, which would yield only 25 billion dollars in total. We are doing what we can to interpret that definition in a broad sense, in order to find what is required to pay pensions to disabled veterans and families of the dead.

M. Loucheur. We are ready to accept the literal interpretation, even if it excludes pensions. I would prefer the pure and simple application of the Fourteen Points to what is proposed.

Mr. Davis. I should regret very much not coming to an agreement with you; I ask you to accept our mediation and both of you to make concessions.

M. Loucheur. If one admitted the absolute priority of reparation proper, one would arrive at a proportion of 1 to 4 between England and France. England offers 3 to 5; she proposed 33 to 50 and, today, 30 to 50. I myself, am at 1 to 2.4, and it is I who have taken the greatest step.

Mr. Davis. Couldn't you agree on 56 per cent for France, 28 per cent for Great Britain, and 16 per cent for the others?

Lord Sumner. Does this mean that the United States Government, regarding this ratio as fair, would support its application?

Mr. Davis. Yes, if President Wilson agrees with me, as I hope he does.

M. Loucheur. I would prefer the strict application of the Fourteen Points, and I can't go beyond 55/25. M. Clemenceau has the right, if he wishes, to make a greater concession for political reasons.

Mr. Davis. I see that Lord Sumner's last proposal was 50/30; M. Loucheur's 55/25. That of the United States is 55/28. It seems to me that we can agree.

Lord Sumner. I am very much obliged to the delegates of the United States for their efforts at conciliation. In spite of the noticeable reduction that their proposal imposes upon us, what they consider to be fair carries great weight with me. I also wish to deal with France in a friendly spirit. I cannot admit for a moment that her damages are actually twice ours. But, in a spirit of understanding, I would recommend to Mr. Lloyd George to accept the proposal made by the delegates of the United States.

Mr. Davis. I hope that M. Loucheur will give proof of the same spirit of conciliation; we can propose nothing more.

Mr. Lamont. Can't M. Loucheur recommend our proposal?

M. Loucheur. In my soul and conscience, I can't recommend what isn't fair. I have made a great step forward; I regret that it was not more appreciated, especially by our American friends, and I regret having to give the appearance of intransigence, when I have actually gone beyond my instructions and beyond what I consider as conforming strictly to justice.

VI

Conversation between President Wilson and MM. Clemenceau, Lloyd George, and Orlando*

MARCH 27, 1919, 11 A.M.

Mr. Lloyd George. Have you read the memorandum[1] which I sent you regarding the general peace terms?

M. Clemenceau. I intend to reply to it in writing; but it must first be translated into French for the President of the Republic.[2]

President Wilson. I hope you agree in principle with Mr. Lloyd George on the moderation which must be shown towards Germany. We don't wish to destroy Germany, nor could we do so; our greatest error would be to give her powerful reasons for wishing one day to take revenge. Excessive demands would most certainly sow the seed of war.

Everywhere we are compelled to change boundaries and national sovereignties. Nothing involves greater danger, for these changes run contrary to long-established customs and change the very life of populations whilst, at the same time, they affect their feelings. We must avoid giving our enemies even the impression of injustice. I don't fear future wars brought about by the secret plottings of governments, but rather conflicts created by popular discontent. If we ourselves are guilty of injustice, such discontent is inevitable, with the consequences it entails. Hence our desire to negotiate with moderation and fairness.

Mr. Lloyd George. I have a historical precedent to cite. In 1814, after the defeat of Napoleon, Prussia, whose chief representative in this case was Blücher, wanted to impose crushing terms upon France. Wellington, who had good sense, took an opposite position and was supported by Castlereagh, who had earlier been one of France's bitterest enemies. Both felt it would be a great error to seek to destroy France, whose presence was necessary for civilization and European stability. Such was the position taken by

---

*Not represented in H.

[1] The so-called Fontainebleau Memorandum, printed, among other places, in *PWW*, Vol. 56, pp. 259-70, in which Lloyd George and other British delegates reviewed all the problems of the peace settlement with Germany and advocated somewhat less harsh terms than the British and French had heretofore proposed, mainly in order to prevent a Bolshevik takeover of Germany.

[2] Raymond Poincaré.

the representatives of England towards France; and if their opinion had not prevailed, France would have been half destroyed, with no other result than to deliver all of Europe to the Germanic powers.

Germany has learned a lesson as hard as any in history. The fall of the Napoleonic empire in 1814 cannot be compared, for the campaign in France was a glorious conclusion to Napoleon's wars; whilst last November the Germans capitulated without even attempting a last stand.

M. Clemenceau. I said yesterday that I agree completely with Mr. Lloyd George and President Wilson about the manner in which to treat Germany. We must not abuse our victory; we must treat peoples with consideration and fear provoking a surge of national consciousness.

But I venture a fundamental objection. Mr. Lloyd George is excessively afraid of the consequences if the Germans should refuse to sign the treaty. I remind you that the Germans surrendered without even waiting for our troops to enter Germany, no doubt fearing the atrocious reprisals of which we were incapable. This time we must expect them to stand out: they will argue, they will dispute every point, they will talk of refusing to sign, they will play up incidents such as the one which has just taken place in Budapest and those which may occur tomorrow in Vienna; they will contest or refuse all they can refuse. You read the interview with Count Bernstorff in yesterday's newspapers:[3] he speaks with the arrogance of a victor. But we mustn't fear them any more than is necessary. We must be aware of possible danger; but, after having obtained victory at the price of so many sacrifices, we must also, assure ourselves of its fruits.

After all, the resistance of the Germans hasn't always been what we expected. You took their entire war fleet from them; yet they were very proud of it, and their Emperor had told them, "Our future is on the sea." We had envisaged the possibility of a desperate opposition on the part of the Germans once they were deprived of their fleet; you remember the observations made by Marshal Foch on this subject when we were drafting the terms of the Armistice. In fact, nothing happened. We are now seizing their merchant fleet—in order to feed them, it is true. But they have foreseen the possibility that they wouldn't be fed, for the *Berliner Tageblatt* reports today that, in that event, Germany would manage to live despite the blockade.

[3] About this interview, see *PWW*, Vol. 56, p. 317, n. 1.

I come to President Wilson's precept, which I accept, but which I apply to the Germans only with certain reservations. We must not—says President Wilson—give the Germans a feeling of injustice. Agreed, but what we find fair here in this room will not necessarily be accepted as such by the Germans.

There is surprise that France is opposed to the immediate admission of Germany to the League of Nations. Only yesterday, I received a new report of the atrocities committed in France. Unfortunately, we have come to know the Germans at our own expense; and we know they are a people who submit themselves to force in order to impose their own force upon the world. I remind Mr. Lloyd George of a conversation I had with him at Karlsbad seven or eight years ago: I conveyed to him my uneasiness over the future of Europe, and I mentioned the German threat. Mr. Lloyd George hoped that Germany would be wise; unfortunately, he has had his eyes opened.

The Germans are a servile people who need force to support an argument. Napoleon said before his death: "Nothing permanent is founded upon force." I am not sure of that; for it is enough to look at the great nations of Europe and the United States itself to have doubts. What is true is that force can't establish anything solid unless it is in the service of justice. We must do everything we can to be just towards the Germans; but, as for persuading them that we are just towards them, that is another matter. I believe we can do something to spare the world from German aggression for a long time; but the German spirit will not change so quickly. Look at the German Social Democrats, who called themselves the brothers of our Socialists and yours: we have seen them in service of the Imperial government, and today they serve Scheidemann, surrounded by the old Imperial bureaucracy, with Rantzau[4] at its head.

Notice that no one in Germany makes a distinction between the just and the unjust demands of the Allies. There is no resistance stronger than that which shows itself against assigning Danzig to Poland. However, to make amends for the historical crime committed against the Polish nation, we are compelled, in bringing that country back to life, to give her the means to live. We must not forget the crimes committed in particular by Germany against Poland, following the great crime of her partition in the nineteenth century, and by scientific methods, so to speak. We remember the children whipped for having prayed to God in

---

[4] That is, Count von Brockdorff-Rantzau.

Polish, peasants expropriated, driven from their lands to make room for occupants of the Germanic race.

Perhaps each of us has similar expropriations on his conscience, in a more or less distant past; but here we have deeds that took place under our very eyes, and those who have committed them are before us. The Social Democrats are with them, for they supported their government during four years of war.

I pay tribute to Mr. Lloyd George's spirit of fairness, when he expresses the desire to give Poland as few German subjects as possible. But I do not accept the sentence in which he says that, on the question of communications between Danzig and the interior, we must leave aside all strategic considerations. If we followed this advice, we would leave a sad legacy to our successors. We must accept the inevitable difficulties in the principle of self-determination if we wish to safeguard this principle itself.

An example haunts my mind: that of Austria. We speak of everyone disarming: I want it very much; believe me, the spirit of conquest, which was once the spirit of the French people, is dead forever. But if we reduce our armaments, and if, at the same time, Austria adds seven million inhabitants to the population of Germany, the power of our German neighbors will increase in a manner very threatening to us. Is it a flagrant insult to the rights of peoples to say to the Austrians: "We only ask you to remain independent. Do what you wish with this independence; but you must not enter into a German bloc and participate in a plan for German revenge"?

My principles are your own; I am only arguing about their application. May I say to President Wilson: don't believe that the principles of justice which satisfy us will also satisfy the Germans. I know them; I have forced myself to go to Germany nearly every year since 1871. I wanted to know the Germans, and, at certain times, I hoped that mutual understanding could be reached between our two peoples. I can tell you that their idea of justice is not our own.

After the greatest effort and the greatest sacrifices of bloodshed that history has ever seen, we must not compromise the result of our victory. The League of Nations is offered to us as a means of giving us the security we need. I accept this instrumentality, but should the League of Nations be unable to give military sanctions to its decrees, that sanction would have to be found from another quarter. I note that, on the sea, that sanction is already in effect: Germany has no more fleet. We must have an equivalent on land. I don't have preconceived opinions about the methods to employ. I implore you to understand my state of mind about this, just as I am making an effort to understand yours. America is far away, protected by the ocean. Not even Napoleon himself could touch England. You are both sheltered; we are not.

No man is further than I from the militaristic spirit. I am ready to do anything to arrive at a solution which would be better than the military solution. But we cannot forget that, in our great crisis, the military did much to save us. Let's not make the error of not taking their advice at a moment like this. On the day of danger and of trial, they would say to us: "It is not our fault if you didn't listen to us."

One last word. We are right to fear Bolshevism amongst the enemy and to avoid provoking its development; but we must not spread it amongst ourselves. There is a sense of justice amongst allies which must be satisfied. If this sentiment was outrageously thwarted, either in France or England, great danger would result. It's good to want to spare the conquered; but we must not lose sight of the victors. If a revolutionary movement was to appear somewhere because our solutions appear unjust, let it not be in our own countries. I wish to give only a simple indication here.

Mr. Lloyd George. I am in agreement on many points with M. Clemenceau, but certain of the positions he takes seem to me full of peril. I know something about the Bolshevik danger in our countries; I have fought it myself for several weeks now, and I congratulate my colleagues for having had less trouble with it than I do. I combat Bolshevism, not by force, but by searching for a means to satisfy the legitimate aspirations that have given birth to it.

The result is that trade unionists like Smillie, the secretary-general of the miners,[5] who could have become formidable, end up by helping us to avoid a conflict. The English capitalists—thank God—are frightened, and that makes them reasonable. But concerning the peace terms, what could provoke an explosion of Bolshevism in England would not be the reproach of having asked too little from the enemy, but of having asked too much. The English worker doesn't want to crush the German people with excessive demands. It's rather amongst the upper classes that you will find an unlimited hatred of the German. Moreover, a marked change of attitude has taken place in this regard since Germany gave up its old political system. If our terms seem too moderate, I will have great difficulties in Parliament, but they won't come from the common people.

I do not agree with what M. Clemenceau has said about the

---

[5] Actually, Smillie was president of the Miners' Federation of Great Britain.

opinions of the military. Their assistance is essential in time of war. But in matters of state, they are the last people I would consult. I admire and like Marshal Foch very much; but on political questions, he is a child. I wouldn't take his advice about how to insure the greatest possible security to nations. Let's remember that Moltke, who was undoubtedly an eminent military leader, perhaps led Bismarck in 1871 further than he would have gone himself. In the end, Germany fell victim to the idea of a strategic frontier, which led it to mutilate France.

Likewise, we had a school of officers who sought to give the Indian Empire what was called a scientific frontier. Gladstone did not believe in scientific frontiers. But Disraeli, in the name of this doctrine, allowed the occupation of Afghanistan, from which we were eventually obliged to withdraw under disastrous conditions. Since then, Afghanistan, respected by us, has become a most useful buffer state. This leads us to the discussion between Wellington and Blücher about which I spoke a moment ago.

I received a letter from General Smuts,[6] who is an impartial soul and whose loyalty to us I insist upon recalling. He is one of the best generals who fought against us in the Boer War. He invaded the Cape Colony with a few hundred men; he had thousands at the time he surrendered to us. During the present war, I have only to recall the role which he played in helping us to suppress the uprising fomented by Germany in South Africa.

---

[6] Smuts' letter of March 26, 1919, is printed in William Keith Hancock and Jean van der Poel, eds., *Selections from the Smuts Papers*, 7 vols. (Cambridge, 1966-1973), IV, 83-87. Smuts severely criticized the policies pursued by the conference in drafting the treaty with Germany and, citing a number of specific examples, called for a radical softening of its terms before they were submitted to the Germans. Smuts argued: "I am seriously afraid that the peace to which we are working is an impossible peace, conceived on a wrong basis; that it will not be accepted by Germany, and, even if accepted, that it will prove utterly unstable, and only serve to promote the anarchy which is rapidly overtaking Europe. I say nothing about the long delays of our Conference work, and the rapid growth of dissatisfaction in all the Allied countries. Our daily communiqués with their record of small details which appear to the world to be trivialities and futilities, are enough to raise great discontent. But it is about the sort of peace we are preparing that I am alarmed.

"To my mind certain points seem quite clear and elementary: 1. We cannot destroy Germany without destroying Europe; 2. We cannot save Europe without the co-operation of Germany. Yet we are now preparing a peace which must destroy Germany, and yet we think we shall save Europe by so doing! . . . My fear is that the Paris Conference may prove one of the historic failures of the world; that the statesmen connected with it will return to their countries broken, discredited men, and that the Bolshevists will reap where they have sown."

His letter, as he himself says, is unpleasant. He talks much about Danzig; he believes that the terms we wish to impose are the opposite of what a statesman should impose. I admit my own grave fears concerning Danzig. We're going to give Poland two million Germans. The Poles will govern badly and will take a long time to conduct business in the western manner. There will be disturbances; the Germans in Poland, if they revolt, will be defeated. If Germany wants to intervene, will you send troops to keep the Germans of Poland under the yoke? The Poles, it is true, will tell us: what good is it to have given us these territories if you don't help us to defend them? I'm certain that public opinion, both in America and in England, would not support us if we intervened in such circumstances. The League of Nations, the treaty which we will sign, will be likewise flouted. I do not believe in a treaty whose future execution could not be assured. If you are not determined to assure the execution of this clause, what good is it to place it in your treaty?

Whatever happens, we are going to impose a very hard peace on Germany: she will have no more colonies, no more fleet; she will lose six or seven million inhabitants, a great part of her natural resources—nearly all her iron, a notable portion of her coal. Militarily, we are reducing her to the status of Greece and, from a naval point of view, to that of the Argentine Republic. And on all these points, we are entirely in agreement. Moreover, she will pay, according to the estimates, five or ten billion pounds sterling. Setting our terms at the lowest level, they will be such as no civilized nation has ever been compelled to accept. If you add to all this terms of minor importance, which could be considered unjust, it will perhaps be the straw that breaks the camel's back.

What did France resent most: the loss of Alsace-Lorraine or the obligation to pay five billions in indemnity? I already know your answer. What struck me most on my first trip to Paris was the statue of Strasbourg in mourning. Germany must not be able to erect such statues in her cities through any fault of ours.

M. Clemenceau. Nor do I want that.

Mr. Lloyd George. The Germans have certain fine qualities of character. They fought very bravely. I believe they will accept all the rest, including a very heavy indemnity; but what will wound them most is the idea of abandoning millions of Germans to Polish domination. It has been very painful for France to see Frenchmen pass under German domination; but the French would at least consider the Germans their equals. It's not the same with the Poles in the mind of the Germans. It's this type of feeling that might prevent them from signing the peace treaty.

I would prefer a solution making Danzig a free port and leaving the Poles in Poland and the Germans in Germany. General Smuts writes very aptly: "Poland cannot exist without the good will of Germany and of Russia." When we all go home, the Poles will stay there by themselves, isolated in the middle of enemies who surround them on all sides.

M. Clemenceau. What's your conclusion?

Mr. Lloyd George. My conclusion is that we must not create a Poland alienated from the time of its birth by an unforgettable quarrel from its most civilized neighbor.

Do not believe that our most extreme democrats don't understand the necessities of the present situation. In a conversation I had yesterday with Lansbury, one of our most notorious pacifists, I told him I would be ready to promise France that, in case of German aggression, we would place all our forces at her disposal. Lansbury told me that he approved. But we must avoid sowing the seeds of war ourselves.

—The letter from General Smuts is read. He greatly fears the imposition on Germany of excessive terms and is alarmed about what is being said about Danzig and the left bank of the Rhine, as well as about the figures for indemnities, and maintains that it is in collaboration with Germany, and not against her, that it will be possible to keep new nations such as Poland and Bohemia alive. "Germany," writes General Smuts, "will remain, despite everything, a dominant element in continental Europe, and it would be folly to believe that we can reconstruct the world without her assistance."

M. Clemenceau. I am willing to believe that General Smuts, who has proved his loyalty to England, does not speak merely as a friend of Germany. But I want the French point of view also to be taken into account.

VII

Conversation between President Wilson and MM. Clemenceau, Lloyd George, Orlando, and Tardieu*

MARCH 27, 1919, 3:30 P.M.

Mr. Lloyd George. I have a few words to say about our plan to send a commission to Ottoman Asia. I just spoke with one of our agents in Mesopotamia, whose views are rather different from those of General Alby concerning the feeling of the Arabs towards France. He also believes it is better not to stir up trouble in that whole region by sending a commission there. It would only be able to collect insufficient information, since oriental people are wary and don't open up to newcomers straightaway.

President Wilson. Despite everything, I would prefer an inquiry conducted impartially. If we fear delaying the final restoration of peace by too lengthy an inquiry, we can instruct the members of the commission so as to limit their task precisely.

Mr. Lloyd George. Emir Faisal also seems to have changed his position. We received a petition from the inhabitants of Iraq, to whom we offered the possibility of being ruled by an Arab emir. They replied in polite oriental phrases that, while they were very grateful, they preferred the direct administration of Europeans.

President Wilson. I insist that we adhere to our decision about the inquiry. Dr. Bliss, who has seen these people close at hand for a number of years, and who, for that reason, identifies with them, tells me that the inquiry will make a good impression upon them.

M. Clemenceau. I agree with President Wilson, whilst wanting the inquiry to be carried out without wasting time.

Could we now take up the question of the left bank of the Rhine?[1]

*Not represented in H.

[1] One of France's fundamental war and peace objectives was the establishment of an autonomous buffer state in the Rhineland under French control. During Wilson's absence from Paris on his visit to the United States from late February to mid-March 1919, Clemenceau and Tardieu began to put heavy pressure on Colonel House and Sidney E. Mezes, head of the research group in the American delegation known as The Inquiry, to consent to the establishment of a Rhenish republic, and House seems to have crumbled under the pressure, despite Wilson's explicit instructions to him to hear no talk of the proposal. House yielded

President Wilson. It seems to me that we have already come much nearer on this question. We agree to forbid all military installations, not only on the left bank of the Rhine, but also within a zone of fifty kilometers on the opposite bank. We can extend this stipulation to include strategic railroads and forbid the assembling of armed forces in the entire region, even for maneuvers; and we could add that any violation of these provisions would be considered a hostile act. If we add to this a military guarantee by Great Britain and, I hope, the United States, acting under the authority of the League of Nations, to come to the immediate assistance of France in case of unprovoked aggression by Germany against France, it seems to me you would have satisfaction.

---

most specifically after Tardieu brought the question to a head on February 26 by distributing a memorandum by the French government. It demanded permanent inter-Allied occupation of the Rhine bridgeheads and the establishment of a "free Rhine State" to "act as a barrier and buffer between Germany and the Western Democracies." While House equivocated, the British came out in strong opposition to the French demand. House informed Wilson about this and other matters on Wilson's arrival back in France on March 13, and Wilson gained the impression that his chief confidant had yielded to French pressure on the Rhineland and other questions. One of the first things Wilson did upon his arrival in Paris on March 14 was to summon the American peace commissioners to a meeting in the Hôtel Crillon and to make known his absolute opposition to the project for a Rhenish republic.

Up to this point, the British had supported Wilson but had let him take the lead in opposing the French. However, on the same day that Wilson laid down his instructions to the American commissioners—March 14—Wilson and Lloyd George agreed upon a common strategy. It was a counterproposal of an Anglo-American guarantee, to be embodied in a treaty or treaties with France, that Britain and the United States would come to the aid of France in the event of unprovoked German aggression against that country if France abandoned her demand for a Rhenish buffer state. There were intermittent discussions of this matter from this point on. Foch, for example, kept strongly urging the necessity for France to have a strategic frontier on the Rhine, and he was supported by many French generals and politicians, including President Poincaré. However, by the time the question comes up here, Clemenceau and his cabinet had yielded their demand for a Rhenish republic and were now concentrating their attention on the promised Anglo-American security treaty and long-term occupation of the Rhineland.

For documents and notes relating to this matter see *PWW*, Vols. 55 and 56, *passim*; *PPC*, Vols. IV and V, *passim*; and Miller, *My Diary at the Conference of Paris*, *passim*. See also Tardieu, *The Truth about the Treaty*, pp. 145-232, and Lloyd George, *The Truth about the Peace Treaties*, I, 384-434. The best scholarly discussions are Harold I. Nelson, *Land and Power: British and Allied Policy on Germany's Frontiers, 1916-1919* (London and Toronto, 1963), pp. 198-248; Louis A. R. Yates, *The United States and French Security, 1917-1921* (New York, 1957), pp. 27-97; and Walter A. McDougall, *France's Rhineland Diplomacy, 1914-1924: The Last Bid for a Balance of Power in Europe* (Princeton, N. J., 1978), pp. 33-96.

> In addition to the securities afforded in the Treaty of Peace, the President of the United States has pledged himself to propose to the Senate of the United States and the Prime Minister of Great Britain has pledged himself to propose to the Parliament of ~~the United States~~ Great Britain an engagement, subject to the approval of the Council of the League of Nations, to come immediately to the assistance of France in case of unprovoked attack by Germany.
>
> Woodrow Wilson

WILSON'S PLEDGE TO FRANCE

(Received from P.-R. Mantoux and J.-A. Mantoux.)

M. Clemenceau. What Mr. Lloyd George has already said to me on this subject satisfies me, and if others don't agree with me, that won't prevent me from going ahead. But what I could not accept would be a temporary guarantee.

President Wilson. We have sought to avoid a formula which, by substituting the action of a group of states on a permanent basis for that of the League of Nations, would seem to admit that the guarantee of the latter would always remain insufficient. But, in our mind, this problem is closely linked to that of the effective action of the League of Nations.

M. Clemenceau. Couldn't we write the guarantee which you offer into the Covenant of the League of Nations?

President Wilson. We cannot insert clauses aimed at one nation in particular into a covenant which sets forth general principles. But we are ready to do what is necessary so that, while awaiting the action provided for by the Executive Council in case of unjustified aggression against a member of the League, two or more nations would be authorized to act without delay. The plans of action could even be studied in advance.

M. Clemenceau. I am ready to accept, if aggression is defined as the entry of German forces into the fifty-kilometer zone beyond the Rhine.

M. Tardieu. In case of aggression, we must have the right to transport our troops up to the Rhine, which is our line of defense.

President Wilson. What we have to fear is a state of nervousness, which will probably last for a generation or more, and the danger of a premature action. Incidents occurred for years on the border between the United States and Canada after we agreed to leave it without fortifications of any kind.

M. Clemenceau. That is why we have proposed the establishment of a Franco-Anglo-American commission, which would establish the fact of aggression.

President Wilson. Mr. Lloyd George has proposed to entrust this task to the Council of the League of Nations.

M. Clemenceau. I fear this would only lead to delays.

Mr. Lloyd George. We are ready to give France a promise of immediate and unlimited support in case of aggression. Here it would be necessary to review the correspondence exchanged before the war between M. Paul Cambon and Sir Edward Grey, which foresaw and, it seems to me, promised cooperation of this kind if France was attacked without provocation.[2]

—Marshal Foch and Generals Bliss, Sir Henry Wilson, and Diaz are introduced.

Marshal Foch. We received a telegram from General Nudant on the reception by the German representatives at Spa of our commu-

---

[2] Lloyd George here referred to the secret agreement of November 1912 between the British Foreign Secretary, Sir Edward Grey, and the French Ambassador in London, Paul Cambon. This agreement was the outgrowth of Anglo-French negotiations over possible military and naval cooperation in the event of unprovoked aggression by Germany against France, which had taken place off and on since the signing of the so-called *Entente cordiale* in 1904. The agreement of 1912 stipulated that, "if either Government had grave reason to expect an unprovoked attack by a third Power, or something that threatens the general peace, it should immediately discuss with the other whether both Governments should act together to prevent aggression and to preserve peace, and if so, what measures they would be prepared to take in common." In 1911, the British had moved their battleships from the Mediterranean to the North Sea, while the French had moved theirs from Brest to the Mediterranean. In 1913, King George V and Sir Edward Grey paid a state visit to Paris, and discussions of Anglo-French cooperation in the event of a general European war were carried on from that time to the outbreak of the World War. By 1914, there was at least an informal agreement between the two countries that the British would protect the northern French coast in the event of a Franco-German war.

nication about transporting Polish troops by way of Danzig.[3] (*Reading of the telegram.*)

President Wilson. I would have liked for this communication to have been delivered directly by Marshal Foch, and I had understood that was what would be done; that would have given it much more solemnity and weight.

Mr. Lloyd George. I agree with the President here.

Marshal Foch. General Nudant is my executive agent in Spa. It is through him that I transmit all communications from the Allies to the German government. I couldn't go to Spa simply to hand a piece of paper to a subordinate.

President Wilson. Is there not still time to ask the Germans to send a plenipotentiary to Spa who would meet with Marshal Foch? I thought that would be the procedure.

M. Clemenceau. We can send a telegram worded as follows: "In order to hasten the solution, Marshal Foch, under instructions from the Associated Governments, invites the German government to send a plenipotentiary to Spa to consider with him the execution of the measure decided upon."

President Wilson. We must at the same time clearly indicate to the Germans that we are not settling the fate of Danzig today. Today we only wish to avail ourselves of the right, which belongs to us under the Armistice, to send Polish troops, considered as Allied troops, into Poland by way of Danzig.

M. Clemenceau. I ask Marshal Foch to keep this point well in mind. Since the question of Danzig hasn't yet been finally decided upon at the conference, it's essential to tell the Germans that, for the moment, it is only a matter of using the port of Danzig for the transportation of Polish troops.

I now ask Marshal Foch to give us his report on the question,

---

[3] The issue being discussed here was the transport by sea, by way of Danzig, of the Polish army in France commanded by Gen. Jósef Haller and consisting of some 65,000 men, mainly to protect Poland against Bolshevik attack. An earlier inter-Allied mission, headed by Gen. Joseph Noulens, had conferred about this matter with German representatives at Posen, but the Germans had claimed that they had no authority to act on the Allied request and had insisted that it be discussed by German representatives and the Permanent Inter-Allied Armistice Commission at Spa, Belgium. As will be seen, the Council of Four insisted that it had the right to send Gen. Haller's army to Poland by way of Danzig, because it was an *Allied* army and the Armistice Agreement gave the Allies the right to send their troops anywhere in Germany. See the notes of the meeting of the Supreme War Council, March 21, 1919, *PWW*, Vol. 56, pp. 129-48, and Kay Lundgreen-Nielsen, *The Polish Problem at the Paris Peace Conference: A Study of the Policies of the Great Powers and the Poles, 1918-1919* (Odense, Denmark, 1979), pp. 125-61, 193-97, 225-33.

which we examined the day before yesterday, of the aid to be provided to Rumania.

—Reading of the document (*summary*): To stop the Bolshevik infiltration, it is necessary to create a barrier in Poland and in Rumania, thereby closing the breach at Lemberg, and to cleanse the points behind it which could be infected, such as Hungary, whilst assuring the maintenance of communications by way of Vienna.

Concerning Rumania specifically, the necessary measures are planned in detail to send to her army the supplies and clothing which it lacks. This army will be placed under the command of a French general. Vienna would be occupied by Allied troops under American command.

President Wilson. Part of this plan refers to what we discussed the other day; but the whole plan seems to aim at something more. It is essential to distinguish between the two proposals.

We agree on the assistance to be given the Rumanian army and on the evacuation of Odessa, which is linked to our action in Rumania. But this document goes much further. It mentions Lemberg. In the quarrel between the Ukrainians and the Poles,[4] it is difficult for us to intervene without having a better understanding of our position vis-à-vis the Ukrainians or the Bolsheviks who are besieging Lemberg. "To close the breach at Lemberg" at this time means to take the part of the Poles against the Ruthenians.[5]

As for the idea of effecting a junction between Polish and Rumanian forces to face eastward, this is the prelude to a march towards the east, and that leads us to the question of military intervention in Russia. We have considered this question more than once, and each time we have arrived at the same conclusion: that we must not consider military intervention.

As for the occupation of Vienna, it seems to me that nothing in the armistice gives us the right to do that.

---

[4] This conflict, which continued off and on during the entire period of the peace conference, was a struggle between the Poles and Ukrainians for control of the eastern part of the province of Galicia. The fighting centered about the provincial capital of Lemberg (now L'vov, U.S.S.R.) The Council of Ten, on March 19, 1919, had sent a telegram to the commanders in chief of the Polish and Ukrainian forces requesting them to conclude a truce immediately, as a prelude to a settlement of the conflict by the Supreme Council. See PPC, IV, 404-12, and Lundgreen-Nielsen, pp. 217-20.

[5] Ruthenia was a part of Galicia, or Austrian Poland. Ruthenians lived in the northeastern Carpathian Mountains and were Ukrainians.

General Sir Henry Wilson. The armistice gives us the right to occupy all strategic points in Austria-Hungary, as we see fit.

President Wilson. Undoubtedly, but we are to occupy them to assure the execution of the armistice and not for an objective outside the armistice, such as this one. Can't we limit ourselves to the immediate object which we had in view the day before yesterday, that is, to measures necessary to strengthen Rumania, without preparing an offensive action against anyone?

The phrase used by Marshal Foch was: "The Rumanian citadel must be reinforced." The evacuation of Odessa was considered as the means of transferring resources, whose use at Odessa could not lead to any satisfactory result, to Rumania, in order to bring her means of defense up to strength.

Mr. Lloyd George. I would ask Marshal Foch if, when he speaks of establishing a barrier, he wishes to take precautions against a military danger from the Bolsheviks, or against danger of another kind.

Marshal Foch. Against an epidemic disease, we create a *cordon sanitaire*: we place a customs officer every 200 meters, and they prevent people from crossing. If we also fear an armed invasion, we create a stronger barrier. My advice is to create a barrier against both dangers, which does not mean preparing an offensive.

M. Orlando. I ask permission to read two telegrams which we have from our Italian commissioner in Vienna about the situation. The first informs us that a dispatch from the revolutionary government of Budapest has been received in Vienna, inviting the Viennese proletariat to follow the example of the Hungarians. The Viennese revolutionaries have decided to form a workers' council, all set to seize power; demonstrations have taken place in front of the city hall and in the streets of Vienna.

In Budapest, the business establishments have been closed by order of the government, and it is forbidden to remove merchandise from them on pain of death. It is possible to save the situation only by an occupation of Budapest by Allied troops, on the condition that these troops include neither Czechs, Rumanians, nor Poles.

The moderate elements in Vienna fear Bolshevism and are making overtures to us in favor of the occupation of Vienna by Italian troops.

The second telegram reports a conversation with a member of the government who is not a Socialist: he considers Bolshevik infiltration likely unless the people's guard is disarmed. The government is weak; but in order to stabilize the situation, it would be enough to send to Vienna two American regiments, which would be greeted with relief by the great majority of the population. A declaration by the Allies on the subject of victualing would produce a useful effect, but would serve no purpose if it followed a Bolshevik triumph.

General Diaz. Bolshevism is a popular movement which appears wherever food is lacking and central authority is weak. It spreads along lines of communication, where small cells are formed and soon grow and combine. Its progress appears to be linked to the present success of the Russian Bolshevik movement. Sending troops without holding on to lines of communication would be very unwise, since these troops could be cut off from their base and placed in a most dangerous situation.

The fermentation now taking place is not happening only in Vienna, but even as far away as the Slovene regions—everywhere, in a word, where people suffer lack of food. By occupying Vienna in strength, we hold the lines of communication and stop this threatening advance. We must give the people the impression that we bring food, order, and security. Otherwise, they will throw themselves instinctively on the side of disorder.

If Vienna is occupied, I ask that Italian troops be entrusted with this mission, since it is Italy which fought against Austria.

General Sir Henry Wilson. The political leaders should decide whether or not they wish military action against Bolshevism. If this decision is taken, the plan presented by Marshal Foch is the best we have. The longer we delay, the more difficult the solution to the problem will become. The Bolshevik incursion into Hungary has already lengthened the border to be patrolled by several hundred kilometers.

General Bliss. The word "Bolshevik" comes up so often in these debates that it obviously sets the tone for all that has just been said. If we replaced it by the word "revolutionary," perhaps that would be clearer. Bolshevism is the form that the revolutionary movement takes in backward countries which have suffered grievously. Furthermore, we hear it said sometimes that Russian Bolshevism is a German product, at other times that it is an essentially Russian movement, which is coming to invade Europe from the East. If it was certain that it comes from Russia, it is obviously there that it should be killed. But the problem is more difficult.

A *cordon sanitaire* could stop the Bolsheviks, but not Bolshevism; to create a true barrier, it would be necessary to deploy very considerable forces all the way from the Baltic to the Black Sea. I don't believe this course should be taken without being sure there is no other means of action. I see two other courses: peace, with a determination of boundaries, since uncertainty about them causes much disturbance and agitation among the populations; and, in the second place, lifting the blockade and thereby allowing the entire world to go back to work.

—Marshal Foch repeats his proposals: the occupation of Vienna is absolutely necessary to maintain our communications with Bohemia, Poland, and Rumania.

Marshal Foch. The overall plan that I submit to you tends to construct a barrier against Bolshevism; this isn't an offensive, but a defensive barrier, behind which the necessary cleansing will be done.

—Marshal Foch and Generals Bliss, Diaz, and Sir Henry Wilson withdraw.

President Wilson. We again find ourselves on familiar ground; isn't it a question of whether it is possible to organize armed resistance against Bolshevism, which means: have we not only the required troops, but also the material means and the public sentiment to support us?

The word "Bolshevik" covers many different things. In my opinion, to try to stop a revolutionary movement with ordinary armies is like using a broom to sweep back a spring tide. The armies, moreover, can be impregnated by the very Bolshevism they would be ordered to fight. A germ of sympathy exists between the forces that one would like to set against each other. The sole means of countering Bolshevism is to make its causes disappear. Moreover, it is a perilous enterprise; we don't even quite know what the causes are.

In any case, one of the causes is the uncertainty of the populations about their future boundaries and the governments they will have to obey, and, at the same time, their misery due to lack of food, transportation, and employment. The only way to kill Bolshevism is to establish boundaries and open all doors to trade.

As for the occupation of Vienna by American troops, that is impossible, because I believe the armistice doesn't authorize us to send our troops to Vienna. I am steadfastly opposed to the reestablishment of an eastern front, which is being proposed to us once again.

The question we wanted to consider was much more limited: that of victualing Odessa. We asked Marshal Foch if it would be better to transfer to Rumania those resources necessary to maintain our troops at Odessa, without any hope of a favorable outcome. We receive as a reply to this question a plan which envisages the establishment of a continuous line from the Baltic to the Black Sea. He speaks to us about "cleansing" Hungary, which is to say crushing Hungarian Bolshevism. If this Bolshevism remains within its borders, that is not our concern. The only problem we intended to solve today was that of sending help to Rumania.

M. Orlando. This question is in fact different from that of intervention in Russia. In Russia, we had to choose between two equally logical and defensible policies. The first was intervention: to go as far as Moscow if necessary and crush Bolshevism by force. The second was to regard Bolshevism as a *de facto* government and establish relations with it, which would be, if not cordial, then at least more or less normal. We have done neither, and thus we have suffered the most distressing consequences of both policies at one and the same time. Without making war, we are in a state of war with Russia. So far, when all is said and done, the Russian or Ukrainian Bolsheviks are only defending their own territory.

I won't comment on the question of Lemberg, which might be either a Ruthenian or a Polish city. At this moment, it is not a question of intervening in Russia, but of defending our allies and assuring our communications with them. Since, from a political point of view, we agree about our duty to support our allies, there remains only a military problem to be solved. We must defend Rumania: the question may arise tomorrow with regard to the Czechs. The occupation of Vienna may become a military necessity. It wouldn't be justified for purely political reasons; but if our military advisers tell us Vienna is absolutely necessary to insure our communications with the Rumanians and the Czechs, I personally believe we would shoulder a great responsibility by refusing to go to Vienna. Moreover, I picture the occupation of this city as an inter-Allied enterprise; and I don't support the opinion expressed by General Diaz. I repeat only that, if this is a military necessity,we would incur a great responsibility if we refused.

M. Clemenceau. President Wilson has expressed my opinion. I am asked to equip or rebuild the Rumanian army; this is the question to which we must confine ourselves.

Mr. Lloyd George. There has been talk of suppressing the revolution in Hungary. I don't see why we should do that: there are few countries so much in need of a revolution. This very day, I had a conversation with someone who has visited Hungary and who knows it well; he tells me that this country has the worst system of landholding in Europe. The peasants there are as oppressed as they were in the Middle Ages, and manorial law still exists there.

—*After an exchange of views, it is decided that Marshal Foch will be asked to confine his proposals to the measures necessary for the reinforcement of the Rumanian army, including the evacuation of Odessa and the sending of the provisions destined for this city to Rumania.*

VIII

Conversation between President Wilson and MM. Clemenceau, Lloyd George, Orlando, and Klotz*

MARCH 28, 1919, 11 A.M.

M. Clemenceau. M. Klotz is going to explain to you the official view of the French government on the general matter of reparations to be asked of the German government.

M. Klotz. In the Armistice Agreement, we compelled the Germans to accept a clause worded as follows: "Reparation for damages." We must analyze this term and determine the amount of reparation due.

Today we don't know the price of materials and labor, and it is very difficult for us to know what repairs will cost. The diversity of the figures which have been submitted to us shows how imprudent it is to commit ourselves to estimates which will be considered by some as exaggerated, but which might, however, in reality be low.

I have prepared a study analyzing and classifying the damages. If the list is too long, or if there are omissions, we welcome all observations which may be offered. I made no attempt to give precise figures: I have indicated qualities and not quantities. Who will determine the figures? If our governments do it today,

*Not represented in H.

they could be mistaken either to the detriment of their own people or to the detriment of their associates. Regional commissions must be established, working according to fixed rules, as well as a central inter-Allied commission, which will collect and evaluate the figures.

We want only our due. What is not subject to debate is that we are entitled to reparations; they will be estimated at their exact value. The document which I present to you only foresees a down payment made by the enemy as partial payment on his debt for a year or two. Later, the commission will determine annual payments according to the debt decided upon and will fix the duration of payments.

—M. Klotz explains the outline of his plan.[1]

M. Klotz. The advantage of this system is its absolute straightforwardness amongst ourselves and even towards the enemy himself. We cannot, at this time, fix the figures without a great element of doubt. If we state a total sum, the Germans might say to us that it is excessive. This system is more flexible; we only ask for a down payment. We anticipate a method of fixing the total amount of damages according to the definitions given and of determining the number of annual payments.

If we can agree on this basis, there will be no discussion about the figures on the day we find ourselves face to face with the enemy negotiators. They have already accepted the principle in the text of the Armistice Agreement; the debate can only center on the nature of losses admitted to the list of damages, and it will thus be limited and facilitated.

—M. Klotz reads the articles defining material damages and, at Mr. Lloyd George's request, the article defining damages to persons.

President Wilson. We mustn't enter here into a consideration of details but decide on the principles. The idea is to determine the nature of damages for which reparations are due without fixing any figure, whilst obliging the Germans to agree to pay our bill in proportion as it is presented to them. If I clearly understood your general proposal, that is the question we are going to discuss.

---

[1] Klotz's plan is printed in Burnett, *Reparation at the Paris Peace Conference*, I, 726-54. It attempted to detail all possible German reparation liabilities and the means of forcing the Germans to meet them. The Four were discussing Annex I (*ibid.*, pp. 732-34) in three chapters. The first chapter defined the geographical areas where damages qualifying for reparation occurred. The second established categories of damages to property for which reparation could be claimed. The third defined damages to persons for which reparation was due.

Mr. Lloyd George. I also believe we should leave the study of the details to the specialists. I consider the proposal presented to us as new and very important. To fix a principle and leave the determination of the figures to arbitrators who will, moreover, hear the views of the Germans—I am not averse to that. I believe one of our financial advisers, Mr. Keynes, has already made a proposal of this kind.

—Mr. Keynes is introduced.

Mr. Keynes. Our uncertainty chiefly concerned Germany's capacity to pay. We proposed to tell the Germans: "Here is what you owe; but we haven't yet determined how much you are able to pay." It is this second point that we will have to discuss with them.

M. Klotz. The plan I present to you today is similar to the judicial procedure in the case of a railroad accident: the victim immediately receives a sum which allows him to pay the doctor, and then damages and interest are fixed by expert opinion.

President Wilson. My objection is that this system would be tantamount to asking Germany to give us a blank check. Suppose we went before one of our legislative assemblies and said: "We can't determine the amount that such and such large public works will cost; we ask you for authority to undertake them, and we will tell you afterwards what they cost." The American Congress would never vote for a motion of this kind. Nothing is more difficult than to know the cost of projects for which there is no strictly limited appropriation. There will be large contracts for repairs, and it would be dangerous not to limit their cost. Germany will think it more severe to accept an unlimited obligation than to consent to pay even a very considerable sum.

This amounts to asking Germany to place at our disposal indefinitely all that she possesses. I understand that we ask Germany to make a down payment; but we mustn't forget that the first years will be the most difficult and those during which, as we have all acknowledged, it will be necessary to allow Germany the time and means to recover economically.

Mr. Keynes' proposal is very different. He says: let us agree on what Germany owes us. None of us knows what she is able to pay; but we are ready to talk with the German representatives in order to discover how much and in what way Germany will pay. In a case of insufficient means, the burden of proof would be upon her. That is very different from what is being proposed to us.

Mr. Lloyd George. I acknowledge this difference; but there is no contradiction between the two proposals, and they can even be easily combined. I should say that my first impression of the plan presented by M. Klotz is favorable.

I accept the objection made by President Wilson against a procedure which would consist of presenting the bill for our expenditures progressively. We can't each undertake our own reconstruction and then come and say: here is what this has cost us. But we can say to the Germans: "We know you are not in a position to reimburse us for all that the war has cost us, as we would have the right to require. That is why we spoke in the Armistice Agreement only of reparation for damages. We define damages by distinguishing between damages to property and damages to persons, and we give you precise details about the meaning of these terms. As for saying what this sum is, that is impossible for us at present. We are appointing a commission which will determine the figures; you will be given a hearing, and the approximate figure at which the commission arrives will be that which you will have to pay."

I see great advantages in not announcing today the total figure of what Germany owes us. You may be sure that, whatever the figure, many people in England, as well as in France, will exclaim at once: "It is too small!" M. Klotz's formula gives us a way to avoid discussions which might ensue in our respective parliaments. If our parliaments should disapprove because we haven't asked enough, what will happen to the governments which succeed us in attempting the impossible?

Another reason to welcome this project is that I dislike discussions amongst us about the proportional percentages of our claims; they are unpleasant, and they cause us to argue about such or such a figure. I prefer to have a commission which will study the facts. What is more important than the proportion of 1 to 2, or whatever else, as you please, is the maintenance of a good understanding between France and England. We intend to continue our alliance with you, to come to your immediate aid in case of aggression—and you know we generally do even better than we promise. We told you to expect the help of six British divisions at the beginning of the war, and we sent you up to sixty. Our American cousins rather resemble us in this. I attach supreme importance to good relations between ourselves and to everything that can preserve them.

This doesn't contradict what Mr. Keynes has said. Let's suppose the commission arrives at some total figure—five billion pounds sterling, for example; it remains to be seen how much the Germans can pay and how this sum should be divided into annual payments. At this point Mr. Keynes' system might be applied.

M. Orlando. As for the principle, I adhere completely to M. Klotz's plan. It offers the great advantage which Mr. Lloyd George has just indicated, that of avoiding discussions, very dangerous as well amongst us—for each will say that he is receiving too little—as with the Germans, who will say that they are being asked for too much. The Germans won't be able to refuse to sign a clause which is only the detailed explanation of the obligation they have already taken in signing the Armistice.

President Wilson's objection regarding the danger of a seemingly unlimited obligation is serious. But it is better to wait until the Germans make it themselves; and there would be a way to overcome it, which would be to fix a maximum figure of payment. However, I don't think we should do this now. It is better to stand purely and simply upon the text accepted in the Armistice Agreement.

The Germans will tell us: "Our means of payment are limited." Undoubtedly, but the moral advantage will be ours, for Germany, having agreed to repair damages which she caused, would be declaring herself incapable of paying what she should. On the other hand, if we fix a figure right now, Germany will say that the figure is excessive and that we seek to enrich ourselves by war. We thus place on our side not only the reality, but also the favorable appearance, of justice. If Germany says she can't pay, it will be up to her to prove it.

Mr. Lloyd George. We have to plan for a means of taking decisions if there are differences of opinion amongst our representatives in the commission. I would propose to accept as an arbitrator a person who would be appointed by the President of the United States.

President Wilson. I must reserve my judgment on the plan that has been presented to us. I see certain difficulties with it, and I haven't yet been able to study the details. I fear that this commission we will establish, like the one at Spa,[2] will only report continually about the ingenious means used by the Germans to elude their obligations. Imagine the correspondence we now receive from Spa continuing for thirty years!

Mr. Lloyd George. The estimate of damages and of payment are two different things. The commission envisaged by this plan would have as its job to determine the sums due. That doesn't

---

[2] That is, the Permanent Inter-Allied Armistice Commission.

mean that we would abandon the system mentioned earlier of having a commission fix, from year to year, the amount of the annual payments and the sum of the total payments.[3]

[3] At the end of this meeting, Wilson, Clemenceau, and Lloyd George discussed for the first time France's claim to the Saar Basin. Lloyd George met Colonel House for lunch immediately after the meeting, and House recorded the gist of their conversation as follows:

"It seems that the long expected row between either Clemenceau and the President, or Lloyd George and Clemenceau, had actually come. I am sorry it should have happened to be the President rather than Lloyd George. They came near calling one another names. The trouble arose over the question of the Western Boundaries and of the Sarre Valley. The President told Clemenceau that the French were bringing up territorial questions that had nothing to do with the war aims of anybody, and that no one had heard of their intention to annex the Sarre Valley until after the Armistice had been signed. Clemenceau grew angry at this and said that the President favored the Germans. The President replied that such a statement was untrue and that Clemenceau knew that it was.

"Clemenceau then stated that if they did not receive the Sarre Valley, he would not sign the Treaty of Peace. To this the President replied, 'Then if France does not get what she wishes, she will refuse to act with us. In that event do you wish me to return home?' Clemenceau answered, 'I do not wish you to go home, but I intend to do so myself,' and in a moment he left the house.

"George said the President was very angry." E. M. House Diary, March 28, 1919, printed in *PWW*, Vol. 56, p. 349.

In the evening of March 28, Wilson told Ray Stannard Baker what had transpired during the morning session of the Big Four. Baker observed that Wilson was "impatient & somewhat discouraged," and he continued:

"It seems that they were near an open rupture. The French brought in their claim to the Saar valley & stated their historical rights, reaching back to 1814. The President said at once, & plainly, that he considered that the French claim to the territory & the people as contrary to the terms of the Armistice & to the fourteen points upon which they had all agreed. At this Clemenceau broke out: 'Then I must resign.' To this the President said he could make no comment, but suggested that if M. Clemenceu were not prepared to abide by the solemnly accepted terms of the Armistice that he (the President) might as well go home. To this Clemenceau responded hastily that he did not of course suggest any such action.

"The 'four' have had to consult their experts, and it is likely that the whole thing will now go over until next week." R. S. Baker Diary, March 28, 1919, printed in *ibid.*, pp. 353-54.

Several months later, Baker added the following account:

"Once in the Council of Four Clemenceau accused Wilson of pro-Germanism. W. very angry: could not eat his luncheon. Made a great speech in the afternoon in reply on the situation in Europe, saying he was not for an easy peace but a just peace & painting a picture of what Europe would be like if an unjust peace were imposed upon Germany. Clemenceau got up & came over to him with tears in his eyes & said: 'I agree with you, Mr. President: I agree with you.' Lloyd George echoed, 'And I too.' " R. S. Baker Diary, Nov. 5, 1919, printed at that date in *ibid.*, Vol. 63.

For other corroborative evidence of this episode, see the memorandum by

R. Lansing, March 28, 1919, and the extracts from the diaries of V. C. McCormick, March 28, 1919, and G. L. Beer, March 30, 1919, printed in ibid., Vol. 56, pp. 351-52, 353, 434.

IX

Conversation between President Wilson and MM. Clemenceau, Lloyd George, Orlando, and Tardieu*

MARCH 28, 1919, 4 P.M.

M. Tardieu. The regions of the Saar[1] and Landau[2] have been French lands for a long, long time. Landau was part of the king-

*Not represented in H.

[1] The French demands concerning the Saar Basin had been spelled out in great detail by Tardieu in a memorandum which formed the basis of his following presentation. These demands consisted of the cession to France of that part of the Saar Basin which lay south of the frontier of 1814 and which included its main cities, coal mines, and industries; and administrative and economic control over the remainder of the basin, including full ownership of its mines. As early as February 21, the British and American experts had agreed to French ownership of all the mines and to some kind of French "supremacy and administration" over the entire Saar Basin, but they had argued against the subjection of the local inhabitants to French institutions and had opposed the outright annexation of any territory.

Tardieu's memorandum had earlier been distributed to the Big Four, who presumably had copies of it in front of them during the following discussion. It is printed in Tardieu, The Truth about the Treaty, pp. 251-62, as part of the general discussion of the Saar question, on pp. 250-79. Other accounts by contemporaries include Charles H. Haskins and Robert H. Lord, Some Problems of the Peace Conference (Cambridge, Mass., 1920), pp. 132-50, which also discusses the history of the Saar Valley in some detail; and the essay by C. H. Haskins on "The New Boundaries of Germany" in House and Seymour, eds., What Really Happened at Paris, pp. 56-63. For diary entries, letters, and memoranda by the chief British expert on the Saar question, see James W. Headlam-Morley, A Memoir of the Paris Peace Conference 1919, Agnes Headlam-Morley, Russell Bryant, and Anna Cienciala, eds. (London, 1972), passim. A large number of documents on the Saar settlement are scattered throughout several volumes of Miller's My Diary at the Conference of Paris. The major developments of this question are well documented in PWW, Vols. 56-60, and PPC, V-VI. For detailed discussions, see Harold W. V. Temperley, ed., A History of the Peace Conference of Paris, II, 176-84; Birdsall, Versailles Twenty Years After, pp. 224-37; and, especially, Nelson, Land and Power, pp. 249-81.

[2] A city in the Palatinate northwest of Karlsruhe, which had passed to France

dom of France after 1648. Sarrelouis was built by Louis XIV. The two regions also took part in the Revolution, and their representatives were at the *fête de la Fédération*,[3] among those who swore in the name of all the French provinces to unite voluntarily to form but one single nation. In 1793, Landau suffered a famous siege and held out heroically. The city was eventually relieved, and the Convention declared by a solemn vote that Landau had deserved well of the the Fatherland. It was at this time that Saarbrücken became French, amidst the immense enthusiasm which has been described by Goethe,[4] and the petitions of the people preserved in our national archives provide enduring testimony to it.

—M. Tardieu reads aloud several of these documents.

M. Tardieu. If we only had isolated documents, they would be of little value. But it is the unanimous sentiment of the entire population of every part of these territories that is expressed there. The following years gave these countries a new reason to attach themselves to France, as a result of the excellent administration of Napoleon. It was then that the mines of the Saar were discovered and developed. Napoleon created a school of mines and had maps of the coal basin drawn.

When Sarrelouis and Saarbrücken were annexed by Prussia, it was an agent of the Westphalian mine owners, himself a native of the Saar region, who was the adviser to the Prussian state to prepare the annexation. One of the first clauses of the act of cession provided that the maps of the coal beds be handed over to the Prussian administration. In 1814, the Allies deemed it impossible to take the Saar region from France; and to bring them to this decision it required the return from Elba, Waterloo, and the strong insistence of Prussia, which knew the value of this territory.

Here, then, are regions which became French voluntarily and which were separated from France by force, not in 1814, but in 1815. The opinion of the English plenipotentiaries, which has been preserved, was expressed in Castlereagh's words drawing attention to the danger of taking from France populations deeply

---

in 1648 and had formed a French enclave until 1815. The French were not only reclaiming the city but also the territory to its south to incorporate it into Alsace.

[3] A celebration across France on July 14, 1790, to mark the first anniversary of the destruction of the Bastille.

[4] Tardieu was in error here. There is no reference in any of Goethe's writings to the reception of the French armies by the inhabitants of Saarbrücken in 1793.

attached to her. Metternich wrote: "Prussia has taken neither justice nor decency into consideration."

Many inhabitants of the ceded territories emigrated during the following years; those who stayed called themselves "Prussians by force," *Musspreussen*. French consciousness manifested itself many times in both Sarrelouis and Landau. At the time of the Crimean War, demonstrations in favor of France took place, as well as many enlistments in the French army. In 1865, William I, visiting the Saar Basin, was received very coldly there. In 1866, Chlodwig von Hohenlohe, the future Chancellor of the Empire, wrote about Landau: "These populations would not object if events should return them to France."

Finally, a still more precious piece of testimony is that of the great Prussian historian, Treitschke, who, acknowledging the age-old fidelity of these peoples to France, saw therein proof that they were true Germans—for fidelity, he said, is a Prussian virtue.

President Wilson. I would like to know at what period the different parts of this territory were acquired by France. What is the proportion of those which belonged to her from the seventeenth century?

M. Tardieu. About two thirds. Saarbrücken became French only in 1793. I should point out, in addition, that the frontier of 1792 was more extensive than that of 1814.

The recent reception of French troops in Sarrelouis and Landau has been the same as in Alsace, and the extreme caution imposed on the French authorities couldn't prevent them from affirming the desire of the populations to be reunited to France. The question arises in other parts of Europe which have been taken by conquest from their former owners: we have here two little bits of French land, united to France by their own will, separated from her against their will, and their desire to return to France has endured.

No doubt one finds there elements of the population who represent the conquerors of the last century. But must one sacrifice the indigenous population out of consideration for them? These are territories that border France and that France considers her own. In other words, the systematic colonization of these areas by Prussia should not be invoked against the old inhabitants—the victims of this colonization—but should, on the contrary, be counted as an argument in their favor. Such is the historical aspect.

From an economic point of view, France has three reasons to

claim these territories: in the first place, the relations of Alsace-Lorraine with the Saar Basin, which has always provided it with the coal upon which its industrial life is based; in the second place, France's situation with regard to coal. Now, just after the war and after the return of Alsace-Lorraine, our annual consumption has risen to seventy-five million tons, whilst our production has fallen to twenty-four million. There will therefore be a deficit of fifty-one million tons, which is more than two thirds of our needs. If we are not to be abandoned to economic dependence upon foreign producers of coal, especially Germany, we must be able to exploit the Saar Basin to our profit.

In the third place, it must be recalled that the destruction of our mines in the North was carried out by the Germans according to a systematic plan. Our basins in the departments of the Nord and the Pas-de-Calais supplied industries which the Germans considered competitors. The documents in our hands show that the destruction of our mines was part of a plan of economic warfare, and this destruction was complete: 220 pits, all the surface installations, have disappeared—which represents a production of twenty million tons; a working population of 100,000 inhabitants was reduced to unemployment.

—M. Loucheur is introduced.

Mr. Lloyd George. What is the annual production of the Saar Basin?

M. Tardieu. 17,500,000 tons, including 4 million in Lorraine proper; 4.5 million beyond the frontier of 1814; and 9.5 million in the territories ceded to Prussia in 1815.

This cession, so well justified from the point of view of reparation, won't have the effect of depriving Germany of absolutely essential resources. In fact, in 1913 Germany produced 191 million tons of coal, without counting lignite. The Saar Basin, if we subtract the part included in the former Department of the Moselle, produced only about thirteen millions.

M. Loucheur. In addition, the basin's production, except two million tons, is consumed either on the spot or in Alsace-Lorraine.

M. Tardieu. As for the transfer of the mines to the French state, that is an easy thing, for before 1814 these mines were the property of the state; they passed into the hands of the Prussian state, and even today, out of 116,000 hectares of mining land, 114,000 are owned by the state. It is thus possible to accomplish the cession without violating private interests.

Under Prussian rule, the interests of the Saar Basin were sacrificed to the interests of the Westphalian Basin. Prussia opposed the canalizing of the Saar and the Moselle valleys, and the Canal des Houillères, which serves this region, only opens on to French territory. It was Germany herself which, in order to protect Westphalia, allowed the transport routes to be directed exclusively towards Nancy and Strasbourg.

In summary, our claims fall neatly into two categories. In the first place, we ask for our historical frontier populations united to France by their own will, separated from her by force, and subsequently mingled with German populations by systematic colonization. In the second place, we ask that Alsace-Lorraine be able to live, that France not be in a state of excessive dependence upon foreign countries for her coal needs, and that reparation be made to us for the systematic destruction of our mines in the North. To do that, this coal basin, first discovered and developed by French engineering, must be returned to France.

M. Loucheur. From the industrial point of view, the Saar and Lorraine form a single entity. Half of the cast iron going to the Saar steel mills comes from Lorraine proper. All the iron ore used in this region comes from the mines of Lorraine. So true is this that, a few days ago, an important metallurgist from the Saar told one of my representatives: "Germany made war for ore; today we must go over to the side which has the ore." Without the Saar, the serious deficit of coal that France suffers would be considerably increased by the needs of the industries of Alsace and Lorraine.

—MM. Tardieu and Loucheur withdraw.

Mr. Lloyd George. Here is a new proposal[5] which was handed to me this morning by some of our English experts who reached agreement with some of your American experts. Their conclusion is that the historical argument is dubious, and that the solid basis of the French claim to the Saar Basin is the principle of compensation. The solution they propose is to place all the mines in a small autonomous state, the mines themselves becoming the property of France by way of reparation. The region would enjoy complete autonomy; it would have its own legislation, its schools, its police; it would not be subject to the military law of either France or Germany. Above local authority, French sovereignty could be established, which would be comparable to

[5] This "new proposal" was, in fact, the plan agreed upon by the British and American experts on February 21. See Miller, *My Diary at the Conference of Paris*, XIX, 59-60, and Nelson, *Land and Power*, pp. 251-53.

British sovereignty over the Isle of Man and over the Anglo-Norman islands which are, in truth, perfectly independent small states, which weren't even subject to conscription during the war.

Considering the systematic destruction of the French mines, those who drafted this report declare that it doesn't seem adequate to establish a purely temporary rule in the Saar region.

I learned about this proposal only this very day. If we are inclined to accept it in principle, it would be necessary that the final plan be presented by France. It seems to me that this deserves study.

M. Clemenceau. I agree.

Mr. Lloyd George. I should say that, concerning Landau, our experts are opposed to the annexation of this territory. You must understand the spirit of the British people: they fear doing anything which might repeat against the Germans the error committed by Germany herself when she annexed Alsace-Lorraine.

President Wilson. I might observe that France never raised this question with us before the beginning of the present negotiations; it is thus a question which must be added to those for which we were prepared to seek solutions. In my mind, it is part of the entire economic problem raised by the war.

From an economic point of view, the Saar region must be treated as a unit, for this unit now extends beyond the small region included between the borders of 1814 and those of 1815.

It is a fact that the Germans have ruined the mines of northern France and have deprived France for a certain number of years of the production of twenty million tons. It is a fact that this damage was caused systematically, and obviously some means of compensation must be found. Repairing the mines of the North will take a long time; however, the approximate number of years required can be calculated. We have to find compensation in kind, and, if possible, in the Saar region. Up to this point, no difficulty.

But it is desirable to preserve the unity of this industrial region; it should not be carved up in such a way that the coal it produces would be used only in part of its area. The areas that use this coal must remain together. My principle accepted, France, if she has these mines at her disposal, will be obliged to allow the coal to be transported north as well as south, as previously. But if the owner of these mines, whoever it is, agrees to this, then the question of ownership becomes a mere question of sentiment.

I am ready to work out a plan: (1) to assure France compensation in kind during the period necessary to repair the French mines; (2) to assure the integrity of this industrial entity, the Saar region. Both can be done without annexation and without violation of our principles. We mustn't forget that these principles obligate us to Germany, towards which we took definite commitments at the time of the Armistice. If we don't wish to place ourselves in the wrong and break our word, we mustn't interpret our own principles too generously to our own benefit. I say this solemnly: let us avoid acting in a manner that would risk creating sympathies for Germany; neither let us seek to interpret our promises with a lawyer's cunning.

Mr. Lloyd George. Please allow me to protest on behalf of the lawyers.

President Wilson. The question being asked here also applies to other parts of Europe—in the Danzig region, at Teschen,[6] where the dispute between the Czechs and Poles recalls in many ways this problem of the Saar. Mr. Lloyd George said the other day: if you try to establish borders according to historical or strategic—and, I will add, economic—considerations, there will be no limit to the claims. We must hold to the principles we have enunciated, and, in that way, we won't be wronging France.

M. Clemenceau. Maybe, provided France agrees.

President Wilson. There is no nation more intelligent than the

---

[6] The Duchy of Teschen, in southeastern Silesia, which had remained under the Bohemian Crown after the rest of Silesia had been ceded to Prussia in 1742. It had rich coal deposits and a substantial heavy industry and was an important railway center connecting northern and southern Europe. Inhabited by a mixture of Polish, Czech, and German populations, it had been claimed during the war by both Poland and Czechoslovakia as part of their future states, and, in late January 1919, serious clashes between Czech and Polish troops had taken place in the area. After hearing spokesmen for both sides on the issue on January 29, the Council of Ten had established a provisional demarcation line between the Czech and Polish forces and, on February 3, had sent an inter-Allied commission to Teschen to prevent further conflict in the region, to study the situation, and to suggest terms for an equitable settlement. Earlier discussions by the conference of the question of Teschen and documents relating to it are printed in PWW, Vols. 54-56; PPC, III-IV, passim, and XII, 312-29, 351; and Miller, *My Diary at the Conference of Paris*, passim. For detailed accounts, see Temperley, *History of the Paris Peace Conference*, IV, 348-63; Piotr S. Wandycz, *France and her Eastern Allies, 1919-1925: French Czechoslovak-Polish Relations from the Paris Peace Conference to Locarno* (Minneapolis, Minn., 1962), pp. 75-103; Dagmar Perman, *The Shaping of the Czechoslovak State: Diplomatic History of the Boundaries of Czechoslovakia, 1914-1920* (Leiden, 1962), pp. 97-120, 228-75; and Lundgreen-Nielsen, *The Polish Problem at the Paris Peace Conference*, pp. 247-52, 400-401, and passim.

French nation. If you allow me to explain my point of view frankly to her, I have no fear of her judgment. Undoubtedly, if they saw that we were not applying the same principle everywhere, the French people would not accept a solution which appeared unfavorable to them; but if we show them we are doing our best to act justly everywhere similar problems arise, the sense of justice which is in the heart of French people will rise to answer me: "You are right." I have such an exalted idea of the spirit of the French nation that I believe she will always accept a principle founded on justice and applied with equity.

The annexation of these regions to France does not have a sufficient historical foundation. One part of these territories was French for only twenty-two years; the remainder has been separated from France for over one hundred years. I realize that the map of Europe is covered with ancient injustices which cannot all be redressed. What is just is to assure France the compensation which is due her for the loss of her coal mines and to give the entire Saar region the guarantees it needs for the utilization of its own coal. If we do that, we will do all that could reasonably be asked of us.

M. Clemenceau. I will keep in mind the words and excellent intentions of President Wilson. He eliminates sentiment and memory; it is here that I have a reservation about what has just been said. The President of the United States fails to recognize the basis of human nature. The fact of war cannot be forgotten. America did not see this war at a close distance for its first three years; during this time we lost a million and a half men. We have no more manpower. Our English friends, who lost less than we, but still enough to have suffered much, will understand me.

Our trials have created a profound feeling in this country about the reparation which is due us; and it isn't only a matter of material repairs: the need for moral redress is no less great. The doctrines just invoked, if they were interpreted in all their rigor, would allow refusing us even Alsace-Lorraine. In reality, the Saar and Landau are part of Lorraine and Alsace.

Our great enemies of 1815, against whom we fought for so many centuries—the English—insisted after the fall of Napoleon that Prussia should not take the Saar Basin. A generous gesture towards a people who suffered so much would not be in vain. It is a mistake to believe that the world is governed by abstract principles. These are accepted by certain parties, rejected by others—I do not speak of supernatural doctrines, about which I have nothing to say. But I believe there are no human dogmas; there are only rules of justice and common sense.

You seek to do justice to the Germans. Don't believe they will ever forgive us; they only seek the opportunity for revenge. Nothing will extinguish the rage of those who wanted to establish their domination over the world and who believed themselves so close to succeeding.

I will never forget that our American friends, like our English friends, came here to help us in a moment of supreme danger; and I'll tell you the argument I hold in reserve for the French, if I can't manage to convince you. I will say to them: "Suppose the English and Americans had offered terms before coming to our help; would you have accepted them or not?"

I hand over my argument to you, I place myself in your hands, to prove to you how much I feel all that we owe you. But you will do justice to humanity by recognizing a sentiment which is something other than your principles, but is no less profound.

Likewise, when those young men, Lafayette and Rochambeau, went to help the Americans fighting for their independence, it was not cold reason, it was not deeds of war—after all ordinary—which created the memory of their intervening; it was a mental impression, a profound sentiment that has bound our two nations forever. The world is not led by pure principles.

I am old. In a few months, I will leave political life forever. My disinterestedness is absolute. As Mr. Lloyd George said the other day, there is no finer role than to succumb in defending a just cause. I don't wish for a finer end; I don't wish anyone a finer end. I will support before Parliament whatever agreements we arrive at amongst ourselves. But here, amongst us, allow me to tell you that you will miss an opportunity to forge one more link in the chain of affection which binds France to America.

I won't change your opinion, I fear; you consider yourself bound by your word. I would observe nevertheless that these 350,000 men, of whom at least 150,000 are French, do not constitute a nation. You don't want to make an exception to the principle? You will certainly be forced to do so by the facts. How will you tear the Germans of Karlsbad away from Bohemia without destroying Bohemia itself? Peoples who fought against each other for centuries have remained mingled as in battle. In the Balkans, you won't be able to create a Greece which contains no Bulgarians, a Serbia which contains no Albanians.

I respect your sentiment, which is very honorable. Your role is grand. But you are going against your own goal. You will not sow hatred; but you will encounter bitterness and regrets. This is the reason we must arrive, not at a mathematical justice, but at a justice which takes feeling into account.

You are ready to do us justice from an economic point of view; I thank you for it. But economic necessities aren't everything. The history of the United States is a glorious history, but short. A century for you is a very long period; for us it is a small thing. I have known men who saw Napoleon with their own eyes. We have our own conception of history which cannot be quite the same as yours.

I simply ask you to think about what I have just said when you are alone and to ask yourself conscientiously if it doesn't contain a part of the truth.

President Wilson. I thank you for the very fine words you have spoken; I am conscious of their gravity. I don't have excessive confidence in my personal judgment. But before terminating this discussion, I would like to return to a single point.

I believe as you do that sentiment is the most powerful force in the world. Someone once told me: "The mind is the sovereign of the world." I replied to him: "If that is so, it is a sovereign which reigns but does not govern."

There is a passion for justice throughout the entire world today. Even some errors and crimes which have been committed came from a false view of what is right. The feeling that brought together in battle peoples from all points of the earth is the feeling that they were fighting together for justice. That is why I have sometimes said here that we represent not so much states as the opinion of the world. This enthusiastic yearning for just solutions will change into cynical skepticism if we give the impression that we have fallen short of the rules of justice we have proclaimed.

You have said that, in pushing logic to the extreme, one could say of Alsace and Lorraine what I said of the Saar. I don't believe this would be possible except by abusing pure logic. The world had its eyes turned towards Alsace-Lorraine for half a century; for half a century, the world never thought of Alsace-Lorraine as German territory. Of all the questions that we have to settle today, this is perhaps the only one whose solution has never seemed in doubt.

I greatly fear the transformation of enthusiasm into a despair as violent as Bolshevism, which says: "There is no justice in the world; all that can be done is to take revenge by force for injustices previously committed by force." What I seek is not to stray from the path being followed by this great world movement towards justice. I wish to do nothing that would allow it to be said of us: "They profess great principles, but they admitted exceptions wherever sentiment or national interest made them wish to deviate from the rule."

I apologize for having spoken thus. It is painful for me to oppose you; I couldn't do otherwise without shirking my duty.

M. Clemenceau. My response when Luxembourg was discussed[7] shows that I don't seek territorial acquisitions. Nor did I ask for the frontier of 1792. You speak of justice, but the people of Landau who sent their petitions to President Poincaré are also men who have a right to justice. One cannot satisfy everybody. By seeking general satisfaction, you run the risk of sowing the seeds of general discontent.

Mr. Lloyd George. I agree with the declaration of principle so forcefully presented by President Wilson, and the country which I represent is bound in honor not to stray from those principles. The Armistice Agreement established the foundations of the peace, and it differed in that regard from the usual armistice agreements. Nothing would do more harm to a great country than not to keep the word which it has given, even to an enemy. Great Britain declared war on Germany in 1914 in order to honor its signature to a treaty that guaranteed the neutrality of Belgium. If we violate a promise given to the Germans a few months ago, how can France depend upon our word when we promise her support in case of aggression?

The question is whether territorial annexations constitute a violation of our commitments. I think that they do, and this applies to questions other than that of the Saar. I took this position first on questions that did not concern France, for example, when the other day, it was a question of the boundaries of Poland.[8] When we are face to face with the Germans, we cannot run the risk of

[7] The only substantive top-level discussion about the future of Luxembourg had taken place during the presentation of the Belgian territorial claims in the Council of Ten on February 11, 1919. However, the minutes of that meeting do not show any response by Clemenceau. See the minutes of the Council of Ten, Feb. 11, 1919, 3 p.m., printed in *PPC*, III, 966-68.

[8] On March 19, 1919, when the Council of Ten had discussed the report by the Commission on Polish Affairs about the suggested boundaries between Poland and Germany and Lloyd George had strongly argued against a settlement that would include more than two million Germans in the future Polish state. See the minutes of the Council of Ten, March 19, 1919, 3 p.m., printed in *PWW*, Vol. 56, pp. 88-95.

giving them the right to say to us: "You have gone back on your word."

I remind you of the enthusiasm on all sides that greeted the signing of the Armistice. After that, we saw the birth and growth of appetites. I don't believe one can substitute appetites for principles, and this applies to small as well as to great nations. At the time of the Armistice, there were no murmurs of protest against the clauses we signed; I saw only great rejoicing everywhere.

M. Clemenceau. People everywhere had suffered for a long time.

Mr. Lloyd George. Almost at the same time that President Wilson did so, in January 1918,[9] I, in the name of the British government, made a statement of our war aims.[10] I said then that the wrong done to France in 1871 had to be redressed, but not a word about the Saar Valley. And yet I received a congratulatory telegram from M. Clemenceau the next day.

Now I hear for the first time about this question of the mines—after the signing of the Armistice.

I don't believe we can be accused of lacking generosity towards France. We did our best to support her. Hundreds of thousands of our young men died on French soil. Our personal feeling for France became a passion.

You wish to redress the injustice of 1815? Remember that, when the Germans took Alsace in 1871, they said that it had been taken from them in 1648. But the resentment that the annexation of Alsace created was justified by the fact that, since 1648, the Alsatians had become French at heart. This error must not be repeated. The English people are haunted by fear of creating new Alsace-Lorraines.

The proposal contained in the report of which I just spoke gives France nearly everything she wants. France doesn't want to absorb populations against their will. On the other hand, she has the right to compensation. The arrangement suggested would not place these people under French domination. They are obviously

[9] Wilson's Fourteen Points Address of January 8, 1918, printed in *PWW*, Vol. 45, pp. 534-39.

[10] On January 5, 1918, before a conference of the Trades Union Congress at Caxton Hall in London. The full text of this address is printed in David Lloyd George, *War Memoirs of David Lloyd George*, 6 vols. (Boston, 1933-37), V, 63-73. For a succinct summary of its main points, see *PWW*, Vol. 45, pp. 487-88. An item-by-item comparison of this speech with Wilson's Fourteen Points Address can be found in Sterling J. Kernek, *Distractions of Peace during War: The Lloyd George Government's Reaction to Woodrow Wilson, December, 1916-November, 1918* (Philadelphia, 1975), pp. 72-77.

Germans; a few manifestations in honor of President Poincaré are not enough to prove the contrary. But we can give them an autonomous government, with the mines going to France; I believe she has a right to them.

President Wilson. She has a right to the use of the mines.

Mr. Lloyd George. I would go as far as ownership. I believe we must have a conference with the experts who drafted this document.

President Wilson. I want that also. We must see them separately and ask them to explain their report to us. But I believe that we violate the principle of self-determination as much by giving one people an independence it does not request as by making them pass under the sovereignty of another. The sole principle I recognize is the one of the consent of the governed, and that is why the conclusions of the report of which you have just spoken seem debatable to me.

Mr. Lloyd George. There are cases in which equally respectable principles collide. We, too, recognize the right of self-determination. To reconcile them, each side must consent to some sacrifice.

M. Orlando. Allow me to make a statement. When the representatives of the Yugoslavs addressed a protest to France,[11] which noted that Italy, being a party to the case, should not at the same time be a judge, they thought that every gentleman and every man who represents a highly civilized country would understand immediately that it was impossible to be judge and party at one and the same time. I feel this limitation so much that I hesitate to intervene in a discussion where principles affecting our own interests might be involved. I am not sure of being free enough to judge.

This reservation made, I would like to say that economic reasons should be excluded as principles in determining sovereignty. Likewise, the historical argument in and of itself must be excluded; otherwise, Italy could, if she wished, claim all the former territories of the Roman Empire.

M. Tardieu has made the most of the feeling of these people, of their desire to be reunited to France; this falls within the principles of justice proclaimed by President Wilson. We agree on the Fourteen Points; but just as the principles which they proclaim

---

[11] For this protest against the possible determination of the frontiers of Italy without the consultation of Yugoslavia by the Supreme Council, see N. P. Pašić to G. Clemenceau, March 6, 1919, printed in *PPC*, IV, 320-21.

will not prevent considerable territories being taken from Germany in order to solve several great problems, so they should not prevent us from finding a solution to this relatively limited problem.

About the feeling of the people, naturally I have nothing to say. But Mr. Lloyd George proposed a compromise which would permit this feeling to be expressed. We should, in my opinion, question the specialists who have studied the matter closely.

X

Conversation between President Wilson and MM. Clemenceau, Lloyd George, and Orlando*

MARCH 29, 1919, 4 P.M.

—Marshal Foch and Generals Weygand, Sir Henry Wilson, Bliss, and Diaz are heard about the question of transporting Polish troops by way of Danzig.

President Wilson. We must take care to show that we are not deviating from the terms of the Armistice. The Armistice authorizes us to send troops to Poland to maintain order. The Germans must be informed that it is for this reason, and to protect Poland from the Russian Bolsheviks, that General Haller's troops are being sent to Warsaw. I believe we will avoid difficulties by leaving no doubt on this point.

Mr. Lloyd George. It isn't in the interest of the German government to prevent us from forming a barrier against Bolshevism.

President Wilson. I couldn't speak with such certainty on this last point.

Mr. Lloyd George. In any case, the German military leaders, from whom surely come most of the difficulties we face right now, greatly desire to protect themselves against Bolshevism.

M. Clemenceau. How shall we reply to the Germans about the landing ports they suggest to us?

Marshal Foch. They have added Stettin to the list, which is much

*See H., *PPC*, V, 15 ff.

further west. They offer all the ports that one could want, except Danzig.[1]

M. Clemenceau. Let's be clear: we must not renounce Danzig.

Mr. Lloyd George. We must stand fast about Danzig, even if we should only have a small portion of the Polish troops pass through there. But we can use other ports; that will only speed up the transport.

Marshal Foch. Then I will accept Königsberg and Stettin.

M. Clemenceau. With Danzig.

Marshal Foch. The last German telegram sent to Spa says: "We can take no responsibility for measures which, if they were not accompanied by adequate guarantees, would provoke civil war in our own country."

President Wilson. What they are asking for, then, are guarantees.

Mr. Lloyd George. The truth is that the maps of the western boundary of Poland, published prematurely,[2] have done the greatest harm. Sir Henry Wilson has just received a telegram from General Franchet d'Esperey asking him to ask us to do everything possible to avoid the publication of maps showing changes in the Bulgarian boundary. "Otherwise," he writes, "it will be impossible to maintain order in that country." Publishing those maps was madness; coming so long before the final decision, they could only provoke a very dangerous situation.

Marshal Foch. The German government will tell us: "Land at Danzig at your own risk."

M. Clemenceau. We can study the question of the guarantees to be given the German government for the behavior of the Poles during their passage across German territory.

Mr. Lloyd George. We must tell the Germans: "This has nothing to do with the problem of Danzig's future, for which we are still studying the solution. We are only invoking Article 16 of the Armistice Agreement to have Allied troops pass through Danzig

---

[1] For the text of the German note, see *PPC*, V, 17-18.

[2] Lloyd George was referring to the publication, in several Paris papers, of the first report of the Commission on Polish Affairs on the boundaries between Poland and Germany, which had recommended the transfer of large parts of German territory, including the city of Danzig, to Poland. After it had been presented to the Council of Ten on March 19, 1919, the report and its accompanying maps had appeared in full in *Le Temps*, *Le Journal des Débats*, and *L'Echo de Paris* on the following day. Lloyd George had vigorously protested against this leak and had blamed the French delegation for it. See the minutes of the Council of Ten, March 19, 1919, 3 p.m., and March 21, 1919, 6 p.m., printed in *PWW*, Vol. 56, pp. 88-95, 148-52.

without stopping there. Our only goal is to send these troops to Poland against Bolshevism."

President Wilson. The Germans have the right to a clear explanation of this.

Mr. Lloyd George. We must add: "These troops are Allied troops, in conformity with Article 16 of the Armistice;[3] they fought in Allied armies on the western front." I insist upon that because it has not been sufficiently emphasized.

Marshal Foch. Other guarantees are possible. We can have the trains accompanied by Allied officers and Allied agents placed in the stations to prevent political demonstrations and disorder during the passage. Otherwise, in the event some incident takes place, it will be impossible to know whether it was Germans or Poles who started it.

M. Clemenceau. If we agree on all these points, we can draft the text of the instructions that will be sent to the Polish troops. There will be agents on the spot to guarantee order, as the Marshal proposes, and I ask the Marshal to inform the German government of our intentions without delay.

Mr. Lloyd George. Do you mean that the Marshal will communicate with the Germans without meeting with them personally?

Marshal Foch. I await their plenipotentiary.

President Wilson. It is better to wait for him and to speak with him directly.

M. Clemenceau (*to Marshal Foch*). You will telegraph thus to the Germans: "We will give all explanations to your plenipotentiary."

Marshal Foch. We must ask that this be a true plenipotentiary, which is to say that he must have full powers.

Mr. Lloyd George. If they send Hindenburg, that would be an interesting interview.

Marshal Foch. He wouldn't eat me.

President Wilson. The date for the meeting must be fixed.

Marshal Foch. I propose the fifth or the sixth. The Germans mustn't be given a pretext to complain that we haven't allowed them enough time to have their experts come from Königsberg or elsewhere.

M. Clemenceau. That is late.

President Wilson. We must choose the earliest possible date.

Mr. Lloyd George. Things will deteriorate if this affair drags on;

---

[3] The German government had maintained that, in the Armistice Agreement, it had pledged to let only Allied troops pass through Danzig and said that it did not consider Polish troops part of the Allied forces.

they are deteriorating both in Germany and in our press. The sooner the better.

Marshal Foch. Then we will fix the date for the third.

—Mr. Lloyd George reads the minute of the decisions just taken,[4] drafted by Colonel Hankey.

Marshal Foch. And if the Germans reply that they accept none of that?

Mr. Lloyd George. We won't tolerate it.

Marshal Foch. Should I then threaten them with a rupture of the Armistice?

Mr. Lloyd George. It seems to me there is nothing else to do.

Marshal Foch. Then I would like to be told what I can threaten them with.

Mr. Lloyd George. Tell them: "Your refusal breaks the Armistice, and the Allied governments will immediately consider what measures to take." We have already reached a decision along these lines. As for the measures to be considered, it might be the occupation of Danzig, which would be both a naval and military operation, the occupation of Westphalia, or tightening the blockade. The governments will have to choose.

Marshal Foch. Must they be told, as in the text just read, that the question of Danzig won't receive its final solution before their plenipotentiaries are at Versailles?

Mr. Lloyd George. I think it is important to say this because of the distressing coincidence which has occurred between the indiscretions of the press concerning the western boundary of Poland and our discussion about sending troops into Poland to maintain order. It absolutely must be shown that these two questions are distinct.

President Wilson. I understand Marshal Foch's difficulty. He wonders whether we should use language which will lead the Germans to believe they will be able to discuss our terms at Versailles, or whether we intend to present them with a settlement which they must accept without change.

Mr. Lloyd George. My text states simply that the question will not receive its final answer so long as the representatives of the Allies and the Germans have not met at Versailles.

M. Orlando. In that case, it would be simpler and briefer to say: "The question won't be decided before the signing of the peace treaty."

---

[4] It is printed in PWW, Vol. 56, pp. 411-12.

M. Clemenceau. I prefer this text.

Mr. Lloyd George. I think it is indeed clearer.

Marshal Foch. Then I must give them no guarantees about the future of Danzig. But the mere fact that I won't offer them these guarantees will allow the Germans to say: "You wish to stay there."

M. Clemenceau. You have only one reply to make: "This question does not concern me."

Mr. Lloyd George. Or rather: "It is a question that is still under discussion."

Marshal Foch. I am leaving for Spa. The German plenipotentiary might try to prolong things. A time limit must be set for the conversation, forty-eight hours, for instance.

Mr. Lloyd George. That seems sufficient to me.

—*The time limit is adopted.*

Mr. Lloyd George. A parenthetical note: the Germans have troops at Libau, where they are fighting the Bolsheviks, and with success.[5] They report to us that, if we give them locomotives, they will drive the Bolsheviks out of Riga. What do you think of that?

---

[5] Under the terms of the Armistice, the German troops which had occupied Lithuania, Latvia, and Estonia during the war were to remain in the area until the Allies deemed the conditions for their withdrawal appropriate. Lacking a clear policy toward the Baltic states and unwilling to commit any of their own forces to the defense of the area against the advancing Bolshevik armies, the Allies, and particularly Great Britain, had, in fact, hoped that the remaining German troops might serve in the establishment of an anti-Bolshevik barrier in the Baltic. Two days after the signing of the Armistice, the Red Army had, indeed, attacked the Baltic states. While the Estonians had been able eventually to repel the invasion, Bolshevik forces had overrun most of Latvia by early 1919, had captured the city of Riga, and had moved into Lithuania. In response, the German authorities in Latvia and the provisional Latvian government had agreed to reinforce the remaining German troops at Libau by volunteers drawn from Germany and to organize them in free corps units in an effort to drive the Bolsheviks from Latvia. At the same time, a group of Baltic Germans had organized the *Baltische Landeswehr*, a militia supplied with arms and equipment from German army stores, and the German government had moved additional troops into the area. Under the command of Maj.-Gen. Count Rüdiger von der Goltz, these combined German forces had launched a major counteroffensive in February and, by late March, had retaken much of Latvia.

The attitude of the Allies toward these German efforts had been very ambiguous. While welcoming the German military success against the Bolsheviks, the Allies had grown highly suspicious of German political motives and the apparent designs by Germany to reestablish hegemony over the Baltic states. Thus, the Council of Ten had turned down an earlier request by the German High Command for permission to ship additional troops and supplies to Latvia. However,

President Wilson. We can't give them to them. By doing that, we would become allies of the Germans against our former allies, who haven't attacked us.

Mr. Lloyd George. One word, before the Marshal's departure. I hope he will succeed in this negotiation. If the Germans give him a refusal, we absolutely must carry out the Armistice; but we don't want a rupture over a decision which is small in comparison with the more serious ones that we have to impose on the Germans. We must do all we can to succeed with using force, all the while reserving the right to use it if the Germans prove intractable.

President Wilson. We invite Marshal Foch in a friendly way to be a diplomat rather than a soldier—as far as possible.

General Weygand. A telegram has just been transmitted to us from Kowno, where we have an officer, Colonel Reboul. It asks us whether, in conformity with the Armistice, the Allied governments shouldn't prevent the Germans from withdrawing from Lithuania. At present, the Germans are fighting the Bolsheviks in Lithuania, side by side with the Poles. If they withdraw, as they seem disposed to do, the Bolsheviks will gain ground, and the Armistice compels them to stay where they are.

M. Clemenceau. Answer that the Armistice must be respected.

—Marshal Foch and the generals withdraw.

M. Orlando. An Italian officer has just arrived from Budapest bearing a letter from Prince Borghese.[6] The latter, appointed Minister

---

except for the dispatch of an American investigative mission, the Allies had so far largely ignored the situation in the Baltic and had failed to establish any policy to deal with developments in the area. See *PPC*, IV, 27, 190-92, 207, 212. For documents pertaining to the Baltic question, see Miller, *My Diary at the Conference of Paris*, XVI-XVIII, passim, and *FR 1919, Russia*, pp. 666-749. The activities of the American mission are documented in *PPC*, XII, 136-227, and described in detail in Robert Hale, *The Baltic Provinces: Report of Mission to Finland, Esthonia, Latvia, and Lithuania on the Situation in the Baltic Provinces*, 66th Cong. 1st sess., Sen. Doc. No. 105 (Washington, 1919). For discussions of the Baltic situation and its treatment by the peace conference, see Georg von Rauch, *The Baltic States—the Years of Independence: Estonia, Latvia, Lithuania, 1917-1940* (London, 1970), pp. 39-75; Warren E. Williams, "Die Politik der Alliierten gegenüber den Freikorps im Baltikum 1918-1919," *Vierteljahrshefte für Zeitgeschichte*, XII (April 1964), 147-69; and Stanley W. Page, *The Formation of the Baltic States: A Study of the Effect of Great Power Politics upon the Emergence of Lithuania, Latvia, and Estonia* (Cambridge, Mass., 1959), passim.

[6] For its text, see the memorandum by V. E. Orlando, March 25, 1919, printed in *PWW*, Vol. 56, pp. 725-79.

Plenipotentiary at Belgrade, left that city after the incident, which you know about, concerning his letters of credence,[7] and he was returning to Italy by way of Budapest and Vienna. Having stopped at Budapest, where one of his sisters lives, he found himself there during the so-called revolution, and he sends us a very interesting letter, which I can have translated if you wish.

The important point is that the new government approached Prince Borghese, stating to him that the revolutionary movement had been provoked by political more than social causes, that his movement was socialist, but not Bolshevik, and that it desired to have friendly relations with the Entente.[8] They asked Prince Borghese to deliver a kind of statement or memorandum to us.[9]

[7] The Serbian government had refused to recognize Prince Borghese's credentials because they had not been addressed to the King of the Serbs, Croats and Slovenes.

[8] Prince Borghese also stated that the Hungarian officials had told him that the resignation of the Károlyi government had been precipitated by the Allied "ultimatum" of March 20, and that the only reason for their appeal to the Bolsheviks had been the apparent abandonment of Hungary by the Allies; that they "eagerly desired not to break off relations with the Entente, and hoped to renew them under better conditions"; and that, although willing to make certain territorial concessions, they would oppose, by force if necessary, the surrender of any purely Hungarian areas that were indispensable for the independent existence of the country.

[9] Béla Kun, "AIDE MÉMOIRE FOR PRINCE BORGHESE," March 24, 1919, printed in *PWW*, Vol. 56, pp. 242-43. It reads, in part, as follows:

"The New Government of Hungary, the Council of the Commissioners of the People, recognise the validity of the Treaty of Armistice signed by the former Government and do not think that the non-acceptance of the note presented by Colonel Vix has infringed it.

"By asking Russia to enter an alliance with the Republic of the Councils of Hungary, the Government has not thought that this step might be interpreted as an expression of its desire to break all diplomatic intercourse with the Powers of the Entente, and still less as a declaration of war on the Entente. The alliance with Russia is not a formal diplomatic alliance, it is at the most—if we may use the expression—an 'entente cordiale,' a natural friendship justified by the identical construction of their respective constitutions, which, in the thought of the Hungarian Government, does not in any way imply an aggressive combination. The new Hungarian Republic, on the contrary, has a firm desire to live in peace with all the other Nations and to devote its activities to the peaceful social reorganisation of its country. . . .

"The Government of the Republic of the Councils of Hungary declare themselves ready to negotiate territorial questions on the basis of the principle of self-determination of the People, and they view territorial integrity solely as in conformity with that principle.

"They would gladly welcome a civil and diplomatic mission of the Entente in Budapest and would guarantee to it the right of extraterritoriality and undertake to provide for its absolute safety."

Prince Borghese replied that he was in Budapest in a purely private capacity. But he couldn't refuse to transmit the memorandum by way of this officer whom I mentioned to you.

I had the same hesitation as Prince Borghese about communicating this document to you. But I thought it better to show it to you. I add that we haven't assumed any kind of obligation towards the Hungarians.

President Wilson (*after reading*). This is a very interesting document, and I believe what it says. Can't we discuss immediately the question of sending an inter-Allied mission to Budapest, as requested by the signer of this memorandum?

Mr. Lloyd George. After all, I don't see why we should treat the Magyars differently from the Croats. The Croats, like the Magyars, fought us until the very end, and very vigorously. The Magyars have never been the enemies of France or England. Undoubtedly they have statesmen like Tisza, who bear great responsibility, but they were supported only by a very limited electorate. We maintain relations with the Croats and the Slovenes, who have on their consciences the death of a very great number of Allied soldiers. Why not enter into conversation with the Magyars as well?

M. Clemenceau. We could, however, await the return of the representatives we had in Budapest. They tell us that the Hungarian revolutionaries have imprisoned Colonel Vix.[10]

M. Orlando. A curious thing, which makes one believe in telepathy, is that Mr. Lloyd George has just said precisely what the Hungarians said to Prince Borghese: the Croats and the Poles are accepted as friends of the Allies; why not the Hungarians?

Mr. Lloyd George. Some Poles fought against us in France up until the final days.

M. Clemenceau. It would be better not to take a decision before we have had an opportunity to consult our Foreign Ministers.

President Wilson. I don't know whether they aren't a bit bound by the particular point of view of the chancelleries, the idea of precedents, etc.* * *

Mr. Lloyd George. Let's take a decision; let's not deal with Hungary as with Russia. One Russia is enough for us.

M. Clemenceau. Take note that this Hungarian government has made an offer of alliance to the Bolsheviks.

---

[10] Although the Hungarian government had tried to delay the departure of Vix and the other members of the French military mission, they had left Budapest on March 26, and there is no evidence that any of them had actually been imprisoned, even temporarily. See *PPC*, XII, 422-24.

President Wilson. By taking it at its word, we can do something useful for peace.

M. Clemenceau. First, I would send some men there to look at the situation. To send a regular mission right away to extend a hand to the Hungarians—I don't know if we can do that.

President Wilson. After all, haven't we sent missions of inquiry far and wide?

Mr. Lloyd George. We even have missions in an enemy country, in Vienna, for example.

M. Clemenceau. I remind you that our representative in Budapest, Colonel Vix, was arrested by the new Hungarian government.

M. Orlando. Our officer says that they have released him, and that he has left for Belgrade.

M. Clemenceau. In any case, I would prefer to wait for news about this matter before sending another representative there.

Mr. Lloyd George. I would be glad to send a man like Smuts. (*To M. Clemenceau*) I know that you don't like him after the letter I read you.

M. Clemenceau. I respect him; but I would prefer that you send someone else there.

President Wilson. I have a comment to make about our meetings. We must explain to the representatives of Japan why we have been meeting without them. I fear offending them.

M. Clemenceau. The truth is that we are meeting in order to study a small number of special questions in which Japan happens not to be concerned.

President Wilson. Undoubtedly; but shouldn't we say this, to avoid offending them?

M. Clemenceau. I agree with you. On the other hand, I do believe there are questions which it would be better to discuss amongst ourselves. Nothing is easier than to inform them of the nature of these questions, and it would be good to add that we will invite them here at the first opportunity.

Mr. Lloyd George. Their presence will be necessary when we discuss the future of the German colonies.

M. Clemenceau. When can we resume study of the Klotz plan for reparation?

Mr. Lloyd George. I am ready.

President Wilson. So am I.

Mr. Lloyd George. I asked my experts to sift out the principles of the Klotz proposal. I believe they saw the American experts before drafting the document I will show you.[11]

---

[11] It is printed as an appendix to the notes of this meeting.

I call attention to the importance, from the point of view of British domestic politics, of not abandoning our claim to the totality of war costs, while admitting the obligation imposed upon us by the practical necessity to limit ourselves to a more modest demand. We should begin by indicating the immensity of the expenses of every kind that the war imposed upon us. They amount, for all Allied and Associated governments, to more than 750 billion marks.

President Wilson. This includes our war debts, for which we have no right to ask reimbursement, according to our commitments preceding the Armistice.

Mr. Lloyd George. I do not intend to ask for this reimbursement; I restrict myself to stating the facts. In Article 3 of the document which you have before you, it is indicated that damages caused to persons include losses suffered by dependents of a combatant by reason of his death or mutilation.

President Wilson. That is a point which the Germans could argue and upon which legal experts might differ.

Mr. Lloyd George. Let's be clear about this: we can't leave the interpretation of such clauses to lawyers.

President Wilson. I will reread to you the letter sent by the Allied governments to the government of the United States explaining the kind of reparations demanded: "All damages caused to the civilian populations of the Allied and Associated States and to their property."

Mr. Lloyd George. That formula would allow us to ask more than I will ask.

President Wilson. I don't deny that; but it is better to repeat in your document the wording of our correspondence of the month of November.

Mr. Lloyd George. Article 4 specifies our definition of damages caused to persons. You will notice that we ask no reparations for failure to earn and all other indirect damage.

M. Clemenceau. I believe we must indicate some priorities in Article 8.

Mr. Lloyd George. We think this priority will take the form of a proportion to be determined.

M. Clemenceau. I reserve my judgment on that.

President Wilson. I must observe that Article 4, on damages caused to persons, appears to extend the definition given in Article 3, and I renew my objection to Article 1, which sets forth the total of Allied expenditures. Is there truly any advantage in saying: "You owe us all that, although we would not claim it from you?

Why not simply say, without giving figures, that the losses are so colossal that Germany couldn't pay them all?

Mr. Lloyd George. Undoubtedly, on the condition that we don't renounce our right to total reparation, limited only by material possibilities, which we have acknowledged by claiming only reparation for damages done to civilians and their property.

{ A P P E N D I X }[12]

1. The loss and damage to which the Allied and Associated Governments and their nationals have been subjected as a direct and necessary consequence of the war, imposed upon them by the aggression of the enemy states by land, air and sea, is upwards of £30,000,000,000.

2. Notwithstanding the indisputable claim of the Allied and Associated Governments to full compensation, they recognize that the financial and economic resources of the enemy states are not unlimited and that it will therefore, so far as they can judge, be impracticable for the enemy states to make complete reparation.

3. The Allied and Associated Governments, however, require that the enemy states should at least make good, at whatever cost to themselves, the value of the material damage done and of the personal losses and injuries, including those to the civilian dependents of combatants which the enemy states have caused.

4. Each of the Allied and Associated Powers ought to receive from Germany a just reparation in respect of the death and disablement or permanent injury to health directly caused to any of its subjects by hostilities or by operations of war, whether on sea or land or in the air, or by the acts of enemy forces, populations or authorities in occupied, invaded or enemy territory. For each Power interested this reparation may always be measured by the rate of pensions or allowances now established in its territories.

5. Each of the Allied and Associated Powers ought to receive from Germany a just reparation in respect of all property belonging to the State or to any of its subjects with the exception of military works or material, which has been carried off, seized or destroyed by the enemy, or damaged directly in consequence of hostilities or of any operations of war:

(a) by immediate restoration of property carried off which

[12] Printed in *PWW*, Vol. 56, pp. 418-20.

can be identified in specie, with just compensation if it has been damaged;

(b) by payment of the full cost of replacing, repairing or reconstructing such property carried off, seized, damaged or destroyed, as cannot be identified in specie, or by payment of its value.

6. The amounts to be paid, the time and mode of payments and the securities to be given therefore shall be determined by an Inter-Ally Commission after examining into the claims and giving to Germany just opportunity of being heard.

7. Compensation may be required, either in the form of payment in gold or securities or in the form of mineral deposits, delivery of commodities and chattels and other reparation in kind, to be credited by the recipient power at a fair value at the time of delivery. The "ton for ton" and other analogous principles being adopted.

8. Each of the Allied Powers interested will receive out of each payment as and when it is made by the enemy a rateable share in proportion to its losses above mentioned.

9. In order to enable the Allied and Associated Powers to proceed at once to the restoration of their industries and economic life pending the full determination of their claims, Germany shall pay in such instalments and in such manner (whether in gold, securities, commodities or ships as they may fix) in 1919 and 1920 the equivalent of £1,000,000,000 sterling to include a due provision for the maintenance of the Armies of Occupation and for indispensable supplies of food.

10. This scheme will be developed along the above lines in further discussion.

(29.3.19)

XI

Conversation between President Wilson and MM. Clemenceau, Lloyd George, Orlando, and Klotz*

MARCH 31, 1919, 11 A.M.

M. Clemenceau. M. Klotz has asked to be heard on Mr. Lloyd George's memorandum about reparation.

M. Klotz. The memorandum drafted by Mr. Lloyd George appears satisfactory to the French government in its general lines. We are grateful to him for having made this useful contribution to our discussion. The last article certainly indicates that it will be necessary to amplify the aforesaid plan; we must arrive at formulas which can be written into the peace treaty.

Don't you think that Articles 1 and 2 are rather meant for ourselves than for the enemy? It seems to me there would be a serious disadvantage in having such formulas discussed by the enemy. But we can notify the enemy of them in the form of a statement, without including them in the preliminary articles.

M. Clemenceau. It is a matter of form and of wording. But I believe it is important to state that our right to compensation is unlimited, and that it is we ourselves who have set a limit, whilst taking account of the possibilities.

Mr. Lloyd George. We must remember that the formula used at the time of the Armistice had already been drafted along these lines and with that intention. From the political point of view in France and in Italy, as well as in England, it is very important to indicate that our right is unlimited, and that the formula we have adopted represents a voluntary limitation on our part.

President Wilson. The document presented by M. Klotz has changed the entire status of the problem of reparation. Let us be careful about adopting a text which, by its imprecision, could lead to infinite discussions with the Germans in the future. I asked Messrs. Baruch, Davis, and Lamont to study this text, and they must get together with your specialists. I feel very strongly that they should see together what difficulties the plan before us could expose us to.

Mr. Lloyd George. I will put them in touch with Mr. Montagu, who has a more flexible mind than Lord Sumner and who is above all accustomed to looking at problems from the political angle.

*Does not appear in H.

President Wilson. I must make my intention very clear: whilst escaping certain difficulties by the adoption of a new plan, I want to avoid throwing ourselves into other difficulties. We have to study this closely and be careful to avoid acting rashly.

M. Clemenceau. We will also send you our specialists.

Mr. Lloyd George. M. Klotz must be present, all the more since he has a personal interest in this plan, since he presented it himself.

M. Klotz. I am going to ask you questions according to the order of the articles. My comments will, moreover, be of unequal importance.

Article 3, concerning damages to persons, contains these words: "including those which affect civilians dependent upon combatants." Does this include indemnities and family allowances?

Mr. Lloyd George. Certainly.

M. Klotz. I notice one omission: there is no provision to reimburse expenses we have incurred to feed and evacuate people from invaded regions and to succor refugees. Without any possible doubt, that constitutes damage inflicted upon civilians because of the war.

M. Clemenceau. Would not England, which has contributed to the victualing of Belgium, have something additional to claim under this article?

Mr. Lloyd George. We did indeed participate in the victualing of Belgium. I should like to know President Wilson's opinion.

M. Klotz. I would also include under this heading damages caused to the inhabitants of invaded regions because of the deprivation of the free use of their property. I ask President Wilson if he doesn't consider that this constitutes damages to the civilian population.

Concerning the expenses for victualing, we know the part America has taken. Without the aid of the Allies and America, the people whom we helped would be dead from hunger. The nature of the damage is unquestionable.

President Wilson. I believe we shouldn't go to such pains to make such complete catalogues of our claims. We know very well that what we will receive can only pay for what we can formulate according to the most restricted definitions.

M. Klotz. I will point out that these categories retain their importance as far as distribution is concerned. We must take account of certain damages suffered exclusively in the invaded areas.

About Article 5, I have to present a rather important observation. Shouldn't it be said here that the estimate of damages will be made by an inter-Allied commission, as we have agreed? I suggested this procedure in the memorandum I gave you. This question concerns the Germans, who could rightly say: "Will it be enough for each of you to give figures without comparison and without warranty?"

Mr. Lloyd George. I am entirely in agreement with you; but if you read Article 6, you will see that the commission is mentioned there, and that it is said that it will scrutinize the claims beforehand. It is therefore unnecessary to insert this clause into another part of the text.

We spoke the other day of an arbitrator who might be designated by the President of the United States; it seems that there are difficulties with this procedure, and that the arbitrator would have to be designated by the Chief Justice of the United States.

M. Klotz. I find further down the words "guarantees of payment." If this concerns economic and territorial guarantees, the governments must specify them now; this task cannot be left to a commission.

Mr. Lloyd George. The word which has been translated as "guarantees" is "*sécurités*," which means rather "*cautions*" in French, in the financial sense of the word. It goes without saying that guarantees for execution of the financial clauses can only be stipulated by the governments.

M. Klotz. Furthermore, Germany must commit herself in advance to accept the decisions of the inter-Allied commission.

M. Clemenceau. Germany will have signed the treaty.

M. Klotz. Yes, but the subsequent decisions of the commission will come long after the signing of the treaty, and the commission will be invested only indirectly with the authority of the governments. I would prefer that it be written here that the decisions of the commission will have self-executing force.

As to Article 8, I will point out that thefts were committed by the enemy, restitution of which has been provided for. Isn't it necessary, if there is a distribution amongst us, that what has been stolen and can be restored in kind be left outside the distribution? Otherwise, we would be allowing all concerned to receive a proportional share of what has been stolen from only one of us.

Mr. Lloyd George. I have no objection to that amendment.

M. Klotz. Article 9 provides that the Germans make a down payment of one billion pounds sterling. In my opinion, we could say 1.2 billion pounds sterling, which is 6 billion dollars, or 30 billion francs. But I would withdraw from this article the charge of this credit for German victualing, except for the sums already pledged. We can indeed predict exactly neither the amount nor the duration of payments necessary under this heading, and it seems to me inopportune to inflate our figures of sums intended to meet Germany's needs. In my opinion, we must separate and not link these two questions.

Mr. Lloyd George. There is much to be said in favor of this, and I accept this point of view, which doesn't prejudice our discussions with the Germans about their needs and about the means to meet them.

M. Klotz. I note an omission in Article 6. There is mention of a payment which will take place at certain periods. I would prefer to reword it as "by annual payments."

Mr. Lloyd George. Of course; the payment could not be made otherwise. That is a matter of wording.

M. Klotz. The document I have just examined treats only reparation for damages. But there will be other financial clauses in the preliminaries; these are the ones that have been studied by the Financial Commission under the chairmanship of Mr. Montagu. These are, for example, the questions of debts and contracts, the cession of German properties abroad, such as the Baghdad Railroad; the exclusion of Germans from international financial commissions, for example the one concerning the Ottoman debt; the expenses of prisoners of war; the order in which Germany will have to meet her debts—taking account of her prewar debts; Germany's confirmation of her renunciation of the financial clauses of the treaties that she had concluded since 1914. It is merely a matter of authorizing the Financial Commission to prepare the text of articles that will have to be included in the treaty.

M. Clemenceau. I think everyone agrees about that.

M. Orlando. Under the heading of reparation, we mustn't forget the compensation owed for issuing paper money which was counterfeited or issued arbitrarily.

—M. Klotz withdraws.

President Wilson. On the question of the Saar, I have a proposal to make along the lines of what was said the other day. It would be serious to do anything which taints a principle to which we are committed. Here is a draft which has been prepared, taking into account the particular importance and difficulty of the case.[1]

---

[1] Drafted by Haskins and Headlam-Morley, the American and British experts, respectively, on the Saar Basin, it is printed in PWW, Vol. 56, p. 420. Wilson summarizes it fully and accurately.

1) Complete ownership of the coal mines in the entire Saar Basin would be awarded to France.

2) All economic facilities would be guaranteed for the exploitation of these mines: no tax, no duty, including customs duties, could be made an obstacle. The mobility of labor will have to be assured in the entire region and in the neighboring regions. Freedom to develop means of land and river communication will be complete. We must seek the political and administrative means to allow the establishment of this state of things with all desirable guarantees.

I continue to see great difficulties in the establishment of a separate state. The above-mentioned guarantees are necessary in order to give France full use of the mines, which will give her rightful compensation for the destruction of her coal mines in the North. But we can't say to these people: "You must accept the form of government which will impose upon you." That is what must be avoided as far as possible, although it must be admitted that it is inevitable, especially in countries where different populations are mixed, that some elements will find themselves detached from their national group and joined to the neighboring group.

M. Clemenceau. Leave me your document; we will study it.

Mr. Lloyd George. I agree in principle with what President Wilson has just proposed.

M. Clemenceau. I will have much to say about President Wilson's document. I am willing for France to have ownership of the mines, but not under conditions which would lead us into perpetual conflicts with the Germans in the future.

We shall have to study another question—that of the occupation of German territories as a guarantee of the payment of indemnities.

Mr. Lloyd George. I am not much in favor of occupation. Since the Germans have almost no merchant fleet left and only an insignificant navy, we still have the weapon of the blockade to compel them to carry out the treaty.

M. Clemenceau. We couldn't be satisfied with that; we aren't so sure of its effectiveness, and public feeling in France wouldn't forgive us for not having imposed upon the Germans the same effective guarantees that they themselves imposed on us in 1871.

President Wilson. Would you think of occupying German territories until complete payment of everything that Germany owes?

M. Clemenceau. No, but for a certain time, which could be divided into several periods, with a gradual reduction of the occupation.

President Wilson. You conceive of this occupation as an Allied occupation?

M. Clemenceau. That's what I would like. But if we can't obtain it, we will ask you to give France a mandate.

Mr. Lloyd George. We cannot dream of keeping conscription in England in order to occupy German territories; British public opinion would never tolerate it.

President Wilson. On the question of reparation, the text we discussed a short time ago[2] avoids stipulating the total sum of our claims and the total sum Germany can pay. What troubles me is this:

When the Germans arrive at Versailles, the first thing they will do will be to ask these two questions. If we can't answer them, they will say: "You want to impose an indefinite obligation upon us. We want to know today the amount Germany is committing itself to pay." The least they have the right to ask is a very precise definition of the grounds for compensation. Do we agree on these definitions? We must be able to answer the Germans, or else we will appear divided amongst ourselves in their presence, and those amongst us with the most limited definitions will appear to side with the Germans.

M. Klotz wishes to avoid figures. Mr. Keynes says correctly that we can only guess somewhat randomly as to what these figures will be. In any case, it is essential to agree completely about the grounds for compensation and to be able to tell the Germans: "Here is our common and single interpretation."

—President Wilson reads aloud a letter from Mr. Baruch pointing out all the resources for payment of which Germany will be deprived due to her territorial losses.[3]

[2] That is, the Lloyd George plan.
[3] B. M. Baruch to WW, March 29, 1919, printed in PWW, Vol. 56, pp. 421-24. Baruch concluded: "We must therefore realize that we are dealing today with a much weaker Germany than the one we knew before the war, and we must recognize that any indemnities based on pre-war conditions would be impossible. To talk of these indemnities in exaggerated terms would result in raising false hopes in the minds of the peoples of the Allied nations that would react in a serious manner."

XII

Conversation among President Wilson, MM. Clemenceau, Lloyd George, Orlando, Marshal Foch, and Generals Weygand, Sir Henry Wilson, Bliss, and Diaz*

MARCH 31, 1919, 3 P.M.

—Marshal Foch reads aloud a report on the Rhine as the necessary military frontier of the western powers.[1]

Marshal Foch (*commenting on the map*). This map shows you that no strategic frontier exists between the Rhine and the Meuse; neither mountain nor river; nature has offered no obstacle other than the Rhine. In all his reports written before the war of 1870, Marshal von Moltke considered the line of the Rhine as Germany's frontier, for defense as well as for attack. If we should give up the Rhine, not only would we lose the trump card in our hands, but we would also place it in the enemy's hands.

I ask permission to reply in advance to an argument I foresee. One would like to avoid creating, in an inverse sense, a new Alsace-Lorraine. I beg you to reread the treaty of 1871[2] to see the difference between the treatment of Alsace-Lorraine by the Germans and the arrangement we can contemplate for the left bank of the Rhine.

By the Treaty of Frankfurt, France renounced all her claims to Alsace-Lorraine in favor of the German Empire. Germany was to possess those territories in perpetuity, with all sovereignty and ownership. When I ask for the yielding of the left bank of the

*Does not appear in H.

[1] It is printed in *PWW*, Vol. 55, pp. 502-10. Foch's memorandum rehearsed at length the history of German militarism and aggression and argued that only the establishment of a defensive coalition of the western powers, the Allied occupation of the left bank of the Rhine, and the creation of autonomous buffer states in that area would provide security for Belgium and France from future German invasions. Foch concluded: "The fortune of war has placed the line of the Rhine in our hands, thanks to a combination of circumstances and a co-operation of Allied Forces, which cannot for a long time be reproduced. The abandonment to-day of this solid natural barrier, without other guarantee than institutions of a moral character and of distant and unknown difficulty, would mean, from the military point of view, the incurring of the greatest risk."

[2] The Treaty of Frankfurt, signed on May 10, 1871, which concluded the Franco-Prussian War.

Rhine, I conceive of the possibility of leaving the territories to the west of the river masters of their own administration.

In order to understand better the importance of a strategic frontier for the western powers, I simply remind you that, without Russia, the assistance of the maritime powers in 1914 would have been of no avail.

M. Clemenceau. Have you anything to add?

Marshal Foch. Militarily, the results we have obtained are guaranteed only by our occupation of the line of the Rhine. If we give it up, the situation could be reversed, and we will have only an unreliable peace.

Mr. Lloyd George. Let's suppose that Germany, in 1914, had had the least idea that not only Great Britain, but also America, would come to the aid of France and Belgium. Would there have been a German general in his right mind who would have advised his government to go to war?

Then again, do you believe the German generals would give such advice to Germany when her army will be reduced to such a degree that it will be no stronger than the British army?[3]

Marshal Foch. To the first question, I answer: if we go back to 1914—supposing Russia did not exist—an officer of the German General Staff could have made the following calculation: "We have enough forces to throw the French back from the Meuse, beyond the Seine, beyond the Loire, before the English have time to intervene effectively; all the more reason for us to have enough time to defeat the English and what remains of the French before the Americans make their appearance."

As for the reduction of German forces, we will pursue it, but we will never be certain of it. We can't build upon what is not in our hands. The Germans can elude the stipulations that will be imposed upon them in all sorts of ways.

I conclude, therefore, that a German general, counting on the troops known to him, but not to us, may think himself in a position to put the French army out of action before the English could appear, and the English army before the arrival of the Americans.

Mr. Lloyd George. But do you think that Germany could reconstruct an army comparable to that of 1914 without anyone knowing about it?

Marshal Foch. I can say neither yes nor no. It isn't impossible.

---

[3] Article 2 of the military terms of peace, approved by the Council of Ten on March 17, 1919, stipulated that the future German army was not to exceed 100,000 men. See *PWW*, Vol. 56, pp. 14-16.

"Comparable to the army of 1914," perhaps not; but we don't know what resources the Germans may find in Russia.

Mr. Lloyd George. Before the war, we had good reason to watch everything Germany did from the naval point of view. Now, we were always informed about all her construction, and we even knew with what types of guns she equipped her warships. If there was an error in our information, it was rather in excess of the realities.

President Wilson. Likewise, the American War College was completely informed about all changes in the German army.

Marshal Foch. We know what we know. In war, you can't build upon what you think you know about the enemy, but only upon your own strength. I repeat what I have already told you: I have never numbered my enemies.

President Wilson. How long would the occupation which you have in mind last?

Marshal Foch. The peace can only be guaranteed by the possession of the left bank of the Rhine until further notice, that is to say, as long as Germany has not had a change of heart.

President Wilson. What contingents do you have in mind for the occupation?

Marshal Foch. As the disarmament of Germany is gradually completed, one could reduce the army of occupation, beginning with twenty divisions and ending with ten or twelve.

M. Clemenceau. What is the present strength of Allied forces on the left bank of the Rhine?

Marshal Foch. Forty-five divisions, of which three are cavalry.

Mr. Lloyd George. And that, at the moment when the military power of Germany is at its lowest!

M. Clemenceau. How many men does that represent?

General Weygand. Nine hundred thousand combatants.

Mr. Lloyd George. I learn from an American source that at the present time the Germans can only assemble, for all practical purposes, around 100,000 men.

President Wilson. What is the strength of a division in your calculations?

Marshal Foch. The full French division has 17,000 men.

General Weygand. Which makes 20,000 men with the rear echelon.

M. Clemenceau. How many annual contingents must be kept under arms in order to maintain this army of occupation?

Marshal Foch. One can maintain it with three classes. In the memorandum I have read you, I showed our reasons for occupying the Rhine. In a second memorandum, which I ask permission to read you, I show that any other solution is not only less certain, but more costly.

—Reading of the second memorandum.[4]

President Wilson. I thank Marshal Foch for the strong and luminous manner in which he has presented his views.

Mr. Lloyd George. I would like to ask General Wilson a question. Marshal Foch seems to believe that the Channel tunnel would not assure us of more rapid transportation than in 1914.

General Sir Henry Wilson. I believe Marshal Foch sees the tunnel as an alternative to transport by sea. Obviously, everything would be changed if one were added to the other.

Mr. Lloyd George. It seems to me that in that case you could double the speed of the transports?

General Sir Henry Wilson. That depends upon the condition of the French railroads and their congestion at the time of a mobilization.

—Marshal Foch and Generals Weygand, Sir Henry Wilson, Bliss, and Diaz withdraw.
—Hearing of M. Paul Hymans, Foreign Minister of Belgium.

M. Clemenceau. We will ask M. Paul Hymans to let us know what he wants to say to us.

M. Hymans. I was summoned a short time ago by M. Tardieu, who told me that you expected to hear me speak about the question of the border between Belgium and Germany. But I am not prepared.

M. Clemenceau. Didn't you yourself ask to be heard?

M. Hymans. Indeed, I asked to be heard by the "Four," but that was

---

[4] Printed in *ibid.*, pp. 445-48. Foch repeated many of his previous arguments and again emphasized that the Rhine was the barrier which was indispensable for the nations of western Europe and the safety of civilization. France and Belgium, he insisted, would not be secure if the Rhineland was merely neutralized, even if this neutrality was guaranteed by an Anglo-American-French alliance. In the event of a German attack, British and American forces could not arrive in time to prevent the German armies from again overrunning Belgium and northern France, and even a Channel tunnel would not assure that troops could be moved more efficiently than in 1914. Thus, Foch concluded: "I instantly [insistently] beg the Allied and Associated Governments, who, in the most critical hour of the War entrusted me with the leadership of their Armies and the welfare of the common cause, to consider that, to-morrow just as to-day, that welfare can only be ensured in any lasting manner, by making the RHINE our military frontier, and by holding it with Allied forces. We must, therefore, maintain our present indispensable position."

because I had to speak to you about general questions relating to the future of Belgium. It would not be fair if we were not present here during the discussion of the distribution of indemnities. The same observation applies to the question of the Rhine, which concerns Belgium as much as any other power. If there is an occupation of the left bank of the Rhine, Belgium will be compelled to take part in it. We wouldn't wish to hear it said one fine day that the great powers took such and such a decision without consulting us.

My position is delicate: I never see you. During the last two months, I have asked twice to see Mr. Lloyd George; I haven't met him.

Mr. Lloyd George. I apologize if that is the case; I was never informed about it.

M. Hymans. I believe I have been very discreet. It would be only fair to allow me to discuss questions affecting the future of my country with you.

President Wilson. I think there has been a misunderstanding here; M. Hymans must understand that, if only the four of us meet, it is only to move more quickly and at the same time to avoid those indiscretions which have several times caused difficulties, for example the case of the Polish boundaries. We seek a settlement amongst ourselves of some difficult questions.

M. Hymans. On the question of indemnities, you heard M. Loucheur, and we have the right to be heard also. My country will find itself in a terrible situation if it is not helped immediately.

Mr. Lloyd George. England is also in a very unsatisfactory condition.

M. Hymans. Excuse me! You have raw materials, you have machines, your industries are working, you can sell and buy.

Mr. Lloyd George. We have a million unemployed.

M. Hymans. Everything is relative. In our country, there is not just hardship, but complete paralysis and misery, and in a country which was one of the richest in the world. You must hear me as you have heard M. Loucheur and M. Lebrun.

President Wilson. So far we have only considered how to make Germany pay. Thus, you haven't been excluded from a discussion about what Belgium should receive. Until now, the question of distribution has been discussed only by a commission on which you are represented.[5]

---

[5] Wilson was of course in error here. See the discussions during meetings V and VIII, on March 25 and March 28, respectively.

M. Hymans. That commission will accomplish nothing; it is you who will decide, and it is you who must hear us.

Another question: we ask for a revision of the Treaty of 1839.[6] We have discussed this question for three years with the French and English governments. We have talked with Sir Edward Grey, Mr. Balfour, the French Ministers of Foreign Affairs. Six months ago, we informed the Allied governments of our intentions; at no time did they make any objection or any suggestion. I came to explain the views of Belgium at the conference. You listened to me; but I received no advice from you; I don't know your opinion. We need to know what you think; we need your advice. This silence and the way we are treated are creating a distressing impression in Belgium, which could turn against the Allies.

Mr. Lloyd George. You don't have any right to speak thus of France and Great Britain. English soldiers died by the hundreds of thousands for the liberation of Belgium. Australia sent you men

---

[6] That is, the three interrelated treaties signed on April 19, 1839, which had established the boundaries and the neutrality of Belgium. Most of the Belgian claims, submitted to the conference in a memorandum on January 17, involved the revision of the Treaty of 1839: the release of Belgium from the obligation of neutrality; the cession by Holland of Dutch territory on the left bank of the Scheldt (Dutch Flanders) to insure free access to the sea for the ports of Antwerp and Ghent; the transfer to Belgium of the southern part of Dutch Limburg in exchange for the acquisition by Holland of German territory in East Friesland and Gelderland; the establishment of some kind of union between Belgium and Luxembourg; and the annexation of the small German districts of Eupen and Malmédy and the neutral territory of Moresnet. For the Belgium memorandum and various abstracts and summaries of it, see Miller, *My Diary at the Conference of Paris*, IV, 427-96.

On February 11, the Belgium plenipotentiaries set forth these claims in the Council of Ten, which referred the matter to the newly created Commission on Belgian Affairs. The commission recommended on March 8, and the Council of Ten agreed, that the Treaty of 1839 should be revised, that Belgian neutrality should be abandoned, and that Holland should be invited to participate in negotiating a new arrangement. As to Belgium's territorial demands, the commission, in its report of March 19, concluded that Moresnet, Eupen, and Malmédy be ceded to Belgium and that some "rectifications" in favor of Holland of the German-Dutch frontier in compensation for Belgian claims to Dutch Flanders and Dutch Limburg were desirable.

The reports and recommendations of the commission, along with the minutes of its meetings, are printed in *ibid.*, pp. 4-210, and a large number of documents covering various aspects of the Belgian question are scattered throughout several of Miller's volumes. For earlier discussions in the Council of Ten, see *PPC*, III, 957-69, and IV, 141-44, 270-71. See also Haskins and Lord, *Some Problems of the Peace Conference*, pp. 48-71. The standard scholarly treatment is Sally Marks, *Innocent Abroad: Belgium at the Paris Peace Conference* (Chapel Hill, N. C., 1981).

all the way from the other end of the world, and she lost four times as many as you did.

M. Hymans. If we didn't have more soldiers, that was because our country was occupied. You don't know what an invasion is. You haven't seen your country under the boot of a conqueror for several years. We are waiting for the help which you promised us.

Mr. Lloyd George. It seems to me that we gave Belgium a promise which cost us the lives of 900,000 men. If you speak to us in this way, we won't listen to you any longer.

M. Hymans. I simply ask you to listen to me when it is a matter of my country's interests.

President Wilson. Regarding the Treaty of 1839, I will say to you that we don't know how to act so long as Holland hasn't been approached. I learned before my recent trip to America[7] that the Dutch were ready to discuss it; but they were wounded by the idea that one could treat them summarily and forget their neutral status. I have the impression that to plead your cause first before the "Ten" was to approach the matter from the wrong side. If you had come to me first, I would have told you: "I want to listen to you only in discussion with Holland."

M. Hymans. By approving the commission's report, the conference declared that there was ground for revising the treaty of 1839; it declared that France and England would invite Holland to discuss the question with them and with us. What I ask today is that, after having heard our statements, you don't leave us without a reply and without advice.

President Wilson. You suggested an exchange between Dutch Flanders and German territories west of the Ems. I don't understand how these German territories could be given to a country which didn't participate in the war. This case cannot be compared to that of Schleswig, which was once taken away from Denmark.

M. Hymans. I only ask you to hear me when you discuss the distribution of indemnities and the question of the left bank of the Rhine.

—M. Hymans withdraws.
—Messrs. Pichon, Balfour, Sonnino, and Lansing are introduced.

M. Orlando. I repeat what I said last Saturday in our Council of Four. An Italian officer arrived from Budapest bearing a letter from Prince Borghese who, as you know, was appointed Minister

---

[7] Wilson had left for the United States on February 15 to attend to urgent matters in Washington. He had returned to Paris on March 13.

to Belgrade but was obliged to leave because his letters of credence were not accepted. On his return, he stopped in Budapest, where one of his married sisters lives, and he was there when the revolution took place.

A member of the new government asked to see him and explained to him that this government did not want to break with the Entente. Prince Borghese replied that he was not qualified to receive overtures, but that he couldn't refuse to transmit a written statement if it was signed by all the members of the provisional government. It is this statement which was brought to us by the officer I just mentioned. This document expresses the desire for good relations with the Entente and asks that an inter-Allied mission be sent to Budapest.

President Wilson. In short, the Hungarians appeal to us so as not to be excluded from the League of Nations.

M. Pichon. I consider it absolutely impossible to respond to this overture of the Hungarian provisional government. That would be the worst of mistakes. What are the circumstances? Following bloody conflicts between Rumanians and Hungarians in Transylvania—a region which we have acknowledged should belong to Rumania—we decided to interpose a neutral line between the combatants. We informed Budapest that the drawing of this line did not prejudice our final decision about the Rumanian-Hungarian boundary.

What happened? That still remains obscure, although the departure of Count Károlyi and the change which followed lead us to suspect that the fall of the preceding government was not involuntary. A republic of soviets was proclaimed. Our missions were expelled, and the first act of the new government was to turn to Lenin and to tell him that it was ready to march with him. Today, the provisional government of Hungary writes us that there is no alliance between it and the Soviet Republic. That is not very clear.

It goes without saying that I have no desire to intervene in the internal affairs of Hungary. But in the document we have just read, we are asked to enter into conversation about territorial questions. The territorial questions concern peoples oppressed by the former Hungarian government—the Slovaks, the Transylvanians, the people of the Banat, of Croatia, and of Bosnia—to whom we have promised freedom.

We can't forget that the Hungarians are amongst our bitterest enemies. The responsibility of the Hungarian government in the origins of the war was dreadful. It is enough to recall the role of a man like Tisza. Hungarian policy guided the monarchy's, and the Hungarians fought to support it. This is an enemy which is offering to negotiate with us, and to negotiate about the interests of nationalities we have promised to liberate. If we accept this offer, we will alienate ourselves from those nationalities who are or will be our allies; they would not understand it if, whilst we are busy here determining their boundaries, we should go and discuss them with the Hungarians. As for Rumania especially, we are bound more than ever to support her now that we consider her a barrier against Bolshevism.

I cannot agree to enter into negotiations with Hungary on territorial questions. When this government protests that it has no alliance with Russia, I can't forget that its leader, Béla Kun, was Lenin's friend and accomplice. Are we to enter, against our allies, into relations with a government of soviets? Would that be the preface to negotiations with Russia? In that case, we would be embarking on a new course, which, as far as I am concerned, I cannot accept.

Mr. Lansing. It seems to me that we have a certain responsibility for what has happened in Hungary. We tried to be fair in establishing a demarcation line between Rumanians and Hungarians. The question is whether the line itself is fair.

It was the Rumanians who first crossed the line fixed by the Armistice. When it came to stopping hostilities, our experts drew a line following fairly exactly the ethnographic configurations; but we asked Hungary to withdraw one hundred kilometers to the west of that line. The effect of that decision was to lead them to believe that their boundary would be that of the Rumanian treaty of 1916. No government in Hungary could accept that, and that's what threw the country into Bolshevism.

M. Pichon. I recall that this was a decision of the conference. The question has been thoroughly studied. Generals have come to report the results of that study to you. We have acted with full knowledge of the case. What we have done displeases Hungary. But if the conference is today incapable of imposing its decision upon an enemy state, we can't hope to make peace anywhere.

Hungary answers us with revolution, with the expulsion of our missions. We are bound to Rumania, whom we have promised to liberate the Transylvanian peoples. We have drawn a line we believe to be just. Are we going to repudiate Rumania? That would be an unpardonable error.

Mr. Lloyd George. Can't we separate the question of the neutral zone from the decision to be taken today? M. Pichon has said that we have tried to be fair, and that is true. But the determination of a neutral zone can always cause misunderstandings. We said that the Hungarians would be informed that the decision taken would not prejudice the final drawing of the boundary. I don't know if this has been said to them clearly enough.

Mr. Balfour. It was a mistake if we neglected to do that. Besides, I don't know whether we ought to look there for the cause of events in Budapest. What I read in the newspapers shows me that the Bolshevik government has a nationalistic side, which would seem rather contradictory. The message from the Hungarians doesn't say much about territorial questions.

M. Pichon. I beg your pardon.

—M. Pichon rereads the text of the message.

Mr. Balfour. Either this is only a commonplace remark, or we cannot accept it. I see nothing in these proposals which would place Hungary in a different situation from that of other enemy countries. It could be helpful for us to send a mission to Budapest, and we certainly have an interest in knowing what is truly behind all this. You suspect Count Károlyi of having used Bolshevism for his own ends. To discover what truth there is in that, the best thing to do is to send men there who will look around.

Baron Sonnino. My impression is that Colonel Vix failed to say clearly enough that the determination of the neutral zone didn't settle the boundary question. What tends to prove this is that the statement published at that time by Károlyi says the contrary. I read afterwards a second statement from Vix, saying to Károlyi: "That is not correct, we are not fixing the boundary at this time." But it is possible he said it too late. We must do everything possible to clarify the situation.

With M. Pichon, I think we can't use a procedure with Hungary different from that which we are using with Germany or Bulgaria. Bolshevik blackmail must not procure an advantage for the Hungarians—that would be a very dangerous precedent. But no doubt must be left about our intentions; we must repeat that the line of demarcation has no other object than to avoid a collision.

M. Pichon. I accept this.

President Wilson. We are talking as if we intended to enter into diplomatic relations with Hungary in order to fix boundaries. That is not what we want to do. But we can send a mission to Hungary to find out what the Hungarians think. It is impossible, I agree with M. Pichon, to enter into normal relations with them, otherwise the other enemy states could ask for the same privilege. But we must avoid driving one country after another into Bolshevism by having too harsh an attitude.

The same danger exists in Vienna. If we had to trace a line of demarcation there, Vienna might plunge into Bolshevism the next day. If similar events repeat themselves, we shall have no peace, because we will not find anyone with whom to conclude it.

Concerning Hungary, we want to separate her from Austria. It won't serve any purpose to tell her: "We wish to have nothing to do with you; we are pure and white as the snow; none of us has ever had anything whatsoever to do with revolutionary governments." As for myself, I am ready to enter into conversation with any rascal whatever, if what he proposes to me is acceptable and my honor remains intact.

We can't consider sending diplomatic agents to Budapest, but rather a confidential agent, having the requisite experience and authority, who would go to tell the Hungarians: "I have no powers from the Associated governments, except on one point. You tell us that you wish to explain your position: do it; we don't understand what is happening amongst you. You say you don't have an alliance with Bolshevism; explain to us what you have done."

It is possible, as Mr. Lansing and Baron Sonnino have said, that we are not without responsibility for events in Budapest. Above all, the situation must be clarified. The government of Budapest is not laden with the crimes with which we reproach the Russian Bolsheviks. It is probably nationalistic. It is a government of soviets, because that is the fashionable revolutionary mode, and there may be many types of soviets. We have only to say to the provisional government of Hungary: "We have read your memorandum, and we come to ask you what you have to say."

Mr. Lloyd George. May I observe that, according to the terms of the armistice, nothing compels the Hungarians to withdraw from the territories into which the Rumanians have advanced? One article authorized us to take possession of them; it is the one enabling us to occupy strategic points to maintain order. In the armistice with Hungary signed by Generals Henrys and Michitch, an article stipulates that a representative of the Allies will be attached to the Hungarian food ministry. If we send someone there under that title, we are only doing what conforms to the armistice.

M. Clemenceau. I wouldn't be surprised if Colonel Vix had this role.

Mr. Lloyd George. It's not a question of sending someone there to negotiate questions of boundaries; that belongs only to the conference. But there is a misunderstanding to be cleared up which is very similar to the one over Danzig. The Germans believed that sending Polish troops by way of Danzig would mean that Danzig was going to be taken from them straightaway. Likewise, the Hungarians think we want to take from them all the territory bounded by the line of demarcation.

The King of England received from Archduke Joseph, who is not a Bolshevik, a letter expressing the Hungarians' fear of seeing their territory divided among the Rumanians, the Czechs, and the Serbo-Croats.[8] It is a rather moving document, which conveys the idea of a current of national despair. Count Károlyi was a tired man, who threw the helve after the hatchet, and Bolshevism only filled a void.

The Austro-Hungarian armistice was drawn up a bit hastily; it doesn't contain the equivalent of Article 34 of the German Armistice.[9] We might try to fill that gap by designating someone to speak in our name to the Hungarians, just as Marshal Foch speaks in our name to the Germans.

I don't criticize the decision taken about the neutral zone; I consider it reasonable. But I strongly support what President Wilson said. It would be pointless to send a subordinate there; it must be a man who has authority.

Don't forget that these peoples are terribly afraid of us. They know that we have destroyed two great empires, and that we can do them much harm. We must speak to them firmly and send not just some colonel, but a man of weight, capable of representing us and of making himself perfectly understood.

Mr. Balfour. Could he not visit centers other than Budapest?

M. Clemenceau. Don't we have two different proposals before us? President Wilson wishes to send someone to Budapest to con-

---

[8] In his letter of December 21, 1918, Archduke Joseph of Hapsburg had asked King George to demand that all the invaders of Hungary leave that country, and he had suggested a political and economic alliance between Hungary and Great Britain. See Thomas L. Sakmyster, "Great Britain and the Making of the Treaty of Trianon," in Béla Király et al., eds., *War and Society in East Central Europe, Vol. VI, Essays on World War I: Total War and Peacemaking, A Study on Trianon* (Brooklyn, N. Y., 1982), p. 120.

[9] In addition to specifying the duration of the original Armistice Agreement with Germany, the article had established a permanent International Armistice Commission under the military and naval high command of the Allied armies "to assure the execution of the present convention under the most favorable conditions." See Harry R. Rudin, *Armistice, 1918* (New Haven, Conn., 1944), pp. 431-32.

duct an inquiry. Mr. Lloyd George wishes to send a military leader to impose our will.

President Wilson. To avoid the appearance of a diplomatic negotiation, it might be better to send a soldier of high rank there, who also has the personal qualities of a diplomat.

Mr. Lloyd George. I would be inclined to send General Smuts, who is a statesman as well as a military leader.

M. Pichon. What I have opposed is the idea of establishing diplomatic relations with Hungary. But is it possible to send someone to Budapest without first demanding satisfaction for the highhanded measures taken against the missions we already had there, along the lines of what Mr. Lloyd George himself has just described as a reasonable measure?

Baron Sonnino. The first thing to do is to impose respect for the neutral zone.

President Wilson. If it seems after an inquiry on the spot that there are grounds for changing the neutral zone, our representative could make such recommendations as he deems advisable on this subject.

Baron Sonnino. That is a dangerous procedure. If, after a defiant refusal, we appear to give in, there is no reason for the same thing not to happen everywhere, at Teschen, for instance.

President Wilson. Personally, I am not sure that the determination of that neutral zone was wise. Maybe the delimitation was not exactly what it should have been. As for the treatment of Allied missions in Budapest, we would have to know exactly what happened.

Mr. Lansing. We are told that the provisional government of Hungary had them arrested only in order to insure their safety.

Mr. Lloyd George. We must first obtain information.

M. Orlando. I will point out that the Hungarian document opens with a helpful statement: "The new Hungarian government acknowledges the armistice agreement." It would be odd on our part if we didn't take formal notice of this declaration. As for the treatment of the missions, the Italian mission at Laibach was expelled by the Croats. I don't see why we should make such a distinction amongst the different peoples of Austria-Hungary; except for the Czechs, whom I respect, all the others were our enemies. One of the reasons for the revolt of the Hungarians is the feeling that other nationalities had to make only a few demonstrations in order to be treated as allies by us.

They also say they don't believe that their refusal to accept the note presented by Colonel Vix constitutes a violation of the armistice agreement. I compare this attitude to that of the Germans at Posen who refused to discuss the question of the transit of Polish troops and, by invoking the text of the Armistice Agreement, asked that it be discussed at Spa. In this case, we admitted that the German observation was justified.

I accept the proposal of Messrs. Lloyd George and Wilson to send an important person to Budapest to clear up the ambiguity. General Smuts seems to me to have the desired authority. We must first demand the reestablishment of our missions, with all necessary reparation.

Baron Sonnino. Mr. Balfour proposed that General Smuts might also visit Vienna. I would oppose that. It is better to treat the Hungarian question as a special question, all the more so because we already have agents who are in contact with us in the most important places of the former Austro-Hungarian monarchy.

M. Clemenceau. Then we agree to send General Smuts to Hungary. He will conduct an inquiry about the treatment of our missions and study the question of the neutral zone.[10]

Mr. Lloyd George. If Baron Sonnino has an objection to General Smuts going to Vienna, I should like him to be permitted to go at least to Bucharest, if he believes he has some chance of thus facilitating the settlement of the questions between the Rumanians and Hungarians.

---

[10] Smuts was also instructed to explain to the Hungarian government the reasons for the establishment of the neutral zone and "to make it clear that the policy was adopted solely to stop bloodshed and without any intention of prejudicing the eventual settlement of the boundaries between Hungary and Roumania." In addition, Smuts was authorized to make any adjustments in the boundaries of the neutral zone that he deemed necessary. "RESOLUTION IN REGARD TO THE SITUATION IN HUNGARY," April 1, 1919, printed in PWW, Vol. 56, pp. 465-66.

XIII

Conversation between President Wilson and MM. Clemenceau, Lloyd George, and Orlando*

APRIL 1, 1919, 11 A.M.

TRANSPORT OF THE POLISH TROOPS

President Wilson. I have received information from a confidential source about the present state of mind of the German government.[1] It genuinely fears seeing the passage of Polish troops through Danzig provoke a violent conflict in the region. The passage of Paderewski has already given rise to some tumultuous demonstrations.[2] To avert this danger, the German government would go so far as to accept the transport of Polish troops by German railways, starting from the Rhine bridgeheads. If the Germans admit in writing our right to have Polish troops pass through Danzig, it would be possible to send only a small contingent there in order to establish this right clearly. Couldn't we instruct Marshal Foch along the lines I have just indicated?

Mr. Lloyd George. Sir Joseph Maclay always told us that this was the right way to solve this problem; in fact, it is very difficult to find the necessary tonnage at a time when Italy lacks coal and Australian troops are complaining about not having been repatriated quickly enough, to the extent that there was a mutiny among them in which thirty soldiers were shot dead.

M. Clemenceau. We will have a certain number of Poles pass through Danzig to establish our right. That is acceptable; but we will have to draw Poland's western border some day.

*Does not appear in H.

[1] See the two memoranda by Brig. Gen. Dennis Edward Nolan, the chief of the Intelligence Department of the American Expeditionary Force, printed in PWW, Vol. 56, pp. 492-94.

[2] Paderewski, who had spent the war years in the United States as the representative of the Polish National Committee, had returned to Poland in early January 1919 in an effort to unite the various Polish factions and establish a broad national government. On his way to Warsaw, he had landed at Danzig and had proceeded to Posen on December 26, where his arrival had precipitated a Polish revolt against the German authorities which had developed into a month-long conflict between Polish militia groups and the German army. See Lundgreen-Nielsen, *The Polish Problem at the Paris Peace Conference*, pp. 113-16.

Mr. Lloyd George. Is it necessary to decide the fate of Danzig immediately?

M. Clemenceau. Failing that, I don't see how you can draw the boundaries of Germany.

President Wilson. The opinion of most of the experts is that the Poles must have the power to control Danzig. Bismarck once said to Crespi: "The resurrection of Poland is impossible unless Thorn and Danzig are taken from Prussia, and unless the German Empire is dismembered." It is better not to raise this formidable question in connection with the transport of the troops.

Mr. Lloyd George. I would be inclined to accept the German proposal to transport the troops by land.

President Wilson. Whilst making the Germans acknowledge their obligation to permit troops to pass through Danzig.

M. Clemenceau. I can accept this.

President Wilson. I have other information about the German frame of mind; it concerns reparations. In fulfillment of the commitment they have already taken in the Armistice Agreement, they would agree to reconstruct all the buildings destroyed in France and Belgium at their own expense and to provide the manpower.[3]

Mr. Lloyd George. There is something to be said in favor of this proposal. I believe there will be a shortage of labor. In England, we can't build the workers' housing we need because of it. The proposal seems practical to me.

President Wilson (*after reading aloud the note which had been communicated to him*). I don't know what use we can make of this document, which is not official.

M. Clemenceau. We can propose this to the German government ourselves, adding that the same requirement would apply to other reparations, such as those for agriculture, railways.

—President Wilson reads the draft of a resolution on the transport of the Polish troops by German railways.[4]

M. Clemenceau. If we adopt this document, it is we who are pro-

---

[3] See the first of the two memoranda cited in n. 1 above.

[4] It reads as follows: "In case the German authorities will say in writing that they fully admit their obligation under the terms of the Armistice to permit the transportation of General Haller's forces through Danzig and Thorn, Marshal Foch is instructed to entertain a proposal for the direct and immediate transportation of those troops by rail to Poland from one of the points under allied control on the Rhine." *PWW*, Vol. 56, p. 496.

posing passage by land to the Germans; I would prefer that the Germans do it.

President Wilson. The wording can be changed along those lines by authorizing Marshal Foch simply to consider, if it is presented to him, a proposal to transport General Haller's troops by rail, starting from the Rhine bridgeheads.

—Marshal Foch and General Weygand are introduced.

M. Clemenceau. President Wilson has received information indicating that the Germans are ready to provide General Haller's troops with facilities for passage by their railways, starting from the line of the Rhine. That seems acceptable to me, on condition that we obtain written acknowledgment from the Germans of our right to have Polish troops pass through Danzig.

That would have some advantages. The first is that we could transport troops in ten days instead of two months; the second is that we would have the Polish troops there when our decision on the subject of the future of Danzig, which might provoke disorders, will be finally known.

Marshal Foch. You think this scheme is advantageous: I think it places the Poles in the jaws of the wolf. The trip all the way across Germany is long. All along the route, the Poles will be at the mercy of the Boches. If the Germans want to let them pass, they will pass; but the Germans can stop them. They can also say that such and such a local soviet is stopping them, and that they themselves can do nothing.

Nevertheless, one can consider the proposal.

M. Clemenceau. The difficulty is that, if we take our decision about the fate of Danzig before the Polish troops arrive in Poland, we run the risk of grave disturbances. Once we have sent Polish regiments to Warsaw, we can then say to the Germans: "Danzig is no longer yours."

President Wilson. It is not very easy for soviets to stop troops who wish to pass. The Russian soviets tried to do it with the Czechoslovaks; it turned out badly for them.

—M. Clemenceau rereads the text of the resolution proposed by President Wilson.

General Weygand. The transport of Haller's troops would require at least 400 trains.

President Wilson. What! For 25,000 men?

General Weygand. Altogether, there will be up to 80,000 men. At a rate of fifteen trains per day, the transport would require one month. Moreover, some of the divisions will be ready only by May 1. That is the sense of the observation I wished to make.

President Wilson. I am surprised by the figure you give me. We had understood that it would be a matter of sending 25,000 men to Poland.

General Weygand. General Haller's army is composed of six divisions, with nondivisional elements equivalent to a seventh division. At fifty trains per division, that makes 350 trains, and fifty more must be provided for additional matériel.

Mr. Lloyd George. How many divisions will be ready before May 1?

General Weygand. Two or three.

Mr. Lloyd George. Between now and May 1, we will have taken our decision on the fate of Danzig. The important thing is to act immediately. Two or three divisions must be sent to Poland as soon as possible.

M. Orlando. When French and English divisions were transported to Italy, one division a week was sent, and communications were difficult.

M. Clemenceau. Yes, we have only two rail lines between France and Italy, which really amount to one and a half.

Marshal Foch. Undoubtedly, the Germans will ask us for cars and locomotives. I am not leaving for Spa until tomorrow evening. We are going to study the question in its quantitative aspects; I can inform you about the result of this study before my departure.

—Marshal Foch and General Weygand withdraw.

President Wilson. I wish to say a word about the subject of the victualing of Bavaria, which I have already discussed with M. Clemenceau. Mr. Lansing, who has been said to oppose the plan, makes no political objection; but M. Pichon didn't inform him sufficiently about the political aspect of the project, the special aim of which is to help Dr. Muehlon and his party.[5] The objec-

---

[5] This "project," which involved the separate and accelerated food shipment from French surpluses to Bavaria, had been submitted by Pichon to the Council of Foreign Ministers on March 27. While Pichon had emphasized the economic aspects of the plan, he had made it obvious that its principal objective was to foster the latent Bavarian separatist movement and to diminish the "political influence of Prussia" on Bavaria. During the meeting, both Hoover and Lansing had strongly opposed the scheme, and, contrary to Wilson's assertion, Lansing had informed Wilson shortly before this meeting of the Big Four of his political objections to the French plan. To Wilson, these French efforts seemed to be connected with another, but apparently unrelated, discussion among German

tion comes from Mr. Hoover, who reminded us of the commitments we have taken towards Germany,[6] and who thinks we cannot provide Bavaria with what is proposed without violating our obligations.

M. Clemenceau. What we ask is not that Bavaria receive more, but that she be victualed through Switzerland, which will give her [Bavaria] a feeling of independence.

President Wilson. This is something that might disrupt Mr. Hoover's distribution system.

M. Clemenceau. Can't anything be done to overcome this difficulty?

President Wilson. I will explain the situation to Mr. Hoover and ask him to take account of the political considerations.[7]

—Brief exchange of views on the question of the left bank of the Rhine. President Wilson states that, according to the last deliberations of the League of Nations Commission,[8] the Council of this organization will be assisted by a military and naval general staff. It will be the task of the Council to give this general staff all necessary instructions to prepare plans of action in case of aggression. The British and American guarantee which has been envisaged would be operative until the security provided by the League of Nations is considered sufficient.

---

emigrés in Switzerland and self-appointed American representatives in Bern, who had been in contact throughout the war. Their somewhat harebrained scheme called for a repudiation by Wilson of the present German leadership and its replacement by a new, pro-Wilson government. One of the persons involved in these talks was Dr. Wilhelm von Muehlon, a former official in the German Foreign Office and a former director of the Krupp firm in Essen, who had been one of the leading German opponents of the war and had long been in touch with American agents in Switzerland. See *PPC*, IV, 515-21, and Klaus Schwabe, *Deutsche Revolution und Wilson-Frieden: Die amerikanische and deutsche Friedensstrategie zwischen Ideologie and Machtpolitik 1918/19* (Düsseldorf, 1971), pp. 480-83.

[6] In the so-called Brussels Agreement, negotiated between German and Allied representatives on March 14 and 15, 1919, Great Britain, France, and the United States had promised to sell to Germany 370,000 tons of foodstuffs a month until September 1.

[7] See WW to H. C. Hoover, April 2, 1919, printed in *PWW*, Vol. 56, p. 543. In his reply, Hoover repeated his opposition to the French plan and pointed out that the question had been "repeatedly agitated up" by the French Minister at Bern, who was "constantly endeavoring to create a Separatist spirit in Bavaria." H. C. Hoover to WW, April 3, 1919, *ibid.*, pp. 574-75. The matter was finally disposed of when the Supreme Economic Council, on April 7, rejected the French plan. See *PPC*, X, 103.

[8] At the meeting of the commission on March 24, 1919. See *PWW*, Vol. 56, pp. 222-33.

XIV

Conversation between President Wilson and MM. Clemenceau, Lloyd George, and Orlando*

APRIL 1, 1919, 4 P.M.

President Wilson. I saw the American financial experts at two o'clock, and I told them, recalling the exchange we had here: "If, when we are face to face with the Germans, we tell them it is impossible for us to indicate the figure of what they owe and what we believe them capable of paying, they will certainly reply: 'At least tell us what the purpose of the reparations will be.' " To reply to this question, we must draw up a classification by categories amongst ourselves, without losing sight of the formula we adopted: "Reparation for damages to the property and persons of the civilian populations." It is understood that this formula should include pensions.[1]

It is a matter of establishing a list to which we put our names in common. From that time on, we will be in a position to reply to the question that the Germans certainly will ask us. We agree to exclude everything that is not direct damage, such as the failure of business to make profits.

Mr. Lloyd George. We can tell the Germans that, if they refuse to

---

*Does not appear in H.

[1] For accounts of this meeting, see the memorandum by J. F. Dulles and the extracts from the diaries of V. C. McCormick and T. W. Lamont, all dated April 1, 1919, printed in PWW, Vol. 56, pp. 498-502. The inclusion of pensions and separation allowances in the categories of damage had been demanded by the British who had realized that, after the renunciation of their claim for reparation of war costs, the ratio of distribution of the German payments among the Allies would be very unfavorable to Great Britain and the dominions. In fact, if reparations were to be strictly limited to direct damage to civilians and their property as stipulated in the Pre-Armistice Agreement, Great Britain, rather than receiving the 30 per cent of the German payments demanded by Lloyd George, would be eligible for not more than 20 per cent, while the dominions would have virtually no claim at all to reparation. Although Wilson had initially opposed the inclusion of noncivilian damages, he had been persuaded to acquiesce in the British demand by General Smuts, who, in a memorandum of March 31, had presented a closely reasoned argument for the compatibility of pensions and separation allowances with the reservation on civilian damages in the Pre-Armistice Agreement. For detailed discussions of the controversy surrounding this question, see Birdsall, *Versailles Twenty Years After*, pp. 250-53; Tillman, *Anglo-American Relations at the Paris Peace Conference*, pp. 244-46; and Trachtenberg, *Reparation in World Politics*, pp. 68-84.

accept one of our categories, for instance pensions, we will resume our unlimited right of claims for all damages suffered, whatever they may be.

President Wilson. Our categories must include compensation due for the deportation of workers.

Mr. Lloyd George. Undoubtedly, and for the outrages against the crews of the merchant fleet.

President Wilson. I have reviewed the proposals relating to Danzig. They are four in number.[2]

The first would make Danzig a free city, somewhat like the Hanseatic cities of the Middle Ages, with sufficient territory surrounding her, but limited so as to include an almost exclusively German population. On the other hand, the border of East Prussia would be extended westward in order to include in that province the Germans of the lower Vistula. The Poles would keep the left bank of the river and would have a small balloon-shaped territory on the right bank between East Prussia and the Republic of Danzig.

The second plan gives Danzig to the Poles, whilst extending the territory of East Prussia as above.

The third is the commission's plan, which you know.[3]

The fourth has just been presented by an expert of the British delegation, Mr. Headlam-Morley. Germany would cede Danzig, along with its territory, to the League of Nations, and the League of Nations would give it to Poland on the condition that it be assured relative autonomy. The Council of the League of Nations would fix the final borders of this little state, as well as those of East Prussia.

This exhausts all the possibilities, it seems to me.

The danger of the first plan is that it would give the Germans of Danzig the temptation to reunite with Germany. The second, with its concession to East Prussia and the cession of Danzig to the Poles, is a compromise. The last has the same character and the advantage of having the League of Nations intervene as a guarantor of the proposed arrangement; but it has the disadvantage of leaving in suspense part of the decisions to be taken.

Mr. Lloyd George. I would rather prefer a combination of the first

[2] For these plans, see the memoranda by S. E. Mezes of March 31 and April 1, 1919, printed in *PWW*, Vol. 56, pp. 471-73, 505.

[3] That is, that Poland receive the city and port of Danzig, as well as the province of Marienwerder and other territories in East Prussia to insure Polish control over the Danzig-Mława-Warsaw railway.

and fourth plans. I don't dislike the idea of reviving the free cities. They flourished at a time when, it seems, international law was more respected than today.

President Wilson. It is above all military methods that have changed.

Mr. Lloyd George. I would conceive of an independent city of Danzig, with a large enough territory to give it a breathing space. I would place this small state within the customs borders of Poland, which would make it impossible for Germany to use it to strangle Poland economically.

The inhabitants of Danzig would know that their future is bound to the economic future of Poland. Indeed, all their opportunities for trade lie on that side. By making them independent, you will give them an interest in the prosperity of the Polish state, to which we would gradually attach them by the economic bond. I am persuaded that the same thing will happen in the Saar Basin, when the latter is united without political ties to France by its interests. I would see to it that all the interests of Danzig's inhabitants are turned towards Poland, whilst leaving to them all the German laws and institutions they want to maintain.

My great concern is to avoid putting too many Germans in Poland. According to the commission's report, the province of Marienwerder alone would include 420,000. I would leave this province to East Prussia, whilst giving Poland absolute right to the railways.

President Wilson. Couldn't the fate of these German-speaking regions be decided by a plebiscite?

Mr. Lloyd George. If there is a plebiscite, I will accept the decision of the people.

President Wilson. The question is how the Poles will receive this plan. When I earlier mentioned to M. Dmowski the possibility of Danzig being a free city, he hit the ceiling.[4] In this case, we must give the Poles sovereignty over the river whose western bank they will occupy. Only a small part of the Vistula would flow along German territory of East Prussia.

Mr. Lloyd George. The railroad from Danzig to Thorn would remain in Polish territory.

M. Orlando. Would the territory of Danzig be in direct contact with Polish territory?

---

[4] For a detailed account of the conference between Wilson, Dmowski, and Paderewski at the White House on September 18, 1918, see Louis L. Gerson, *Woodrow Wilson and the Rebirth of Poland, 1914-1920* (New Haven, Conn., 1953), pp. 94-96.

Mr. Lloyd George. Certainly. (*Mr. Lloyd George shows the map.*)

M. Clemenceau. We cannot take a final decision on this subject without the Poles being present.

President Wilson. No, but we can agree amongst ourselves beforehand.

Mr. Lloyd George. I believe it would be vain to hope to satisfy the Poles.

President Wilson. They must accept the solution that we deem reasonable.

M. Clemenceau. They won't accept it without difficulty.

Mr. Lloyd George. If they don't accept it, let them do better on their own. My advice is to decide upon a plan and then to summon the Poles.

President Wilson. Do we agree to create a free state around Danzig?

Mr. Lloyd George. Yes, but under the authority of the League of Nations.

President Wilson. What structure do you conceive for this authority?

Mr. Lloyd George. I would rather favor seeing the League of Nations represented in Danzig by a High Commissioner. That would prevent the Germans from intriguing in this little state. This High Commissioner could play a part similar to that of our Governors-General in Canada and Australia, whose presence doesn't prevent the inhabitants from governing themselves freely.

President Wilson. The union of the province of Marienwerder to East Prussia must be added, with freedom of transit guaranteed to the Poles; this could be settled by plebiscite. I must say that this solution is, on the whole, the one that I have always preferred.

Mr. Lloyd George. Our Foreign Office has always advised us along these lines. After all, we don't owe much to the Poles, who fought as much against us as for us. We must avoid anything that would make it difficult for the Germans to sign the treaty.

President Wilson (*to M. Clemenceau*). What are your thoughts on this last point?

M. Clemenceau. I am not very sure you would succeed by this strategy in coaxing the Germans.

President Wilson. We mustn't allow ourselves to be influenced too much by the Polish state of mind. I saw M. Dmowski and M. Paderewski in Washington, and I asked them to define Poland for me, as they understood it, and they presented me with a map in which they claimed a large part of the earth.

Mr. Lloyd George. What I ask is that we don't put in the treaty articles for which we are not prepared to go to war in the future. France would make war tomorrow for Alsace if it was contested. But would we make war for Danzig?

President Wilson. Furthermore, we shouldn't violate the principles we ourselves have set forth as the basis of the peace. All we have promised to Poland is access to the sea; and, at the same time, we have always declared that we would respect ethnographic lines as much as possible.

If you really wish it, I will have Professor Haskins study this question anew.

Here is a document which Mr. Norman Davis sent me.[5] There is agreement amongst our financial representatives to accept, in its general outlines, the plan which Mr. Lloyd George submitted to us: the Germans recognize their debt according to our formula and a permanent commission is established to examine claims and determine Germany's capacity to pay, with the right to fix annual payments, etc.

A date is suggested for the announcement of figures: it would be May 1, 1921.

Mr. Lloyd George. I am told that the experts don't agree because M. Klotz, on the contrary, wants the annual payments to be stipulated in the peace treaty.

—M. Loucheur is introduced.

M. Loucheur. Your financial delegates are studying the question of reparations. The English and the Americans have come to terms, and we will arrive at a general agreement. I hope we will be able to bring you our conclusions at noon tomorrow.

However, we need precise instructions about the categories of damages admitted for reparation. Since we accept the principle offered by the American delegation, agreement should be easy.

President Wilson. I believe the question of the Polish boundaries is nearly settled.

M. Clemenceau. I wasn't very favorably disposed towards adopting this type of solution. But after having listened to you, I am inclined to go along with you, whilst I think the greatest precautions must be taken if we wish to avoid throwing the Poles into confusion.

[5] It is printed as an appendix to the notes of this meeting.

President Wilson. We must consider the agenda for the coming days. Peace with Germany will not remove all the causes of possible difficulties. I greatly fear those that might arise from the developments related to all these nationalities in Central Europe. If we are not very careful, they will be an inexhaustible source of disorder and war.

I propose to ask our territorial commissions to review their reports and to change them if need be along the lines indicated by our fundamental principles. Then we can finish rapidly.

Mr. Lloyd George. We can, I hope, be ready on all the great questions in a week. During the time required for the work of the Drafting Committee, we could tackle amongst ourselves the questions of the nationalities of Austria-Hungary, as well as the Bulgarian and Turkish questions.

M. Orlando. It is necessary, from the Italian point of view, that our decision on the eastern boundary of Italy not be delayed. For the Italian people, this is a question of self-respect, to which must be added our concern for national security. It would create a bad impression if the Italian people learn that the German questions are completely settled and the Austrian questions are postponed.

Mr. Lloyd George. I am quite ready to discuss this question next week, when we will be working on the final wording of our decisions on the German treaty. We also have the report on the question of responsibilities[6] that we could consider here.

President Wilson. I have a word to say on this subject. Charles I was a contemptible character and the greatest liar in history; he was celebrated by poetry and transformed into a martyr by his execution. The same for Mary Stuart, whose career was not in the least exemplary.

Mr. Lloyd George. Concerning Mary Stuart, the poetry could be explained otherwise: she was a very seductive woman.

President Wilson. Napoleon who—by different methods, I concede—tried, exactly like the German Emperor, to impose his domination upon the world, was surrounded by legend because of his captivity at Saint Helena.

Mr. Lloyd George. It wasn't only Saint Helena that created the Napoleonic legend.

I would like to see the man responsible for the greatest crime in history punished for it.

---

[6] That is, the report of the Commission on the Responsibility of the Authors of the War and the Enforcement of Penalties, which had been submitted on March 29, 1919.

President Wilson. He has drawn universal contempt upon himself; isn't that the worst punishment for a man like him?

—An exchange of views takes place about the Turkish questions. It is agreed that Turkey need only be informed about her territorial boundaries on the Armenian side. On the Greek side, they can be extended beyond strictly ethnographic lines, in such a way as to give the ports on the western coast some breathing space. Constantinople and the area of the Straits would be placed under a separate mandate of the League of Nations. It remains to be decided whether Turkey will be independent or itself placed under a mandatory different from the one for Constantinople.

{ A P P E N D I X }[7]

APRIL 1, 1919.

1. The Allied and Associated Governments recognize that the financial resources of the enemy States are not unlimited, and, after taking into account permanent diminutions of such resources, which will result from other treaty clauses, they judge that it will be impracticable for the enemy states to make complete reparation for all loss and damage to which the Allied and Associated Governments, and their nationals, have been subjected as a direct and necessary consequence of the war imposed upon them by the aggression of the enemy states.

2. The Allied and Associated Governments, however, require that the enemy states, at whatever cost to themselves, make compensation for all damages done to the civilian population of the Allied and Associated Powers and to their property by the ag-

---

[7] Printed in *PWW*, Vol. 56, pp. 504-505. The British, French, American, and Italian financial experts had met on March 31 to discuss Lloyd George's proposal on reparation. After the conference had adjourned to permit the French to submit amendments to Lloyd George's plan, the British and American advisers had continued their negotiations and had drawn up the following tentative accord. They had also agreed that an "interpretation document" should be prepared to explain to the Germans the categories of damage under which the Allied and Associated Powers would seek reparation, subject to Germany's capacity to pay as determined by the Permanent Reparation Commission. It had been understood that among those categories should be the cost of pensions and the cost of damage to property. See the memorandum on Anglo-American progress on reparations, April 1, 1919, printed in *ibid.*, pp. 502-503. For documents relating to this question, see also Burnett, *Reparation at the Paris Peace Conference*, I, 756-804 *passim*.

gression of the enemy states by land, by sea, and from the air, and also from damage resulting from their acts in violation of formal engagements and of the law of nations.

3. The amount of such damage for which compensation is to be made shall be determined by an Inter-Allied Commission, to be constituted in such form as the Allied and Associated Governments shall forthwith determine. This Commission shall examine into the claims and give to the enemy states a just opportunity to be heard. The findings of the Commission as to the amount of damage shall be concluded and communicated to the enemy states on or before May 1, 1921; and a schedule of payments to be made by the enemy states shall be set forth covering a series of years not to exceed 30, and in general to be based upon the reasonable capacity of the enemy states to pay.

4. The Inter-Ally Commission shall further determine from time to time any necessary modifications in the time and mode of payments to be made by the enemy states, after giving them a just opportunity to be heard. Payment may be required and, with the approval of the Commission, accepted in the form of properties, chattels, businesses, rights, and concessions in ceded territory or in territory outside the enemy state, ships, gold and silver, bonds, shares and securities of all kinds, foreign currencies or the currency of the enemy state, or in German Government bonds.

5. In order to enable the Allied and Associated Powers to proceed at once to the restoration of their industries and economic life, pending the full determination of their claim, the enemy states shall pay in such installments and in such manner (whether in gold, commodities, ships, securities or otherwise) as the Inter-Allied Commission may fix, in 1919 and 1920, the equivalent of Ł1,000,000,000 sterling. Out of such payment provision shall be made for the maintenance of the Allied Armies of Occupation, and for indispensable supplies of food and raw materials for the enemy states. The balance shall be credited on account of the sum that may be determined to be due as compensation for damages.

6. The successive instalments paid over by the enemy states in satisfaction of the above claims shall be divided by the Allied and Associated Governments in proportions which have been determined upon by them in advance, on a basis of general equity, having regard to all relevant circumstances.

XV

Conversation between President Wilson and MM. Clemenceau, Lloyd George, and Orlando*

APRIL 2, 1919, 11 A.M.

—Reading of a memorandum from the Japanese embassy asking that no question concerning that country be discussed without the presence of the Japanese delegates.

President Wilson. We can only accept this observation, which is presented in a most polite form.

Mr. Lloyd George. We might reply that we are meeting amongst the four of us to study purely European questions, and that the delegates of Japan will be welcome when we touch on the kind of question that interests them.

M. Clemenceau. I am in full agreement with you, and I think our reply should be worded with the greatest courtesy.

QUESTION OF THE TRANSPORT OF THE POLISH TROOPS TO WARSAW

—Marshal Foch and General Weygand are introduced.

Marshal Foch. I wish to speak to you about the way I should conduct the negotiations at Spa on the subject of the transport of the Polish troops. I have received three instructions—on March 24, March 29, and April 1. There are some differences amongst these texts.

On the twenty-fourth, it was decided to demand that the Germans assure free passage for General Haller's troops through Danzig in conformity with Article 16 of the Armistice, and to warn them that a refusal would constitute a breach of the Armistice. This decision was communicated to them.

On the twenty-ninth, it was decided that the Germans would be invited to send a plenipotentiary to Spa; that I would demand of him, in the name of the powers, the passage of Polish troops through Danzig; but that I would be authorized, without renouncing Danzig, to accept the passage of a portion of these troops by way of Königsberg and Stettin.

*Does not appear in H.

Yesterday, April 1, you gave me rather different instructions, as follows: "If the Germans acknowledge in writing their obligation to allow Polish troops to pass through Danzig, in conformity with the Armistice Agreement, Marshal Foch will consider the transport of these troops across Germany by rail."

We seem to be abandoning Danzig, especially if we compare this text with those of March 24 and March 29.

President Wilson. There is no contradiction between these successive decisions. We have constantly sought to uphold our right. Our instructions have only changed because of circumstances. The essential principle has not been changed.

Marshal Foch is authorized, not to propose, but to take into consideration—if it is proposed by the Germans—the solution which consists of transporting Polish troops by German railways. We know the Germans are inclined to make this proposal, which will have the great advantage of surmounting the difficult question of tonnage.

Marshal Foch. Then the fundamental terms of my negotiation is our right to have these troops pass through Danzig.

President Wilson. It is not a matter of actual passage, but of our right to have them pass through.

Marshal Foch. That right is recognized by the Armistice; we don't have to claim it, but to impose it.

M. Clemenceau. If I understand the Marshal rightly, what he means is this: "I must open the negotiations by demanding passage through Danzig."

Marshal Foch. I am not going to Spa to win a right which I possess, but to win an advantageous and practical execution.

Mr. Lloyd George. It is most important to get these troops to Poland as soon as possible. Our goal isn't to seek a quarrel with the Germans, but to see that General Haller's troops arrive promptly in Warsaw.

Marshal Foch. Do we have any information about the Germans' proposal? Have they made a proposal, strictly speaking?

President Wilson. The information I have received comes from a source which I do not know directly but which has allowed the officers who represent me in Germany to provide this piece of information. There is nothing official about it. It is an indirect report which informs us that the Germans are ready to make the proposal.

Mr. Lloyd George. The utilization of Stettin allowed us to double the landing facilities offered by Danzig; this new proposal would allow the entire transport to be made in one third the time. Each change in our first resolution has thus represented progress.

—Reading by General Weygand of a dispatch from General d'Anselme announcing that the military situation at Odessa is restored, but that, because of the lack of provisions, which has forced us to share the supplies of the army of occupation with the population, evacuation has been ordered. It will begin with the Allied civilian population and will continue with the troops, who will retire behind the Dniester.

M. Clemenceau. I would remark that this decision seems to precede the reception of the order which we ourselves had sent, which proves how necessary was the decision we took.

Marshal Foch. I return to the question of the Polish troops. The transport of these troops by railway across Germany can't be made without guarantees. For instance, the trains must be accompanied by Allied officers; the Germans must provide the rolling stock and the personnel. If the proposal is made, it shouldn't be accepted with eyes shut and without conditions. I think I have the right, if these conditions are not accepted by the Germans, to refuse the solution?

President Wilson. I would point out that the troops to be transported are Allied troops.

Marshal Foch. I mean it would be advisable to place Allied officers in the trains, who would be there in case of an incident between the Poles and the Germans.

Mr. Lloyd George. I see senior officers there.

President Wilson. What is the point of your comment about the rolling stock?

General Weygand. We must know whether it will be provided by us or by the Germans. If the Germans are to provide it, precise promises must be extracted from them. If it is we who send cars and locomotives across Germany, we must be assured that this rolling stock will come back to us. There are similar stipulations to be made with regard to personnel.

President Wilson. If they provide the rolling stock, we will undoubtedly have to pay for it, because the Germans are not obliged to provide us with cars for this type of transport.

Mr. Lloyd George. I believe it would be better to provide the rolling stock ourselves, as we would be doing if these troops were transported by sea.

M. Clemenceau. But the Germans will provide the coal, for it couldn't be done otherwise.

President Wilson. Since this proposal is a German proposal, they have every interest in presenting it with satisfactory terms, in order to make it acceptable.

Marshal Foch. I would like your instructions on another point.

When the convention of February 16[1] was concluded, we included a clause aimed at stopping hostilities between the Poles and Germans. The execution was entrusted to an inter-Allied commission in Poland. Hostilities did stop, in fact; but the Noulens mission didn't succeed in negotiating with the Germans. Must we take this business up at Spa and again ask the questions already asked by M. Noulens at Posen? Such as it is, this problem is not pressing, but it has remained without a definite solution.

Mr. Lloyd George. It is not worth the trouble, since we are approaching the date when the preliminaries of peace will give a real solution. From a practical point of view, there is no urgency, since hostilities have ceased.

Marshal Foch. I also have to inform you of a request made by the German financial commission which has just arrived in France.

General Weygand. Herr Melchior, head of that delegation, asks that he be allowed to establish daily communications with the German government by means of a German courier who would be covered by diplomatic immunity. This courier would circulate either between the Château de Villette and Berlin, or between Villette and Spa. We have already provided for a courier service from Villette to Spa, protected by French gendarmes. But Herr Melchior asks to have his own courier, with diplomatic immunity.

M. Clemenceau. What does Marshal Foch think of this?

Marshal Foch. So long as the peace hasn't been signed, I don't wish to have a German courier free from all control on territory occupied by our armies.

Mr. Lloyd George. Is this request so unreasonable? Minor vexations without a serious object must be avoided; and all a courier could do would be to take scraps of information about our conference to Germany.

M. Clemenceau. I concur in Marshal Foch's objection, since there is already a functioning courier system.

President Wilson. It is we who invited this commission to come to France; we can grant it certain facilities.

M. Clemenceau. If the Marshal consents, I also consent. But do they have a complaint about the gendarme who carries their mail?

Mr. Lloyd George. I understand their feeling rather well, although I believe your gendarmes do transport their dispatches most scrupulously. Herr Melchior is a capable man, and we must not wish

---

[1] That is, for the third extension of the Armistice.

for his departure. We have nothing to gain by petty harassments. Herr Melchior knows that the French gendarme can always open the dispatch, even if he doesn't do so, and that restricts his correspondence. Couldn't we grant him the courier he asks for and add that this courier must be accompanied by a French gendarme?

M. Clemenceau. I would gladly accept that solution.

Marshal Foch. Then there will be a German courier accompanied by a gendarme. But will he have the right to send entire carloads, like other diplomatic couriers? In any case, he could carry whatever he wanted; we don't know what he might do, what people he might meet, or what system of espionage he might be the agent of. We have introduced a German into our midst; by this decision, we could give him the right to send and receive whatever he wishes, and to correspond about any subjects that pleased him.

M. Clemenceau. We give him the same right if the letters are carried by a French gendarme.

Marshal Foch. Yes, but he would then be on his guard.

M. Clemenceau. My opinion is that you should keep an eye on anything transported in this manner. If abuses occur, you should be able to warn us and even to arrest the courier.

Marshal Foch. He must be under my orders.

President Wilson. If he does anything irregular, the gendarme accompanying him makes a report. That should be enough; he must have the right to pass freely.

M. Clemenceau. If he wants to stop en route without justification, or if he takes a route other than that which he himself has requested, the gendarme could arrest him immediately and warn you by telegraph.

XVI

Conversation between President Wilson and MM. Clemenceau, Lloyd George and Orlando*

APRIL 2, 1919, 4 P.M.

President Wilson. It seems our troublesome friends the Poles raise a new difficulty about the truce they have to conclude with the Ukrainians. They refuse to sign it, except with stipulations which prejudge the terms of the armistice. Our adviser, Dr. Lord, proposes to send a telegram reminding them of our previous decision and our proposal to follow the existing truce with an armistice to be negotiated in Paris, under the mediation of the conference. But the first condition should be that the text of the agreement to suspend hostilities must contain nothing which prejudices the provisions of the armistice.

—*The text of the telegram is adopted.*[1]

THE QUESTION OF RESPONSIBILITIES

Mr. Lloyd George. I would like to discuss the question of responsibilities with you. Our commission declared itself against bringing to trial those who are in different degrees responsible for the declaration of war.[2] Personally, I regret this decision, but I accept

*Does not appear in H.

[1] Addressed to the Polish Minister of Foreign Affairs, it reads as follows: "It will be recalled that in its note of March 19th the conference suggested to both the Polish and Ukranian Governments that a suspension of arms should be arranged in Eastern Galicia pending the discussion at Paris of an armistice under the mediation of the Allied and Associated Governments. To further those objects the conference has decided to appoint an armistice commission to hear the representatives of the two belligerents and this Commission will begin its sittings in Paris as soon as it is informed that a truce has been concluded and that accredited Polish and Ukranian representatives are ready to present their views. To save time it is suggested that representatives be appointed from the Polish delegation now in Paris." Printed in *PWW*, Vol. 56, p. 530, n. 2.

[2] Lloyd George was objecting because the majority report of the Commission on Responsibility had not specifically called for the trial of the former German Emperor for the high crimes of violation of treaties, aggression, etc., even though that report had recommended trial of all former enemies guilty of violations of "usages established among civilised peoples," "the laws of humanity," and "the dictates of public conscience." The American members of the commission, Lan-

it. In my opinion, if we could hold the high and mighty men who unleashed such a scourge—the greatest of all—responsible for this greatest of all crimes, there would be less danger of war in the future.

On the other hand, responsibility has been admitted for the violation of treaties which caused the death of millions of men. The same for acts against individuals, atrocities of all sorts committed under orders, the kidnaping of girls for forced prostitution, the destruction of ships on the high seas by submarines, leaving ships' crews in boats hundreds of miles from shore. In the text of the treaty, we will demand that the enemy acknowledge our right to judge these crimes and promise to deliver the culprits to us. We must also have the right to demand the production of all German documents which would be necessary for the tribunal's use.

Finally, the commission proposes the establishment of a court of justice in which all the belligerent nations, great and small, would be represented, and which would pronounce judgments.

President Wilson. You know that the representatives of the United States signed a minority report. I believe certain recent proposals, such as the one renouncing prosecution of the authors of the war, bring them a little closer to your advisers than before.

Mr. Lloyd George. I have to inform you of Japan's objection to the admission of the Kaiser's responsibility: the Mikado is a god who cannot be held responsible.

I am also told that the Americans don't want to create a precedent which could be invoked against the President of the United States.

President Wilson. I don't believe that. In fact, it is Congress that declares war in the United States. However, I acknowledge that actual, if not legal, responsibility belongs to the President, if it is he who advises war, as I did. At the time of the Spanish-American conflict, on the other hand, President McKinley was opposed to war; Congress decided on it against his advice.

It is difficult for us to determine today what the Kaiser's responsibility is. It is probably very great. However, certain accounts represent him as signing the orders reluctantly and saying to those who advised him: "You will regret what we are doing."

---

sing and James Brown Scott, had long and strongly fought against the inclusion of any provisions for the criminal prosecution of William II for alleged violations of treaties, responsibility for war atrocities, etc. They embodied their points of view in reservations to the majority report. About the majority report and the American "reservations," see *ibid.*, n. 4.

Mr. Lloyd George. All we want to do is to punish those responsible, whoever they may be.

President Wilson. I ask that we don't link the American objection with the Japanese objection, which, from our point of view, rests on a ridiculous principle.

Mr. Lloyd George. I don't know; after all, the Japanese principle is the English principle—that the King can commit no crime. If the question of the origins of the war should arise in England, it is Mr. Asquith who would be responsible, and not King George. However, the case of the German Emperor is entirely different, because he had direct executive power.

President Wilson. I have doubts about our right to set up a tribunal composed only of the belligerents. The parties to the dispute would be at the same time the judges.

Mr. Lloyd George. I don't consider England and the United States as injured parties. Both of us made war for justice.

President Wilson. We have done justice by arms; but arms have not delivered to us the culprits we want to punish.

Mr. Lloyd George. I argue that we are claiming them by virtue of the success of our arms. Their case is similar to that of prisoners who, in conformity to the laws of war, may be judged by military tribunals if crimes they have committed are discovered after their capture.

President Wilson. It would create a dangerous precedent to try our enemies by judges who would represent us. Suppose, in the future, a single nation is victorious over another which had attacked it in violation of international law. Would it alone judge those who were guilty of crimes against international law, of which it had been the victim?

Mr. Lloyd George. Not at all; in that case, the League of Nations, conforming to the fundamental rules we have given it, must intervene, and it is not Belgium or France which judges its offenders; we judge with them, and we intervene in order to vindicate justice.

If we want to give the League of Nations a chance to succeed, it must not appear to be a paper document. It must be able to punish crimes against international law from this time forward. The violation of treaties is precisely the kind of crime directly involving the League of Nations.

President Wilson. We have to think about that. But I will point out that, up to now, the responsibility for international crimes has been solely a collective responsibility. It is unfair to make an act of this type a personal crime after it was committed. That would be to give retroactive force to the principles we pose, contrary to all legal tradition.

Undoubtedly certain crimes committed would be crimes punishable within each of the nations involved. But these are not crimes for which an international tribunal existed at the time they were committed. If you declare that, in the future, crimes recognized as such within each nation, if they are committed during an international conflict, can be punished by an international tribunal, you will substitute personal responsibility for collective responsibility, alone recognized in the past. But you cannot act according to this principle before it has been acknowledged.

Mr. Lloyd George. In time of war, one has always acknowledged the right of belligerents to punish violations of the laws of war summarily. We didn't challenge it even amongst our enemies, except when they invoked it wrongly, as against Captain Fryatt.[3]

President Wilson. Is it just to include in the peace treaty a usage customary during hostilities?

Mr. Lloyd George. We can say that no state of peace will exist until the culprits have been delivered to us. That is what Austria said to Serbia in 1914, whilst attributing to her a crime of which she was not guilty.

President Wilson. Suppose the Austrian version of the crime of Sarajevo had been true; the entire world would have acquiesced if Austria had demanded from Serbia the condemnation of the culprits by Serbian courts. If we could secure a promise from Germany that she herself would judge the culprits, there would be no ground for the objections I have made.

What I want to avoid is leaving to historians any sympathy whatsoever for Germany. I want to consign Germany to the execration of history and to do nothing to allow it to be said that we went beyond our rights in a just cause. We must prevent history from reproaching us for having judged before establishing the legal principle for the sentence.

Mr. Lloyd George. My opinion is that history can also condemn us for our weakness. We would have an absolute right to obtain punishment for these crimes if the culprits were in our hands. These are crimes for which no equivalent can be found in the Napoleonic wars, nor in any war of the last two centuries. Napoleon was punished for having ravaged the world by his ambi-

---

[3] Charles Fryatt, captain of an English merchantman, who had been shot on July 27, 1915, by order of a German court-martial. Fryatt was accused of having tried to ram a German submarine, contrary to the rules of international law.

tion, but not for having committed international crimes like those for which we blame the Germans.

President Wilson. I recently reread the documents on the war of 1870, and it seems to me that the conduct of the Germans at that time resembles that for which we blame them today.

M. Clemenceau. There is no similarity. They were brutal in 1870; but we could not blame them for crimes committed under orders, and there was not, during the war or immediately afterward, the same hatred of the German soldier that you would find today amongst the belligerents.

Mr. Lloyd George. We are facing crimes committed under orders, one of the most striking examples of which is submarine warfare. I would go so far as to say that it would not be worth the trouble to make peace if one believed that all these crimes would go unpunished. I see no disadvantage, moreover, in having the League of Nations establish this tribunal.

President Wilson. Unless we wait a long time to go through the process, the judgment will be passed in an atmosphere of passion. For myself, every time I read documents on atrocities committed, I saw red, and I was very careful not to take a decision in such moments, in order always to be able to judge and act according to reason.

Mr. Lloyd George. The truth is rather that our capacity for indignation is almost exhausted on account of hearing the frightful stories we have been hearing for five years. In fifty years, they will judge more severely than today.

President Wilson. You think me insensitive. But I struggle constantly against emotion, and I am compelled to put pressure on myself to keep my judgment sound.

M. Clemenceau. Nothing is done without emotion. Was not Jesus Christ driven by passion on the day when he drove the merchants from the temple?

Mr. Lloyd George. I see a great disadvantage in saying solemnly: "Here is the principle we establish, and the next time we shall do terrible things; but this time we will be content to set forth this principle." The world would not take us seriously.

M. Clemenceau. The first tribunal must have been summary and brutal; it was nevertheless the beginning of a great thing.

Mr. Lloyd George. If what we call the Concert of Europe had had common sanctions at its disposal, it could have kept the peace. If the League of Nations is to possess in future the power we wish for it, it must demonstrate from the beginning that it is capable of punishing crime.

President Wilson. I agree with you about crimes committed, but I want us to act, ourselves, in a manner which satisfies our consciences.

XVII

Conversation between President Wilson and MM. Clemenceau, Lloyd George, and Orlando*

APRIL 3, 1919, 11 A.M.

Mr. Lloyd George. I wonder if it wouldn't be advisable to hold a Plenary Session soon to approve the report of the Commission on International Labor Legislation, which has finished its task.[1] That would make a very good impression and enable us to give the debate the desirable scope.

M. Clemenceau. In fact, I think that could be beneficial before May 1.

Mr. Lloyd George. We can try to schedule this Plenary Session for the earliest possible date, but without being diverted from our present discussions. They must be pushed forward without a break.

President Wilson. Professor Haskins, Mr. Headlam-Morley, and M. Tardieu, who met to study the plan we had outlined about Danzig, have reached agreement.[2]

Mr. Lloyd George. We were already agreed amongst ourselves, except for the reservations made by M. Clemenceau.

M. Clemenceau. I have thought it over, and I am inclined to fall in with your opinion. The essential thing is to reach a solution ac-

---

*Does not appear in H.

[1] This report recommended the establishment of what became the International Labour Organization as an adjunct of the League of Nations to recommend minimal standards for hours, wages, and working conditions of the workers of member states. About this matter, see James T. Shotwell, *The Origins of the International Labor Organization*, 2 vols. (New York, 1934), II, 368-78 (for the report), and *passim*.

[2] It was embodied in the memorandum by S. E. Mezes, dated April 1, 1919, printed in *PWW*, Vol. 56, p. 505. Wilson had already explained the plan in detail in the meeting of April 1, 1919, 4 p.m.

ceptable to the Poles. I don't want to break with them, and you know they are not always accommodating.

President Wilson. In sum, the point is to create in Danzig and the territory inhabited by Germans immediately surrounding it a small state economically bound to Poland by a customs union. In the province of Marienwerder, the areas inhabited by Germans would be consulted by plebiscite and could, if they desired it, be united to East Prussia. In that case, the Vistula would be placed under the regime of international waterways, such as our special commission contemplates. The Germans could obtain the right to establish in peacetime direct rail service across the territory of Danzig towards East Prussia and Russia.

Mr. Lloyd George. An equivalent right must be provided for Polish communications between Danzig and Warsaw, for the Mława line will cross the area of Marienwerder.

M. Clemenceau. On the whole, I don't dislike this plan.

Mr. Lloyd George. Then we agree. What is M. Orlando's opinion?

M. Orlando. I also agree.

M. Clemenceau. Have we taken a decision on the subject of the rest of the German-Polish border?

President Wilson. We have accepted the commission's report, reserving the right to consider it again when we take comprehensive decisions on the German boundaries.

Mr. Lloyd George. I had no comment to make concerning the commission's report, except on the question of Danzig.

I wish to say a few words to you about the interview I had last evening with the King of the Belgians.[3] I found him full of common sense and moderation. He claims no territories. Concerning Luxembourg, he only wants to strengthen relations between that country and Belgium, perhaps by a customs union.

M. Clemenceau. The German dynasty must also disappear.

Mr. Lloyd George. I believe there would be a great advantage in hearing the King of the Belgians here if, according to the reservation he himself made, the [Belgian] Constitution allows him to do so. We could invite him by letter.

President Wilson. I believe it would be more respectful to visit him about the matter.

M. Clemenceau. I am prepared, if you wish, to go to Versailles, where it seems he is residing.

President Wilson. I shall see him today at two o'clock.

M. Clemenceau. In that case, the simplest thing is for the President to speak to him in our name.

---

[3] Albert, King of the Belgians.

President Wilson. Which commissions haven't yet completed their reports? I know that the Financial Commission is still debating some difficult points, notably concerning the responsibility of the new states formed out of the dissolution of Austria-Hungary.

Mr. Lloyd George. Really, I find it rather unfair, if Poland includes the better part of Silesia, for her not to bear her share of what the enemy owes us. She has indeed little intention of doing so, no more than the Czechs and the Yugoslavs, who are all vying with one another to reject responsibilities in order to begin their existence without a burden of debt. It is a little hard also to think that Danzig, which is a very flourishing city, will pay nothing because we will make her a free city.

President Wilson. I propose to ask the commissions to complete their still unfinished reports by next Monday at noon.

M. Clemenceau. That would be very desirable.

Mr. Lloyd George. I also believe it would be in our interest, before finishing with the German questions, to know immediately the point of view of the Italian government on the question of the Adriatic.

M. Orlando. The question in general terms is well known. As for our point of view, we regard the Treaty of London[4] as a compromise which the mixture of nationalities in the Adriatic region forced us to accept. The question of Fiume arose later, for reasons I can explain to you.

M. Clemenceau. Wouldn't it be best to hear M. Orlando on this subject?

Mr. Lloyd George. Yes, we are listening.

M. Orlando. Italy renounced Fiume in order to reach the compromise of which I have just spoken. We then believed that Austria-

---

[4] Between Italy and Great Britain, France, and Russia, signed at London on April 26, 1915. It provided for Italian entry into the war on the side of the Entente in return for such territories as the South Tyrol, Istria, Trieste, the Dalmatian islands, the southern part of Dalmatia, and the Dodecanese Islands. However, on account of Russian insistence, the treaty provided that the Adriatic port of Fiume, then under Hungarian control, should go to Croatia. Italy declared war on Austria-Hungary on May 23, 1915, and on Germany on August 27, 1916.

The subsequent controversies provoked by Italian claims in the Adriatic and Mediterranean areas continued to preoccupy the Council of Four to the very end of the peace conference and the Allied and Associated Governments until 1920. René Albrecht-Carrié, *Italy at the Paris Peace Conference* (New York, 1938), is an excellent study of this matter; many documents not available to Albrecht-Carrié are published in *PWW*, Vols. 56-64. A study that concentrates on Wilson's role in these controversies is Sterling J. Kernek, "Woodrow Wilson and National Self-determination along Italy's Frontier ...," *Proceedings of the American Philosophical Society*, CXXVI (Aug. 1982), 243-300.

Hungary would survive the war; no one considered a total dissolution possible, and it was thought impossible to leave this great continental state without an outlet to the sea; the necessary outlet was Fiume.

This question is not unrelated to that of Danzig. The countries which form the true hinterland of Fiume are all of Hungary, a part of Bohemia and Austria, and Croatia. Italy understood the necessity of giving up this Italian city: but the situation has changed and, with it, the status of the problem.

Several reasons intervened. The most important is the national reason. Austria-Hungary was a country in which several nationalities lived side by side. This mixture itself created a sort of equilibrium in which Italians could find certain guarantees. In Fiume, Italian interests were relatively well respected because of the equilibrium created by the rivalry between the Hungarians and the Croats.

Mr. Lloyd George. Are there many Hungarians in Fiume?

M. Orlando. A certain number, and the rivalry between the two interests was such that the city had been established as an autonomous entity between Croatia and Hungary. That balance has now been finally destroyed, and the consequence is that the Italian element in Fiume risks being submerged. It is no longer only a question of renouncing political union with an Italian city, but also of condemning the Italian element to death.

As for the economic argument which we took account of in 1915—knowing that Fiume is the outlet of vast hinterland—that argument now speaks in our favor. Of the merchandise which passes through the port of Fiume, no more than 7 per cent is of Croatian origin. All the rest is Hungarian, Bohemian, or Austrian. Thus Fiume is not the natural outlet of Yugoslavia, but of other more distant countries. It is impossible to give Fiume to all these countries at one and the same time. That being the case, it is natural enough to allow the national claim of Italy to prevail. The administration of the city by Italy will give more guarantees to the different peoples who form the clientele of Fiume than a Yugoslav administration would do. Italy can have no other interest than the prosperity of the city.

Thus the economic argument, in the new situation created by the dismemberment of Austria-Hungary, reinforces the national argument. Moreover, Italy is ready to accept all stipulations which would establish and guarantee the freedom of international trade in the port of Fiume.

Another aspect of the question is that the Yugoslav countries have no lack of outlets to the sea. Poland, deprived of Danzig, has no other port. In spite of that, we have been prevented from giving Danzig to Poland by concern about handing over this purely German city to the Poles. The Yugoslav state, on the contrary, will have several hundred kilometers of coast with magnificent ports such as Cattaro, Ragusa, Spalato, Mitrovic, which is the best port of Montenegro, and, in the [Gulf of] Quarnero, Porto Re, Buccari, and Segno, which has for a long time been a port used by the Croats. Thus one cannot say that the Yugoslavs need to own Fiume in order to have access to the sea. Finally, Fiume is at the extremity of their territory. That is why Fiume is much more a Hungarian port than a Croatian port.

If it was only a matter of the port, I would prefer to destroy the port of Fiume and to construct another port for the Yugoslavs at Italy's expense, rather than renounce having this Italian city unite with Italy.

Mr. Lloyd George. What would happen if Fiume was a free city under the control of the League of Nations?

M. Orlando. I would accept that solution for the port, but not for the city.

If we look at it simply from the economic point of view, what reason could one invoke if not distrust of Italy? To make Fiume a free city is to prepare for the absorption of the Italian element by the Croats who surround the city.

President Wilson. I am so especially interested in this problem that there is no solution which I have not studied. I sent the most competent and disinterested man I could find to Fiume to inform me about the feelings of the population. I have his report in my hands.[5] He assures me that there is a true unanimity in favor of autonomy in Fiume. Opinions differ as to the degree of this autonomy, up to and including complete independence.

I was very much struck by the conversation I had, shortly before my recent departure for America, with several leading people of Fiume, members of the municipal administration. They told me they wanted to be placed neither under the jurisdiction of Italy nor under that of the Yugoslavs, and they showed me a zone to be established around the city in order to create an autonomous territory.

Undoubtedly this local opinion must be subordinated to our international view, should a contradiction between the two exist; but this contradiction doesn't exist. The dismemberment of Aus-

---

[5] Lt. Col. Sherman Miles. His report is printed in PPC, XII, 479-83.

tria-Hungary makes it more desirable than ever that no particular nationality be in exclusive possession of an outlet common to the peoples of the former monarchy. Free competition between Trieste and Fiume will be much more fruitful if these two cities are not placed under the same jurisdiction. It will be in the interest of all the peoples for whom Fiume is the outlet to work towards its development. Trieste has a clientele which will not abandon it.

What M. Orlando has just said about the other ports which the Yugoslavs can use did not convince me, because, although these ports are very fine, they have only difficult communications with the interior.

I earnestly beg M. Orlando to take under serious consideration the plan to make Fiume a free city without customs ties to any of its neighboring states. In that way, Fiume would not be the port of the Yugoslavs, but of all the interior. This solution seems to me the best one by far. I wouldn't like to ask guarantees of a great nation like Italy. We have complete confidence in her; we wouldn't wish to seem to be imposing terms upon her.

M. Orlando. I take occasion to express my gratitude to President Wilson for what he has said, and for the careful study he has made of the question. But I beg him to consider the political situation of the representatives of Italy. One can show deference and personal respect towards a man one esteems by allowing him the right to decide about his own interests. But when one speaks, not for oneself, but for a nation, one does not have that possibility, and one is constrained to remain within the confines of the national mandate. I must say this to justify the opposition which I am compelled to express against the opinion of a man whom I respect.

The economic difficulty is not insuperable. If access to other ports is costly, that won't stop us, for modern engineers have solved greater problems. If, on the other hand, Croatian trade is not profitable enough to justify or pay for the necessary works, the argument is in our favor.

For us, the question is above all a matter of sentiment. If, however, we consider it from the economic point of view, I would say to you that the question of Fiume is very closely related to that of Trieste. I would accept their competition if I didn't fear that it would be manipulated in some way. We have reason to believe, without being able to furnish proof, that the Czechs and Yugoslavs have a secret agreement to use Fiume in preference to Trieste. If this agreement was carried out, it would divert part of the commerce of Trieste to the port of Fiume. But that is secondary. For the Italians the question of Fiume is a question of sentiment. We don't wish to abandon our brothers, whose liberation was the great goal of our national war.

You tell me that the people want autonomy. It is difficult to believe that without absolute proof. I can tell you that the deputy of Fiume and the mayor of the city, who are both in Paris, tell me that they won't hear of its establishment as a free city. That is a possibility they reject absolutely. If I could be sure that Fiume prefers this solution, that would not fail to have much influence upon my decision. But all I know leads me to think it is not so.

President Wilson. You say you fought to liberate your compatriots of Fiume. Yet you declared war after having signed a treaty providing that Fiume would remain outside Italy.

—Mr. Lloyd George reads a letter from Mr. Balfour: the King of the Belgians will attend the meeting of the heads of governments tomorrow, accompanied by M. Hymans who, "like well-bred children, will be seen but not heard."

XVIII

Conversation between President Wilson and MM. Clemenceau, Lloyd George, and Trumbić*

APRIL 3, 1919, 4 P.M.

M. Clemenceau. We have heard a statement from M. Orlando on the question of Fiume; we wished to hear a representative of the Yugoslavs on the same subject.

M. Trumbić. I am ready to answer your questions, although I was designated for this mission barely an hour ago.

The city of Fiume is a Slavic city. Today a majority of the population is Italian-speaking; but that is above all the result of the favor accorded that element by the Magyar domination since 1868. It is also the consequence of the growth of the port of Fiume.

If we go back to 1848, we see that, at that time, the city had

*Does not appear in H.

only 12,600 inhabitants, of whom 11,600 were Slavs and only 1,000 Italians. In 1868, Fiume passed under the political power of Hungary through the well-known forgery of the Hungarian-Croatian Convention. I recall that incident. After Sadowa, the Imperial government was obliged to accept dualism, when Hungary became an autonomous state. In 1868, an agreement between Hungary and Croatia gave the Croats a species of autonomy, which they enjoyed until the present war. In fixing the territorial line between the two countries, the Croatian commission and the Hungarian commission could not agree on the question of Fiume, and the article of the convention, Article 66, stated the disagreement purely and simply. The text was approved in this form by the Parliament of Pest and by the Parliament of Zagreb, and signed by the Emperor. But the Austro-Hungarian Foreign Minister had pasted in the place of Article 66, which stated that no agreement could be reached about Fiume, another text which assigned that city to Hungary. I have brought you a photograph of the forged document, and we have the original text, without falsification, preserved in the archives of Croatia.

After that, the Magyars seized the city of Fiume, removing all Croatian authorities, even eliminating Croatian-speaking schools after ten years. The Slavic population had access to only one secondary school which, being located in the suburb of Sušak, on the other side of the Resina River, was in Croatian territory. At that time, there were no Magyars in Fiume, only Croats and Italians. The latter were used by the Magyars as an instrument of their policy, because they were anti-Croat.

The government of Pest tried to make Fiume a great port, constructed a railroad, wharves, docks, which created a certain sympathy for the Magyars amongst the elements of the population associated with those works. Until the present war, the Italian element had no political aspirations; irredentism did not exist in Fiume. The Italians were only one of the elements in the local game played by the Magyars. The latter handed over the schools to the Italians and gave them first place in the city, with the sole aim of excluding the Croats. It was thus that the Italian element grew and prospered, animated by a Hungarian political spirit, or as an instrument of Hungarian policy.

Mr. Lloyd George. When was the railroad constructed?
M. Trumbić. Between 1870 and 1880.
Mr. Lloyd George. Fiume was not a great port before this time?
M. Trumbić. No, the port grew only afterwards.

Mr. Lloyd George. It was the Hungarian government which had these works done?

M. Trumbić. It was the government of Budapest, acting as the common government of Hungary and Croatia, with funds voted by both parliaments.

Official statistics show that in 1880 there were 11,175 Slavs and 9,920 Italians in Fiume; in 1890, 13,478 Slavs and 13,012 Italians; in 1910, 24,212 Italians, forming the majority, 15,696 Slavs, 6,493 Hungarians, and 2,315 Germans. I would call your attention to the appearance of these two new elements, which explains better what I said about the growth of the Italian population, which was attracted by the development of the port.

These figures only apply to the city of Fiume proper, excluding the suburb of Sušak which, although an integral part of the same conglomeration, is administratively separate and is part of Croatia.

The Italian element of Fiume is an artificial creation. The Italians are not an indigenous population; that is essentially Slavic. The Italians are immigrants, who came to work on the port and the railroad. Under Magyar rule, the Slavic element was subjected to a complete political boycott. The municipal charter of the city was drawn up in such a way as to exclude the Croats from the management of affairs; the electoral laws deprived them of any chance of having a seat on the municipal council, which until now consisted entirely of Italians and Hungarians acting in concert.

It was to weaken the Slavic element that the suburb of Sušak was separated from Fiume. Sušak counts 11,705 Slavs and 658 Italians, a few families. Fiume with Sušak, according to the statistics provided by the Italo-Magyar municipality itself, had a population before the war of 27,392 Slavs, 24,870 Italians, 6,492 Magyars, and 2,315 Germans. Thus we can conclude that the city of Fiume must not be considered an Italian city; the Italian element is interesting from a demographic point of view, not from a political point of view. Rijeka—that is the original name of the city, translated into Italian as "Fiume"—belongs to Croatia, of which it is a geographical part. Moreover, it is surrounded on all sides by exclusively Slavic populations, as the ethnographic map shows.

The Slavic element has always maintained a primary economic position in Fiume, and its preponderance is well demonstrated by the following facts. The city of Fiume, in the strict sense of the word, numbers 2,756 property owners; 1,193 are Yugoslavs. The most noteworthy buildings in the center of the city and on the wharves belong to Yugoslavs. The shipping companies of Fiume are the following: (1) the Hungarian-Croatian Company for Coastwise Trade—forty-two vessels, 15,506 gross tons; (2) the Hungarian-Croatian Company for Free Shipping—six vessels, 22,606 tons; these enterprises are completely Croatian in capital, officers, and crews; the name given them can be explained by the fact that the Hungarian government granted them a subsidy for the postal service and for the export of Hungarian flour; (3) the Oriental Company—six vessels, 26,405 tons; (4) the Levant Company—eleven vessels, 39,436 tons; (5) the Atlantica Company—ten vessels, 41,550 tons; (6) the Adria Company—thirty-two vessels, 74,555 tons. Several small businesses should be added, which together have eight vessels.

I said that the first two are almost exclusively Yugoslav; the last three have principally Hungarian capital, but with Yugoslav participation; in the Oriental Company, this participation is important. If we take all these companies together, the capital is divided in the following proportions: Hungarian capital, 68 per cent; Yugoslav capital, 28 per cent; Italian capital, 6 per cent.

The merchant fleet of Fiume employs 283 captains and 269 engineers; 199 captains and 169 engineers are Yugoslavs. As for the crews, they are recruited from the coastal region, and they are 98 per cent Yugoslav. In Fiume's banks, the ratio of Yugoslav to Italian capital is ten to one.

President Wilson. What is the nature of the trade of Fiume? What is the origin of the merchandise? What is the proportion which comes from Yugoslav lands? What are the relations with the different countries of the hinterland, such as Hungary and Bohemia?

M. Trumbić. In 1913, the commerce of Fiume reached a level of approximately 2,100,000 [metric] tons—927,500 entering and 1,180,000 departing. It is impossible to say exactly what belongs properly to Yugoslav lands, because of the dual regime which permitted distinctions only between Austrian and Hungarian areas. But I can say that the coastal traffic, purely Yugoslav, because all the coastal region is inhabited by our peoples, reached a level of approximately 330,000 tons.

The principal export—27 per cent of the total—is lumber. Now, this product comes almost exclusively from Croatia, with a small portion coming from Carniola; this is a Yugoslav export. The division in the official statistical documents between Hungary and Austria does not enable us to distinguish specifically what comes from Bohemia.

On the other hand, I can give some figures on imports. English coal—160,000 tons—was destined almost exclusively for the commercial fleet and railroad of Fiume. Rice from India—120,000 tons—was destined for the rice-husking factory of Fiume. Australian ore—5,500 tons—was allotted to the lead foundry of Martin Sitza. Oil seeds—27,000 tons—went to the oil and chemical factories in Fiume. Phosphates from India and North Africa were destined for the agriculture of our countries.

Serbian trade did not pass through Fiume, because Serbia, boycotted economically by Austria, sought its outlet towards Saloniki. In our unified state, Fiume would serve the trade of Croatia, Slovenia, Serbia, the Banat, the Backa; it is the only outlet to the sea for these regions.

Mr. Lloyd George. What are the outlets for Hungary and Bohemia?

M. Trumbić. Of necessity, the port of the Hungarians is Fiume; the port for Bohemia, an industrial country and especially rich, is Trieste. The eastern part of the Czechoslovak Republic will gravitate towards Fiume through Pressburg. The principal items in Fiume's export trade are timber and wine; both are in the hands of the Yugoslavs. Of twenty-seven commercial establishments which conduct commerce in timber, sixteen are Yugoslav, the others belonging mostly to Hungarians. The wine trade is in the hands of the Dalmatians and the Slavs of Istria. The most important establishment of the entire coastal area is the firm of Boubokovitch in Lesina.

Fiume's trade is only at the beginning of its development. Our new state will enable it to take wing by the construction of a new railway network linking the Banat, the Backa, Serbia, and Bosnia, and by the elimination of artificial obstacles which have impeded the port's trade. It is a well-known fact that the Germans, when they built their railroad, established a system of rates designed especially to favor Hungary, particularly the city of Budapest, whilst sacrificing Croatian interest. For example, to send a sack of flour from Sziszek, which is located about two hours east of Zagreb, to Fiume, it was necessary to pay more than to send it to Budapest, which is much further away. In fact, it was arranged so that the first railway journey was divided into two zones, whilst the second passed through only one.

President Wilson. What are the possibilities of the development of a port such as Spalato?

M. Trumbić. Very small: there is no railroad to Spalato; moreover, a series of mountain ranges parallel to the coast would make its construction very difficult and very costly.

I would like to say a word about the banks. I have already indicated that the ratio between Slavic and Italian interests is as ten to one. Four great banks of Fiume are in the hands of Yugoslavs; together they have a capital of twenty-nine million crowns, with reserves of eight million. Their annual turnover in 1917 was 2.5 billion crowns. The major Italian bank, the Cooperative Bank, had a turnover in the same year of only 246 million, with a capital of only two million crowns.

Mr. Lloyd George. Do these Yugoslav banks have branches in different parts of Croatia?

M. Trumbić. I don't think so; but there are branches of the Zagreb banks in Fiume.

President Wilson. I understand that the companies are Croatian, but are the capital and deposits principally Yugoslav, or do they contain an Italian element?

M. Trumbić. These businesses are almost exclusively Yugoslav. The Italians do business with or deposit their capital in Italian or Hungarian banks. That is the natural consequence of the political situation. I didn't mention the Banca Commerciale di Fiume and the Hungarian Realty Bank. The first was created by the Commercial Bank of Budapest, and the second is the creation of the Hungarian Discount Bank.

The local agencies of the Croatian banks of Zagreb do much to encourage business in Fiume. For instance, the agency of the First Savings Bank of Zagreb had an annual turnover of two billion crowns in 1917. The entire economic life of Fiume proves that it is the Croatian people who provide this city with the greatest part of its capital. Hungary did everything it could to suppress Croatian activity through licit or illicit means; but it didn't succeed.

Mr. Lloyd George. What do the Italians do?

M. Trumbić. They are shopkeepers, employees; they form part of the employees of the port and railroads.

Mr. Lloyd George. This doesn't correspond to the figure of 24,000 Italians for the city of Fiume.

M. Trumbić. It mustn't be forgotten that this figure is the statistic established by the Italo-Hungarian municipality, figures based, not upon nationality, but upon habitual language. A well-known custom is to enter a house and say "Good morning" in Italian. One is answered in Italian, which everyone knows how to speak in our country. Having been born in Spalato, I myself speak it like an Italian. So it is written on the list that the family is Italian.

The same thing happens in Austria with regard to the German language. It is the system used everywhere to the advantage of the language of the nation which holds power.

Cordial relations between Italians and Magyars were reinforced by memories of 1848; the two peoples then both fought against the Hapsburgs. The great Hungarian patriot, Kossuth, died in Italy. The Magyars had no reason to fear the Italian population of Fiume, which formed only a small island, whilst they feared the Croats. On the other hand, during the time of the Triple Alliance, the Hungarian government made concessions to the Italians in order to avoid offending Italy. It was the Croats who paid the price and were constantly accused of being the instruments of Pan-Slavism and of the Russian drive towards the Mediterranean.

President Wilson. Italian spokesmen dispute these statistics. What is the source of yours?

M. Trumbić. I have drawn them from official Hungarian sources and, for those concerning banks, from information gathered right on the spot.

XIX

Hearing by MM. Clemenceau, Lloyd George, Orlando, and Colonel House* of His Majesty, the King of the Belgians, accompanied by M. Paul Hymans, Minister of Foreign Affairs of Belgium**

APRIL 4, 1919, 11 A.M.

M. Clemenceau. We beg Your Majesty to let us know what he has in mind.

The King of the Belgians. We believe that Belgium, if the promises which have been made to her are carried out, has the right to priority in reparations. The invasion caused her to lose nearly all her means of production. Raw materials and most of the indus-

*For the indisposed President Wilson.[1]
**Does not appear in H.

[1] Wilson had just come down with a viral infection. See *PWW*, Vol. 56, pp. 557-58.

trial machinery were carried off. The Belgian state was forced to pay war levies to the enemy totaling 2.6 billion, and this figure amounts to 3 billion if forced contributions by cities are added. Belgium lost, not only nearly all the machinery of its great industrial establishments, but also half its livestock.

Mr. Lloyd George. What is the condition of your coal mines?

The King of the Belgians. Even in peacetime, Belgium imported more coal than it exported. It is a country which lives by its exports, since eight tenths of its people are involved in industry.

Mr. Lloyd George. What is the nature of the war levies that the cities had to pay? Did a part represent works done for their benefit?

The King of the Belgians. Not at all: they were penalties. For example, the people of Brussels had to pay two million because they gave an ovation to Cardinal Mercier. The city of Brussels paid fifty million francs on different occasions. Tournai, which has only 30,000 to 40,000 inhabitants, paid around thirty million francs during the war. Many small cities paid one or two million. That is what raises the figure of our war levies from approximately 2.5 billion to 3 billion.

Colonel House. We have contemplated the possibility of the actual reconstruction by the Germans of all buildings destroyed. But sums paid as war levies should obviously be repaid by pure and simple restitution.

The King of the Belgians. At present, we have in Belgium 800,000 unemployed and more than 1,600,000 people on state assistance. It is as if there were in the United States twelve million unemployed and twenty-five million persons supported by allowances. If we can't be helped at once, Belgium will find itself in a very grave situation. The state debt is increasing enormously, without any compensation in sight.

France, which has suffered much, it is true, has at least a great part of her territory intact and in a state of production. Eighty-five per cent of Belgian production is paralyzed. There is not enough manpower for the necessary works of repair in France; but in our country, there is more manpower than work.

M. Clemenceau. Your mines didn't stop working?

The King of the Belgians. No.

M. Clemenceau. Has the work in them been completely resumed?

The King of the Belgians. Yes, but I remind you again that our coal needs have always surpassed our production, particularly of long-burning coal, which our steel mills import from England.

Colonel House. Isn't it possible to use this labor in the reconstruction of the devastated regions?

The King of the Belgians. It is difficult to use in the building trades men trained, for instance, in the textile industry.

Mr. Lloyd George. Wouldn't it be possible to recover your stolen machines? The Germans are very systematic and write everything down.

M. Clemenceau. They are indeed systematic thieves. We were able to recover many objects stolen from France, thanks to the way in which they had been registered.

The King of the Belgians. In fact, there are commissions of recovery in Mainz and Wiesbaden; but their work can only yield rather slow results.

We are completely lacking in raw materials, in metals for our metallurgy, in wool and cotton for our textile industry. During their occupation and withdrawal, the enemy emptied Belgium. They took foodstuffs in considerable quantity. That is why, moreover, there are so many marks in Belgium; for they paid for a part of what they took. These marks represent, so to speak, the liquidation of Belgium, and we are obliged to reimburse our citizens at a rate of 1.25 francs, which is a very disadvantageous operation for the state.

Mr. Lloyd George. The *Frankfurter Zeitung* had the audacity to speak of this German money left in Belgium as a great kindness by Germany. Can greater impudence be imagined?

The most important thing to know at this time is what can be put in the terms of the peace treaty between us and Germany; the question of distribution is one to be settled amongst ourselves and doesn't concern the Germans.

The King of the Belgians. You have received a memorandum from the Belgian government indicating what we claim.

Mr. Lloyd George. I should inform Your Majesty that we have arrived at a provisional arrangement about the kind of damages for which we will ask reparation. We divide these damages into damages to property and damages to persons, and we put into the second category the losses by death or mutilation that necessitate pensions.

The King of the Belgians. This classification would be very unfavorable to us; damages to persons have very little place in the sum of our claims, because Belgium, having been invaded very rapidly, was unable to raise an army. Otherwise, instead of 150,000 men under arms, she would have had 800,000.

Mr. Lloyd George. We would prefer to have living men than to receive pensions for the dead.

The King of the Belgians. What I say is only to indicate that there is a factual reason, independent of our will. I will point out, moreover, that an indemnity to persons always takes the form of annuities, whilst it is impossible to put destroyed businesses back on their feet without capital.

Mr. Lloyd George. They tell me that France lost up to 58 per cent of her young men between the ages of twenty and thirty. It is a terrible figure. No material reparation could ever suffice to compensate for such losses.

The King of the Belgians. It is indeed frightful. I believe Serbia lost even more.

M. Clemenceau. Probably.

Mr. Lloyd George. On the first point, that is on the one concerning damages to property, the Germans seem inclined to repair them directly.

M. Clemenceau. I recall one of President Wilson's Fourteen Points, which promises complete reparation to France and Belgium.

Mr. Lloyd George. Does Your Majesty see another category of losses to be reimbursed? We mentioned the restitution of sums extorted in the form of war levies, machinery, raw materials, foodstuffs, livestock; all that is included in our categories.

The King of the Belgians. There are also damages to railroads and public works.

Mr. Lloyd George. We have provided for these. However, military works, such as your forts at Liège destroyed by German guns, are not included.

The King of the Belgians. Does your classification include public improvements, forests?

Mr. Lloyd George. Yes, as well as orchards and all agricultural resources.

If Belgium has other suggestions to make to us, we will be happy to know them. This classification exhausts what the Germans will have to know. The distribution of payments remains a matter amongst ourselves.

M. Clemenceau. Another question which must be settled by the preliminaries of peace with Germany is the question of Malmédy.

M. Paul Hymans. This small territory is composed of the districts of Malmédy and Eupen. Eupen is a small German city, but the great forest adjoining it sits astride the German-Belgian border. The Belgian portion of this forest was destroyed by the enemy during the war, so that possession of the other portion would be compensation for Belgium; and this cession is only imaginable if it includes the small city where exploitation of the forest is concentrated.

As for Malmédy, it is a Walloon city of 4,600 inhabitants who speak French; before the war they had French schools and French newspapers. The same applies to the villages surrounding Malmédy. The border has to be drawn in such a way as to give us the railway from Malmédy to Eupen, which otherwise would cross a portion of German territory. Altogether, this is not much and doesn't represent more than 10,000 souls.

M. Clemenceau. Does Your Majesty wish to speak to us about the question of the Scheldt?

The King of the Belgians. It was the events of 1914 that called into question the validity of the Treaty of 1839. The essential clause of this treaty was the neutrality of Belgium, which was violated by German aggression.

Two questions are connected to the Treaty of 1839—the security of Belgium and the interests of Antwerp. I was surprised to see that the British Admiralty seems to prefer the *status quo*, that is the possession by Holland of the banks of the Scheldt. The Admiralty seems to consider it as inevitable that Belgium would be invaded in case of war and prefers, in that eventuality, that Holland close the Scheldt.

Mr. Lloyd George. The Admiralty is reasoning as it did in 1793. But I see nothing in the Tardieu report[2] about the Scheldt.

M. Paul Hymans. The Tardieu report concludes simply in favor of the revision of the Treaty of 1839 and the invitation to Holland to consider this revision with the Allies.

The King of the Belgians. The conference approved this report and accordingly agreed to bring up the matter again.

Mr. Lloyd George. It is certain that the arrangements concerning the Scheldt, such as they were in 1914, are absurd. We were compelled to blow up some English ships in the Scheldt, which we would have had time to withdraw, simply so as not to violate Holland's neutrality. It is true that Grey, who was then Foreign Secretary, was particularly scrupulous. I don't know if I would have been as much. It is an absurd situation. Belgium must have free access to the sea by way of the Scheldt without having to ask Holland's consent.

M. Clemenceau. There is no difficulty there.

Mr. Lloyd George. No; the territorial question is another matter.

The King of the Belgians. The worst effects of the Treaty of 1839 were not felt until nearly seventy-five years after its signing. But it contained a series of provisions favorable to Holland and un-

---

[2] That is, the report of the Commission on Belgian Affairs of March 8, 1919, about which, see n. 6 to XII.

favorable to Belgium. For example, it was impossible to create a navigable canal between Antwerp and the Meuse, because Holland told us that the construction of a railway had exhausted our rights.

Concerning Limburg, the important thing is to know whether Holland can defend it.

Mr. Lloyd George. It is certain that she hasn't done so, and that she allowed the Germans to pass in retreat with all their supplies under questionable circumstances.

Couldn't the question of the Scheldt be settled by our Commission on Navigable Waterways?

M. Paul Hymans. There would be some disadvantage in bifurcating the Belgian claims, the same question being treated here in some respects, and, in other respects, by the Commission on Navigable Waterways.

Mr. Lloyd George. The commission is concerned with assuring free passage on international rivers.

M. Paul Hymans. The Scheldt is not, properly speaking, an international river, since from an economic point of view it is exclusively Belgian. We are asking for sovereignty over this river.

Mr. Lloyd George. I would approve of anything to give Belgium free use of the Scheldt.

Undoubtedly Your Majesty wishes to speak to us about the problem of the occupation of the left bank of the Rhine?

The King of the Belgians. What I would have to say depends upon the arrangement contemplated for that area.

Mr. Lloyd George. What we contemplate is a complete disarmament of the left bank of the Rhine and of a zone extending up to fifty kilometers on the right bank.

The King of the Belgians. That seems a sound plan to me.

M. Clemenceau. I must observe that our border, which touches the Rhine in Alsace, diverges from it by up to 100 kilometers, and there is the danger that a German army could be only fifty kilometers from the river, while we would be twice as far from it.

I have thought of different solutions, notably to increase this distance of fifty kilometers; but I rejected that. We say to President Wilson: in case of invasion, the French and Belgians will be compelled to give battle before you have time to arrive. President Wilson replies: "It is absurd to reason as if the Germans could build up an army from 100,000 men to a million men without anyone noticing it." This reply is acceptable, but on condition that Germany be watched. If she increases her army from 100,000 to 120,000 men, or even her artillery from 1,000 to 1,500 guns, we would perhaps not declare war for that; but it would be necessary, if this movement should grow, that we should be able immediately to warn England and America of a violation by Germany of the treaty she had signed. We must be able to ask the English and Americans to come to ascertain the fact and to join us in taking the required decisions. Failing this, I would only have a scrap of paper in my hands.

I favor making practical provisions, in such a way as not ourselves to provoke the danger we fear. Our military leaders are against a surveillance of this kind; I have to fight against them. President Wilson doesn't like the idea of permanent commissions watching the military condition of Germany. I don't favor permanent commissions, but we must have means of immediate inquiry if necessary.

Colonel House. I must say that I don't share President Wilson's feelings about commissions. In my opinion, if a power is only doing what it has the right to do, it has no reason to take offense at any inspection whatsoever.

Mr. Lloyd George. Yes, on condition that the inspection be universal. But we must agree that inspection by a foreign power in a single country, for perhaps fifty years, could cause some difficulties.

The King of the Belgians. One objection against the occupation is the following: Germany won't be very dangerous before twenty or twenty-five years; it is precisely when Germany will have recovered that the occupation will end.

Mr. Lloyd George. Then I understand that Your Majesty doesn't favor a prolonged occupation of German cities?

The King of the Belgians. All the military leaders I see, including your generals, tell me that the German army no longer exists. The danger is not for the coming years, but much later, and Belgian public opinion wouldn't favor a prolonged occupation.

Mr. Lloyd George. About this, English public opinion is the same.

M. Clemenceau. Neither do I ask for such a prolonged occupation.

The King of the Belgians. In addition, we have no interest in making the Rhenish provinces suffer, which might lead them to envy Saxony or Bavaria, and where purely German sentiment might be reinforced by that.

M. Clemenceau. On the contrary, we have an interest in treating the Rhineland relatively well.

M. Orlando. The only policy to follow in Germany is to try to profit from the divisions between Catholics and Protestants, and the Rhineland is Catholic.

The King of the Belgians. I will raise the question of Luxembourg myself. Negotiation is going on between us and the government of Luxembourg; and we would be happy to see France approve of this negotiation and to declare that its success would conform to the interests of the two countries in question and of all of Europe.

M. Clemenceau. May I ask what Belgium's intentions are? I have understood that she wanted the annexation of Luxembourg.

M. Paul Hymans. We have simply asked that France favor the free rapprochement of the two countries.

M. Clemenceau. You can't ask me to tell the people of Luxembourg: "I want you to become Belgians." They must be left their freedom of choice. You know very well that I am not claiming Luxembourg for France.

I consider the present government of Luxembourg to be German, and I don't want to enter into relations with it. That is why I didn't send a plenipotentiary there. You have done so; that is very well. I ask only one thing: the disappearance of the German dynasty.

Concerning the fate of Luxembourg, the conference should be approached by Luxembourg herself. I ask nothing for France. I ask that Luxembourg say what she wants. I won't send anyone there; I am ready to withdraw the last French soldier. You have acted differently; you have acted in Luxembourg, and you have provoked protests.

The King of the Belgians. There have also been protests against the French propaganda.

M. Clemenceau. A French general intervened in Luxembourg's affairs; I punished him. This defines my position. I will be happy if Luxembourg becomes Belgian; but this change must be made by the Luxemburgers.

The King of the Belgians. We didn't seek out the people of Luxembourg; it was the government of Luxembourg which entered into negotiations with us.

M. Clemenceau. The only thing I don't accept is for M. Hymans to ask me to invite Luxembourg to talk with Belgium. That is a pressure I cannot agree to apply. What I want myself is to withdraw my troops from Luxembourg and to play no role whatever in that country. I complain about the conduct of your government, which wants to force our hand. If Luxembourg were Belgian, I repeat that I would be very glad.

The King of Belgians. The acquisition of Luxembourg would give France a bad frontier. On the other hand, if Luxembourg is reunited to Belgium, the violation of any part of Luxembourg's border will immediately entail the participation of the Belgian army.

M. Clemenceau. I just don't want anybody to force my hand.

The King of the Belgians. I should remind you that, several times during the course of the war, we received assurances concerning Luxembourg from President Poincaré, M. Ribot, and other French statesmen. In the past, Luxembourg was united to Belgium. Some Luxemburgian deputies sat amongst Belgian deputies after the revolution of 1830.

M. Clemenceau. Don't ask me to throw the people of Luxembourg into the arms of the Belgians; I don't know their feelings. All I know is that we had 1,500 Luxemburgian volunteers in the French army, and that there were only 170 in the Belgian army. However, I am not saying that in order to claim Luxembourg.

The King of the Belgians. The Luxemburgian colony in Paris consists of 30,000 persons, and the volunteers for the French army undoubtedly came from it. The invasion of Belgium was so rapid that Belgian Luxembourg itself could not provide us with soldiers.

M. Clemenceau. The advice I gave to M. Hymans, when he came to Paris, was to let things work themselves out. He didn't listen to me, he caused agitation there. The only thing I don't want is for the reunion of Luxembourg to Belgium to take place in such a way as to seem to be a setback for France.

The King of the Belgians. There has been French agitation in Luxembourg.

M. Clemenceau. I already told you how I punished the general who interfered in Luxembourg's affairs. I said to M. Hymans: "I shall inflict punishment if you inform me of other acts." He didn't inform me of any.

Believe me, it is easy for us to agree.

Mr. Lloyd George. This matter has to be settled, but how?

M. Clemenceau. At the conference, President Wilson and Mr. Lansing proposed a plebiscite. M. Hymans said that the time was not favorable and that it would be better to wait. If you have a decent way to solve the problem, indicate it. I don't want to do anything about Luxembourg. Belgium's friendship for France is worth ten Luxembourgs. But I ask you to do the thing as it should be done.

Mr. Lloyd George. What is the method?

M. Clemenceau. I haven't suggested it. But I refuse to negotiate with the present government of Luxembourg, which is a German government.

The King of the Belgians. There has been change of leadership. Herr Eyschen is no longer in power.

M. Clemenceau. I only ask you to help me to overcome all the obstacles to what you desire. Undoubtedly the best way is to consult the population, which can be done under American occupation, with General Pershing responsible for the maintenance of order.

The King of the Belgians. The misfortune is that there is no clear orientation; the people of Luxembourg await an indication from the great powers.

M. Clemenceau. Just now, you are speaking for them. It is probable that, if one put to them, purely and simply, the question of what they want to become, they would reply: "We wish to remain what we are." But if one asked them: "Do you want to be attached to France or to Belgium?", we don't know what they will say.

Mr. Lloyd George. What is the language of Luxembourg?

The King of the Belgians. The official language is French, but the popular language is a low-German dialect.

Mr. Lloyd George. What is the political system?

M. Paul Hymans. Since 1867, Luxembourg has been independent and neutralized. Hence the danger it constitutes for its neighbors.

M. Clemenceau. I hope Your Majesty will forgive me for the frankness of my language. From the first day, I have said to Belgium that I ask nothing for France, and I have added: "If you remain quiet, no difficulty will arise between us." I want to reach agreement with you, but I also want to avoid 150 deputies coming to tell me: "Luxembourg wished to be French; you have not allowed that, you have given it to Belgium." I am with you, but what takes place must not give the appearance of a defeat for France.

XX

Conversation between MM. Clemenceau, Lloyd George, Orlando, and Colonel House*

APRIL 4, 1919, 4 P.M.**

M. Clemenceau. I have just studied the report of the competent commission of experts on the boundary between Bohemia and Germany.[1] The settlement is very complicated and makes all

*For the indisposed President Wilson
**Does not appear in H.

[1] About this report and its very complicated genesis, see Perman, *Shaping of the Czechoslovak State*, pp. 121-82.

sorts of changes, some of which include cessions of territory to the Germans; that seems very useless to me. The simplest thing is to maintain the border as it was before the war and to leave to Bohemia and Germany the task of making territorial exchanges between themselves as they deem appropriate.

As for the question of the Germans of Bohemia, that has nothing to do with the peace preliminaries between us and Germany.

Mr. Lloyd George. It is indeed a question related to the division of the former Austrian Empire. I agree with you that the old frontier between Bohemia and Germany should be respected. As for the question of Teschen, that is also part of Austrian questions.

Colonel House. That solution seems the best to me. On the subject of Teschen, we could establish a commission which will report to the League of Nations.

M. Clemenceau. The question of Ratibor and of Upper Silesia, which concerns both Poland and Bohemia, could be treated at the same time as the Polish questions.

Thus we conclude—reserving the opinion of President Wilson—to maintain purely and simply the old border between Bohemia and Germany.

—An exchange of comments about the agenda takes place. Colonel House proposes that the financial experts be heard tomorrow at eleven o'clock, in order to reach a decision in the afternoon. The meeting will be held at the Place des États-Unis, so that Colonel House can immediately ascertain President Wilson's opinion.

—M. Orlando makes known that, in a conversation between the English, American, and Italian delegates and the German financial commission at the Château de Villette, the Germans insisted especially upon the necessity of provisions informing Germany clearly about the obligations which will be imposed upon her. "Germany," they say, "will work and do what she can to pay; but she could not bear to remain in uncertainty about her obligations."

—Colonel House believes that the moment has come to take a decision, and that it is possible to do it quickly.

XXI

Conference among MM. Clemenceau, Lloyd George, Orlando, Colonel House, Baruch, Davis, Lamont, Lord Sumner, Klotz, Loucheur, De la Chaume, and Crespi*

APRIL 5, 1919, 11 A.M.

REPARATION

M. Clemenceau. I ask M. Klotz to report to us about the state of the question.

M. Klotz. Following the conversation which took place here the other day, a memorandum was drafted through the good offices of Mr. Lloyd George.[1] The French delegation presented certain observations on this memorandum; the American delegation then studied the text, with the French annotations, and proposed a new draft.[2] It was then the object of a common discussion of the English, American, French, and Italian delegations. The observations formulated by our delegation brought out some rather important differences. I will explain the Anglo-American plan, with the French observations.

Article 1 of the Anglo-American text is a declaration of principle, which has political significance. According to this article, the Allied and Associated Powers acknowledge that the enemy's resources are not unlimited, and that consequently it will be impossible for him to furnish complete reparation for all damages done. Is it appropriate to place a clause of this kind in a financial agreement, which should be composed of precise stipulations? I don't believe it would be politically advisable to place such a statement here, although it might be well to insert it—in a form to be studied—in general preamble. I fear, if it is put amongst the financial clauses, it could only create an unfortunate impression.

Mr. Lloyd George. I have some sympathy for the point of view that M. Klotz expresses. This Article 1 is insufficient to allow us to face the political difficulties we can expect from both British and French public opinion.

*H., PPC, V, 21ff.

[1] Printed as an appendix to X.
[2] Actually, the Anglo-American draft printed as an appendix to XIV.

I transmitted to M. Clemenceau an account of the debate which took place in the House of Commons on this question of reparation, and he could see the violence of feeling which arose. Mr. Bonar Law wrote to me, after this session, that Parliament showed itself very dissatisfied with his statements.[3]

The English public, like the French public, thinks the Germans must above all acknowledge their obligation to compensate us for all the consequences of their aggression. When this is done, we will come to the question of Germany's capacity to pay; we all think she will be unable to pay more than this document requires of her.

M. Clemenceau. I don't entirely agree with you about that. But undoubtedly Germany won't be able to pay all she will owe.

Mr. Lloyd George. It is important to state clearly that, if the definition of reparation claimed by us is limited, it is only because we admit the sheer impossibility of a complete payment.

Colonel House. I believe we can agree about that.

Mr. Norman Davis. It wasn't the American delegation that wanted to introduce that sentence into the text. In drafting it, we were trying to respond to the desire expressed by Great Britain and France.

M. Clemenceau. Then we must indicate in this sentence that Germany *acknowledges* the totality of her debt. It is not enough to say that we affirm it.

Mr. Lloyd George. We must say that the Allies affirm their claim to and that the Germans acknowledge their debt for the entire cost of the war.

Colonel House. That would be contrary to our agreement prior to the Armistice and to the note which you addressed to the American government. We mustn't draft this text in such a way that it appears to violate our own commitments.

Mr. Norman Davis. We can write that Germany is morally respon-

---

[3] The debate took place on April 2. It was the most recent onslaught in the continuing offensive by a group of Conservative M.P.s against Lloyd George's alleged lack of resolve on the question of obtaining a full indemnity from Germany. This latest attack had been precipitated by the publication in the London *Westminster Gazette* of March 31 of what has become known as the "moderation interview." In this off-the-record interview, Lloyd George repeated many of the points of the Fontainebleu Memorandum. He called for "moderation" in the peace negotiations, a "practical treaty," and a "sane peace." Most inflammatory to the hardliners was Lloyd George's assertion that the Allies could not go on "stripping Germany bare" and that the question of indemnities beyond the mere reparation of material damages could not even be considered. See *PWW*, Vol. 57, pp. 6-7.

sible for the war and all its consequences and that, legally, she is responsible for damages to property and persons, according to the formula adopted.

M. Clemenceau. It is a matter of wording; I believe we can find a way out.

M. Klotz. I have some important observations to make about Articles 2 and 3. Mr. Lloyd George's memorandum dated March 29 and the American memorandum of April 1 affirmed Germany's responsibility for damages caused to property and persons, "whatever the financial consequences might be for the enemy." Now, what is presently proposed is to limit the actual payments to Germany's capacity to pay over thirty years.

Mr. Lloyd George. That limitation doesn't seem to me to proceed from the text I have before me.

M. Klotz. I beg your pardon. Let us suppose that the inter-Allied commission concludes that the sum due from Germany is 50 billion dollars but that, on the other hand, it estimates that Germany can only pay 40 billions or 30 billions in thirty years. According to this text, the difference, that is, 10 billions or 20 billions, would be irretrievably lost to the Allies.

Mr. Lloyd George. It is pointless to debate with me about something I don't support. Let us suppose that Germany can pay 60 billion dollars in forty years, or only 50 billions in thirty years. I am not proposing that we reduce her debt to 50 billions. Note that Article 4 says that the period of payment can be prolonged if that is necessary. If then Germany can pay everything in forty years, I won't reduce the total so that the payment might be completed in thirty years.

I just said a word about this to Lord Sumner; he thinks Germany should pay in thirty years, but if she can't manage to fulfill her obligations within that time, the commission can prolong the period of payment.

M. Loucheur. We are completely in agreement with Mr. Lloyd George. But in our discussions amongst the experts, the British delegation didn't support this point of view. I will explain.

The estimate of damages is made. A total of 50 billion dollars is reached. Our commission says: "In thirty years, Germany will be able to pay only 40 billions." What has been said is that, in this case, the difference—10 billions—would be lost to us.

Lord Sumner. I believe there is a misunderstanding arising from the terminology used. Mr. Montagu accepted the limit of thirty years because he understood that Mr. Lloyd George desired this figure. The French delegates say: "If, in thirty years, everything is not paid, will the remainder be abandoned?" I answer: no, because of the power given to the commission to prolong the duration of payment and to accept payment in German treasury bonds if necessary. It is not our wish to enable Germany to evade us by not paying what she owes in thirty years.

M. Loucheur. If you had expressed yourselves as clearly as that, our discussion of today would not have been necessary. I must do justice to the American delegation, which left no doubt about the meaning of its statements. Article 4 doesn't apply to that loss of 10 billions, which I envisage hypothetically. Let's suppose that the commission declares that Germany can only pay 40 billion dollars in thirty years, instead of the 50 billions she owes us. It was observed that perhaps Germany would not manage to pay these 40 billions which the commission will have said was her capacity to pay over thirty years. Our colleagues then said: "The commission will have the power to prolong the period until the complete payment of the 40 billions. But the 10-billion difference between the commission's estimate of her capacity to pay and the sum actually due from Germany will be lost to us."

Mr. Davis. In fact, this text was drafted by the British delegation, and here is how I understand it. Two years from now, the commission must declare the total sum due us. If it finds that this sum exceeds Germany's capacity to pay within thirty years, it will decide what Germany should pay according to that capacity. But that last sum will have to be paid in full, even if it is later found necessary to prolong the period of payment.

Mr. Lloyd George. I don't think there is a real divergence between our views. In 1921, we will not only have studied but will have determined all our claims. I suppose that the total will reach 70 billion dollars, but that the commission will conclude that it is impossible for Germany to pay more than 50 billions; we will have to be satisfied with these 50 billions. Once this conclusion has been reached, we can consider the period over which this sum should be divided.

Mr. Davis. That's it.

Mr. Lloyd George. I agree with the French delegation. Obviously, if you say to the commission: "You must restrict yourselves to seeking what Germany can pay in thirty years," you are imposing a limit on it.

M. Loucheur. Mr. Lloyd George seems to be admitting that the commission will be able to limit the total figure according to Germany's ability to pay.

M. Clemenceau. I wouldn't leave that right to the commission without the governments being consulted.

Mr. Davis. There is no real difference between a period of thirty years and a period of forty years, because of the role of compound interest, and we should try to present the Germans with something acceptable.

M. Klotz. Yes, but it must also be acceptable to the French, who will never admit that part of the financial responsibilities which Germany will have acknowledged be thrown back on them. I acknowledge, as you do, that it is highly desirable that Germany be able to acquit herself in thirty years; but if that is impossible, we shouldn't be the victims.

The commission must be able to grant extensions. I don't think we can arrive at a satisfactory total estimate as early as 1921. It would require superhuman genius to know at that date what Germany will be able to pay during the next thirty years. In my opinion, it will be in 1930 or 1940 that the commission, faced with an acknowledged and justified inability, will be authorized to grant delays. I recall the formula of the memorandum of April 1: "We must determine the enemy's debt, whatever financial obligations it imposes upon him." This principle having been stated, if the commission judges an extension necessary, it will have to turn to the governments.

Colonel House. All our experts seem to agree in thinking that a period of thirty years should be the basis of all our calculations. The commission fixes the sum to be paid during this period; if that sum is not paid within thirty years, the commission can distribute the payments over forty or fifty years. If that really is it, what are we debating?

M. Loucheur. There is still something unclear. The commission meets. What will it do? According to the American delegates, it will determine the sum that Germany can pay in thirty years.

Mr. Lloyd George. Is that what Colonel House thinks?

Colonel House. Yes.

M. Clemenceau. Will the commission be instructed to declare the amount which, according to its estimates, Germany is capable of paying in thirty years?

Mr. Davis. That's it.

M. Loucheur. Then the difference between that sum and the actual amount of damages is lost to us?

Mr. Davis. What we are now proposing to have the commission do in two years is simply what we have tried to do amongst ourselves—namely, to determine what Germany can pay and, consequently, what one can demand of her.

M. Clemenceau. I don't accept the way you state the question.

M. Orlando. I have a precise objection to make to Mr. Davis. I am examining this text as a lawyer, and I read in it: "The Allied and Associated Governments demand that the enemy make compensation to the very limit of his capacity." This sentence signifies clearly that the limit of our claims is none other than the limit of Germany's capacity to pay.

Now, when we come to expressing this capacity in figures, we cannot take account solely of the present wealth of Germany, but of her future capacity, which depends upon her power of production. It follows that the capacity for payment, when we have a long period in mind, is related to the will of the debtor. It would be dangerous to adopt a formula which would, as it were, reward bad faith and a refusal to work.

Mr. Lamont. It seems to me that our discussion revolves entirely around a purely theoretical point. We are proposing to entrust to the commission the very task we have undertaken here. In our discussions, we always admitted that it wasn't worthwhile to consider a period longer than thirty or thirty-five years. What I hear now contradicts what we said amongst ourselves.

Mr. Lloyd George. Since there are doubts about the meaning of the text submitted to us, and about which much could be said, I think, in favor of Mr. Davis' interpretation of it, I propose to change the draft in the following way: the commission will fix Germany's total capacity to pay and will draw up a plan for periodic payment over thirty years, with the right to change the annual payments and to extend the period if that is necessary. First of all, it must be stated that Germany must pay in order to try to obtain what she can pay in thirty years, and, if she cannot manage to do that, to reserve the right to prolong the period.

M. Loucheur. I understand that Mr. Lloyd George contrasts total capacity with capacity to pay in thirty years.

M. Klotz. Here is how I understand the thing: (1) the commission establishes the amount of the debt; (2) the commission estimates the total capacity to pay and divides the sum over a period of thirty years; (3) if the payment is not completed in thirty years, the commission can prolong that period.

Mr. Davis. I think it preferable that thirty years remain the limit.

Mr. Lloyd George. I have to present a fairly strong argument against this idea. We will all be in a rather bad state for a number of years, and Germany will need ten years to get back on her feet. We can't really say what Germany's capacity to pay will be! We don't know what Germany will be able to pay in the next thirty years.

Mr. Davis tells us: "Germany must know where she stands and

what she will pay." But the Germans know very well what they have destroyed; they know better than we the condition of the devastated regions, for they have stayed there longer. They know what ships they have sunk; they know what pensions we have to pay. So they have an approximate idea of what they owe. If they say today that they themselves will rebuild destroyed houses, that eliminates one of the most uncertain elements from the calculations.

Colonel House. In that case, why name a commission? Why not simply draw up such a list?

Mr. Lloyd George. The commission will have to be concerned with compensation for the lives of sailors lost at sea, for the restitution of stolen or damaged property. But obviously its work concerns only part of the reparation due.

Colonel House. As Mr. Davis said a short time ago, if the period contemplated is too long, the accumulation of interest will make payment nearly impossible.

Mr. Lloyd George. I admit the importance of this observation. Perhaps there is no advantage in prolonging the payment for a hundred years instead of fifty years. But because of the circumstances in which we find ourselves, there will be a great difference between the next thirty years and a period of fifty years, for instance.

Colonel House. Haven't all the estimates of capacity to pay been made according to the estimates of Germany's wealth in 1914, when she had Alsace and Lorraine, Silesia, and her entire merchant fleet?

Mr. Lloyd George. No; Lord Sumner's report took account of the difference resulting from the loss of Alsace-Lorraine, the mines of Silesia, the merchant fleet, etc.

Colonel House. It seems to me that a few minutes ago we were close to a conclusion.

Mr. Lloyd George. We thought so; but now I no longer think so.

Colonel House. President Wilson always believed that our estimates were all based on a period of thirty years.

Mr. Davis. That is what I had thought, and we think on the other hand that, by admitting the right to reimbursement for pensions, we won't obtain any tangible difference, except perhaps in regard to the distribution, and that because Germany's capacity to pay is limited.

M. Clemenceau. No one can say today what that capacity is.

Mr. Lloyd George. I have fought against those who go on repeating that Germany can pay all that the war cost; but I don't want her to pay less than the extreme limit of the possible.

Colonel House. Perhaps it would be better to make no mention of the time period.

Mr. Lloyd George. I will have a text drafted on the following main lines: the Reparation Commission will estimate Germany's future capacity to pay. At the same time, it will prepare a plan for annual payments within the limits of the total sum due us, determining what, according to its opinion, Germany should pay over thirty years. Believe me: Germany won't create the anticipated difficulties about payments; she knows that she has to pay, and she is prepared to face the situation.

Colonel House. Why, in that case, not say simply that Germany acknowledges her obligation to pay reparations for damages caused to property and persons, without enumerating all the categories that have been suggested and without indicating the limit of thirty years? A text of this kind can be drafted in three lines.

M. Klotz. We could also return to the first Anglo-American text.

M. Clemenceau. I propose to adjourn the rest of the debate in order to discuss a text written in accordance with Mr. Lloyd George's suggestions.[4]

[4] This was a plan to define the composition and powers of the proposed Reparation Commission which Lord Sumner had just drafted. The Sumner draft empowered the commission to determine Germany's capacity to pay reparation obligations. Sumner's draft is printed in Burnett, *Reparation at the Paris Peace Conference*, I. 822-24. Its details will become evident in the subsequent discussions in the council.

XXII

Conference among MM. Clemenceau, Lloyd George, Orlando, Colonel House, McCormick, Baruch, Davis, Lamont, Lord Sumner, Klotz, Loucheur, De la Chaume, Chiesa, Crespi, and Count Aldrovandi*

APRIL 5, 1919, 4 P.M.

REPARATION

Mr. Lloyd George. I see in the American text[1] presented to me that reparation is due for the consequences of acts committed in violation of express agreements and of principles recognized by international law. This was aimed especially at the invasion of Belgium. But this text would allow claims to compensation for all losses suffered by trade as a result of the submarine warfare and a host of things to which we have renounced claim. It was not I who proposed this text: I note that it allows claiming all that the war has cost.

Colonel House. We can eliminate this article by inserting in another form the provision necessary for Belgium.

Mr. Lloyd George. I don't believe a special clause is necessary to cover the case of Belgium. Yesterday, we heard the King of the Belgians explain to us the damages for which Belgium is asking reparation; I saw nothing there that wasn't included in our own list. It seems to me impossible to distinguish the damage done to Belgium from the damage done, for example, to France; and the formula which is proposed to us would open the door to anything on earth.

Mr. McCormick. According to the principle stated and the declarations made, Belgium alone has the right to complete reimbursement for all her war costs.

Mr. Lloyd George. It is we who have paid Belgium's war costs: France and Great Britain provided the money required for her army and her government, and even a civil list for her King. Are

*H., *PPC*, V, 31ff.

[1] The council had before it the document printed as an appendix to the notes of this meeting. Lloyd George referred to Paragraph 6 of the American annex to this draft.

we to draft an express formula to assure to Belgium a compensation which would be refused to France and Great Britain? That is impossible.

If you would be so kind as to reread our list,[2] you will find it much more precise and complete; it includes in detail the categories of damages.

Colonel House. We accept your formulas if they assure the restoration of Belgium.

M. Klotz. Two texts have been presented—an English text and an American text. The American text was adopted by France, with the reservation that two additions be made to it, and by Italy, under the reservation of one addition. We have studied it minutely, word by word. If we adopt a new English draft, we will have to recommence that detailed study. That is why I believe it better to keep the American text as the basis of discussion, whilst reserving to Great Britain the right to present all helpful observations and to make the additions she will judge necessary.

Colonel House. The two texts were presented at the same time and have been studied. As for myself, I am ready to come round to the English text.

Mr. Lloyd George. Does M. Klotz accept the interpretation given by Mr. McCormick of Article 6, namely that this article would allow Belgium, and not France, to receive full compensation?

Our method of defining in detail damages caused to civilians is such as to satisfy the public much better.

M. Loucheur. It is true that we have discussed only the American text in detail, without, however, seeing in it the interpretation just given to the question of the privilege accorded to Belgium. We don't refuse to take up the English text, but it would be necessary to study it carefully. That could be done in half an hour amongst the financial specialists.

M. Clemenceau. I ask that we return to the discussion of the proposal drafted by Mr. Lloyd George at the end of this morning's session.[3] I don't acknowledge the right of a commission to fix Germany's capacity to pay. I would say this: Germany owes me X for damages caused to property and to persons. This sum X can be reduced by the governments in the course of time if they find it right to do so; but I am not prepared to agree that it be reduced at the present time. We shall see what is possible and what is not; we shall take account of the element of interest, which I am

---

[2] That is, the British annex.
[3] See n. 4 to the notes of the previous meeting.

inclined to renounce if we deem it necessary. The door will be wide open to liberal solutions.

But I ask in the name of the French government, and after having consulted my colleagues, that the peace treaty fix what Germany owes us and indicate at least the kind of damages for which reparation is due us. We shall reserve to ourselves the freedom to make adjustments. We shall fix a period of thirty years, as most of us want to do, and we shall give the commission a mandate to require payment of all that Germany owes us during these thirty years. If that is acknowledged to be impossible, the commission will have the right to prolong payments beyond thirty years.

Mr. Lloyd George's text seems to leave to the commission the right to fix a figure below what is due us; that I could not accept.[4]

Mr. Lloyd George. Could M. Klotz read his proposal?

M. Klotz. I will reply to the question asked this morning by Colonel House: "Why not limit ourselves to declaring that Germany will have to compensate for damages to persons and to property, without fixing a period of payment?" If Germany's capacity to pay requires that payments be divided over a period of fifty years, we are ready to give her fifty years. Let us suppose that the commission arrives at a figure of 60 billion pounds sterling [dollars] for the total of Germany's debt to the Allies; it will determine whether that can be paid in thirty years, or whether it will take forty.

M. Clemenceau. That is not very clearly expressed.

M. Klotz. I mean that the capacity to pay should be taken into account, in order to fix the number of annual payments.

Colonel House. It seems to me that M. Clemenceau's conclusion is close to the American proposal.

M. Loucheur. Here is what M. Clemenceau said: what is due is due; the commission has no right to declare that Germany will pay less. The governments, on the other hand, reserve to themselves the right to reduce the sum they claim. The commission will have only the right to change the length of the period of payment. We will suggest to it a period of thirty years to which it will be held, on the condition, however, that the total can actually be paid in thirty years.

Mr. McCormick. In other words, all will be paid, whatever period is necessary.

---

[4] At this point, the council decided to submit the Sumner draft to a subcommission for study.

Mr. Davis. This leads us away from the principles which have served as the basis of our work for three months. We had always spoken of taking into account, on the one hand, what is due, and on the other hand, the capacity to pay, which we always considered to be less than the debt. We have constantly worked with the idea that Germany would have to pay what she could pay in thirty years or, at most, thirty-five, for after that, the accumulation of interest would become so enormous that the problem is impossible to solve.

Regarding the capacity to pay, we have made estimates which varied, at least in the American delegation, between a minimum of 25 billion dollars and a maximum of 35 billions. These figures were determined without taking any account of the [German national] debt; we only tried to imagine a Germany in good shape and able to pay. We then concluded that it was better not to fix a figure at all. But by working on this new basis, we are ending up by abandoning our constant principle, which was this: Germany must pay what she can pay. At the same time, we are renouncing the attempt to fix a minimum and a maximum between which the commission can operate. If none of this remains in our proposals, we are abandoning our principles.

Mr. Lloyd George. I will observe that we were indeed trying to find out what Germany could pay, without trying to establish categories of damages which should be compensated. By doing that, we were doing our best to satisfy the principles laid down by President Wilson, in their strictest interpretation. We had to reach a solution: hence the choice of the other method.

Mr. Davis today wants to superimpose the limits that both methods would impose upon us. May I tell him that the difficulties which he fears do not exist? If we allow Germany to pay in goods, reconstruct buildings herself, restore machinery, we solve a great part of the problem. For Germany, the difficulty is not finding money, but money which can serve for payments abroad; through payment in kind, payments abroad are considerably reduced, and this almost eliminates the question of the capacity to pay.

—(Reading of the text.)[5]

[5] That is, the Klotz text, or redraft. At one point, in response to House's suggestion in the previous meeting, Klotz submitted a revision of Articles 2 and 3 of the Anglo-American accord of April 1. Klotz's version (some words are different, probably on account of translation from French into English) follows:

"Note: Words inserted in the original draft are underlined. Words omitted

M. Klotz. Articles 2, 3, and 4 should be corrected as a consequence of the change made in Article 1.

I have a word to say about Article 5, with reference to the down payment. I am not questioning the amount of this down payment; but the formula used seems to me impolitic and dangerous. The same figure will include compensation for us and sums destined for the maintenance of the army of occupation and the victualing of Germany. It is not very politic to say to the peoples who have suffered most: here are 25 billion [francs] that we are getting immediately—then to deduct from this sum what is necessary to maintain the armies and to pay for food destined for Germany.

If the army of occupation was maintained in its present state, in two years its maintenance would cost 14 billions. Add to this what is necessary for the victualing of Germany; practically nothing would remain for our invaded populations. That formula would be impolitic, not only as far as the French people are concerned, but for the German people as well; it will appear to them that a huge sum is being required, when in reality one third or one quarter would be destined for their own use. It seems to me preferable to divide the total under two distinct headings.

Mr. Lloyd George. Your figure for the expenses of the army of occupation is exaggerated, because that army won't remain long at its present strength.

M. Loucheur. We agree to leave Germany enough to buy food and raw materials. We only think that the figure must be fixed for these purchases; otherwise, Germany could spend the greater

---

from the original draft are in brackets.

"(1) The Allied and Associated Powers require <u>and the Enemy Powers accept</u> that the Enemy States at whatever cost to themselves make compensation for all damages done to the civilian population of the Allied and Associated Powers, and to their property by the aggression of the Enemy States by land, by sea, and from the air, and also for all damages resulting from permanent injury to the health of any of their nationals [and for all damages resulting from the acts of the enemy in violation of formal engagements and of the law of nations].

"(2) The amount of damages <u>as set forth in the specific categories annexed hereto</u>, for which compensation is to be made, shall be determined by an Inter-Allied Commission to be constituted in such form as the Allied and Associated Powers shall forthwith determine.

"This Commission shall examine into the claims and give to the Enemy States a just opportunity to be heard.

"The findings of this Commission as to the amount of damages shall be concluded and communicated to the Enemy States on or before May 1st, 1921.

"The schedule of payments to be made by the Enemy States shall be set forth <u>by this Commission</u>, taking into account <u>in the fixation of the time for payment</u> their capacity for payment." Printed in *PWW*, Vol. 57, pp. 27-28.

part of the 25 billions on them and get out of working. We must allot her, say, five billions, and from the rest, which will be reserved for us, deduct the expenses of the army of occupation.

Mr. Lamont. You recall that this wording was previously suggested by the British delegation. You had already made the same objection; but it was answered, further on in the same text, that a reservation is made which gives us a complete guarantee, for it is said that the sums spent for Germany will have to be recognized as necessary by the Allied and Associated Powers.

M. Loucheur. Yes, but I remember the recent discussion on the victualing of Germany. In order not to repeat this discussion endlessly, I would prefer a lump sum.

Mr. Lamont. Germany has no more interest than we in dissipating all she owns.

Mr. Lloyd George. If you give Germany a fixed sum, I believe it will go against what you are seeking. The Germans will spend that sum and will come and tell us afterwards: "You didn't give us enough; we can no longer buy raw materials to reconstruct your houses." So they must be given a supplement. Five billion francs is a large sum. I prefer that they come to ask us in detail, and that they be required to justify their request each time.

M. Loucheur. I see a danger in encouraging the Germans to make repeated demands on us.

M. Klotz. I return to the danger of seeming to inflate the sum we are asking the Germans to pay immediately. I would prefer to say that we are demanding 20 billions from them, instead of 25 billions, without fixing the figure for the victualing of Germany. The Economic Commission would examine their requests as its work proceeds, according to established rules. If we kept this text, we would seem to be demanding more from the Germans than we are actually demanding, and our people would be disappointed when they compared the announced figure with what is reserved for them.

Mr. Lloyd George. I prefer a system which enables us to keep control of German purchases in our hands; our draft gives us this control. I prefer that to giving a lump sum to a government which we don't even know.

M. Klotz. Another question: it seems to me absolutely essential to specify guarantees. Between individuals of whom one is indebted to the other, mortgages or securities are required. This is not a matter of military guarantees; but are there no guarantees which could be found in the revenues of railways, ports, and customs? The American delegation says that it has no mandate to discuss these questions. I believe a provision along these lines should be inserted in the treaty.

Mr. Lloyd George. I don't see what we would gain by that. If we seize the customhouses, what will we get?

The truth is that we must anticipate the problem of how to compel Germany to fulfill her obligations. But it seems to me useless to concern ourselves with customhouses and ports. It is up to the governments to see what they want to do if Germany refuses to carry out the treaty or if, without refusing, she doesn't carry it out. But I would place nothing about this subject in the specifically financial articles of the preliminaries. We can study the question of whether we have to accept German bonds as a means of payment. That is another question, to be handed over to the financial experts.

I am surprised to see nothing about the subject of direct restoration or reconstruction.

Mr. Baruch. If Germany commits herself to paying sum X and gives her signature, I don't see what we can gain by requiring guarantees of the type suggested by M. Klotz.

Mr. Davis. The real sanction is the occupation of a part of German territory until the first payment.

M. Clemenceau. Like Mr. Lloyd George, I want to have the restoration of buildings expressly mentioned.

M. Loucheur. That question is especially important for France, Belgium, and also for Italy. It actually means the right to choose amongst the kinds of payment. We must be able to demand, not only the reconstruction of buildings, but also certain supplies which are necessary for us. One vital supply for France and Italy is coal. Even if France can exploit the entire Saar Basin, her coal deficit will be 18 million tons, taking into account all that Great Britain normally provides her. If we turn to Germany, she can refuse to provide us with coal or propose to sell it at an exorbitant price. What will we do then? The same applies to certain materials necessary to our industries in the east of France.

We have asked Italy to inform us about her coal needs. This question is no less important for her than for us. We must be able to claim from Germany supplies and works such as the reconstruction of railways, bridges, roads. What we ask is that it be clearly stated in this text that we have the right to choose the kinds of payment, in such a way as to insure us direct reconstruction of destroyed cities and the supplies necessary to our industry.

M. Clemenceau. I propose that you bring us a precise text on that, which we can examine on Monday.

{ A P P E N D I X }[6]

TEXT TENTATIVELY AGREED UPON BY THE BRITISH
AND AMERICAN DELEGATES.

1. The Allied and Associated Governments affirm the responsibility of the Enemy States for causing all the loss and damage to which the Allied and Associated Governments and their nationals have been subjected as a consequence of the war imposed upon them by the aggression of the enemy states.

2. The Allied and Associated Governments recognize that the financial resources of the enemy states are not unlimited and, after taking into account permanent diminutions of such resources which will result from other treaty clauses, they judge that it will be impracticable for enemy states to make complete reparation for all such loss and damage. The Allied and Associated Governments, however, require that the enemy states, to the extent of their utmost capacity, make compensation for all damage done to the civilian population of the Allied and Associated Powers and to their property by the aggression of the enemy states by land, by sea, and from the air.

(See Annex for interpretation clause prepared by the British.)

3. The amount of such damage for which compensation is to be made shall be determined by an inter-allied commission, to be constituted in such form as the Allied and Associated Governments shall forthwith determine. This commission shall examine into the claims and give to the enemy states a just opportunity to be heard. The findings of the commission as to the amount of damage defined in Article 2 shall be concluded and communicated to the enemy states on or before May 1st, 1921. The commission at the same time shall also draw up a schedule of payments up to or within the total sum thus due, which in their judgment Germany should be able to liquidate within a period of thirty years, and this schedule of payments shall then be communicated to Germany as representing the extent of her obligations.

4. The inter-allied commission shall further have discretion to

[6] Printed in *ibid.*, Vol. 56, pp. 536-39.

modify from time to time the date and mode of the schedule of payments fixed in clause 3 and, if necessary, to extend them in part beyond thirty years, by acceptance of long period bonds or otherwise, if subsequently such modification or extension appears necessary, after giving Germany a just opportunity to be heard. Payment may be required and, with the approval of the commission, accepted in the form of properties, chattels, businesses, rights, and concessions in ceded territory; of ships, of gold and silver, of properties, chattels, businesses, rights and concessions, of bonds, shares and securities of all kinds, of foreign currencies or the currency of the enemy state, or of German Government bonds.

5. In order to enable the Allied and Associated Powers to proceed at once to the restoration of their industrial and economic life, pending the full determination of their claim, the enemy states shall pay in such instalments and in such manner (whether in gold, commodities, ships, securities or otherwise) as the interallied commission may fix, in 1919 and 1920 the equivalent of $5,000,000,000 gold towards the liquidation of the above claims, out of which the expenses of the army of occupation subsequent to the Armistice, shall first be met, provided that such supplies of food and raw materials as may be judged by the Allied and Associated Governments to be essential to enable Germany to meet her obligation for reparation may, with the approval of the Allied and Associated Governments, be paid for out of the above sum.

6. The successive instalments paid over by the enemy states in satisfaction of the above claims shall be divided by the Allied and Associated Governments in proportions which have been determined upon by them in advance, on a basis of general equity, and of the rights of each.

7. The payments mentioned above do not include restitution in kind of cash taken away, seized or sequestered, nor the restitution in kind of animals, objects of every nature and securities taken away, seized and sequestered, in the cases in which it proves possible to identify them in enemy territory. If at least half the number of the animals taken by the enemy from the invaded territories cannot be identified and returned, the balance, up to a total of half the number taken, shall be delivered by Germany by way of restitution.

8. The attention of the four Chiefs of the respective Governments is to be called to the following:

APRIL 5, 1919

(a) That necessary guarantees to insure the due collection of the sums fixed for reparation should be planned; and

(b) That there are other financial clauses which this conference has not been charged to deal with.

U. S. ANNEX TO CLAUSE 2.

Personal Injury
(1) Personal injury to or death of civilians resulting from military operations or mistreatment by the enemy.

Pensions
(2) Damage to the civilian population resulting from the absence, incapacitation or death, in military service, of persons upon whom they are dependent and which damage is met by pensions or payments of like nature made by the State. (French scale to govern.)

Damage to Labor
(3) Damage to civilians resulting from their being forced by the enemy to labor without just remuneration, or to abstain from labor.

Damage to Property
(4) Damage to non-military property and property rights caused by military operations or illegal act of the enemy or war measures in the nature of requisitions or sequestrations, taken by the enemy.

Fines, etc.
(5) Damage in the form of levies, fines and other similar exactions imposed by the enemy upon the civilian population.

Violations of law and engagements
(6) Damage resulting from acts in violation of international law (as found by the Commission on Responsibilities) and in violation of formal engagements.

Note: Where the State or other public authority has already itself made compensation for the damage, it may present the claim in its own behalf.

APRIL 2ND.

G. B. INTERPRETATION OF CLAUSE 2.

Compensation may be claimed under Clause 2 under the following categories of damage:

I.

a) Damage caused to civilian victims of acts of war (including bombardments or other attacks on land, on sea or from the air and all the direct consequences thereof and of all operations of war by the two groups of belligerents wherever arising) and to the surviving dependents of such victims.

b) Damage caused to civilian victims of acts, cruelties, violence or maltreatment (including injuries to life or health as a consequence of imprisonment, deportation, internment, or evacuation, of exposure at sea, or of being forced to labour by the enemy) committed or ordered by the enemy wherever arising and to the surviving dependents of such victims.

c) Damage caused to civilian victims of all acts of the enemy in occupied, invaded or enemy territory, injurious to health or capacity for work or to honour and to the surviving dependents of such victims.

II.

a) All pensions and compensations in the nature of pensions to naval and military victims of war, whether mutilated, wounded, sick or invalided, and to the dependents of such victims.

b) Cost of assistance by the State to prisoners of war and to their families and dependents.

c) Allowances by the State to the families and dependents of mobilized persons, or persons serving with the forces.

III.

Damage in respect of all property belonging to any of the Allied and Associated States or to any of their subjects, with the exception of military works or material, which has been carried off, seized, injured or destroyed by the acts of the enemy on land, on sea, or from the air, or damaged directly in consequence of hostilities or any operations of war.

XXIII

Conversation between MM. Clemenceau, Lloyd George, Orlando, and Colonel House*

APRIL 7, 1919, 3:30 P.M.

Present are: Marshal Foch and Generals Weygand and Sir Henry Wilson.

Mr. Lloyd George. Before we tackle the financial question, I would like to submit to you a list of questions whose solution could be entrusted to our Foreign Ministers.[1]

—(*Reading of the list.*)

Mr. Lloyd George. It seems to me that it might be necessary to add here: insertion in the treaty of a clause annulling the treaties of Brest-Litovsk and of Bucharest.

Colonel Hankey. That question is already in the hands of a commission.

M. Clemenceau. I approve that list; but I would like to replace "solution" by "study." The ministers will study, but we have to reserve to ourselves the final right of decision if there is a disputed point.

M. Orlando. On No. 7 of the list—the obligation imposed upon Germany to acknowledge the treaties which will be signed by the Allied and Associated Powers with Austria-Hungary, Bulgaria, and Turkey—I would make the following observation: as far as possible, the signing of the Austro–Hungarian treaty should take place at the same time as the German treaty is signed. That coincidence has a great importance from the Italian point of view.

Mr. Lloyd George. Even if all these treaties should be signed on the same day, a clause of the kind I have just indicated would be necessary.

I acquaint you with a telegram we have just received from General Smuts.[2] He has failed. He declares that the Hungarian government, which he was supposed to visit, has no authority beyond the environs of Budapest. He asks to return. I suggest that he visit the French headquarters on the way in order to be able to make a complete report to us on the situation.

*H., *PPC*, V, 39ff.

[1] It is printed in *PWW*, Vol. 57, pp. 76-77.
[2] It is printed in *ibid.*, pp. 77-79.

M. Clemenceau. There could only be benefits in doing that.

Mr. Lloyd George. He could also go to Rumania so he could report to us as many facts as possible. He will undoubtedly have to take some decisions.

M. Clemenceau. We are agreed.

Mr. Lloyd George. We have also received a report from our military representative in Berlin. He thinks the Spartacists[3] are making progress, and he proposes an Allied occupation; that is always the solution of the military.

M. Clemenceau. The information we have received is very similar.

Mr. Lloyd George. According to the same report, the organized troops the German government has at its disposal are not more than 80,000 men—25,000 in Berlin, 6,000 in Halle, 6,800 in the Ruhr Basin, between 8,000 and 10,000 in Silesia, and the remainder on the Polish border. Berlin is thought to be able to hold out for a month.

Do these figures correspond to Marshal Foch's?

Marshal Foch. We don't have exact figures, but these don't contradict what we know.

Mr. Lloyd George. A Spartacist coup is expected this week.

—Marshal Foch presents his report on the negotiations at Spa concerning the transport of Polish troops.[4]

---

[3] The German Communist party organized by Karl Liebknecht and Rosa Luxemburg, both of whom had been assassinated. The feared Spartacist uprising in mid-April did not occur. See, e.g., Eric Waldman,*The Spartacist Uprising of 1919 and the Crisis of the German Socialist Movement* (Milwaukee, Wis., 1958).

[4] "REPORT ON THE NEGOCIATIONS OF APRIL 3RD AND 4TH 1919 AT SPA." This "report" actually consisted of the minutes of the meetings between Foch and the German delegate, Matthias Erzberger. According to Erzberger, the German government acknowledged the "absolute necessity" of sending Haller's army to Poland. However, as the Council of Four had anticipated, Erzberger then brought up the suggestion that he had already unofficially conveyed to Wilson: instead of sending Haller's forces to Poland via Danzig, where the German government could not guarantee the absence of disturbances, the troops could be transported safely from the Rhine bridgeheads across Germany by rail. Foch immediately accepted the proposal, but he insisted that the German government explicitly recognize the legal right of the Allies, according to the Armistice Agreement, to have their troops disembark at Danzig. The remainder of the negotiations was taken up almost entirely with the question of whether Haller's troops were, in fact, Allied troops and as such had the theoretical right to pass through Danzig.

The formal agreement between Foch and Erzberger stipulated the general terms which would govern the transport of General Haller's army to Poland. On the question of whether these troops could, in principle, pass through Danzig, Foch and Erzberger reached a compromise: the Allies affirmed this right, but the German government did not explicitly acknowledge it. Thus, the first paragraph of the protocol reads as follows: "By Article XVI of the Armistice Convention of

M. Clemenceau. Mr. Lloyd George can read the report of the negotiations at his leisure.

Marshal Foch. I think it would be worthwhile, because it shows the present temperature of the German government.

Mr. Lloyd George. This document is too interesting not to be read attentively.

(*Perusing it*) They want the French to occupy Budapest! And Vienna! Anything we like, except Germany. Naturally, Erzberger is very hostile towards the Bolsheviks; he is a Catholic. * * * Ah! But he is very friendly!

Very interesting. I believe Marshal Foch has established his qualifications as a great diplomat. We should congratulate him on his skill and success.

Marshal Foch. Several practical matters remain to be settled.

General Weygand. It was decided that the Allies would designate officers who would accompany the trains in order to assure the transport under the best conditions.

Mr. Lloyd George. Agreed. How many will you need?

General Sir Henry Wilson. Eighty-three.

M. Clemenceau. Are the Americans also ready to provide some?

Colonel House. I think there is no difficulty about that.

General Weygand. The plan for transport is ready. The execution, on account of necessary preparations, will begin on the fifteenth

---

11th November 1918, Germany is bound to authorize the passage via Danzig of allied troops, and consequently (according to the Allies' understanding of the matter) that of General Haller's troops also."

An attached "ANNEX to the Protocol of 4th April, 1919," spelled out in detail the arrangements for the implementation of the agreement.

In his private conversation with Foch on April 3, before the opening of the official negotiations, Erzberger stated that, if the Allies "really" intended to establish a barrier against Bolshevism by sending Haller's army to Poland, the German government would do all it could to assist in this endeavor. However, the German government believed that the danger of the spread of Bolshevism was greatest in South Central Europe. Whereas in the Baltic region and in Poland, anti-Bolshevik forces were effectively holding the line, the "southern wing of the forces opposed to Bolshevism" in Rumania, Bessarabia, and Hungary was not capable of fulfilling its mission. In Hungary, Bolshevism was already victorious; in Bessarabia, a country of great landowners, the ground was favorable for the outbreak of Bolshevism. Erzberger concluded: "The German Government thinks that, if the Marshal wants to defeat Bolshevism, it is necessary for the French Authorities to settle in BUDAPEST. There is in that direction a great danger lest Bolshevism should spread through VIENNA and BAVARIA, and reach the RHINE and ITALY. The German Government is convinced that the southern wing of the forces actually opposed to Bolshevism are unemployable." See *PWW*, Vol. 57, pp. 74-75.

of this month and continue until June 15. I don't know whether the Polish government has been notified.

M. Clemenceau. I saw M. Paderewski at the Quai d'Orsay; he is informed about what has taken place at Spa.

General Weygand. Isn't it necessary to inform him officially of it?

M. Clemenceau. Marshal Foch can see him in our name.

Mr. Lloyd George. Agreed.

General Weygand. There is also the question of the Russian prisoners of war. Marshal Foch is only transmitting to you the conclusions reached by the generals who represent France, England, and the United States in Berlin. They propose to ask the German government to send the prisoners back to Russia, unless the latter themselves might not want to return to their country.

Mr. Lloyd George. I believe these Russians are equally dangerous in Germany and in Russia.

M. Clemenceau. I also have many Russians to send back; this is no small problem.

THE QUESTION OF REPARATION*

—The members of the Reparation Commission are introduced.

M. Clemenceau. I request a reading of the text, article by article.[5]

M. Klotz. I believe it will suffice to examine the articles on which we have observations to make.

Article 2 presents two difficulties. First of all, it is again declared that the enemy's resources are not unlimited. We have already expressed our objection to that wording. It seems unfortunate to us, in any case, to place a sentence of this kind at the head of the financial articles of the treaty; it could be placed somewhere else. The impression it would produce here would be very unfavorable.

Second. For the formula "whatever the financial consequences that this reparation might entail for the enemy," this one has been substituted: "up to the very limit of his capacity to pay." I propose to return to the first formula. It strikes a note we wish to keep.

M. Clemenceau. I have an observation to make. The day before yesterday, we adopted a text; I would like to have it in front of us.

*H., *PPC*, V, 44ff.

[5] Of the document printed as the appendix to these notes. This was a further revision of the reparation clauses prepared by Lamont, Keynes, and Loucheur on April 5.

Mr. Lamont. In the text submitted to you, all that has been added to the text of the day before yesterday is underlined.

Mr. Lloyd George. I don't favor removing from this text the indication of the enemy's inability to pay all that he owes. We have to justify somehow the action of the British and French governments, which find themselves compelled to accept less than complete compensation for the costs of the war. We must clearly establish that we have adopted a limiting formula, not because it would be unjust to claim it, but because it is impossible to obtain it.

M. Clemenceau. It must be said in a preamble, but not in the financial clauses of the treaty.

M. Klotz. Likewise, the enemy must be required to acknowledge, not only what he can pay, but also what he owes. I share Mr. Lloyd George's opinion of the importance of explaining the position of the governments; but, like M. Clemenceau, I believe this should be done in a preamble.

Mr. Lloyd George. I agree with you on the second point. I have already said that Germany must acknowledge all her debt. But I would observe that the second sentence no longer makes sense if we omit the first.

M. Klotz. In any case, the wording is poor. To say that the enemy states do not have unlimited resources is to express a truism. No state has unlimited resources. It is better to say that the enormity of the debt surpasses all possibilities of payment.

Mr. Lloyd George. The best thing is to omit, purely and simply, the words "up to the very limit of their capacity." What remains is enough and agrees with the precise commitment taken at the time of the Armistice.

M. Clemenceau. Here is the new wording I propose for Article 2: "The Allied and Associated Governments, recognizing that the financial resources of the enemy states, in the situation in which they find themselves at the conclusion of the peace, are not adequate to assure complete reparation of the losses and damages referred to in Article 1, require that Germany compensate for all damages enumerated in the appended annex."

Mr. Lloyd George. I regret that we have spent so much time on a mere question of wording. But allow me to say to you that, from the point of view of public opinion, I do not find this draft felicitous. Our public opinion, like yours, demands reparation as complete as possible. Imagine the effect of this formula: to take into consideration the enemy's situation at the time of the conclusion of the peace—such wording is vaguer and less satisfactory than that which had been presented to us. The public will say: "It isn't the enemy's situation on the day after the peace, but a rather long period—ten years, twenty years—that must be contemplated in order to know what he must pay us."

The only thing we must take into account—because it is a permanent fact—is the loss by the enemy of his iron mines, of part of his coal mines, of his colonies, of his merchant marine. All that has a direct influence upon his capacity to pay.

I earnestly beg you not to hold us up on questions of wording. With what the Americans accept, that is, the elimination of the words "up to the very limit of his capacity" and the addition, further on, of the indication that his resources are not adequate—underlining this—to compensate for the damages, I believe this text will meet our needs.

Colonel House. We favor neither the one nor the other of these two clauses. If you wish to eliminate them both, the Americans won't object.

—*Final draft of Article 2:*

"The Allied and Associated Governments recognize that the financial resources of the enemy states are not adequate after taking into account permanent diminutions of such resources which will result from other treaty clauses to make complete reparation for all such loss and damage. The Allied and Associated Governments, however, require, and the German government undertakes, that she will make compensation for damage done to the civilian population of the Allied and Associated Powers and to their property by her aggression by land, by sea, and from the air, as defined in the annexed schedule."

—*Article 2, thus worded, is adopted.*

M. Klotz. In Article 3, it is said, after the sentence relating to the conclusions of the Reparation Commission which must, at the latest, be presented on May 1, 1921: "The commission shall thereupon draw up a schedule of payments." What does the word "thereupon" mean? If it means "after May 1, 1921," that is too late. The system of payment must be notified at the same time as the amount of the damages. I would replace "thereupon" by "concurrently."

—*(Adopted.)*

At the end of the same article, it is said that "any remaining balance unpaid may, within the discretion of the commission be postponed for settlement in subsequent years; or may be handled otherwise, in such manner as the Allied and Associated Governments, acting through the commission, shall determine."

Mr. Davis. This was written at the request of M. Clemenceau, who wished to reserve the right of the governments.

M. Klotz. Yes, but the power to postpone the payments is granted to the commission.

Mr. Lamont. It was always understood that the commission would have this right.

M. Klotz. Undoubtedly, but will the commission decide by majority or by unanimous vote? It is a question which concerns not only us, but also the enemy.

Mr. Lamont. We thought this would be settled in the protocol establishing the commission.

M. Clemenceau. It is very important that the taxpayer know that it won't be possible to take a decision involving his interests without the consent of his government.

Mr. Lloyd George. If, before agreeing on a text like this one, the method of voting in the commission has to be studied, we will never get finished. I believed I understood that we had, last Saturday, entrusted MM. Klotz, Keynes, Lamont, and Crespi with the drafting; it is to them that a question of this type should be referred.

M. Clemenceau. Can we simply say here that the commission will be able to take a valid decision only unanimously?

Mr. Lloyd George. I concur.

M. Orlando. So do we.

Colonel House. Without offering any opposition, I am obliged to reserve the judgment of President Wilson.

M. Klotz. There is a question of sovereignty here that no people can abandon. Decisions affecting the interests of our respective countries to such an extent can only be taken by common agreement. Suppose that one of us, Italy for instance, should be in a minority and that the commission takes a decision that this country should judge to be contrary to her interests. Could she accept it?

Mr. Lloyd George. Three governments have just expressed their views in favor of unanimity; I believe we can move on.

M. Klotz. In Article 4, I see in the new draft that the commission will have the powers required to change the kinds of payment. This is something new. I recall that Mr. Lloyd George said the other day: "The true question is to know how the governments can compel Germany to pay." This is a political question, which has no place in the financial clauses. At the same time, Mr. Lloyd George said it could be useful to ascertain whether Germany would have to acknowledge her debt immediately by an issue of bonds. Shouldn't we have a more precise text about this than these few words? I am not asking that this technical question be discussed today, but that it be assigned to a small committee, which would present a text as soon as possible.

Mr. Lloyd George. I continue to think that this possibility must indeed be studied. Lord Sumner has proposed to insert a clause along these lines in the protocol establishing the commission. All that can be done in the text which we have before us is to authorize the commission to pursue that course.

Mr. Davis. The question is one of those which will be asked in the course of the negotiations with the Germans, and we don't have the time now to prepare a plan for the emission of German bonds.

Mr. Lloyd George. Like M. Klotz, I am of opinion that we must indicate the principle here. I would put a few words in Article 3 giving the commission the right to determine the period and the kinds of payment.

M. Klotz. I request that we go further. All this affects our future— for all of us. People don't live on hope alone; beginning tomorrow, budgets have to be made. Since the enemy must pay, and since we can take no material pledges worth the trouble, we must at least have the enemy's signature, something to put in our safes at once. Germany would certify her debt in writing in the form of bonds. These bonds, demanded immediately under the heading of certificates of indebtedness, would be equivalent to the acknowledgment a creditor demands of his debtor who is unable to pay him immediately. If the debtor is not insolvent, this paper is negotiable. By such means we can allow our countries to live whilst awaiting the final settlement.

Mr. Lloyd George. I agree with you completely. I am going to read you the proposal that Lord Sumner has prepared for the protocol establishing the commission: "The latter will fix a sum, corresponding approximately to the probable minimum of the payments, and will ask Germany to make a first issue of bonds corresponding to that sum, which will serve as collateral for payment of the debt."

It is pointless to insert this draft here; we must indicate only the principle.

M. Klotz. That draft is excellent. But since there is here an obligation imposed upon Germany, Germany must know it when she signs the treaty. Can't we make the protocol establishing the commission Annex 2 of these reparation clauses and put here: "The commission can prescribe the kinds of payment such as they are defined in Annex 2"?

Mr. Lloyd George. It is too much to ask for today. Our American friends haven't yet studied this plan. But we agree, I believe, to give this power to the commission in general terms.

M. Klotz. I believe the protocol establishing the commission should be included in an annex to the treaty.

Mr. Lloyd George. No, that protocol is our business only.

M. Klotz. We will be setting a figure for the bond issue. This figure has to be communicated to the Germans.

M. Loucheur. I have an observation to present on Article 7. The text has been accepted by the delegations. But President Wilson removed a sentence referring to compensation for livestock taken or requisitioned and which cannot be restored directly. M. Clemenceau asks me to say that he reserves the right to take that question up directly with President Wilson.

At our last meeting, it was agreed that I would prepare a report on the kinds of payment amongst which we would have the right to choose—this especially concerns coal—and on the question of payment by direct repair or restoration of buildings or business establishments destroyed and damaged. The study of that question hasn't advanced very far, and it must be postponed.

Mr. Baruch. The question has already been studied, at least as far as coal is concerned.

Mr. Lloyd George. There are two different questions here, which, in my opinion, must be studied separately. The question of reconstruction, on the one hand, and the question of a guarantee of a supply of coal, on the other hand, must be submitted to two different committees.

Mr. Baruch. In that case, it would be best to withdraw the question of coal from the subcommission which has dealt with it up to now.

Mr. Lloyd George. I see here a special additional article on Belgium. I hope no one will insist on the insertion of that article.

Mr. McCormick. It is better to discuss this point whilst considering the categories.

—(Reading of the categories.)

Mr. Lloyd George. I read in Article 2, Paragraph e, that pensions will be calculated on the basis of the French scale. I would like to have this studied again. I don't propose that the nation which pays the most generous pensions should receive more. The question is whether we shouldn't take the English scale for pensions as the uniform basis. That seems to me well worth considering.

You will certainly have in France, as we have had in England, a movement to increase pensions. If you accept compensation on the most modest basis for the future, any increase will be at your own expense. That is why I propose to take the British scale as the identical basis for all the nations concerned.

Mr. McCormick. When that article was discussed in our commission, it seemed understood that the Prime Ministers agreed on the formula adopted. In fact, Italy and Serbia have pensions lower than the French pensions. That is why the French figures were adopted as the average.

Mr. Lloyd George. If President Wilson has the impression that we are agreed on the principle, I don't insist.

Mr. McCormick. I will observe that the French have already raised the scale of their pensions, and it is the new scale that we will use as a basis.

Mr. Lloyd George. In Article 2, Paragraph b, I read: "Damage caused to civilians by being compelled to abstain from all work as the only alternative to doing military work for the enemy or employing themselves on his armaments." This formula opens the door to unlimited claims, particularly in Belgium. Since the entire Belgian population was imprisoned in its territory by the invasion, there isn't a single Belgian who could not come and say to us, without any possible verification, that he has the right to compensation under this formula. We will find ourselves faced with an enormous totality of claims that we will be unable to verify.

M. Klotz. It must be admitted, however, that there are cases where compensation is certainly due. Let us take as an example a factory fallen into the hands of the enemy who wants to use it to manufacture shells. The head of the establishment refuses. The consequence is unemployment, and the establishment does whatever it can to prevent the workers from starving to death. There are grounds, in this case, for compensation. But I think, like Mr. Lloyd George, that proof would have to be required.

M. Clemenceau. Like Mr. Lloyd George, I believe it is very dangerous to open the door to unlimited demands.

Mr. Lloyd George. It could be done if this concerned only France, where a great part of the male population was under arms from the beginning of the war. But I fear that this version would expose us to endless claims in Belgium.

—(Paragraph b of Article 2 is deleted.)

Mr. Lloyd George. Article 4, thus worded: "interference with non-military property caused by acts of war * * * or war measures" disturbs me somewhat. All business losses caused by war operations could easily be included here. For instance, the owner of a destroyed farm could say that this farm yielded him nothing for three years and could ask compensation for this loss. Now, I know farmers from a fiscal point of view; they estimate their revenue very differently when it is a matter of paying taxes or of winning a lawsuit.

Similarly, for sunken ships, one could then ask—which we don't dream of doing—compensation for loss in freight, for the wages of the crews, etc. The bombardments which took place on the eastern coast of England ruined all the seaside resorts on that coast for three years. Shall we admit this kind of damage as cause for compensation? The action of the submarines cut off the Australian trade entirely. It would be good news to Mr. Hughes to learn that the Germans would pay the price of all the wheat which, having been impossible to export, was eaten by rats.

I believe we should stick to the formulas which insure reparation for damages to persons and to property, but that we should exclude business losses.

M. Loucheur. We agree on the latter. But the prewar value of destroyed property must bear interest from the date of the Armistice, November 11, 1918, in view of the fact that immediate payment is impossible.

Mr. Lloyd George. Would you extend this arrangement to ships?

M. Loucheur. Yes.

Mr. Lloyd George. I am no advocate of that. That would lead us very far, especially if we count the interest on the capital of the shipping companies.

M. Loucheur. We can fix a uniform interest rate of 5 or 6 per cent.

Mr. Lloyd George. Even so, I fear that this method of inflating the figures would lead us too far.

M. Loucheur. Take the case of the mines in the north of France: it will take ten years to put them back in working order. If, meanwhile, the mining companies don't receive the interest on what is owed them, how will they pay their bondholders?

Mr. Lloyd George. All right. But, if some cases of this type must be admitted, I think we should define them carefully. A text would have to be drawn up.

Mr. McCormick. The American delegation abandons this Article 4, provided Belgium is sufficiently protected by the final text.

Mr. Lloyd George. I wouldn't like us to appear to be giving special treatment to Belgium and granting her what we are not granting France. France has suffered much more than Belgium. The latter has the right to equality, but I wouldn't accept a clause giving her privileged treatment. I see nothing that Belgium has the right to claim which is not mentioned in this text. As for defending the violated right, all we are doing here has no other objective.

M. Klotz. I have an addition to propose. The loss resulting from the necessity of redeeming the enemy's currency in reconquered territories and of reimbursing civilian and military prisoners for it must give rise to compensation. In fact, in all the territories he invaded, the enemy immediately imposed the mark at a rate of 1.25 francs. In the reconquered territories, we had to redeem all these marks at the same rate, despite their depreciation. The Belgian government is doing the same in Belgium. Isn't it fair that we be reimbursed for the difference?

I propose that that question be referred to the committee which will study the question of the interest due in the case of the mines, according to M. Loucheur's proposal.

Lord Sumner. Three different cases must be distinguished: that of prisoners, that of invaded and reconquered lands, and that of Alsace and Lorraine. The first raises no difficulty. The other two raise a political as well as a financial question.

I would remark that the Rumanians, the Serbs, the Poles would have much to claim under the same heading. In that case, that would become a considerable question, and the British, American, and Japanese delegates agree in thinking that it would be dangerous to admit the proposed clause. In any case, the question must not be handled by the financial experts, but by the heads of governments, taking political considerations into account.

Mr. Lloyd George. It seems to me almost impossible to accede to that request. To whom would you give the compensation? To the men who originally received those marks you are redeeming? No, because the paper has passed from hand to hand, while depreciation was increasingly felt. The last person who received those marks received them at their depreciated value. If we grant the compensation asked, it won't go to those who suffered the loss, but to others, and that, in the end, would amount to hundreds of millions of pounds sterling. We can't know where that will lead us.

M. Klotz. In Belgium and in northern France, the Germans posted notices from 1914 on, establishing the forced exchange of the mark at a rate of 1.25 francs, and suddenly, at the end of the occupation, the rate fell to .70 francs. I would observe that, even if we follow Mr. Lloyd George's reasoning, it remains nonetheless true that the French and Belgian governments are paying the difference and, consequently, are suffering a loss. It was impossible not to act in this way; the two states made up the difference and, consequently, are being robbed. I ask that what they have lost be repaid them.

M. Clemenceau. France was robbed, and what she is claiming is restitution. She asks nothing for Alsace, but she asks restitution for the invaded regions. In short, the loss has been absorbed by the French state, which has a right to compensation. I ask that this question be referred to a committee.

—(*Adopted.*)

Mr. Davis. Can you indicate for us a figure for the difference paid by the French government?

M. Clemenceau. One billion, without taking Alsace and Lorraine into account.

Mr. Lloyd George. I come to the special clause for Belgium, which I can't accept.

Mr. McCormick. All we want to do is to honor the commitment taken in our name by President Wilson in the seventh of his Fourteen Points. When Article 4 of the document under consideration was deleted, we said that we would reserve the rights of Belgium. If Belgium declares herself satisfied with the text when it is presented to her, we will have nothing to say: but until then, we reserve judgment.

Mr. Lloyd George. When the Belgian delegates see this text again, they can present all the observations they wish, and we will do justice to them if they are legitimate. But I refuse to insert an article into this text which would seem to grant Belgium something that would not be granted to France.

{ A P P E N D I X }[6]

REPARATION

1. The Allied and Associated Governments affirm the responsibility of the Enemy States for causing all the loss and damage to which the Allied and Associated Governments and their na-

[6] Printed in *PPC*, V, 55-58.

tionals have been subjected as a consequence of the war imposed upon them by the aggression of the enemy States.

2. The Allied and Associated Governments recognize that the financial resources of the enemy States are not unlimited, and, after taking into account permanent diminutions of such resources which will result from other treaty clauses, they judge that it will be impracticable for the enemy States to make complete reparation for all such loss and damage. The Allied and Associated Governments however, require, and the German Government undertakes that to the extent of her utmost capacity, she will make compensation for all damage done to the civilian population of the Allied or Associated Powers and to their property by her aggression by land, by sea and from the air.

3. The amount of such damage (as set forth under the specific categories attached hereto) for which compensation is to be made by the enemy States, shall be determined by an Inter-Allied Commission, to be constituted in such form as the Allied and Associated Governments shall forthwith determine. This Commission shall examine into the claims and give to the enemy States a just opportunity to be heard. The findings of the Commission as to the amount of damage defined as above shall be concluded and notified to the enemy States on or before May 1st, 1921, as representing the extent of their obligations. The Commission shall thereupon draw up a schedule of payments providing for the discharge for the entire obligation within a period of 30 years from May 1, 1921. In the event, however, that within the period mentioned, Germany shall have failed to discharge her obligation, then any balance remaining unpaid may, within the discretion of the Commission, be postponed for settlement in subsequent years: or may be handled otherwise in such manner as the Allied and Associated Governments, acting through the Commission, shall determine.

4. The inter-allied Commission shall thereafter, from time to time, consider the resources and capacity of Germany and, after giving her representatives a just opportunity to be heard, shall have discretion to extend the date, and to modify the form of payments, such as are to be provided for in Clause 3: but not to cancel any part, except with the specific authority of the several Governments represented upon the Commission.

5. In order to enable the Allied and Associated Powers to proceed at once to the restoration of their industrial and economic life, pending the full determination of their claim, Germany shall pay in such instalments and in such manner (whether in gold, commodities, ships, securities or otherwise) as the inter-allied commission may fix, in 1919 and 1920, the equivalent of $5,000,000,000 gold towards the liquidation of the above claims, out of which the expenses of the army of occupation subsequent to the Armistice shall first be met, provided that such supplies of food and raw materials as may be judged by the Allied and Associated Governments to be essential to enable Germany to meet her obligations for reparation may, with the approval of the Allied and Associated Governments, be paid for out of the above sum.

6. The successive instalments paid over by the Enemy States in satisfaction of the above claims shall be divided by the Allied and Associated Governments in proportions which have been determined upon by them in advance, on a basis of general equity, and of the rights of each.

7. The payments mentioned above do not include restitution in kind of cash taken away, seized or sequestrated, nor the restitution in kind of animals, objects of every nature and securities taken away, seized or sequestrated, in the cases in which it proves possible to identify them in enemy territory.

8. The attention of the four chiefs of the respective Governments is called to the following:

(a) That necessary guarantees to ensure the due collection of the sums fixed for reparation should be planned: and

(b) That there are other financial clauses which this conference has not been charged to deal with.

Compensation may be claimed under Clause 2 under the following categories of Damage.

I. (a) Damage to injured persons and to surviving dependents by personal injury to or death of civilians caused by acts of war (including bombardments or other attacks on land, on sea or from the air, and all the direct consequences thereof and of all operations of war by the two groups of belligerents wherever arising).

(b) Damage caused to civilian victims of acts of cruelty, violence or maltreatment, (including injuries to life or health as a consequence of imprisonment, deportation, internment or evacuation, of exposure at sea or of being forced to labour by the enemy) committed or ordered by the enemy wherever arising and to the surviving dependents of such victims.

(c) Damage caused to civilian victims of all acts of the enemy in occupied, invaded or enemy territory injurious to health or capacity for work, or to honour, and to the surviving dependents of such victims.

(d) Damage caused by any kind of maltreatment of prisoners of war.

(e) As damage caused to the peoples of the Allied and Associated Powers all pensions and compensations in the nature of pensions to naval and military victims of war, whether mutilated, wounded, sick or invalided, and to the dependents of such victims, the French scale to be adopted.

(f) Cost of assistance by the State to prisoners of war and to their families and dependents.

(g) Allowances by the State to the families and dependents of mobilised persons or persons serving with the forces.

II. (a) Damage caused to civilians by being forced by the enemy to labour without just remuneration.

(b) Damage caused to civilians by being compelled to abstain from all work as the only alternative to doing military work for the enemy or employing themselves on his armaments.

III. Damage in respect of all property wherever situated belonging to any of the Allied or Associated States or to any of their peoples, with the exception of military works or materials, which has been carried off, seized, injured or destroyed by the acts of the enemy on land, on sea or from the air or damaged directly in consequence of hostilities or of any operation of war.

IV. Interference with non-military property directly caused by acts of war on land, on sea or from the air or illegal acts of the enemy or war measures in the nature of requisitions or sequestrations taken by the enemy.

V. Damage in the form of levies, fines and other similar exactions imposed by the enemy upon the civilian population.

(VI. The U.S.A. para. 6 is dropped and their note also.)

XXIV

Conversation between MM. Clemenceau, Lloyd George, Orlando, and Colonel House*

APRIL 8, 1919, 11 A.M.

—Mr. Lloyd George reads aloud a dispatch from General Smuts.[1] The General was unable to persuade the Hungarian government to accept a changed line of demarcation, which would have allowed its troops to be moved eastwards, while respecting the boundary laid down by the Commission on Rumanian Affairs. It seems impossible to satisfy the Hungarians without breaking our word to the Rumanians.

M. Clemenceau (*to M. Orlando*). Your government proposes that we occupy Vienna. We received a formal letter on this subject from the Italian Ambassador.[2]

M. Orlando. We received a telegram from our legation in Switzerland informing us that the proclamation of a republic of soviets in Vienna is probable for the fourteenth of this month, unless Vienna is occupied by the Allies.

Mr. Lloyd George. Whom do you propose to send to occupy Vienna? If we followed these suggestions, why shouldn't we occupy all of Europe? Our representatives in Berlin speak the same language to us; there would be no reason to stop.

I want to present to you a list of questions which absolutely must be settled before we invite the Germans to come to negotiate with us.[3] I wonder if we aren't trying to settle too many questions before meeting the Germans. After all, we have enough time to determine the borders between the Czechs and the Poles or between the Rumanians and the Serbs. But as for the Germans, we only have to inform them of what we are taking from them. We will dispose of it in due course as we judge best. If we don't proceed in this way, we will be here forever.[4]

*H., *PPC*, V, 59ff.

[1] It is printed in *PWW*, Vol. 57, pp. 108-109.

[2] Marquis Guglielmo Imperiali, Italian Ambassador in Paris.

[3] For which see, *PWW*, Vol. 57, pp. 109-13. It included all outstanding issues and questions.

[4] Both the British and American delegations were at this time growing increasingly impatient with the slow progress of the conference. Two days earlier, Wilson had signaled his own frustration over the interminable delays, for which he squarely blamed the refusal of the French delegation to settle the questions of the Saar Basin and the Rhineland in conformity with the principles of the Four-

teen Points. Convinced that only a "bold stroke" could overcome the French crisis, Wilson decided on April 6 to take dramatic action. He called Dr. Grayson to his sickbed and, according to Grayson, told him the following:

"The President said: 'While you have me on my back I have been doing a lot of thinking, thinking what would be the outcome on the world if these French politicians were given a free-hand and allowed to have their way and secure all that they claim France is entitled to. My opinion is that if they had their way the world would go to pieces in a very short while. I hope that I can get things in hand and that we can work them out when I get up. But if we don't within a specified time, I am going to tell all of the Peace Commissioners plainly what I am going to do. And when I make this statement I do not intend it as a bluff. I am trying to formulate in my mind the exact procedure I am going to take.' He added: 'I wish you would communicate with Admiral Benson and find out what the movements are of the U.S.S. GEORGE WASHINGTON. If she is in an American port, order her to proceed to Brest, France, at once.' 'When I decide, doctor,' he said, 'to carry this thing through I do not want to say that I am going as soon as I can get a boat; I want the boat to be here.' " Grayson Diary, April 6, 1919, printed in *ibid.*, pp. 50-51.

In his meeting with the American commissioners later in the day, Wilson made it clear that, if no progress was made in the next few days on the question of France's eastern borders, he would tell Lloyd George and Clemenceau that, "unless peace was made according to their promises, which were to conform to the principles of the Fourteen Points, he would either have to go home or he would insist upon having the conferences in the open." House Diary, April 6, 1919, printed in *ibid.*, p. 53. That same night, Admiral Benson, as instructed by Grayson, sent a telegram to the Office of the Chief of Naval Operations, inquiring about the earliest possible date that the *George Washington* could sail from the United States and about its "probable earliest date of arrival" at Brest. The President, Benson added, desired that the movements of the vessel be expedited. Printed in *ibid.*, pp. 61-62.

When the news about Wilson's orders for the return of the *George Washington* was released to the press, American newspapers treated the episode as a major sensation and generally understood it as a "warning" or an "ultimatum" by Wilson to his colleagues in the Council of Four. Although the heavily censored French press minimized the significance of the incident, the fact that its implications alarmed the French government was clearly reflected in the news reports of April 7 and 8. In the wake of Wilson's announcement, the Paris papers, which, in the past weeks, had emphasized the differences between the French and American positions and had painted a pessimistic picture about the fate of the conference, suddenly denied emphatically that any real disagreements existed and predicted that the negotiations would be completed within several days. Moreover, the French authorities also realized immediately the importance of minimizing France's annexationist aims. Thus, in the afternoon of April 7, shortly after the news about the *George Washington* had been given out, a semiofficial statement in *Le Temps* declared that France had "no annexationist claim . . . to any territory inhabited by Germans." In an obvious allusion to the Saar Valley, the statement further pointed out that this pertained "particularly to the regions lying between the boundaries of 1871 and 1814." For a detailed discussion of the reaction to Wilson's announcement, see *ibid.*, pp. 63-65, and George Bernard Noble, *Policies and Opinions at Paris, 1919: Wilsonian Diplomacy, the Versailles Peace, and French Public Opinion* (New York, 1935), pp. 322-28.

I have received a telegram from the War Office informing me that the situation in Germany is deteriorating and that a catastrophe is feared. We have an interesting report on this subject from General Haking. General Wilson, who collects this information, thinks everything is falling apart there. Today, we learn of the proclamation of a soviet republic in Bavaria.[5] The danger is that when we ask the German delegates: "Whom do you represent?", they won't know what to answer. Time is working against us. That is why we must move ahead without too much attention to detail.

M. Clemenceau. I agree with you; but I don't think that advancing the date when the Germans will be summoned here will change the situation much. They told us that the solution of the question of victualing would greatly improve Germany's condition: food is beginning to arrive, and things are going from bad to worse. All we can do is move ahead as quickly as possible.

Colonel House. If people who represent no one come before us to negotiate, what will we do?

Mr. Lloyd George. We must think about that. General Wilson correctly tells me that it is up to Marshal Foch to consider how we must answer that question. We must also put it to our admirals. Assuredly, we have to begin to think about it straightaway.

Must we proceed to an occupation? Will it be necessary to renew the blockade? In any case, we must have a plan in readiness

---

[5] Following the assassination of the Bavarian Prime Minister, Kurt Eisner, on February 21, 1919, the political situation in Bavaria had been characterized by utter chaos and confusion, the absence of any single source of power and authority, and the lack of any consensus among the various moderate and radical left-wing parties and revolutionary councils which determined the fate of the Bavarian Republic in the spring of 1919. For weeks, Munich witnessed a fierce struggle between proponents of a parliamentary form of government and advocates of a socialist soviet republic ruled by workers', soldiers', and peasants' councils. Finally, a medley of radical leaders seized the initiative and, in a meeting on April 5, 1919, decided to establish a Bavarian soviet republic. Proclaimed on April 7, the first Bavarian Soviet Republic was headed by Independent Social Democrats, leaders of the Bavarian Peasants' League, and a number of socialist intellectuals without party affiliation. Ironically, the Communists refused to endorse what they called a "pseudo soviet republic," created by a revolution "proclaimed from a green table." As it turned out, the first soviet regime in Bavaria, which was marked above all by confusion and disarray, lasted but six days. As a result of an abortive *Putsch* by the moderate left, the Communists seized power and, on April 13, proclaimed the second Bavarian Soviet Republic. After a bloody civil war, it was overthrown by 35,000 Free Corps troops under the command of the Berlin government in early May. For a detailed discussion, see Allan Mitchell, *Revolution in Bavaria, 1918-1919: The Eisner Regime and the Soviet Republic* (Princeton, N. J., 1965), pp. 273-331.

so that we have only to take a decision. I suggest we ask our generals and admirals to prepare these plans, based on different possibilities: (1) if we have no one before us with whom to sign; (2) if the Germans refuse to sign.[6]

Colonel House. What will you do?

Mr. Lloyd George. We might have to occupy Berlin. But I don't know whether that will serve any purpose.

M. Clemenceau. I think it will; the Germans are a servile race.

M. Orlando. Personally, I don't favor occupations, whatever the opinion of certain representatives of Italy. But if it comes to that, I will remind you of what Erzberger told Marshal Foch, when we drew attention to the weakness of our right wing: it is useless to be very strong on the side facing Germany, if Bolshevism turns our Austrian flank. If we want to do something in that direction, it must be done with a certain symmetry and not leave one of our flanks exposed.

Mr. Lloyd George. We agree to consider what we must do, not only if Germany falls apart, but also if the situation deteriorates in Austria and neighboring countries.

M. Clemenceau. I am not much worried about symmetry from the strategic point of view; but I am very much concerned about the necessity of maintaining our military and political situation. We must not ask Marshal Foch: "Do you favor the occupation of Berlin or Vienna?" but: "From the military point of view, what measures would you advise if we have no one before us to sign the peace treaty, or if the enemy refuses to sign it, or if Germany can sign, but not Bavaria, supposing that it doesn't recognize the authority of the central German government?"

Colonel House. Can't we set a date now for meeting the Germans?

M. Clemenceau. We would risk having them wait if we are unprepared.

Mr. Lloyd George. Let's wait until Thursday to take a decision.

M. Clemenceau. I am afraid we have enough to do for this entire week. Aren't there still points to be decided concerning the military terms to be imposed on Germany?

Mr. Lloyd George. Nothing very important. There are only a few questions of first rank: that of reparation first, that of responsibilities, to which the English public attaches a very great importance. For it wouldn't for an instant allow to go unpunished the

---

[6] At this point, the council decided to instruct Marshal Foch and Admiral Wemyss to prepare reports as to what action they would advise, from a military and naval point of view, in the event that any of the Central Powers was unwilling or unable to sign the peace treaty. See PWW, Vol. 57, p. 104.

crimes of submarines, the ill-usage of prisoners, the violence committed against civilians, the abominable treatment of women and girls in invaded countries, the use of asphyxiating gas and other methods of warfare contrary to international law.

The questions the Economic Commission is studying are of primary importance; since the members of that commission are far from agreeing, things must be taken in hand and settled promptly.

On the question of the Saar, the report I have received from one of my advisers concludes that the plan submitted to us is not practicable; that was my conviction, but I didn't want to prevent consideration of this plan. We have to return to the plan of which I have already spoken. You can't grant ownership of the mines to France, with very extensive powers over the means of communication, etc., if, on the other hand, sovereignty remains with Germany. This would be a perpetual source of friction, with very serious risks of war.

I myself favor an arrangement that would establish a sort of Luxembourg in that region. The advantage of that arrangement is that you don't make the inhabitants French against their will, which we wouldn't accept. You leave them their language, their legislation, the right to govern themselves. I would apply this arrangement to a region more extensive than the Saar Valley, strictly speaking. We must include the entire industrial region whose economic life depends upon the mines and even go as far as the Moselle, for the question of the navigable waterways and canals to be built between the coal basin and the Moselle is a vital question.

I would grant this country independence, under the authority of the League of Nations. A customs union would attach it to France. In fact, there are no natural economic ties between this region and Germany; all its relations are with Alsace and Lorraine. If we say to the inhabitants: "You will not be French, and you will govern yourselves freely," no injustice is done them; and we mustn't forget that this country was mostly French until the beginning of the nineteenth century, that it was taken from France by force, despite the opposition of English statesmen at the time.

Mr. Haskins was no less impressed than our own representatives by the advantages of this arrangement. Our expert, Mr. Headlam-Morley, is very hostile to annexation to France but doesn't think we can make this region viable if we don't establish it as a political entity. There would be another advantage in having a kind of buffer state there, larger than Luxembourg, with a population of at least 600,000 inhabitants.

It is essential to make it part of the French customs system. Without Alsace and Briey, this area cannot live. I am convinced that, if a plebiscite took place a few years from now, those people wouldn't ask to return to Germany.

Colonel House. That statement seems to me very reasonable, and I wish to inform President Wilson about it immediately.

M. Clemenceau. I must remind you that President Wilson admitted, in the plan he transmitted to us, that there might be reason to study an administrative and political solution making it possible for the economic arrangement he contemplated to function.

Mr. Lloyd George. There is a strong analogy between this case and that of Danzig, and I think the same arrangement, or a similar one, will succeed in both cases. The life of Danzig depends entirely upon its commercial relations with Poland, just as the life of the Saar depends upon its economic relations with France, including Alsace and Lorraine. I would like to be able to extend this solution to Fiume as well.

M. Orlando. That is impossible!

Mr. Lloyd George. Three different plans have been submitted to me.[7] The first assumes that sovereignty remains with Germany, with economic administration in the hands of France. I reject that solution, for the reason I stated.

The second solution is the one I have just explained: local sovereignty under the authority of the League of Nations, with a local parliament, and a mandate given to France, which would appoint a governor while respecting local institutions. The country would be attached to France by a customs union. It would be completely disarmed, and its inhabitants could perform no military service. Ownership of the coal mines would belong to France, which would deduct the necessary administrative costs of the region from the output of these mines.

[7] They are printed in *ibid.*, pp. 113-17. The first two plans had been combined under the heading of A. & B. The combined plan left sovereignty over the Saar region to Germany but transferred administration of the area to the French, or transferred sovereignty to France and gave administration to the French. The third plan "C" established a separate state under the mandate of France.

XXV

Conversation between President Wilson and MM. Clemenceau, Lloyd George, and Orlando*

APRIL 8, 1919, 3 P.M.

M. Clemenceau. Mustn't we hear M. Paderewski on the question of the Polish boundaries?

President Wilson. If we transform these conversations into hearings, as we have done several times, I fear we will fall back into all the drawbacks of the procedures which we wished to change by meeting as the Four.

M. Clemenceau. It seems to me difficult not to hear M. Paderewski. I have seen him, and I think he will agree to the arrangement we have in mind for Danzig; but he is making strong objections to the assignment of Marienwerder to Germany because of the railway line that would be cut by the German boundary.

President Wilson. I think it better for each of us to hear M. Paderewski. As for the question of Marienwerder, I would remark that the use of the railway must in any case be guaranteed to Poland, just as we will guarantee to Germany the right to cross the territory of Danzig from the East to the West.

THE QUESTION OF RESPONSIBILITIES

President Wilson. Shall we discuss the report[1] article by article?

Mr. Lloyd George. It is better to proceed more broadly and to distinguish clearly between two categories of punishable acts. First, criminal acts, properly so-called; second, general orders contrary to international law. For example, the order given to submarines instituted actual piracy. Two hundred years ago, our privateers didn't sink ships without warning and didn't abandon crews to their fate.

President Wilson. I think you agree with me that the perpetrator of a purely negative act, for example, the officer who, by refusing to obey an order, would have been able to prevent a criminal act,

---

*Does not appear in H.

[1] That is, the majority report, with the reservations of the American members, Lansing and Scott, about which, see XVI, n. 2.

and who didn't do so, committed a crime from a moral point of view, but not from a legal point of view.

Mr. Lloyd George. We could begin with submarines. According to all established laws, their activity was nothing but piracy. According to the laws of war, we would have had the right to shoot all enemy sailors who took part in the submarine war. But we thought they had obeyed orders, and we preferred to make them prisoners and to wait until we could punish those who had given the criminal orders. The man, or the two or three men, who ordered the submarine campaign are obviously guilty. But this does not render certain crimes nugatory, like that of the commanders of submarines who fired upon shipwrecked crews.

President Wilson. There is general responsibility—that of Admiral Tirpitz, if you will—and responsibilities for execution, such as that of the officers who gave the inhuman orders of which you speak.

Mr. Lloyd George. In short, all those who are the source of criminal action are responsible.

It should be the same concerning ill-usage inflicted upon prisoners. If an order came from Berlin, the man who gave it must be punished. But given the unequal treatment of prisoners in the different camps, I am convinced that most often it was the head of the military district or of the camp who was responsible.

President Wilson. Mr. Lansing doesn't disagree with his colleagues concerning criminal acts, strictly speaking; what he finds difficult is to know how to judge them and according to what law. Shall we establish a tribunal which will make its own law by choosing among national laws? Mr. Lansing says that we have established courts-martial in each country, which judge crimes of this type; we might conceive of the fusion of these courts-martial—an international court-martial—on which French, English, Belgians, Italians, etc., would sit, with this tribunal applying laws in force either in the place where the crime took place or in the victims' country of origin. But I fear it would be difficult to catch the true culprits, because nothing is easier than to destroy the trace of orders given. I fear we may lack evidence.

Mr. Lloyd George. The man who committed the crime is responsible if he can't show the order from his commander.

A more difficult case is that of the violation of treaties. Here it is a matter of a crime against international law. Actually, the Treaty of 1839 created a league of four nations which guaranteed the neutrality of Belgium. The man who broke the pact and thereby caused the unspeakable sufferings of the entire world is the worst of criminals. We can treat him in two ways: either order his internment as a political measure, as the Allies did to Napoleon in 1815, or put him on trial. The method doesn't much matter to me, provided the man be punished and placed where he can't harm anyone; at the same time, we must set an example and prevent intrigues which might enable him to regain dangerous power. Send him to the Falkland Islands or Devil's Island. Do whatever you wish—it doesn't much matter to me.

M. Clemenceau. A solemn judgment is what will make the greatest impression.

President Wilson. What I want to do is to dishonor the Kaiser and avoid creating any kind of sympathy in his favor. If you refuse, according to the conclusions of the commission, to try him as the author of the war, which is to say, as the author of the decision which led immediately to the invasion of Belgium, you accuse him only for the method that he used to carry out his policy of violence. Unfortunately, there are many precedents in past wars.

Mr. Lloyd George. Not so; there is nothing like the invasion of Belgium in the War of 1870, nor in the wars which we have witnessed between Japan and Russia, between the United States and Spain. Those were open conflicts that were resolved by the appeal to arms, but without violation of an international treaty by those who themselves had guaranteed it.

M. Clemenceau. The German Emperor must be tried. The violation of law in the case of Belgium was so flagrant that the conscience of the peoples would not be satisfied if that act were treated in any other way than as a crime against public law.

President Wilson. It is indeed a crime, but one for which no sanction has been provided, because there is no legal precedent. Today, we are founding the regime of the League of Nations, from which new rules and formulas of international law will emerge. But today we have to create the principle and the penalty.

M. Clemenceau. The violation of a treaty calls for a sanction against the nation which is judged guilty of it. But if one man is responsible for what that nation did, will it satisfy us to know that three or four million Germans were killed and to allow the culprit to go free?

Mr. Lloyd George. Suppose the Kaiser alone, in peacetime, had crossed the frontier of Belgium with gun in hand and had fired on the inhabitants: the first Belgian policeman on the spot would have had the right to arrest him and to have him hanged; and because, instead of doing it himself, he sent a million men into Belgium, he should go unscathed?

M. Clemenceau. That's what our peoples would never understand.

President Wilson. Perhaps it would not be understood in the United States either; but I can only do what I believe is right, regardless of whether public feeling is for or against the judgment of my conscience.

Mr. Lloyd George. War between nations is justifiable according to precedents. But unprovoked aggression, without any grievance against the nation attacked, because it was advantageous to cross its territory, and despite a solemn commitment treated like a scrap of paper, is indisputably a crime.

President Wilson. What I seek is the severest lesson. I say: this is an unspeakable crime; but we didn't want to lower ourselves to the level of the criminal by abandoning principles of law, and we have treated him so as to spare him nothing of the universal contempt which should overwhelm him. We may have the right to take political precautions against a political danger; but we mustn't exalt the culprit by summoning him before the highest tribunal we can conceive. The worst punishment will be that of public opinion.

M. Clemenceau. Don't count on it.

Mr. Lloyd George. I also have my doubts on this subject. No sovereign was more contemptible than James II, whom we chased out in order to replace him by a Dutchman. But James II in exile became the symbol of legitimacy, and he had partisans who later sought to create disorder in England.

William II was the greatest commercial traveler of Germany and of the world. We remember his speeches on the merchant marine and all he did for the economic development of his country. The industrialists and businessmen in Germany will remember him with regret; they will think: "In his time, Germany was great and wealthy," and who knows what feelings and actions might follow? What we do must be a lesson for kings and for all those who have responsibility for government.

President Wilson. What would you propose to do?

Mr. Lloyd George. I would bring him to trial solely for violation of the Treaty of 1839. The tribunal would hear witnesses who would explain how the treaty was violated, who would recall the atrocities committed in Dinant, in Louvain, and I would then say to the court: "Judge!"

President Wilson. How would you envision the makeup of this tribunal?

Mr. Lloyd George. Members must be chosen from the highest jurisdictions of our different countries—from the French, Belgian, and Italian high courts of appeal, from the High Court of Appeal of Great Britain, from the American Supreme Court. But, in my opinion, Belgium must be the public prosecutor. As for us, we only came to Belgium as defenders of law, and I can guarantee you that, if we take judges from our courts, they will act with perfect impartiality. They are men of high conscience, without any responsibility to Parliament or public opinion.

President Wilson. This tribunal would be too large if each great power had three representatives.

Mr. Lloyd George. We must limit ourselves to the great powers, which would each have one representative. Belgium could play the role of public prosecutor.

President Wilson. In this case, I would add Serbia. Another question is whether the verdict must be by unanimous vote.

M. Clemenceau. In tribunals, a majority is sufficient.

Mr. Lloyd George. In our country, the jury must decide unanimously.

M. Clemenceau. In our country, the jury renders its verdict by majority.

M. Orlando. In Italy, also.

President Wilson. In all international transactions, the rule is to require unanimity.

Mr. Lloyd George. Yes, for deciding on matters at interest. But the problem we are considering is entirely different. Think about the effect that would be produced by the acquittal of the Emperor of Germany by one vote against four, and I wouldn't completely trust our Japanese friends. If we gave to a single vote—that of Japan—the right to pronounce the acquittal of the Kaiser, it would have a very bad effect in Europe.

President Wilson. It seems to me that we have sorted out this question in its main outline. I would like to hear M. Orlando's opinion.

M. Orlando. I appointed two delegates to the commission: one a professor of law in the University of Rome, the other a counselor to our High Court of Appeal, both legal experts of great ability. I left them entirely free. They accept the conclusions of the majority; I therefore accept them also. But if I must express my personal opinion, I think we have no right to punish. I repeat that I leave the matter to the considered opinion of my legal experts, and that is why I have refrained from participating in your discussion up to now. But, in my opinion, crime is essentially a violation of the domestic law of each national entity, a violation of a subject's obligation towards his sovereign. To create a different precedent is a serious thing.

One can say that practical necessity forces us to create law.

Undoubtedly! But we should fear the consequence of a violation of established principles. We could find ourselves faced with difficulties which we won't know how to resolve because we are no longer sure of our principle. The Italian government supports the commission's conclusions. But since you ask my personal opinion, I give it to you frankly.

President Wilson. I asked M. Orlando to answer us as a lawyer. We have distinguished between two clearly different cases. The first is the violation of recognized laws of war, with penalties provided when those guilty of such acts are captured during hostilities. For crimes of this type, I suggest the creation of a military tribunal to apply the established rules. Here we can base ourselves upon known principle and procedure. The second question is that of the responsibility of heads of state, and the Kaiser in particular; here, we are venturing into completely unexplored territory.

But what does M. Orlando think about the first point?

M. Orlando. I heard Mr. Lloyd George's observation when he said, speaking of the crews of submarines: "We had the right to hang those men as pirates." According to the laws of war, that would have been justified. But can we apply in peacetime a law which assumes a state of war and ongoing hostilities? Moreover, we will have the greatest difficulty in determining responsibility. A general who takes prisoners can recover their orders on the battlefield, if they are carrying any. But we are no longer at war; will we be able to trace these orders to their source?

What we have the right to do is to require the Germans themselves to judge those who are accused of certain crimes. But I am unable to conceive of an international court established in peacetime to judge by applying a wartime principle.

As for the heads of state, it seems to me that there would be less hypocrisy in imposing a punishment on them by the peace treaty on whatever grounds you wish; but I am unable to understand how we can summon them before a tribunal. Until now, heads of state have been considered in all they do as representatives of collectives. It is the collectivity that is in fact responsible for their errors; it is the people who pay for them, and it must be said that, in the case before us—that of Germany—the people and the sovereign are surely one. But we would be establishing a completely new principle if we wanted to punish as an individual a man who was acting as the instrument of the collectivity.

M. Clemenceau. We have examples: Louis XVI in France, Charles I in England.

APRIL 8, 1919

M. **Orlando.** In both cases, the issue was a domestic one. In the international field, the law you are trying to establish can't be based on any precedent.

M. **Clemenceau.** Was there a precedent on the day when liberty was given to men for the first time? Everyone must assume his own responsibility, and I assume mine.

I don't understand M. Orlando's argument. He asks: are we going to apply the laws of war in peacetime? For me, one law dominates all others: that of responsibility. Civilization is the organization of human responsibilities. M. Orlando says: "Yes, within each nation." I say: "In the international field." I say this along with President Wilson who, by establishing the foundations of the League of Nations, has had the honor of transferring the essential principles of national law into international law.

What we want to do today is essential if we want to see international law established. None of us doubts that William II bears responsibility for the war. I agree with M. Orlando on the solidarity of the German people with their sovereign. However, there is one man who gave the order, whilst the others followed it. We are told: "It is better to exile him and to expose him to the scorn of the world, without convicting him." It is a sanction which can be defended; it is not the one I prefer. Today we have a perfect opportunity to carry into international law the principle of responsibility which is at the basis of national law.

There is no precedent? There never is a precedent. What is a precedent? I'll tell you. A man comes; he acts—for good or evil. Out of the good he does, we create a precedent. Out of the evil he does, criminals—individuals or heads of state—create the precedent for their crimes. We have no precedent? But that is our best argument. Was there a precedent in recent generations for the atrocities committed by the Germans during the present war—for the systematic destruction of wealth in order to end competition, for the torture of prisoners, for submarine piracy, for the abominable treatment of women in occupied countries? To those precedents, we will oppose a precedent of justice.

Our judges, who will meet in the tribunal we propose to establish, will be accustomed to applying different laws. We will ask them to unite their consciences in a concept of equity. We shall assemble the greatest judges in England, France, America, and Italy. We shall tell them: "Seek amongst yourselves the principles upon which you must rely in order to judge the greatest crime of history."

If necessary, I will resign myself to a solution which is not mine. But I beg the heads of state to reflect that, if they follow my advice, they will do for their own glory an unprecedented thing—I admit it—in establishing international justice, which up to now has existed only in books, and which we will at last make a reality.

President Wilson. A practical question arises. We don't have the legal means to compel Holland to deliver the Kaiser to us.

Mr. Lloyd George. No, but we can tell Holland that if she refuses, she won't be admitted into the League of Nations.

President Wilson. Referring to crimes by individuals, M. Orlando said: "Beware of applying in peacetime a wartime principle against the violation of the laws of war." In his capacity as a lawyer, what does he think it possible to impose upon the Germans in the peace treaty? Can we extend, so to speak, the procedure of wartime in the period following the war?

M. Clemenceau. It would be too easy for the criminals if peace annulled all responsibilities. Believe me; amongst the peoples who have suffered for these five years, nothing would sow so many real seeds of hatred as an amnesty granted to all the criminals.

Mr. Lloyd George. We have the right to say that, for us, the war won't be ended so long as the enemy hasn't handed over those who are judged guilty of certain crimes. Along with the question of reparation, this is the one of greatest concern to English public opinion, and we couldn't sign a peace treaty which left it unresolved.

President Wilson. Ideas are beginning to become clearer about this. Nevertheless, you will allow me, because of the special competence of Mr. Lansing in the field of international law, not to take a final decision without speaking with him.

Mr. Lloyd George. In England we have called together six or seven of our greatest authorities on matters of international law, including Sir Frederick Pollock. They concluded unanimously in favor of arraigning the Kaiser, as well as all those who committed crimes against international law. The British government bases its opinion on the conclusions of these legal experts

M. Orlando. I must add that, after having read the commission's report, I discussed the conclusions with the Italian delegates whom I just mentioned. We had a serious, even stormy discussion. But they kept to their point of view, and I didn't want to impose mine upon them.

In my opinion, the only principle which justifies our action is M. Clemenceau's. I accept M. Clemenceau's views, because they raise us above legal technicalities; it is history that is taking place here, it is no longer law. If we consult the code, we will have great difficulty in finding what we seek there. If we speak only about international morality, it is different.

I still insist that Italy has as much to say on this subject of crimes committed as the other Allied nations. The number of Italian ships sunk by submarines on the high seas constitutes a higher proportion of our merchant fleet than do the losses suffered by the English merchant marine. One hundred thousand Italians died in the enemy's prisoner-of-war camps, victims of the ill-usage they suffered.

THE QUESTION OF THE SAAR

President Wilson. Since we seem to be agreeing on this question of responsibilities, I would like to speak to you about another question which we have to resolve—that of the Saar Basin.

I have received a new report from my experts.[2] It seems to them, and to me, very difficult to establish a semi-independent state in that region. It would be a mistake to create a new political entity there unless it is absolutely necessary.

I have received M. Tardieu's plan concerning the economic aspect of the question.[3] It seems very practical to me; but certain elements are missing, as is indicated in the document which I now submit to you.[4]

I would propose, not to end German sovereignty over the territory of the Saar, but to establish there—in order to settle all the litigious questions which could arise from the economic point of view on account of the special situation granted to France—a permanent arbitration commission charged with interpreting the treaty and making the regulations necessary for its proper execution. That commission would be composed of five members—a Frenchman, a German, and three members appointed by the League of Nations. The expenses of the commission would be divided between France and Germany. Upon the expiration of a period of fifteen years, the inhabitants would be consulted about their future political status by means of a plebiscite, this plebiscite taking place by district and commune, according to a method of voting determined by the League of Nations. It is this consultation which would finally decide the territorial sover-

[2] From David Hunter Miller and Charles H. Haskins, which Wilson summarizes below. For the report, see *PWW*, Vol. 57, pp. 119-20.
[3] It is printed in *ibid.*, pp. 55-59.
[4] Printed in *ibid.*, p. 118.

eignty over the whole and over all the parts composing that region. If certain districts should return finally to Germany, that power could repurchase ownership of the mines by payment in gold.

M. Clemenceau. The main thing is to make exploitation possible. I don't think this arrangement would give us the required security.

President Wilson. Its great advantage is to eliminate the political difficulty raised by an immediate transfer of sovereignty.

Mr. Lloyd George. My advisers are clearly of opinion that the functioning of the economic arrangement proposed by M. Tardieu is incompatible with German sovereignty.

President Wilson. According to M. Tardieu, France would have the police in the region.

Mr. Lloyd George. It is almost annexation to France. But Germany would retain title to sovereignty and could intervene, no longer to do anything positive or useful there, but in order to disorganize and disturb everything.

President Wilson. I continue to repeat that I am opposed to the arbitrary creation of an independent state in the Saar Valley. This case cannot be compared to that of Luxembourg, which is a small historical entity. Rather, I would compare it to the Pittsburgh area, if this same problem arose there. There you have a large industrial district, with a floating population, Italian workers, for example, who are only transient. No common political tradition, nothing upon which an independent society could be established.

The difficulties that appear to be feared seem to me to be largely imaginary. In certain industrial districts of the United States, large private companies have their own police, which operate in the factories and coal basin, without any conflict with local or federal authorities. The arbitration commission which I propose to establish will prevent or settle disputes on questions of ownership or exploitation; and, in the end, a plebiscite will decide the fate of the region.

M. Clemenceau. Would a customs union with France be established?

President Wilson. All industrial operations would be carried out under the French customs system.

M. Clemenceau. We will study that; but I fear such an arrangement could only lead to endless disputes.

President Wilson. I ask you now not to let world peace be hung up on this question of the Saar.

M. Clemenceau. No, but world peace requires that we first establish justice amongst ourselves.

President Wilson. In my opinion, we have spent too much time discussing questions which exclusively concern the four powers represented here.

Mr. Lloyd George. They are, after all, the ones which together carried the burden of the war.

XXVI

Conversation between President Wilson and MM. Clemenceau, Lloyd George, and Orlando*

APRIL 9, 1919, 11 A.M.

President Wilson reads a text on the question of responsibilities:

"1. All persons guilty of crimes against the laws of war to be tried by military tribunals in the usual way and sentenced, if convicted, to the usual punishments. In case the crime was against the nationals of only one of the belligerents, the trial to be by the military tribunals of that belligerent. In case the crime was against the nationals of several of the belligerents, the trial to be by a military tribunal made up out of the personnel of the military tribunals of the belligerents affected. The accused in every case to be entitled to name his own counsel.

"2. Request to be made of Holland to deliver the ex-Kaiser into the hands of the Allied and Associated Powers for trial before a special tribunal, that tribunal to consist of five judges, one of such judges to be appointed by each of the five Powers here named; namely, the United States of America, Great Britain, France, Italy and Japan; the offense for which it is proposed to try him not to be described as a violation of criminal law but as a supreme offense against international morality and the sanctity of treaties. The punishment to be determined upon is left to the tribunal selected, which is expected to be guided by the highest motives of international policy with a view to vindicating the solemn obligations of international undertakings and the validity of international morality."[1]

*Does not appear in H.

[1] This document prepared by Wilson, was signed by him, Lloyd George, Clemenceau, and Orlando on April 9. Marquis Saionji, a Japanese plenipotentiary, signed the document later. See PWW, Vol. 57, p. 631.

President Wilson adds: I remind you of the objections which were made by the Japanese delegation; but, it seems to me, they don't exactly run counter to this text.

Mr. Lloyd George. Although it hasn't been expressly stated, at the root of the Japanese objections is the idea of divine right; it is a notion that Europe has abandoned forever.

President Wilson. In any case, the Japanese representatives must take part in our decision. Shouldn't they be summoned?

Mr. Lloyd George. I think it is better to wait, in order to present to them at the same time all questions of a general nature in which Japan is interested.

I think the formulas proposed to us by the President cover all cases of violation of international law which we want to punish. It will be easy for us to prove that these crimes are not, as the Germans have alleged, merely reprisals against our actions, nor are they justifiable as new methods of warfare. Concerning poisonous gases, for example, I could show you in indisputable documents that, during the Crimean War, the British government rejected a proposal suggesting the use of sulfurous gas. That proposal, made again at the beginning of the war of 1914 by Mr. Winston Churchill, was rejected a second time as contrary to principles we did not want to abandon.

Hence the Germans don't have the right to say that they introduced a new element into the war by means of an invention which we regretted not having made ahead of them; we had the invention, and we refused to use it.

THE QUESTION OF THE SAAR

Mr. Lloyd George. We have all received a copy of M. Tardieu's memorandum in reply to the proposal made yesterday by the President of the United States.[2] It is a document whose argument has much force, and it deserves careful reading.

President Wilson. What makes the solution of this problem difficult is that the only certain justification of anything we can do in the Saar Basin is France's right to reparation for her economic losses; that doesn't justify a change of territorial sovereignty.

Mr. Lloyd George. In this problem, there is something besides the simple question of reparation: there is the past. I recall once

[2] It is printed in *ibid.*, pp. 155-59. The Tardieu memorandum criticized the new Wilson plan mainly on the ground that it created an administrative structure that was unworkable and was bound to lead to endless disputes between France and Germany.

again the English government's repugnance in 1815 at allowing Prussia to annex this territory. There is the fact that part of the people of this district have retained anti-Prussian sentiments.

I note that M. Tardieu accepts a plebiscite in his memorandum; it is a great concession, it opens the way for you to agree to place the Saar Valley under a special political administration.

—*The question is postponed until the afternoon session.*

THE GERMAN-POLISH BOUNDARY

Mr. Lloyd George. We have received information about the work of the small special committee which last studied the question of the Polish boundary.[3] I see that, in the small state which we propose to create around Danzig, there will be 324,000 inhabitants, of whom only 16,000 will be Poles. In the region of Marienwerder, whose fate will be settled by a plebiscite and which can, if the population so decides, be joined to East Prussia, there are 169,000 inhabitants, the number of Poles being no more than 26,000. This justifies the policy we have supported.

President Wilson. This text gives the Poles the necessary guarantees for their communication with the sea.

Mr. Lloyd George. We are devising equivalent guarantees for German communications between West Prussia and East Prussia and, for the Poles, between Danzig and Warsaw.

M. Orlando. How many Germans would remain on Polish soil after the change of the border proposed by the committee?

President Wilson. There are more than two million.

M. Orlando. Let us say 2,200,000. If you subtract 450,000 around Danzig and from Marienwerder, nearly 1,800,000 will still remain in Poland.

President Wilson. I concede that it can't be otherwise, since these German populations are scattered, and their presence is due in large measure to systematic colonization.

Mr. Lloyd George. That is inevitable. What we want to avoid is taking from Germany territories which have always been part of East Prussia, even when Poland was independent.

—*Reading of the text concerning Danzig: the city, with the surrounding territory, will be made into an autonomous state under the authority of the League of Nations. It will be attached by a customs union to Poland,*

[3] Composed of Haskins, Headlam-Morley, and Tardieu. This committee had not yet made its formal report, but had agreed on its provisions concerning Danzig and Marienwerder. See Nelson, *Land and Power*, pp. 185-87.

which will in addition have ownership of the railways, free use of the port of Danzig, and the control of the foreign relations of the state thus established.

—Reading of the text concerning the region of Marienwerder: the fate of this region will be settled by a plebiscite, which will take place by universal suffrage, including women, and by commune, the area being first evacuated by German and Polish armies and placed under the provisional administration of an inter-Allied commission.

—M. Paderewski is introduced.

President Wilson. At this time, we are doing our best to arrive at a settlement of Polish affairs in such a way as not to provoke grave dangers in the future. We are striving to follow lines indicated by ethnography and to secure Poland's indispensable communications with the sea, without including more Germans than necessary in the Polish state. Our wish is to establish the Polish state on a foundation that will give it as few enemies as possible.

The plan we have prepared can be summarized as follows, and I assure you that there is no question that has been studied more conscientiously: Danzig will cease to belong to Germany and will form, along with the adjacent territory, a different and autonomous political entity. It will be included in the Polish customs union and subordinated to Poland for all its foreign relations. We have provided secure guarantees for Poland's free communication with the port of Danzig. Polish sovereignty will be established over the course of the Vistula, over the railway parallel to this river, and over the territory lying on its left bank. The free use of the railway from Danzig to Mława will be assured to the Germans, allowing East Prussia to communicate with Germany proper.

Concerning the concentrated German group which is located to the southeast of Danzig, we propose to apply the same principle as in the southern part of East Prussia: a plebiscite will allow the population to decide its own fate for itself.

Our concern is to spare Poland the dangers which the existence of a *Germania irredenta* would cause her. We know from past experience that there is no more serious and lasting cause of international conflict. We ask you for your observations on the advantages and disadvantages of this plan.

M. Paderewski. I am not very well prepared for this discussion; I didn't expect to be called today. But I am authorized to express the feeling of my country. The Polish Diet, which is probably the most democratic assembly in existence in the world today, conveys to you its respect and complete confidence. It begs me to transmit its best wishes.

It wants, first of all, a complete alliance with the Entente; it also wants to have the territorial guarantees necessary for our very existence. Unfortunately, we know the Germans better than you do; we have been their neighbors and victims for seven centuries. Please believe me: however little is taken from Germany, there will always be a *Germania irredenta*.

The Germans are playing a rather crafty diplomatic game at the moment, and we are in danger of being its first victims. Danzig is indispensable to Poland, which cannot breathe without this window on the sea. Patriotic feeling has allowed the Polish government to maintain order in Poland. Our country is surrounded by a furious assault of disorder and violence; it stands as the fortress of political order in eastern Europe. But our situation is only maintained thanks to our confidence in you. If that confidence should be betrayed, the disappointment, the despair which would result, could lead to a catastrophe and open the doors to Bolshevism.

Poland must be strong, and she cannot be strong without Danzig.

If we study the districts inhabited by German peoples along the length of the Mława line, we see that, according to the statistics, the district of Stuhm has a Polish population of 47 per cent. But if one takes as a basis the number of Polish-speaking children in the schools—a more authentic figure—that proportion rises to 59 per cent. In the district of Marienwerder, the Polish children constitute 47 per cent of the school population.

Mr. Lloyd George. Isn't that an argument in favor of a plebiscite?

M. Paderewski. Those people are still frightened; they don't feel strongly enough that we are victorious over the Germans.

Mr. Lloyd George. Guarantees of a free vote would be assured. We are providing for the evacuation of these territories by all military forces, the temporary establishment of an inter-Allied administration. If your figures are correct—and I have no intention of contesting them—the plebiscite would go in your favor.

M. Paderewski. In that entire region, German civil servants and soldiers comprise 11.45 per cent of the population. In the district of Rosenberg—the most Germanized—the Polish population constitutes only 17 per cent of the total; but, on the other hand, 19 per cent are civil servants and soldiers.

With regard to the city of Danzig, if it is consulted, not by German officials, but under conditions that would permit it to express itself freely, I am convinced that it would vote for annexation to Poland; that is in its economic interest.

Mr. Lloyd George. If it is impossible for you purely and simply to annex Danzig, would you accept a popular referendum as a last resort?

M. Paderewski. Our Diet, which is an assembly of peasants and workers, with a small number of representatives from the petite bourgeoisie, has very democratic feelings and wants no conquests. But it unanimously demands Danzig; it's the voice of the Polish people, of whom I am the servant. The representatives of Poland are making the incorporation of Danzig into the Polish state a condition *sine qua non*, like the reunion of Upper Silesia to our territory, like the reintegration of Lemberg. They also want federation with Lithuania.

Mr. Lloyd George. On this last question, I believe there has been no report presented.

M. Paderewski. For us, the question of Danzig is a matter of life or death.

President Wilson. Our intention is to place Danzig entirely at the disposal of Poland. We would like to make it a free city, such as it was in the Middle Ages, within the customs frontier of Poland, which will have in every respect the same economic rights in the port of Danzig as if she had sovereignty there.

Mr. Lloyd George. It is a sort of home rule for Danzig. Foreign relations being in your hands, Danzig has less autonomy vis-à-vis Poland than Canada has vis-à-vis England.

M. Paderewski. But Danzig would remain in the hands of the Germans, and consequently of Germany, to which it would return in the end.

President Wilson. Didn't you say—and we also believe it on the basis of our information—that the economic interest of Danzig's population must lead it to the side of Poland?

M. Paderewski. We must take national feeling into account; Germany is not yet knocked out.

Mr. Lloyd George. Really?

M. Paderewski. She challenges you over the passage through Danzig; she uses revolution and Bolshevism as means towards her ends.

President Wilson. Do you believe that Germany, for a political goal, can long employ methods which ruin her?

M. Paderewski. The instinct for obedience amongst the Germans is an amazing thing; they are capable of making or of stopping revolutions on order. In eastern Poland, we see German troops, as they withdraw, themselves preparing quarters for the Bolsheviks.

Germany can give up Danzig; she has an entire series of great ports—Emden, Bremen, Hamburg, Stettin, Königsberg; that is enough for her 60 million inhabitants. And are the 25 million Poles not to have a single port?

President Wilson. On the contrary, we want to insure you the use of the port of Danzig, while establishing a system of government there which creates the least possible danger for the future.

M. Paderewski. We are prepared to treat the Germans well who will reside on Polish territory; we won't imitate their persecutions.

President Wilson. Our desire is to leave Germany with no pretext to seek a quarrel with you.

M. Clemenceau. Wouldn't you consent to a plebiscite?

M. Paderewski. I am prepared for all the plebiscites that one might wish in order to settle the difficulties we will have with our friends—towards Lithuania, or towards Bohemia—but not with our enemies.

The question wouldn't be resolved, moreover, even if we had Danzig, if you didn't at the same time give us the territory through which the route which links Danzig to Poland passes; isn't it better, if we must choose, to sacrifice 300,000 Germans rather then 25 million Poles?

Mr. Lloyd George. If Danzig preferred to be Polish, or if, fearing the creation of a port at a neighboring point on the coast, she turned voluntarily to you, that would be the best solution. What we don't want is to create an Alsace-Lorraine question in Danzig, so that Germany could assume the posture of a victim.

President Wilson. Won't you be satisfied if you have special guarantees for the use of the railways?

M. Paderewski. We know the Germans too well to rely on any guarantees they may accept. We have seen them be always the same, ever since the tenth century; we have been familiar with their scraps of paper for a long time. I might remind you of the story of the grand master of the Teutonic Order, who having signed a treaty with several Pomeranian and Polish princes of the coastal region, invited them to a banquet during which he had them assassinated. That is the kind of treaties we have made with Germany in the past.

I ask you to ponder what I have told you and to inform me of your conclusions.

President Wilson. We were anxious to hear you, and I thank you for having responded to our appeal.

XXVII

Conversation between President Wilson and MM. Clemenceau, Lloyd George, and Orlando*

APRIL 9, 1919, 3:30 P.M.

THE QUESTION OF THE SAAR

President Wilson. I have read the three plans presented by the British delegation on the question of the Saar. All three entail Germany's renunciation of sovereignty over the Saar Basin. In my opinion, this would prejudice the result of the popular referendum which is to take place fifteen years after the signing of the peace treaty. I consulted Professor Haskins about this matter, and it seems to me that any plan that eliminates German sovereignty and substitutes that of the League of Nations, with a mandate conferred upon France, would only provide an ambiguous solution to the problem.

Moreover, as I have already said very frankly, I am afraid of a solution of this type for reasons of principle. However, I don't want to hold inflexibly to the letter of the principle if a reasonable solution can be reached. What I would reject is an arrangement which would prejudice the outcome of the plebiscite.

I propose to require Germany to leave this region for fifteen years under the administration of a commission appointed by the League of Nations and responsible to it. The people would keep their laws, their present institutions, with the commission having power to institute changes necessitated by the special economic arrangement established by the treaty. At the same time, I would give this commission the functions of a court of arbitration to settle all disputes arising from the application of the treaty, whilst it would have legislative and executive power over the entire region.

Fundamental rules would be established to insure to the people complete religious freedom, respect for their educational institutions, etc. In short, Germany's sovereignty would be suspended for a period of fifteen years, and, at the end of that period, the people would decide their fate for themselves by a plebiscite.

*Does not appear in H.

The other solutions proposed remove the country from German sovereignty without placing it under French sovereignty, and give it a French governor appointed by the League of Nations. I prefer the arrangement I have just explained, which places the country under a provisional administration while awaiting the result of the plebiscite.

Mr. Lloyd George. It seems to me that this plan answers the objections raised by M. Tardieu in the memorandum he presented to us about the earlier plan.

M. Clemenceau. I understand that German sovereignty would be suspended and administration assigned to the League of Nations. But in this case, why should the League of Nations not give a mandate to France?

Mr. Lloyd George. I would point out to you that the entire economic life of the region would already be in France's hands.

President Wilson. I am seeking with all my strength a solution which satisfies you and satisfies me; I see none acceptable with the abolition of German sovereignty. The statements we have made, the commitments I have undertaken, promise France reparation for the wrong done her in 1871. Perhaps it would have been better to have said: "The wrong done to France in Alsace-Lorraine," or any other formula which would have included the violation of the rights of France in 1815. But only the Treaty of Frankfurt was mentioned, and we are bound by what we have said.[1]

I cannot return to the United States and say to the American people: "After consideration, we found it convenient to go back on our word." They would answer me that we had committed ourselves by the terms of the Armistice and by the statements we made at the time it was signed.

I ask you to help me find a path in your direction. I have taken many steps to meet you; do not make it impossible for me to help you as much as I can.

Mr. Lloyd George. The most important thing for France is to have the coal of the Saar.

M. Clemenceau. That depends upon which public opinion you are thinking of; it is obviously true of the French industrialists. But the rest of France attaches another importance to the Saar region.

Mr. Lloyd George. A solution must be reached which gives France the coal of the Saar without creating new causes for conflict in

---

[1] "VIII. . . . and the wrong done to France by Prussia in 1871 in the matter of Alsace-Lorraine. . . ."

the future. The document criticized by M. Tardieu didn't fulfill that condition, and M. Tardieu's criticisms were fair. But the same objections don't apply to what President Wilson has just proposed. Germany's sovereignty would be suspended during the period of the fifteen years which will precede the plebiscite. During these fifteen years, France will have time to recover economically and, at the end of that period, the Saar region will be so closely tied to France by its interests that it will go voluntarily to her.

M. Clemenceau. I make no objection to this plan. I would only like to have it carefully studied by my advisers.

Mr. Lloyd George. It might be interesting to hear the impressions of the experts immediately.

—MM. Tardieu and Headlam-Morley are introduced.

M. Clemenceau. President Wilson is going to explain a new solution to the Saar problem.

President Wilson. The decision we have to take must be based upon our public commitments. We declared that "the wrong done to France in 1871"—and not "in 1815"—must be redressed. I want to act scrupulously towards Germany, for the very reason of her own lack of scruple.

The latest solution proposed would actually give the region to France, with a plebiscite which would be hardly more than a formality. There is an objection to that which I find insuperable, and here is what I propose.

German sovereignty would be suspended for fifteen years and transferred, in fact, to the League of Nations, which would be represented in the Saar region by a commission which would receive a clearly defined mandate. Except for the economic administration, conferred on France under terms which you know, the people would keep their laws, which the commission could change as required to accommodate them to the necessities of French economic control. At the same time, it would act as a court of arbitration. At the end of the fifteen-year period, a plebiscite would take place to settle the question of sovereignty in a final manner.

I said to M. Clemenceau that I am compelled to remain faithful to my Fourteen Points, but without inflexibility, and going as far as possible to meet your legitimate wishes. We are not prejudging the question of sovereignty; we are leaving it in suspense.

M. Tardieu. The commission would have administrative power?

President Wilson. And legislative.

M. Tardieu. How does this plan differ from one of Mr. Lloyd George's proposals, which would transfer administration to the League of Nations?

Mr. Lloyd George. One of our proposals did in fact envisage the administration of the region by the League of Nations, with Germany theoretically retaining sovereignty.

M. Clemenceau. The difference is that here the sovereignty is transferred to the League of Nations for fifteen years.

President Wilson. It is not necessary to use the word "sovereignty." We would only say that the administration of the region passes into the hands of the League of Nations for the contemplated period.

Mr. Lloyd George. Isn't it necessary to have M. Tardieu and Mr. Headlam-Morley study your text?

President Wilson. What I bring you is only an outline. I asked Professor Haskins to formulate the plan with all the necessary details. It is better to discuss a well-defined text. As I see it, the essential point is to leave the question of sovereignty open and to assure respect for local institutions, except as it might perhaps be necessary to accommodate them to the necessities of the new economic order.

M. Clemenceau. In your system will it be possible to remove Prussian civil servants?

President Wilson. The commission will have all powers.

Mr. Headlam-Morley. But wouldn't the inhabitants be under a dictatorial regime? Would they have a voice in education and all their local interests?

Mr. Lloyd George. It would be very advantageous to give them the beginnings of local autonomy on local questions; nothing will help them more to detach themselves from Prussia. A people which has acquired these kinds of rights doesn't want to be deprived of them.

President Wilson. It is very difficult for us to decide here, in this room, what will best suit these people. Let us give the commission power to organize a system of local government agreeable to the people themselves. Would they like an assembly? Would they be content to have organizations to deal with educational questions or other questions of local interest? It is the right of those people themselves to make this known.

M. Tardieu. They won't be represented in the Reichstag?

President Wilson. No, no more than in the French chambers.

M. Tardieu. We will confer, Mr. Headlam-Morley and I, and we will come back to present our report to you.

M. Clemenceau. I foresee a satisfactory agreement on these terms.

President Wilson. The most important thing is to adjust this plan to the economic terms upon which we have already agreed.

—MM. Tardieu and Headlam-Morley withdraw.

THE VICTUALING OF RUSSIA

—President Wilson reads aloud the report which has been submitted about M. Nansen's proposal,[2] suggesting the organization of the victualing of Russia by neutral nations.

—The greatest difficulty appears to be tonnage.

Mr. Lloyd George. From the political point of view, the most important question is that of distribution in the interior of Russia. I don't see any organization which can take charge of this distribution, except the Bolshevik government. Would M. Nansen care to give Lenin the power that would be conferred upon him by the

---

[2] For the Nansen plan, see F. Nansen to WW, April 3, 1919, PWW, Vol. 56, pp. 575-76. Nansen was Fridtjof Nansen, a famous Norwegian Arctic explorer and oceanographer. He had recently come to Paris because of his concern over the Russian situation and the plight of the prisoners of war of all nations.

The Nansen plan proposed that a commission of Norwegian, Swedish, and possibly Danish and Swiss members be organized along the lines of the Belgian Relief Commission to collect and deliver foodstuffs and medical supplies to Russia.

Herbert Hoover and Colonel House originally conceived of what became the Nansen plan, and Nansen's letter to Wilson of April 3 was originally drafted by House, Hoover, and other members of the American delegation. At this point in this meeting, the council had before it a proposed reply to Nansen that had been drafted by William Christian Bullitt of the American delegation, with a few changes made by David Hunter Miller and Gordon Auchincloss. This draft reply, which would be sent to Lenin alone, responded positively to Nansen's suggestion but pointed out that there would be great difficulties involved in getting food to the warring parts of Russia. The distribution of the food, the draft reply went on, should be left to the people of Russia themselves. However, in order for the Nansen plan to have any chance of success, all hostilities in Russia should cease, and the transfer of all troops and war materials of all kinds to and within Russian territory should be completely suspended. Printed in PWW, Vol. 57, pp. 93-94.

Although the Mantoux notes do not reveal the fact, the Big Four approved this draft with a few changes on April 17. Nansen then incorporated both his letter to Wilson of April 3 and the reply of the Big Four in a telegram to Lenin on April 17, but he was not able to transmit the telegram until about May 4, because the French, British, and others refused to send it. For Nansen's telegram to Lenin, which was sent from Berlin, see ibid., pp. 438-40.

For a discussion of all these events, see John M. Thompson, *Russia, Bolshevism, and the Versailles Peace* (Princeton, N. J., 1966), pp. 246-60.

distribution of hundreds of thousands of tons of wheat to the Russian peoples?

President Wilson. I don't think the Russians will oppose that. Lenin will be only too glad to find someone to assume this responsibility. M. Nansen thinks that it is possible to establish an organization of this type. He only asks us to accept the principle and to help him as much as we can. I can understand the interest of the neutrals in that matter: they can establish very interesting commercial relations with Russia for the future.

FINANCIAL INTERDEPENDENCE

Mr. Lloyd George. Another point we must think about inserting into the treaty is the interdependence of debts. Germany must know to what countries she owes reparation.

President Wilson. Since we will ask Germany to pay everything she is materially capable of paying, I think the problem of distribution can remain amongst ourselves.

M. Orlando. As far as Italy is concerned, I would point out that German submarines sank our ships in the Mediterranean, that a great number of our prisoners died in German camps, that the bomber planes which devastated our cities were German planes. At the beginning of the war, the Emperor of Austria gave the order not to bomb open cities; from the moment of their appearance, the German aviators hastened to do it. The Austrian high command having forbidden them to do it, they protested violently; it was a German prisoner who boastingly recounted it.

After the disaster of Caporetto,[3] the Germans took half the plunder.

I admit that, by right, the question of the interdependence of debts should be debated amongst ourselves. The Germans will certainly have no right whatever to protest; we consider that interdependence in crime entails interdependence in obligations.

Mr. Lloyd George. I don't want to make an objection; I would simply like to indicate a question which the Germans might ask. Italy suffered losses before declaring war on Germany; must Germany be held responsible for them?

M. Orlando. Even if this question is answered as the Germans might like, the matter is of no great importance. The war was so long that that makes no great difference.

[3] The Battle of Caporetto, which began on October 24, 1917. In this offensive, an Austro-German army overran Italian lines and pushed to the Piave River. The Italians lost 300,000 men taken prisoner and more than that number in deserters.

Mr. Lloyd George. What was the date of your declaration of war against Germany?

M. Orlando. June 1916.

Mr. Lloyd George. Germany could repudiate all responsibility for the first thirteen months from the end of May 1915.

President Wilson. This question must be settled once for all amongst ourselves.

—*Reading and approval of the text on responsibilities considered during the previous session.*

XXVIII

Conversation between President Wilson and MM. Clemenceau, Lloyd George, and Orlando*

APRIL 10, 1919, 11 A.M.

THE QUESTION OF THE SAAR

President Wilson. The text which was to specify the suggestions I made yesterday is in our hands,[1] and, for my part, I approve it.

M. Clemenceau. I read in Article 1 that sovereignty remains with Germany. I would like to replace this sentence by another which would indicate that sovereignty is transferred to the League of Nations.

I would like to make my feelings clear to you, as I am doing my utmost to understand yours. I have no hatred against the Germans as individuals, and I hope that in the future, if the Germans behave decently, it will be possible for the two nations to be reconciled. But we can't wipe out our memories. For us, this question is not simply one of economic interest. Sarrelouis was established by Louis XIV, and Landau suffered a historic siege at the time of the Revolution during a German invasion. Your starting point is the principle of reparation. Mine is reparation—and something else. That matters little, provided we arrive at the same goal.

*Does not appear in H.

[1] It is printed as an appendix to the notes of this meeting.

Mr. Lloyd George. As was said yesterday, the simplest thing is not to use the word "sovereignty" here and to write simply: "Germany surrenders the administration of that region to the Allied and Associated Powers as trustees of the League of Nations."

President Wilson. I will point out that the Allied and Associated Powers don't constitute a legal personality, while the League of Nations will. I would prefer to write that Germany renounces the administration of that region in favor of the League of Nations.

M. Clemenceau. Wouldn't this seem to leave sovereignty to Germany?

Mr. Lloyd George. It seems to me that the formula is satisfactory.

M. Clemenceau. Not to me.

M. Orlando. It is a question of words. The word "administration" in French and Italian has too narrow a meaning, which corresponds to that of the German word "Verwaltung." If we wish to avoid an ambiguity, which M. Clemenceau fears, "administration" must be replaced by "government."

—*This proposal is adopted.*

—MM. Haskins, Headlam-Morley, and Tardieu are introduced.

President Wilson. We want to avoid raising the question of sovereignty. Do you see any drawback in eliminating this word, and in replacing "administration" by "government"?

Mr. Haskins. I see no objection.

—Reading of the text by M. Tardieu (*summary*):

The League of Nations appoints a commission entrusted with the government of the region. This commission is composed of five members, one of whom is French and one a native of the region. These five members are appointed for one year and are eligible for reappointment. The League of Nations appoints the president.

The commission possesses all the rights of government. It appoints and dismisses officials. It can create all the administrative and representative bodies deemed necessary. The use of state property other than the mines is transferred to the League of Nations, *in return for compensation. (After an exchange of views, this last phrase is deleted.)*

Except for the clauses relating to the mines and means of communication, the local laws will be maintained. The commission can allow the formation of local assemblies elected by universal suffrage, women included. The inhabitants cannot be represented in any assembly outside the territory under discussion. The commission will be entrusted with the protection of the interests of the inhabitants in foreign countries.

At the end of a period of fifteen years, a plebiscite, by commune or district, by universal suffrage, for both sexes, will decide the final fate of the area.

M. Clemenceau. According to this text, the "inhabitants" would be given the right to vote at the time of the plebiscite: there could be foreigners amongst them.

M. Tardieu. The vote is reserved to persons domiciled in the Saar region at the time of the signing of the peace.

Mr. Lloyd George. I would favor specifying a shorter period of residence. You have every advantage in allowing Italian or Slavic workers, who are numerous in all the great German industrial regions, to participate in the plebiscite. Many will vote in your favor.

M. Tardieu. The labor in the Saar region is overwhelmingly of local origin. I don't see why foreign elements, which have come to work temporarily in the mines, should have the right to vote, and I fear Germany might take advantage of this clause to introduce into the region elements which would be hostile to us.

M. Orlando. I agree with M. Tardieu; the right to vote must belong to citizens, not to immigrants; the latter are not qualified to decide the fate of an area to which they have only recently come to settle. On the basis of such an arrangement, Germany could use all the means of bribery of which she is a past master.

Mr. Lloyd George. I don't agree with that. I remember that a question of this kind was raised in the Transvaal, before the South African War. That war could not be avoided because President Krüger demanded a residence of fourteen years—instead of seven, the figure demanded by the British government—to grant newcomers the right to vote.

M. Tardieu. If the compulsory period of residence is reduced to five or seven years, I believe there will be a systematic invasion of German elements.

—Reading of the article providing, in the case of a return of part of the territory to Germany after the plebiscite, for the repurchase of title to the mines by payment in gold.

M. Clemenceau. France must have the right to keep ownership of the mines and to sell only if she wishes.

Mr. Lloyd George. One of our main reasons for supporting M. Tardieu's arguments and objecting to the previous plan is the desire not to separate ownership and sovereignty; we have acknowledged that that could lead to frictions and continual dangers. If government was restored to Germany and ownership remained with you, these dangers could not be avoided.

M. Tardieu. That is a very strong argument. But in fifteen years, the relations between France and Germany might be very different from what they are today. Moreover, whilst it is true that acknowledgment of our right to sell preserves, by the same token, our right to ownership, I must remark that the coal of the Saar is necessary for us as coal and cannot be replaced by gold. If this necessity is acknowledged, we must be assured of a supply of coal; and a stipulation to this effect must be part of the treaty.

President Wilson. I hope relations between France and Germany can improve. But the reasons for conflict, if sovereignty and ownership do not correspond, will remain the very ones you have pointed out to us.

As for providing coal, we are told that the coal of the Saar was consumed entirely in the region or in the factories of Lorraine. There is no reason to assume that that will change.

Mr. Lloyd George. This coal seems to be of such quality that it transports poorly and can only be used in a rather limited area. The coal mines of the Saar can find their market only in Lorraine. Further north, they would meet the crushing competition of coal from Westphalia. Moreover, in fifteen years France will have recovered the use of her mines in the North. I don't see the usefulness of a stipulation such as M. Tardieu suggests.

M. Tardieu. We could impose the obligation to continue to supply coal upon Germany.

Mr. Haskins. Those supplies will be governed by the force of circumstances. Exchange between the iron ore of Lorraine and the coal of the Saar will continue, whatever the provisions of the treaty.

M. Tardieu. But meanwhile I take the liberty of insisting on the guarantee which seems necessary to me.

President Wilson. The strongest obligation is the economic obligation, and it exists in this case. It would be an error to transform it into a political obligation which would last for fifty years or more. What would you do if Germany made an agreement and then refused to keep it? Would you declare war on her for that?

M. Clemenceau. I don't know in advance, if the plebiscite should divide this region, what proportion of the coal would return to Germany. My opinion depends upon concrete facts, about which I would still like to consult my experts. I ask you for twenty-four or forty-eight hours in which to give you a final answer. I am sure we will reach an agreement.

Mr. Lloyd George. Think also about what I have said concerning the right to vote. As a friend of France, I advise you to require only a residence of five years. There will be Italian workers, for example, coming in great numbers to work in the region; don't you think they could be a favorable electoral element?

M. Orlando. May I take the liberty of declaring myself against the right of Italians to vote in that region. They are Italian citizens; why should they participate in the exercise of a right which should be reserved to the real inhabitants?

—Before breaking up, the meeting studies the map of the Saar Basin. *It is agreed that the boundary of that region will be drawn along the boundary of the present coal basin, with the changes required to allow it to include established administrative units.*

{ A P P E N D I X }[2]

PARIS, 9th APRIL, 1919.

THE SAAR BASIN.

Draft Proposals.

A. In order to award to France compensation for the destruction of the coal-mines in the north of France and as a part payment of the amount due for reparation from Germany to France, the full ownership and exclusive right to the exploitation of the coal-mines in the Saar Basin is ceded to France.

B. In order to assure the rights and welfare of the population and to secure to France the necessary freedom of exploitation of the mines, Germany agrees to the clauses set out in Annex I and II.

C. In order to make in due time permanent provision for the government of the Saar Basin in accordance with the wishes of the population, France and Germany agree to the clauses set out in Annex III.

ANNEX I.

This is identical with the Economic and Administrative articles already communicated. They will be subject to such changes as will be necessary if Annex II is approved.

---

[2] Printed in PWW, Vol. 57, pp. 196-99. Words in angle brackets deleted by Wilson; words in italics added by him. Wilson made these changes in response to the action of the council. The draft had been prepared by Headlam-Morley and amended by him, Haskins, Miller, and Tardieu during the morning of April 10.

ANNEX II.

1. Germany, ⟨while preserving her sovereignty,⟩ renounces in favour of ⟨the Allied and Associated Powers as trustees of⟩ the League of Nations *as trustee* all her rights of ⟨administration⟩ *government* over the territory defined in Article I.

2. The League of Nations shall appoint a Commission to administer the district.

3. The Commission will consist of five members chosen by the Council of the League of Nations, of whom one shall be a citizen of France, one ⟨a German subject, the latter⟩ a⟨n⟩ *native* inhabitant of the Basin of the Saar *who is not a French subject*, and the others chosen from three countries other than France or Germany. The members of the Commission shall be appointed for one year; they can be removed and replaced by the Council of the League of Nations.

4. The Chairman of the Commission shall be appointed for one year from its members by the League of Nations; he can be reappointed; he will be the executive of the Commission.

5. The Commission shall have all those powers of ⟨administration and police⟩ *government* hitherto belonging to Germany, Prussia or Bavaria, including the appointment and dismissal of all functionaries and the creation of such administrative bodies as it deems necessary. In particular, it will have full control of the administration of railways and canals. The decision will be given by a majority vote.

The use of the property in the Saar Basin belonging to the Imperial German Government, or the Government of any German State will pass to the Administration of the Saar Basin, subject to reasonable compensation.

6. The territory shall be governed subject to the provisions of Annex I. in conformity with the existing law; amendments necessary, whether for general reasons or for bringing the said laws into accord with the said provisions, shall be decided and put into effect by the Commission after consultation with the local representatives in such a manner as the Commission shall determine. No law or amendment thereto can affect or limit the provisions of Annex I.

7. The local civil and criminal courts of the territory will continue. Civil and criminal courts will be appointed by the Commission to judge appeals against the decisions of the said local courts and to decide all matters which cannot be determined by the local courts. The Commission will determine the competence of this last named jurisdiction.

8. The Commission will alone have the power of levying taxes in the district; these taxes will be exclusively applied to the local needs of the district. The present fiscal system will be maintained as far as possible. No new tax will be imposed without consulting the elected representatives.

9. The inhabitants will retain their present nationality, but no hindrance shall be placed in the way of those who wish to acquire a different nationality. They will preserve under the control of the Commission their local assemblies, their religious liberties, their schools, their language. The right of voting for local assemblies will belong without distinction of sex to every inhabitant above the age of 20 years. On the other hand there will be no right of voting for a representative whether in the Reichstag or in the Prussian or Bavarian Chambers or in the French Chamber.

10. Those of the inhabitants who desire to leave the district will have every facility for retaining their real estate or for selling it at a fair price and for freely taking their moveable property with them.

11. There will be no compulsory military service or voluntary recruiting or fortifications. A local gendarmerie for the maintenance of order may alone be established.

12. The Commission shall have power to arrange under conditions which it shall determine for the ⟨representation⟩ *protection* abroad of the interests of the inhabitants of the territory.

13. The Commission shall have power to decide all questions which may arise regarding the interpretation of these articles.

ANNEX III.

1. At the termination of a period of fifteen years, there shall be held a plebiscite in the above defined territory under the control of the Commission. The vote shall be held by communes or districts. In the vote there shall be no discrimination on the ground of sex. None shall be admitted to the vote except inhabitants domiciled in the territory at the time of the signing of the present peace. The regulations as well as the date for the voting shall be fixed by the Executive Council of the League of Nations in such a way as to secure the liberty and secrecy of the vote.

2. The League of Nations shall decide on the sovereignty of the territory in conformity with the wishes of the inhabitants thus expressed. Germany agrees to cede to France, in accordance with the decision of the League, all that territory to which the decision of the League applies.

3. On such of the said territory as shall remain German under the result of the decision of the League of Nations, the property rights of the Government of France under these articles shall be taken over as a whole by Germany at a price payable in gold which shall be determined by three appraisers or a majority of them, one of whom shall be appointed by Germany, one by France, and one who shall be neither a German nor a French citizen by the League of Nations.

4. The price so fixed shall be payable within [blank] after the determination thereof and unless the said price so fixed shall be then paid by Germany to the Government of France, the territory which would otherwise remain German shall thereafter be occupied and administered by France as an integral portion of French territory.

5. The provisions of the foregoing article shall be subject to any agreement which may have been reached between France and Germany with regard to the rights of France before the time fixed for the payment above mentioned.

6. As soon after the plebiscite as possible the League of Nations shall make regulations for bringing to an end all provisions for a special regime in the territory in question, having due regard to personal and property rights.

The value of the property ceded to France under these articles shall be credited as a part payment of the amount due for reparation from Germany to France. This value shall be determined by ⟨a mixed⟩ *the Reparation* Commission appointed by the Council of the League of Nations, on which both France and Germany shall be represented and which shall make its decisions by majority vote.

XXIX

Conference among President Wilson and MM. Clemenceau, Lloyd George, Orlando, and the financial experts: Messrs. Baruch, Davis, Lamont, and McCormick (United States of America); Mr. Bonar Law and Lord Sumner (British Empire); MM. Klotz, Loucheur, and Sergent (France); MM. Crespi and D'Amelio (Italy)*

APRIL 10, 1919, 4 P.M.

THE QUESTION OF REPARATION

President Wilson. What is the point we have to discuss?

M. Klotz. The other day, Lord Sumner presented in this meeting a text[1] that was taken under consideration and referred to a subcommission. In that subcommission, Lord Sumner agreed that it was possible to admit certain amendments. The representatives of France proposed such amendments on three principal points; I am going to submit them to you.

Mr. Davis. I believe the subcommission could come to an agreement on these points.

President Wilson. It seems that the final effort of the subcommission hasn't been made. Is it worthwhile to bring this question before us before it has been completely studied by the subcommission?

Mr. Lloyd George. It involves points of principle. The first is this: will the United States be represented on the commission entrusted with the execution of the financial clauses of the peace treaty?

Second: Do we agree on the issue of German bonds?

Third: Will unanimity be required for the decisions of the Financial [Reparation] Commission on all questions which involve the essential interest of the states?

On these three points, it seems to me that it is the governments which must decide.

*H., PPC, V, 71ff.

[1] See n. 3 to XXI.

President Wilson. I can answer immediately on the first point: if the arrangements for that commission seem acceptable to us, we will participate in its work.

Mr. Lloyd George. That point is then settled.

As for the question of the unanimity of the vote, France, Italy, and Great Britain agreed the other day in the affirmative. Colonel House believed that he had to reserve the opinion of the President of the United States. If we can agree on this point right now, only the third question remains—the one concerning the bonds. This latter is also a question of principle. As soon as we have resolved it, it won't be difficult for our experts to draft their text.

President Wilson. You speak of a unanimity of the vote: on what questions?

M. Klotz. When it is a question of the total or partial remission of the sums owed by Germany.

—On this subject, Mr. Lloyd George reads the minutes of the preceding financial session, drafted by Colonel Hankey. It is a matter whether, if the question arises at any time of remitting part of Germany's debt, the decision could be taken by the majority of the powers represented on the commission or only unanimously.

President Wilson. The constitution of the commission is still being studied by our delegates. I just said that, if this constitution seems to me to be established upon an acceptable foundation, the United States will participate in the work of that commission. But the subcommission's report isn't ready yet, and our participation will depend upon the merits of the plan, as it appears to us. That is why I am not yet in a position to tell you whether or not the decision in the case you mention must be or must not be taken unanimously.

My opinion is that the decisions must be taken by majority vote, except in the case of a complete cancellation of part of the debt. What surprises me, because this appears to be your own desire as well, is that our experts haven't seen to what extent we have agreed.

M. Loucheur. Does what the President of the United States just said mean that, when it is a question of deciding on the kinds of payment, a majority decision will suffice? For instance, will a majority be able to decide that half of the payments can be made in marks?

Mr. Davis. We think the kinds of payment can be determined by majority vote.

Mr. Bonar Law. But, then, that amounts to giving the majority the right to cancel a part of the debt. For such would be the effect of a decision which would allow payment in paper marks instead of gold.

President Wilson. I am not sufficiently familiar with the details of this discussion to take part in it. I am not disposed to express my opinion when I have only an incomplete document before me. What I can say to you right now is that there must be no remission of the debt without a unanimous vote.

M. Clemenceau. It is not I who asked that this discussion take place this evening; I should have thought, on the contrary, that it would have been desirable to postpone it.

Mr. Lloyd George. We didn't say it would be helpful to hear the arguments presented on each side by our experts, who have debated for months. But if they are not given guidance by decisions of principle taken by the heads of governments, they can find no way out of their controversies. It is up to us to assume the responsibility for certain decisions. If we send the experts back to their work without having given them any guidance, they won't agree, because they will clash, as before, on questions of principle which they cannot possibly resolve themselves. It would be best to give them instruction after a short conversation amongst ourselves.

President Wilson. I see no objection to discussing the question of bonds immediately if we have a chance of reaching a conclusion. I didn't hear it said that the subcommission is in such disagreement on this subject that it despairs of finding a way out.

Mr. Lloyd George. Here is what I would suggest. I have already proposed it to President Wilson in a private conversation. Instead of stipulating in the peace treaty the amount of bonds to be issued, I would give a mandate to the Financial [Reparation] Commission entrusted with the execution of the treaty to determine the amount of the issue when it has all the claims in hand. The French interest and the British interest are, from this point of view, identical. I know very well that we will be reproached if we fix a figure right now. What has been proposed is 150 billion [French francs]. Our members of Parliament will exclaim straightaway: "That's all, then, that you are demanding of Germany?"

I wish to avoid this. That's precisely the result you obtain by leaving the task of fixing the figure to the commission according to the instructions it will receive. That is the opinion of Mr. Bonar Law, just here from London, who has been facing the very opposition of which I am thinking at this moment.

M. Klotz. In short, it is only a matter of determining the first installment of the total sum to be collected. As far as our parliaments are concerned, what we have to fear is being asked this question: "Where are your guarantees?" When I proposed to you to take the customhouses, ports, and railways as guarantees, Mr. Lloyd George said he didn't want such kinds of guarantees. Do we have others? The commission will fix a figure. But what guarantee do we have that, when this figure is communicated to Germany two years from now, Germany won't reject it? In the interval, how, by what means, will we prepare our budgets of 1920 and 1921? We must be able to base them on something other than promises.

If we announce the figure of 150 billion francs, we satisfy public opinion, for we are taking care to say that it is only a payment on account. Between private persons, in the absence of mortgages, the creditor asks the debtor to give him an acknowledgment of debt, a document which bears a signature and which is negotiable. We need a guarantee of that kind. From this point of view, a promise to pay 150 billions imposed upon Germany will satisfy public opinion immediately. If we announce no figure, we will be blamed for having built a fine locomotive without putting coal in it.

Mr. Lloyd George. You are not exactly answering my observation. Like you, I am in favor of the issue of bonds; I feel as strongly about that as you do, and I believe a figure must be announced. I am only proposing to reserve this task for the commission, which must carry it out, not at the end of its work, but from the moment of its establishment, or, more exactly, as soon as it has received all the claims, and before scrutinizing them in detail. I agree completely with you on the necessity of that issue to give us the guarantee we need.

M. Clemenceau. In your opinion, shouldn't our commission of experts have completed its work by the time the preliminaries of peace are signed?

Mr. Lloyd George. That depends upon the promptness with which all parties can submit their documents.

President Wilson. What will be done with the bonds once issued?

M. Klotz. Our proposal is that these bonds remain in the treasury of the commission. It would be very dangerous to place an exorbitant sum at the disposal of any one of us within a short time. But each nation will know its rights all the same and can use the bonds as collateral for the credits it seeks to obtain during the first two years. On the day of the signing, Germany will give us bonds for 150 billions. The commission won't distribute them but will reserve for each of us the quantities required to get credit. In short, these bonds won't be negotiated, but the commission will allow them to be pledged in part.

Mr. Lamont. Our subcommission is not in disagreement about that. We are divided on the figure; but M. Klotz admits that 150 billions was simply a figure submitted for discussion. The only difference of opinion between us is that, according to M. Klotz, the figure must be announced immediately, while Mr. Lloyd George proposes that the commission announce it.

President Wilson. I don't doubt, any more than Mr. Lloyd George does, the necessity of an issue of bonds to support the credit indispensable to the reconstruction of the countries which have suffered from the war. But there is a great drawback in including an arbitrary figure in the text of the peace treaty, since we don't yet have all the claims before us.

In the peace treaty, the Germans will have to accept the power of the commission with all its consequences. If we demand that the sum be set in the preliminaries of peace, we will only appreciably delay the signing.

Mr. Lamont, who just spoke to me, adds that the commission could be required to meet one week after the signing of the preliminaries.

M. Clemenceau. But when will it make its decision known? The study of the documents might compel us to wait six months for it.

President Wilson. At this time, France is the only country which has not provided us with its complete figures.

M. Clemenceau. France suffered losses so heavy and so varied that it is perhaps less easy for her than for others to know the extent immediately. On the other hand, we want to study our estimates closely, so that no one can reproach us for having exaggerated them. In short, it is only a matter of fixing a figure which will obviously be less than the total we are entitled to claim. If we hesitate to announce this figure, it will be a great disappointment to public opinion. It will believe that we wish to spare the Germans. I see no valid reason for not announcing this figure. I fear the deplorable effect which, in France certainly, would result from this silence. However, if at least a date was set on which this figure would be known, public opinion could be appeased. But no figure and no date—that I cannot accept.

Mr. Lloyd George. Concerning your claims, you can provide provisional figures rapidly. That would suffice for the immediate work that we could ask of the commission. I don't see what would prevent the commission from being provided with all the necessary figures within one week after its establishment, and it could take an immediate decision. There are figures which can be established by simple addition, such as those of the pensions included in our different budgets. The commission could then determine the total amount of the down payment demanded in a very short time.

M. Clemenceau. You don't mean to let the Germans discuss the amount of the issue?

Mr. Lloyd George. No, that concerns the commission alone.

President Wilson. I must confess that I don't know where I am. After long discussions, we had concluded that it was better not to try for the moment to fix the figures; whatever they are, they may indeed cause disappointment. Today, we are absolutely insistent on returning to the figures.

Mr. Lloyd George. This time it is not a matter of fixing the figure of what Germany must or can pay us, but only the amount of a down payment.

President Wilson. I think we now agree in thinking that the amount of the issue would have to be determined by the commission at the earliest possible date. But how can we fix this date now without knowing when the commission will have in hand the documents necessary to take its decision?

Mr. Lloyd George. I would give it two weeks from the time of its establishment.

M. Clemenceau. I could accept this. But I don't understand the difficulty there might be in fixing the amount of the down payment. One steals from me my watch, my paintings, my furniture. The thief is apprehended; it isn't difficult to fix a sum before an appraisal; that happens every day, it is the practice of the courts. In a spirit of conciliation, I would go as far as to accept what Mr. Lloyd George has just proposed, if President Wilson agrees with him on this.

President Wilson. I have already said that I agree. But another question arises: will the amount of the issue be determined by a majority of the commission?

Mr. Lloyd George. Undoubtedly.

President Wilson. We would like it to be done unanimously.

M. Clemenceau. I have two observations to make on that. First, it is much more difficult for a commission than for a small meeting of political leaders to take a decision unanimously, and I am convinced that two weeks would be far from enough for it to reach it.

In the second place, we know that your experts have proposed the payment of a part of the debt in paper marks. A decision of this kind would have a disastrous effect on public opinion, which would see in it a renunciation of a part of the debt. Something must be placed in the text which limits the power of the commission.

Mr. Lloyd George. Let us set aside that last question, if you will, so that we can speak only about unanimity. I believe that the necessity of a unanimous vote would be fatal to our plan. It would be much better to fix the figure straightaway. If a single power raises opposition, an indefinite delay can follow. Belgium, for example, whose claims are rather exaggerated, can refuse to agree with the other powers, except under certain conditions, by requiring in advance that a certain part will be reserved for her. I don't wish to give that temptation to any one of us. To write the principle of unanimity into this text would be to ruin the text itself.

President Wilson. The object of the issue of bonds is to furnish collateral to support loans. Without doubt, you will try to place them in large measure in the United States. Suppose that the quantity of bonds is excessive; that will reduce the value of the collateral and will have a bad effect on those from whom you seek credit. Our bankers will hesitate to lend on the security of paper of dubious value. I must say that, if it is the majority which fixes the amount of the issue, it would be unwise on the part of the United States to participate in the work of that commission, which doesn't respond to any American necessity.

Mr. Lloyd George. You know very well that America must participate in it for cardinal reasons, and it is absolutely essential that a great impartial power be represented on that commission.

President Wilson. The amount of the issue will have an influence on world credit. We can consider ourselves as being outside the problem, and that is why we won't expose ourselves to being placed in a minority in the commission.

Mr. Lloyd George. I grant you that the United States is probably the country which we will look to most to obtain credits. But one will also turn to Great Britain, because she will provide other countries with Australian wool, machine parts, since production of the United States is inadequate. It is obvious that, if there are too many bonds on the market, they will fall in value, but it is the country which counts on them as collateral that will suffer first from this. Our bankers, like yours, will only take the bonds if it pleases them, that is, if they think they have any value. If France or Belgium or Great Britain throw too many bonds on the market, it is those powers themselves which will suffer the consequences.

President Wilson. It is not in the interest of the world, and it is not in our interest, for the credit of France to fall to nothing. If our bankers refuse a collateral too widely distributed, your countries' credit will fall. Hence the supreme importance of a definite sum which is not excessive.

Mr. Bonar Law. That is perfectly true; but do you think the commission won't have that in mind when it fixes the amount of the issue? After all, that commission will represent the governments and won't forget the rules of common sense. The principle of unanimity would allow any one of the powers represented to halt everything, and it might happen that it could be a power that would not find the figure high enough.

Mr. Lloyd George. We must give the commission power to limit the quantities of bonds being thrown on the market within a given period.

President Wilson. That has to be part of the fundamental terms of operation of the system.

Mr. Davis. The best thing would be, as for all other securities, not to place these bonds on the market before Germany is able to redeem the coupons.

Mr. Lloyd George. We know in advance that Germany won't be able to redeem the coupons for several years. That is no reason not to issue these bonds, if we are convinced that payment will be made later.

President Wilson. Let us suppose that the figure was fixed by a majority and that the United States was of a contrary opinion; don't you believe that the minority report drafted by the representatives of the United States would be enough to make your credit operations in America impossible?

Mr. Bonar Law. Don't you believe that the commission will take that very danger into account and do nothing to provoke it?

Mr. Lamont. Couldn't the difficulty be settled if our little subcommission agreed on a figure? It would be understood in advance that the commission's figure must come close to it.

—*This proposal is accepted.*

XXX

Conversation between President Wilson and MM. Clemenceau, Lloyd George, and Orlando*

APRIL 11, 1919, 11 A.M.

—Mr. Lloyd George explains the reasons why he has to go to England next week: he has to answer critics who are expressing concern about the indemnity settlement and ask for a vote of confidence from them.

M. Orlando. Being in the same situation as Mr. Lloyd George, I would draw your attention to the importance of no longer delaying the consideration of the questions which concern Italy. I have to face the same difficulties in my country as you do. Yesterday, there was a Bolshevik demonstration in the streets of Rome which, it is true, turned against its organizers and ended as a great patriotic demonstration. But that shows the unrest amongst the people. The inevitable postponement of the discussion of Italian questions is creating an unfortunate impression in Italy, and we must avoid prolonging it.

I wish to have a conversation with President Wilson as soon as possible. I would like to know, if Mr. Lloyd George is leaving Paris, when he will return. I myself must attend the opening session of the Italian Chamber on April 23, which has already been postponed once by Royal Decree and which can't possibly be postponed a second time. I can't go to Rome without the Italian questions having been broached.

Mr. Lloyd George. I plan to leave on Tuesday, Monday if I can, and I hope to be able to return on Friday. But these discussions must not be interrupted. Mr. Balfour will represent me here, and he has studied the questions concerning Italy with particular care.

I will return on Friday, unless the House of Commons refuses me its confidence—in which case it will be with Lord Northcliffe or with Horatio Bottomley that you will continue these discussions. * * *

President Wilson. I know better than anyone how little time we have had to study the questions which concern M. Orlando, for I sat with him on the League of Nations Commission yesterday until midnight. However, I did have a conversation with him, and I

---

*Does not appear in H.

promised him to prepare a memorandum, to discuss it with him, and to bring the results of our conversation to you. Perhaps the best time to do it would be in a few days, during Mr. Lloyd George's absence.

Mr. Lloyd George. This question must first be settled between the President of the United States and M. Orlando; for, concerning the boundaries of the Adriatic, France and England are bound by the treaty they signed with Italy.[1]

THE QUESTION OF THE SAAR

M. Loucheur. If, after a period of fifteen years, part of the coal basin of the Saar should return to Germany, France would ask for guarantees to receive the coal necessary for Alsace and Lorraine and the industries of the east of France. Will it be said that she can obtain it by the simple play of free competition? Here is what keeps us from believing it.

During the ten years preceding the war, we were subjected yearly to German blackmail, made possible by our industries' need of coal from the Saar. English coal, which could only arrive in Lorraine by way of the Seine and by long and slow water routes, cost the metallurgical industries four or five francs more a ton than German coal. The Germans played on that difference and used it to impose terms on our steel mills which placed them in an inferior position in relation to their own companies. We do *not* want that to happen again.

Furthermore, Alsace and Lorraine consume, beyond what is produced on their own soil, around eight million tons of coal from the Saar Basin. Without Alsace and Lorraine, France already had a deficit in coal consumption; if she is deprived of the coal needed by the industries of Alsace and Lorraine in fifteen years' time, the situation will be more difficult than ever and will tempt the Germans to exert annoying pressure on her.

What we are asking for is the right of option for the average annual quantity consumed in the three years before the plebiscite, at the same price as on the German domestic market.

Mr. Lloyd George. You are fixing no time limit. Can the same arrangement be made in perpetuity based on the price of the three last years?

M. Loucheur. That is not right; it is not the price but the amount which will be fixed according to the average of the three last

---

[1] That is, the Treaty of London of April 26, 1915.

years. As for the price, we only ask that it be the same for the French consumer as for the German consumer.

President Wilson. What seems to me difficult is the enforcement of such a clause; I see a danger of frictions and conflicts there.

M. Loucheur. I think Germany will execute that clause without difficulty. What would be more serious than the conflict which you foresee would be the halting of the activity of our industries in the East. We are asking for nothing more than the continuation, after the contemplated period of fifteen years, of a *de facto* situation which will have existed during that period. We only wish to protect our industries against what Germany might do in a spirit of revenge. That will do no great harm to Germany, because it is a matter—assuming that the entire Saar Basin returns to Germany—of thirteen million tons out of a production of 240 million tons.

Mr. Lloyd George. It is an arrangement similar to the one we make in England when we obtain water for a large city; we provide what is called "compensation water." It seems to me that that clause contains nothing that can be called humiliating or excessive. The danger would be great if the ownership of the mines belonged to France and the sovereignty to Germany: we all agree on avoiding that. But if Germany acknowledges her obligation to provide France with a certain quantity of coal, and if she finds herself unable to do so for reasons beyond her control—as a result of strikes, for instance—nothing will be easier than for her to explain that to the representatives of the League of Nations. If she should refuse without any justification, she would thereby show her spirit of revenge and her desire to ruin the industries of eastern France; this would be a serious sign which we would have to worry about.

President Wilson. What is the opinion of our experts on M. Loucheur's plan?

M. Loucheur. I haven't consulted the American experts on this subject.

President Wilson. Mr. Lloyd George called to our attention the other day the fact that the coal of the Saar doesn't lend itself to transport over a long distance and can only be consumed in a rather limited area. If that is so, why not simply stipulate that the coal will be sold at the same price in France as on the domestic market? The means of pressure employed by the Germans, if I understand M. Loucheur, has been the difference in price between the coal of the Saar and English coal. A solution must be sought from this angle.

M. Loucheur. I think it is absolutely essential to mention the amount to be delivered.

President Wilson. Don't you think the usual commercial motives will continue to operate? What we want to avoid is allowing the Germans to raise prices arbitrarily. We are preventing that by compelling them to sell this coal to France at the same price as to consumers in their own domestic market. If we fix an amount, and if that amount is not delivered, must the League of Nations intervene?

I see a serious danger in forcing any country to give another country any kind of service for an unlimited period. Suppose the French government proves itself too demanding in the execution of a clause of this kind; suppose Germany shows bad faith: I see difficulties on all sides as a consequence of imposing that provision without time limit.

Mr. Lloyd George. This problem doesn't arise only in the Saar Valley. There are other countries in Europe where we are obliged to provide arrangements of this nature, for example in the Teschen Basin. It would seem to me unjust to take that region from Poland, since the population is Polish, passionately Polish. But the coal is necessary for the industries of Bohemia, which it has always supplied. M. Paderewski makes no objection to a clause like the one suggested by M. Loucheur. He acknowledges that the coal of Teschen is absolutely essential to Bohemia, and he is prepared to accept, without considering it any humiliation, the obligation to provide coal to the Czechoslovak Republic, whilst the Polish population of Teschen is not compelled to separate itself from the Polish nation.

When mines necessary to the existence of one country are located in a neighboring country, that situation imposes a sort of obligation upon the latter. My sole objection concerns the length of the period which should serve as the basis for determining the required amount. We only wish to be just, and we believe we are being scrupulous in giving the people of the Saar the right to become German again at the end of the fifteen years. But that doesn't mean that Germany will be able to deprive France of the coal she needs. That would be as if, in deciding that a mountain will cease to be part of a country where it was formerly included, one gave the new owner the right to divert the river which created the wealth of an entire region.

M. Clemenceau. Will the difficulties foreseen not be the same, whether it is the price which is fixed compulsorily or whether it is the amount to be delivered?

President Wilson. I don't see any principle at stake here, and what I fear is not injustice. I am seeking only the system which can function best and with the least danger of future conflicts.

I am not a prophet, and I would hesitate in a case like this to impose for an indeterminate time an arrangement whose operation could be difficult. I ask you to draft a text which satisfies you, and to do this in agreement with our experts.

Mr. Lloyd George. Couldn't we at the same time instruct them to change the article relating to the plebiscite? Instead of asking the inhabitants only if they want to become French or to become German again, can't they be asked a third question, to wit, whether they want to remain established as a separate state? Born myself in a small country, I believe in the advantages of small communities and the services they can render. I think they are often capable of taking initiatives useful to humanity which would be more difficult for large countries.

President Wilson. You were born in a small country; I was born in a conquered and devastated country,* and that has helped me, believe me, to understand the questions which are raised here. What I fear is giving the League of Nations too much to do, imposing upon it too many duties at one and the same time, and multiplying the number of its officials. Are you sure we will find them?

Mr. Lloyd George. We find men to administer the most backward regions of India in a torrid climate, with low salaries. I don't see why you would fail to find persons to represent the League of Nations in the Saar Basin.

President Wilson. Your civil servants have one of the most powerful motives which act on men: they are serving their country. That motive doesn't yet exist for the League of Nations.

Mr. Lloyd George. I am convinced that the men who will come to the Saar Basin to represent the League of Nations there will be aware of their authority and will never regret having accepted this post.

—*It is decided that M. Loucheur will draw up a final text, along with MM. Tardieu, Haskins, Bennett,[2] Cornwall, and Headlam-Morley.*

*The territory of the southern states after the Civil War.

[2] Mantoux undoubtedly meant Baruch, who did attend the meeting of this committee. The Editors have not been able to identify anyone by the name of Bennett.

THE COMMISSION OF INQUIRY IN THE NEAR EAST[3]

President Wilson. Have you appointed your representatives to the commission of inquiry which is to ascertain the attitudes of the different populations of the Ottoman Empire? Mine are appointed and ready to leave.

Mr. Lloyd George. We haven't appointed ours yet, and I believe there must be a conversation on the subject between M. Clemenceau and myself.

President Wilson. We have taken a formal decision about this, and I don't see how an agreement between France and England can excuse us from sending that commission to Asia. It is a matter of knowing, not whether France and England agree, but what the feelings of the populations are.

M. Clemenceau. Undoubtedly; but it would be helpful to know in advance how France and England can agree on the question of mandates, so we can submit proposals that the populations can accept.

Mr. Lloyd George. The opinions of our representatives differ. You have heard General Alby. Mr. Wilson, who represents us in Mesopotamia, and who knows much better than General Alby the mentality of the near eastern peoples, holds opposite opinions, especially concerning the feelings of the Arabs of Damascus towards France.

—After a short discussion, it is decided that a conversation will take place between the French and English governments on the subject of Syria, Mr. Lloyd George declaring that he dissociates himself from that question, and that he wishes Emir Faisal to understand that he must not rely on a disagreement between France and England.

---

[3] There had been intermittent discussion of an inter-Allied commission of inquiry to the Arab portions of the former Ottoman Empire in the Council of Ten and the Council of Four since at least February 3, 1919. For a review of the discussions of near eastern questions to March 20, 1919, see *PWW*, Vol. 56, pp. 104-18, and Harry N. Howard, *The King-Crane Commission: An American Inquiry in the Middle East* (Beirut, 1963), pp. 1-35. Wilson, on March 20, 1919, suggested the appointment of an inter-Allied commission to "tell the facts as they found them," and Wilson was authorized to draft a "Terms of Reference to the Commission." Wilson's instructions, embodied in a memorandum dated March 25, 1919, are printed in *PWW*, Vol. 56, pp. 272-75. With only tacit approval of the project by Lloyd George and Clemenceau, Wilson, on April 2, appointed Henry Churchill King, President of Oberlin College, and Charles Richard Crane, as the American members of the commission.

XXXI

Conversation between President Wilson and MM. Clemenceau, Lloyd George, and Orlando*

APRIL 12, 1919, 11 A.M.

Mr. Lloyd George. I want to speak to you about the publication of the preliminaries of peace. Before leaving for London, I'll ask you if we agree about the question of whether that publication should take place before or after we meet the German plenipotentiaries.

President Wilson. In my opinion, it would be very unwise to publish this text before the beginning of the negotiations. I would do everything possible to prevent any disclosure.

Mr. Lloyd George. In England, we can issue an order under the powers granted to the government by the Defence of the Realm Act.

President Wilson. I don't have corresponding powers. But I believe I can get the press to abstain from any disclosure of this kind.

Mr. Lloyd George. Do you have this influence over the Hearst press?

President Wilson. Its representative in Paris[1] is perhaps the best of the American correspondents and one of the most public-spirited. I believe it is possible to influence him.

M. Clemenceau. What does M. Orlando think?

M. Orlando. From my point of view, any publication before the start of the negotiations could only have very regrettable effects.

Mr. Lloyd George. Don't you think we should have a conversation about this with the Ministers of Foreign Affairs? We could see them this very morning.

It would be madness to publish the articles of the treaty before the arrival of the German plenipotentiaries. It would make it impossible for them to accept our terms if ever German public opinion flares up.

I have another question to put: for what date will we summon the Germans? Since nearly all the provisions are ready, I would favor summoning them for Friday week, April 25.

M. Orlando. Unfortunately, that is when I have to be in Rome for the opening of Parliament.

*Does not appear in H.

[1] John Edwin Nevin.

Mr. Lloyd George. I had forgotten that. When will you return from Italy?

M. Orlando. I hope the questions which most concern Italy will have been settled in their main outlines before my departure for Rome. That is of particular importance for Italian public opinion; it wouldn't understand why talks with the Germans were beginning before the problems especially concerning us had been taken up.

Once that is done, it is not essential that I be present at the exact moment when negotiations with the Germans begin. M. Sonnino can represent the Italian government here if I arrive two or three days later. The important thing, so far as I am concerned, is that, when the Germans arrive at Versailles, Italian public opinion has the impression that our questions have received a satisfactory solution in principle.

M. Clemenceau. Before summoning the Germans, the question of Danzig must also be settled.

Mr. Lloyd George. Aren't we agreed on its solution?

M. Clemenceau. Undoubtedly, but you have seen M. Paderewski's opposition. If the region of Marienwerder isn't left to Germany, I believe the Poles might resign themselves to the independence of Danzig.

Mr. Lloyd George. It would be contrary to all our ideas to leave within the Polish state a territory so obviously German and one which has always been part of ancient Prussia.

M. Clemenceau. You can't imagine Paderewski's emotion; he even cried.

President Wilson. Yes, but you must take account of his sensitivity, which is very lively.

Mr. Lloyd George. After all, the Poles are assured of independence after a century and a half of servitude. If they think that they can't survive because we refuse them a small territory which contains 150,000 Germans! * * *

President Wilson. I would favor giving M. Paderewski a statement signed by us, explaining our motives, in order to make the Poles understand that we have acted without any desire to favor their enemies, but, on the contrary, in order to protect them from future danger.

Mr. Lloyd George. On the question of Teschen, I lean towards the side of the Poles. The population of that region seems to be Polish by a large majority. On the other hand, it is fair to insure Bohemia a right to the use of the coal under terms similar to those provided for France in case the Saar Basin should become German again. M. Paderewski understands that and acknowledges the vital importance of those coal mines for the industries of Bohemia.

President Wilson. I must tell you how moved I was yesterday by a visit of a group of Polish peasants who came from their country, having traveled sixty kilometers on foot to the nearest station, and whose villages had provided them with the funds required for the trip.[2] They begged me to see to it that the boundary line unites them to Poland—their country—and not to make them subjects of the Czechoslovak Republic. Their simplicity and passion were touching. This is a case of one of those indentations in the drawing of the borders about which it is so difficult for us to decide.

Mr. Lloyd George. We wanted to maintain the boundary between Bohemia and Germany such as it existed before the war. But concerning borders between friendly states, such as Bohemia and Poland, or Rumania and Serbia, I don't see why it shouldn't be possible, in cases where a few doubtful points remain, to give some commissions the mandate to settle these difficulties after the conclusion of the preliminaries of peace.

—Marshal Foch and General Weygand are introduced.

Marshal Foch. I asked to see you to inform you of a telegram I just received from our headquarters in Mainz. They tell me that one of our agents in Weimar says that Dr. Heim, head of the Bavarian Peasants' League in the German National Assembly, asks for a safe conduct in order to enter into contact with a representative of Marshal Foch, to whom he has an important communication to make. I ask for your instructions.

Mr. Lloyd George. It probably concerns some movement against the soviets.

President Wilson. Why does this Dr. Heim address himself to the military authority?

M. Clemenceau. He thinks Marshal Foch will communicate to us what he will say.

Mr. Lloyd George. That could mean that, if the soviets are holding the Bavarian cities, the peasants are hostile to them. It may be interesting to hear what a representative of the peasants has to say.

We have several questions to ask ourselves about our attitudes

[2] For a graphic description of this meeting, see the entry from the Diary of Dr. Grayson printed at April 11, 1919, *PWW*, Vol. 57, pp. 237-38.

towards the German parties. Do we want to intervene in the domestic quarrels of Germany? Do we want to prevent Bavaria from separating from the rest of Germany, if such is her desire? If Austria joined a Bavaria separated from the rest of Germany, wouldn't that be a situation altogether different from the one created by the union of Austria with a unified Germany?

Marshal Foch. I conclude then that I should tell our headquarters in Mainz to give a safe conduct to Dr. Heim and arrange an interview with him, either in Mainz or in Kreuznach.

—Marshal Foch and General Weygand withdraw.
—MM. Lansing, Balfour, Pichon, and Sonnino are introduced.
—President Wilson explains to the Foreign Ministers the question, already studied by the heads of governments, of publicity concerning the preliminaries of peace. The heads of governments agree in thinking that all publicity must be avoided before the opening of the negotiations with the Germans; but they made a point of hearing the Ministers of Foreign Affairs on this subject.
—Mr. Balfour says that, after a first conversation with Mr. Lloyd George, he believes with him that this publicity would have very dangerous effects, both in Germany, where it could provoke a movement which could make negotiations difficult, and in our respective countries, where it might cause more or less violent discussions.

Mr. Lloyd George. There are two ways to avoid publicity. The first is to try to prevent indiscretions, which is very difficult. The second is to prevent publication. We can do this in England, in France, and in Italy. The President of the United States believes he can obtain the same result by using his influence over the press. There remains the question of whether we can communicate the text to the Germans before having communicated it to all the powers represented at the conference. In any case, those who participated directly in the war against Germany must be summoned.

—Mr. Lansing thinks that all the powers which declared war on Germany have to sign the treaty and, consequently, have the right to know the proposed text in advance.

Mr. Lloyd George. A distinction should be made between the countries directly affected by certain clauses of the treaty and those which only have a general interest in it. We are obviously compelled to submit the clauses which involve them to Belgium, to Bohemia, to Poland.

—Mr. Lansing insists on the same right for all the powers at war with Germany, which cannot accept being informed at the same time as the enemy, or after him.

—Mr. Balfour proposes, in the first place, a scrutiny of the clauses of special interest to certain powers, such as Belgium, along with the representatives of those powers, and, in the second place, a plenary and secret session of the representatives of all the Allied and Associated Powers, to which the preliminaries would be explained in their main outlines, without the text being communicated to them in all its details.

—*After an exchange of views, that proposal is provisionally adopted.*

XXXII

Conversation between President Wilson and MM. Clemenceau, Lloyd George, Orlando, and the financial experts: Mr. Davis, Lord Sumner, Lord Cunliffe, and MM. Loucheur, Crespi, and Chiesa*

APRIL 12, 1919, 5 P.M.

M. Loucheur explains the state of the question of the bonds to be issued by Germany. The American delegate, Mr. Norman Davis, thinks Germany could not pay the interest on an amount of bonds exceeding fifteen billion dollars before a certain number of years; he does not deny that Germany must pay in gold, but says that if one issues so many bonds that Germany cannot pay the interest on them, these bonds will have no value, whatever the amount. Mr. Davis' view is correct from the financial point of view, but difficult to explain to the public.

Mr. Davis suggests issuing ten billion dollars in paper marks. That solution seems dangerous to us. We would prefer for Germany, whilst issuing bonds for only fifteen billion dollars in gold, to give us in addition an acknowledgment of a debt of ten billion dollars, the kind and time of the issue being left to the judgment of the commission. Thus, we would arrive at a total guarantee of twenty-five billion dollars in gold, without risking an excessive issue.

*Does not appear in H.

Mr. Davis would prefer to leave the commission entirely free to determine the time and method of future payments, without announcing the amount in gold now.

Mr. Lloyd George fears that the solution proposed by M. Loucheur would be dangerous from the political point of view. The public, noticing that Germany is issuing bonds for only fifteen billion dollars and is merely signing an acknowledgment of debt for the rest, would conclude, wrongly no doubt, that this is all we are proposing to ask of her. It is an impression that could not be avoided.

M. Clemenceau insists strongly that no issue of bonds in paper marks be provided for in the peace treaty. If ultimately Germany cannot pay, it is preferable to cancel part of her debt at that time rather than to declare in advance that paper without assured value will be accepted from her in payment or in guarantee.

Mr. Davis observes that if Germany proves capable of paying the interest on an issue of fifteen billion dollars, that will show that her business is sufficiently recovered to raise her exchange rate. From that time on, the paper mark will rise in value. Thus the bonds will be more easily negotiable than if we had tried to set the issue at an excessive figure.

Lord Sumner presents a text which, after discussion, is adopted and which provides for an issue of bearer bonds for 100 billion marks in gold, in three periods, namely:

(1) Twenty billion marks issued immediately, corresponding to the down payment which will be demanded of Germany at the time of the signing of the preliminaries.

(2) Forty billions, which will be issued after the signing of the peace treaty and which will bear 2 ½ per cent interest until 1921, then 5 per cent, and beginning in 1926, 1 per cent for amortization.

(3) A bond for forty billion marks, which will be transformed into an issue of negotiable bonds only when the Reparation Commission judges that Germany is in condition to pay the interest.

The commission will be able subsequently to prescribe other issues according to the financial means of Germany, up to the amount of the acknowledged debt. The times and the modes of these issues will be left to the judgment of the commission.

XXXIII

Conversation between President Wilson and MM. Clemenceau, Lloyd George and Orlando*

APRIL 13, 1919, 6 P.M.

President Wilson. We have to know if we can even now set the date for summoning the German plenipotentiaries. M. Orlando, to whom I have just spoken, wants no definite decision to be taken on this subject so long as we haven't agreed in principle on the Italian questions.

M. Orlando. It would indeed be impossible for me to accept it. The impression would be disastrous in Italy if I told my compatriots that, five months after the conclusion of the Armistice, all the French questions are settled, whilst there is not even an agreement in principle on the Italian questions. I am very reasonable, and I am not asking that the latter be completely settled before the summoning of the German plenipotentiaries; I am only asking that decisions of principle be arrived at. If there is no serious disagreement amongst us, that could be done in forty-eight hours. It would be enough to set down the bases of the agreement and, between the time the Germans are summoned and the moment they arrive in Versailles, we'll have time to pursue the matter. I would observe that, until now, Italian affairs have never been discussed in this Council of Four.

M. Clemenceau. That is because, in everyone's opinion, the most pressing matter was to settle German affairs. However, I don't mean to contradict what you have just said.

M. Orlando. Four or five days must be devoted to a consideration of Italian questions.

M. Clemenceau. Do you mean all the questions that interest Italy, or only the one of Fiume and Dalmatia?

M. Orlando. That is the most important one.

Mr. Lloyd George. Like you, I think consideration of these questions must not be delayed. But I am anxious that we set the date for summoning the Germans before my departure, which takes place tomorrow.

M. Clemenceau. We mustn't set this date before we are sure of being ready.

*Does not appear in H.

President Wilson. Will we be if we provide for a postponement of ten days?

Mr. Lloyd George. I was just visited by two Belgian ministers, MM. Hymans and Vandervelde. I found the latter very open and very reasonable.

They wished to discuss the question of Luxembourg[1] with me. I told them that we were not ready, and I informed them of the outlines of the treaty we have prepared. They seemed satisfied with what I told them regarding reparations, as well as with our resolution regarding responsibilities and the trial of the Kaiser; they are especially happy about our proposal to reserve the role of prosecutor for Belgium. I proposed to submit to their financial experts the final draft of the text relating to reparation, on which they have, after all, collaborated in the commission.

President Wilson. What do they say about the territorial questions?

Mr. Lloyd George. They would like to receive a letter from us telling them that we are glad to know that they have undertaken negotiations with Luxembourg looking towards a rapprochement of the two countries.

M. Clemenceau. I am prepared to do everything to assist them, except to appear to be making a present of Luxembourg to them.

Mr. Lloyd George. The Belgians view with displeasure a plebiscite in Luxembourg, which I believe must at one and the same time settle the political system of the country and its customs system. They would like us to assist them at this time with a letter expressing our good will towards their negotiations with Luxembourg. Mr. Lansing, it seems, has shown himself favorably disposed. But I told them I could promise them nothing before bringing the question before the Four.

President Wilson. Mr. Lansing was only expressing a personal opinion. Naturally, any decision must be taken in common.

M. Clemenceau. I am not against the union of Belgium and Luxembourg; but it must be done properly. For my part, I cannot throw Luxembourg into the arms of Belgium. I ask to be informed about the state of the question before replying to you.

President Wilson. Let us return to the question raised by M. Orlando. Would he see any objection to summoning the Germans now, to appear within ten days, whilst we commit ourselves to

---

[1] For earlier discussions of Belgium's relationship to Luxembourg, see XII, n. 6.

spending the time required to study the Italian question amongst ourselves this week, before the date when he himself must return to Italy? When the Germans arrive, they will need several days to scrutinize the text we submit to them, and that will give us time to complete, if necessary, our consideration of the problems which interest Italy especially.

M. Orlando. I have the greatest desire to reach agreement with you. But I have two observations to make. First and foremost, it is necessary to emphasize the impression that such a decision would create in Italy. My fellow countrymen know that at the present time the questions which concern us are unresolved. If we now announce that the Germans are summoned for a date in the near future, that will cause the Italians to believe that the questions they regard as vital are seen by the Allies as being outside the general peace. So much the better if that impression is consequently contradicted by events; but at the outset it will be disastrous.

In the second place, I believe our questions can be settled in principle this week, and I hope they will be; they can receive a simple solution. But in what situation would I find myself and in what situation would you place the conference itself if the Germans arrived here before the Italian question was settled? The Italian government would then be in a very perilous situation; the effect would be nearly the same as that of a separate peace, and that would create dangers so grave that I prefer not to explain myself further.

M. Clemenceau. Can you be precise about what you are asking?

M. Orlando. I am asking that the summons of the Germans not be issued before the Italian questions are settled in general outline; that can be done in forty-eight hours and, in that case, the summons could follow immediately, the Germans could still be here in ten days. But I wouldn't like them to be summoned before our agreement in principle had been reached.

Mr. Lloyd George. That is absolutely impossible. I would point out that the first request for an armistice came from Germany. Afterwards, we received news that Austria wished to negotiate. Then we considered the situation, and, in spite of our main concern, which was to stop hostilities with Germany as soon as possible, given the heavy losses which the British, French, and American armies were suffering, we decided in the general interest to conclude an armistice with Austria first.

Today, the terms of the problem are reversed: if it is impossible to lead two horses abreast, one must be allowed to move in front of the other, and there is no doubt that we must deal with Germany first. Don't forget that Italy is also interested in the conclusion of the preliminaries with Germany, if only in the chapter on reparation.

We have spent weeks and months preparing the preliminaries of peace with Germany, because we were all agreed on the necessity of negotiating with that power first. You are not proposing to summon the Austrians, the Turks, the Bulgarians here to talk with them at the same time as with the Germans. We could say about Turkey what you are saying about Austria. We still have hundreds of thousands of British soldiers on Ottoman territory, and we would like to be able to demobilize them. In delaying, however little, direct negotiations with Germany, we run the risk of prolonging the anxiety and uneasiness of the entire world, which Italy shares. From the political point of view, what concerns Italy most is the settlement of the Austrian questions. But from the economic point of view, Italy is interested in the settlement of German affairs.

We cannot further delay summoning the German plenipotentiaries. They will need some time to study the document we will hand them, not only because this document will be long and complicated, but also because it affects the entire life of their people for a period of perhaps half a century. Whilst they proceed with that study, we could consider the Austrian questions and even call the Austrian delegates here. I hope the summoning of the Germans will not be delayed until we have taken our final decisions on Fiume and Dalmatia—questions which have absolutely nothing to do with Germany.

President Wilson. Would M. Orlando be satisfied if we announced that, whilst we are summoning the Germans and are actively continuing consideration of the other questions, the Italian question has priority over all the others? We could add that we have every hope of a prompt solution of the problems that concern Italy.

M. Orlando. I would reply to Mr. Lloyd George that there is no relationship between the question raised today about the peace and the one raised last November about the subject of the Armistice. At the basis of our decision on the date of the Armistice, there was a question of fact. I do believe we received a definite request for an armistice from Austria before receiving one from Germany. But in any case, the problem of the peace is completely different. Now it is a matter of reestablishing law and normal conditions.

Mr. Lloyd George says: "The questions concerning Italy and those which relate to the German peace are separate." Perhaps they are legally; but politically, they are linked. If we talk concretely, not abstractly, I would ask you this question: what would happen if peace was signed with Germany whilst a state of war continued in the Adriatic? England, France, and the United States would be at peace, and there would be no peace for Italy.

I appeal to Mr. Lloyd George's sense of justice and to our mutual friendship during several years of collaboration. Five months have passed since the conclusion of the Armistice; weeks have been devoted to difficult and admittedly necessary discussions about problems such as that of reparation. The representatives of Italy have waited patiently; during this delay, they didn't ask for priority for the questions which especially interest them. At the end of these five months, I ask you for a few days to know at least in what sauce you intend to cook me, and you refuse?

To President Wilson, I would reply: are we certain we can arrive at a general agreement on the Italian questions between the time the Germans are summoned and their arrival? I hope so. But are we sure of it?

M. Clemenceau. No.

M. Orlando. I thank M. Clemenceau for this word. We still haven't deliberated on the questions which interest me; I am in the dark, and I can't say whether the conversation amongst the four of us will allow me to arrive in time.

M. Clemenceau. Don't misunderstand what I just said. I agree with President Wilson in asking for the immediate summoning of the Germans; in the interval, we must, without losing a moment, do what is necessary to be ready when the Germans arrive. Between the moment of their arrival and the beginning of the negotiations, I am ready to study the Italian questions. But I repeat that we haven't a moment to lose if we want to be prepared to talk with the Germans within ten days.

M. Orlando. I repeat my objection. When we are prepared to sign the preliminaries with the Germans, will the Italian questions have received a satisfactory solution, at least in principle? In the contrary case, you would place me in an extremely difficult situation. From the Italian point of view, it is dangerous if the summoning of the Germans is announced when we know nothing about the solutions which concern us. What I am asking you for is an effort of two or three days.

M. Clemenceau. Why won't you agree that our discussion should take place as soon as the Germans have arrived, during the time they need to study the text of the preliminaries? Don't forget that we still have very important points to settle before meeting the

German plenipotentiaries: the text relating to Alsace-Lorraine, the text relating to direct reconstruction of the devastated regions.

M. Orlando. The proposal President Wilson made a short time ago differs from the one M. Clemenceau is now making. President Wilson said: "We will study the Italian questions during the interval between the time we summon the Germans and the time of their arrival." M. Clemenceau proposes to examine them after the arrival of the Germans: that proposal is still more unfavorable to me.

President Wilson. May I say aloud the thoughts which come to my mind? The difficulty that M. Orlando is struggling with is real; it is the same one which worries Mr. Lloyd George in England and M. Clemenceau in France. It is a matter of satisfying a public opinion which is ill-informed and worried. The problem is not foreign to me. In America, too, we are asked: "What are you doing? What is your position? What is happening in those meetings between you and the three statesmen who visit you every day?" Without any doubt, the time has come to reply. I will also be obliged to do it, and in writing, whilst you have the advantage of being able to speak directly to your parliaments.

Would M. Orlando be satisfied if we announced now that all the questions relating to Germany have reached a point of maturity which allows us to summon the German plenipotentiaries within ten days, but that we have decided to delay that summons until we have come to an agreement with Italy on the questions concerning her? This manner of proceeding would have the advantage of informing our public that we are prepared and of announcing at the same time that we have thought it reasonable to acknowledge to our Italian colleague that the Italian questions must be settled urgently.

Mr. Lloyd George. How will this arrangement work? At the time of the final draft of the treaty, certain lacunae will obviously be found which we will have to fill in. There are still certain questions of principle for which we haven't yet worked out a final formula. Do you mean that we shall only summon the Germans after having resolved in detail all the questions of wording, and after having solved the Italian question? I am very sorry, but I can't agree with that view. I am convinced that it is in the general interest to summon the Germans straightaway and thus to prepare ourselves to negotiate with the only enemy state which is still standing.

M. Orlando. I thank President Wilson. He has understood that my feeling is genuine and profound. Since I have always shown myself to be very conciliatory, you will understand that I must have very serious reasons for speaking as I do. I don't believe what I am asking can cause a considerable delay. I am only asking you for a very short time to permit our questions to be considered. If, in three days, we succeed in outlining the solution, we could then summon the Germans for the following week. We are not keeping a transcript, and my memory may deceive me; but I believe I remember that we always meant not to summon the Germans before we had general ideas about the solution of all important questions. I believe I even remember that President Wilson spoke of his concern not to delay the solution of near eastern questions.

I am asking you to place me at least in a position to announce that our questions have been considered by the Allies. Otherwise, the impression in Italy would be terrible. It will be said that problems vital to the Italian people were relegated to the same rank as those of Teschen or Mesopotamia. Italian public opinion is very excitable. I am doing everything possible to calm it; but the consequences of a disappointment of this kind would be very grave. When I appear before the Italian Parliament on April 23, the least that can happen is the fall of the cabinet, the effect of which would certainly not be to hasten the conclusion of the peace. I beg you to accept what President Wilson has proposed.

President Wilson. In any case, you could tell the Italian Parliament that the Italian questions have been and will continue to be considered without losing a moment during the ten-day period from the present. By announcing that we have summoned the Germans at the end of that ten-day period, we would be saying that this won't at all delay the consideration of questions outside the preliminaries of peace with Germany, and that the Italian question is first on the list.

Maybe we won't arrive at a solution of the Italian problems before April 23. In that case, wouldn't it be advantageous for M. Orlando to be able to explain to his Parliament his own point of view, as well as that of the other Associated governments, in order to inform Italy that what is delaying the solution is only the exchange of views necessary amongst friends who wish to do nothing except in a spirit of friendship for the Italian people? I hope it will be possible to set a date now for the Germans and to declare that the Italian question is the first item on our agenda.

I was just going to propose that we have no meeting tomorrow, in order to give me time to consider these problems at length with M. Orlando.[2] By announcing only the day after tomorrow that we are summoning the Germans, we will have the right to say that discussion of the Italian questions has begun.

M. Orlando. I hope our conversation tomorrow can clarify the situation. If the Germans aren't summoned before Tuesday, I can't wait. But that allows me to suspend my judgment only for twenty-four hours more.

Mr. Lloyd George. This means that, if tomorrow, there is no prospect of an immediate agreement on the question of the Adriatic, the German treaty will remain in the air; that's what is impossible for me to accept. To indicate my feelings regarding Italy, I add that I am ready to accept in advance any solution on which President Wilson and M. Orlando manage to agree.

M. Orlando appeals to our feelings of friendship. I ask him to consider our situation. France and Great Britain made war longer than Italy; their losses were heavier: England had twice as many dead and France at least three times. Without speaking of the general interest, we have the right to stress to Italy those considerations which especially concern us.

There is also the matter of allowing world trade to revive; as long as we have no treaty with Germany, the economic life of the entire world will remain at standstill.

M. Orlando. I don't wish to compare our sacrifices, and I accept Mr. Lloyd George's comment, while recalling that, if the number of dead is compared to the population, I believe Italy's losses were heavier than England's.

I understand as well as anyone the interest we all have in making peace with Germany promptly. That is why I have consented

---

[2] Wilson conferred for about two hours with Orlando and other members of the Italian delegation at 11 a.m. on April 14. Orlando brought with him Andrea Ossoinack, former member for Fiume of the Hungarian Parliament. A transcript of their conversation is printed in *PWW*, Vol. 57, pp. 337-43.

At this general meeting, Wilson handed Orlando a memorandum on the question of Italian claims in the Adriatic (printed in *ibid.*, pp. 343-45), which set forth the arguments and proposals that Wilson would repeat many times in the near future: a restatement of the principles and spirit of the Fourteen Points Address; the fact that the dissolution of the Austro-Hungarian Empire had removed the Italian need to control the Dalmatian coast and islands for security reasons, in other words, that new circumstances had rendered the Treaty of London obsolete; what he, Wilson was willing to concede to Italy by way of changes in her northern and northeastern borders (later referred as the Wilson Line); and why Fiume could not be ceded to Italy, but should be included in the Yugoslav customs system, with "a very considerable degree of genuine autonomy" for Fiume.

Wilson told Orlando that he could publish his memorandum in Italy, which the Italian Prime Minister did on April 29, 1919.

for weeks to give priority to the German questions. I gave you weeks, and I am only asking for a few days: I hope this proportion of time bears a relationship to our sacrifices.

President Wilson. Tomorrow we will spend the day discussing the Italian questions amongst the two of us. I would be very happy to be able to announce on Tuesday that the study has been pursued actively and even, if our conversation allows it, that we glimpse the solution. We will say that the Germans are summoned for April 25 because the preliminaries of peace with Germany are ready, and that that very fact facilitates the discussion of other important questions, of which the first is the Italian question. I don't see how we could give you a clearer priority, and I hope this will allow you to face the difficulties you foresee.

M. Clemenceau. I agree to summon the Germans for April 25.

President Wilson. We must do what is necessary to press on with the consideration of the Italian question, without neglecting the finishing touches on the preliminaries of peace with Germany.

M. Orlando. I insist on repeating that I can only suspend my judgment until after our conversation tomorrow. I don't know whether it will be possible for me to say tomorrow evening anything other than what I am saying today.

Mr. Lloyd George. If that is so, you are putting everything in doubt again. As for myself, I am compelled to leave tomorrow morning.

M. Orlando. I'll try to inform you about my position before your departure.

—MM. Haskins, Headlam-Morley, and Tardieu are introduced. They show on the map the last changes in the delimitation of the territory of the Saar, in order to bring the boundary into conformity with administrative divisions.

XXXIV

Conversation between President Wilson and MM. Clemenceau, Balfour, and Orlando*

APRIL 15, 1919, 11 A.M.

THE QUESTION OF LUXEMBOURG

Mr. Balfour. I would like to discuss the question of Luxembourg with you. England has no direct interest in that question. But we see France regaining Alsace-Lorraine and obtaining the coal mines of the Saar: if Belgium, after events which have earned her the sympathy of the whole world, gets nothing of what she asks, the impression will be deplorable—and even more so if Luxembourg becomes French.

M. Clemenceau. I agree with you. I accept every word you have just said.

Mr. Balfour. I saw M. Hymans: he told me that a bill for a plebiscite is to be introduced next Thursday in the Luxembourg Parliament. He would like the great powers to send the Belgian government a letter indicating that they would view with pleasure the success of the negotiations between Belgium and Luxembourg.

M. Clemenceau. I couldn't sign that letter, and if you sign it without us, the impression in France will be unfortunate. I am willing to seek a way to attain what the Belgians want. I don't want to leave Luxembourg as it is; I wish it to be united to Belgium. I only ask that the thing be done in such a way as not to shock French public opinion.

Could we not send an Englishman or an American to Luxembourg—not a Frenchman or a Belgian—to seek information and sound out opinion? There must be nothing in writing; the conference must not be involved. But we must try to find out what the Luxembourg parties think and want, and to prepare a solution by the expression of Luxemburgian public opinion, which no doubt must eventually be consulted by a plebiscite.

Mr. Balfour. Can't we instruct our envoy to express our sympathy for the ideas of a union between Luxembourg and Belgium?

M. Clemenceau. We have to act with tact and say simply that we

---

*Does not appear in H.

are leaving the door open to a union between the two countries—if Luxembourg desires it. I ask you to give me twenty-four hours so that I may have time to speak with M. Poincaré, who favors the union of Luxembourg to Belgium, and also with the Minister of Foreign Affairs. Undoubtedly, we will find a solution. In the meantime, you could write M. Hymans that you can't do what he asks, but that the conference is acting to the best of its ability, with the desire to do nothing against the will of the people of Luxembourg.

Mr. Balfour. This is what I propose to write to M. Hymans: (1) I did not succeed in the mission he entrusted to me; but (2) I found M. Clemenceau in full sympathy with Belgium and with no objection to her aspirations, if they can be realized without doing violence to the feelings of the Luxemburgers; (3) the question will be studied with the greatest care by the great powers, and we have every hope of arriving at a satisfying solution.

The question of the plebiscite remains, and it must be decided, in principle, next Thursday. M. Hymans objects to this plebiscite. I will note that the first question to be asked of the Luxembourg people is whether to maintain the dynasty. Wouldn't it be in our interest to prevent this plebiscite from taking place now?

M. Clemenceau. Certainly, and I won't hear of keeping the German dynasty.

Mr. Balfour. Then we can add that we want the plebiscite to be postponed until we know more about the state of public opinion in that country.

M. Clemenceau. That's it; you could advise M. Hymans of that and, at the same time, one of our governments, preferably the American government—since it has troops there—could send a telegram to Luxembourg along these lines.

—*Mr. Balfour's and M. Clemenceau's proposals are adopted.*

THE QUESTION OF LEMBERG

President Wilson. I have received news to the effect that the Poles are not acting correctly in Lemberg.[1] The Ukrainians complain that the representatives of Poland have dragged out the discussions in order to gain military advantages before the moment of the cease-fire. I have here a letter from the Ukrainian general,

[1] A memorandum by Gen. Francis Joseph Kernan, a member of the Noulens mission, printed in *PWW*, Vol. 57, pp. 275-80.

Pavlenko,[2] saying that the Ukrainians accepted the terms proposed by the Allies for a military truce, whilst the Poles insisted on maintaining a line of demarcation which prejudges the solution of the dispute between them and the Ruthenians, so that it is their fault that hostilities have continued.

I believe this exposition of the facts is true, and that it would be useful to make representations to the Polish government. It would perhaps be as well not to summon M. Paderewski about this: General Bliss, who is receiving reports from General Kernan, in charge of mediating between the Ruthenians and the Poles, is fully qualified to speak in our name to the Polish delegation.

—*This proposal is adopted.*

—*After an exchange of views about the position to be taken towards the secondary powers at the time of summoning the Germans to Versailles, it is decided:*

(1) That the Ministers of Foreign Affairs of the United States, France, Great Britain, Italy, and Japan will receive separately, in groups of three, the delegates of the fifteen other belligerent powers and will inform them of the decision which the heads of governments of the Allied and Associated Governments have reached regarding the date of the convocation (April 25);

(2) They will announce to them that, on April 24—that is, before the first contact with the German plenipotentiaries—a secret session of the representatives of all the belligerent powers will take place, and the complete text of the preliminaries of peace will then be given to them;

(3) The reports of the commissions which have not yet been presented will be communicated in the same session, or earlier if possible.

—Mr. Balfour lists the questions on which final decisions have not yet been taken and which must be settled before April 25. They are the following:

Territorial questions:
—the frontier of Denmark;
—Heligoland;
—the frontier of Belgium;
—Danzig and Marienwerder.

Have we arrived at a precise draft?

President Wilson. I have that draft on my desk.

M. Clemenceau. I will ask you to consider again the question of the

[2] M. Omelianovych-Pavlenko to the Supreme Council, n.d., printed in *ibid.*, p. 356, n. 2.

territory of Marienwerder. If it was decided to make it part of East Prussia, the consequence would be to cut lines of communication vital for Poland. I completely share the point of view of the Poles on that question.

President Wilson. In any case, we must delay consideration of that question until Mr. Lloyd George's return; it is he who has shown the greatest interest in it.

—Mr. Balfour continues:
—reconstruction in kind in devastated regions (that question is under study and is to be the subject of a report by M. Loucheur);
—guarantee of the payment of indemnities (question of the temporary occupation of the left bank of the Rhine);
—the Kiel Canal: on that question, the Commission on Waterways should be consulted. If it has not drawn up its opinion, the question should be referred back to it;
—report of the Commission on Ports, Waterways, and Railways;
—question of the disarmed zone on the right bank of the Rhine;
—disarmament of the left bank of the Rhine.

President Wilson. It seems to me that the draft of the military terms deals with this question.

—Mr. Balfour continues:
—economic terms;
—provisions regarding commercial aviation.

M. Clemenceau. The question of Alsace-Lorraine has to be added because we have drafted nothing concerning it, and there must be something about it in the treaty, if only two lines.

Mr. Balfour. On the question of cables, Japan has something to ask; she wishes to keep the three lines she has seized. One of these lines belongs to a private company, and Japan is prepared to purchase it.

President Wilson. I have an observation to make. All these lines, as well as other important lines in the Pacific, meet on a small island called Yap. I will ask that this island be internationalized; for if it belonged to the Japanese, they could cut communications between different parts of the Pacific whenever they liked, notably between the United States and the Philippines.

Mr. Balfour. There is still the question of Kiaochow.

President Wilson. China doesn't attach merely an economic importance to the cancellation of all foreign concessions in Shantung. Since this province is one of those which evoke the most sacred memories of its history and religion, she is particularly anxious to rid it of foreign influence. On the other hand, what the Japanese want most is not Kiaochow, which they themselves have offered to return to China, but the concessions in Shantung.

My sympathies are with China, and we must not forget that, in the future, the greatest dangers for the world can arise in the Pacific.

Mr. Balfour. When Japan entered the war, China being at that time a neutral state, the Japanese asked to keep what they would take from the Germans. We then consented.[3] Since then, a treaty was concluded between Japan and China.[4] We have asked that it be communicated to us, and so far we haven't received it. The Japanese agree to restore to China what they took from Germany.[5] But they say that, having made the sacrifices which made it possible to recapture the territory of Kiaochow, it must be ceded to them so that they can give it back to China afterwards. There is a question of national pride here.

President Wilson. We must first have the Sino-Japanese treaty in front of us. The Japanese are rather difficult in business. I know by experience that they are very clever in the interpretation of treaties.

M. Clemenceau. This week, we still have to hear the powers directly involved in the treaty with Germany: Belgium, Poland, and Bohemia. A morning must be reserved for each of them.

—It is agreed that a meeting of the Ministers of Foreign Affairs will be called for three o'clock, and that Mr. Balfour will make known there the decisions taken about the communiqué to be given to the secondary powers.

—The question of Schleswig and Heligoland will be studied by the Council of Four at the end of the afternoon.

[3] In an Anglo-Japanese secret exchange of notes of February 16 and 21, 1917. In this exchange, the British and Japanese agreed to divide German territories in the Pacific along the line of the equator, with Japan to acquire the German islands north of that line. For this agreement and the larger subject, see Ann-Yuen Yong Thaddée, *Chine & Japon à la Conférence de la Paix* (Abaye de Saint-André, 1934).

[4] A Sino-Japanese exchange of notes on September 24, 1918, concerning Japanese economic concessions in Shantung Province, about which much more will be said later.

[5] Balfour was confused. He here referred to the Sino-Japanese treaty of May 25, 1915, which resulted from negotiations over Japan's so-called twenty-one demands on China. See Madeleine Chi, *China Diplomacy, 1914-1918* (Cambridge, Mass., 1982), and Arthur S. Link, *Wilson: The Struggle for Neutrality, 1914-1915* (Princeton, N. J., 1960), pp. 267-308. A good monograph on the Shantung question at Paris is Russell H. Fifield, *Woodrow Wilson and the Far East: The Diplomacy of the Shantung Question* (New York, 1952).

XXXV

Conversation between President Wilson and MM. Clemenceau, Balfour, and Orlando. Present are Admirals Benson, de Bon, and Hope.*

APRIL 15, 1919, 4 P.M.

THE QUESTION OF HELIGOLAND

Mr. Balfour. It is obvious that we can't leave the island of Heligoland as it was before the war. It constitutes a threat, not only to the eastern coasts of England and Scotland, but to all the powers with interests in the North Sea. Should it become necessary for England and the United States to come to the aid of France under attack by Germany, Heligoland, even deprived of its fortifications, would remain dangerous. During the war, it was a formidable center for submarines and minelayers. It would remain as a dagger pointed at the naval communications of the neighboring nations.

President Wilson. We all agree about dismantling the island.

Admiral Benson. The question before us is whether the great port created by the German Admiralty should be destroyed and, if so, whether America should participate in that destruction.

Mr. Balfour. About the port, the Admiralty tells us that it was created by the Germans as a naval base, and that it never had any other use. Before the construction of this port, there was a small fishing port at Heligoland, which largely served the small seaside resort which clings to the side of the island.

Will it be said that, by destroying this naval base, we do damage to something legitimately needed during peacetime? I am told that ships can seek a refuge there against storms. But the Admiralty assures us that fishing boats easily found refuge along the island before the port was constructed, and that the disappearance of that naval base will cause them no harm. From the commercial point of view, fisherman have no interest in coming to Heligoland, which is a very small island, at least sixty kilometers from the markets of the mainland.

I conclude that the destruction of the naval base at Heligoland

---

*Does not appear in H.

would not harm the inhabitants of the island in any way, that it would do little injury to navigation, and that it would free the naval communications of neighboring powers from an indisputable danger. Once destroyed, this naval base could be rebuilt only by major and very drawn out construction. On the other hand, if the port, even disarmed, remains as it is, the Germans can, without fortifying it, in a matter of days protect it by mines and restore nearly all its offensive and defensive value.

President Wilson. Isn't the fact that this port served military uses only due to the German government's having reserved it for such uses?

Admiral Hope. As a refuge, this port is useless. In time of storm, ships of a certain tonnage can reach the mouth of the Elbe or Jade Bay without difficulty, and fishing boats find adequate refuge in the small port which existed before the present construction.

Admiral Benson. The reservation I have to make is this: once the island is disarmed, the port can be used for peaceful purposes, and it is better not to embark upon pointless destruction.

President Wilson. My concern is not to destroy anything unnecessarily, in order to avoid giving the impression of gratuitous violence. Since we are doing the essential thing in destroying the fortifications, I wouldn't go so far as to destroy works which could be useful in peacetime.

Mr. Balfour. Here is our navy's argument. In time of war, the most important thing today is to have a submarine base. To protect it, artillery is necessary. This we will destroy. But in the absence of artillery, one can fall back on mine fields, which require only two nights of work to lay, and in an instant they would make the island of Heligoland a formidable threat to all maritime powers.

Admiral de Bon. When we previously studied this question in the Supreme War Council,[1] we made the distinction between the fishing port and the naval port artificially created by Germany as an instrument of war. We find it legitimate to destroy the instrument of war, whilst leaving the fishing port, which is amply sufficient for economic needs. By leaving the artificial port to the

---

[1] Established by the British, French, and Italian governments by the so-called Rapallo Agreement on November 7, 1917, in the wake of the disaster at Caporetto, to coordinate the Allied war effort. Wilson, through Colonel House, agreed on November 16 to appoint a military member, General Bliss. The council, which had military, naval, and political members, sat at Versailles during the war and the peace conference. See David F. Trask, *The United States in the Supreme War Council: American War Aims and Inter-Allied Strategy, 1917-1918* (Middletown, Conn., 1961).

Germans, we would be leaving them what really constitutes the first step towards a complete restoration of their naval base. That seems to me pointless and dangerous.

If this port is considered as other than a fishing port, its existence would have to be justified by its commercial usefulness; but this usefulness is nonexistent since the island is only a pebble in the middle of the sea.

President Wilson. It is as a refuge that the port can be useful.

Mr. Balfour. Does the Admiral think that this port can be very useful as a refuge against storms?

Admiral de Bon. No; for small boats, the only ones which would need that kind of refuge, the natural ports are enough. The only two reasons that could be invoked for not destroying the port are the fear of carrying out a destruction which is not really necessary and, in addition, the difficulty of the work of destruction, which will be considerable.

Mr. Balfour. I could invoke another argument, although I only wish to do it with discretion; it is that of public feeling in England. The island of Heligoland belonged to Great Britain until 1890. We would never have ceded it to Germany if we had known what use she could make of it; but at that time there were no submarines, or mines, or aviation. Lord Salisbury, wishing to settle all sorts of questions pending between Great Britain and Germany all over the world, threw this little bit of change into the balance, thinking that Heligoland had little value for us and a certain sentimental value for the Germans.

Since then, bitter reproaches about this cession have been made against that government, of which I was a member, whilst forgetting the large transaction of which it was part. If today, with the left bank of the Rhine being disarmed, and even with the forced reduction of the German army, Heligoland retains even a dismantled military port, English public opinion won't forgive us for it.

M. Clemenceau. If this port is only a naval base, as our admirals think, there is no reason not to destroy it.

President Wilson. I could answer Mr. Balfour that, in the United States, public opinion will reproach us for having lacked composure in forgetting that we had reduced Germany to the status of a third-rank naval power.

Admiral Hope. The Admiralty has closely studied the question of the possible use of the port of Heligoland for fishing or trade; it has concluded that this port would serve neither. Besides, the proposals we have presented for its destruction leave enough jetties or piers to allow the island to provide more refuge than it offered previously.

President Wilson. I can't hold an opinion contrary to that of the naval authorities; but I believe we are exaggerating the importance of this matter.

M. Clemenceau. It can become considerable in certain circumstances.

Mr. Balfour. Don't our naval experts agree on this point—that Heligoland was the most formidable base of the German fleet during the war?

Admiral Benson. On the contrary, I think that the importance of Heligoland has been exaggerated. In future, its greatest value will undoubtedly be for aviation; in that regard, Heligoland could constitute a danger. But with the naval power of Germany being reduced as it must be, I don't believe the destruction is justifiable.

Mr. Balfour. We are in agreement if Germany, from the naval point of view, remains what we intend to make her by the treaty. But we have no more certainty in that respect than about the army, and I will call to your attention that, despite the reduction of military forces in Germany, we are stipulating that her land fortifications will be destroyed.

President Wilson. Yes, but we don't stipulate the destruction of the railroads in the left bank of the Rhine, although railroads are very important from the military point of view. The question didn't even arise, because rail networks are not made solely for war.

Mr. Balfour. I wonder if that argument doesn't turn against you, for we want the destruction of the detraining platforms on the left bank of the Rhine. The port of Heligoland serves no present commercial need.

President Wilson. If you don't believe in the permanence of the arrangements of the treaty, by which the military and naval forces of Germany must be reduced to limited proportions, you are correct in taking other precautions. But whilst chemical installations can be converted into factories for asphyxiating gases, I don't believe it is possible to construct warships, including submarines, without anyone knowing about it.

Admiral Benson. It is not impossible for submarines, which can be constructed in sections.

President Wilson. I am not convinced of the necessity of this destruction. If it was absolutely necessary, I wouldn't refuse.

M. Clemenceau. I must declare that I can't refuse England the destruction which seems to her absolutely necessary.

Mr. Balfour. My request doesn't seem unreasonable to you?

M. Clemenceau. Not at all; I would act as you do if I were in your place.

President Wilson. I continue to believe that your fears are excessive.

M. Clemenceau. I don't know; I have known the Germans for many years.

Admiral de Bon. As long as the Germans keep this port, they will be able to make it rapidly into an instrument of war.

Mr. Balfour. I recall yet again that no economic interest is at stake, and I am convinced that the Admiralty's arguments are very strong. Moreover, we will be reproached in England for not having gone far enough and for not having asked for the destruction of the entire island.

Besides, the time may come when we are blamed for having been shortsighted, and for not having foreseen the development of aviation, or of some other such danger in future. The role of destroyer is not the one I prefer.

—The naval experts withdraw.

THE QUESTION OF SCHLESWIG

Mr. Balfour. I will explain to you the conclusions on which the commission has agreed with the representatives of Denmark.[2] Northern Schleswig will be divided into three zones. In the first, where the population is purely Danish, a plebiscite will soon take place for that entire region, after its complete evacuation of all German soldiers and civil servants. The second, the region of Flensburg, is Germanized in part, especially the city of Flensburg itself, where the Germans created a port of some importance and where the majority of the population speaks German. In that zone, the plebiscite will take place later and by communes, instead of for the entire area at once. The third region, further south, which extends as far as the city of Schleswig, will be subject to the same kind of plebiscite as the preceding one; but the operation would be delayed there still further. The reason given is that that zone has been completely terrorized by the Germans for a long time. The example of the northern region, followed by that of the middle region, might give it the courage necessary to express its feelings openly.

[2] The Commission on Belgian and Danish Affairs had presented a report to the Council of Foreign Ministers on March 28. See *PPC*, IV, 529-32. The report is printed in Miller, *My Diary at the Conference of Paris*, X, 211-28.

A natural objection to this plan is the following: why apply different arrangements to these three zones? The representatives of Denmark especially insisted that these precautions be taken. The Danes don't wish to be open to reproach for having annexed any part of German territory by force.

If the vote by communes yields such a result that the boundary doesn't take form by itself, an international commission will be entrusted with drawing this border.

I fear difficulties in Flensburg; but the Danes seem more confident than I. They believe the economic interest of that city will lead it to their side. Our experts believe that, despite its apparent absurdities, this plan can work and will yield good results.

President Wilson. The commune which voted in favor of return to Denmark and which would then be located inside German borders would find itself in a painful situation. All I can say is that it is up to Denmark to decide about that, for it is she who suffered in 1864,[3] and if this plan is agreeable to the Danes, I accept it.

—*There follows a conversation about the agenda; it is decided that the border between Belgium and Germany will be discussed tomorrow at 11 o'clock, with a view to a final solution.*

[3] During the war of Prussia and Austria against Denmark.

XXXVI

Conversation between President Wilson and MM. Clemenceau, Balfour, and Orlando*

APRIL 16, 1919, 11 A.M.

President Wilson. There was a question about whether the Commission on Navigable Waterways had presented us with its conclusions concerning the Kiel Canal. I have the text of those conclusions,[1] to which we can return shortly.

I have to inform you of a request of Mr. Hoover who, in view of the fact that Hungary is making the victualing of Central Eu-

*Does not appear in H.

[1] "*Recommendations Regarding the Kiel Canal*," March 11, 1919, Wilson Papers, Library of Congress. Wilson summarizes it well and quotes a significant part of it below.

rope difficult by retaining some of the railroad rolling stock, wishes to be able to tell the Hungarians that their own victualing will depend upon the promptness with which they place the equipment at the disposal of our commission.[2]

—*This proposal is accepted.*

President Wilson. I received a memorandum from Dr. Lord,[3] our specialist on Polish and Baltic questions, which recommends the creation of a commission to study on site the questions relating to the establishment and future of Finland, Latvia, Estonia, etc.

Mr. Balfour. The present situation in that part of Europe is odd.[4] There are German troops on the coast of the Baltic who are fighting against the Bolsheviks and who ask us to help them by supplying them with coal and food and even by allowing them to receive reinforcements from Germany. We agreed to allow provisions absolutely essential to them to go through; but we have refused all reinforcements.

Given the chaos now reigning in those areas, the Germans, by preventing the formation of local armies, and by forcing the countries which they occupy to rely entirely upon their aid against the Bolshevik invasion, are working for the permanence of their influence and domination.

—*It is decided to send the commission of inquiry proposed by Dr. Lord to the Baltic countries.*

M. Clemenceau. I have to propose to you the establishment of a committee of five members to oversee the drafting of the clauses of the treaty and to insure that they will be complete and arrive on time. This committee will report to us on the twenty-third of this month.

Mr. Balfour. I fear that this committee would duplicate the work of the Drafting Committee.

M. Clemenceau. I don't insist.

—*M. Hymans, Sir Eyre Crowe, Mr. Haskins, and M. Tardieu are introduced.*

President Wilson (*to M. Hymans*). We have invited you to come here in order to prepare with you our final decision about the drawing of the German-Belgian border.

[2] H. C. Hoover to WW, with Enclosure, April 15, 1919, *PWW*, Vol. 57, pp. 367-69.
[3] R. H. Lord to J. C. Grew, April 8, 1919, *ibid.*, pp. 137-39.
[4] See X, n. 5.

M. Tardieu. The commission's report[5] concludes in favor of the annexation by Belgium of the territory of Moresnet—left in a state of neutrality between Germany and Belgium by the treaty of 1815—as well as the districts of Malmédy and Eupen.

M. Clemenceau. Would you like to summarize the main points of these conclusions?

M. Tardieu. These territories are inhabited by a rather sparse population, almost exclusively Walloon, which was once united to Belgium and has always retained a sympathy for her. Economic interest draws it towards the neighboring Belgian population. Moreover, the claim of reparation has merit concerning the Hertogenwald Forest, near Eupen, the Belgian portion of which was destroyed during the war.

The figures for the population of these districts are as follows, respectively: Moresnet, 4,600 inhabitants; Eupen, 26,000; Malmédy, 34,000.

M. Hymans. I must ask you for a slight change in our first drawing of the boundary lines; the commission has already taken it up. The goal of this change is twofold. It would allow us, in the first place, to occupy a dominant position near Aix-la-Chapelle,[6] and, in the second place, to have on our territory the entire line of the railroad from Eupen to Malmédy, whose passage across two borders would be a nuisance for the population. That change would affect only 4,000 inhabitants, along with a part of the Hertogenwald.

Mr. Balfour. Are these 4,000 Germans or 4,000 Flemings?

M. Hymans. Four thousand Germans. As for the Flemings, there are none in that area; the nearest populations are Walloon.

Mr. Balfour. Didn't the commission provide for a plebiscite in those districts or, in any case, any opportunity for the inhabitants to make their feeling known? If that is so, it is not in your interest to claim 4,000 more Germans.

M. Hymans. We are only doing it because of the railroad, which plays an important role in the life of these peasant people. The line unites Eupen and Malmédy, and it would be very inconvenient, in going from one city to the other, to submit to customs twice.

Mr. Balfour. We must carefully consider whether the annexation doesn't offer more disadvantages than advantages. Isn't the population of Eupen largely German?

---

[5] About which, see XII, n. 6.
[6] That is, Aachen.

M. Hymans. They speak a low German dialect.

M. Clemenceau. It seems to me that, if there must be a plebiscite, you have no interest in annexing too many Germans.

M. Hymans. The question of Eupen is linked to that of the Hertogenwald Forest. The Belgian part of that forest was destroyed by the Germans; we are claiming the other part as compensation. Now, its exploitation is impossible without possession of the city of Eupen, where all the roads and means of work are concentrated. Besides, Eupen has the same industry as Verviers—wool—and is linked to Verviers by its interests.

Mr. Balfour. Do you take into account the fact that the commission recommended consulting the inhabitants?

President Wilson. The commission proposes that, at the end of six months, a register be opened, where the inhabitants can inscribe their protest or their approval. The result of that consultation will be communicated to the League of Nations, whose decision Belgium accepts in advance.

M. Hymans. We accept that procedure; it is all a matter of good administration. Aside from the undoubted feelings of the Walloons, we know that their interests attach them to Belgium.

President Wilson. Mr. Haskins tells me that the value of the Hertogenwald Forest will be deducted from reparations, like the value of the mines of the Saar from what is due to France. You don't object?

M. Hymans. No.

Mr. Balfour. I notice that the railroad that you wish to see pass only over Belgian territory serves the small city of Montjoie, which would remain in Germany. Isn't that an objection which might be made against you?

M. Hymans. We are not claiming Montjoie, because it is a purely German city, despite its name, which is only a corruption of the original name, Mönchau, "the meadow of the monks."

M. Tardieu. This railway has a military value only for Germany. It served the camp of Elsenborn, near Malmédy.

President Wilson. Doesn't it seem to you that, despite the small number of people concerned—4,000—we would in their case risk departing from the principle that we seek to apply to much greater problems? Aren't we obliged to have as many scruples when it is a question of 4,000 Germans or four million?

M. Hymans. We could emphasize the historical argument and, from this point of view, our claims are very moderate, for we are staying well within the boundary of 1815. On this entire question, I rely on your judgment.

President Wilson. I am looking at it from the point of view of the feelings of the inhabitants and of the interests of Belgium. If you introduce an element making for unrest into these newly united territories, that won't do you any good.

M. Hymans. I agree with you, and we want to have as few Boches as possible in Belgium.

President Wilson. We must avoid pointless difficulties and also avoid seeming to pay little heed to our own principles just because it affects only a small group of people.

M. Hymans. That is true; but there must also be logic in drawing a boundary line. It is rather absurd to see a railroad which serves two cities cross a foreign territory between those two cities.

President Wilson. This problem can be compared to that of the railroad from Danzig to Mława, which crosses through German populations, then a rather large group of Polish populations, then again a German territory, in order finally to enter into Poland proper. We are seeking the solution of these difficulties in a convention guaranteeing transit. We don't believe the fate of a people can be linked to that of a railroad, but that the problem of the railroad should rather be solved in such a way as not to violate the rights of peoples.

M. Hymans. We have sought a logical and practical border, and we believe it conforms to the interests of the populations.

Mr. Balfour. No great economic interest is involved in that change.

M. Hymans. No, except concerning the extension of the Hertogenwald Forest, which would be ceded to us.

As for the small change we are requesting on the side of Aix-la-Chapelle, it is a very small thing; it only concerns a hill which gives us a dominant position in relation to the city.

President Wilson. I don't see the necessity of that dominant position, since there will be no German fortification between your border and a line fifty kilometers beyond the Rhine.

Mr. Haskins calls my attention to Article 8, which provides for changes in the Dutch-German border. That article could compel Germany to accept in advance a territorial change which might ultimately be decided by the League of Nations, in case Holland should demand access to the estuary of the Ems, subject to the agreement of the people involved.

Mr. Balfour. What is the reason for that article?

M. Tardieu. The discussion between Holland and Belgium hasn't yet begun. Since we are on the point of beginning negotiations with Germany, we must try to open the possibility of later exchanges of territories. In this text, the commission has indicated the principle and, at the same time, fixed the maximum of what could eventually be asked of the Germans.

President Wilson. It is dangerous to anticipate negotiations which haven't yet begun. Is it our business to rectify the boundary of Holland, which we neither fought against nor alongside? It would seem to me questionable to insert in our treaty with Germany a clause providing a possible settlement of Dutch-Belgian affairs; we would find ourselves mixed up in something which directly concerns neither Germany nor ourselves.

When M. Hymans first informed us of that question, I told him that we had no means to compel Holland to cede territories, and that the solution of the differences between Belgium and Holland could be sought only by those two powers. It was asserted, it is true, that it was a matter of revising the treaties of 1839, and that this concerns all the powers that signed these treaties. But, on the one hand, all the signatories of the treaties of 1839 are not present, since Holland hasn't yet participated in the discussion; on the other hand, newcomers are involved in this discussion, such as the United States, which are forced to take a different point of view. I consider the question of the boundary between Holland and Germany to be outside those we are settling now.

M. Hymans. When we came to explain our position regarding the Treaty of 1839 to the conference, we thought that it wouldn't be proper not to make this report before all the Allied and Associated Powers, even though, in fact, that question specifically concerns only the signatories of the Treaty of 1839. Holland, invited to negotiate with us, replied that she agreed to come and inform the conference of her views. We would like this hearing to take place soon. It will be followed by negotiations between Holland and Belgium for the settlement of questions concerning themselves. The most important question for our country is that of the navigation of the Scheldt. There lies the future of the port of Antwerp, there lies our military and political security. We are not asking that this problem be solved by annexations; we are asking that it receive a solution; there can be another one besides the territorial solution.

President Wilson. The proposal we are considering at this time contemplates compensations for Holland at Germany's expense; we cannot embark upon that course.

M. Hymans. It must be anticipated that Holland will ask us for compensations; we have the means to provide them; it doesn't seem to me unjust to ask them from the enemy, on the condition always that the people involved wouldn't suffer. But the inhabitants of German Gelderland and Friesland are closely related to their neighbors in the Netherlands. After what the Germans did in 1914, after these four years of war and what they have cost our country, I don't believe it is unfair to ask that compensation from Germany.

Mr. Balfour. In my opinion, the only argument that could justify this policy would rest on the sympathy of the region's inhabitants for Holland. Then it would be a question similar to that of Schleswig. Do we have reason to believe that that sympathy exists?

M. Tardieu. I will recall that our commission had no mandate concerning the negotiations between Holland and Belgium. Our task was to draft articles which would possibly be helpful in negotiations about which we had no information.

President Wilson. The commission did what it had to do. But by providing a plebiscite in German Gelderland and Friesland, you have determined in advance the reply of the Dutch. They will say: "What will be our compensation, if these people refuse to be annexed to Holland?"

M. Hymans. We could make a conditional arrangement with Holland. But if the proposal you are considering is discarded, compensation itself becomes impossible. We are very anxious to establish a friendly agreement with Holland and to preserve the most cordial relations with that country. To that end, we mustn't allow irritating questions to remain between Belgium and Holland. A solution must be found for them, and I don't know how we will find it if we can't arrange any compensation. The proposed solution seems good to me, because it rests on the real affinity of the populations.

M. Tardieu. All the commission sought was to leave the door open to a possible negotiation.

—M. Hymans and the experts withdraw.

President Wilson. I am afraid of this proposal. To make Germany foot the bill in a transaction which has nothing to do with the war seems a bit too much to me.

Mr. Balfour. I must say that I also dislike that very much. The attitude of the Belgians in this question has always been a bit brazen. For example, when I told the Dutch Minister: "Be assured that none of us is thinking of taking territory from a neutral power against the will of the inhabitants," M. Hymans told me, "That is true, but you should not have said it to the Dutch Minister."

President Wilson. I think we agree to discard these new articles and to keep the commission's text as it was before.

I return to the Kiel Canal, about which here are the conclusions of the Commission on Navigable Waterways. It proposes, on the assumption that the Kiel Canal remains in German territory, to insert in the treaty the following clause, without prejudice to the military guarantees which could be stipulated:

"The Kiel Canal will remain under the sovereignty of Germany, subject to the application to this canal and to its banks of rules which will subsequently be formulated for the regime of international navigable waterways, especially of rules concerning the freedom of navigation for persons, property, and flags of all nations at peace with Germany, no distinction being made between German persons, property, and flags and those of other states at peace with Germany. That arrangement will apply not only to commercial vessels but also to warships."

I will observe that this clause will place the Kiel Canal under the same arrangement as that of the Panama Canal. Concerning the fortifications of the canal, I believe that, after consideration, we have decided not to destroy them. It would be rather delicate for us, who have fortified the Panama Canal, to impose different terms on the Kiel Canal, which crosses exclusively German territory.

Mr. Balfour. Without denying the weight of that argument, I will point out that there are also contrary arguments. The Kiel Canal doubles the naval power of Germany, a power which she has, moreover, abused. It might be useful to study this question again.

M. Clemenceau. That's my opinion, and I will communicate on this subject with the Minister of the Navy.[7]

[7] Georges-Jean-Claude Leygues.

XXXVII

Conversation between President Wilson and MM. Clemenceau, Viscount Chinda, Balfour, Lansing, and Baron Sonnino*

APRIL 16, 1919, 4 P.M.

M. Clemenceau. It was thought useful to call together the Council of Four and the Council of Five** to exchange mutual information on our respective activities. Has the Council of Five any questions to refer to the Council of Four?

Baron Sonnino. Several secondary questions are still to be considered: the questions of the prohibition of the opium trade, that of provisions concerning the Suez Canal, and the draft of the general clause of renunciation by Germany of all territories that she holds outside Europe, which will be left in the hands of the five great powers, which will determine their fate.

President Wilson. Are we wrong in thinking that you wished to meet with us to arrive at final conclusions on different questions?

Baron Sonnino. There is the question of the upkeep of the occupation army. The calculation of expenses has been made on different bases, and it is a question of deciding which must be adopted.

M. Clemenceau. Isn't that commission business?

Mr. Lansing. It seems to me that this question had been referred to the Supreme Economic Council.

Mr. Balfour. It was referred back to the Council of Four yesterday.

President Wilson. Does it concern the occupation army before or after the peace treaty goes into effect?

Baron Sonnino. Both.

President Wilson. For the present, the question is settled: the expenses of the occupation army will be charged against the amount of reparations.

Baron Sonnino. General Weygand explained to us the other day that there are two ways to calculate, and that it would be necessary to decide between them. It is a matter of knowing the nature of the expenses which must be covered.

President Wilson. I have always understood that by "expenses of

---

*Does not appear in H.
**Composed of the Ministers of Foreign Affairs of the five Principal Allied and Associated Powers.

the occupation army" we mean the expenses of its maintenance on the territory that it occupies.

Mr. Lansing. On this subject, General Pershing asked Marshal Foch a question which hasn't yet received an answer.

M. Clemenceau. We can only decide on the basis of a report, or after having heard our experts.

Baron Sonnino. The military differ in opinion.

President Wilson. Then let us ask them to tell us what that difference of opinion is.

Mr. Balfour. A discussion on this subject took place at Spa.

—Mr. Balfour reads aloud a few lines from the minutes of that discussion.

President Wilson. Can that question be entrusted to someone who will enlighten us on what we are being asked to decide?

Mr. Balfour. What we need is a summary of the opinions stated, with the reasons supporting them.

President Wilson. Can't this question be referred to the military representatives of the Allied and Associated Powers at Versailles,* who will refer to the minutes which Mr. Balfour has just read and then present us with a statement of the question?

—This proposal is adopted.

Mr. Balfour. Is it really necessary that that question be settled before the signing of the preliminaries?

President Wilson. It is part of the peace treaty.

Baron Sonnino. The Germans accepted the principle of the payment of the expenses of the occupation army when the Armistice was signed. But it is natural that they should wish to know how far their obligation extends.

M. Clemenceau. Do you have other questions to submit to us?

Mr. Balfour. Some secondary amendments to the military clauses have been presented. There is one on which the representatives of the five powers don't agree: it is the one relating to the secrets of certain war industries.

Mr. Lansing. It involves compelling the Germans to reveal the secrets of manufacturing certain products used in the conduct of the war contrary to international law. This is aimed essentially at gases and other chemical products.

The representatives of the United States have declared themselves against that clause. In fact, I don't believe this obligation, if we should impose it upon the Germans, would add much to

---
*The Supreme War Council.

what we already know. Moreover, the knowledge of secrets of manufacture would add nothing to our real means of protection against these dangerous products, which is the prohibition against their manufacture. Finally, one can't demand such information without at the same time asking for the revelation of secrets of industrial manufactures, such as dyestuffs. That is what we don't have the right to do under a military pretext. I don't see, moreover, the military usefulness of our demands if we admit, as our technical advisers keep on saying freely, that our gases are now superior to those of the Germans.

Mr. Balfour. I am told that our military advisers insist on that provision, and I can assure you that they are completely uninterested in anything concerning dyestuffs. They seem, however, to attach great interest to that question, and I can assure Mr. Lansing that the ulterior motives he has just mentioned don't exist in the minds of the men who proposed that clause.

Baron Sonnino. Without suspecting them of any such intention, one could say that the measure we would be taking for military motives would have inevitable economic consequences.

President Wilson. That is precisely what I think; it is not a question of suspecting the English military authorities of any ulterior motive.

Baron Sonnino. Moreover, what is the good of knowing the secret of manufacturing gases if not in order to use them oneself?

Mr. Balfour. It must be known in order to protect oneself—to know, for example, how to manufacture protective masks.

President Wilson. The great objection is the following. It is easy to require the revelation of technical secrets; but how will you ever know if you have obtained them? I have lived for a long time in universities, and I know what goes on in laboratories. There are scientists who, when they engage in research which they consider important, keep their formulas in their heads, for fear their discovery might be stolen from them. German chemists will tell you what they like.

My objection to the insertion of this article is its ineffectiveness. We know enough about German dissimulation and ruses. The Germans will perhaps give you their old formulas, but how will you compel them to reveal the new ones?

Mr. Balfour. I am inclined to agree with you. But since our military seems to attach a certain importance to that clause, we must hear what they have to say. I don't know if there is any answer to the argument President Wilson has just presented. We will see if our experts can reply.

President Wilson. Your experts know better than I do what they want, but I know as well as they do what they have a chance of getting.

Mr. Balfour. I believe we can't refuse to hear them.

President Wilson. I am always ready to hear the military, and I always listen to them with interest. But, even now, I declare myself flatly against that article. We can refer it to the Supreme War Council, which will give us a report.

Mr. Balfour. In laying that question before them, it would be necessary to explain President Wilson's very strong objection, which can be summarized as follows: "No matter what you want, you won't have the true manufacturing secrets," as well as Mr. Lansing's observation, which warns us against an operation having a military interest in appearance only, and carrying above all economic consequences.

THE KIEL CANAL

M. Clemenceau. President Wilson has communicated to us this morning a resolution of the Commission on Navigable Waterways on the subject of the Kiel Canal. I notice that this resolution has already been presented to the Ten and referred back to the commission. Nothing, it seems, has been done since. Don't you think it would be necessary, before reaching a conclusion, for the Commission on Navigable Waterways to confer with our naval advisers?

Mr. Lansing. I propose that the question be sent back to a mixed commission, where our naval representatives will meet with the members of the Commission on Navigable Waterways.

—*This proposal is adopted.*

QUESTION OF MARITIME PRIZES

Baron Sonnino. There still remains the question of prizes. It is a matter of demanding that Germany recognize the judgments pronounced by the prize courts. We have before us two proposals, one by England and one by the United States. The proposal by the United States is more extensive, for it also concerns the prizes taken by the Germans and says that we have the right to contest the decisions of German prize courts. That question is not yet sufficiently developed to make it the object of a decision of the Four.

Mr. Lansing. Moreover, there is the question of prizes taken by the Americans. Since our prize courts automatically cease to exist at the time of the signing of the preliminaries, it is certain that a great number of prizes will not be the subject of any verdict.

THE QUESTION OF RESPONSIBILITIES

M. Clemenceau. I have a communication to make to you about the question of responsibilities. It was said the other day in the Council of Four that, in the trial of the German Emperor, the role of prosecutor should be reserved to Belgium. I had been told that M. Hymans had accepted that idea. Today, I am informed that the Belgian Prime Minister[1] has arrived in Paris and that he is making all kinds of reservations about this proposal. Not only has he no desire to see Belgium take on this role, but, as the representative of a country with a monarchical constitution, he doesn't accept the arraignment of a sovereign.

President Wilson. That changes nothing in the present position of the question. We said that the German Emperor would be tried for violating Belgian neutrality. If Belgium doesn't want to play the role of public prosecutor, we will retain the right to call her as a witness, and I don't believe she will refuse to appear. The idea of entrusting the prosecution to Belgium was not expressed in the text we adopted; it was only discussed in our conversations.

M. Clemenceau. In that case, there is nothing to change in our text.

[1] Léon Delacroix.

XXXVIII

Conversation between President Wilson and MM. Clemenceau, Lloyd George, and Orlando*

APRIL 18, 1919, 11 A.M.

—M. André Tardieu and Lt. Col. Sir Maurice Hankey are introduced.

M. Clemenceau. M. Tardieu is going to propose measures to us to hasten the work of drafting the preliminaries. If we don't take them, we risk being unprepared for April 25.

*Does not appear in H.

M. Tardieu. The Drafting Committee is doing its best; but it can only study and prepare a certain number of articles a day. This number is far below what would be necessary to finish the work on the twenty-third, which is absolutely essential if the document has to be printed for the twenty-fifth. It would be necessary to increase the number of members of that committee, some being able to devote themselves to the study of territorial clauses, others to the study of economic or financial clauses.

President Wilson. I will observe that, in conformity with the instruction we gave some time ago, nearly all the reports of the commissions now include conclusions drafted in the form they are to take in the peace treaty. Such are, for example, the conclusions we have received from the commission on means of communication. In such cases, the work of drafting consists only of inserting completely finished clauses in the treaty.

Mr. Lloyd George. Don't the legal specialists we appointed as members of the Drafting Committee already have the right to obtain assistance from experts? I believe it would be enough to remind them of that right.

Sir Maurice Hankey. The British representative on the Drafting Committee, Mr. Hurst, asks particularly that the heads of governments inform them in precise terms of the decisions they have taken. In some cases, the Drafting Committee finds itself faced with two different proposals. For instance, concerning the recognition by Germany of the decisions of our prize courts, the Council of Five did not arrive at one conclusion, but at two, between which a choice still has to be made.

Mr. Hurst asks especially that the Drafting Committee be informed of the text adopted on the question of Danzig, as well as of that relating to the left bank of the Rhine.

President Wilson. I have the text relating to Danzig[1] on my table.

Mr. Lloyd George. In that case, would you like us to arrive at our decision on that question this morning? About the left bank of the Rhine, you will recall that we have a text which formed part of the military clauses, but which was removed from them because it was thought it should be placed amongst the political clauses of the treaty.

—Reading of this text in the draft of the military clauses.

Mr. Lloyd George. I have an observation to make on this point. It

---

[1] The document is missing; but Wilson paraphrases it below. For a revised version, which incorporated the changes suggested during this meeting, see PWW, Vol. 57, pp. 593-97.

is provided that the people who live on the left bank of the Rhine will be exempt, not only from all military obligations in Germany, but also from all contributions to the German military budget. Is it to our advantage to reduce the taxes those people will have to pay? I don't think this arrangement is necessary.

M. Clemenceau. We will see if it must be kept.

—M. Tardieu and Sir Maurice Hankey withdraw.

President Wilson. You will recall our conversation the other day about the dispute between the Poles and Ukrainians. It was agreed that General Bliss would make representations in our name to M. Paderewski about the uncompromising attitude of the Poles. The General informs me that the Polish and Ukrainian representatives in Paris are prepared to discuss the terms of an armistice according to our suggestion. It is up to us to designate representatives who would participate in the discussion in the name of the Great Powers. Is each of you ready to appoint a delegate to attend the negotiations?

—This proposal is adopted.

THE WESTERN BOUNDARIES OF POLAND

—President Wilson reads aloud the new text on the western boundaries of Poland (question of Danzig and question of Marienwerder):

Danzig and its territory will be established as a free Hanseatic city, under the guarantee of the League of Nations, which will be represented there by a High Commissioner. The territory of Danzig will be included in the Polish customs system, Poland having direction of foreign relations and the possession of the railroads, with free use of the port.

The people of the districts of Stuhm, Riesenburg, and Marienwerder will be consulted by means of a plebiscite, after complete evacuation by German troops, about their attachment to Poland or to East Prussia.

Polish sovereignty will extend over the entire course of the Vistula. Special rights of transit will be guaranteed to the Germans on the railroad which connects West Prussia to East Prussia, and to the Poles on the line from Danzig to Mława.

Mr. Lloyd George. One article of your text speaks of Polish sovereignty over the Vistula; it must be clearly understood that this doesn't give Poland the right to forbid the use of the river to the inhabitants of Danzig.

Another observation: is it necessary to lay out in the peace treaty the detailed operation of the plebiscite? Many details cannot be arranged in a satisfactory manner except on the spot, after a study of local conditions. Wouldn't it be enough to say in the treaty that there will be a plebiscite, that this plebiscite will take place by universal suffrage, the right to vote being reserved to persons actually domiciled in the region for a certain period of time? These essential points being well defined, it would be better to leave the rest to the discretion of the international commission which will organize and oversee the plebiscite.

Apart from this, I am satisfied with this text, and I don't see what else we could do.

M. Clemenceau. I must confess to you that I would like to be able to do otherwise in order to give satisfaction to our Polish friends; but in all sincerity, I don't think it possible to do so.

Mr. Lloyd George. Another article I don't like is the one which demands the dissolution of workers' and soldiers' councils. Its execution isn't easy.

M. Clemenceau. That is what we have done in territories we are occupying.

Mr. Lloyd George. Undoubtedly; but we want precisely to avoid having to occupy that remote region.

President Wilson. As for the expenses of the plebiscite, the text provides that, if they exceed what can reasonably be asked of the area itself, the extra cost will be paid by East Prussia.

Mr. Lloyd George. Wouldn't it be better to write: "by the country in whose favor the plebiscite goes?"

M. Mantoux. M. Tardieu asked me to remind you that the peace treaty with Germany has to mention the border between Germany and Lithuania. The map prepared by the Commission on Polish Affairs reveals a drawing of that border which takes from Germany the strip of territory along the coast of the Baltic Sea north of the Niemen, with the port of Memel.

Mr. Lloyd George. This is a question about which we will have to refresh our memory. Is the population Lithuanian?

—Mr. Lloyd George goes to consult his secretaries and returns.

Mr. Lloyd George. According to the commission's report, I see that the border it drew corresponds to the ethnographic line between Germans and Lithuanians and that, in addition, Memel is the only outlet to the sea available to Lithuania. In these circumstances, I believe we can only adopt the conclusions of the Commission on Polish Affairs.

—*The conclusions of the Commission on Polish Affairs concerning the German-Lithuanian frontier are adopted.*

QUESTION OF KIAOCHOW

President Wilson. This morning I studied the two treaties between China and Japan on the subject of Kiaochow. The first provided, after the cession of Kiaochow to Japan by the peace treaty, its retrocession to China under certain terms: the opening of the Gulf of Kiaochow to Japanese trade, a Japanese concession to be established at a place chosen by the Japanese government.

Since then, China and Japan have concluded another treaty concerning the railroad from Tsinan to Kiaochow by which China recovers the civil administration of the territory crossed by this railroad but shares the policing and administration of the railroad with Japan, as heretofore with Germany.

Mr. Lloyd George. For the moment, we only have to see what is appropriate to put in our treaty with Germany. I don't know why Kiaochow shouldn't be treated in the same way as all other German overseas territories, which, we have decided, are to be handed over by the Germans to the Great Powers to dispose of as they see fit.

President Wilson. That is also Mr. Lansing's opinion, and I think it is the best solution. It would be helpful to have a serious conversation on the subject with the Japanese; it is not in their interest to make an enemy of China; the future of the two countries is closely linked. We must advise the Japanese to be generous towards China and promise them, if they follow our advice, to promote their peaceful relations with the Chinese Republic.

What would allow us to use this language with authority would be to announce that we ourselves are renouncing our spheres of influence in China. I don't believe the retention of these spheres has any great advantage, and, besides, we are interested in the maintenance of peace in the Far East. I fear great danger for the world from that direction unless we are careful.

Mr. Lloyd George. We can study the question, on the sole condition that the principle of the open door continues in China.

President Wilson. Certainly.

Mr. Lloyd George. For my part, I am ready to study that question.

President Wilson. In my opinion, when the Bolshevik fever dies down, Europe will be protected from a great war for a long time, but I fear it is not the same in the Far East. I would readily compare the seeds of conflict that are indistinctly developing there to sparks hidden under a thick bed of leaves, which smolder gradually for months and, invisible, grow little by little, until the moment when those great forest fires explode suddenly, as we sometimes see in America. That is what we must try to avoid.

Mr. Lloyd George. Then we will tell the Japanese that the formula adopted for Kiaochow will be the same as for all German possessions abroad.

President Wilson. If the Japanese are with us, they must submit to the same method as we do.

Mr. Lloyd George. Concerning the spheres of influence, if China is open to the commerce of all nations, I think the English public will accept our renunciation of a purely nominal privilege.

—*Mr. Lloyd George's proposal concerning Kiaochow is adopted.*

Mr. Lloyd George. Mustn't we also consider the question of reparations which are or are not due Poland, Rumania, Serbia, Bohemia? I will observe that two thirds of the Poles fought against us during this war and are claiming their part of the reparation for damages to which they contributed themselves. On the other hand, shouldn't we take into account that they are being amply indemnified by the possession of areas as rich as the coal basin of Silesia? To receive that province freed from its share of the German debt and then to claim still more indemnities is excessive. What does M. Orlando think of that?

M. Orlando. That question touches directly on Italian interests; I have said nothing about it until now because the question is reserved; but obviously the problem is one of those which must be raised. From the political point of view, the territories which were part of the enemy states must be called upon to pay their part of what is owed by those states. First, it would be necessary to ask our financial experts what is the capacity to pay of the territories which constituted the Austro-Hungarian Empire, and then to divide the damages amongst these territories, either proportionately, according to their wealth, or, if that appraisement should appear too difficult, according to the number of their inhabitants. Each state whose territory is increasing at the expense of the former Austro-Hungarian monarchy, such as Serbia and Rumania, will have to bear liability for a contribution corresponding to the capacity of the annexed territories to pay.

Serbia, for example, would have a credit for the reparations due her and a liability for a part of what the Austro-Hungarian Empire would have had to pay if it still existed. The same method would be applied to Rumania or to Poland. We must begin by consulting our experts.

Mr. Lloyd George. Do you want to tell your financial representative to invite his colleagues in our name to meet to study that question?

M. Orlando. He has already spoken to them about it, and they said they were ready to begin that study with him, if they are so instructed by their governments.

Mr. Lloyd George. If we agree, that is the mandate of the governments that I ask you to communicate to them through your financial expert.

—This proposal is adopted.

President Wilson. We also have to return to the question of cables. My great concern is to avoid having the essential communications across the Atlantic Ocean, as well as across the Pacific Ocean, fall under a monopoly. I have already mentioned the case of the cables seized by the Japanese, which they want to keep. These cables cross at the island of Yap, and if that island remains in the hands of the Japanese, mastery of the telegraphic communications of a great part of the Pacific, especially between the United States and the Philippines, would belong to them. We must see to it that the means of communication across a great ocean are not placed under the control of a single nation.

It was decided the other day that the Germans would have the right to raise and use those of their cables which were cut during the war, but which were not rerouted in other directions. It is interesting to know where they could place these cables. If, for example, all rights of this kind in the Azores were reserved to English companies, the consequence would be that America's communications with Europe and western Africa could take place only by English cables, which could lead in the future to tension and difficulties.

Mr. Lloyd George. I must tell you that I don't know about this question. Mr. Lansing has studied it closely and Mr. Balfour is briefed; I propose that they confer and submit their conclusions to us.

—This proposal is adopted.

XXXIX

Conversation between President Wilson and MM. Clemenceau, Lloyd George, and Orlando, and Baron Sonnino*

APRIL 19, 1919, 11 A.M.

THE QUESTION OF THE ADRIATIC

—President Wilson invites M. Orlando to present the Italian claims.

M. Orlando. I would like today to consider the Italian question from the point of view of decisions taken here about other claims. One of the powers represented here did not sign the treaty[1] which binds us to France and Great Britain; I must, therefore, consider the questions which concern us aside from any contractual obligations.

Italy puts forward three essential claims; she believes they conform to the principles that have been invoked when the settlement of analogous questions was at issue. Moreover, I will attempt to make comparisons with other cases in order to show how these principles apply.

The first of our claims is the annexation to Italy of all the territories which are inside our natural borders. Along with Spain and Scandinavia, Italy is the most clearly demarcated country of the continent; her national unity is based upon her geographical unity. The sea surrounds the peninsula on three sides, and the fourth is blocked off by a chain of mountains, the most formidable in Europe. We are asking that our border coincide with the natural boundary of the Alps, that is, with the line of the watershed. We know that this boundary will include population elements who are not Italian-speaking; we don't dream of denying that. I won't go into their numbers. All those who testified before you have declared, one after another, that the Austrian statistics are false, and the most forceful statement on this point was that of the Yugoslavs. I could show you incontrovertible documents which clearly establish that these statistics were falsified against

*H., *PPC*, V, 80ff. It is from this meeting on that Sir Maurice Hankey carried out regularly the duties of secretary of the Council of Four and that Count Aldrovandi accompanied the representative of Italy.

[1] That is, the Treaty of London of April 26, 1915.

the Italian elements; but I don't want to get involved in that debate. The question is whether we will include 100,000 foreigners, more or less, within our borders.

Every time this conference has drawn the boundaries of a state, it has admitted that it was impossible to draw lines in zigzag or to leave enclaves which would dot the map like a leopard's skin. We have admitted that the presence within a national area of certain heterogeneous elements is no reason to refuse a country its natural boundary. This principle has to be applied to Italy. For example, if we draw across the peninsula of Istria the boundary indicated on the map which I see on this wall,[2] we cut up an economic, strategic, and political unit; a boundary drawn in this way would make the defense of Trieste impossible. If the possession of Trieste isn't refused to Italy, Istria must go to Italy—in its entirety—because it forms a unit.

Even if Italy has all she asks, the foreign elements that will be found within her territory will be in a far smaller proportion than those which we have allowed for other nations. Poland, for example, even after the changes recently made in the drawing of her boundary, will have 1,800,000 or 2,000,000 Germans out of a total population of twenty-five millions. Italy, if her demands are satisfied, will have only 600,000 subjects of other nationalities, out of a population of more than forty million inhabitants. Rumania will include some Hungarians. Bohemia will include a considerable proportion of German-speaking inhabitants—between two and three millions out of a total of ten to twelve millions.

Italy believes she has a right to claim the natural frontier that God has given her. If groups belonging to other nationalities find themselves included, that is no reason to refuse Italy what is her right. Suppose there had been only 400,000 or 500,000 Germans between the French border and the Rhine; would their presence have been enough to refuse France the natural boundary which she lacks?

The second point is the question of Fiume. It is also near to being resolved if one considers the natural boundary of Italy, such as it has always been defined: the *limes italicus* of the Romans goes through the Monte Nevoso and touches Fiume. But we are claiming Fiume in the name of the right of self-determination. We aren't insisting enough on what is today a historical fact:

---

[2] The map prepared by the American experts, which projected what was called the American line for Italy's northern and northeastern frontiers.

Fiume itself has manifested its desire, without any intervention by Italy. It was on October 18, 1918, before the armistice with Austria, that the member for Fiume in the Hungarian Parliament made a declaration claiming annexation to Italy for the free city of Fiume from the moment the Austro-Hungarian Empire should fall into dissolution. Thus, it was not Italy which raised the question; it was raised by the Italians of Fiume, who affirmed their right to self-determination.

I see a possible objection. This principle, it will be said, applies to peoples, not to a tiny group, not to a relatively unimportant city. I will note that that objection assumes that Fiume must be treated as an isolated unit and prejudges the question of whether it is an integral part of Italy. But I accept that manner of putting the question. I say that small peoples, as well as great ones, if they form a historical unit, have the same right to decide their own fate. Fiume has its own history of liberty. If it was a question of the Republic of San Marino, I would say to you: in spite of its tiny size, this little state has the right to self-determination. We think, then, that the union of Fiume to Italy conforms to the principle of the free self-determination of peoples.

From the economic point of view, I would invoke the precedent of Danzig. We didn't admit the demand of Poland, which desired the annexation of that city, and we did that because we wanted to respect the rights of the German majority. Thus, in Danzig, the economic factor didn't prevail over the political aspect. Will it be said that Fiume can be made into a free city like Danzig? Italy would answer that this would be to act in a friendlier way towards the Germans, our worst enemies, than towards the Italians, your friends and your allies.

In fact, two arguments are valid for Danzig which are not valid for Fiume. Poland has no maritime outlet other than Danzig; the Yugoslavs, on the contrary, have no lack of them. I could show you that their true natural port is not Fiume. It is impossible to deny that they will have several ports and hundreds of kilometers of coastline. Thus, the first argument, valid for Danzig, fails to apply here.

The second argument of the Poles is that Danzig is essentially a Polish port and can serve only Poland. Fiume, on the contrary, serves Yugoslavia only as an accessory. During our earlier discussion, I said that Croatian commerce constituted only 7 per cent of the trade of the port of Fiume. I have since learned that M. Trumbić, when he came to testify before you, declared this figure wrong and said that the true figure was 50 per cent. I asked the Chamber of Commerce of Fiume to fill out the information we already had about the exact number of merchants in that city; it replied by giving us more detailed figures. The result is that the proportion is indeed 7 per cent. Whether it be 12 or 15 per cent, the fact remains that Fiume is not principally a Yugoslav port. In reality, it is a port which serves Hungary and, in part, Galicia and Bohemia.

If, then, the case of Fiume was likened to that of Danzig, all Italy would think the enemy has been better treated than an ally.

I will add a little proof of the historical independence of Fiume. It is only a small detail, but it has its value in a traditional state such as Austria used to be. In the official coat of arms of the Austro-Hungarian monarchy, there were a great number of small escutcheons, representing all the different units making up that composite whole. Now, among those escutcheons, there was one for Fiume, considered as a distinct unit in the empire.

I come to the third point: this concerns Dalmatia and the neighboring islands. I should also mention the islands off Istria— Cherso and Lussino [or Lussin]—which are Italian islands.

The first argument for the annexation of Dalmatia to Italy is the strategic argument. One does not have to be a sailor to understand it, and besides, I won't engage in a technical discussion here. The eastern coast of Italy is at the mercy of whoever is the master of the other shore of the Adriatic; that is the consequence of the geographical layout of the two coasts. Even if the naval forces of the people across from us were reduced to a minimum, even if they kept only what was necessary for policing the coasts, as is legitimate, it will always be possible for a ship leaving from the mid-Adriatic to raid a city on the Italian coast, bombard it, and take refuge behind the labyrinth of the islands without running any risk. I don't wish to enter into the technical examination of the question; but it would be easy to demonstrate what I am contending.

Besides, there is no better demonstration than the one provided by the present war. The Entente had mastery of all the seas; it must be acknowledged that it didn't have it in the Adriatic. The Austrians, it is true, could not sail there, but neither could we. Despite the crushing superiority of the Italian fleet, reinforced by French and English squadrons, Italian cities were bombarded, and the Italian coast remained in a state of complete insecurity. So, I have the right to say that Italy remains in permanent danger if she doesn't have a defensive base on the coast across from her.

But the strategic question isn't the only one; there is a national question for us in Dalmatia. It has been said here that historical grounds cannot have a decisive influence on our decisions, and I myself have acknowledged that. But there are cases in which history has a profound significance, which it is impossible to ignore. From Dalmatia's origins, until the Treaty of Campo-Formio in 1797,[3] Dalmatia's fate was always linked to that of Italy. It belonged to the Roman Empire. Then, for centuries, it was part of the Republic of Venice. It is separated from the interior by mountains which rise up like a wall and make its gravitation towards Italy inevitable. Not only was Dalmatia Venetian until the Treaty of Campo-Formio, but the majority of the Dalmatian Diet was Italian until 1881. So we are not going back centuries to validate our historical rights.

Recently, we found an Austrian document in Zara, dated 1887, which determined the official language—*Dienstsprache*—of the different communes of Dalmatia. This document from an Austrian source proves that, out of eighty-four Dalmatian communes, nineteen were considered exclusively Italian, and twenty-five officially used both languages. Thus, in more than half the Dalmatian communes, the Italian character of the population was recognized by an official document of the Austrian state. In the cities of Zara, Trau, and perhaps Spalato, there is still an Italian majority today. The Italian character of Dalmatia is still remarkably flourishing. I would ask our allies, our friends: is it possible for Italy, after a terrible war which cost her so much, to abandon these centers of Italian culture and civilization and to condemn them to certain destruction?

The Pact of London was a compromise; we have voluntarily abandoned a rich and important part of Dalmatia, with the cities of Spalato, Ragusa, and Cattaro. We stand by that solution. Thus we are moderate in our claims.

President Wilson. Since I have had several talks with M. Orlando and his colleagues, it is, I believe, desirable that I remind you what I have already said to them. My Italian friends owe me the justice of saying that I never ceased to look at things from their own point of view. It was I who had the responsibility and privilege of making the arrangements which led to the cessation of hostilities and to the conclusion of the Armistice. At that time, we agreed upon well-defined principles which have to serve as the basis for our peace with Germany. It is not possible for us to

---

[3] By which Dalmatia, formerly under the control of Venice, was ceded by France to Austria.

say that we will make peace with Germany on certain principles, and that we will invoke others to make peace with Turkey, Bulgaria, and Austria. So I must assume that we are acting everywhere according to the same principles; the entire question boils down to that.

We are trying to do what has never been done heretofore: we want to lay the foundations of a new system of international relations. That preoccupation has guided us in the solution of all the questions we have successively studied. Never have statesmen had to resolve greater and more difficult problems. But that itself compels us to reject certain claims that would destroy the very foundations that we wish to lay. For example, that makes it impossible for us to distribute territories by taking the idea of strategic frontiers as a guiding principle. It is perfectly just to accept certain claims of that order. When, for example, a country has natural frontiers as clear as those of Spain and Italy, it is impossible not to acknowledge them; it is not only the waters which the mountains divide and redistribute between the neighboring countries, it is peoples, it is all the elements of national life.

So I have no difficulty in agreeing with you on part of your claims. Nature has raised between Italy and neighboring nations a great barrier, whose highest points are easily recognizable; that barrier gives you Trieste and the larger part of the peninsula of Istria. About that, I have no difficulty in agreeing with the representatives of Italy. But farther south, that argument can no longer be invoked in your favor.

From the point where we leave the line of the Alps, we find ourselves faced with another problem. So far, the fate of the countries in question has been linked to that of the Austro-Hungarian Empire. That empire was governed by men who were inspired by the same spirit as the leaders of the German Empire; not only did they submit to the influence of Germany, but they were in her hands. If the Austro-Hungarian Empire had not fallen to pieces, the world would be very different from what it is today. It has disappeared. The only wise and advisable policy is to create friendly populations out of the populations of the former Austro-Hungarian Empire—states ready to enter in full right into our new international organization.

When we wanted to detach the Yugoslavs from Austria, we spoke to them as friends. Now that they have parted from her and have repudiated the former state of things in the Austro-Hungarian Empire, can we treat them as enemies?

As for Fiume, it is possible that Yugoslav interests have only a secondary position there. But that doesn't prevent this port from being of capital importance for the neighboring area, since it is the sole port of easy access and served by a railroad. Moreover, it is, first of all, an international port and, in particular, a Hungarian port. In the recent past, it was Hungary which was most concerned with Fiume. She often had to favor the Italian population there, in order to oppose the Slavic population. One can imagine—although I have no proof of it—that, if Hungary allowed Fiume's autonomy to subsist, it was in order to be able more easily to separate that city from the neighboring populations.

In all that can be said about Fiume, nothing leads to its annexation to Italy. You have compared the case of Fiume to that of Danzig; but there is no analogy there, for we have removed Danzig from German sovereignty, whilst this is a matter of placing Fiume under Italian sovereignty, and Fiume has never belonged to Italy, except during the time of the Roman Empire. If we followed the precedent of Danzig, it would be impossible for us to do what the representatives of Italy wish. As for the economic and strategic arguments, they all led to the union of Danzig with Poland. In order to respect the principles which inspire us, we renounced a scientific solution; we even accepted the risk of seeing the railroad which will unite Warsaw and Danzig cross German territory. We rejected the economic argument, like the strategic argument, in order to satisfy the ethnographic argument. You will recall, however, the force of the arguments presented in the contrary sense by M. Cambon.[4]

I also remind you about our conversation the other day with M. Hymans about the railroad from Malmédy to Eupen.[5] It was impossible to give Belgium the entire length of this small line without annexing some thousands of Germans to Belgian territory, and we refused. To place Fiume under the domination of Italy would be absolutely contrary to the new principle on which international relations must be based.

What is to be done with Fiume? That is another question. Should Fiume be established as a free port? There is no question that its function is chiefly to serve the hinterland. In any case, it is separated from Italy geographically and physically. Its Italian population is only a small island. To unite it to Italy would be an arbitrary act so contrary to our principles that, as for myself, I could not associate myself with it.

[4] In the meeting of the Council of Ten on March 19, 1919, for the minutes of which, see PWW, Vol. 56, pp. 88-95.
[5] See XXXVI.

As for Dalmatia, the argument which is most insisted upon and which Baron Sonnino, since his arrival in Paris, has emphasized to me with great force, is that Dalmatia is necessary for the protection of the Italian coast. Here again, it is a question of whether or not we accept a new order of things. In this new order of things, we unite our forces, and we want to make our policies agree in order to guarantee mutually our independence and territorial integrity. Under the regime of the League of Nations, I cannot conceive of a Yugoslav navy which could become a real threat to Italy. That threat could only exist if the Yugoslavs became the instruments of a great naval power through an alliance having no other goal than to attack Italy.

One of the great results of this conference is to liberate the Balkan peninsula from the intervention of the great powers. In the past, we know how the intrigues of the powers intersected on that ground; we know what role Germany recently played there, and how Constantinople was a center where dangerous intrigues against peace were unceasingly hatched. That situation was due to the fact that the peoples of the Balkans had not attained complete independence, and that a great power like Germany could exercise pressure on them towards certain ends. I am against everything that will give any great European power whatsoever a foothold in the Balkans. The role it would inevitably play in that situation would be deadly to our plans. Intervention in Balkan domestic politics would repeat itself as in the past. That is why one of my great concerns is to keep all the great powers out of the Balkan peninsula.

The strategic argument was invoked in 1815. It was invoked in 1871. The military advisers who imposed strategic boundaries bear responsibility for some of the gravest mistakes committed in the history of the world. I believe it would be a danger to the peace of Europe if Italy insisted upon establishing herself on the eastern coast of the Adriatic. We are creating a great League of Nations, in which one of the principal roles is reserved to Italy. If that isn't enough, if it is also necessary, at the same time, to resort to strategic measures, that is because we are trying to combine two irreconcilable systems. As for myself, I cannot drive both horses at once. The people of the United States won't accept seeing the world fall again into its former state, and the governments which don't understand that will learn from their own peoples that their time has passed.

We have sometimes spoken in this setting as if we were the masters of Europe. We are not; we are in the hands of the people, and I would fear to wrong them by a tragic error.

I have already said this to my Italian colleagues: we are their friends; it is as friends that we wish to act towards them. I don't believe I would be serving the best interests of their country if I accepted their claims to Fiume and Dalmatia. I submit myself in advance to the judgment of history, and I don't fear that it will accuse me of having served the interests of Italy less well than they. I was born far from here, in another world. I recall a time when I worried little about what went on in Europe. I came with my fellow countrymen to help Europe to extricate herself from the old order of things which had led her to catastrophe. If I succeed in this, all our people will be behind me in helping you. If I don't succeed, you can expect nothing from the American people.

Moreover, I will observe that the claim to Fiume is recent. You speak of the right of people to self-determination. But this only concerns a tiny island of people. If we should decide in your favor, there would be those small spots on the map of which M. Orlando has spoken. When we wanted to avoid that in Poland, in Bohemia, we followed historical boundaries. I don't find a historical boundary in the case of Fiume. Not a single one of the arguments which convinced us in other cases applies to this one.

I feel profoundly the gravity of our debate. Be convinced that, if I have committed an error, it is not an error of the heart, but of judgment. My conclusions are those of a friend who wishes to serve you and not to injure you.

Baron Sonnino. President Wilson says that the new order of things is irreconcilable with the strategic argument. I must remark that, by invoking this argument, we have no aggressive thought; we seek only to defend our territory. We have no plan to penetrate the Balkans. But the tragic destiny of Italy has for centuries been to lie open to invasions. Enemy forces waiting in ambush behind the islands of the Adriatic could defy the entire League of Nations, as, during this war, they have defied the fleets of the Entente, three times stronger than theirs. That coast, if it remains outside our possession, will still be a temptation for anyone who wishes to do us harm; or even more, it will be a temptation for Italy to profit from any complication in Europe to rid herself at any price of an intolerable danger. The best organized League of Nations will not give us any more guarantees than the police in our cities; now, the presence of the police in the streets doesn't prevent us from closing our doors at night. That is what we are asking to be able to do in the Adriatic.

We have no desire to get ourselves involved in the Balkans.

Northern Dalmatia is completely separated from the Balkan peninsula by its mountains; all its relations are with the Adriatic coast and beyond the Adriatic. That is what explains the persistence of the Italian character in Dalmatia, in spite of foreign domination. That is what explains why Zara, Spalato, and the other cities on the coast have preserved their Italian character to such a degree. The Italian element always remained so important in that region that, for this very reason, it was treated well by Austria for a long time.

If, after a war which cost us 500,000 dead and one million seriously wounded, we should submit to terms more unfavorable than those which Austria offered us to remain neutral—for Austria offered us several islands in the Adriatic[6]—we could not justify our participation in the war. Then I would feel the most cruel remorse, and I would have the feeling that we committed a veritable crime against our people.

You reassure us by speaking to us of the League of Nations and of the improvement of relations amongst the governments of the world; that is a hope for the future. But can the League of Nations act tomorrow? Could it settle the Russian question tomorrow? It is not enough to sign a pact. Time alone will give this pact its true value. It would be a crime for us to place our signature at the bottom of a pact establishing the League of Nations if we had to accept responsibilities for others and remain ourselves without the guarantees which are absolutely essential to us.

President Wilson. You will have our guarantee.

Baron Sonnino. You will arrive too late to protect us, and, across from us, we have the Balkan states which have neither good faith nor law, and which will see nothing but enemies everywhere.

President Wilson. You speak of the Balkan states as they were, when other powers used them as tools.

Baron Sonnino. I have even less confidence in them than in those other powers. How can one guarantee the future?

I am profoundly moved. I fear that I have done the opposite of my duty during this war.

Mr. Lloyd George. We—M. Clemenceau and I—have to speak from the British point of view and the French point of view, different from President Wilson's because of the treaty which binds us. Would you like to put off this debate?

---

[6] In fact, in the final proposal for a diplomatic settlement with Italy on May 19, 1915, Austria-Hungary had made no mention of any islands in the Adriatic but had merely renounced all claims to the Dodecanese Islands. See Albrecht-Carrié, *Italy at the Paris Peace Conference*, p. 344.

—After a short discussion, it is decided to continue the conversation.

M. Clemenceau. We are presently attempting a hazardous but noble enterprise. We are trying to free the world from savagery and periodic crises, the latest of which surpassed in horror all it had known. Even if we should succeed in this, we cannot change the policy of a great people in an instant. That applies to Italy as well as to France. I will not willingly separate myself from Italy in this grave hour. I will recall that, earlier, when she moved away from us and drew near to states which were hostile to us, I remained her friend despite everything, and that I have more than once manifested my friendship towards her.

President Wilson has put forward powerful arguments. As for us, we are bound to Italy by a treaty. It was not I who signed it; but I won't repudiate France's signature. I will note, however, that this treaty, which gives Dalmatia to Italy, leaves Fiume to the Croats. At that time, Italy put her signature at the bottom of a document which gave Fiume to the Slavs. M. Barzilai said to us in this connection: Austria-Hungary has collapsed much more than we had thought. Undoubtedly; but we are surprised to see Italy claim today what she herself gave to the Croats when we signed our treaty. If Italy asked us for a modification of our agreements, that is a question we could consider. But to ask for the maintenance of our agreements and to want to impose upon us a term which is contrary to them—that is impossible. If it were thus, signatures would no longer mean anything.

I fear our Italian friends are committing a regrettable act in allowing themselves to break with the conference. By doing that, they would not serve the cause of the world, which is their own cause. Upon their return to their country, they will meet with exaltation, enthusiasm; but they will soon come back to cold reality. All the friends of Italy will be alienated from her; they will suffer the effects of it—Italy, too, I fear. It is with profound emotion that, after months of common efforts to insure the peace of the world, we should see one of the peoples which did the most for humanity break away from us. We would suffer greatly from it; Italy would perhaps suffer even more.

If our friends must depart, I hope that, after consultation with their compatriots, they can soon return and agree with us on the basis of reason. My heart will always be with Italy, with her great and noble history, with her genius, more necessary than ever for civilization. But duty speaks loudly. I have, you will acknowledge, bent all my efforts towards conciliation. Italy has our word; we don't dispute it. But she also gave her word in May 1915 to leave Fiume to the Croats. If we are upholding the treaty, let us uphold it.

M. Orlando. I have a brief statement to make. Italy is being reproached for having added to her demands. At the beginning of this session, I said that I would speak as if the Treaty of London did not exist, because I was speaking to President Wilson, who didn't sign it. If I asked my allies for the fulfillment of their obligations under the treaty, I wouldn't claim Fiume from them.

As for the rest, in the deep anguish of my heart, I find the strength to protest against the assumption that, in our position, a concern for popularity could count for something. The enthusiasm which will welcome us if we return to Italy—we'll see what it will be. I understand the tragic solemnity of the moment. Italy will suffer from this decision. For her, it is only a question of choosing between two deaths. She would die if one could think that we had accepted a peace which constituted a violation of her right. Will she die if she is separated from the rest of the world? For myself, I prefer to die with my country.

Henry III [of France] said before the body of a dead enemy: "He is even bigger dead than alive." If this great corpse of Italy should lie on the ground, I hope it doesn't poison the world.

Mr. Lloyd George. I speak as the representative of a country which signed the Treaty of London, and I must state our position. Our government, which signed this treaty, doesn't dream for an instant of repudiating it. There is much force in the arguments presented by President Wilson. But one could say to us—to us, the signatories of the treaty: "If you have scruples about handing over that Dalmatian coast to Italy, you should have expressed them before Italy had 500,000 men killed on your side." We don't have the right to have these scruples today. Great Britain stands by the treaty, but by the treaty such as it is. According to this document, Fiume must become part of Croatia. I don't see how we could consent to violate one part of the treaty whilst fully keeping the other.

Why do you claim Fiume? You invoke the right of self-determination. In that event, it is necessary to apply it everywhere. If you told us that you ask for a plebiscite on this entire coast, and if this plebiscite should give the area to Italy, that would be the end of it. But that is not what you propose. You demand Fiume. But then you must mean Fiume in the narrowest sense, without an inch of the territory around the city. For, if you include the suburbs of the city, the Italian majority disappears, and if you attach the surrounding countryside, it changes into a small minority. M. Orlando's argument, when he said that Trieste couldn't be left under the enemy's guns, applies to Fiume.

I don't see on what principle we could stand in giving Fiume to Italy. We can't say that that city will be treated as a part of Istria; for it can be united to Istria only by including other Slavic populations inside the Italian frontier. We couldn't do it without breaking the very treaty which we signed with Italy, without violating all our principles. I am not forgetting the terrible losses suffered by Italy during this war, but what couldn't be said of France's losses? M. Clemenceau could invoke them to say to us: "I am annexing the left bank of the Rhine," which, as you know, has been a historical frontier for France and which is eagerly claimed today by very active parties. If the Rhine was the frontier of France, that country would still not have the strategic guarantees that the sea gives us. If we admit Italy's claim, then we must start all over again and begin with France, which, bowing before our common principle, renounced its claim to the left bank of the Rhine.

If Italy should leave the conference, it would be a very serious decision. And why would she take it? On account of Fiume? On account of a city where there are 24,000 Italians and where, if you count the population of the suburbs, the Italian majority is very doubtful? Fiume doesn't count from the strategic point of view. Because, in the city of Fiume, separated from its suburbs, there exists an Italian majority, a majority which is of recent date, you would withdraw from the conference? I don't know what the consequences would be in the Adriatic, with these passionate populations behind the coasts; I don't know what the consequences would be in the other parts of the world; I am certain that Italy is wrong, and that her wrong would be much more serious if it resulted in bloodshed.

The policy of nations must be directed, after all, by common sense. To break an alliance which has lasted four years, after the most terrible trials, for this wretched question! I want to make it clear that we won't bear the responsibility for it. We remain faithful to our treaty and, as I said to M. Orlando several weeks ago, the British cabinet has taken the decision to honor its signature, whether we like the terms of the treaty or not.

M. Orlando. I said a short time ago that I would conduct my discussion as if there had been no treaty. If what Mr. Lloyd George has just said means that the conference is deciding in favor of us on the basis of the Treaty of London, with the question of Fiume remaining to be settled as the conference will determine it, this raises the question in a new manner and could require study by my colleagues of the Italian delegation.

President Wilson. This would throw the responsibility on me in a way which would be unfair. I don't know whether my French and English colleagues think the Treaty of London can be reconciled with the peace that we want to establish. But as for myself, who is free of all contractual obligations, I say that it cannot. The Treaty of London is one of those secret treaties against which we have declared ourselves.

Mr. Lloyd George. We made that pronouncement in signing the German Armistice. But I recall that, concerning Austria, M. Clemenceau and I made necessary reservations, precisely because of our commitments to Italy.

President Wilson. I already said that I don't see how we could make peace with Germany on one principle, whilst we invoked others to deal with Austria and the other powers. I am not criticizing the Treaty of London; I know the circumstances in which it was signed. But to say that you are carrying out this treaty would place the government of the United States in an impossible situation.

Baron Sonnino. We are not asking you to adhere to this treaty.

President Wilson. No, but you are asking me to accept what it contains. I am ready to say before the entire world that I cannot act against the principle on which the United States entered the war.

Baron Sonnino. In one of your statements, you accepted the principle of the security necessary to Italy.[7]

President Wilson. I don't admit that Italy can have no security in the Adriatic without that. It would be just as true to say that England will have no security unless she possesses the German naval bases. The sole risk that Italy runs, which England runs as well, is that of a bombardment.

It is inconceivable to me that Italy can part with her friends at a time like this. I beg my Italian friends not to take a hasty decision, to consider everything, not to alienate their country from us and the rest of the world. In my opinion, that would be the most tragic event since the end of hostilities.

[7] Sonnino was here referring to Wilson's message to the Italian people on May 23, 1918, on the occasion of the third anniversary of Italy's entrance into the war. It is printed in *PWW*, Vol. 57, p. 493, n. 12.

XL

Conversation between President Wilson and MM. Clemenceau, Lloyd George, and Orlando, and Baron Sonnino*

APRIL 20, 1919, 10 A.M.

THE QUESTION OF THE ADRIATIC

President Wilson. May I ask M. Orlando if he has some suggestion to make to us?

M. Orlando (*reading a statement*). I must hold to all the declarations we have previously made, whilst reducing the question to its minimal terms. I will respectfully point out to President Wilson that, in order to attain his generous goals of peace amongst the nations, it is necessary, above all, to avoid creating hatred and resentment against injustice. I solemnly affirm that, if Fiume is not awarded to Italy, that would excite in the Italian people such a movement of protest that it cannot fail to result in serious conflicts in the near future. I believe nothing would be more fatal, not only to the interests of Italy, but to the peace of the world.

Nevertheless, since our French and English allies told me yesterday that they don't acknowledge Italy's right to break the alliance, unless the terms on which it was concluded were refused us, I am too conscious of my responsibility not to shield myself against such a reproach. If the conference insures Italy all the rights guaranteed her by the Treaty of London, I won't break the alliance, and I will abstain from any act or any measure which could have that import.

—A silence.

President Wilson. It seems unbelievable to me that the representatives of Italy should take this position. At the center of this war, there were three great powers—France, Great Britain, and Italy. They shared the burden of the war; the entire world understood that it was their common action that saved them from the hegemony of the Central Powers. But, afterwards, other powers intervened which had nothing to do with the Treaty of London, and you must acknowledge that, without them, the war could not have been brought to a successful conclusion, or at least that vic-

*H., *PPC*, V, 95ff.

tory would have been considerably delayed. I don't believe I am exaggerating the importance of the military and financial assistance that the United States gave the Allies.

When we entered the war, we announced the principles that would control our action, and those principles were acclaimed, not only by the small oppressed nations, but also by the peoples of the great nations, who recognized in them their own deep aspirations. That was because, when I formulated those declarations, which everyone remembers, I did not write them in my name, nor in order to express my personal thoughts; I sought to express the sentiment of the people of the United States—and it coincided with that of all the great peoples of the world. My sole desire was to call to consciousness, so to speak, what the masses dimly felt. What Mr. Lloyd George, in January 1918,[1] and I myself said afterwards,[2] was found to be the correct interpretation of the motives which guided the peoples in that terrible struggle. It was on the basis of the principles thus proclaimed that the United States entered the war and that other nations followed her.

This world conference, in which we are taking part, has the duty to express the sentiment of the world and not to carry out a pact in which only a restricted group participated—allow me to use these words, in spite of the importance of the powers which compose it.

The aim of the principles we enunciated was not to close the door to legitimate aspirations. If you review what are called the Fourteen Points, you will read therein that Serbia was to have free and secure access to the sea and that relations amongst the Balkan states were to be established upon the basis of the free will of the peoples and of historical traditions, with boundaries drawn along clearly recognizable ethnographic lines. Concerning Italy, she was to obtain boundaries which would unite to her peoples of the same language and tradition.

If we don't apply these principles, we will create the same danger that M. Orlando dreads, we will provoke that feeling of indignation and of hatred that will be the most dangerous cause of future conflicts. If Italy declares that she insists upon the terms of the Treaty of London, she is barring the road to peace. The United States cannot associate itself with such a policy.

The Treaty of London was made in circumstances very different from those of the present time. If Austria-Hungary still ex-

[1] About Lloyd George's speech, see *PWW*, Vol. 48, pp. 487-88.
[2] In his Fourteen Points Address of January 8, 1918, printed in *ibid.*, pp. 534-39.

isted, my attitude would not be the same as the one I am taking today. If Italy still had before her such a powerful enemy state, established on the negation of the principle of nationality, I would consider it a duty to award her all the outposts she deemed necessary for her defense. The change which occurred because of the collapse of the Austro-Hungarian Empire cannot affect the position of the signatories of the treaty, who are bound by their word; but it is not the same for the powers which are not themselves bound by any obligation.

I will ask our Italian friends: have you really decided to lessen the probability of peace with Germany, to renew the possibility of war, to alienate yourselves from a nation—ours—whose friendship for Italy amounts to enthusiasm? Are you prepared to say that you won't enter into the new order of things we are preparing, because you cannot, at the same time, maintain the old one? What Italy gains by the terms we accept is sufficiently satisfying and glorious; she completes her unity, she rescues her brothers of the Trentino and of Trieste from foreign domination. Five years ago, it would have been a dream whose realization would have been believed hardly possible. This dream has been realized by the valor of the Italian army and by the combined efforts of the world. It would be incredible to see all that disappear in an instant. This, I declare, would be the supreme tragedy of this war. You would turn your back on your best friends, and I would deplore it profoundly. My heart would be broken; but, as the representative of the United States, having the right only to speak in its name, I have no choice in what I do. I cannot violate the principles whose establishment constitutes the very mandate which was given to me when I came to participate in these negotiations.

M. Orlando. If I have invoked the Treaty of London, I have done it only at the last moment and in spite of myself, in order to reply to the appeal of Messrs. Lloyd George and Clemenceau who, remembering our alliance, have told me that I would be taking on too great a responsibility if I should break the tie which attaches me to powers ready to fulfill their obligations towards Italy. I have done everything to demonstrate Italy's right, whilst remaining within the realm of reason and without invoking any contractual obligation; I would be happy to remain on this ground; no one would regret more than I to seem to be basing myself on a text, because my reasons would not be good enough.

Italy is not intransigent. Has one avenue of conciliation been offered to me? None. President Wilson has just spoken of the

Fourteen Points. Yesterday, he admitted that the points relating to Austria-Hungary have lost their validity because Austria-Hungary has disappeared. This also applies to other points. You were speaking of giving Serbia access to the sea. At that time, the extreme aspirations of Serbia consisted of obtaining the ports of Alessio and San Giovanni di Medua. She hardly dared dream of Ragusa. Today, she has even more than that.

I earnestly beseech President Wilson to remember two things. First of all, if, in the Fourteen Points, the proposals relating to Austria-Hungary cannot be applied after the disappearance of that power, can the clause concerning Italy remain intact? In the second place, as for the application of the Fourteen Points to the problems which concern us, we made unequivocal reservations. Colonel House received our communication about this.[3] We are not bound by any commitment, and we don't believe that President Wilson is either.

President Wilson has said in moving words that this war was fought for justice and right; I beg him to believe that we too think we are placing ourselves on the ground of right and justice. I don't pretend to possess absolute truth. But the idea of justice is a subjective idea, about which one can differ in opinion without ceasing to be sincere. I respect profoundly President Wilson's feeling; but he can also believe in our good faith, and I can use the same arguments as he to tell him that it is impossible for me to make a peace which would be contrary to right and justice. I say that only to apologize for my opposition.

President Wilson has said with obvious sincerity that his heart is broken at the thought that we could withdraw. I thank him for that. My heart is even more broken than his. I experience the same feeling as he in thinking of the friendship and loyal affection which exists, not only between two peoples, but between two men; beyond that, I experience a feeling of anguish which, happily for him, he is spared. I sense all the horror of the difficulties to which my country is going to be prey; but I am too convinced that we are acting for right and justice not to be ready to brave all the consequences, up to and including death, for we are dying, I and my country, for a just cause.

President Wilson. Be assured that I don't misunderstand the mo-

---

[3] Actually, during the Pre-Armistice negotiations in London, Orlando had tried from time to time to enter reservations to Points 9, 10, 11, and 12, but he had been out-manueuvered by Colonel House and Lloyd George and failed to have any reservations accepted. See Albrecht-Carrié, *Italy at the Paris Peace Conference*, pp. 60-66.

tives behind your action. Between us, there is only a difference of judgment and policy.

I have always thought, and I have always acknowledged, that Italy was not in any way bound by the Fourteen Points. But for myself, I cannot make peace with Germany on the basis of one principle and peace with Austria on the basis of another principle. We must endeavor to draw boundaries everywhere according to ethnographic and national lines.

Mr. Lloyd George. I fear we are facing the gravest situation which has arisen since the beginning of the conference. We have had to resolve some hard problems; but half a dozen solutions have always come to mind. Here, I see none clearly. On one side, there appears to me the danger that Italy should conclude that she cannot join us in our work of peace, and, on the other, the danger that the United States should refuse to accept the application of a treaty which she judges contrary to the principles for which she entered the war. Both alike would be serious. Personally, I am not free, since I have the duty to respect the commitment taken by my country.

—M. Orlando shows signs of the liveliest emotion.[4]

Mr. Lloyd George. The pact we signed was kept by Italy; she gave us her resources and the blood of her soldiers. I would tarnish the honor of my country if I hesitated to carry out commitments taken, although no one feels more than I the force of the arguments presented by President Wilson.

Italy is in a difficult position, with the Germans in the Tyrol and the Slavs on the Adriatic. I understand M. Orlando and M. Sonnino's state of mind. The latter especially took upon himself the responsibility of rejecting the offers of Austria and of Prince Bülow in 1915; it was he who advised his compatriots to join us. I don't know in what position he will be towards his people if he is compelled to say to them: "After having lost 500,000 dead, after having had more than one million wounded, after having crushed our country with debts, I cannot bring back to you much more than what Austria offered to us for not going to war."

The only proposal I can make is to have a conference amongst the signatories of the Treaty of London. I repeat that, if there is

[4] "At the conclusion of the President's remarks Orlando got up out of his chair, walked over to the window, and sobbed and wept." Grayson Diary, April 20, 1919, printed in *PWW*, Vol. 57, p. 513. See also the entry from Hankey's diary for April 20, 1919, printed in Stephen Roskill, *Hankey, Man of Secrets*, II, 81.

no alternative, I shall respect the commitment taken by Great Britain. But I propose that we meet—the representatives of Italy, M. Clemenceau, and I—to study together President Wilson's declaration and see what reply we should make to it.

President Wilson. I believe it is my duty to mention everything that might offer a chance for conciliation. If the fate of Fiume is settled according to the provisions of the Treaty of London, if the boundary envisaged by that treaty is provisionally accepted, the territories that it includes being delivered to the five great powers, which will then decide their fate, do the representatives of Italy believe they can give their consent? I must add that it would be impossible for us to guarantee to them that these territories will remain finally with Italy. I recall, however, that, from the strategic point of view, there is a concession that I have already declared myself ready to make to Italy: it is the possession of the island of Lissa. I admit that this is a relatively small thing. But I would not be frank if I let you hope for the consent of the American nation to the final cession to Italy of all the territories in question.

The advantage of the provisional solution I propose is that it would allow us to see how events develop, and perhaps to prepare an acceptable final solution.

Mr. Lloyd George. I would like to have time to think about it, and I repeat my proposal of a meeting tomorrow amongst the powers signatory to the Treaty of London.

Baron Sonnino. We must do everything possible to find a way out of this. I must confess that I don't see any. M. Orlando is ready to reply to Mr. Lloyd George's invitation and to consider with him and M. Clemenceau whether there is a way out. It is our duty to do it.

For my part, I see my death in all of this—I mean my moral death. I have ruined my country whilst believing that I was doing my duty. Moreover, I don't want to insist any longer on something personal to me.

Mr. Lloyd George. You have the right to speak about the offer you rejected in order to come over to us.

President Wilson. I have never doubted the sincerity of your statements when you told me that Italy has no imperialistic intentions. I acknowledge that you have always spoken only of protecting yourself against the danger which might come to you from the Yugoslav coast. I have great respect for you, Baron Sonnino—for the firmness of your views and the obvious sincerity of your intentions. If I saw any way to get out of this difficulty to your satisfaction, it would be a true joy to me. I would consent to any solution of that kind that might be offered, in the interest of Europe and out of consideration for you.

But don't believe that you are guilty towards your country; I believe you have worked for her glory as well as for her true interest.

Baron Sonnino. I thank you for having acknowledged that the Italian government is not imperialistic. We have no desire to dominate other races. We wish only to protect ourselves, and, in the Balkans, we wish only to protect ourselves against Balkan complications. We are neighbors of the Balkan peninsula, and we can do nothing about that. What we want is to be in the position of not finding ourselves dragged into Balkan affairs; if we are not protected, as we must be, we will inevitably be drawn into these quarrels, because, if we have the Serbs as enemies, we will have to seek to win the support of either the Bulgarians or the Rumanians. These intrigues and counter-intrigues will have no end.

We have no other thought than a defensive thought. Remember that Italy suffered centuries of invasions; it is not surprising that we should try to close our door still open on this side.

President Wilson. If I believed this would close your door, I would support you in this. On the contrary, I think it means opening it.

Baron Sonnino. The Treaty of London gives us no means for an offensive policy. But it must be recognized that the war has strongly excited the sentiment of nationalism; we are seeing twenty new nations suddenly appearing. We took care to leave the Croats, not only the coasts, but very adequate defenses. The government of the world would be very easy if it were possible to apply to it simply one or two principles. It has been necessary, in the solution of problems other than our own, to make laborious and complicated compromises.

—*It is agreed that a meeting of the powers signatory to the Treaty of London will take place tomorrow, Monday, April 21, at 10 o'clock.*

—M. Clemenceau reads a telegram from Herr von Brockdorff-Rantzau, in which the German government announces that, on April 25, it will send to Versailles three representatives from the Wilhelmstrasse, Herren von Haniel, von Keller, and Schmidt, to receive the text of the peace preliminaries and to take it home immediately.

Mr. Lloyd George. We cannot meet with these messengers. This manner of proceeding would be a sign of insolence, if it wasn't perhaps a sign of impotence. I am going to read you a report from our military representative in Berlin,[5] which throws some light on this incident.

—Reading of the report: The present German government is not inclined to sign the peace treaty; but it is very weak, and its fall could plunge Germany into complete disorder, barring a prompt reconstruction through an agreement with the left-wing Socialists and the creation, besides the National Assembly, of an assembly representative of the councils of workers and soldiers. The author of the report believes that we could take an initiative through the intermediary of Switzerland that might precipitate this change.

Mr. Lloyd George. I propose simply to refuse to meet mere messengers of the German government and to demand the sending of plenipotentiaries. That can contribute to the fall of this government; we would have a great interest in that if it is not capable of signing the treaty in the name of the German people.

—*Drafting of a telegram in this sense.*

[5] It is printed in *PWW*, Vol. 57, pp. 521-24. The report made even more apocalyptic predictions than the summary below indicates: the establishment of either a military dictatorship backed by the right wing or a soviet government probably leading to a Bolshevik dictatorship. The author of the report, Captain Thomas Gibson, thought that it would be easier to negotiate a treaty with a new government composed of Majority and Independent Socialists.

XLI

Conversation between the representatives of the powers signatory to the Treaty of London on April 26, 1915: Messrs. Lloyd George and Balfour, MM. Clemenceau and Pichon, and M. Orlando and Baron Sonnino.*

APRIL 21, 1919, 10 A.M.

THE QUESTION OF THE ADRIATIC

M. Clemenceau. I am trying to find how we can escape the difficulty; I see no way out. As for us, the treaty binds us; if our Ital-

*Does not appear in H.

ian friends declare that they will adhere to the letter of the treaty, we must keep our word.

Mr. Lloyd George. Undoubtedly, but it would be a serious thing if the United States didn't sign the treaty with Austria-Hungary. The German populations of the Alto-Adige and the Yugoslav populations of the coast of the Adriatic will remain equally discontented; both will believe that, if they stir things up, the United States will be behind them. If the President of the United States can't sign the treaty, I see a peril from these two sides. On the other hand, I don't see how Europe can put itself back in working order if the United States doesn't oil the machinery. We have made plans to assure ourselves of the support of American credit, and all our financial advisers agree on the danger of a complete stagnation of business in Europe if this credit isn't available to us. It is a situation comparable to that of South Africa after the Boer War. England lent that country thirty million pounds sterling—which, incidentally, were never repaid—to allow the recovery of economic activity. Without that, South Africa would have remained in the situation of a devastated and ruined country for years.

The present problem in Europe is the same; it is essential that America stay with us all the way. It was difficult to bring her over to us. All things considered, President Wilson has in the course of these negotiations gone much further in our direction than we had at first thought possible. He has come over to our views on the question of indemnities, on the question of the Saar Basin, on many others besides. In this Italian problem, I see a favorable outcome if it is possible to make a concession which facilitates his adhesion. In the contrary case, we can only repeat to you that we will carry out the treaty if you ask us to. Please believe that we are only speaking as friends who wish to come to the aid of friends.

M. Clemenceau. I accept all that Mr. Lloyd George has just said, and I could take it as my own words. I believed that an arrangement would be possible in the matter of Fiume; but I have lost that illusion. When the Italians foreshadowed a renunciation of the treaty in order to consider the question in its entirety, that led to no amelioration. When, for his part, President Wilson suggested a provisional solution which left the problem in abeyance, no favorable result followed.

I had a new conversation yesterday evening with the President of the United States; his position is quite firm. The only advice I can give you is this: if you want Fiume, see what other concession would be possible for you. I think I find an argument for

President Wilson in the negotiations which Italy had with Austria before the rupture of the Triple Alliance. But what Austria offered to Italy in 1915 and nothing is nearly the same thing. No one has the right to say that Italy would receive no more today if she should come out of this war with all of the Trentino, the Isonzo Valley, Trieste, and Istria.

Baron Sonnino. When I spoke of the negotiation with Austria, I neglected to say that, one month after the break, Austria continued her advances through the intermediary of the Vatican.

M. Clemenceau. Were you ever offered Trieste? I sought an argument in that direction for President Wilson; I didn't find any. Even if today you obtained only a few points in Dalmatia, you would be in what seems to me an excellent position with regard to Italian public opinion.

For my part, I renounced asking the frontier of 1814 for France; I renounced asking the permanent occupation of the left bank of the Rhine, and I did that against the opinion of important people, and at my own risk. So I can offer myself as an example. If Italy participates in the rest of the negotiations, she will gain numerous advantages, believe me, more considerable than she would have been assured of obtaining at the beginning of the war.

I rely on your wisdom in this matter. Mr. Lloyd George, M. Pichon, and I, we speak as friends of Italy when we say to you: this way only does a solution lie; accept it, otherwise we are hastening towards the most deplorable consequences: isolation, the work of the war left unfinished, and a powerful ferment of disorder sown in Europe.

Baron Sonnino. President Wilson was categorical about Fiume: he says no. About the rest, he tells us: "Place these territories in the hands of the five powers, and I don't promise you that they will then give them back to Italy."

The terms we are asking for are those on the basis of which we entered the war. We lost half a million dead; our country is ruined, and all the advantages we expected are being taken away from us. When, in the armistice agreement,[1] the very frontier defined by the Treaty of London was indicated as the boundary of the occupation, all Italy believed that the cause was finally won, and there was no American protest at that time.

Mr. Lloyd George. Did President Wilson know about the treaty at that time?

Mr. Balfour. Yes.

---

[1] The agreement concluded between Italy and Austria-Hungary at Villa Giusti, near Padua, on November 3, 1918.

Baron Sonnino. Put yourself in the position of the Italian public. The United States only took part in the war, as far as we are concerned, by lending us money. There was only one American regiment in Italy, which lost only a single man dead. I don't give you that as an argument, but to make you understand the Italian public's impression. We negotiated with you; a third party arrives which declares that it doesn't recognize our agreements.

The League of Nations is invoked; let it go, if it can, and put Russia in order! Let it settle Balkan affairs! One can't change human nature that way.

As for myself, I have always taken pains to calm public opinion. When I went to Rome, after the signing of the armistice, and when they came to my windows to cheer me, I hid, because I strongly sensed that a time of troubles was beginning.

America said nothing to us for five months. Now, after having made concessions right and left to legitimate interests, she wants to recover her virginity at our expense by invoking the purity of principles. How could we accept? We would have disorder and anarchy in our country; I don't see how we could avoid it. All that President Wilson just told us is this: "Place all this in our hands, and I will not give it back to you." That would change the memory that I treasure of these five years into a long remorse. I don't believe I can be reproached for not having been faithful to the Allies.

Mr. Lloyd George. You won't be offended if I make a suggestion to you? I read your memorandum,[2] which contains very strong arguments. The main one is that of Italy's security. The danger which you fear comes from the islands behind which an enemy fleet can always hide. On the other hand, the difficulties I fear would come only from the occupation by Italy of the mainland. You would never have peace in that part of the world.

Baron Sonnino. The peoples of the Balkans will have enough to do amongst themselves.

Mr. Lloyd George. You would be compelled to maintain a considerable garrison in Dalmatia and to be always on your guard. My proposal is that Italy occupy the islands which lie along the coast, whilst offering to the Slavic population, if it wishes, to be transported and settled on the mainland, which the war has so depopulated. If you have only the islands, that won't impose a heavy military burden on you. Such is the friendly suggestion I venture to make to you.

---

[2] That is, Orlando's long statement at the beginning of the meeting on April 19, 11 a.m.

Baron Sonnino. This question of the islands will raise the same objections, and, as for the difficulties which you fear, I believe they would disappear within two years.

Mr. Lloyd George. Do you believe that? There are 600,000 Croats in Dalmatia against 40,000 Italians.

Baron Sonnino. We are not asking for all of Dalmatia.

M. Orlando. I want to explain to you the reasons for our firmness which, within certain limits, must be absolute.

The first is a reason of practical utility, in the general interest. If I returned to Italy bringing a peace which provoked an uprising of the population, I would render a serious disservice to the entire world. If President Wilson's opinion prevails, there will be a revolution in Italy, don't you doubt it. Recently brawls took place in Rome and Milan between Bolsheviks and patriots. It was the Bolsheviks who were defeated; in Milan two of them were killed. Now, this nationalistic element, which is so worked up now, would make revolution if the peace seemed bad to it, and this time the Bolsheviks would be on the same side, because they will always be for revolution in whatever way and under whatever pretext it begins. A satisfied Italy would remain absolutely firm and calm; an Italy disappointed and discontented—that will mean revolution and a danger for the entire world.

If I return to Rome alone against the entire world, whilst saying to our people as after Caporetto: "Arise! Have courage! The country can still be saved!", I will perhaps be able to hold together the nationalistic elements. For that I am counting on the deep patriotism of the Italian people. Then you will have Italy in a terrible state, but standing; the evil will be less, not only for her, but also for you yourselves.

I could not accept President Wilson's proposal, even as a basis for discussion. The line drawn by President Wilson is the one which was published in 1917 by *New Europe*, which is a kind of official publication of the Yugoslavs.[3] Now, in the eyes of the Italian, the Croat is exactly what the Boche is in the eyes of the French. Imagine how the French would regard a proposal iden-

---

[3] Sir Arthur John Evans, "Diagrammatic Map of a Future South Slav State," *The New Europe: A Weekly Review of Foreign Politics*, IV (Oct. 11, 1917), 415-16. The foldout map faces p. 416. It showed Fiume, all of Dalmatia, and all of the islands off the coast of present-day Yugoslavia as part of the "future South Slav State." Evans was a distinguished archaeologist with a strong interest in the future of Yugoslavs. Robert William Seton-Watson and Thomas Garrigue Masaryk had founded *The New Europe* in October 1916 mainly to promote the cause of the independence of Czechoslovakia. It was published in London through October 1920.

tical to the one which the Germans themselves could make to them.

Last January, President Wilson showed me his boundary line and asked me what I thought of it. I answered him: "It is impossible." I begged him to consider that, faced with such a proposal, I could only withdraw from the conference. President Wilson stopped the interpreter and said to him: "Does M. Orlando really mean that, in this case, he would withdraw from the conference?" I answered: "Yes, that is precisely what I mean."

For three months, I found myself in a false position. I collaborated with you on the solution of the problems of the peace whilst President Wilson and I shared the memory of that conversation. Mr. Lloyd George proposes to us to seek conciliation, and I recognize the fertility of his mind. If our allies can, with President Wilson, arrive at an arrangement which I could decently present to my country, I am quite ready to follow them. But I think that painful conversations are no longer useful. If Mr. Lloyd George and M. Clemenceau wish, with President Wilson, to make a compromise proposal not putting in question the annexation of Fiume, we wish with all our hearts for the success of their endeavors. If it doesn't succeed, it will be best for the world that we bring an equivocal and agonizing situation to a close. We will ask for the carrying out of the Pact of London, and it will be up to our allies to give us satisfaction. Until then we will be isolated.

M. Pichon. Do you have no other proposal to make?

M. Orlando. It is a matter of finding what to pay for Fiume.

Mr. Lloyd George. In that case, I see no hope. For on Fiume, I agree with President Wilson. I stand by the Pact of London absolutely. But the Pact of London provided that Fiume would be given to the Serbs and they know it, and they were our allies. We cannot violate our word to them, any more than to you.

M. Clemenceau. We gave Fiume to the Serbs along with you; Italy's signature is at the bottom of the treaty, and I cannot take that city from them.

Mr. Lloyd George. That clause is as much part of the treaty as the others.

Baron Sonnino. If you managed to work out a plan of conciliation, we could see what we would have to give up. I will recall, on the subject of Serbia, that, when offers were made to Bulgaria to attract her to the side of the Allies, part of Macedonia was held out to her. The Allies offered Croatia to Serbia in compensation. But Serbia refused to agree to that arrangement, and the Allies replied that, in that case, they were withdrawing their offer. So we can say that Fiume was promised to the Croats, but not to the Serbs.

M. Clemenceau. That makes no difference today, and I have promised.

Mr. Lloyd George. I receive information from our General Staff that, if Fiume is taken from the Croats and the Serbs, they will not hesitate to fight.

I don't know whether it is useful to insist on the suggestion I just made, which was to ask President Wilson to consent to the cession of the islands to Italy, the mainland remaining with the Yugoslavs?

Baron Sonnino. Without Fiume?

Mr. Lloyd George. Without Fiume.

M. Orlando. That is impossible.

Baron Sonnino. Then we would be renouncing Dalmatia without compensation. We cannot accept that. The question of security is undoubtedly the first; but there is also a national question in Dalmatia. The cities on the coast, the civilization, are Italian.

Mr. Lloyd George. Isn't a large majority of the population Slavic?

Baron Sonnino. Not in the cities. We cannot forget the national and historical reasons which bind us to them. Is it not President Wilson himself who said that the national consideration must take precedence over the economic consideration? Then, why not take account of the 24,000 Italians who live in Fiume, when we are concerned with the fate of 4,000 or 5,000 Germans on the border of Belgium?

Mr. Lloyd George. I beg to point out to you that the comparison is not valid. The Germans on the Belgian border form one body with the rest of the German people, and it is not the same with the Italians of Fiume.

Mr. Balfour. We must take into account the difficulty in which President Wilson finds himself. He will have to justify himself before American public opinion for having consented to the annexation of the entire southern Tyrol to Italy, including the German valleys.

Mr. Lloyd George. There is no point in arguing amongst ourselves, but only in seeking a way to obtain the adhesion of the United States to the treaty. If we don't obtain it, it will be serious.

Mr. Balfour. I don't believe we realize how serious it will be. M. Orlando fears revolution in Italy. But suppose Italy falls out with the United States. I don't see how the economic life of the country will be able to continue, and, in that case, how will you avoid social revolution? The danger seems to me at least as great as if you returned to Rome with a treaty which, in my opinion, would be perfectly satisfactory. The life of Italy would become an insoluble problem, and the situation would then become dreadful.

M. Orlando. I acknowledge the truth of what Mr. Balfour says; but I don't believe that one of the two dangers is more serious than the other, and I still have a hope of avoiding revolution if I remain with my country. We are a sober people, and we know the art of dying of hunger. The danger being equal, I prefer to stay on the side of justice and honor.

XLII

Conversation between President Wilson and MM. Clemenceau and Lloyd George*

APRIL 21, 1919, 4 P.M.

THE QUESTION OF THE ADRIATIC

Mr. Lloyd George. Has the President of the United States seen my proposal? It would consist of giving Italy the islands off the Dalmatian coast. Philip Kerr has just had a conversation with the Yugoslavs. They say that, if Italy took Fiume, they would fight. If Italy installs herself in Dalmatia, a guerrilla war would follow. It doesn't seem that they are equally concerned about the islands.

President Wilson. On the subject of the island of Cherso, M. Trumbić says that, if Italy possessed it, she could create all the difficulties she might want in the Gulf of Fiume.

Mr. Lloyd George. What difficulties could she create?

President Wilson. In any case, the Yugoslavs are very touchy in this respect.

Mr. Lloyd George. It would suffice to stipulate that the waters surrounding these islands could not be treated by Italy as territorial waters, and that they will be free to the shipping of all flags, except in case of war.

M. Clemenceau is convinced that the Italians won't accept this arrangement. What would perhaps bring M. Sonnino towards us would be a concession in Asia. Have you seen the map of Asia Minor which was prepared yesterday?

*H., *PPC*, V, 106ff.

President Wilson. Do you believe that would be enough to bring him back?

Mr. Lloyd George. I believe so. I am well aware of his situation. He took the decision to make war with a poor country behind him. Italy doesn't have many natural resources. She has no mines. Think about all that France will have in iron ore, potash, etc., merely in Alsace and Lorraine.

President Wilson. I don't know whether Italy would find great resources in Anatolia; but the real difficulty is that the Greeks and other peoples fear having the Italians as neighbors. A very colorful and venerable person, the Patriarch of Constantinople, who came to see me the other day, expressed to me, with the reserve of an ecclesiastic, a very marked feeling against the possibility of seeing the Italians become his neighbors.

Mr. Lloyd George. You remember that M. Vénisélos proposed to give Italy a mandate over all of Anatolia.

President Wilson. Italy lacks experience in the administration of colonies. She would ask for territories only to satisfy her ambition.

Mr. Lloyd George. The Romans were very good governors of colonies.

President Wilson. Unfortunately, the modern Italians are not the Romans.

Mr. Lloyd George. What if we should give them an extended sphere of economic influence in Asia, without putting administration in their hands?

President Wilson. That would seem to me dangerous with such people as the Turks.

Mr. Lloyd George. No, they are a docile people, who have never cut railroads, nor anything of the kind.

President Wilson. I also fear direct difficulties with the Italians if we have a mandate in their vicinity. But I have a particular horror of paying them compensation for something which should never have belonged to them.

Mr. Lloyd George. I would agree with you if Italy was moved only by ambition. But it must be recalled that she entered the war on the basis of certain promises, and M. Sonnino would be hanged from a lamp post if he returned without those promises having been kept.

M. Clemenceau. I saw the Italian *Green Book*:[1] what Austria offered her was nothing.

[1] Italy, Ministry of Foreign Affairs, *Diplomatic Documents Submitted to the Italian Parliament by the Minister for Foreign Affairs (Sonnino), Austria-Hungary, Session of the 20th May, 1915* (London, 1915).

President Wilson. The Italian ministers could say to us: "We are going to take the advice of our Parliament on this question." Then they could return.

Mr. Lloyd George. They cannot face their Parliament without bringing anything to it. I know what would happen at home if we went before the House of Commons without having settled the question of indemnities.

President Wilson. Can't they say, in order to justify themselves in the eyes of their people: "We held out strongly, but so far the solution has not been found?"

Mr. Lloyd George. Believe me: parliaments—I have had some experience with them—behave like undisciplined crowds if they are not led with a firm hand; they readily take the bit between the teeth, and it would be fatal to give them free rein.

President Wilson. What will Italy do if M. Orlando and M. Sonnino go and tell her: "We have left the conference"?

Mr. Lloyd George. There will be an explosion, delirium, and nothing will do more to encourage the Germans to believe that we are quarreling amongst ourselves. What has already been said is partly the fault of our press.

President Wilson. I think that the only line of action we can follow is this. Colonel Hankey should write a text on the basis of our proposal, take it to M. Orlando, and ask him if his colleagues and he want to take it under consideration.

Mr. Lloyd George. We will tell them that if they want to study this plan, there is a chance of working things out, but that it is the limit beyond which you can't go.

President Wilson. I don't much like to make a compromise with people who aren't reasonable. They will always believe that, by persisting in their claims, they will be able to obtain more.

Mr. Lloyd George. It seems to me that M. Sonnino, despite his obstinacy, would be more tractable. This morning he said: "If we could have the cities of the coast * * *."

President Wilson. We come back to the difficulty.

Mr. Lloyd George. These cities are Italian.

President Wilson. They contain an Italian element predominant in culture, but not in numbers, whatever the justifiable suspicion concerning the Austro-Hungarian statistics.

Mr. Lloyd George. Can I tell Baron Sonnino that, if Asia Minor is divided into spheres of influence regarding economic development, Italy will have her large part?

President Wilson. Yes, under a mandate of the League of Nations. But, on the other hand, it will be necessary for the Turks to have

APRIL 21, 1919

some sort of government, and, from this point of view, their territory cannot be divided.

Mr. Lloyd George. To govern all of Anatolia will be a considerable task.

President Wilson. The division of the country would present great difficulties.

M. Clemenceau. Didn't the Italians say this morning that there was no agreement possible if they were not given Fiume?

Mr. Lloyd George. M. Sonnino didn't say that.

President Wilson. Colonel House just learned from Italy that public passion is concentrated on Fiume, more than on Dalmatia.

Mr. Lloyd George. We will help M. Sonnino to get around the question of Fiume by saying: "I was compelled to hold fast to the line of the Treaty of London."

President Wilson. But he won't have what the Treaty of London promised him. What resulted from your discussion this morning?

Mr. Lloyd George. What I proposed to you: it is the only solution in sight.

President Wilson. They must be told that if that suggestion seems to them open to discussion, we are prepared to meet with them and to study it with them. It is a matter of giving them the outposts of the islands, so as to respond to their concern for the security of the Italian coast. That means, moreover, that they would have control of all of Yugoslavia from the naval point of view.

—Lt. Col. Sir Maurice Hankey is sent to the Hôtel Edouard VII to communicate verbally Mr. Lloyd George's proposal to the Italian plenipotentiaries.

President Wilson. Since it is I who am creating the obstacle to the solution, and since I am forced to do this by my proposal, a time will come when I will have to explain my position and America's. Towards this end, I have prepared a document which I am going to read to you.[2]

—Reading of the document: The circumstances have changed since the Treaty of London was signed. On the one hand, some powers entered the war which not only did not sign this treaty but did not know about it beforehand. On the other hand, Austria-Hungary has disappeared and has been replaced by small nations which have the right to fair treatment and friendly relations. The treaty with Germany will be based on the principles which led the United States to declare war against that

[2] Wilson's statement is printed as an appendix to these notes.

power; it is impossible for us to negotiate with Austria-Hungary or with the states which replaced her by grounding ourselves on other principles.

Fiume must be an international port by reason of the function which this city plays with regard to the hinterland. It is for that very reason that the Treaty of London gave Fiume to the Croats. The strategic argument lent force to the Italian claims on the Dalmatian coast when it was a matter of Italy protecting herself against Austria-Hungary. But Austria-Hungary has disappeared, the coast will be dismantled, and the new states will be subjected to limitation of armaments under the control of the League of Nations.

Italy undoubtedly took part in the war gloriously; but she is not without compensation, since she is recovering the Italian territories of the Trentino and of Istria up to the watershed, and since she will finally achieve her unity within the natural boundary of the mountains surrounding her.

America is the friend of Italy. The ties of sympathy which united the two countries have been reinforced by the blood shed for the same cause. But our action was guided by principles which I am obliged to respect. For us, the question is not a question of self-interest; it is a matter of the right of peoples to self-determination and of the right of the world to a secure and lasting peace.

Mr. Lloyd George. That is a fine document, which will be useful if the Italian ministers end by going home and taking back to their fellow countrymen only part of what the Treaty of London promised them.

President Wilson. I think this statement will also respond to the necessities of the circumstances if the Italians reject our proposals.

Mr. Lloyd George. The document could indeed produce a helpful impression in Italy, but only after a certain period of time. For the moment, we must expect only madness.

President Wilson. The Italians can't accuse the United States of being an interested party.

Mr. Lloyd George. No, but of siding with the Yugoslavs against them.

President Wilson. Our tenet is that the Slavs have the same right to independence and national unity as the Italians themselves.

Mr. Lloyd George. Yes, but if a word must be said for the Italians, the Slavs have to admit that Italy's sacrifices contributed much to their own liberation, and that didn't prevent the Croats from fighting against us to the end. Except for the Czechoslovaks, the Slavs of Austria played a rather questionable part.

President Wilson. It is difficult for us free peoples to understand the state of mind of races which have been oppressed and held under terror for a long time.

Mr. Lloyd George. Despite so many persecutions and capital sentences, the Czechs took another position.

President Wilson. Bohemia had a more independent position in the empire. We have to understand the situation of populations gradually humbled by oppression.

Mr. Lloyd George. How did the Poles of Austria fight?

M. Clemenceau. I really don't know.

President Wilson. About the Poles, I must tell you that I received a report from General Bliss,[3] which indicates that they intend to send General Haller's army to Lemberg. This is contrary to our plans. Shouldn't we inform M. Paderewiski that, having accepted in principle the conclusion of a cease-fire and an armistice, he must stop hostilities and not allow General Haller's troops to be sent to Lemberg, nor used to relieve other troops, who would receive that same order? If our agents are not listened to, we could, if necessary, threaten to stop the victualing.

Mr. Lloyd George. We must avoid throwing the Poles into the arms of the Bolsheviks.

President Wilson. Do you see an objection to my proposal?

Mr. Lloyd George. We can't allow General Haller's army to be sent to Lemberg.

M. Clemenceau. I am of the same mind as you, and I propose to approve President Wilson's suggestion.

President Wilson. What is your news from Germany?

M. Clemenceau. Bad. News received in Lyons by radio denies that the German financial delegates have taken a conciliatory attitude which foretells the signing of most of the clauses of the treaty. That is the gist of it. Tomorrow we'll have the Germans' reply to my telegram, and we'll see if they are trying to continue their game.

Mr. Lloyd George. In reality, the German government is weak; it is most probable that it will fall. Is it too early to anticipate what we will do if it refuses?

President Wilson. That is difficult, because we don't know how it will refuse; instead of refusing purely and simply, it can adopt dilatory tactics.

Mr. Lloyd George. I think our summons will bring it down to earth. If it doesn't feel strong enough to send us plenipotentiaries, it

---

[3] See T. H. Bliss to WW, April 18, 1919, *PWW*, Vol. 57, pp. 461-64.

will have to be reconstituted, and that is what we should want.

President Wilson. We have the right to say to those who present themselves to us: whom do you represent?

Mr. Lloyd George. We must act vigorously. After all, hostilities are only suspended; the war can be resumed after a previous notice of forty-eight hours. It is better to make these people face the hard reality if they are trying to play tricks on us. Then they will fall, and they'll be replaced by others with whom we can talk. After having defeated those great German armies commanded by Hindenburg and Ludendorff, we can't allow ourselves to be trifled with by politicians of the fourth rank.

President Wilson. Maybe, but the real problem is this: how will we have peace? No one wants the war to be prolonged indefinitely.

M. Clemenceau. No, none of us; but we can force them to peace by occupying their territory.

Mr. Lloyd George. I'm not so sure about that. The Germans have a thick skin and will tolerate an occupation better than the French would.

President Wilson. Besides, there are people in Germany who fear for their property and would prefer a foreign occupation to a revolution and Bolshevism.

M. Clemenceau. If you tell them, if it is necessary: "You will have war in forty-eight hours," you'll see the effect.

—Lt. Col. Sir Maurice Hankey returns from his mission.

Sir Maurice Hankey. The Italian Ministers refused to consider what I took them; they were absolutely inflexible. I explained the proposal to them and asked them if they would agree to talk on that basis. I saw M. Orlando and M. Sonnino: both replied negatively. They asked me if I could give them the plan in writing. I answered no. They say that, even looking at it solely from the point of view of defense, they cannot accept. To tell the truth, what they mean by defense is not only military defense, but the defense of Italian nationality on the coast facing them.

President Wilson. That is not what M. Sonnino said, and that proves that there is no limit to what they are asking.

Sir Maurice Hankey. M. Sonnino went so far as to say that that proposal marked a retreat, since the idea of Fiume established as a free port seemed abandoned. Perhaps this was only a bait for a new discussion.

Mr. Lloyd George. If the Yugoslavs keep Dalmatia, Fiume can be established as a free city. Besides, I would see a great disadvantage in making it into a Croatian city with Croatian customs.

President Wilson. I have thought about this last point: I am still inclined to support the plan to make Fiume a free city, because this plan is good for the interests of the hinterland. I never closed the door to that proposal.

Mr. Lloyd George. What is your impression, Colonel Hankey?

Sir Maurice Hankey. I have the impression that the Italians are bluffing a little and that they think you are weakening.

President Wilson. What I can best do is publish my manifesto in the newspapers of tomorrow morning.

M. Clemenceau. If you publish it, there will be nothing doing any longer after that. When the business is dead and buried, say why, but not before.

President Wilson. But then I will be too late. In order to clarify the situation, I can say that it seems to me important to state the views of the United States.

Mr. Lloyd George. It will unleash a tempest in Italy. Everything will be topsy-turvy.

President Wilson. Meanwhile, the situation remains ambiguous, and the United States appears to be taking an unreasonable position.

Mr. Lloyd George. Two months ago, the French press spoke of me as badly as the Italian press can speak of you. I thought it better to keep quiet, and I was glad I did.

President Wilson. But there was a reasonable government here with which we could talk. That is not the case in the matter with which we are dealing.

M. Clemenceau. I thought the Italians would return.

Mr. Lloyd George. My advice is not to budge, to act a little like them, giving them rope, and to confine ourselves to informing them that we are going on to another subject.

M. Clemenceau. I think that will soon bring us a visit from M. Sonnino.

President Wilson. If the Italians publicly announce their views tomorrow, I don't want to let them fire the first cannon shot, so to speak.

Mr. Lloyd George. I would let them be.

M. Clemenceau. You will read articles tomorrow in our newspapers, but they will not represent French public opinion, I can guarantee you that.

Mr. Lloyd George. In England, no one is much concerned about this question.

M. Clemenceau (*to President Wilson*). Wait forty-eight hours and, if there is good reason, say: "Here are my position and reasons."

President Wilson. After the debate is over?

Mr. Lloyd George. If you do it before, you will cause an explosion; you'll raise all Italian public opinion up against you.

President Wilson. I haven't yet presented my point of view to the Italian people, and I confine myself to saying that, afterwards, they won't ask us for what we cannot grant.

Mr. Lloyd George. Yes, but your statement makes no allusion to our efforts at conciliation, to the last suggestions we have made. It would make all compromise impossible for us. It is better to say these things only when all the doors have been closed. I would coolly invite the Italians to come to discuss the question of Kiaochow with the Japanese tomorrow.

M. Clemenceau. They won't come. I recall that, when we spoke of sending the invitation to the Germans to come to Versailles, M. Orlando said, "I enter my reservations about my participation as long as the Italian questions haven't been settled."

President Wilson. Indeed, M. Orlando said that he couldn't participate in the negotiation with Germany before the Adriatic question was settled.

Mr. Lloyd George. I warned the Italians of the consequences that would follow from the financial point of view if they were not represented here when we discuss the question of reparation with Germany. My advice is to invite them to participate in our discussions as if nothing had happened.

President Wilson. I had an interview with Baron Makino,[4] and I reminded him of the decision of the conference on the application of the mandate system to the Pacific islands. I indicated to him the reservation that I had to make concerning the island of Yap. As for Kiaochow and the concession in Shantung, the Japanese say that their rights are established by treaties and that to place these rights in the hands of the five powers would be equivalent to a dispossession. I replied that we only wanted to favor an arrangement accepted equally by Japan and China, which would in no way be an infraction of the treaties already signed.

The position of the Japanese is very inflexible. They refuse to consent to that. They say they are ready to give up Kiaochow on the sole condition that a Japanese concession be established in the bay and that the bay itself be open to international commerce. As for the railroad between Tsingtao and the Huang Ho, they are

---

[4] For another report of this meeting, see K. Matsui to Y. Uchida, April 22, 1919, *ibid.*, pp. 581-85.

asking for a partnership with China on equal terms. I observed that that would create a situation of real inequality, because it is not China which will provide the capital. They answered by citing precedents. In short, they insist on maintaining their treaty as it is.

Mr. Lloyd George. Is there a clause which has to be placed in the treaty with Germany?

President Wilson. Only in one respect. The Japanese are asking that Germany cede to them all her rights in China, and they declare that they will then carry out their treaty with the Chinese Republic.

Mr. Lloyd George. Why shouldn't they accept what we ourselves have accepted in the Cameroons, in New Guinea, in South-west Africa, etc.?

President Wilson. I submitted my plan to them for renouncing all spheres of influence and all special rights for foreigners in China. They said that they *were* inclined to that concession.

Mr. Lloyd George. Yes, but after they have received what they demand today.

President Wilson. I must say that the special rights that would be established by common consent would include the right of military occupation, which is a formidable right in the hands of Japan, and the right of extraterritoriality. It would be very important for Japan to renounce them at the same time as all of us.

Mr. Lloyd George. Undoubtedly; but I would like to avoid, if possible, an inequality of treatment between South Africa and Japan, an inequality all the more obvious as South-west Africa is at the doors of South Africa.

—President Wilson reads aloud the two treaties between China and Japan.

Mr. Lloyd George. If the Japanese don't agree that these German possessions should be treated in the same way as the others, which will be subjected to the mandate system, it is as if they were saying to us: "We have no confidence in you." What they want is to escape the control of the League of Nations.

President Wilson. This morning they said they would interpret that procedure as putting their good faith towards China in doubt. I said to them that the peace of the Far East was in their hands, that China cannot resist, and that her prosperity is beneficial to the entire world. Isn't it in their interest to convince the Chinese that they are coming amongst them as friends? They approved my words.

Mr. Lloyd George. They always accept the principles. When you come to the application, it is different. They don't want to receive anything from the hands of the League of Nations. Nevertheless, we can call their attention to the fact that it was Germany's defeat in the West which allowed them to keep their gains. If we are not firm on this point, what can I answer Mr. Hughes if he in turn asks to escape from the mandate system.

M. Clemenceau. Be careful that Japan doesn't break with you. If you are prepared for that, all right; but she'll break.

President Wilson. The Japanese told me with all oriental courtesy that, if we didn't take their side on this article of the treaty, they couldn't sign the rest.

Mr. Lloyd George. Dear! Dear!

M. Clemenceau. If that doesn't bother you any more than that, I can't seem to be more bothered than you.

President Wilson. We must hear the Japanese tomorrow morning.

Mr. Lloyd George. Unless the German reply takes all our time. I propose that M. Clemenceau, if he hasn't received the answer from the Germans, invite the Japanese for tomorrow. If the German reply arrives in the meantime, I would prefer not to involve the Japanese in the discussion.

M. Clemenceau. Will you invite the Italians?

President Wilson. It is difficult in view of the position they have taken.

M. Clemenceau. It is better to show them that our work is continuing.

Mr. Lloyd George. I propose to advise them simply that we are placing the Japanese question on the agenda, unless the German reply arrives and requires discussion.

{ A P P E N D I X }[5]

In view of the capital importance of the questions affected, and in order to throw all possible light upon what is involved in their settlement, I hope that the following statement will contribute to the final formation of opinion and to a satisfactory solution.

When Italy entered the war she entered upon the basis of a definite, but private, understanding with Great Britain and France, now known as the Pact of London. Since that time the

---

[5] Printed in *ibid.*, Vol. 58, pp. 5-8. The text printed here is that of Wilson's statement issued on April 23. The draft that he read to Clemenceau and Lloyd George, printed in *ibid.*, Vol. 57, pp. 542-44, is only slightly different in wording.

whole face of circumstance has been altered. Many other powers, great and small, have entered the struggle, with no knowledge of that private understanding. The Austro-Hungarian Empire, then the enemy of Europe, and at whose expense the Pact of London was to be kept in the event of victory, has gone to pieces and no longer exists. Not only that. The several parts of that empire, it is now agreed by Italy and all her associates, are to be erected into independent states and associated in a League of Nations, not with those who were recently our enemies, but with Italy herself and the powers that stood with Italy in the Great War for Liberty. We are to establish their liberty as well as our own. They are to be among the smaller states whose interests are henceforth to be as scrupulously safe-guarded as the interests of the most powerful states.

The war was ended, moreover, by proposing to Germany an armistice and peace which should be founded on certain clearly defined principles which should set up a new order of right and justice. Upon those principles the peace with Germany has been conceived, not only, but formulated. Upon those principles it will be executed. We cannot ask the great body of powers to propose and effect peace with Austria and establish a new basis of independence and right in the states which originally constituted the Austro-Hungarian Empire and in the states of the Balkan group on principles of another kind. We must apply the same principles to the settlement of Europe in those quarters that we have applied in the peace with Germany. It was upon the explicit avowal of those principles that the initiative for peace was taken. It is upon them that the whole structure of peace must rest.

If those principles are to be adhered to, Fiume must serve as the outlet and inlet of the commerce, not of Italy, but of the lands to the north and northeast of that port: Hungary, Bohemia, Roumania, and the states of the New Jugo-Slavic group. To assign Fiume to Italy would be to create the feeling that we had deliberately put the port upon which all these countries chiefly depend for their access to the Mediterranean in the hands of a power of which it did not form an integral part and whose sovereignty, if set up there, must inevitably seem foreign, not domestic or identified with the commercial and industrial life of the regions which the power must serve. It is for that reason, no doubt, that Fiume was not included in the Pact of London but there definitely assigned to the Croatians.

And the reason why the line of the Pact of London swept about many of the islands of the eastern coast of the Adriatic and around the portion of the Dalmatian coast which lies most open to that sea was not only that here and there on those islands and here and there on that coast there are bodies of people of Italian blood and connection but also, and no doubt chiefly, because it was felt that it was necessary for Italy to have a foothold amidst the channels of the Eastern Adriatic in order that she might make her own coasts safe against the naval aggression of Austria-Hungary. But Austria-Hungary no longer exists. It is proposed that the fortifications which the Austrian Government constructed there shall be razed and permanently destroyed. It is part, also, of the new plan of European order which centres in the League of Nations that the new states erected there shall accept a limitation of armaments which puts aggression out of the question. There can be no fear of the unfair treatment of groups of Italian people there because adequate guarantees will be given, under international sanction, of the equal and equitable treatment of all racial or national minorities.

In brief, every question associated with the settlement wears a new aspect,—a new aspect given it by the very victory for right for which Italy has made the supreme sacrifice of blood and treasure. Italy, along with the four other great powers, has become one of the chief trustees of the new order which she has played so honourable a part in establishing.

And on the North and Northeast her natural frontiers are completely restored, along the whole sweep of the Alps from northwest to southeast to the very end of the Istrian peninsula, including all the great watershed within which Trieste and Pola lie and all the fair regions whose face nature has turned towards the great peninsula upon which the historic life of the Latin people has been worked out through centuries of famous story ever since Rome was first set upon her seven hills. Her ancient unity is restored. Her lines are extended to the great walls which are her natural defence. It is within her choice to be surrounded by friends; to exhibit to the newly liberated peoples across the Adriatic that noblest quality of greatness, magnanimity, friendly generosity, the preference of Justice over interest.

The nations associated with her, the nations that know nothing of the Pact of London or of any other special understanding that lies at the beginning of this great struggle, and who have made their supreme sacrifice also in the interest, not of national advantage or defence, but of the settled peace of the world, now unite with her older associates in urging her to assume a leadership which cannot be mistaken in the new order of Europe. America is Italy's friend. Her people are drawn, millions strong, from Italy's own fair countrysides. She is linked in blood as well as in affection with the Italian people. Such ties can never be broken. And America was privileged, by the generous commission of her associates in the war, to initiate the peace we are about to consummate,—to initiate it upon terms she had herself formulated, and in which I was her spokesman. The compulsion is upon her to square every decision she takes a part in with those principles. She can do nothing else. She trusts Italy, and in her trust believes that Italy will ask nothing of her that cannot be made unmistakably consistent with those sacred obligations. Interest is not now in question, but the rights of peoples, of states new and old, of liberated peoples and peoples whose rulers have never accounted them worthy of right; above all, the right of the world to peace and to such settlements of interest as shall make peace secure.

These, and these only, are the principles for which America has fought. These, and these only, are the principles upon which she can consent to make peace. Only upon these principles, she hopes and believes, will the people of Italy ask her to make peace.

Woodrow Wilson

XLIII

Conversation between President Wilson and MM. Clemenceau and Lloyd George*

APRIL 22, 1919, 11 A.M.

M. Clemenceau. I have received the Germans' reply.[1] They will leave only on the twenty-eighth. They don't indicate the exact

*H. PPC, V, 112ff.

[1] A. P. Nudant to F. Foch, April 21, 1919, printed in PWW, Vol. 57, pp. 590-91, conveying a message from the German government, which advised that it was sending a newly appointed delegation "with all the necessary powers." The new delegation consisted of Count Ulrich Karl Christian von Brockdorff-Rantzau, Minister of Foreign Affairs; Otto Landsberg, Minister of Justice; Johann Giesberts, Minister of Posts and Telegraphs; Robert Leinert, President of the Prussian Diet; Carl Melchior, a German banker and head of the newly constituted Democratic party; and Walther Max Adrian Schücking, Professor of Inter-

time of their arrival at Versailles. We have to agree amongst ourselves on the freedom of movement that it is appropriate to allow them. We cannot allow them to communicate with just anyone.

Mr. Lloyd George. Undoubtedly; but they must be free to communicate with their government.

M. Clemenceau. It would be impossible to act otherwise. What I want, above all, is to prevent possible incidents, including mass demonstrations which could be provoked by agitators.

President Wilson. I would let them know that they will have the freedom of movement required for the conduct of the business with which they are directly entrusted.

M. Clemenceau. Do you want to draft the formula?

President Wilson. They will have complete freedom of movement for the accomplishment of their mission and free communication by telegraph with their government.

—*The text drafted by President Wilson is adopted.*

—M. Clemenceau submits for Mr. Lloyd George's and President Wilson's final approval the text of the articles of the treaty relating to the disarmament of the left bank of the Rhine and the occupation of this territory as a guarantee of the execution of the treaty.[2]

Mr. Lloyd George. That occupation would last fifteen years!

M. Clemenceau. I could reduce that period. We will have difficulty even so in having it accepted in France.

Mr. Lloyd George. You mustn't think that we'll leave British troops in Germany for fifteen years.

M. Clemenceau. I must be able to write in this text that the occupation will be carried out by international troops. All I am asking you for, if absolutely necessary, is to leave me one battalion and a flag.

Mr. Lloyd George. You know how impatiently England is waiting for the abolition of compulsory military service. The problem is

---

national Law and a member of the Reichstag. For a fuller description of this group, see Alma Luckau, *The German Delegation at the Paris Peace Conference* (New York, 1941), pp. 54-61.

[2] They stipulated that the left bank of the Rhine and a fifty-kilometer-wide zone east of the Rhine be permanently demilitarized by Germany; declared that any violation of these provisions would be regarded as a hostile act against the signatories of the treaty; provided for the occupation by "international forces" of the bridgeheads and the left bank of the Rhine for periods of five, ten, and fifteen years; and stated that the evacuation of the area depended upon Germany's faithful execution of the treaty terms. These articles are printed in *PWW*, Vol. 57, pp. 591-92.

different for France because it is an institution to which your people are accustomed.

M. Clemenceau. I don't know if the word "international" is found in President Wilson's copy.

President Wilson. Why not say that these territories will be occupied for a fixed period of time, without any other indication?

M. Clemenceau. The Germans will ask by whom. I will also be asked that here. If I don't have your flag beside mine on the left bank of the Rhine, I won't be able to go before our Parliament.

Mr. Lloyd George. These fifteen years: are they indicated here as an absolute limit? Can't it vary with the payments made by Germany?

M. Clemenceau. No, unless Germany refuses to pay. If the League of Nations states that Germany is not fulfilling her commitments, we can prolong or even renew the occupation.

Mr. Lloyd George. All right; I accept.

President Wilson. You also have my assent.

M. Clemenceau. The third document that I bring you is the plan for the treaty between France, on the one hand, and England and the United States, on the other, to guarantee France against aggression.[3]

President Wilson. It is better to have two separate texts, a Franco-English treaty and a Franco-American treaty.

Mr. Lloyd George (*after having read the text*). All right. We accept this text.

M. Clemenceau. My fourth document concerns the boundaries of Austria.[4]

Mr. Lloyd George. No objection.

THE QUESTION OF KIAOCHOW AND OF SHANTUNG

—The delegates of Japan, Baron Makino and Viscount Chinda, are introduced.*

M. Clemenceau (*to President Wilson*). This morning I reread our

*H., *PPC*, V, 123ff.

[3] Actually, Clemenceau presented the draft of a single Franco-American treaty that he and Wilson had agreed to on April 20. It provided that the United States would come immediately to the aid of France "as soon as any unprovoked movement of aggression against her is made by Germany." This pledge was to be subject to the approval of the Council of the League of Nations and would continue in effect until the contracting powers agreed that the League itself afforded "sufficient protection." Printed in *ibid.*, p. 592.

[4] "Germany recognizes the independence of German Austria within the frontiers as defined by the present treaty." *Ibid.*

treaty with Japan:[5] it binds us, as well as Great Britain, to her. I wish to stress this.

Baron Makino (*reading a statement*). On August 15, 1914, Japan sent an ultimatum to Germany, calling on her to surrender to her the leased territory of Kiaochow, so that she could restore it to China. Germany not having answered within the stated time, military action followed, carried out in cooperation with Great Britain. Kiaochow was taken in November 1914.

In January 1915, the first negotiations took place between China and Japan on the subject of Kiaochow and the rights possessed by the Germans in Shantung Province, in such a way as to make it impossible for Germany to recover her position in China after the war and again to become a danger in the Far East. From that negotiation resulted the convention of May 25, 1915. By this transaction, Japan declared herself ready to give Kiaochow back to China at the end of the war, on the condition that the bay be open to international commerce, that a Japanese concession be established in that bay, and that a later agreement settle the fate of the properties and privileges of the Germans in China.

At the beginning of 1917, Japan, in agreement with the Allies, made every effort to induce China to end her neutrality. In March 1917, the Chinese Republic broke diplomatic relations with Germany and declared war on her in the month of August. In September 1918, that is, more than three years after the convention of May 1915, a new exchange of notes took place between Japan and China, which settled the questions left in suspense by the former convention. Japan promised to end the civil administration it had established along the Tsingtao railroad. It was agreed that the police along the line would be made up of Chinese, but with Japanese instructors and administrators. The administration of the line, as well as the construction of new lines, was to be on half shares between China and Japan. At the same time, China placed a loan of twenty-five million yen in Japan.

Japan is thus ready to restore Kiaochow on terms which seem hardly unjust to her if one considers what was done to take that place from the Germans. The treaty of 1918 only completed the one of 1915. To follow any other procedure than one which consists of executing these treaties would be contrary to the agreements undertaken on both sides.

The representatives of China say that that country's declara-

---

[5] Actually, an exchange of notes between the French and Japanese governments of February 19, March 1, and March 6, 1917.

tion of war against Germany annulled, *ipso facto,* the lease which had been granted Germany at Kiaochow. In reality, the lease was nothing other than a cession, pure and simple, for a period of ninety-nine years.

We are convinced that you will do justice to Japan by taking account of the efforts she has made during this war, and in such a way as to cause no injury to her national honor.

—There follows the reading of the text proposed to be inserted in the treaty with Germany.[6]

President Wilson. Did the cables, which this text mentions, belong to the Germans by treaty?

Baron Makino. Yes, they were the property of the German government.

President Wilson. I have already explained to you as best I could the result of the conversation I had yesterday with Messrs. Clemenceau and Lloyd George. I told you what I myself thought. I would now like my colleagues present here to inform you of their feelings.

Mr. Lloyd George. We are in the same situation towards Japan as we are towards Italy: we have taken commitments which we must keep. Concerning Kiaochow, we are bound by the agreement of 1917, signed by our Ambassador in Tokyo. The remain-

---

[6] The text reads as follows:

"*Article 1.*

"Germany renounces, in favour of Japan, all the rights, titles, or privileges—particularly those concerning the territory of Kiaochow, railways, mines and submarine cables—which she acquired, in virtue of the treaty concluded by her with China on the 6 March, 1898 and of all other arrangements relative to Shantung Province.

"The Tsingtao-Tsinan Railway, including its branch lines together with its accessories of all kinds, stations, shops, fixed materials and rolling stocks, mines, establishments and materials for exploitation of the mines, [are], and shall remain, acquired by Japan, together with the rights and privileges appertaining thereto.

"The submarine cables of the State of Germany, from Tsingtao to Shanghai and from Tsingtao to Chefoo, with all the rights, privileges and properties appertaining thereto, shall equally remain acquired by Japan.

"*Article 2.*

"The rights of movable and immovable properties possessed by the State of Germany in the territory of Kiaochow, as well as all the rights which she is entitled to claim in consequence of the works or equipments set up, of the expenses disbursed, or of the contracts concluded by her, either directly or indirectly, and concerning the territory, are, and shall remain, acquired by Japan."

Printed in *PWW,* Vol. 57, pp. 609-10.

ing question is whether the final fate of the territory of Kiaochow has to be mentioned in the treaty we are signing with Germany.

By the Anglo-Japanese treaty of 1917, the English government pledged itself to support the Japanese claims to Kiaochow and in Shantung. The Japanese made the same promise concerning the claims of the dominions south of the equator. I think there is no reason, in the treaty with Germany, to say how the territories taken by Japan will be distributed, no more than those that will go to the dominions. It must be enough for us to say that Germany loses these territories. What they will become is our own business. We will ask for mandates from the League of Nations for Australia and New Zealand, and I am sure we will have Japan's support in that.

Baron Makino. Certainly, for all the islands located south of the equator.

Mr. Lloyd George. This doesn't concern Germany; it is a matter to be settled amongst ourselves. I am ready to support Japan in what she asks. But, if she insists that her right be mentioned in the treaty with Germany, Australia and South Africa will ask to be treated in the same manner. Then it will be necessary to proceed at once to the distribution of the mandates, to determine the very functioning of the system, and we don't have time to do that before our negotiations with Germany.

Viscount Chinda. Do you have in mind applying the same system to Kiaochow as in the southern part of the Pacific? I will point out that the mandate system concerns people incapable of governing themselves and, consequently, doesn't apply to Kiaochow. If you wish simply to delay the solution, by making Germany sign only a clause of renunciation, that is only a question of time. But we have the order of our government not to participate in the signing of the treaty if the territories and rights that we claim are not placed purely and simply at our disposal in such a way as to allow us to carry out our obligations towards China.

Baron Makino. Our treaty with China must be carried out. Its terms are known in China. If it is considered as nonexistent, it would be a very serious matter for Japan.

Viscount Chinda. The question is simple: a definite agreement exists between China and Japan; so there is no cause for a long discussion, and we cannot be convinced that a dilatory solution can be of any advantage at all.

President Wilson. It is necessary to define your relations with

China clearly. The text you have read us is very clear concerning Kiaochow. It is not quite the same for the railroad.

Viscount Chinda. The treaty uses the expression of joint enterprise between China and Japan: those are sufficiently explicit terms.

President Wilson. Those are very general terms. It would be necessary to follow them with a more detailed definition, with an indication of practical regulations which will be their direct consequence. I see that the police will be organized by Japan along the line. There will be Japanese at each station, as well as at the school where this police force will be trained: the treaty doesn't say clearly what their role will be.

Viscount Chinda. They will be instructors. There are numerous precedents for that in China.

Mr. Lloyd George. The Chinese customs are organized and directed by foreigners.

President Wilson. Yes, but that is a consequence of the past relations of China with the European powers.

Isn't Japan asking for other concessions than the railroad?

Viscount Chinda. There are mines, three to be exact; they belong to the same company as the railroad.

Baron Makino. These mines first belonged to a separate company. The exploitation of the coal did not yield great results. It was then that this company was merged with that of the railroad.

President Wilson. Was the goal of the exploitation to provide coal for the railroad itself?

Baron Makino. Principally.

President Wilson. Are the concessions limited to the existing mines, or do they anticipate a right to prospect?

Viscount Chinda. There are altogether three mines, one of which is not in a condition to produce. The two others are linked to the railroad. There is no other concession. One of the three mines is an iron mine.

President Wilson. Is the ore of good quality?

Baron Makino. Exploitation of it did not begin seriously before the war.

President Wilson. I am told that there are large deposits of iron ore in that region.

Mr. Lloyd George. The difficulty that I fear for us is this. Mr. Hughes will not fail to say: "Kiaochow is put in the treaty; why not put there the cession of New Guinea to Australia?"

President Wilson. The case is not the same. Here it is a matter of a German concession, under a special arrangement, in a country which was neutral at the beginning of the war. It is not the same thing to take one of her colonies from Germany.

Viscount Chinda. The Germans did nothing to exploit the iron mine I mentioned. That seems to indicate that its value is questionable.

Baron Makino. As for the joint exploitation with China, it is not the first time we are trying it. We are exploiting forests on half shares; the management, as well as the profits, are divided between us. That works perfectly.

President Wilson. Are you imposing any restrictions whatever on the use of the railroad? My concern is to maintain the open door in China.

Baron Makino. We are imposing no restrictions.

President Wilson. Once again, it is I alone who find myself in the position of judging with complete independence. Messrs. Clemenceau and Lloyd George are bound by their commitments. Personally, I am not so sure that England and Japan, when they negotiated together, had an obvious right to dispose of the islands of the Pacific.

Mr. Lloyd George. They were German islands, property of the enemy.

President Wilson. Peace in the Far East rests on good relations between China and Japan. That is what concerns me. I see that we are in the presence of firm commitments, which don't leave us with a free hand. But if Japan doesn't show the whole world her desire to help China attain the same independence and freedom of development as other nations, if she doesn't show that she wants, not to impose herself on her, but to help her with capital and technical superiority, she will create suspicions and elements of hostility in China. It must be acknowledged that the relations of mutual trust between Japan and China, which must be established between them for the future peace of the Far East, do not exist now. What I fear, if Japan holds strictly to the letter of the treaties, is that she would appear to be thinking only of her rights, without taking into account corresponding duties. We must try today to concentrate less upon the rights that one or the other of us has and more upon the duties incumbent upon us, each towards the others.

The fundamental idea of the League of Nations is "one for all." The conception that we are trying to introduce in the world is that nations must act, not as rivals, but as partners. I would like to see Japan, the most advanced nation of the Far East, take a position as the champion of this new idea in the part of the world where her position is so eminent. She can have no finer role there, nor one which promises her more success; this is what I covet for the Japanese nation.

What I would like is for the treaty to provide for the cession of the rights which formerly belonged to Germany in China to the five powers acting as trustees. The five powers would then see amongst themselves how the treaties existing between Japan and China, on the one hand, and Japan, France, and Great Britain, on the other, should be executed, and how they could be changed if necessary, not by external pressure, but by the consent of the interested parties themselves. That procedure would not violate any commitment taken.

It would be useful, first of all, to have more complete details about the administration of the railroad and the mines.

I have another proposal to make: it is that we agree that all the powers which have extraterritorial rights in China, the right to land troops, etc., renounce them at the same time, so as to place China on the same footing as the other great nations, and cease to impose foreign sovereignties upon her soil. There are, you know, many inflammable elements in China, and we must guard against starting a fire there one day which no one could extinguish. For no power in the world could restore order in a country where 400 million souls live. You know, on the other hand, what the feeling of the Chinese is regarding Shantung, to which they are attached by so many of their most ancient and sacred traditions. I fear that, in acting without precaution, one might provoke amongst the Chinese a movement based on what is deepest within the soul of a people.

I must add, moreover, that I respect all international agreements, even when I should prefer that they had not been signed, and that I am not at all proposing to hold them null and void.

Baron Makino. The best elements of Japanese public opinion agree in wanting good relations with China. What Japan wants is a friendly agreement with that country and the open door for her commerce. I am convinced that this is the only policy which benefits both countries.

In the past, international relations with China have not always been conducted according to principles of justice. It is better not to try to search for the first guilty party; one began, the other followed. As for us, the guiding principle of our policy will be based henceforth on equity and the desire for friendly relations.

Marquis Yamagata, who is one of our principal capitalists, said to me recently that, in all our enterprises with China, we must act so as to share the profits equally with the Chinese. If we have the open door in China, that is all we ask.

President Wilson. I am happy to learn it, and I do not doubt your good intentions. It is necessary only to find a means of making them become evident.

Baron Makino. Our treaty contains nothing more; what sovereignty Germany possessed disappears. Only the economic terms accepted by China remain in our hands. Our Foreign Minister[7] gave a speech at the opening of the session [of the Diet] in January, in which he insisted on our desire to do everything that can assist the economic prosperity of our neighbors.

What especially wounds the Chinese is the right of extraterritoriality of foreigners; it is the presence of foreign troops in China; it is the privilege that foreigners have of submitting only to their own jurisdiction; it is the payment of the Boxer indemnity. I believe our government is completely ready to discuss these questions with the great powers. These are problems that can be solved and whose solution will contribute much to end a dangerous feeling of injustice in China. We will be very happy to meet with you on this ground. China could gradually, like Japan, recover all her sovereign rights concerning the courts, etc.

President Wilson. What is the nature of the concession you are asking for Japan in Kiaochow? Will it give you extraterritoriality?

Baron Makino. Yes, since it is the system generally applied in China at the present time. If the general question of the special rights of foreigners is settled amongst ourselves afterwards, all that will disappear at once.

President Wilson. Now I see much more clearly where we stand. Do you want to meet here with the Chinese? Or would you prefer to explain yourselves directly to them? Since they are members of the conference, we cannot arrive at a final decision outside their presence and without their consent.

Baron Makino. It is right to hear them. But we do not wish to debate with them. When there are preconceived ideas on both sides, time is necessary in order to dissipate them. I greatly regret the misunderstanding which exists; but we could not make it disappear in this way.

Mr. Lloyd George. Does that mean that Japan would prefer to see the Chinese apart from us, or even to meet them here?

[7] Yasuya Uchida.

Baron Makino. I mean that we do not wish to debate with them.

President Wilson. In that case, we must see the Chinese without delay.

Mr. Lloyd George. Shouldn't we take advantage of this opportunity to explain to the Japanese plenipotentiaries what we have done here in these last days? We have settled questions in which Japan is not interested, such as that of Danzig, that of the Saar. The only question which concerns Japan is that of reparation.

Baron Makino. Yes.

President Wilson. You are represented on the Reparation Commission?

Baron Makino. Certainly.

Mr. Lloyd George. Yes, but that commission has only debated without concluding. Since then, we have formed a small group of experts which is arriving at conclusions.

President Wilson. These gentlemen can see M. Loucheur, M. Crespi, Mr. Norman Davis, and Lord Sumner.

Baron Chinda. Have they determined the part reserved for Japan?

President Wilson. We have made no allocation. It didn't seem possible to determine now either the sum due from the Germans or their capacity to pay. So we have concentrated our effort on finding the best way to arrive at these two figures; we believe we have succeeded. What would be best for you to do is to get in touch with Mr. Norman Davis, who will acquaint you with the details.

As Mr. Lloyd George said, we have settled the question of the Saar, which will allow France to be compensated for the loss of her mines in the North, the question of Danzig, that of Schleswig. That of the Kiel Canal, which might interest you, is still not yet completely settled.

Baron Makino. We have our representatives on all the commissions. What we lack sometimes is knowledge of the decisions taken here.

President Wilson. You have the right to know them and to take full part in them every time it is a matter of a general question in which you are interested.

Viscount Chinda. When are you summoning the Chinese delegates? We don't want to appear before you as suitors.

President Wilson. The Chinese are a little afraid of you, and I also think it would be better if we hear them alone, to permit them to express themselves freely.

Viscount Chinda. That is very desirable. What we don't want is a direct discussion with them.

President Wilson. We will inform them of your statements of this morning.

Baron Makino. We are insisting on the form of the restitution of the territory of Kiaochow to China. This restitution must be made directly by Japan. Our government regards this as essential.

XLIV

Conversation between President Wilson and MM. Clemenceau and Lloyd George*

APRIL 22, 1919, 4 P.M.

Mr. Lloyd George. I saw M. Orlando, accompanied by a secretary, a short time ago; he told me that he couldn't participate in our conversations. I asked him if he wouldn't be at the conference; he answered me in the negative. I observed to him that, in that case, Italy could not present Germany with her demand for reparations. Does she want to have herself represented by one of us? He seemed embarrassed. I stressed to him that, if no compromise was possible, the situation could not be more serious. We will keep our commitments according to the Treaty of London; but if America refuses to sign, that will be a disaster for all of us. He appeared rather moved.

I came back to the suggestion we had made about the islands. What particularly concerns M. Orlando seems to be the fate of the three cities of Zara, Sebenico, and Spalato.

President Wilson. That is not their real preoccupation.

Mr. Lloyd George. Taking one more step, I would propose to establish these three cities, or at least the first two, as free cities, with a plebiscite at the expiration of a period of fifteen years.

President Wilson. The Italians ought to make us a proposal along these lines.

Mr. Lloyd George. If they do, what will your attitude be?

President Wilson. Believe me: such a proposal, even if accepted, won't assure peace on the Dalmatian coast. These cities will soon be submerged by the Yugoslav element and, in addition, the Italian population will remain dangerously agitated.

*H., PPC, V, 135ff.

Mr. Lloyd George. We have to take account of the present situation in Italy.

M. Clemenceau. Didn't the government itself create it?

President Wilson. I have spoken with people who know the Italians better than I. Their conversation has led me to believe that, if I publish my document tomorrow, with a preamble explaining that it is better that each of us makes known his attitude, there will be a great sensation in Italy for the moment; but it will not lead to an immediate decision, and, in conformity with the Italian temperament, this moment of agitation will be followed by a depression in morale, with a feeling of hopelessness.

It must not be forgotten that Italy sends millions of men to America, that tens of thousands of Italians from the United States come to visit their families each year, that there is a continual flow of money from the United States to Italy. When the man in the street sees what we have to say, he will reflect and think that a new settlement can take place on the basis of new principles. Then a sudden change in Italian public opinion could occur.

Mr. Lloyd George. I fear a crisis we can no longer control, and that crisis could bring Giolitti back to power.

THE QUESTION OF SHANTUNG

—MM. Lou Tseng Tsiang and Wellington Koo, delegates of China, are introduced.*

President Wilson. You know the interest we are taking in the question of Kiaochow. We saw the Japanese this morning. The question is complicated on account of the commitments taken. It seems that, before China entered the war, there was an exchange of notes between China and Japan, on the date of May 25, 1915. Japan promised, after the cession of the territory of Kiaochow by Germany, to restore it to China; the Chinese government replied that it took note of that declaration. Another exchange of notes took place in 1918, in which the Japanese set terms which China accepted. In the interval, France and England had made treaties with Japan in which they pledged themselves to support the claims of Japan at the peace conference concerning the German concessions in China and the German islands in the North Pacific, and Japan agreed for its part to support the British claims in the South Pacific.

*H., *PPC*, V, 138ff.

Mr. Lloyd George. You must remember that, at that time, the submarine campaign had just been intensified. All our torpedo boats and destroyers were in the Atlantic. We had to ask Japan urgently to send us destroyers, and Japan made as advantageous a bargain as she could. At that time, we were in a very difficult situation.

President Wilson. You see how embarrassing the situation is. Mr. Lloyd George has just explained to you the circumstances in which England signed this treaty with Japan; M. Clemenceau says that his commitment towards Japan is even more explicit.

When you explained your situation at the Quai d'Orsay,*[1] you stressed the argument that your declaration of war against Germany had had the effect of annulling your treaty with that country. That is true; but it did not annul your treaty with Japan, and in particular the convention you signed after having declared war.

My proposal consists of putting the disputed territories and rights in the hands of the five great powers, acting as trustees. They would try to obtain in a friendly way a modification of the treaties. At the same time, they would conclude amongst themselves an agreement of general renunciation of spheres of influence in China, of rights of extraterritoriality, of all the privileges granted up to now to foreign powers on Chinese soil, so as to place China on an equal footing with the other powers.

Japan opposes the first part of that proposal. We are embarrassed on account of the treaties which bind France and England.

When I asked the Japanese what the exact meaning was of the terms placed on the retrocession of Kiaochow, they told me it was a matter of three mines, which are in the hands of the Tsingtao railroad company.

These three mines, as well as the railroad itself, would be exploited jointly by China and Japan. The Japanese declare themselves prepared to end the civil administration in the region served by the railroad, to leave troops only at the terminal stations. These troops themselves would be withdrawn if a general renunciation of the privileges of foreigners in China was consented to by all the powers.

The Japanese add that their sole desire is to enter into cooperation with China. You will tell us what can be done with their proposal.

---

*Before the Council of Ten.

[1] On January 28, 1919. Koo's remarks to the Council of Ten are printed in *PWW*, Vol. 54, pp. 315-18.

M. Wellington Koo. The treaties which we signed with Japan were the consequence of a sort of ultimatum.

Mr. Lloyd George. What was that ultimatum?

M. Wellington Koo. In January 1915, after the capture of Tsingtao, the port was opened to trade. The Chinese government asked for the withdrawal of Japanese troops, which were occupying the interior up to a distance of 200 to 250 miles from the sea. Japan made a pretext of this request as an unfriendly act to present China with a demand in twenty-one points. The first of these demands stipulated that Japan would thereafter provide political advisers to the Chinese government.

We resisted as best we could. On May 7, 1915, Japan, weary of the slowness of the conversation, delivered a veritable ultimatum demanding a reply within twenty-four hours, in the absence of which she reserved the right to take such measures as she might deem appropriate. This ultimatum threw China into a state of consternation. Europe was absorbed by the war and could do nothing.

Mr. Lloyd George. Didn't you appeal to the United States?

President Wilson. Yes; we protested against Japan's attempt to violate the sovereignty of China. The Japanese had tried to keep the thing secret. But it came to our knowledge.

M. Wellington Koo. Secrecy had been imposed upon us under dire threats. Even when America was informed, she knew only eleven out of the twenty-one demands made.

The treaty we signed was the forced consequence of the ultimatum; consequently, it is very different from a treaty freely consented to. Japanese troops remained in Shantung Province; their presence there caused incidents and disorders. Complaints arose without end, and China asked several times for the withdrawal of these troops. Japan ignored these requests. On the contrary, she established a civil Japanese administration along the railroad, for a distance of 250 miles, with Japanese courts and a Japanese police force enforcing the observance of Japanese laws and regulations.

A dangerous agitation exists in Shantung Province. The Chinese government fears that it will only end in violence. It would gladly welcome a friendly solution.

Mr. Lloyd George. Did the Germans have police along the railroad?

M. Wellington Koo. No; the line was protected by Chinese troops.

Mr. Lloyd George. So Japan, by your treaty, obtains more than Germany herself had.

If you had to choose between the execution of your treaty with

Japan and the transfer, pure and simple, of the rights and privileges of Germany to Japan, which would you prefer?

M. Wellington Koo. Japan is so close to us and so strongly established in Manchuria, where she has troops and holds the Peking railway, that the presence of the Japanese in Shantung would create a much more serious situation for us than the one which the presence of the Germans created. Peking would be between the two jaws of a vise.

Mr. Lloyd George. But if it was a matter—and it is thus that the question stands for Great Britain and for France—of choosing between the transfer of the rights of the Germans to Japan and the execution of the Sino-Japanese treaty, which would you choose?

M. Wellington Koo. If we had signed the treaty of our free will, there could be an alternative here.

Mr. Lloyd George. I repeat the question. We ourselves are not bound by the Sino-Japanese treaty. Would you like to consult your colleague about that?

M. Wellington Koo. I just consulted him. In the Sino-Japanese treaty, the restitution made by Japan is purely nominal. If one compares the two treaties, I think that, altogether, the one with the Germans was more limited. I must insist on the serious situation which would be created even in case Japan only received rights equivalent to Germany's.

We are asking only for what is necessary to maintain peace in the Far East. The painful experience of the last three years in Shantung Province has sufficiently enlightened us. I would like to make you understand the necessities of the situation.

President Wilson. This morning I tried to speak as if I represented Chinese interests myself. I insisted upon the capital importance of the settlement of this question for the peace of the Far East and the world. It is essential for all of us that China be treated on a footing of equality, with the door open to the commerce of all nations, in the interest of other countries and in her own interest.

Today, we find ourselves in a very delicate situation. The United States protested in due course against the twenty-one demands Japan wanted to impose on you.

Mr. Lloyd George. I remember that Sir Edward Grey also did so.

President Wilson. We are also trying today to extricate ourselves as best we can from a questionable situation. The United States alone is not bound by any prior commitment. Since this war began by the protest of the western nations against the violation of a treaty, we must, above all, respect treaties, although I deplore the circumstances in which you were led to sign your treaty with Japan in 1915.

Mr. Lloyd George. The situation was different in September 1918, when the second Sino-Japanese treaty was signed; for, at that time, victory was on our side.

M. Wellington Koo. The treaty of 1918 only rounds out the one of 1915.

—President Wilson reads the convention of 1918.

Mr. Lloyd George. Our treaty with the Japanese only provides for the transfer of the German rights to Japan. I would like the two arrangements to be studied and compared by the experts, who could tell us which of the two is more favorable to China. We would also give the Chinese delegates time to make that study. For us, this is the only alternative, since we are bound to Japan by our signature.

If the transfer, pure and simple, of the rights and privileges of Germany to Japan is the solution least unfavorable to China, that is all we are bound to grant to Japan. We are not compelled to assure her the benefit of a treaty signed behind our backs and under threat of an ultimatum.

President Wilson. I recall what the character of that ultimatum was. In the twenty-one demands, Japan demanded the right to provide the Chinese government with political advisers, to participate in the policing of all the large cities; she asked for a monopoly—for half—of the sale of arms and munitions, a preponderant role in the exploitation of the mines of all central China. The Chinese had to accept part of these terms.

Mr. Lloyd George. Are they still in effect?

M. Wellington Koo. Yes; that is why we are asking the conference to support us.

President Wilson. Japan, along with China and ourselves, will be one of the members of the League of Nations. All the members of the League mutually guarantee their territorial integrity and national independence. In this way, China will have a protection she never before possessed, and we, for our part, will have a right to intervene in the Far East which did not belong to us heretofore. When we protested in 1915, Japan, in conformity with international law, could say to us: "This does not concern you." But the act which establishes the League of Nations says that everything that endangers the peace of the world is the business of all the participant powers, and that the intervention of any one of them cannot be considered an unfriendly act. This system will make its effects felt in the Far East.

I am ready to recommend very warmly the proposal of a general renunciation of the special rights of the foreign powers in

China. I recall that Japan declares herself ready to accept that proposal. The consequence would be the disappearance of Japanese troops, Japanese courts, etc., and we would in future have a means of action. It is a hope for the future, if we can do no better for the present.

The present difficulty is that, whatever the origin of the Sino-Japanese treaty, whatever the reservations we could make about an agreement obtained by threat, the same doubt does not exist concerning the Franco-Japanese and Anglo-Japanese treaties. Even if your treaty was annulled, these would stand. Now, they allow Japan to claim what Germany formerly possessed. That is what leads us to ask you if you prefer the execution of your treaty or that of the Anglo-Japanese and Franco-Japanese treaties?

Mr. Lloyd George. I would like to have this question studied by three experts, French, English, and American.

—*This proposal is adopted.*[2]

M. Wellington Koo. I have two things to say. In the first place, I insist on the fact that China stands at the crossroads. A great part of the nation wishes to cooperate with the western powers, and that is equally the desire of the present government. But if we fail to obtain justice at the conference, that can throw us into the arms of Japan. There is a party in China which favors Asia for the Asians. If we fail in our mission, I fear that the effect of the reaction that will follow might be very strong.

In the second place, the obligations taken by France and England under the pressure of certain circumstances, at a critical moment—are they still applicable today? Circumstances have been changed by the fact that China became your ally. On the other hand, the principles on which the peace must be founded are incompatible with Japanese ambitions.

While thanking you, I cannot insist too strongly on the serious consequences that can result. It is a question of whether we can guarantee a peace of half a century to the Far East, or if a situation will be created which can lead to war within ten years.

President Wilson. These are serious considerations. But the respect for treaties by the powers which signed them is not a denial of justice. The principles we support here cannot have the effect of destroying valid treaties; they cannot be invoked to annul obligations accepted earlier. I do not admit that respect for treaties could be considered an injustice.

[2] About this committee and its report, see XLVIII, n. 4.

In the past, China has been treated unjustly; that is what we wish to redress in the future. But the sole solution to the present difficulties is the entry of China into the League of Nations. It is not the individual protest of states, it is the opinion of the world which must operate. The world is full of sympathy for the great Chinese people and knows that its own future depends on what these 400 million men will become and what they will think. But it is necessary not to confuse justice and the repudiation of treaties, even unfortunate ones.

M. Wellington Koo. The commitment you took was connected only to the circumstances of the war.

Mr. Lloyd George. We cannot embark upon that course. These are commitments we took solemnly, when it was a matter of saving the world, including China, from German domination. Nothing would have prevented Germany, if she had conquered us, from then taking possession of China. Remember that the expression "the mailed fist" was first used with regard to China.

At a grave moment, when the life of our peoples was in danger, we had to appeal to Japan. Not only did we have the cooperation of the Japanese fleet in a critical period, but without Japan we would not have taken Kiaochow. It is impossible for us to say to the Japanese: "We were happy to find you in time of war; but now, good-by."

Our sympathy for China is undeniable. We understand the difficulties of the situation in Shantung Province; we are ready to do for you all that the treaties allow us to do, we are ready to welcome China into the League of Nations and to give her all the protection that that League can offer. I am convinced that China has before her a future at least equal to her glorious past. But we cannot consider treaties as scraps of paper which can be torn up when one no longer needs them.

President Wilson. I admit that those were unfortunate agreements. But they were signed to save the world and China from German domination.

M. Wellington Koo. Their justification is only in the European situation.

Mr. Lloyd George. If Germany had been victorious here, she would have been mistress of the world. America? America was not ready to resist her; the world was at her feet.

President Wilson. Germany did not merely want everything included in the Hamburg-Baghdad plan.[3] She knew about and in-

---

[3] Actually, the plan for a German-controlled railroad from Berlin to Baghdad,

tended to exploit the famous riches of the Far East. A long time ago, the Kaiser set himself up as the enemy of your race, and we all remember his famous speech on the Yellow Peril. He would not have tried to govern France and England; it would have been enough to vanquish them to seize all that pleased him afterwards. One of the results of this war was to save the Far East in particular.

All we can advise is that you study the alternatives we are offering you.

—The Chinese delegates withdraw.

President Wilson. I realize the apparent contradiction between my stand on this question and my position on the Italian question. But the difference is that Austria-Hungary has disappeared. If she still existed, I would not oppose the execution of the Treaty of London. And the Yugoslavs and Italy are admitted, like us, to the League of Nations.

Concerning Japan, we must do what is required to make her join the League of Nations. If she stood aside, she would do everything she wanted to do in the Far East. You heard them this morning say clearly that they won't sign the treaty if the obligations contracted towards them are not honored.

Mr. Lloyd George. The way they terrorized the Chinese to force them to sign their treaty is one of the most unscrupulous acts in all history, especially against a gentle and defenseless people.

President Wilson. Yes, but I am above all concerned not to dig a chasm between the East and the West.

Mr. Lloyd George. That is the strongest argument, and the Chinese don't sufficiently see that, without us, they would be at the mercy of the Germans today.

THE QUESTION OF THE ITALIAN BOUNDARIES*

M. Clemenceau. Are we returning to the question of Zara and Spalato?

Mr. Lloyd George. I would like another discussion with the Italians, to see whether they would accept my plan, with free cities

*Does not appear in H.

---

which was to be the spearhead of German economic and political penetration of the Balkans and the Middle East. The standard work on this subject is Edward Mead Earle, *Turkey, the Great Powers, and the Bagdad Railway: A Study in Imperialism* (New York, 1923).

on the Dalmatian coast and a plebiscite at the end of fifteen years.

M. Clemenceau. You wouldn't place these cities under their administration?

Mr. Lloyd George. No, but under that of the League of Nations. President Wilson tells us that the Yugoslavs have a majority in these cities.

President Wilson. What I said was that the Italian majority was doubtful, although, certainly, the dominant element at least by culture is the Italian element.

Does your plan include the cession of the islands?

Mr. Lloyd George. Yes; Italy would have the outer line of islands; Fiume would be a free city.

M. Clemenceau. What would its customs arrangement be?

Mr. Lloyd George. We would establish it as a free port for all commerce in transit. From the point of view of strategic protection, Italy would receive satisfaction by the possession of the islands. Zara and Sebenico would be free cities like Fiume.

President Wilson. The island of Cherso commands Fiume's roadstead.

Mr. Lloyd George. That is why it constitutes a protection for the Italians.

President Wilson. With all due respect to the Italians, that's a bad joke.

M. Clemenceau. We don't owe them Fiume.

Mr. Lloyd George. Fiume would be a free port for the use of Hungary and the other countries of the hinterland.

President Wilson. I fear a compromise like this one; I fear the consequences. I dread dangerous contacts; I sense the probability of intrigues and conflicts, with the question of Montenegro[4] and with the presence of two religious and three different ethnic groups in these territories.

Mr. Lloyd George. Serbs, Croats, and Slovenes have the same language and the same literature.

M. Clemenceau. It is true that the island of Cherso bars the route of Fiume.

Mr. Lloyd George. Yes, but if the Italians adhere to the Treaty of London, we have promised them those islands. Thus, as far as we are concerned, we have nothing more to say.

[4] The Serbs had invaded and seized Montenegro, expelled its King, Nicholas I, and incorporated the little kingdom into the new Yugoslav state in December 1918. Nicholas was in Paris during the peace conference and addressed several piteous appeals to Wilson for support. The Big Four eventually acquiesced in the Yugoslav takeover.

President Wilson. Sir Maurice Hankey transmitted a proposal to them yesterday. Here is another one. If this is also transmitted to the Italians, they will think it enough to hold fast and that we will end up saying they are right. As for myself, I am not inclined to make new proposals to them.

Sir Maurice Hankey. I must point out that the Italians practically never make a proposal. They wait for one to be made to them.

Mr. Lloyd George. What we really have to decide is whether we want to have M. Orlando or M. Giolitti here within a week.

President Wilson. Giolitti wouldn't last.

Mr. Lloyd George. Who knows? In any case, at the most crucial moment, Giolitti would intrigue with the Germans.

M. Clemenceau. We mustn't forget that the Italian Chamber is basically Giolittian.

Mr. Lloyd George. Do you want to let me make a new attempt?

President Wilson. Let me publish my document; that can only clear the air.

Mr. Lloyd George. Yes, but as a storm would. Our poor Europe is like a land sown with mines; if you step on them, everything blows up. I think my plan is not impractical, because the Yugoslavs are much less interested in the islands than in the mainland.

M. Clemenceau. We'll let you act.

Mr. Lloyd George. It would be a catastrophe if the European powers and the United States separated over this unfortunate affair. To tell the truth, I fear much more the problem which could be raised by the presence of a German element in the Italian Tyrol.

President Wilson. There is a fatal antagonism between the Italians and the Slavs. If the Slavs have the feeling of injustice, that will make the abyss unbridgeable and open the road to Russian influence and the formation of a Slavic bloc hostile to western Europe.

Mr. Lloyd George. I don't think this feeling would be provoked by the cession of a few islands.

President Wilson. Why not make the cities we have just mentioned free cities without a plebiscite? I would fear a systematic immigration. We can, it is true, stipulate that the right to vote will be confined to the present inhabitants of those cities.

Mr. Lloyd George. We can leave the decision to the League of Nations.

M. Clemenceau. Who will make the proposal to the Italians?

Mr. Lloyd George. I would very much like to try it. Undoubtedly they will say that we have forced their hand.

M. Clemenceau. That doesn't worry me.

Mr. Lloyd George. Nor me, if we keep peace amongst ourselves.

President Wilson. You will surely admit that it was I who caused America to enter the war, who educated and gradually shaped American public opinion. I did it whilst standing on the principles you know. Baron Sonnino led the Italian people into war to conquer territories. I did it by invoking a principle of justice; I believe my claim takes precedence over his.

Mr. Lloyd George. In reality, the Italian claim is based primarily on a question of security; it doesn't aim at the conquest of territories or of great cities, for we are dealing with hardly more than rocks.

President Wilson. What M. Sonnino says to the Italian people is this: "We cannot abandon our brothers." He doesn't speak to them of strategy; that argument is for our use. M. Orlando sent me two beautiful volumes showing that Dalmatia, on account of its artistic traditions, should be Italian. it is by these methods that they create popular feeling.

Mr. Lloyd George. I fear much more the difficulties in the Tyrol than those over these little islands.

XLV

Conversation between President Wilson and MM. Clemenceau and Lloyd George*

APRIL 23, 1919, 11 A.M.

Mr. Lloyd George. If Italy is not represented when we open the negotiations with Germany, it will be impossible to inscribe her on the list of powers which have the right to reparation.

President Wilson. I believe we should treat Italy in the fairest and even the most liberal way when we deal with Austria.

Mr. Lloyd George. Undoubtedly. I must say that I persist in thinking it imprudent to have the Germans of the Valley of the Adige included within Italy's boundaries, and I shall perhaps have to make some observations on this point. But in any case, I don't see how we could ask the Germans for reparation for Italy if she isn't present.

President Wilson. I received a memorandum from a Yugoslav who

---

*H., PPC, V, 149ff.

has a teaching position in the United States, M. Pupin.[1] Its conclusion is that, if the Yugoslavs have the impression that they have not been treated justly, they will throw themselves on the side of the Slavic world against the western world. What we have to fear is a coalition of which Russia would be the spiritual leader.

Mr. Lloyd George. There is indeed a danger from that side.

President Wilson. Isn't it better to risk exciting the temporary discontent of Italy than the permanent hostility of all the Slavs?

President Wilson. I have to acquaint you with a message from Mr. Hoover.[2] His representatives, who are everywhere in Germany, say that it is impossible to do anything in that country before the people have absolutely essential foodstuffs and jobs. Scarcity, in the most general sense of the word, is the soil on which Bolshevism grows. No one in Germany knows what will happen to him the next day, and that is the main reason for the instability from which we ourselves have so much to fear. The conclusion of Mr. Hoover and his representatives is that it is imperative to lift the blockade.

Mr. Lloyd George. I have to remind you that the same malaise and paralysis of business exists in countries which are not under the blockade: France suffers from it, as well as Belgium and England herself.

M. Clemenceau. The Germans are coming next week to receive our proposals for peace. It would be a sign of weakness, and they would interpret it as such, to lift the blockade before their arrival.

I must inform you about a telegram intercepted by us that the German government addressed to its representatives at Spa; there is talk of sending German journalists to Versailles at the same time as the plenipotentiaries. I believe we must oppose that.

Mr. Lloyd George. You can't act on the basis of an intercepted document.

M. Clemenceau. No; I merely suggest, if these journalists present themselves and can account for themselves in no other capacity, to send them back to Germany. Besides, my opinion is that Brockdorff-Rantzau is only coming to Versailles to cause a break.

Mr. Lloyd George. Perhaps; but it isn't the same with Melchior.

President Wilson. The most critical question for them is the economic question. If they feel the treaty chains them from the economic point of view, they will refuse to sign. All we ought to

---

[1] His memorandum is printed in *PWW*, Vol. 57, pp. 499-502.
[2] H. C. Hoover to WW, April 21, 1919, printed in *ibid.*, pp. 566-67.

demand is that Germany not create a regime unfriendly to one of the signatories of the peace treaty.

M. Clemenceau. I have to acquaint you with another rather annoying affair. Incidents have occurred concerning the transit of Polish trains across Germany: cars have been pillaged, notably in the station at Glogau.

Mr. Lloyd George (*after reading the telegram*). It isn't very surprising that a famished population throws itself on food cars.

M. Clemenceau. What should we do?

Mr. Lloyd George. Give instructions to Marshal Foch to call seriously the attention of the Germans to these incidents.

President Wilson. I am now receiving complaints from all sorts of people who think they have a claim to present or a grievance to make known. I received a communication of this kind from the Minister of Foreign Affairs of Persia.[3] He recalled that Persia asked to participate in the conference; that, during the war, at the request of the Allied Powers, she maintained a benevolent neutrality; that that neutrality was violated by the enemy; and that Persia suffered the horrors of war. Having received no reply to the first message written to this effect, the Minister of Foreign Affairs sends me a note[4] about the claims that Persia would like to present to the peace conference. He insists on the right of Persia to national independence, to the restitution of territories which were occupied, and to reparation for damages. If the Persians cannot be admitted to the peace conference, they ask at least to be heard.

Mr. Lloyd George. We must wait to settle this question until we come to the discussion of the peace treaty with Turkey; it has no place in our present debates.

Sir Maurice Hankey. May I remind you that Mr. Balfour expressed an opinion against hearing the representatives of Persia.

President Wilson. In any case, we must answer them.

Mr. Lloyd George. I will see Mr. Balfour on this subject. He must have good reasons, for he is a man of very moderate judgment. Allow me to consult him on this question.

M. Clemenceau. What are we going to do about the Italians? We must reply to them. You know what M. Barzilai proposes. The Italians continue to insist on the possession of Fiume.

Mr. Lloyd George. Mr. Balfour has drafted a rather satisfactory doc-

---

[3] Mochaverol-el-Memalek to WW, March 19, 1919, Wilson Papers, Library of Congress.

[4] Mochaverol-el-Memalek to WW, April 8, 1919, enclosing two pamphlets setting forth the claims of Persia. *Ibid.*

ument setting forth the point of view of the signatory powers.[5] He declares himself in the clearest possible way against the annexation of Fiume by Italy.

President Wilson. I will also have to publish my statement.

PUBLICATION OF THE PRELIMINARIES

M. Clemenceau. The question of the publication of the preliminaries of peace has already been raised. In any case, we will be compelled to publish them as soon as they are in the hands of the Germans; otherwise, they would come back to us via the German press.

Mr. Lloyd George. The Germans will only publish them if they want everything to fail, and, if we publish them prematurely, we shall have embarrassing and dangerous discussions in the press.

M. Clemenceau. I believe, however, that, when our peace terms are known, they won't make a bad impression on the public; they can defend themselves.

Mr. Lloyd George. There are newspapers which have taken their stand and which don't care whether those terms are truly good or bad.

M. Clemenceau. I must confess that the opinion of those newspapers doesn't matter to me. What we can't risk is having our own compatriots read the text of the treaty in the *Berliner Tageblatt*.

Mr. Lloyd George. If Bismarck had published the text of the treaty[6] before it was signed, would the negotiations have succeeded?

M. Clemenceau. First, the Germans had made no mystery of their intentions, and, next, I must tell you that, although I voted against the treaty of 1871, there was absolutely nothing else to do.

President Wilson. It will be impossible to read the complete text of the preliminaries to the plenipotentiaries of the Allied and Associated Powers.

THE ITALIAN QUESTION

—Mr. Lloyd George reads Mr. Balfour's draft of a letter to the Italian government.

President Wilson. Why give arguments against the departure of the

---

[5] It is printed as an appendix to the notes of this meeting. Balfour's draft was delivered as a letter from Clemenceau and Lloyd George to Orlando on April 24.

[6] That is, the Treaty of Frankfurt.

Italians before they have firmly declared their intention to leave?

Mr. Lloyd George. They indicated that their departure was imminent.

President Wilson. They withdrew from these discussions, but they didn't say they were withdrawing from the conference. This letter assumes that their decision is taken. Now, if we want to turn them away from a fatal decision, it is better not to treat the question as if it were settled.

Mr. Lloyd George. Moreover, Mr. Balfour's letter gives no answer to the last message I received from M. Orlando.[7] I also fear that Mr. Balfour did not sufficiently stress our resolve to honor the commitments we have taken under the Treaty of London. It is, rather, an appeal to Italy herself to free us from one part of these commitments.

President Wilson. Undoubtedly; but there is nothing more honorable than such an effort.

Mr. Lloyd George. What we must avoid is to have the Italians say that we went back on our word to them by accepting the letter of the treaty but putting pressure on them to change its clauses.

President Wilson. The responsibility for the situation rests on me.

Mr. Lloyd George. Not entirely, because, as regards Fiume, we are with you; or rather, it is mainly from us that the objection comes, and I am convinced that, if there is a break, it will be over Fiume.

President Wilson. What will you do if they say to you: "We are demanding the execution, pure and simple, of the Treaty of London," and if they compel you thus to separate yourselves from the United States?

M. Clemenceau. It mustn't come to that. We'll tell them: "Keep those territories if you can."

Mr. Lloyd George. We can do it. But they will stay in Fiume, and that is against the treaty. As for everything aside from Fiume, it is impossible for us to say that we had qualms of conscience after

---

[7] It read as follows: "ITALIAN PROPOSALS I. The line of the Alps (Brenner) to the sea, East of Volosca. II. Fiume under the sovereignty of Italy. Italy will establish in the port of Fiume free zones in accordance with the terms of articles 8, 9 and 10 of the Peace clauses drawn up by the Commission of Ports, Waterways, and Railways and will extend to Fiume those facilitations which may be arranged for later on in a general convention with reference to free ports. III. Italy will have all the islands mentioned in the Pact of London except Pago. IV. Zara and Sebenico will be placed under the League of Nations with Italy as Mandatory Power." Printed in *PWW*, Vol. 58, p. 14. About the negotiations between Lloyd George, Orlando, and others at this time, see Albrecht-Carrié, *Italy at the Paris Peace Conference*, pp. 131-41.

the victory, whereas we didn't have any when Italy's cooperation was necessary for us.

On Fiume, I am prepared to follow you completely and to cut off imports of coal into Italy if necessary.

President Wilson. When we make our treaty with Austria, it will be necessary to fix the boundaries carefully. Then it will be a question of whether you stay with Italy or whether you side with the United States. I cannot consent to give Italy what would be the cause of a dangerous separation between the Slavic world and western Europe. We face an alternative: either we draw the southern Slavs towards western Europe and the League of Nations, or we push them towards Russia and Bolshevism.

The Italians must realize that there is no possible comparison between the so-called necessities of the defense of Italy and the general peace of Europe. The Slavs have behind them the immense reservoir of the populations of Asia, whose position and destiny will be the great problem of the future. There are 800 million men there, against whom our 200 million would seem a small thing. Must we alienate half of Europe from ourselves for a strategic boundary which, in the opinion of the American experts, is of no importance?

Mr. Lloyd George. What matters is not one boundary or another, but the sanctity of treaties. Say, if you wish, that the Treaty of London should never have been signed. It was done by Mr. Asquith and M. Briand. Sir Edward Grey did not really like it, and the English cabinet did not like it when it found out about it. But, after all, our signature is at the bottom of that treaty.

President Wilson. I wouldn't at all be scandalized if I saw France and England repudiate a treaty concluded in a world situation completely changed today.

M. Clemenceau. I am not inclined to do anything like that. But what I ask myself is whether the Italians, by withdrawing from the conference, are not withdrawing from the treaty.

Mr. Lloyd George. We can tell them: "We decided with you that Fiume should go to the Croats; if you don't accept that, the treaty no longer exists, and if you keep Fiume, you are violating the treaty."

President Wilson. And what will you do if they answer you: "We abandon Fiume"?

Mr. Lloyd George. In that case, we are caught; we will have to carry out the treaty.

President Wilson. And you will be compelled to break with us.

APRIL 23, 1919

M. Clemenceau. I tell you they'll never give up Fiume.

President Wilson. The Treaty of London is a deal I never would have approved of, and with which I cannot associate myself.

Mr. Lloyd George. You can be satisfied with refusing your signature.

M. Clemenceau. My point of view is that, if the Italians withdraw from the conference, they are breaking the treaty.

Mr. Lloyd George. They can be told that to withdraw from the conference is to break the alliance, for they adhered to the London Treaty of 1914,[8] which binds us for the war and the conclusion of peace.

M. Clemenceau. I think we must agree about the procedure to follow when the Germans are here. I propose that all the objections they have to make about the terms of the treaty be presented in writing. That is the only way to manage. If we begin to make and listen to speeches, there'll be no end to it.

Mr. Lloyd George. What have we decided about the publication of the treaty?

M. Clemenceau. It is impossible not to publish it.

Mr. Lloyd George. Remember that the first impression is the one that counts. This document, whose length will be very considerable, must not be handed over to ordinary journalists who will take parts from it at random. Moreover, they won't find there the treaty of guarantee given to France by America and England.

M. Clemenceau. I said a short time ago that we were preparing a summary. We'll submit it to you.

Mr. Lloyd George. This summary must be very well done. I wonder whether there wouldn't have to be one for each country, because the concerns of the public are different in your country and in ours.

President Wilson. The important thing is indeed the wording of this summary.

M. Clemenceau. I'll submit it to you.

Mr. Lloyd George. We must also warn the journalists that we will give them this document at the time of the communication of the terms of peace to the German delegates, and that any infraction would entail serious consequences.

---

[8] A treaty signed by the then members of the Entente Allies in London on September 5, 1914, usually known as the Pact of London, by which each signatory agreed not to make a separate peace. Italy adhered to this treaty in a supplement to the Treaty of London of April 26, 1915.

{ APPENDIX }⁹

PARIS. 23.4.19.

FIUME AND THE PEACE SETTLEMENT.

We learn with a regret which it is difficult to measure that, at the very moment when Peace seems almost attained, Italy threatens to sever herself from the company of the Allied Nations, through whose common efforts victory has been achieved. We do not presume to offer any opinion as to the effects which so momentous a step would have upon the future of Italy herself. Of these it is for the Italian people and its leaders to judge, and for them alone. But we, who have been Italy's Allies through four anxious years, and would gladly be her Allies still, are bound to express our fears as to the disastrous effects it will surely have upon us, and upon the policy for which we have striven.

When in 1915 Italy threw in her lot with France, Russia and the British Empire in their struggle against the Central powers, Turkey and Bulgaria, she did so on conditions. She required her Allies to promise that in case of victory they would help her to obtain in Europe the frontier of the Alps, the great ports of Trieste and Pola, and a large portion of the Dalmatian coast with many of its adjacent islands. Such accessions of territory would enormously strengthen Italy's power of defence, both on land and sea, against her hereditary enemy, and would incidentally result in the transfer of over 200,000 German-speaking Tyrolese and over 750,000 Southern Slavs from Austrian to Italian rule. Under this arrangement Fiume was retained by Great Britain, France and Italy herself for Croatia.

Such was the situation in April, 1915. In November, 1918, it had profoundly changed. Germany was beaten; the Dual Monarchy had ceased to exist: and side by side with this Military revolution, the ideals of the Western Powers had grown and strengthened. In 1915 the immediate needs of self-defence, the task of creating and equipping vast Armies, the contrivance of new methods for meeting new perils, strained to the utmost the energies of the Allies. But by 1918 we had reached the double conviction that if the repetition of such calamities was to be avoided, the Nations must organise themselves to maintain Peace, as Germany, Austria, Bulgaria and Turkey had organised themselves to make war; and that little could be expected, even

⁹ Printed in *PWW*, Vol. 58, pp. 86-90.

from the best contrived organisation, unless the boundaries of the States to be created by the Conference were framed, on the whole, in accordance with the wishes and lasting interests of the populations concerned.

This task of re-drawing European frontiers has fallen upon the Great Powers; and admittedly its difficulty is immense. Not always, nor indeed often, do race, religion, language, history, economic interests, geographical contiguity and convenience, the influence of national prejudice, and the needs of national defence, conspire to indicate without doubt of ambiguity the best frontier for any State:—be it new or old. And unless they do, some element in a perfect settlement must be neglected, compromise becomes inevitable, and there may often be honest doubts as to the form the compromise should take.

Now as regards most of the new frontier between Italy and what was once the Austrian Empire, we have nothing to say. We are bound by the Pact of London, and any demand for a change in that Pact which is adverse to Italy must come from Italy herself. But this same Pact gives Fiume to Croatia, and we would very earnestly and respectfully ask whether any valid reason exists for adding, in the teeth of the Treaty, this little city on the Croatian coast to the Kingdom of Italy? It is said indeed, and with truth, that its Italian population desire the change. But the population which clusters round the port is not predominantly Italian. It is true that the urban area wherein they dwell is not called Fiume; for it is divided by a narrow canal, as Paris is divided by the Seine, or London by the tidal estuary of the Thames, and locally the name, Fiume, is applied in strictness only to the streets on one side of it. But surely we are concerned with things, not names; and however you name it, the town which serves the port, and lives by it, is physically one town, not two; and taken as a whole is Slav, not Italian.

But if the argument drawn from the wishes of the present population does not really point to an Italian solution, what remains? Not the argument from history; for up to quite recent times the inhabitants of Fiume, in its narrowest meaning, were predominantly Slav. Not the arguments from contiguity; for the country population, up to the very gates of the city, are not merely predominantly Slav, but Slav without perceptible admixture. Not the economic argument; for the territories which obtain through Fiume their easiest access to the sea, whatever else they be, at least are not Italian. Most of them are Slav, and if it be said that

Fiume is also necessary to Hungarian and Transylvanian commerce, this is a valid argument for making it a free port, but surely not for putting it under Italian sovereignty.

There is one other line of argument on this subject about which we would ask leave to say a word. It is urged by some, and thought by many, that the task of the Great Powers is not merely to sit down and coldly re-arrange the pieces on the European board in strict, even pedantic, conformity with certain admirable but very abstract principles. They must consider these great matters in more human fashion. After all (so runs the argument), the problems to be dealt with arise out of a Great War. The conquerers in that War were not the aggressors: their sacrifices have been enormous; the burdens they have to bear seem well-nigh intolerable. Are they to get nothing out of victory, except the consciousness that State frontiers in Europe will be arranged in a better pattern after 1918 than they were before: and that nations who fought on the wrong side, or who did not fight at all, will have gained their freedom through other peoples' losses? Surely the victors, if they want it, are entitled to some more valid reward than theoretical map-makers, working in the void, may on abstract principles feel disposed to give them.

There is something in this way of thinking which at first sight appeals to us all; and where no interests are concerned but those of the criminal aggressors, it deserves respectful consideration. But in most cases of territorial redistribution it is at least as important to enquire what effects the transfer will have on the nations to whom territory is given, as upon those from whom it is taken: and when, as in the case of Jugo-Slavia, the nation from whom it is taken happens to be a friendly State, the difficulty of the problem is doubled.

We do not presume to speak with authority on the value of the strategical gains which Italy anticipates from the acquisition of the islands and coastline of Dalmatia. They seem to us to be small; though, small as they are, they must greatly exceed the economic advantages which will accrue to Italian trade from new opportunities, or to the Italian Treasury from new sources of revenue. We cannot believe that the owners of Trieste have anything to fear from Fiume as a commercial rival, or the owners of Pola from Fiume as a Naval base.

But if Italy has little to gain from the proposed acquisition, has she not much to lose? The War found her protected from an hereditary enemy of nearly twice her size by a frontier which previous Treaties had deliberately left insecure. Her Eastern seaboard was almost bare of harbours, while Austria-Hungary possessed on the opposite side of the Adriatic some of the finest harbours in the world. This was her condition in 1914. In 1919 her Northern and Eastern frontiers are as secure as mountains and rivers can make them. She is adding two great ports to her Adriatic possessions; and her hereditary oppressor has ceased to exist. To us it seems that, as a State thus situated has nothing to fear from its neighbours' enmity, so its only interest must be to gain their friendship. And though memories belonging to an evil past make friendship difficult between Italians and Slavs, yet the bitterest memories soften with time, unless fresh irritants are frequently applied; and among such irritants none are more powerful than the constant contemplation of a disputed and ill-drawn frontier.

It is for Italy, and not for the other signatories of the Pact of London, to say whether she will gain more in power, wealth and honour by strictly adhering to that part of the Pact of London which is in her favour, than by accepting modifications in it which would bring it into closer harmony with the principles which are governing the territorial decisions of the Allies in other parts of Europe. But so far as Fiume is concerned the position is different. Here, as we have already pointed out, the Pact of 1915 is against the Italian contention; and so also, it seems to us, are justice and policy. After the most prolonged and anxious reflexion, we cannot bring ourselves to believe that it is either in the interest of Jugo-Slavia, in the interests of Italy herself, or in the interests of future peace—which is the concern of all the world—that this port should be severed from the territories to which economically, geographically and ethnologically it naturally belongs.

Can it be that Italy on this account is prepared to separate herself from her Allies? The hope that sustained us through the perilous years of War was that victory, when it came, would bring with it, not merely the defeat of Germany, but the final discredit of the ideals in which Germany had placed her trust. On the other hand, Germany, even when she began to entertain misgivings about the issues of the campaign, felt sure that the union of her enemies would never survive their triumph. She based her schemes no longer on the conquest of Europe, but on its political, and perhaps also on its social disintegration. The Armistice might doubtless produce a brief cessation of hostilities: but it would bring no repose to a perturbed and over-wrought world. Militant nationalism would lead to a struggle between peoples;

militant internationalism to a struggle between classes. In either event, or in both, the Conference summoned to give us peace would leave us at war, and Germany alone would be the gainer.

This, or something like this, is the present calculation of a certain section of German politicians. Could anything more effectually contribute to its success than that Italy should quarrel with her Allies, and that the cause of quarrel should be the manner in which our common victory may best be used? We are calling into being a League of Nations; we are daily adding to the responsibilities which, under the approaching Treaty, it will be called upon to assume; yet before the scheme has had time to clothe itself in practical form, we hasten to destroy its credit. To the world we supply dramatic proof that the association of the Great Powers, which won the War, cannot survive Peace; and all the world will ask how, if this be so, the maintenance of Peace can safely be left in their hands.

For these reasons, if for no other, we beg our Italian colleagues to reconsider their policy. That it has been inspired by a high sense of Patriotism we do not doubt. But we cannot believe either that it is in Italy's true interests, or that it is worthy of the great part which Italy is called upon to play in the Councils of the Nations.

G. Clemenceau.
D. Lloyd George.

XLVI

Conversation between President Wilson and MM. Clemenceau and Lloyd George*

APRIL 24, 1919, 11 A.M.

Mr. Lloyd George. I saw M. Orlando again this morning. I would like to prevent him from doing anything which could really separate our countries. If he goes to Rome, he will be met there by a surge of public opinion, and he won't be able to make any concessions, especially concerning Fiume. I told him that. I warned him that we wouldn't consent to cede Fiume to Italy and, if Italy kept Fiume, that would put an end to the Treaty of London. That made a great impression on him. He has prepared a sort of man-

*H., PPC, V, 202ff.

ifesto in reply to President Wilson's open letter.[1] I said to him: "If you speak about Fiume in that statement, that will close the door to negotiations." He promised me to change the text in such a way as to avoid this danger.

I urged M. Orlando very strongly not to leave. He told me that if he left, he would leave Baron Sonnino here. I replied that his very presence in Italy would be enough to provoke a disturbance extremely dangerous for the success of our discussions.

Do you see any problem if we make a statement to the press saying that the discussions are continuing and that we are seeking a way to find a satisfactory solution to the question?

President Wilson. The question is whether I can be a party to a compromise. I will ask you to observe that nothing in my manifesto separates me from you.

Mr. Lloyd George. You criticize the Treaty of London rather sharply, and you say it should never have been signed.

M. Clemenceau. I have nothing much to say against that.

President Wilson. My argument is that the circumstances which justified the treaty have completely changed since then.

M. Clemenceau. Unfortunately, it is impossible for me to take this point of view.

Mr. Lloyd George. That would mean that Italy has succeeded so well that she must not profit from her victory.

President Wilson. That is not what I meant. But I showed that the annexation of Dalmatia no longer makes sense after the fall of Austria, which can hereafter no longer threaten Italy.

Mr. Lloyd George. It is impossible for us to discuss the Treaty of London, which we signed. But I will gladly set all dignity aside if I can arrive at an acceptable arrangement. Think about what the Germans can make out of the departure of the Italians when they arrive here in a few days.

M. Clemenceau. I don't attach a very great importance to that.

---

[1] In his manifesto, or reply, of April 24, Orlando expressed surprise at the publication of Wilson's statement and argued that a direct appeal to the people "almost in opposition to their Governments" certainly had to be considered "an innovation in international intercourse." It was even more regrettable, he maintained, that this procedure, which heretofore had been used only against enemy governments, was now employed against a "loyal friend" and at the very moment when the Allied and Associated Powers were in the middle of serious negotiations with the Italian government. Orlando then addressed the specific issues raised by Wilson, repeated his position on the questions of Italy's boundaries, Fiume, and Dalmatia, and again insisted on the justice of the Italian claims. Orlando's reply is printed in Albrecht-Carrié, *Italy at the Paris Peace Conference*, pp. 501-504; see also the news report printed in PWW, Vol. 58, pp. 97-101.

Mr. Lloyd George. I disagree.

President Wilson. All I wanted to do was to inform the Italian people of my true position, in view of all that has been said by a venal press. But I surely believe it desirable to give the representatives of Italy time to reflect. I sincerely hope that M. Orlando can stay here at least a week and that some agreement may thereby become possible.

Mr. Lloyd George. I will ask you to treat him with respect and consideration. We have nothing to lose by giving him an opportunity to think again about the risks of the situation and how he can disentangle himself from it.

President Wilson. Yes, but he must understand your position and mine.

Mr. Lloyd George. I left him in no doubt about our position on Fiume.

M. Clemenceau. In that case, I would do best not to reply to the letter addressed to me by M. Orlando;[2] that would only make things worse.

Mr. Lloyd George. You can write him a personal letter; but you must try at the same time to treat him with discretion and to make some accommodation possible. Unfortunately, I fear that the harm already done prevents peace from being concluded.

M. Clemenceau. I expect the Germans to refuse. But that difficulty won't last longer than a few weeks.

Mr. Lloyd George. I am not sure of that. I fear this refusal very much.

President Wilson. If we omit from the treaty secondary details which, whilst without any real importance for us, are such as to alarm the Germans, that will make the signing easier.

Mr. Lloyd George. I again propose to send a communiqué to the press indicating that we made an effort to persuade M. Orlando not to leave before a new conversation.

M. Clemenceau. I see no objection to that.

President Wilson. As for myself, I was going to write to him to beg him to stay.

Mr. Lloyd George. For his part, he has consented to publish his statement in a form that won't close the door to an acceptable solution.

I was categorical on the question of Fiume.

---

[2] Orlando, on April 23, addressed a communication to Clemenceau, as President of the conference, stating that, as a result of the publication of Wilson's statement, the Italian delegation had decided to leave Paris in the afternoon of April 24. *New York Times*, April 24, 1919.

APRIL 24, 1919

—*Mr. Lloyd George's proposal is adopted**

Mr. Lloyd George. I come back to the question of the publication of the preliminaries.

M. Clemenceau. The Germans are announcing in the newspapers—this time no longer in a confidential telegram—that they are sending seven journalists to the peace conference. What should we do?

President Wilson. I detest the idea of seeing them here. But I hardly know what is advisable.

Mr. Lloyd George. If they are told they will be subject to the same rules as the plenipotentiaries and will have no communication with the outside world, their presence offers no great danger. They will be confined to sending telegrams to Berlin, as the plenipotentiaries themselves will be.

As for the publication of the terms of peace in our countries, I must say that there are people in Germany who want peace, others who don't want the treaty to be signed. The first are in favor of secret negotiations; the others are for publicity. One of our representatives in Germany, Mr. Gibson, tells me that, if the terms of the peace are published in advance, that will only strengthen the extreme nationalist movement in Germany. Moreover, that will make it impossible for us, vis-à-vis our public, to make concessions on secondary points, such as the form of bond issues, on which we could satisfy the Germans to some extent.

Couldn't we try to find out if the German government is inclined to publish the terms of the treaty once it knows them, and what the probable effect of that publication will be in Germany? In comparison to the danger I fear, facing the clamor of the newspapers is nothing. We can say firmly that it is contrary to the interest of the peace to publish the text of the preliminaries in advance.

President Wilson. I have always said that it was hardly desirable to publish it, but that it was inevitable. In these circumstances, the best we can do is to have a well-done summary, in order to avoid false interpretations. Without a communication from us, be assured the newspapers will publish more or less complete information.

Mr. Lloyd George. Ah! That's not the same thing! From the moment you publish an official document, all remaining doubts will disappear.

*After the session, the communiqué to the press was postponed at M. Orlando's request.

President Wilson. M. Clemenceau spoke of a summary; if it is written in sufficiently general terms, it could answer your objections.

M. Clemenceau. For my part, I believe publication is inevitable, and I am convinced that the Germans will publish the treaty as soon as they have it in their hands. The consequence would be that the French or English reader would read the document coming from Germany; it is a risk we cannot run.

Mr. Lloyd George. I am not sure they will publish it.

M. Clemenceau. Believe me, that is a great error.

Mr. Lloyd George. Then they don't want to have peace?

M. Clemenceau. No German government at the present time can truly make peace.

President Wilson. I have information from one of our representatives about the attitude of Brockdorff-Rantzau, with whom he had a conversation.[3] First, he said he doesn't see why he should bother to receive a document about which no discussion will be allowed. You see there is an impression on this subject which does not correspond to our true intentions.

He also says he can never sign a peace which would crush Germany; in particular, he insists on the impossibility of depriving his country of the coal mines of the Saar and Upper Silesia. When our representative asked him if it was possible for Germany to live without having peace, he didn't reply, but indicated that Germany might move towards Russia. It is rather remarkable that he made no protest about Alsace and Lorraine, and that he said little about indemnities.

Our representative's impression is that the solution which we worked out for Danzig will be accepted by Germany.

Rantzau's opinions seem to be rather widespread in Germany; it is possible that the German people will be consulted by referendum about the terms of the peace.

M. Clemenceau. In that case, I rest easy; they'll vote for peace.

President Wilson. My informant said to Brockdorff-Rantzau that the economic recovery of Germany is acknowledged by the powers to be a necessity in the interest of the world, but that refusal of the peace would have very grave consequences for Germany. He listened without saying a word.

My conclusion is that Brockdorff-Rantzau represents an extreme opposition to our views. He is prepared to accept all the consequences rather than yield. But there is a sizable public to

[3] A report by Ellis Loring Dresel, dated April 20, 1919, printed in *PWW*, Vol. 58, pp. 44-46.

the rear of him which will accept all our terms in order to have peace and to start earning its living again. That is the universal impression of our missions spread all over Germany. It is especially the state of mind of the countryside. There is some Bolshevism in the cities.

It seems to me important that German public opinion be informed of our intention to allow the German plenipotentiaries to have their say. Like M. Clemenceau, I think this discussion will have to take place in writing. Concerning publication, I share the opinion of both Mr. Lloyd George and M. Clemenceau. I would gladly be against publication, but I believe it is impossible to avoid it.

Mr. Lloyd George. We can stop publication in France and England, and, if the document can get to the United States only by mail, it will take at least eight or ten days to go and as many to return. M. Pichon has unfortunately announced, without warning us, that publication will take place on Monday.

M. Clemenceau. We can't do otherwise than publish a summary.

President Wilson. I recall that we agreed on the communication of a summary of the treaty to the delegates to the conference. That communication was to take place behind closed doors and in strict confidence. I don't remember any other decision. In any case, there is no question of publishing the entire text.

Mr. Lloyd George. We can prevent publication if we wish.

M. Clemenceau. We can't prevent it in Germany.

Mr. Lloyd George. No, but then we can throw the onus on the Germans; I don't want to allow them to say that we made peace impossible through a publication which we permitted. I would like you to hear Mr. Gibson on this subject.

President Wilson. The question is who will control the German delegation, Brockdorff-Rantzau or Melchior.

M. Clemenceau. Then we limit ourselves to the publication of a summary.

Mr. Lloyd George. The summary will be enough to create the danger I dread. The certainty that Germany will have to lose Silesia and Danzig will be enough to provoke a serious opposition. I don't want to act in such a way as to make it impossible for any German government to sign the peace treaty. Couldn't we try to find out what the German government itself thinks about the publication of the treaty? If they said themselves that publication would make conclusion of the peace impossible, we would be assuming a serious responsibility in deciding to publish it.

President Wilson. Can't the difficulty be avoided by publishing a summary written in very general terms? For example, it could be said that the borders of Germany had been drawn according to ethnographic lines, without any other particulars.

M. Clemenceau. We can try.

President Wilson. Everything depends upon the nature of the summary. It can be written now; for if it is only a matter of a general statement, we don't need to wait for the final drafting of all the articles.

M. Clemenceau. How long will a document of this kind run?

Mr. Lloyd George. As for myself, I see no drawback in publishing in full our agreement with France to guarantee her against the danger of an invasion. That publication will make a useful impression in Germany; it will show that we are sticking together.

President Wilson. General Pershing[4] tells me that Marshal Foch's orders prescribe preparations for a military advance.

Mr. Lloyd George. It is only the result of our recommendations; we must make plans in case the Germans should refuse to sign.

M. Clemenceau. What will we do with M. Orlando? I think preferable not to send a reply to the letter I received from him; but I will put my signature at the bottom of Mr. Balfour's letter.

President Wilson. Will M. Orlando make new proposals?

Mr. Lloyd George. He is to meet with his colleagues today, and they'll let us know what they have decided. I believe they will accept the suggestion to make Fiume a free city. When I spoke to him about it, he merely asked me what Fiume's diplomatic representation would be. He would have desired, naturally, that it be secured by Italy. I believe it is an easy problem to settle; the city of Fiume can have itself represented as it likes.

—President Wilson reads the text prepared by the commission on the administration of the Kiel Canal.[5] Two different proposals were presented for the settlement of conflicts. The Anglo-American-Italian-Japanese proposal provides for the establishment of a German organization which will study the differences in the first instance, with appeal to the League of Nations. The French proposal provides for the immediate establishment of an international commission.

President Wilson. What militates in favor of our proposal is that we must avoid multiplying these international commissions and

[4] He meant General Bliss. See *ibid.*, p. 57.
[5] That is, the report of the subcommission on the Kiel Canal of the Commission on the International Regime of Ports, Waterways, and Railways. It is printed in *ibid.*, pp. 65-67.

have recourse to them only when other instrumentalities have failed to give satisfaction.

M. Clemenceau. I must tell you that what concerns me most is the question of the fortifications of the Kiel Canal. I would like Admiral de Bon to be heard on this subject.

President Wilson. We have provided for free access to the Kiel Canal for the merchant ships and warships of every nation at peace with Germany; if the canal lacks fortifications, Germany at war with any power whatever might find herself unable to fulfill this commitment.

THE QUESTION OF THE SAAR

Mr. Lloyd George. I have in hand the report of Professor Haskins:[6] according to the observations made by the French delegates, the northern boundary of the Saar region, such as it has previously been provided for, doesn't coincide with the natural boundary of this district, which is rather well marked by hills and by a narrowing of the river. The difference between the two lines represents thirty-two square kilometers and 4,000 inhabitants who are, moreover, attached to the Saar region by their jobs. The American representative wants this question to be submitted to our judgment, and the experts propose first of all to go to the site next Sunday.

The British delegate agrees with Mr. Haskins, and he is of opinion to accept the French proposal.

President Wilson. The experts agree; but they prefer to go first to the site; I believe they should be encouraged to do so.

Concerning the Saar, there is a question that continues to trouble me. The production of the basin is only seventeen million tons; the production of which France was deprived in the North was twenty-one million tons. Now the coal from the Saar is consumed in the neighboring region; consequently, the losses suffered by France in another region cannot be compensated for in that way.

M. Loucheur insists strongly that Germany be compelled to sell the amount of coal needed by French industries at the market price. The difficulty is this: we have already taken several of her coal basins from Germany; we must avoid placing her industries in a situation which would not allow her to recover and pay us what she owes us.

[6] Haskins' and Headlam-Morley's report is printed in *ibid.*, p. 67.

M. Clemenceau. It is a question of figures.

President Wilson. M. Loucheur must be heard on this subject, and, at the same time, our experts must be summoned.

Mr. Lloyd George. I would also like you to hear Mr. Gibson, who is returning from Berlin.

—Count Aldrovandi is introduced and makes it known that the Italian ministers will come to a meeting in the afternoon to study the question of the Adriatic once again.

XLVII

Conversation between President Wilson, MM. Clemenceau, Lloyd George, and Orlando, and Baron Sonnino*

APRIL 24, 1919, 4 P.M.

Mr. Lloyd George. I will ask M. Orlando what he desires to tell us.

M. Orlando. I have studied the situation, and I must declare that it is very serious so far as we are concerned. I have already had two telephone conversations with Rome. I find myself in a very painful situation on a question which now takes precedence over the territorial question: I mean the effect produced by the publication of President Wilson's statement.

I also insist on saying that my esteem, admiration, and feelings of personal friendship for President Wilson, which I have always sought to show him in our conversations, assure me, before hearing him once again, that his intentions towards me could be nothing but friendly. But in politics, the impression produced on the public has an importance which often surpasses that of reality itself.

The publication of this document, which, in its form, is friendly and courteous, gives the public the impression that it is an appeal made to peoples in general. The consequence, even if that consequence was not desired, is to cast doubt upon my authority as the representative of the Italian people. Such is the impression produced in Rome, and that creates a very delicate situation for me. I find it necessary to return to the sources of my

*H., *PPC*, V, 210ff.

authority. If I have decided, after mature deliberation, to leave for Rome, it is not because of the territorial question; it is not that there was any idea of a rupture in my thought. But I must return to my people, to explain the situation to them and to establish the authority on which I can stand to act at the conference.

I repeat that, at this time, the territorial question is cast into the background. If you agreed to the terms which appeared acceptable to me yesterday, I would say to you that I am still compelled to return to Italy. An uncertainty about the plenitude of my power prevents me from knowing whether I have the right to accept or to refuse anything today.

President Wilson. I can only bow before M. Orlando's statement. The cordial sentiments he expresses towards me are reciprocated. I have nothing but consideration and respect for the motives which move him, and I hope nothing will alter this mutual feeling. It was never in my mind to appeal to the Italian people over his head; if I appeared to do that, I regret it. I gladly avail myself of this occasion to say right now what caused me to make the publication in question.

My position—you will render me this justice—has not changed. Now, during these months of discussion, I saw erroneous and tendentious interpretations spreading amongst the public. The French press and the Italian press, which, moreover, have their echo in the press of the United States, have often presented my position and that of the American government in a light so false that I felt compelled to indicate my true position and its justification; the latter rests upon the principles which have been the soul of all our common action. I believed it necessary to dispel a cloud of slander and misunderstanding, the responsibility for which I am very far from attributing to our colleague, M. Orlando. He will acknowledge with me that the state of mind of nations is affected by these mendacious representations.

I am reassured, and I am happy to hear M. Orlando express himself as he has about his trip to Rome; he is going there to seek instructions, not to break. It would be a serious and perhaps irreparable act if Italy withdrew from our negotiations with Germany, and I am glad to learn there is no question of that. I understand the reasons why M. Orlando wants to meet the Italian people face to face. I hope he will make his intention, which is not to break with us at a crucial moment, well understood to them.

M. Orlando. I thank President Wilson for his noble statement and for the good grace with which he has given his explanations to us. I said spontaneously that I would exclude any idea of an unfriendly intention towards our allies and associates. I thank the President for having understood the true reasons for my departure.

To speak with all frankness—and frankness is the only way to thank President Wilson for what he has just said—even if the prejudicial question of my authority had not arisen, it would probably be better for me to try to reestablish contact with the Italian people. I recall, some time ago, a conversation in which President Wilson himself invited me to go to Rome to explain the situation to our Parliament. Today, it is an absolute necessity. President Wilson's message, whose meaning he has just explained to us, makes this no longer merely a necessity recognized by us, but a public necessity obvious in everybody's eyes.

There have been differences amongst us. Experience has shown that no solution was in sight. I have the duty to warn the Italian people; perhaps I have delayed too long. I will explain to our Parliament the situation as it results from our conversations. I will tell it what we can do to agree with President Wilson, and the alternative which the execution of the Pact of London, in agreement with our allies, offers us.

I speak as a friend to friends. I am not trying to find out who is responsible for the present situation. But the fact is that Italy has made a national question out of the question of Fiume. Now, about that question, not only the United States, but also our allies oppose our claims. It is pointless to reopen the discussion. I must inform Italy; she will see if she can resign herself to this sacrifice. At least the situation will become clarified.

President Wilson. May I ask M. Orlando if he would like to call attention to the opinion of the United States on the Treaty of London? We think this treaty was not made in such a manner as to insure good future relations between Italy and her Slavic neighbors; we believe it to be dangerous for the peace of the world. So the question of the Treaty of London is one of those that I must reserve. Although declaring that I wish to lend myself to any reasonable solution, I have the duty to express clearly the reservation I just mentioned.

M. Orlando. I will make that statement to the Chamber. I will explain in all loyalty President Wilson's reasons; I will recall what he told me in our private conversations and the memorandum he sent me,[1] which I will read to the Parliament.

---

[1] That is, Wilson's memorandum of April 14, 1919, summarized in XXXIII, n. 2.

M. Clemenceau. I will also ask M. Orlando to hear my views on the question of Fiume once again. The Treaty of London committed us to Italy; but it also committed us to the Slavs, who, according to that treaty, should have Fiume. I can't go back on my word either to Italy or to the Yugoslavs.

Mr. Lloyd George. I would like to go a bit further. A great new event occurred: the entry into the war of the United States, free of commitments and free of the necessities which led us to take commitments. That justifies a change of the Treaty of London as regards Fiume, if it is absolutely necessary. As for myself, I feel free to undertake a change of this kind if Italy, for her part, consents to renounce certain provisions of the treaty concerning Dalmatia.

What we would propose would be, instead of giving Fiume to the Croats, to make it into a free city governed by its inhabitants, with a free port open to all neighboring populations. Within that limit, I consider myself free to consent to a change of the Treaty of London, if our allies—it goes without saying—accept it along with me.

I don't dispute the necessity M. Orlando feels to return to Rome now. I myself had to return to London—to face a political situation obviously less difficult than his. If this week was similar to so many others we have spent together, the departure of M. Orlando for a few days would be of no great importance. But we are expecting the Germans in Versailles next Tuesday. Germany is the only one of our enemies still standing. When will M. Orlando return?

M. Orlando. I can summon the Italian Parliament for the twenty-eighth.

Mr. Lloyd George. Whilst we are putting the final touches on the clauses of the treaty, where is Italy? Yesterday, in a financial discussion, questions were asked on which the Italian and English experts had reached common conclusions; but no representative of Italy was any longer there to support us. The economic clauses of the treaty are now going to be submitted for our approval; in England, that is one of the subjects of most concern to the majority of our public—much more than other problems which interest scarcely anyone but the newspapers and some politicians specializing in foreign affairs. It also has a vital importance for Italy. Take, for instance, the question of coal, without which Italy cannot live. We will hear M. Loucheur on this point; but will we have M. Crespi here? Are we qualified to ask for millions of tons for Italy if Italy is not represented? Does Italy want us to settle these questions over her head?

Excuse me if I speak to you in such a direct manner. After all, the economic and financial future of Italy is at stake. We are considering plans for international credit; will Italy be included or will she be excluded?

Will Italy make peace with Germany at the same time as we? Will she come later to make separate claims? We need to know.

M. Clemenceau. I have another argument to stress. If Italy is not there when the Germans arrive, they will conclude that our alliance is broken, and that will obviously reduce the chances of peace.

President Wilson. I hope this won't happen.

M. Orlando. I am taking note of M. Clemenceau's and Mr. Lloyd George's statements. This is not the time to discuss all this in detail. I will explain the situation to Parliament, and I will repeat to it what has been said to me. I acknowledge the seriousness of the questions of a practical nature raised by Mr. Lloyd George. But they must be classified under two distinct headings. First, what will happen in the interval between the present time and the arrival of the Germans?

About that, I will say that the general terms of the treaty are decided; and I, for my part, have accepted them. Some important questions obviously remain undecided; but I can say that I have confidence in my allies, who will support Italian interests with all the greater care if we are not present. The judge is sometimes more benevolent when the accused has no lawyer. Besides, I can consult my colleagues about this matter and seek a way to have us represented. M. Crespi will stay in Paris.

The second question, which is more serious, is that of our presence when the Germans are here. I read in the newspapers that Germany is asking for a new postponement of the meeting.

M. Clemenceau. I know nothing official about that. All they have made known is that they won't leave before the twenty-eighth; so they won't arrive before the end of the month.

M. Orlando. I hope our decision will be taken before May 1. So the question is one of those which can be reserved. I agree with you on the importance of not giving the Germans the impression that our alliance is not as firm as ever. But I believe the fundamental question I find myself faced with is of such great importance that, in order to resolve it, it is better to risk the difficulties which Mr. Lloyd George has just alluded to.

M. Clemenceau. I ask you a question point-blank: will Italy be represented when we meet with the Germans, or not?

M. Orlando. That depends on the decisions which will be taken in Italy between now and May 1.

President Wilson. But the Italian territorial questions don't, after all, affect the peace with Germany. There would be no contradiction if Italy participated in the German treaty, whilst making her reservations about the treaty that we are to draw up with Austria.

Mr. Lloyd George. I repeat that, if Italy is not present, we cannot present claims in Italy's name. If M. Orlando is not here on May 1, and if he doesn't have the consent of his Parliament, how could we speak in his name?

M. Clemenceau. We would be compelled, moreover, to change all the wording of the treaty, since it was made with Italy's participation.

Mr. Lloyd George. The first question the Germans will ask us is: "Whom do you represent?" We won't know what to reply, unless M. Orlando declares to us in writing that we can act in his name.

M. Orlando. I believe that, if Mr. Lloyd George's objection is considered by itself, he is correct. I agree with him; it is not possible to propose terms to the Germans in the name of a power which is not represented. Naturally, I will study the situation carefully, and our decisions will be taken in view of all the necessities of the circumstances. But I insist on repeating: if Italy is not represented, she has no right to anything.

As for the changes that our absence would entail in the text of the treaty, I don't think they are considerable; for the only questions which concern Italy in the treaty with Germany are those of reparations and the financial and economic questions. But they could remain almost as they are; there would only be one participant less.

I am considering the objection which preoccupies Mr. Lloyd George in connection with the one which President Wilson formulated. Can't Italy—the President said—participate in the peace with Germany, even if the questions between Italy and Austria are not settled?

I have two replies to make. I don't want to go into the interpretation of the Treaty of London, nor of the act of September 1914.* But I believe that, in the spirit of these two acts and of the alliance itself, the peace can only be a general peace. Now, there would be no general peace if the entire world was at peace and Italy remained at war. Without entering into long considerations, I will say that, from the point of view of equity, not only amongst allies but also amongst associates, peace must be general.

In the second place, I grant to President Wilson that the peace

---

*By which the Allied Powers at that date pledged themselves not to conclude a separate peace.

with Germany can indeed be considered apart from the peace with Austria. But at the request of President Wilson himself, the fundamental statute of the League of Nations was added to the peace treaty, in order to be signed at the same time. One essential article of the Covenant of the League of Nations is the reciprocal guarantee of territories belonging to the signatories. So Italy would be obliged to guarantee the territorial integrity of other states, whilst her own boundaries would still be undetermined, and she would not be assured of what she regards as her territorial integrity.

The League of Nations is essentially an arrangement to avoid wars. If Italy adheres to it, whilst a danger of war still exists by the fact of the uncertainty of her borders, she can only receive the territories that she considers to be hers through the intermediary of the League of Nations, instead of acquiring them as the immediate and direct recompense for her services in the common victory.

It is thus very difficult for us to sign the peace treaty with Germany if questions properly Italian are not previously resolved.

Mr. Lloyd George. If M. Orlando goes, it will be important to prepare a communiqué for the press.

Baron Sonnino. As M. Orlando said, we are going to explain the situation in its main outlines to the Italian Parliament. But that will be difficult for us if we don't know exactly the intentions of our allies and associates. Two days ago, it seemed there was some prospect of compromise. What is the final state of the question in your own minds? Mr. Lloyd George has told us that, on Fiume, he was ready to accept a change of the Treaty of London if Italy made concessions on another side. M. Clemenceau didn't seem to associate himself with that view.

Mr. Lloyd George. I am certain that I didn't go beyond the ideas on which I had agreed with my colleagues. I proposed to you to make Fiume a free city, which is very different from its cession to the Yugoslav state.

M. Clemenceau. On that matter, I state that Mr. Lloyd George's view is my own.

Baron Sonnino. What does President Wilson think?

President Wilson. In my memorandum to M. Orlando, I declared myself prepared to make Fiume a free city.

Baron Sonnino. In President Wilson's memorandum, the frontier of Istria is not the one which is provided for by the Pact of London. Does President Wilson consent to the boundary of the Treaty of London? If I am asking all these questions, it is so as to say nothing inaccurate to the Italian Parliament.

President Wilson. In my memorandum, I explained clearly the position of the government of the United States. In any statement you make to the Italian Parliament, it will be best to refer to that memorandum.

Baron Sonnino. That will add to the difficulty.

M. Orlando. We must give an account to Parliament. We have President Wilson's memorandum, on the one side, and the statements of the Allies on the other. But can I indicate that there exists amongst the "Three" a basis of agreement, a possibility of compromise? If you can't reply to this question today, you can send me your answer tomorrow. Otherwise, if I say: "The Allies are adhering to the Pact of London," I will be told: "You won't have the signature of the United States." Is there a compromise plan accepted in principle by the representatives of France, Great Britain, and the United States?

President Wilson. I must reply that I am not free myself to suggest infractions of the principles to which I am bound. I have the right, on the other hand, to consider suggestions made to me. I must in truth say that I have seen no middle course yet.

Mr. Lloyd George. This is not altogether right. M. Clemenceau and I have insisted upon an intermediary solution; we have proposed one which was not preferred by President Wilson, but which he showed himself disposed to take under consideration. If I am wrong, he should tell me so. My impression is that, if Italy abandons the Treaty of London as it relates to Dalmatia, with Zara and Sebenico, however, becoming free cities, the question of Fiume would be settled as I said a short time ago, and a barrier of islands would be ceded to Italy to give her the strategic protection that she asks. I thought I understood that, if Italy accepted a proposal of this kind, we could arrive at a solution.

President Wilson. If I misled you, I am sorry. But all I said when you presented this plan to me was that we must see if our Italian colleagues were disposed to discuss it; they replied to us that they were not. I then reserved my position. If I seemed to go further, I regret it.

Mr. Lloyd George. I had the impression that you would not stand in the way of that solution, if it was accepted by Italy.

President Wilson. Above all, I wanted to persuade my Italian colleagues that I was prepared to study and discuss any reasonable proposal. But I never committed myself positively to accept such or such a particular solution.

Mr. Lloyd George. I believed that the reservations made by you on certain points meant that you were prepared to accept the plan in its main outline.

Baron Sonnino. What has just been said refers to a plan made the day before yesterday. We replied, day before yesterday, that we couldn't negotiate on the proposed basis. Yesterday, the Italian delegation studied the question again and prepared a proposal of conciliation; we communicated it to Mr. Lloyd George. If sovereignty over Fiume were given to Italy, we offered to renounce Dalmatia, except for Zara and Sebenico, which would be placed under an Italian mandate under the authority of the League of Nations. We would also ask for the islands mentioned in the Treaty of London, except the island of Pago, and the border of Istria as it was determined by the Treaty of London. Mr. Lloyd George replied that, as to sovereignty over Fiume, the plan was unacceptable, but that the remainder was acceptable to him.

President Wilson. Were you told that that was the impression produced on all of us by your proposal?

Mr. Lloyd George. After our conversation yesterday morning, I believed a proposal of this kind could be studied. But I must say that I raised an objection to the mandate demanded by Italy over Zara and Sebenico.

Baron Sonnino. In the afternoon, we said: "You don't want Italian sovereignty over Fiume; tell us what you would put in its place." We have had no answer.

Marquis Imperiali came to see Mr. Lloyd George at four o'clock and asked him what the arrangement for Fiume would be. You answered that Fiume would be a free city under the control of the League of Nations.

Mr. Lloyd George. Yes. I added that the city of Fiume would itself take charge of its diplomatic representation abroad, a question raised by the Italian delegation, which wanted to attach Fiume to Italy from the diplomatic point of view.

Baron Sonnino. We were beginning to discuss that last reply when the printed text of President Wilson's manifesto was brought to us. We said at once: "This changes the entire situation."

Today, what I would like to know are the final terms accepted by our two allies and by President Wilson. It would be pointless for us to go before the Italian Parliament and say: "Some accept this; the other accepts only that."

Mr. Lloyd George. My role of conciliator is a thankless role. I always risk being accused of having misinterpreted the thought of others. Nevertheless, I venture again to ask our Italian colleagues a question: if the three of us present a certain proposal to them, can't they undertake to present it to the Italian Parliament?

Baron Sonnino. We are only asking that you give us the opportunity to inform the Italian Chamber of your position.

Mr. Lloyd George. I am putting myself in President Wilson's place: it is difficult for him to commit himself and to accept a compromise if you yourselves are not committed.

I have some experience in arbitrating labor conflicts, and, when I had to play the part of the arbitrator, I always spoke to the parties in the following way: "Do you want to take the responsibility, not of accepting, but of recommending to those whom you represent, a solution which seems fair to me?" This is the way we have to proceed.

Baron Sonnino. If you ask us that question, we will answer you: "Yes, on condition that the proposal seems acceptable."

M. Orlando. I must say that Mr. Lloyd George has just spoken as I myself would speak. I don't believe I have the power today to accept a solution, whatever it might be. If I spoke otherwise, I would be contradicting what I said just now. All I ask now is whether the French, British, and American governments are agreed on a compromise. The response has been "no"; so I know what I wanted to know.

On the other hand, if I understood correctly, Zara, Sebenico, and the islands were mentioned; but nothing was said about Istria. For us, it must be completely Italian up to Volosca.

Baron Sonnino. Mr. Lloyd George tells us only: "Are you in a position to recommend to the Italian Parliament such a compromise as we will present to you?" I say: "Yes, if your compromise is acceptable." In these circumstances, we could make a final proposal.

Mr. Lloyd George. Unless the members of the Italian government commit themselves as much as we ourselves do, any solution is impossible.

Baron Sonnino. If the proposal you make is acceptable, we can, not accept it—for we lack the authority to do that after President Wilson's manifesto—but promise to recommend it to our Parliament.

M. Orlando. Undoubtedly; but since no proposal of that kind is presented to us thus: * * *

President Wilson. M. Orlando has said: "I will go and ask my people if I have the required authority to settle the question." What he needs to know are the positions taken by the Allies on the one side and by the United States on the other. Supplied with this information, he transmits it to his Parliament and asks it: "Do you confirm me in my authority?" I believe that we must leave it at that, and that there is no reason to present a solution in the nature of a compromise at this time.

Baron Sonnino. I believe that way of proceeding is dangerous. Suppose we are given full authority in Rome to settle the question. If we return and don't arrive at a solution, the situation will be worse than it is today. If we knew your views on the compromise, the chances for a final arrangement would be much greater.

M. Orlando. I agree with President Wilson. The events of these last days, however unfortunate, have had the advantage of clarifying the situation, which it is better to face up to. Why put pressure on President Wilson to obtain a proposal from him which he doesn't want to make? What will happen when we are in Rome? I don't know. I must warn you loyally that I will never tell Parliament: "Tell me what I must do," without myself giving it some indication. I will make my opinion known; that is the duty of a head of government. If I have the confidence of Parliament, then I will see what I have to do. If not, another government will replace us and enter into relations with you.

Perhaps, instead of the awkward schemes we are vainly seeking, the Italian people will find something else and give President Wilson a reason that is acceptable from his point of view to reach a settlement or change his action. The hours we have just spent are bitter hours for us; but, I repeat, the situation is clarified.

President Wilson. That is a very clear position, and one I understand. What would the Italian Parliament think if, on the day after my message, I accepted a proposal which would be the opposite of what I stood for?

Baron Sonnino. Yet the Italian government can't tell Parliament: "Give me your confidence" without submitting a plan of action to it. Once published, this plan, with all the agitation that this debate will provoke, will bind us, and thereafter any compromise will be more difficult. If we could say to the Italian Parliament that there is an agreement amongst the Allied and Associated Powers on the general outlines of a certain transaction, and if, on our side, we judged this proposal acceptable, we could go before Parliament and say: "The only probable solution is along these lines." What I am looking for is the line of the possible and the practical.

Mr. Lloyd George. Unfortunately, this conflict is a conflict of principles. I have nothing to say against President Wilson's principles; I myself fought for them, and it was in their spirit that our armies fought. But there is also the principle of respect for treaties, for which my country entered the war. It is permissible to make a compromise when it is a matter of reconciling two equally honorable principles. I believe that is the character of the compromise I suggested.

I don't know the Italian Parliament; but I have some experience with another Parliament. I know very well that I would never set foot there without knowing where I stood. If I went before the English Parliament to say, on the question of indemnities: "I ask you only to have confidence in me," I shouldn't feel very comfortable about what might follow.

President Wilson. But that is almost what you have done.

Mr. Lloyd George. Parliament knows very well my position and the commitments I have taken. But if I went to tell it, on this question or on any other: "I stand between three or four possible solutions: I will do my best," they would reply to me: "We'll have confidence in you when you have confidence in yourself." I fear it would be dangerous for the Italian ministers to leave for Rome without knowing where they stand.

President Wilson. A very clear path of conduct is open to them: they must inform the Italian Parliament that the Allies and America agree not to allow the cession of Fiume to Italy. On that, you don't consider yourselves bound. Apart from Fiume, there remains the whole question of Dalmatia and the islands, on which, on the contrary, France and England are bound by their treaty. The government of the United States deems the execution of this treaty contrary to the principles which motivate it, but it understands the difficulty of the Allies and is prepared to consider any reasonable arrangement.

Baron Sonnino. However, we can't tell the Italian Chamber that, on the one hand, the treaty excludes us from Fiume, and, on the other hand, that America is depriving us of Dalmatia because she doesn't recognize the treaty. The Chamber will send us packing.

M. Orlando. I will say this: concerning Fiume, the three powers agree in refusing it to us. As to the Treaty of London, President Wilson envisages the possibility of a deal, taking into consideration the difficult position created for the Allies by the obligations they contracted.

President Wilson. Until now, the Italian Parliament has never correctly known the position taken by the government of the United States. I insist on saying that our position is not solely negative. In my statement, I took care to mention that, insofar as Italy's security is concerned, we stipulated the limitation of naval armaments on the coast facing the Italian coast, the destruction of all Austrian fortifications, the protection of national minorities, etc. I want the Italian Parliament to know exactly what I said and what I think. Then we will see whether the Italian Prime Minister must resume the discussion by rejecting what we can propose to him, or whether it will be possible to arrive at a compromise.

XLVIII

Conversation between President Wilson, MM. Clemenceau and Lloyd George, and the economic experts*

APRIL 25, 1919, 4 P.M.

President Wilson. M. Loucheur has a short report to give us on the conference he had with the small powers about reparations.

M. Loucheur. Their observations can be summarized in a few words.

Belgium claims reimbursement for her war costs; she asks for restitution of or compensation for certain works of art taken from her. She also wants certain changes in the categories.

Serbia essentially asks to be represented on the Reparation Commission.

Brazil asks for the same treatment as the United States concerning the German ships that she seized.

Portugal asks for reimbursement of her war costs and the right to keep the seized vessels.

All of them ask to be heard by the Supreme Council. Since Belgium has the most important presentation to make, it would undoubtedly be desirable to hear her separately.

—*This proposal is adopted.*

Mr. Lloyd George. I am always afraid of this question of the ships. As for Brazil and Portugal, I have already told you my point of view.

THE ECONOMIC CLAUSES[1]

President Wilson. The differences amongst our experts are not very numerous. There is a point which concerns the United States, because it is a question of principle: it concerns the treatment, on the territory of the Allied and Associated Powers, of the subjects

*H., *PPC*, V, 229ff.

[1] The articles prepared for inclusion in the preliminary treaty by the Economic Commission. Its leading members were Baruch, Lamont, Sir Hubert Llewellyn Smith, Sir George Foster of Canada, Clémentel, Jean Morel, and Crespi. About the work of the commission, see, for example, Baruch, *Making of the Reparation and Economic Sections*, pp. 79-123.

of enemy states.[2] We would like for the special postwar arrangement to end automatically at the end of three or five years, and for the length of that period to be extended only by a decision of the League of Nations. We prefer that arrangement to the one which would, on the contrary, give the League of Nations the task of fixing the term, with the power to reduce it to five years.

Sir Robert Borden. The only discussion we have had relates to this time limit. The question is whether the period will be prolonged until the League of Nations ends it, or whether, on the contrary, it will end unless it is prolonged by a decision of the League of Nations.

M. Clémentel. This problem arises with regard to two categories of facts: in the first place, on the matter of tariff rates; in the second place, on the matter of foreigners located inside our country and also of merchant ships.

Concerning tariffs, we accepted the limitation of the special treatment which will follow the war for a period of five years, unless renewed by the League of Nations. It appears to us, moreover, that this renewal is very unlikely, since the decision can only be taken unanimously.

On the second point, our position is very different. We must remember, not only what France suffered during the war, but also the economic enterprises of the Germans before the war. After a period of only five years, it will probably be impossible to make this country forget the abominable treatment it suffered and to allow the Germans to come here as before the war. Nevertheless, that is what would happen if the period ended automatically at the end of five years, failing a contrary decision taken unanimously by the League of Nations. Then we would expose ourselves to seeing our nationals expelled from Germany as a reprisal, because it would be impossible for us to receive the Germans.

It seems to me that the countries which suffered invasion and devastation have the right to special treatment. So we accepted, concerning the status of Germans in Allied countries, the reversal of the system adopted for tariffs. The anticipated arrangement will continue, unless a decision of the League of Nations ends it. Psychologically, it would be impossible for us to contemplate at the end of five years the obligation to receive the Germans as before the war. There would be a revolt of public feeling, and it could result in a dangerous situation. It is better to leave the task

[2] This article referred to German commercial travelers.

of limiting the period to the League of Nations according to its judgment.

President Wilson. M. Clémentel goes too far in supposing that unanimity could not be obtained in the decisions of the League of Nations. But if he is correct, the clause he proposes would have a permanent effect; for the decision of the League which must put an end to it could never take place.

M. Clémentel. We ourselves understand very well that such an arrangement cannot be prolonged indefinitely. What we have proposed is to fix a maximum period. Twenty years has been spoken of; no doubt it must be less. But if the limit is too short, the effect in France will be deplorable. We could accept a maximum of ten years.

M. Clemenceau. I support the maximum of ten years for countries which suffered invasion.

Mr. Baruch. I must say that the representatives of the United States have always thought that five years was already more than was desirable; we had hoped that five years would be accepted as a maximum.

M. Clémentel. You must realize the fact that different countries were not affected in the same way by the war. The devastation and ordeals of France are without parallel. It cannot be imagined that there is the same state of mind in countries which have not suffered and in those where the consequences of the war and the ravages it has caused will remain visible for a century. Five years is a period which might be appropriate in most cases; but we ourselves could be granted a longer period.

Sir Robert Borden. I will propose a compromise to you. A maximum of five years has been proposed on the one hand, a maximum of ten on the other. We could say: minimum of five years, maximum of ten years; in the meantime, a commission of the League of Nations, deciding by majority vote, will fix the effective limit.

President Wilson. One aspect of this question is always present in my mind. When the Germans arrive in Versailles, they will represent a very unstable government; they will wonder, concerning each clause: "Do we dare sign it?" They know they are running the risk of being repudiated if they agree to clauses absolutely unacceptable to the nation they represent. The consequence might be their replacement by a government which would represent tendencies far more dangerous from our point of view. So we must study a question like this one from a dynamic point of view, so to speak, to see what will unleash the least force against the equilibrium we are trying to establish.

This is a matter of special restrictions on the liberty of individuals, which can be prolonged, without reciprocity, for ten years. The German negotiators will represent a country prostrate from an economic point of view, one which is going to hand over to us its ships, its property abroad, which will have lost some of its greatest sources of wealth. We are going to compel her to open her doors to foreigners for a relatively long period of time without reciprocity. This is not unrelated to the question of reparations; Germany cannot pay in gold the sums we will demand of her unless her balance of foreign trade is in her favor. She cannot pay us if her foreign trade is not more prosperous than before the war, for prewar profits would be inadequate. We are risking, then, not being paid if we ourselves take measures which will prevent Germany from recovering. And, if this risk is known, the bonds which will be guaranteed by her future payments will be worthless and unable to play the role we hope to give them as a means of credit.

What we want is peace. We also want the Germans to pay what they owe and to assist in the economic reconstruction of the world. Germany must restore what she has taken and rebuild what she has destroyed. But if we make her unable to do that, the penalties we want to impose on her will be purely nominal; on the contrary, we want them to be real. We don't want to place Germany in such a situation that we could obtain only imaginary sanctions against her.

M. Clémentel. I fear there is a misunderstanding about what I am suggesting. The clause relating to tariffs would remain as it is, the limit being fixed at five years, if the League of Nations so decides at the end of the fourth year. But for the status of persons, a question arises which is, above all, moral: it is not necessary that the Germans should come to clash with the French, in whose country they can do nothing useful for themselves or for their country for a number of years.

Sir Robert Borden's proposal satisfies us. We are making a concession by accepting a figure between five and ten years to be fixed by a decision of a majority of the proposed commission.

President Wilson. However, M. Clémentel, I don't believe a unanimous vote of the League of Nations would be impossible.

Mr. Lloyd George. Do you accept the compromise suggested by Sir Robert Borden, including the decision to be taken by majority vote?

President Wilson. I don't like this text very much, and I believe we risk nothing by saying that the limit will be five years, unless prolonged by a decision of the Council of the League of Nations.

But I wish, every time I can, to yield to the wishes of our French colleagues. I realize the great difficulty of their situation, and I don't forget the sufferings of their country. In spite of the risk of jeopardizing the signing of the treaty, I accept the compromise proposed by Sir Robert Borden.

Mr. Lloyd George. It seems to me that we have nothing more to say on this point.

Mr. Taussig. The question I have to ask relates to the interdependence of debts. It is a question, for instance, of whether Italy can keep German properties for the payment of reparations due from Austria.

Mr. Lloyd George. If the principle of interdependence is accepted, there is no way to escape that conclusion.

President Wilson. That presents no difficulty when it is a matter of public property. But will you accept it for private property?

Sir Hubert Llewellyn Smith. Concerning private property, it allows compensation for the nationals of enemy countries by their own governments.

President Wilson. In short, since it is a matter for France and Great Britain, which alone have an interest in this question, of possibly sacrificing for Italy's benefit a part of what would come to them, I can make no objection. But I find the principle ill-founded.

Mr. Lloyd George. It is difficult to discard a proposal of this kind in the absence of our Italian colleagues.

—The economic experts withdraw.

THE QUESTION OF THE KIEL CANAL*[3]

—Admirals de Bon, Benson, and Hope are introduced.

Mr. Lloyd George. The first point I want to draw to your attention relates to the destruction of the fortified works on the Kiel Canal (Article 8). The French and Italian admirals favor the destruction of these works. We deem that that question has already been treated as part of the matter of coastal defenses; we have decided they should be preserved because of their defensive character. This applies to the fortified works of the canal on the side of the Elbe. On the side of the Belt, the works would be destroyed because they command the Belt, which is an international navigable waterway. On the other hand, I believe that, with or without

*H., *PPC*, V, 235ff.

[3] The council again had before it the report on the Kiel Canal cited in XLVI, n. 5.

fortifications, the Germans can easily forbid access to the canal by exploding a mine.

Admiral de Bon. The French delegation thinks there is no reason not to destroy the fortifications on the side of the Elbe. If the canal is to become an international route of communication, it is desirable to make it entirely free.

As for the possibility of instantly destroying part of the canal by exploding a mine, I will observe that this method of defense would deprive the Germans of use of the canal. That is what we want, for the canal can be a formidable instrument of war in their hands. From the commercial point of view, traffic on the canal can amount to eleven million tons a year. In these circumstances, it must become an avenue of international transit as important as the Belt, and it would be natural to treat it in the same way. It is said besides that the fortifications could be rebuilt promptly; this reasoning applies equally to the Belt, where the interdiction is categorical. I haven't yet seen an argument which doesn't apply in the one case as in the other. On March 6, we reported our views on that question, and they were accepted by Messrs. Lansing and Balfour.

President Wilson. I don't see the importance of this question from a commercial point of view, for, in time of peace, the fortifications are of no consequence.

Mr. Lloyd George. We said that would allow Germany to defend her ports. I don't see how we can forbid her to defend the entrance of the Kiel Canal on the side of the Elbe.

Admiral Benson. It could also be said of the fortifications on the side of Kiel, that, if they disappear, a great part of the German coast will remain defenseless. If it was decided that they are to be destroyed that was because, given the range of modern guns, they command a part of a natural navigable waterway which, according to the principles we have advanced, must be without any fortification.

Mr. Lloyd George. I hope the French delegation will not insist.

President Wilson. The treatment planned for the Kiel Canal seemed fair to us. It is similar to that of the Panama Canal, where our agreement with Great Britain provides free passage for all, except in time of war. We have fortified the banks of the canal without any objection.

M. Clemenceau. On the other hand, the Suez Canal is not fortified, and no one has the right to fortify it.

Mr. Lloyd George. If Germany was at war with us, obviously we couldn't use the canal. In that case, what point is there in destroying defensive fortifications?

M. Clemenceau. There can be an advantage in preventing Germany from using the canal.

President Wilson. We mustn't forget that this canal is entirely on her territory.

Admiral de Bon. The case is very different from that of the Suez Canal, but only because the Suez Canal is an international canal: that is precisely the arrangement we wanted to establish at Kiel.

Mr. Lloyd George. In short, Admiral Benson finds that the plan goes too far, and Admiral de Bon that it doesn't go far enough. The British Admiralty is between the two extremes.

Admiral de Bon. There is a contradiction between the rules we have set for international waterways and the manner in which we propose to treat the Kiel Canal.

President Wilson. Not at all: the same rules will apply in both cases. The only disputed point is whether we will allow the defensive fortifications at the western entrance of the canal to remain.

—*The amendment proposed by Admiral de Bon is not adopted. The article is maintained without change.*

Sir Maurice Hankey. Concerning Article 7, there are two texts to choose between.

Admiral de Bon. It concerns the commission which will have surveillance over the canal. Your text provides that this commission will be German, and that it will be possible to appeal to the League of Nations. We propose to establish an international commission immediately.

Mr. Lloyd George. Is it worth the trouble to create an international commission to administer a canal which is purely German? This canal has little chance of becoming very important from a commercial point of view. Ships will continue to pass through the Danish Straits, because the saving in time by passing through the canal is inconsiderable, and there will be tolls to pay.

M. Clemenceau. I reckon we don't have to insist on our text.

Admiral Hope. There remains the question of the interned German ships and of those for which we are going to ask delivery: must we stipulate their destruction?

Mr. Lloyd George. We must confine ourselves to saying that they will be handed over, without saying what we will do with them.

Admiral Benson. I insist that the fate of these ships be decided in the text of the peace treaty. That would make the situation clearer and the negotiation easier.

Mr. Lloyd George. Like you, I am in favor of destruction. But we don't have time to settle that question amongst ourselves before the arrival of the Germans. You know that our French colleagues will make certain objections. Let us confine ourselves, for the moment, to demanding that these ships be handed over to us. Then we will debate their fate, and, undoubtedly, we can arrive at a decision before the signing of the peace treaty.

President Wilson. We can obligate ourselves to do it during that time.

Admiral Benson. Any distribution of these ships amongst the Allied and Associated Powers would result in the increase of armaments.

Mr. Lloyd George. If I wanted, I could make a proposal to the American navy which would result in a considerable reduction of armaments. But I daresay you wouldn't accept it. I repeat that I believe, as you do, that it would be better to sink those ships; but the question cannot be settled amongst us before next Tuesday.

President Wilson. Why are the French opposed to the destruction of the German warships?

Admiral de Bon. First, it does away with things of considerable value and increases the losses suffered. Besides, if these ships are divided amongst us, they won't bring us very much military force; but they'll be very useful to us in time of peace to carry our flag in different parts of the world and to represent our authority there. For five years, France, whose entire effort was concentrated on wartime work necessary for the army, built no ships. Our fleet suffered losses which could not be repaired, while the fleets of our allies increased in considerable proportions. So it is in the national interest to be able to use a certain number of German ships.

Mr. Lloyd George. It should also be acknowledged that, in time of peace, the military burden carried by France prevented her from constructing many warships. There are grounds for compensation.

President Wilson. We will say to the Germans, if they ask what will become of the ships, that we cannot reply to their question before the signing of the peace treaty.

Mr. Lloyd George. As for myself, I think they will be little concerned about it.

Admiral Hope. Should we specify the destruction of the submarines in the treaty?

Mr. Lloyd George. Why stipulate it there? That question concerns us only.

President Wilson. Here, I will be more insistent, because I am against the use of submarines in general.

Mr. Lloyd George. We have already demolished a great number of submarines handed over to us. We can say that we will demolish the others. We agreed about that.

M. Clemenceau. No, I opposed it. What are we doing with the German submarines in our hands?

Admiral de Bon. We are keeping them.

M. Clemenceau. In any case, it is a question to be studied. It was never settled. What are the English doing with their submarines?

Mr. Lloyd George. We are destroying those which the Germans handed over to us.

M. Clemenceau. Yes, but you are keeping a great number which you yourselves constructed. Now, we have very few; our situation is thus very different.

Let us not mix questions. I have no opinion on the latter. I ask for time to inform myself and, for the time being, let us confine ourselves to stating in the treaty that all these ships will be handed over to us.

Mr. Lloyd George. I think you have no objection to the destruction of all matériel, such as torpedoes, naval shells, etc. This clause is quite similar to a clause adopted for munitions of the army.

—*This measure is adopted.*

—Admirals Benson, de Bon, and Hope withdraw.

THE QUESTION OF KIAOCHOW*

President Wilson. I would like for us to exchange a few words on the Japanese question; it is almost as difficult as the Italian question.

Mr. Lloyd George. Yes, but the Japanese are much more determined; they don't bluff.

President Wilson. What are we going to do? We have the report of our experts on the question that we asked.[4] They say that the transfer to the Japanese of the rights previously granted the Germans would be preferable to the execution of the treaty concluded between Japan and China. Do your treaties with Japan compel France and England to grant the transfer of the German rights to Japan?

MM. Lloyd George and Clemenceau. Yes.

*H., PPC, V, 245ff.

[4] The members of the committee were Edward T. Williams, Jean Gout, and Ronald Macleay. Their report is printed in PWW, Vol. 58, pp. 72-73.

President Wilson. So you can't ask that the German rights be placed in the hands of the five powers?

Mr. Lloyd George. Mr. Balfour proposes to say to the Japanese: "We will assure you the transfer of the German rights; but we are asking you to discuss with us the terms on which you propose to restore Kiaochow to China." The Chinese are proposing a compromise; but I don't believe the Japanese will accept.

President Wilson. Suppose they refuse; we really cannot sanction the treaty between Japan and China. It was obtained by violence and under threat; it gives the Japanese more than the Germans ever possessed, and, moreover, they acquired, not the control, but the ownership of a large part of the bay. I will discuss with them before Thursday the terms on which they will have to restore Kiaochow to China. But we must take into account the fact that, without the intervention of Japan—and I can add our own—Kiaochow would still be German.

What do you think of Japanese cooperation at sea?

Sir Maurice Hankey. The Japanese cleaned up the Pacific and allowed the transport of Australian and New Zealand troops.

Mr. Lloyd George. We can't forget that; we needed those troops badly.

President Wilson. On the other hand, the Japanese declared themselves ready to give up the special rights of foreigners in China if we ourselves did the same. If they accept the transfer, pure and simple, of the German rights to Japan and really want to discuss with us the change of the terms they imposed on China, we can find a solution to the problem.

Mr. Lloyd George. We couldn't agree to give up our special rights in the Yangtze Valley if Japan retained a privileged position in Shantung. What we can propose is a perfect equality of treatment.

President Wilson. The question is whether or not this equality, which would open the Yangtze Valley to the Japanese, would be advantageous to China. What I seek is to liberate China from the chains which weigh on her.

Mr. Lloyd George. The Japanese, be assured of it, are working on a plan of conquest. When it is a question of building railways in China, whilst we confine ourselves to construction, they retain administration of them, they install themselves in the stations and in the countryside. There are 400 million men in China who, if they were organized militarily by Japan, would constitute a formidable mass.

I was struck the other day to see Baron Makino handle with perfect dexterity and a certain disdain the phraseology of the

West about the rights of humanity and the League of Nations. The Japanese are truly the Prussians of the Far East.

President Wilson. We must remember that their country is too small and infertile for their growing population. They found space in Korea and in Manchuria; but that is not enough for them.

Mr. Lloyd George. I will see with Mr. Balfour what we can do.

M. Clemenceau. I believe the Japanese will hold fast to what they call their rights.

President Wilson. They will get satisfaction by the transfer of the German rights. But we will tell them that we want to discuss with them the terms on which they will restore Kiaochow to China, and that in no event will we agree that the rights to be conceded to them will exceed those which the Germans possessed.

—*It is agreed that Mr. Balfour will be instructed to study this question.*

THE QUESTION OF SYRIA

Mr. Lloyd George. On the subject of Syria, must I send my two commissioners there and what instructions must I give them?

President Wilson. It seems to me that we are changing our position on this question every day. I have already sent mine and called them back.

M. Clemenceau (*to Mr. Lloyd George*). You pointed out the dangers of the commission, and you told me: "Let us first agree between ourselves."

President Wilson. If you settle the question between yourselves, it would be a mockery to send a commission to the spot.

M. Clemenceau. I only saw one man who insisted on the commission: it was Faisal; he told me he was certain that Syria would ask the commission to place him at its head.

President Wilson. I don't think it wise to proceed as you want to, and, moreover, we have agreed that the populations would be consulted.

M. Clemenceau. I said that, and I won't go back on my word.

Mr. Lloyd George. There are three parties in Syria; Faisal is not everyone's favorite.

President Wilson. That is not the question. If it is a matter of establishing a mandate of the League of Nations over Syria, can you decide between yourselves to whom that mandate should go?

Mr. Lloyd George. All I have to say is that, as far as the British government is concerned, its absolute decision is not to accept a mandate for Syria. The friendship of France is worth ten Syrias to us.

President Wilson. Nor do I wish a mandate for the United States, but the mandate question cannot be settled simply by an arrangement between the two of you. In my opinion, a question other than the one you are concerned with arises: I think a single mandate for all the Arab countries might be necessary.

Mr. Lloyd George. To tell the truth, these countries have never been united, except in the great empires of antiquity. As for the Bedouins, no one has ever succeeded in governing them. In any case, the members of this commission must be told whether they should leave or not. First I told them to go, then to stay.

M. Clemenceau. I would prefer that this commission leave only after the arrival of the Germans here. That would make the matter easier for me.

XLIX

Conversation between President Wilson, MM. Clemenceau and Lloyd George, and the representatives of the Commission on the International Regime of Ports, Waterways and Railways*

APRIL 26, 1919, 11 A.M.

—Reading of the report of the commission.[1]

President Wilson. As for me, I have no observation to make on this text.

Sir Robert Borden. I am instructed to express to you the commission's wish to continue its task of drafting an international convention of a permanent character, which would extend to all the countries of the world. This work has been prepared by the commission; but it recently received the instruction to concentrate its attention on what had to be made part of the peace treaty with Germany. It asks you for authorization to complete its work, with the intention I just indicated.

*H., *PPC*, V, 251ff.
[1] It is printed in *PPC*, V, 260-90.

President Wilson. Nothing is more desirable.

M. Clemenceau. That's very well.

Sir Robert Borden. One of the clauses of the treaty gives France the right to undertake works on the Rhine, between Basel and Strasbourg, for the utilization of the water power. This right includes the one of supporting the dams on the German bank. The commission is of opinion that there are grounds for compensation for Germany, both because of the use of certain points on the bank which belong to her and for the utilization of the driving power, half of which is provided by German waters.

Mr. H. White. What sort of compensation do you contemplate? A sum paid once, or periodic payments according to use?

Sir Hubert Llewellyn Smith. It's the second method that we contemplated.

M. Claveille. France asks that the right bank be subject to an easement. This easement naturally would give the right to an indemnity, as in any private transaction of the same nature. As for the supporting installations and quais which might exist or which might need to be created on the right bank, they will continue to belong to Germany, with the sole reservation that she must do nothing that might in any way change the flow of the river against our interests.

Mr. H. White. Sir Robert Borden also indicated that there was reason to pay for half of the power produced, since half of the waters belong to Germany.

Sir Robert Borden. The arrangement would be the same as for the St. Lawrence, where that river flows between Canada and the United States.

Brigadier General H. O. Mance. The draft article provides that France is bound to compensate for any encroachment on German property made necessary by the establishment of the works. There indeed remains the question of compensation for the value of the driving power itself. What guided the commission's conclusions is the acknowledged necessity that the works have to be directed by a single country. Moreover, the best plans provided by the Germans themselves place all the works on the left bank, except the dams, one end of which will naturally have to rest on the right bank.

M. Claveille. We were led to ask the question because, until now, all the hydroelectric power used in Alsace came from Germany, principally from the Black Forest. It is a matter of replacing that power, which would now have to cross the frontier, by utilizing the energy provided by the Rhine. The Germans made intensive studies of the question, and we can use them. There will be two dams and a canal dug out of the left bank. Since the expense is carried entirely by France, the power must belong to her. Moreover, our works will considerably improve the navigability of the Rhine between Basel and Strasbourg, and Germany will profit from these improvements on an equal footing with us.

President Wilson. It nonetheless remains that the energy of the river which, normally, should belong to the two riparians, will only belong to one.

Brigadier General H. O. Mance. In any case, it would be necessary to take into account the expenditures which will be made to harness the power and to improve river navigation.

President Wilson. Certainly. What I mean is that the value of the power produced will have to be shared equally between France and Germany, a deduction to be made to the credit of France for the cost of the works carried out to produce that power.

—*This proposal is adopted.*

—*Sir Robert Borden reads from the text.*

Mr. Lloyd George. Should we give Germany the right to claim that compensation in the form of energy?

M. Claveille. Sir Robert Borden's text says that the right belonging naturally to Germany on the river is a basis for sharing. I understand the intention of this text, but it is not clearly expressed. I would prefer to say expressly that the difference between the costs of the works and the value of the product will be shared equally.

Mr. Lloyd George. Very well. But don't you agree to add that the compensation can take place either in money or in power?

M. Clemenceau. I accept this.

Sir Hubert Llewellyn Smith. Article 61A of the text of the international convention prepared by our commission raises the question of the duration of that convention. I believe it is difficult to fix here a time limit different from that which was foreseen for maritime shipping. The opinion of the British delegation is that the two clauses must be put in harmony.

—*The question, along with this recommendation, is sent back to the Drafting Committee.*

Mr. Lloyd George. Article 39 provides that no work can be done on the Rhine without the approval of the commission; but that clause cannot apply to Holland.

M. Claveille. This arrangement was introduced at the request of Belgium, which insisted very strongly, because she wants to construct a canal from the Rhine to the Meuse and fears, if the river is not supervised by the commission, that material obstacles could be put in the way of the realization of that plan.

President Wilson. If Holland doesn't sign the treaty, it goes without saying that this clause cannot apply to her.

Sir Hubert Llewellyn Smith. I strongly believe that she will not sign if that article remains as it is.

President Wilson. How can we give satisfaction to Belgium?

Sir Hubert Llewellyn Smith. Belgium has satisfaction by Article 30 of the Mannheim Convention of 1868, which forbids all riparians to do anything that might impede navigation.

M. Claveille. If Belgium declares herself satisfied, well and good. But Article 30 of the Mannheim Convention is not enough. It only prevents direct obstacles to navigation—bridges obstructing passage, floating mills—and it doesn't compel the riparian to create facilities to prevent the silting up of the river; by neglecting to do this, it is easy to block the entrance of a canal. Hence, the necessity of the intervention of an international commission.

President Wilson. Are we not compelled to limit the application of this article to the territories covered by the treaty?

Mr. Lloyd George. As for myself, I fear this clause may be draconian. Where it concerns that part of the Rhine which is purely German, how can we compel Germany not to build works without the approval of an international commission? For example, if it is a matter of the Mannheim docks, will we say that Germany cannot enlarge them without foreigners being mixed up in it? I would like to avoid that appearance of persecution.

President Wilson. We can say expressly that it involves only works which could create an obstacle to shipping.

M. Claveille. We never had any other intention.

Mr. Lloyd George. I am satisfied.

Sir Hubert Llewellyn Smith. One clause relates to the speed of trains intended to serve purely continental countries, such as Bohemia; it compels Germany to provide services as fast as the best of her own network for the lines crossing her territory. It is perhaps necessary to specify that Germany would not be compelled to take as a basis of comparison train services provided, for example, between two closely neighboring industrial cities, but which don't run over great distances.

—(Adopted.)

Likewise, Article 53 provides an obligation on Germany's part to create, at the will of the Allies, connecting lines allowing the establishment of new train service towards some of the neighboring countries. This article, as it stands, would lend itself to arbitrary applications. If it must be kept, it would be preferable to hand over control to the Council of the League of Nations.

M. Claveille. This arrangement doesn't concern France. It was inserted in the interest of the Czechoslovaks, the Yugoslavs, etc. Since it imposes the costs of establishing connecting lines on the beneficiaries, I think that stipulation will be sufficient to prevent arbitrary multiplications. But I see no objection to having any decision of this kind subject to the approval of the League of Nations.

Sir Hubert Llewellyn Smith. We are providing for the establishment or reconstitution of a commission of the Rhine and a commission of the Danube.

The treaty provides for the digging of a connecting canal, which can only be decided upon with the consent of the Allied and Associated Powers. In this text, I propose to substitute the commission to which the decision would belong by the Council of the League of Nations.

—(Approved.)

—The technical delegates withdraw.

President Wilson.* I have some telegrams about the state of opinion in Rome.[2] The crowd marched tumultuously to the Capitol, and, along the way, stopped to cheer in front of the Japanese embassy: that is rather significant.

Moreover, I have received telegrams[3] warning me of the movement of Italian troops towards Fiume, and warning me that the battleship *San Giorgio* is leaving for Fiume today. That bodes nothing good.

Mr. Lloyd George. I fear M. Orlando will be swept away by the movement he has allowed to develop. He is today in the situation of a secretary of a labor union who has allowed a strike to run wild.

*H., PPC, V, 291ff.

[2] From Ambassador Thomas Nelson Page, all dated April 24, 1919. They are printed in PWW, Vol. 58, pp. 91-93.

[3] From Admiral Benson, repeating a telegram from Rear Adm. Philip Andrews, American naval commander in the Mediterranean, printed in *ibid.*, p. 142.

President Wilson. On the other side, the Rumanians are continuing their offensive in Hungary. Since it is no longer a matter of protecting themselves, I think we must tell them to stop. The aggression seems now to come from the Rumanians, who are in fact more powerful than Hungary in her much reduced condition.

The best way to begin the pacification of all these areas would, I believe, be to fix a date for the opening of our negotiations with the Austrians as soon as possible. That would have a particularly good effect in Vienna, and we must try to avoid having the disorder in Hungary spread to Austria. That is the opinion of Mr. Hoover, who is firm in his own particular point of view and who has much information from his agents.

Do we have a way of stopping the movement of the Rumanians?

Mr. Lloyd George. I believe we must speak to them seriously. Do you want to summon M. Brătianu?

M. Clemenceau. Yes; we'll tell him in a few words what we want and give him the opportunity to make a brief explanation.

President Wilson. What do you think of the idea of inviting the Austrians to be in Versailles on May 15?

M. Clemenceau. What is left to settle, concerning Austria, apart from the question of the Adriatic?

President Wilson. The work of the commissions enables us to settle all the border questions very rapidly. But there remains the question of the distribution of the Austro-Hungarian debt and that of reparations—if it is possible to obtain any. We would have two weeks to arrive at our position on these questions.

Mr. Lloyd George. I don't believe it is necessary to decide the distribution of the Austro-Hungarian debt now. It would be enough to determine principles and establish a commission, whose work will be long and difficult, for it will be necessary to evaluate the relative wealth of each part of the Austro-Hungarian monarchy.

The question of the Danube, the questions of the railways, are settled. The borders are nearly defined by the work of the commissions.

President Wilson. There is still the question of Teschen. M. Kramář and M. Beneš want to see us on this subject.

For our approaching meeting with the Germans, the first question which arises is verification of the credentials. The Germans will present their credentials and will ask for ours. What will we say about the Kingdom of the Serbs, Croats and Slovenes?

M. Clemenceau. It is true that we haven't recognized it up to now, in order to please the Italians.

Mr. Lloyd George. Why not simply present Serbia's credentials?
President Wilson. M. Trumbić won't accept that.
M. Clemenceau. Obviously, the recognition of the Kingdom of the Serbs, Croats and Slovenes at this time will increase the danger from the Italian side. But I don't see how we can avoid it.

Hasn't America recognized the Yugoslavs?
President Wilson. Yes.
Mr. Lloyd George. I propose to decide that, if the Italians are not present at the time the negotiations with Germany begin, we recognize the Kingdom of the Serbs, Croats and Slovenes.

—(Adopted.)

President Wilson. Shouldn't we agree about the time we will allow the Germans to study the treaty and present us with their written observations?
Mr. Lloyd George. I propose two weeks.
President Wilson. That is not much; the document will be very voluminous.
M. Clemenceau. They won't be much more satisfied with this document at the end of fifty days. I propose two weeks. It goes without saying that, if the Germans ask for more time and seem to be interested in arriving at a solution, we can't refuse them an extension. It is understood the communications and replies will take place in writing.

Shall we invite all the belligerents to the opening session? I don't believe it would be possible to do otherwise.
Mr. Lloyd George. That will mean a good many people. I don't know whether we have to include amongst the belligerents the newly formed powers which didn't fight against the Germans, such as Poland and Czechoslovakia.
President Wilson. Before taking a decision on the amount of time we will allow the Germans to study the text of the treaty, I propose to ask each of the commissions, which know the parts of the treaty on which they have worked, how much time it would seem to them reasonable to grant.

—(Adopted.)

Mr. Lloyd George. In the list of questions to be submitted the Germans, which correspond to the different chapters of the treaty,[4] I

---

[4] A note to accompany the presentation of the preliminaries of peace to the German delegation. It outlined the procedure for the exchange of credentials and listed the questions that required written responses, each to be answered in blank number of days. The note is printed in PPC, V, 297-98.

see neither the Covenant of the League of Nations, nor the international labor convention.

President Wilson. They only have to be added.

M. Clemenceau. How will we divide the time which will be granted to the Germans to study the document. We don't intend to allow them to work for two weeks without receiving any reply from them.

Mr. Lloyd George. I believe it will be necessary to fix time limits for each of the principal questions, with two weeks as the outside limit. We're not going to sit here for two weeks without doing anything.

M. Clemenceau. I will have the text recast along these lines.

L

Conversation between President Wilson and MM. Clemenceau and Lloyd George*

APRIL 26, 1919, 3 P.M.[1]

M. Clemenceau. The Germans will be here Wednesday evening; the work can begin on Thursday. What will we do if the Italians are not there?

Mr. Lloyd George. The Drafting Committee must be told to place everywhere, instead of "the Five Powers," "the Principal Allied and Associated Powers," a formula which neither mentions nor excludes the Italians.

—The financial delegates are introduced.

REPORT OF THE FINANCIAL COMMISSION[2]

President Wilson. The American delegation has no new observa-

*H., PPC, V, 299ff; 302ff.

[1] There was a very brief meeting preceding this one, which Mantoux apparently did not attend. The Three received the members of the Drafting Committee, who asked whether the treaty with Germany should be "agreed" or "imposed." After a short discussion, the council decided that "it should be an 'agreed' peace and should be prepared in this form." The council then discussed other matters very briefly. See PWW, Vol. 58, pp. 153-54.

[2] Its principal members were Lamont, Davis, Albert Strauss, Montagu, Keynes, Klotz, and Crespi. Their report seems to be missing. However, its subject matter will become evident in the discussion below.

APRIL 26, 1919

tions to make on the text presented by the Financial Commission, except for some clarifications.

In the second paragraph of Article 4, to the words "payments for food and raw materials," we would add "and such other payments as might take place."

M. Klotz. What other payments do you foresee?

Mr. Norman Davis. In any case, according to another article, they will only be the payments that we ourselves will authorize. But if we didn't introduce these words, we would be closing the door to different purchases which might be necessary.

M. Clemenceau. I accept that amendment.

President Wilson. In the second paragraph of Article 2, before the last line, we propose to insert: "at the current or agreed upon rate of exchange."

Mr. Norman Davis. In that article, it is only a matter of marks for the upkeep of the army of occupation. In principle, these marks are received at the current rate of exchange. But since this rate is not always exactly known, what happens in fact is that one fixes it approximately. The article only regularizes that practice.

M. Klotz. We concur.

One difficulty has been raised by Mr. Keynes about objects handed over in execution of the Armistice: he asks that, when there is no direct restitution of the same object taken from us, the value of the object substituted for it be credited to Germany in the reparation account. When the object is similar to that which was requisitioned or stolen, it should be treated as if it was the object itself. For, in a great number of cases, notably those concerning railway equipment, we haven't had the time to find the objects which we have the right to claim. On this question, we are ready to rely on the judgment of the Reparation Commission, which will study each case.

Mr. Lloyd George. I see no obstacle to adopting the arrangement proposed by M. Klotz. But, in that case, it will be necessary to apply it uniformly to all similar cases, notably to the sunken ships which were replaced by other ships: there, too, there is replacement by similar objects.

M. Klotz. There is no comparison possible between the two cases mentioned, for your ships were sunk and cannot be recovered; the objects we mention were stolen and could, in most of the cases, be recovered if we had the time to look for them. Lacking the time, we are given others which replace them. But I trust the judgment of the commission.

Mr. Lloyd George. The difference doesn't seem real to me. For you also had railway cars destroyed.

President Wilson. I will call to your attention that another clause provides that everything that will be identified later can be claimed: that article gives you complete satisfaction.

M. Klotz. Articles 9 and 10 of the English text relate to the participation of states which will annex German territories, or will be established over them as mandatories of the League of Nations, in the fraction of the German debt assignable to those territories. The English text rejects that participation; the French text allows it within a certain limit. How could Germany fairly be made to continue to assure the payment of the debt assigned to the colonies she has lost? That question is connected to the one of public properties located in those same territories.

Mr. Lloyd George. What is fair, if you take state properties, either in the colonies or in Alsace-Lorraine, is to make an evaluation of them and to place their value to the debit of the state which takes possession. It goes without saying that that cannot apply to works which have been carried out for military purposes. General Smuts, for example, says that South Africa won't agree to pay for the works which the Germans undertook specifically in order to attack South Africa. But, concerning railways, the compensation seemed fair to him. The same principle must be applied everywhere in the same way.

I am speaking moreover, only of public works and of state properties. As for participation in the debt, that is another matter. The debt could have been contracted for a military purpose, and I am not inclined to participate, however little it might be, in the German debt.

M. Clemenceau. In Alsace-Lorraine, we cannot pay for public properties which were ours and which the Germans took from us in 1871; we cannot pay for the forests of Alsace which the Germans took and which are coming back to us today.

Mr. Lloyd George. Agreed for the forests; but you can pay for the railways built since 1871 and for everything that has a commercial value.

M. Clemenceau (*to M. Klotz*). What does that amount to in Alsace-Lorraine?

M. Klotz. Something like two billions.

President Wilson. All we have to do here is determine the principle; the commission will see how it is to be applied.

M. Clemenceau. I would like to see the text proposed by the English experts.

—Reading of the text: In the territories annexed or placed under a mandate of the League of Nations, all property of the German state or states which has an economic value qualifies for compensation. In the case of Alsace-Lorraine, this principle will not be applied to any of the properties which Germany appropriated without compensation in 1871.

M. Clemenceau. According to the text proposed by the French delegation, France recovers public property in Alsace-Lorraine as it is, without indemnity, and she refunds the sum which the Germans, in 1871, deducted from the war indemnity for the payment of the railways of the East.

Mr. Lloyd George. I accept the French text, on condition that the same principle be applied everywhere. I would have preferred, for myself, to establish everywhere the principle of payment for public properties; if you can't accept it, we must have payment nowhere. Otherwise, we would be obliged to pay for railways and other public works in countries where we are only the mandatories.

President Wilson. I see a profound difference between the German colonies and the provinces taken from France in 1871, which the entire world, for forty-eight years, has thought of as the greatest example of a historical injustice. If the principle of payment was established everywhere, with the exception of Alsace-Lorraine, that is what the world would understand best.

Mr. Lloyd George. I cannot concur in that opinion, because I must think of the position of the British dominions. We will have the greatest difficulty in making them pay for German state properties if those which have been—I don't say taken from France in 1871 and restored since—but created by the German state in Alsace-Lorraine, pass to France without compensation. I hope no one will insist on making an exception in this case; otherwise, I anticipate the greatest difficulties.

President Wilson. On the other hand, I find it unjust to take properties without paying for them. If we ask Germany to compensate for damages such as we defined them at the time of the Armistice, and if we don't count the properties we take from her in the reparations, we go beyond the commitment we undertook towards her.

Mr. Lloyd George. I will point out that we could have interpreted the terms of the Armistice much more broadly, and I don't believe we are committing any real injustice against the Germans. The enormous weight of our debt facing us for forty or fifty years would justify us in being more exacting. If it is impossible to establish the principle of payment everywhere, I ask that we renounce it everywhere.

President Wilson. I thought the case of Alsace-Lorraine would be treated entirely separately.

Mr. Lloyd George. If I wished to argue about that, I could say that the economic worth of Alsace-Lorraine has been multiplied four or five times by German effort.

Mr. Norman Davis. We must take into account the local debt of Alsace-Lorraine, which France agrees to assume.

Mr. Lloyd George. I am compelled to ask for the application of the same principle; otherwise, I could not make the solution acceptable to the dominions. I propose not to place public property to the credit of Germany either in Alsace-Lorraine, or anywhere else.

President Wilson. Is that fair?

Mr. Lloyd George. I believe so. I am prepared to accept the other principle; but I will accept the one or the other only if it is uniformly applied.

President Wilson. I still have doubts about that.

Mr. Lloyd George. Australia won't agree that one can deduct the price of German railroads in New Guinea from what is due her for the payment of her pensions. With a population of four million inhabitants, she lost as many soldiers as the United States, and she contracted a debt of 300 million pounds sterling. I could not yield on that point.

President Wilson. We can say that France should not pay in Alsace-Lorraine, because Alsace-Lorraine is being restored to her, and that the mandatories of the League of Nations won't pay, because they are not taking possession of the territories. But in all other cases, compensation will be due.

—*It is thus decided.*

LI

Conversation between President Wilson and MM. Clemenceau and Lloyd George*

APRIL 28, 1919, 11 A.M.

M. Clemenceau. I have to submit to you an amendment to an article of the military clauses which forbids the Germans to provide instructors to foreign armies or to enlist in them. We are asking

*H., PPC, V, 308ff.

that this article be changed in such a way as to enable us to keep our Foreign Legion, which has always included a great number of German volunteers.

—*The amendment is adopted.*

Mr. Lloyd George. Our military experts ask for the insertion into the treaty of an article compelling the Germans to disclose the manufacturing secrets of asphyxiating gases and explosives. According to this report, Germany is several years ahead of us, and our advisers see a serious danger for the future in this.

President Wilson. We have already considered that question, and I told you, referring to my university experience, how impossible it was to know laboratory secrets, whatever the nature of the inquiry you might seek to undertake. It is easy to demand their secrets from the Germans; but how can you compel them to give them up?

Mr. Lloyd George. Can't we compel them, as in the carrying out of any other article of the treaty?

M. Clemenceau. I will put in the treaty what you want; but I don't believe a stipulation of this kind can have any effect.

—Mr. Lloyd George reads aloud the text of the proposed amendment: the production of synthetic nitric acid and ammonia are specially mentioned therein.[1]

President Wilson. What I also fear is that a stipulation of this kind, which cannot attain the objective you have in mind, provides an indirect way of disclosing industrial secrets. The thought that this could be the aim of your military advisers is far from my mind. But there is almost no chemical discovery made for the needs of war which cannot be used even more for the industries of peace.

Mr. Lloyd George. Is that a reason not to protect ourselves?

President Wilson. If you are compelled to trust the word of the Germans, you can also urge them to refrain from making any military use of their chemical discoveries. But I couldn't accept a formula which would allow extending the investigation to other fields.

—*The text is modified along these lines and adopted.*

M. Clemenceau. I return to the question of the procedure when we meet the Germans.[2] As for what we must do concerning Italy, we

---

[1] This proposal and the modified text mentioned below are printed in *PPC*, V, 311.

[2] The council had before it a revised text of the document cited in XLIX, n. 4,

are highly embarrassed, and we also have to take a decision about the recognition of the Kingdom of the Serbs, Croats and Slovenes.

Mr. Lloyd George. Is this urgent? What do they have to do with the Germans?

President Wilson. The question is one of credentials: since they will be present, and since the Germans can ask them for their credentials, that leads you to the necessity of recognizing them.

Lt. Col. Sir Maurice Hankey. I should recall that Mr. Balfour seems rather preoccupied with that possibility; he believes the official recognition at this time of the Kingdom of the Serbs, Croats and Slovenes would be considered as an unfriendly act in Italy.

President Wilson. On the other hand, it is very difficult to leave the Yugoslavs out. Let us remember that the war began with aggression against Serbia.

Mr. Lloyd George. Yes, but, on the other hand, we haven't yet made peace with Austria-Hungary, which is supposed to include the Yugoslav territories.

President Wilson. The trouble is that the representatives of Serbia no longer have Serbian credentials. Their credentials are drawn up in the name of the Kingdom of the Serbs, Croats and Slovenes.

Mr. Lloyd George. I wouldn't like to do anything to increase the danger of an explosion in Italy. Can't we wait?

M. Clemenceau. If it wasn't for the Italian situation, I would recognize them. But I am of opinion, with Mr. Lloyd George, that we must avoid creating a new cause of agitation at this time, and that it is better to wait.

President Wilson. However, a German legal expert might say that, if the Yugoslavs sign the treaty without having been officially recognized, Germany can one day contest the validity of the treaty which contained an unknown or invalid signature. About that question, couldn't the Foreign Ministers have a talk with M. Vesnić?

—(Adopted.)

President Wilson. The other day, the question was asked whether the Poles and the Czechoslovaks would be asked to sign the peace treaty with Germany. In fact, they haven't acted as belligerents against Germany.

Mr. Lloyd George. No, but we have to fix the boundaries between

---

with the time schedule for the German counter-proposals now filled in. It is printed in PPC, V, 321-22.

their territories and Germany's; they must be admitted to the signing.

—*It is decided that the Czechoslovak and Polish delegates will be present at the negotiations with the German plenipotentiaries.*

Sir Maurice Hankey. The question has been asked whether the invitations should be limited to the actual belligerents or extended to all the powers which declared war on Germany.

President Wilson. It seems to me impossible to make that distinction, which could give offense. I think we must admit those who declared war on Germany. In any case, it would be impossible to exclude a great power like Brazil.

Mr. Lloyd George. Moreover, Brazil sent us several destroyers. One of them even prevented one of our ships from being sunk.

—*It is decided that Brazil will be added to the list of powers which will be present at the opening of the negotiations with Germany.*

President Wilson. The text in front of me provides a period of forty-eight hours for the reply of the Germans after we have replied to their observations on the text of the treaty. It seems to me impossible to set a rigid time period; isn't it better to write that we will set it in each case?

M. Clemenceau. I much prefer that wording.

—(Adopted.)

Mr. Lloyd George. Along the same lines, the question arises whether we can, as we thought, fix in advance the number of days granted to the Germans to give us their reply on such and such parts of the treaty. Upon reflection, I think that, before speaking out on any part of the treaty, the Germans will first take a decision on the whole. The questions of indemnities, of territorial frontiers, of colonies, cannot be separated at the start from one another. This leads us to say to them: "You have two weeks to study the entire document and to present us with your observations. If you have something to say to us before the end of that period, we will be prepared to study it."

M. Clemenceau. What will we do during these two weeks?

Mr. Lloyd George. We have to settle the terms of the treaty with Austria.

M. Clemenceau. I believe this arrangement is much better than the one which was contemplated. I myself had concluded that it would be impossible to fix a time table for the Germans as rigid as the one we had foreseen.

Mr. Lloyd George. At the same time, I see an important advantage in not giving them, by the number of days assigned to such and such parts of the treaty, an idea of the relative importance that we attach to the different questions.

M. Clemenceau. I am informing you of the result of the conversations which M. Loucheur,[3] according to our instructions, had with the representatives of the small powers about the reparation question. Serbia asked to have a voting delegate on the Reparation Commission.

President Wilson. There is much to be said in favor of that request. We mustn't forget that the war began in Serbia.

Mr. Lloyd George. Yes, but I don't know if Serbia will have any right to reparation, since she is annexing countries which are repudiating all the Austro-Hungarian debt, and since the debit and the credit will have to be put side by side.

M. Clemenceau. I favor granting Serbia what she asks.

President Wilson. I don't see a decisive practical argument in her favor; but the argument of sentiment is very strong.

Mr. Lloyd George. In this case, how could you resist a similar demand by Rumania?

President Wilson. We could say that Rumania entered the war much later and that she was compelled to withdraw before the end. But, undoubtedly, the distinction would be more or less arbitrary.

Mr. Lloyd George. We must recall that voting will be by majority in the Reparation Commission. We must not put people on it who are not called there by interests of the first order. I fear the risk to which that might expose us, and I would like to consult our specialists about it.

President Wilson. We can tell Serbia that the reparations due her are rendered in the form of territories free of all debts.

Mr. Lloyd George. In any case, we must speak with them about the matter. Like you, I don't forget that the Serbs were the first victims of the war, and they fought very well, much better than the Belgians.

THE QUESTION OF KIAOCHOW

Mr. Lloyd George. I must inform you about an interview which took place Saturday between the Japanese representatives and Mr. Balfour.[4]

---

[3] Loucheur's memorandum is printed in *ibid.*, pp. 322-24.

[4] Balfour's report of this conversation is printed in *PWW*, Vol. 58, pp. 175-76.

The Japanese denied that the arrangement claimed by them was more advantageous than that from which the Germans profited. They called to our attention that they proposed to evacuate militarily all of Shantung, including the zone of fifty kilometers occupied by the Germans around Kiaochow. They repeat that they intend to restore Chinese sovereignty in that province; the occupation of the railway line by Japanese troops is, they say, a temporary measure.

Their demands are essentially economic. What they want is a Japanese concession in the Bay of Kiaochow and the transfer of the German rights over the railway and the mines, which belong to the same company. The other lines they propose to construct with Japanese capital will be established under the same conditions as other railways constructed in China by foreign capital.

National pride stands in the way of the Japanese accepting a revision of their treaties with China. But they are willing to pledge themselves to us not to oppose the establishment of an international concession in the Bay of Kiaochow and to restore Chinese sovereignty in Shantung in all its plenitude.

What is your impression of that conversation?

President Wilson. There is certainly a change for the better.

Sir Maurice Hankey. Mr. Balfour also informs you that the Japanese approved the summary you just heard read.

President Wilson. Can we tell the Japanese that we will leave them in possession of all the rights previously conceded to the Germans on condition that they don't exercise their temporary right of military occupation? Note that nothing would so easily inflame American public opinion as the idea of an injustice done to China in Japan's favor. The news I receive from America shows, not only that public opinion supports me strongly in the position I have taken on the Italian question, but also that it expects me to take the same position on the Japanese question.

Mr. Lloyd George. We must speak to the Japanese about it; Japan is a great power, it must be treated as such.

M. Clemenceau. We must speak to them frankly and show them the bases on which we believe we can agree with them.

President Wilson. In that case, I would propose that we see them tomorrow.

M. Clemenceau. What have we decided about the presence of the Serbs on the Reparation Commission?

Mr. Lloyd George. We have agreed to consult our specialists, who will tell us what might be the effect of Serbia's participation in the work of that commission.

M. Clemenceau. In order to respond to the demands of Belgium, do we have to see the Belgians?

President Wilson. Certainly. But we will say to Belgium that she cannot obtain reimbursement for all her war costs: that would make us violate commitments we have taken.

M. Clemenceau. Brazil also asks to keep the German ships she requisitioned.

Mr. Lloyd George. I am against it, as you know. Brazil took ten times more tonnage than Germany sank of hers. I think these ships must be placed in common with all those we will have to distribute amongst ourselves. The same rule must apply to Portugal, which makes a similar request of us.

President Wilson. That seems fair to me. It might have been different if they had played another role during the war; then I would be compelled to request the same treatment for them that you have accepted for the United States.

M. Clemenceau. I come to an important amendment to the text of the treaty. In the event Germany fails to meet her commitments, we have demanded that she be subjected to an investigation by the League of Nations. There will be no permanent control committee; but each of us can apply to the League of Nations and request an inquiry. The Council of the League will decide if there are grounds for that investigation.

But the text says that the decision will be taken unanimously. We cannot accept that wording, because one vote would be enough to stop everything, and we ask that the vote be taken by majority.

President Wilson. In that case, an amendment would have to be introduced into the Covenant of the League of Nations to indicate that unanimity will be the rule "except in cases stipulated either in the Covenant or in the peace treaty."

M. Clemenceau. I couldn't accept, you understand, that the opposition of a single power could prevent the investigation from taking place.

—*It is decided that:* (1) an amendment will be introduced into the Covenant of the League of Nations so as to allow, in the cases stipulated, a vote by majority; (2) an amendment will be introduced into the peace treaty, stipulating that all decisions of the Council of the League of nations to institute an inquiry into the execution of the clauses of the treaty will be taken by majority vote.[5]

---

[5] These amendments are printed in *PPC*, V, 319.

President Wilson. You recall that we had agreed on the creation of a commission to study the Baltic questions. Should that commission meet in Paris or on site? Mr. Lord thinks it will serve us best if it gathers all the information and meets in Paris.

—*This proposal is adopted.*

President Wilson. Mr. Hoover sends me a letter which impresses me very much.[6] He asks that we recognize the independence of Finland immediately. That country is now isolated from the world. Her ships have no recognized flag and cannot sail. It is impossible for the Finns to find credit abroad, and they can possess no passports to travel. At the same time, the food situation in Finland is very bad. If we don't recognize it soon, the Finnish government will be in great danger.

Mr. Lloyd George. I would recall that it can only blame itself. Its sympathies were only too much on the side of Germany. After the Russian Revolution, it created a German-Finnish army, and the principal reason for our expedition to Murmansk was to prevent the junction of the Finns and the Germans, on the one side, and the Bolsheviks on the other. Today, the Finns have abandoned the Germans, they have abandoned the Bolsheviks, and they come to us.

President Wilson. All right; but all they ask is the recognition of their state.

M. Clemenceau. I believe we can agree on that without any drawback.

Mr. Lloyd George. Mr. Balfour is here; he says the Japanese are expecting to be received today.

—*Mr. Balfour is introduced.*

Mr. Balfour. I saw the Japanese on Saturday. Baron Makino came back to see me yesterday evening at seven o'clock and, in a very delicate way, gave me to understand that Japan needed a decision. He said to me: "We cannot join the League of Nations, in spite of the great interest we take in its founding, without having protested against the refusal to adopt the principle of the equality of the races.[7] But we cannot accept at one and the same time the

---

[6] H. C. Hoover to WW, April 26, 1919, printed in *ibid.*, pp. 357-59.

[7] During the discussions of the League of Nations Commission, which drafted the Covenant, the Japanese had tried to gain the inclusion of an article affirming the principle of racial equality as a basic principle in relations among nations. Opposition to the proposal came principally from Lord Robert Cecil, who spoke for Australia, which feared that the application of the proposed article might

refusal of this principle and the rejection of our claims to Kiaochow. Before the meeting on Monday, we ask you to tell us where we stand on that latter question." I replied to him that the explanations given by the Japanese delegation were not such as to displease the heads of government. But the Japanese expect to be heard this afternoon.

Mr. Lloyd George. If not, what will they do?

Mr. Balfour. I think they will make a protest against the refusal to accept the principle of racial equality. But if they aren't satisfied on Shantung, they could go much further.

President Wilson. Would they go as far as to withdraw from the League of Nations?

Mr. Balfour. Not if they expect a solution acceptable to them on the Kiaochow problem.

President Wilson. I can't return to America saying that I abandoned China. If the Japanese give up Kiaochow and content themselves with economic rights without any military advantage, we then would have the feeling that they are giving China better terms than the Germans did.

Mr. Balfour. That is what the Japanese promise.

President Wilson. That is not quite the opinion of our experts.

Mr. Balfour. Whatever the policy of Japan may have been in 1915, don't forget that it is not the same today. The government has changed; the military party is no longer in power. The men we are dealing with are ready to agree with the western powers to grant China reasonable treatment.

President Wilson. That is all very well. But I would like to see that in black and white.

Mr. Balfour. They will give you the same assurances as those in the memorandum which I sent you and which summarizes our conversation.

President Wilson. They want to keep their troops on the railway line?

Mr. Balfour. Temporarily.

President Wilson. What I will ask them is to be content with eco-

---

threaten its policy of total exclusion of oriental immigrants. When the Japanese presented a resolution for inclusion of the racial-equality article on April 11, 1919, Wilson, chairman of the League of Nations Commission, declared that the resolution had not passed because it had received only majority and not unanimous support. For documents relating to this subject, see the index references to Japan in PWW, Vols. 54-57. For the discussion at the meeting of April 11, 1919, see ibid., Vol. 57, pp. 259-66.

nomic rights. Later we can propose a general renunciation of special rights for foreigners in China.

Mr. Balfour. I think we can obtain assurances from the Japanese that they are content with purely economic advantages. They are prepared to give you the most explicit assurances. Authorize me to write to them that the statement of their intention to renounce all sovereignty has satisfied you, and that you object only to the military occupation of the railway and the organization of the police by the Japanese.[8] Lastly, I propose that you have a short conversation with them on this subject before the Plenary Session which takes place at three o'clock.

President Wilson. Very well; we may come to terms if there is agreement on the last point. But I don't want this question to be settled hastily, and I would prefer to see them tomorrow at leisure.

[8] Balfour's letter is printed in PPC, V, 325-26.

LII

Conversation between President Wilson and MM. Clemenceau, Lloyd George, Balfour, Baron Makino, and Viscount Chinda*

APRIL 29, 1919, 11 A.M.

President Wilson. I asked our Japanese colleagues to be here at ten o'clock, and I have just had an hour-long conversation with them. I told them that we take it that Japan is ready to restore to China everything that Germany possessed by virtue of the lease on Kiaochow, with the exception of a residential concession, which would be granted to Japan in the bay, and of the economic rights previously granted to the Germans. As I understand it, this would not include either the right to occupy militarily the railway line, or the right to establish and train the police force.

I called to the attention of our Japanese colleagues that, if they insisted on these last two points, they would be asking for more than the Germans ever possessed outside the leased territory proper. It would seem natural that the railway company should

*H., PPC, V, 327ff.

have the right to organize the line's police force. But I would oppose the insertion into the treaty of a clause which would appear to impose Japanese control beyond the strictly economic field.

Viscount Chinda. The Germans owned the line with extraterritoriality, which includes the right of policing.

Mr. Balfour. Didn't you tell me in our conversation that the land over which the railway passes will remain under Chinese sovereignty?

Viscount Chinda. The right of extraterritoriality exists for the railway.

President Wilson. Why? If the Americans constructed a railway in China, they would have only the rights of private property over this railway.

Viscount Chinda. By treaty, China agreed that we should participate in the policing of the line.

President Wilson. She agreed to give you more than she had previously conceded to the Germans?

Mr. Balfour. In my conversation with our Japanese colleagues on Saturday, didn't they say that Japan should succeed Germany in the railway company? The latter owned the majority of the shares; it seems obvious to me that that would not be enough to confer extraterritoriality. To grant extraterritoriality to a purely commercial enterprise seems to me to be a completely new principle.

President Wilson. I am also convinced that a deed of property can give no such right. Did Germany possess it?

Baron Makino. She did in fact.

President Wilson. You yourself acknowledge that she didn't have it in law.

Viscount Chinda. In all concessions granted to foreigners in China, the right of extraterritoriality exists.

President Wilson. In that case, it is a matter of places where the civilian life of a foreign population is protected by extraterritoriality. What I don't admit is that the same arrangement can be extended to administrative personnel dispersed along a railway line.

Viscount Chinda. Germany had the policing of the line. It must not be assumed that that police force will intervene outside the railway.

Mr. Lloyd George. In England, we have police who are placed under the authority of railway companies by a special arrangement with the Home Office. Likewise, on the docks, there are detachments of police who are under the authority of the administration of those docks. In the case we are concerned with today, couldn't we make an arrangement of the same kind? This would be no more a derogation of sovereignty for China than for England in similar cases.

President Wilson. The difference is that the railway company of Kiaochow would be in the hands of a foreign government. In the case you cite—and a similar one exists in the United States—the policeman remains legally under the authority of the local or national government.

If the majority of the stock of the company is in Japanese hands, Japan can without difficulty determine the arrangement for the policing of the line. Why insist that it must be the Japanese government that does what a Japanese majority of stockholders could easily do? It is an encroachment on the political rights of China, which changes nothing in the practical result.

Viscount Chinda. In fact, that can amount to the same thing; but the Chinese government could create difficulties.

President Wilson. What we are seeking is to remove all appearance of political domination from your action.

Viscount Chinda. This concerns an arrangement which China voluntarily accepted.

President Wilson. That is precisely what China disputes.

Viscount Chinda. I will note that there is reason to distinguish between the twenty-one demands and the railway convention, which is much posterior, since the latter dates from September 1918.

President Wilson. The convention is the consequence of the demands, in spite of the change of circumstances and, I acknowledge, of the disposition of the present Japanese government.

Viscount Chinda. I can assure you that, in the second case, no pressure was applied.

Baron Makino. When we speak of providing instructors for the police, that is obviously a vague term which can be abused. But we have no intention of doing what the Germans did in Turkey along that line.

President Wilson. It is difficult for me, considering public opinion in the United States, to accept such a settlement. I am looking for another way. I cannot hide from you the fact that American opinion is suspicious. I strongly desire to find a way out, whilst taking into account the position taken by the present Japanese government. But if the Japanese government insists on possessing rights that Germany herself did not have, I could not justify my approval in the eyes of the American public. They would say to me in the United States: "We never dreamed that you would support the claims of the Japanese to Kiaochow; now, you go further, you are granting them privileges Germany herself did not possess." By insisting on a right which would exceed that of providing instructors and policemen if they are asked of you, you are placing me in a difficult position.

Mr. Balfour. I am a bit surprised at what I hear when I recall our conversation of Saturday; our Japanese colleague indeed told me that China would regain her complete sovereignty in Shantung and that Japan would claim only economic rights. The only point of dispute seemed to be the temporary military occupation of the line. Now I no longer know where we stand.

Baron Makino. I do believe the question of the railway police was mentioned in our conversation of Saturday.

Mr. Balfour. The great point is the sovereignty of China. If it is clearly acknowledged, the rights of the administration and direction of the railway claimed by Japan are quite reasonable and similar to those that other groups of foreigners enjoy in China. I thought the only question pending was how long the temporary arrangement for policing and military occupation would continue along the Tsingtao line.

Baron Makino. I regret that misunderstanding; but we always asked to participate in the policing of the line and to provide instructors.

President Wilson. If you accept the military evacuation of Tsinan, why attach so much importance to that police question?

Baron Makino. About the military occupation, I am a bit surprised to have found the idea in your minds that it could be permanent. The concentration of Japanese troops on the railway line, which has attracted your attention, is precisely one of the steps towards a complete evacuation. On this point, then, there is no disagreement. There remains the question of the police force.

President Wilson. I will recall that, in those unfortunate twenty-one demands, there was one that provided for the establishment of a Japanese police force in certain regions or certain cities. That demand caused, you will remember, great irritation. If you insist, you won't avoid having the arrangement which you wish to institute along the Kiaochow line being associated with the memory of the twenty-one demands.

Viscount Chinda. There is a very great difference. It is not a matter of establishing a police force in a province or in a city, but only along the railway, and for its protection.

Mr. Lloyd George. Great Britain undertook to support the transfer of the rights of Germany to Japan. At the same time, she wishes to agree with the views of the United States. Can't we succeed here by applying the arrangement which is followed for the protection of railways in England and America? I understand very well that the Japanese don't have absolute confidence in the Chinese local administration. But if it was said that the railway police will belong to the company, including the training of the policemen, that would give you all you need.

I regard what Viscount Chinda said as very important—that is, that the control and protection of the line are all that Japan wants.

Viscount Chinda. From the practical point of view, the solution you propose would be satisfactory; but it compels us to revise our treaty with China, and it is on this point that we fear Japanese public opinion.

Mr. Lloyd George. Why not say that the clause of the treaty relating to the railway—which it is pointless to change—will be interpreted in the way I indicate?

President Wilson. We have to explain ourselves frankly: the convention of last September went beyond the German rights.

Viscount Chinda. That is not our opinion. Mr. Lloyd George's proposal is quite acceptable; but the revision of the treaty with China would place the Japanese government in a very difficult position.

President Wilson. American public opinion wouldn't admit an extension of the rights of Germany in favor of Japan.

Viscount Chinda. The difficulty is that you are interpreting the policing of the railway as an infringement on Chinese sovereignty. We don't think it is.

President Wilson. I accept the surveillance of the line by the company. What I dispute is the right of the Japanese government to make it a condition of the retrocession of Kiaochow to China.

Mr. Lloyd George. The Sino-Japanese treaty confines itself to saying that Japanese will have to be employed on that police force. I understand the attitude of the Japanese government, which cannot appear to be repudiating its treaty with China. But such as it is, the text has nothing excessive in it.

I propose once more to say that the Japanese employed on the police force will be appointed by the directors of the railway company; that amounts to the same thing, for the latter won't fail to communicate on this subject with their government.

President Wilson. I must explain my point of view once more: we are being asked to insert in the treaty with Germany an arrangement which would have the effect of increasing the rights previously possessed by the Germans in favor of the Japanese.

Mr. Lloyd George. Did the Germans have instructors for the railway police?

Viscount Chinda. They were called "advisers." For us, the possession of the railway entails extraterritoriality.

President Wilson. That is what I dispute. Extraterritoriality can only be applied to concessions; but in that case the entire civilian life and organization are involved.

Mr. Lloyd George. The text of the German lease of Kiaochow provides only for a Chinese police force along the railway.

Baron Makino. The question in itself is perhaps not very important. But we cannot appear to be renouncing our treaty with China.

Mr. Lloyd George. I regret having to insist so much. Couldn't we say, by way of interpreting the article in question, that the nomination of the policemen will belong to the directors of the company? That changes nothing in the treaty itself.

—Mr. Balfour presents a draft of a declaration: Japan respects the sovereignty of China in Shantung; her only desire is to succeed the Germans in the enjoyment of their economic rights. The clauses referring to the police aim solely at insuring the security of the railway.

Mr. Lloyd George. I would add a sentence about the intention to confer the task of organizing the police force on the railway company, as certain companies in America and England do.

President Wilson. There remains this difference, that our companies can enlist no foreigners in their police force. You would find no precedent in the West.

Mr. Lloyd George. Yes, but in many cases China employs foreigners, notably in the customs service.

President Wilson. Undoubtedly, but she chooses them herself, and voluntarily. I recognize with you that China is not in a normal condition.

Mr. Lloyd George. China's stagnation justifies a great part of what foreigners have done there. The Chinese are like the Arabs, a very talented race, but at a stage that doesn't allow them to progress further. China would have been destroyed by the Taiping Rebellion if Gordon hadn't been there to organize her army.[1] It must

---

[1] The Taiping Rebellion, 1850-1864. Maj. Charles George ("Chinese") Gordon, a British soldier of fortune, was involved in helping the Imperial army to put down the rebellion in 1863-1864.

be acknowledged that China isn't in the same situation as the great powers represented in this conference.

President Wilson. What I am saying is that I couldn't allow the United States to accept the sanction of the Sino-Japanese convention if it continued to give the Japanese, on certain points, more than the Germans possessed by virtue of their lease.

I believe what Baron Makino said about the military occupation.

Baron Makino. I said that the troops would be withdrawn.

Mr. Lloyd George. Can't we confine ourselves to stipulating, in the treaty with Germany, that the Germans' rights are transferred to Japan, and put off the details relating to the method of this transfer?

President Wilson. It is impossible to do that without knowing in advance what arrangement will follow the treaty.

Mr. Balfour. I will reread the draft of the declaration that we would ask the Japanese delegates to sign. It provides, in the first place, for the reestablishment of China's sovereignty over the entire Shantung Province; (2) the institution of a police force along the railway line, in the interest of the railway exclusively; (3) the appointment of the personnel of that police force by the railway company.

—The Japanese delegates examine the text of the statement.

President Wilson (*after a moment of conversation with the Japanese delegates*). Our Japanese colleagues tell me about their difficulty in appearing to abandon the treaty that Japan signed with China. Can't they declare that, in order to promote the success of the League of Nations and contribute to the peace of the world, they will gladly be content with the purely economic rights that will be granted them? Such a statement to their Parliament would only enhance their dignity, since Japan would only be bowing before the common ideal of civilized nations.

Baron Makino. For my part, I don't believe the arrangements we have requested for the railway police imply a derogation of China's sovereignty. It is a matter of insuring the protection of the railway in the interest of the company that will use it. I don't see where the offense lies against the national integrity of China, which herself employs so many foreigners in her public services.

President Wilson. According to the provision suggested by Mr. Balfour, the railway company would have the *option* of enrolling Japanese to serve in the police force: that formula would remove my objection. If the Japanese delegation wishes to have time to study this draft declaration, it could give us its reply this afternoon.

Baron Makino. And you would want our interpretation of the treaty to be published?

President Wilson. That is necessary for American public opinion.

Viscount Chinda. Yes, but that would have the opposite effect on Japanese public opinion.

President Wilson. Even with the preambles I propose?

Viscount Chinda. I fear a real danger from that direction.

Mr. Balfour. May I suggest the possibility of making such a statement in the form of an interview? In that way it would have the appearance of spontaneity, which might prevent the impression you fear.

—At the end of the session, M. Clemenceau raises the question of the credentials which will have to be presented by the German delegates in the name of Bavaria and Saxony.

—*It is decided that research will be done on the question whether these credentials are to be required.*

LIII

Conversation between President Wilson and MM. Clemenceau and Lloyd George*

APRIL 29, 1919, 4 P.M.

M. Clemenceau. Here is the question that comes up on the subject of the prisoners of war.[1] We are agreed on the obligation to return the prisoners to Germany upon ratification of the treaty; but, according to the commission, this question is connected to that of the labor to be provided by Germany for the reconstruction of the devastated regions.

*H., PPC, V, 327ff.

[1] The Three were reviewing, at the request of the Council of Foreign Ministers, a draft of articles on prisoners of war prepared by the Commission on Prisoners of War. Articles 1 and 6 were in dispute. Article 1 related to the use of certain prisoners of war in the reconstruction of the devastated areas; Article 6 related to the detention of certain German officers to insure the delivery to the Allies for trial of all prisoners of war accused of war crimes and atrocities. The draft clauses are printed in PPC, V, 339-42.

President Wilson. Mustn't we treat the two questions separately?
M. Clemenceau. That is my opinion.

—M. Cahen-Salvador, president of the Commission on Prisoners of War, is introduced.

M. Cahen-Salvador. The commission thought, in the event you decided that we can require Germany to provide us with labor for the work of reconstruction, it would be desirable to combine the transport of prisoners of war to Germany and that of German workers to France. That combination would have the effect of delaying the freeing of German prisoners of war.

M. Clemenceau. We don't have to get into this business of train schedules. Once the peace is signed, we must free the prisoners of war; is it necessary, in the clause relating to the prisoners, to speak of the labor which will be provided later?

M. Cahen-Salvador. The two questions are connected, for the prisoners of war are right now working on the reconstruction of the devastated regions. We have tried to keep two simultaneous operations parallel.

M. Clemenceau. When the war is over, and the peace is signed, we cannot keep the prisoners; that would be slavery. As for German manpower, that is a question we will consider at Versailles.

M. Cahen-Salvador. Will you not compel Germany to provide manpower?

M. Clemenceau. No, it is a subject of negotiation.

President Wilson. That is really what we mean.

M. Clemenceau. We cannot do what the commission proposes. We shall return the prisoners of war, purely and simply, and then we'll make an agreement about manpower.

Mr. Lloyd George. What is proposed here was done as a matter of course two or three thousand years ago.

President Wilson. I see in the report that M. Cahen-Salvador presents to us a clause which would give us the right to retain German officer prisoners of war as hostages to guarantee the delivery by the Germans of individuals charged with crimes against international law. That, again, would take us back two thousand years.

Mr. Lloyd George. I can't conceive of the usefulness of a clause of this kind towards the present government of Germany.

President Wilson. Moreover, what would we do with these hostages? We certainly don't intend to shoot them if the Germans don't deliver the accused individuals to us; we could do nothing with them, and the result would be nil.

M. Clemenceau. We can keep only those against whom there is a presumption of crime.

M. Cahen-Salvador. The proposal in question was made by the British delegation.

Mr. Lloyd George. I feel myself all the more free to reject it.

M. Cahen-Salvador. The idea was this. Numerous crimes, of which we have proof, were committed against our prisoners of war in Germany. In cases of this kind, if the sanction is not effective, that will be a true weakness of the policy adopted by the Allied Powers. Amongst our prisoners of war, we have German officers who belong to that military caste which bears the responsibility for the crimes committed. We demand that the culprits be handed over to us individually. If they are not handed over, the sanction we apply preserves the principle.

Mr. Lansing opposed this plan by using, as was done a moment ago, the word "hostages." The idea of taking hostages was absent from the minds of those who proposed that clause. They wanted only to provide us with a means of hastening Germany's delivery of the real culprits. If one objects to the arbitrary retention of German officers who are prisoners of war, one could keep only those who committed offenses against discipline; in short, it is a favor done to them to release them immediately.

Mr. Lloyd George. I cannot support that proposal.

M. Clemenceau. It is not possible to punish a man for the crime of another. We will prosecute the criminals. We have, or we will have, the names of those who mistreated our prisoners. As for the means of pressure, we are using the same ones in this case as for the execution of all the other clauses of the treaty. But I don't accept the method which is proposed to us.

—M. Cahen-Salvador withdraws.

M. Clemenceau. We have to take a decision on the clauses of the treaty relating to Luxembourg.

President Wilson. What is this about?

M. Clemenceau. Only to say that Luxembourg has nothing to do with Germany, and that all the treaties giving Germany advantages in Luxembourg are and will remain abrogated.

Mr. Lloyd George. Have the Belgians seen this text?

Sir Maurice Hankey. They are represented on the commission.

—*The text relating to Luxembourg is approved.*

M. Clemenceau. I return to a question which has already been raised—that of the credentials of the Serbs, Croats and Slovenes.

After examination, it was acknowledged that, by accepting these credentials, we are by that very fact recognizing the Kingdom of the Serbs, Croats and Slovenes, without needing to make any formal statement.

Mr. Lloyd George. This extricated us from the difficulties that we feared.

—The delegates of Belgium, MM. Hymans, Van den Heuvel, and Vandervelde, are introduced.*

President Wilson. Will M. Hymans explain to us the observations of the Belgian delegation on the clauses relating to reparation?

M. Hymans. Soon after having learned of the text accepted by the great powers, we wrote two letters to M. Clemenceau on April 24.[2] The first requested the insertion of two or three new clauses in the treaty. The second asked that an arrangement be made amongst the Allies in order to permit Belgium to receive, by priority, an advance of two and a half billion [Belgian] francs out of the first payments made by Germany; these two and a half billions will not be used for the reimbursement of sums lent to Belgium by the Allies during the war.

The new clauses requested are the following:

(1) reimbursement of Belgium's war costs;
(2) reimbursement of the costs of feeding the Belgian population;
(3) reimbursement of the expenses of establishing the Belgian government on French territory. These expenses were covered by loans made by the Allies, the repayment of which we would like to speed up.

We add here compensation for the loss suffered by the Belgian government at the time of the redemption of marks introduced into Belgium by the Germans at the forced rate of 1.25 francs and reimbursement of the interprovincial loan made in order to pay the indemnities imposed on Belgian cities or provinces by Germany. We must also mention aid to the communes for their extraordinary war expenses, which amount to about one billion francs.

Is it necessary to recall the special situation of Belgium created by the international statute under which she lived before the war and the violation of her neutrality by Germany? By the Declara-

*H., *PPC*, V, 344ff.

[2] About these letters and the following discussion, see Marks, *Innocent Abroad*, pp. 190-91.

tion of Sainte-Adresse,³ France, England, and Russia committed themselves, from the beginning of the war, not to lay down arms until Belgium had recovered her complete independence and been amply indemnified. President Wilson's seventh point promises Belgium the most complete restoration.

The situation of our country is such that we could not take responsibility for bringing back to her a treaty which didn't grant her the favorable treatment we are asking. Belgium is waiting. Our industries have stopped and everyone asks: "Will we receive what was promised us?" Without that assurance, it is impossible to revive our economy. The danger would be great if the problem remained without solution. Our working class has behaved admirably since the Armistice; but it is anxiously awaiting your decisions.

Mr. Lloyd George. M. Hymans has just asked two different questions. One is easy to settle: Belgium asks to receive by priority two and a half billions from the first payments the Germans will make; there is no problem there, and the sum seems very reasonable to us. But in the second category of questions, the difficulty is great.

Is M. Hymans asking that the costs of the war be reimbursed to all the Allies, or to Belgium alone, by a privileged clause? M. Hymans knows that we all have parliaments to which we are responsible. Before the British Parliament, I had to resist a demand of this kind, and to make it understood that it was impossible to make the Germans pay all we had spent during the war. Once this principle is laid down, I don't see how one could make an exception for Belgium. Undoubtedly, the French Parliament, as well as the British Parliament, would protest against this preferential treatment; we couldn't meet all the claims that might arise.

We know the sufferings and merits of Belgium; I am entirely of opinion that we must grant her the advance she asks of us. But to reimburse all her war costs is impossible.

M. Hymans. They would not amount to more than five billions.

Mr. Lloyd George. In certain respects, it would be advantageous to us to give you satisfaction. It was we who lent that money, and we would rather the Germans returned it to us. But I don't believe our people would understand if a privileged treatment was granted to one of the belligerents. Isn't the case of Serbia similar to yours? She was completely invaded and devastated, even more than Belgium; she can present us with the same request, The next day it will be Rumania. France too was invaded, and

³ The declaration was actually signed on February 14, 1916. *Ibid.*, pp. 22-24.

she has suffered terribly. But she renounces claiming reimbursement of her war costs. If we begin to reopen the list of categories, it will have to be done for everyone on an equal footing. I don't dispute Belgium's priority for the one hundred million pounds sterling that she claims immediately. But I don't see how we could admit to our list special Belgian claims which couldn't be admitted for other countries.

M. Van den Heuvel. Mr. Lloyd George just said that there is a distinction to be made between the two parts of our request; that he sees no difficulty in granting us the first part, which asks a first payment of two and a half billion francs for Belgium, but that he foresees great difficulties for the second part. What does it involve? M. Hymans spoke of the reimbursement of our war costs. What do we mean by that? By that we mean the expenses caused by the war, rather than war costs proper. Our war costs, in the strict sense of the word, including pensions, do not amount to more than 3.3 billions. But the war and invasion imposed other expenses on us.

When the Germans came into our country, the government had to move to Le Havre. Hence expenses which were not war costs in the strict sense of the word. Feeding the Belgian population cost very dearly. It must not be forgotten that the great mass of that population of seven million inhabitants stayed in Belgium and was only fed with aid from abroad and from the Belgian government. Germany, which had the duty to feed those people, did not do it; we had to do it ourselves, with your aid—and we have particularly to thank the United States for the cooperation she gave us. But the Belgian government itself had to do much; its expenses under this heading amounted to 2.75 billions.[4]

That, and the costs of the administration of our government in Le Havre, are the consequences of the war, although they may not be war costs, strictly speaking; it is legitimate to claim reimbursement for them from the Germans. France and England were very willing to lend us the money we needed—hence a debt of five and a half billion francs. That sum was only used for the objects I have just indicated. If we cannot claim reimbursement for them, we will remain debtors of our allies without any compensation on the part of Germany. Our creditors could, if they wished, ask Germany for that money; by forbidding us to do it ourselves, they would prevent us from reimbursing them.

The list of reparations first established acknowledged our

---

[4] For an excellent account of all this, see George H. Nash, *The Life of Herbert Hoover: The Humanitarian, 1914-1917* (New York and London, 1988).

right; but the articles which gave us satisfaction have been deleted. Thus the means of paying our creditors was taken away from us.

I could understand if Mr. Lloyd George said that he accepts the payment of our victualing and of our costs of administration, whilst setting aside the reimbursement of our war costs proper, since France, England, and the United States have been obliged, for their part, to renounce this reimbursement. In reality, certain war expenses, and not the least important, will be reimbursed: they are the costs assignable to military pensions. Nothing is more legitimate; one cannot deny that pensions are an important part of the charges resulting from the war. Why aren't we asking, purely and simply, for the reimbursement of pensions? It is because we are in a special situation. Mr. Lloyd George said: "What will I reply to my Parliament if I am asked what the special privilege granted to Belgium means?" Couldn't one rather ask the opposite question if that privilege was refused us?

In the eyes of the entire world, there is an essential difference between Belgium's situation and that of all other countries. In Belgium's case, the cause of the war has an exceptional character. Serbia was spoken of; what comparison can be made between the way in which the war began in Serbia and the way it began in Belgium? As a consequence of our international status before 1914 and the violation of our neutrality, our situation is such and so obvious that we, so to speak, served as a standard for all the nations which, one after another, entered the war. The atrocities committed by the invader, the loyalty with which we fulfilled our commitments, made Belgium's name a veritable symbol.

Not only was the cause of the war different, but the obligations of the powers towards us have no equivalent in any other case. One never had to take the same obligations towards Serbia that one took towards us. We were told more than once: "You will be amply indemnified." Mr. Lloyd George himself made a statement along these lines in his address of January 5, 1918. The first of the peace terms—constantly placed at the top by all the politicians of the Entente—was the complete restoration of Belgium, not only from the political point of view, but from the economic point of view. It has to extend to everything that was to be repaired in our country.

I believe I have answered Mr. Lloyd George's objections.

Mr. Lloyd George. The guarantee given by the British government cannot go beyond the limit of the possible. That limit is Germany's capacity to pay. What did the Belgian experts say about this subject?

M. Loucheur. M. Despret, who represented Belgium on our Reparation Commission, always agreed with us about the limit of Germany's capacity to pay.

M. Vandervelde. I won't go back to the details. But I am aware of the seriousness of the hour for our country, aware of the seriousness of the refusal of requests presented with extreme moderation, the sole object of which is to get Belgium out of an untenable situation.

At the present time, we have 800,000 unemployed who live on an allowance of seven to fourteen francs per week. The cost of living in Belgium is three times what it was in 1914. Nevertheless, order and calm still reign there. What has maintained them is, first, the strong organization of our workers' party, which I am proud to say is the most powerful guarantee of order in our country; in the second place, the formation of a government of national unity for the economic reconstruction of the country. If we want order to be maintained, this government must be able to live. If satisfaction is not given us today, the existence of the Belgian government will become impossible.

I cannot be suspected of extreme views. I represent the socialist working class, which is opposed to all demands that could be called imperialistic. All the Belgian Socialist party asks is the freedom of the Scheldt in time of war as in time of peace, a free reconciliation between Luxembourg and Belgium, and the fulfillment of the solemn promises made to Belgium by the Declaration of Sainte Adresse and in President Wilson's Fourteen Points.

I am told that you will agree to grant us the two and a half billions we are asking out of the first German payments. But you are surprised that we should ask for special treatment for our war costs; you answer us that, if you grant them to us, all the others would ask to be treated in the same manner. I am extremely surprised at this reply. Can you compare Serbia to Belgium? When you entered the war, you did Serbia an immense service, and she comes out of this war with considerably augmented territories and cuts the figure of a great power. By entering the war, it was Belgium that rendered an immense service to the Allies.

If you speak of Rumania, of Italy, I will recall that they stipulated benefits for themselves by treaty; these benefits have been granted to them. It would be a deep disappointment for the Belgian people if they thought that, because they did not put a price tag on their aid, they will remain without right to reparation.

Our war was not even a war of national defense. It was caused by the violation of a right and by our fidelity to the obligations connected to this right. Hence the obligation of the powers towards us. When I heard it said a moment ago: "There is no reason to grant Belgium special treatment," I remembered what I heard in Russia at the beginning of the revolution. The most extreme Russian pacifists—those who set forth the statement "no annexations, no indemnities"—admitted only a single exception, and that exception was in Belgium's favor. Chancellor von Bethmann Hollweg acknowledged before an open session of the Reichstag that Germany had wronged Belgium and owed her reparation. If you show yourselves less fair than the Russians and the Germans, what could we say to the Belgian people?

Mr. Lloyd George assures us that he could not make the British Parliament understand the privileged treatment that would be granted us. We would have much trouble in making the Belgian Parliament understand why it had been refused us. What we are asking for is not an advantage; it is the very condition of our existence. In the speech I made a few days ago in the Plenary Session about working conditions, I said that the Belgian workers, having to choose between the English method and the Russian method, had chosen the English method. Mr. Lloyd George told me that he was proud to see that the Belgian workers acknowledged the excellence of the British method. But for that to last, it is absolutely necessary that you help us; the future of our workers and of our very country is involved here.

—After consultation with the financial experts:

M. Hymans. We have thought about the proposals made to us: they would allow two and a half billions of the first German payments to go to Belgium. Moreover, the cost of provisioning the Belgian population would be entered in the list of damages entitled to reparation. But we know nothing of the percentage that will be granted us of the whole of Germany's payments, nor the time necessary for those payments.

M. Clemenceau. You are here in the same situation as we; we know no more about it than you.

M. Hymans. In these circumstances, the Belgian government, which held a cabinet meeting on this subject, could not change its position without a new consultation. We therefore have to refer the matter to our government and Parliament. I have nothing more to say.

President Wilson. But we are going to meet with the Germans immediately. We fear you might be absent at that time.

M. Hymans. We are not leaving the conference. But we must refer the matter to our Parliament before taking a decision. We cannot assume the responsibility alone.

President Wilson. If your Parliament doesn't approve the proposal, what will happen? What you just said is serious. I hope our Belgian friends will think again. Belgium is asking what we have unanimously acknowledged to be impossible; we are making no exception against her. We have the most sincere desire to fulfill our obligations to the Belgian people.

Concerning the reimbursement of war costs, I will recall that the Armistice was based on certain statements which I was authorized to make to the Germans in the name of all the Allied and Associated Powers. In those statements, we gave a definition of damages entitled to reparation, and that definition binds us. I don't see how we could deviate from it.

M. Hymans. There is something that doesn't seem to me to strike sufficiently the minds of the statesmen present here: it is the fact that Belgium entered the war against her will and without advancing any claim. She entered the war by the fact of the violation of her neutrality by Germany. Germany demanded passage of her, and Belgium, faithful to her international obligations, refused it. In that way, she rendered a great service to the entire world, and she did it without laying down any terms.

Thus, Belgium had to make war. For that reason, she was compelled to borrow; she owes five to six billions to her allies, and she could not ask of Germany, which violated the law towards her, the compensation which is due her?

Isn't it true that the Belgian cause was like the flag of the Allies from the moral point of view during the entire war? That is why France, England, and Russia took commitments towards us, the equivalent of which exists for no other power; they promised us not to make peace without the complete restoration of Belgium. We could bring before you here a hundred declarations which—all of them—say: "The first of our claims is the restoration of Belgium." And our people would be faced today with a treaty in which it would appear to them that there is nothing for them, except reparation defined in the strictest limits, as for the other belligerents? We cannot accept responsibility for that. Our duty is to take the question before our Parliament. In what is perhaps the gravest circumstance in our history, can we turn to the Belgian people and say: "You must be content with that"? We cannot do it.

Once informed, the country can agree, if it wishes to. Perhaps it will be compelled to do so because it is a small country. But small though it is, it is aware of its rights, and we cannot let it to be said that we abandoned it.

M. Clemenceau. I will remind you that you won't be in a situation inferior to that of any other country. Your moral standing remains very high. You say you will have nothing; but you will have what we ourselves will receive. If I myself had taken an intransigent position, as you are doing at this time, I would have had several opportunities to break up the negotiations. But I am thinking, above all else, of the necessities of the present hour and of those of the future. Can we say that we are going towards peace tomorrow? We can only sign a treaty of peace. Peace must be carried out, must be lived, and to do this our peoples must stay hand in hand, failing which we risk falling into the ravages of anarchy, sad examples of which we unfortunately see.

I wasn't always satisfied with the solutions I had to accept. But, thinking of the higher interest, I said nothing. I don't know what promises were made to you that are not being kept today. On the other hand, I remember a discussion last summer with the Belgian Chief of Staff, at the Supreme War Council, which I prefer not to return to. Do you find that we did not give you enough consideration? If you come to ask us to help you, I don't say no.

Our parliaments, as you know, all believe we won't be given enough. Some newspapers, sometimes supported by persons in very high places, tell me every day that I am not doing enough for my country. I am doing my duty, and that is enough for me.

Be certain that you won't find us indifferent to your difficulties. We are convinced that we have done nothing against the rights of Belgium. The necessities of tomorrow will bind us as much as those of yesterday, and I am thinking, above all, of tomorrow's peace. It would be a pity to see you leave here slamming the doors. I believe you will do well to consider the situation of your country in the light of the political forces of tomorrow.

M. Hymans. In order to have the support of the Belgian people, who would be deeply disappointed with what we would bring them today, we must be able to promise them something more. After all, France is recovering Alsace-Lorraine; she will have the coal mines of the Saar. Belgium will have nothing.

M. Clemenceau. You forget that France also has her devastations, for which you will not easily find the equivalent.

M. Hymans. All we are asking for amounts to about five billions. Our debt to you amounts to five or six billions.

Mr. Lloyd George. What is the meaning of your protest? Does it mean that, if Belgium isn't satisfied, she will make a separate peace.

M. Hymans. It simply means that we cannot sign before having put the question before our Parliament.

Mr. Lloyd George. Will you be here Saturday?

M. Hymans. We cannot say.

Mr. Lloyd George. But in that case, we couldn't present any claims to Germany in your name.

M. Clemenceau. The question arises in an even more urgent manner: the Germans are arriving this evening. The day after tomorrow, they will present their credentials to us and will ask us for ours; what shall I answer for Belgium?

M. Hymans. If our demands are late, it is not our fault. It is only since last Friday that we have had the text of the provisions relating to reparation before us. We answered you quickly in our two memoranda of April 24. If we were not heard earlier, we are not responsible for that.

M. Clemenceau. I am not making any reproach. I am only stating that the authenticity of credentials will be examined on Thursday.

M. Hymans. We shall hurry.

Mr. Lloyd George. I wish very much that we could demand that Germany pay for the Belgian war debt. But I don't favor asking her to pay for the cost of victualing.

—After consultation, it is decided that the representatives of Belgium will telegraph their government and ask for an immediate reply.[5]

[5] The reader will have noticed that Wilson, who was Belgium's strongest friend at the conference, participated hardly at all in this lively debate. He had suffered what was almost certainly a small stroke the day before and was presumably barely able to follow the conversation. About Wilson's illness of April 28, see the essays printed as appendixes in *PWW*, Vol. 58. For a fanciful and highly satirical account of this meeting by Keynes, see Marks, pp. 192-95.

LIV

Conversation between President Wilson and MM. Clemenceau and Lloyd George*

APRIL 30, 1919, 10:30 A.M.

M. Clemenceau. Today M. Jules Cambon will have Brockdorff-Rantzau informed that he will expect him tomorrow morning at

*H., *PPC*, V, 352ff.

the Trianon Palace with his credentials. We'll see what these papers will be, and if there is reason to raise the question of Bavaria and Saxony.

Mr. Lloyd George. It would be better if M. Jules Cambon was accompanied by the representatives of the other powers. For instance, we could be represented by Lord Hardinge. We could speak to M. Cambon about it.

—M. Cambon is summoned.

—Reading of a clause of the preliminaries of peace fixing the boundaries within which Germany will be permitted to establish airfields.[1]

President Wilson. I don't believe this text takes sufficient account of the fact that aviation will be one of the great means of transportation of the future.

Mr. Lloyd George. I also believe that we cannot compel Germany to have airfields situated only at great distances from her borders, and I would propose to reduce the distance fixed to that which was provided for the disarmed zone of the right bank of the Rhine—fifty kilometers.

President Wilson. But, then, that would be useless. Besides, I don't see the utility of this measure in any case. I propose to omit the article.

M. Clemenceau. For my part, I see no problem in that.

Here is another article which provides for the payment by the Germans of the expenses of the control commissions which will function to assure the execution of the treaty.

President Wilson. What will be the duration of these payments?

Sir Maurice Hankey. The existence of the commission is provided only for a period of a few months.

—*The article is adopted.*

Mr. Lloyd George. We have a memorandum from the Japanese in which they ask to sit on the Reparation Commission. The objection I have to make is the same as for Serbia: it would be one more vote on the commission without an important corresponding interest. It is dangerous to multiply the votes in a commission which decides by majority.

President Wilson. M. Loucheur proposes that Serbia be admitted in the place of Belgium when the commission discusses questions relative to Austria-Hungary. Japan would take the same place

---

[1] Article 41, in the aerial terms, which prohibited the establishment by Germany of airfields and dirigible sheds within 150 kilometers of any frontier.

when questions relative to maritime losses, which concern Belgium only very little, are discussed.

—*This proposal is adopted.*

Mr. Lloyd George. What shall we do about Italy? The question is pressing.

M. Clemenceau. Must the Italians be notified that we are making contact with the Germans tomorrow?

Mr. Lloyd George. I would tell them nothing. They made no reply to the compromise proposal I made to them, but I am convinced they will end by accepting it. In his speech in Montecitorio, M. Orlando said that we had proposed to establish Fiume as a free city in exchange for concessions in Dalmatia; this opens the way to the compromise I hope for.[2]

President Wilson. As far as I am concerned, I declare that Italy can have all she can obtain by a plebiscite. On that condition, I don't see any harm in her occupying all the territories she wants.

Mr. Lloyd George. The Italians are invoking an argument other than that of the will of the people; they are speaking of Italy's security.

President Wilson. That is an argument which doesn't hold. It would obviously be very dangerous for them to refuse plebiscites, because it would mean admitting the weakness of their claims.

[2] Orlando's speech to the Italian Chamber of Deputies which sat in the Palace of Montecitorio. Orlando had delivered the same speech to separate sessions of the Italian Chamber of Deputies and the Senate in the afternoon and evening, respectively, of April 29. Wilson's public statement of April 23 on the Italian territorial claims, he declared, had made it necessary for him to renew his mandate from Parliament and the nation before continuing negotiations in Paris. After appealing for "calm and serenity" on the part of all concerned, he proceeded to a detailed exposition of his negotiations on Italy's territorial claims with Wilson and with Lloyd George and Clemenceau since mid-March. He asserted that it was only after meeting with Wilson on April 14 and after reading Wilson's memorandum of that date that he had realized that their positions were irreconcilable. He said that Clemenceau and Lloyd George remained prepared to honor their commitments to Italy made in the Treaty of London, but could not accept Italy's claim to Fiume. He was somewhat vague as to the course he proposed to follow in the future: he declared, on the one hand, that Italy must and would remain loyal to its wartime allies, but he made it clear, on the other hand, that Italy would not accept a peace settlement which did not essentially meet all of her just claims. Following his speech to the Chamber of Deputies, that body passed a resolution of confidence in the government by a vote of 382 to forty. The Senate passed a similar resolution unanimously. Summaries with quotations appear in the London *Times*, May 1, 1919, and in the *New York Times*, April 30-May 1, 1919.

M. Clemenceau. A dispatch which we received indicates that the Italians are sending a battleship to Smyrna.

Mr. Lloyd George. This is dangerous, and it would seem that the Italians want to cause a crisis. It is better that we don't concern ourselves with them.

President Wilson. They are supported by their Parliament.

Mr. Lloyd George. Remember that Baron Sonnino was against the trip to Rome and in favor of a compromise. If he should return here, and if we didn't manage to agree, that would be worse than anything, and we, bound by our treaty, would be in a very difficult situation. If they don't want to come, for goodness sake let's leave them where they are. If they come to ask us to carry out purely and simply the Treaty of London, we are compelled to do it. I am not anxious for that to happen. The present situation is bad but not irreparable.

For the moment, it seems to me impossible to present Italy's claims to Germany.

President Wilson. In the conversation I had with M. Orlando before all of us became engaged in the debate, he stated to me that, if Italy could receive only what I was inclined to grant her, she would be compelled to dissociate herself from us, and in this case she would find herself, he said, outside the law. I said to him: "Nothing would be more tragic when we are dealing amongst friends." He replied that that seemed inevitable to him, since he only had the choice between dying honorably or living by a shameful compromise.

The Italian question leads us to another, about which we have not yet taken a decision—that of financial interdependence. Must we say that Germany, Austria-Hungary, Turkey, and Bulgaria are jointly responsible for damages?

Mr. Lloyd George. In any case, it would be necessary to compare the damages with the acquisitions made by certain states. Serbia, Rumania are acquiring considerable territories which were part of the Austro-Hungarian monarchy and which will come to them free of all debt.

President Wilson. It is certain that, if you admit the principle of interdependence, it tends to reduce what France or Great Britain themselves can receive.

Mr. Lloyd George. In any case, Germany must know exactly, at the time we are negotiating with her, what she is held responsible for. Mustn't we take the opinion of our experts on that question?

President Wilson. It is they who have referred the matter to us.

Mr. Lloyd George. Then I would be inclined to accept the principle, whilst stipulating that the calculation will be made in debit and credit, as M. Orlando proposed. Thus, Serbia would have the right, on the one side, to reparation for the damages caused to her by the invasion, and, on the other side, it would be calculated what the union to Serbia of large territories, which are repudiating any participation in the Austro-Hungarian debt, represents from the financial point of view. Then we will see on which side the difference lies.

M. Clemenceau. Will we allow Italy to claim reparation for all her damages from Germany?

Mr. Lloyd George. That wouldn't be very fair.

For the division amongst us of payments made by Germany, I propose to decide that it will be made in proportion to the claims which will be approved by the Reparation Commission. This conforms absolutely to the principle we accepted and has the advantage of not making us announce publicly any set proportion before the necessary investigations have taken place.

—*This proposal is adopted.*

M. Clemenceau. On the question of interdependence, I ask to consult my financial advisers, and I will give you my answer tomorrow.

—President Wilson reads the text of the articles of the treaty relating to China.[3]

Mr. Lloyd George. I will see how our claim concerning Shameen is justified. I don't understand very well what that means.

M. Clemenceau. Likewise with us for the German properties in China, which this text claims in our name.

President Wilson. I have to present to you the request of the press, which would like to see something of the presentation of the preliminaries of peace to the German delegates. It appears that admission of the journalists has been provided for only behind a hedge, from which they could see the Germans march past; they ask to be present at the presentation of the document, if it is possible.

M. Clemenceau. It seems to me quite impossible to admit them to the room where the presentation will take place. We can think

[3] These provided for the return to China by Germany of all concessions heretofore enjoyed by Germany, except for German concessions in Shantung Province and certain properties in Shameen, or Canton. These articles are printed in *PWW*, Vol. 58, pp. 255-57.

about how they might be given the opportunity to see a bit more than from behind the hedge.

Mr. Lloyd George. Perhaps they could be put in the room that adjoins the one where the Supreme War Council met, which is separated from it by a glass partition. But I don't like the idea of exhibiting the German plenipotentiaries as in a menagerie, and, despite my small sympathy for them, I understand the objection they could make to it.

M. Clemenceau. I also fear that exhibition might be in very bad taste.

President Wilson. If I insist, it is because the representatives of the press are bent on it, and I fear we will have difficulties.

Mr. Lloyd George. These difficulties mustn't be exaggerated. In a question like this one, the public is not behind the press.

M. Clemenceau. Perhaps they could be admitted to the great hall of the Trianon Palace from which they would see the German plenipotentiaries, as well as ourselves, enter and leave the room. That question must be studied by the Secretariat.

—M. Jules Cambon is introduced.

M. Clemenceau. We are asking you to see Brockdorff-Rantzau tomorrow for the presentation of credentials, with your colleagues on the Committee on the Verification of Powers. How many are you?

M. Jules Cambon. Four: Marquis Salvago Raggi, Mr. Balfour, who is represented by Mr. Barnes, Mr. Henry White, and myself.

Sir Maurice Hankey. According to the rules of the conference, it must be plenipotentiaries who present the credentials.

M. Clemenceau. Then the best thing is to say that M. Cambon will be accompanied by Messrs. White and Balfour. There can be no question of an Italian representative, since Italy, for the moment, is absent. Do that tomorrow morning and come in the afternoon to report to us about what took place.

Mr. Lloyd George. Mustn't we also try to know the intentions of the Germans concerning the publication of the treaty, in order to regulate our own conduct according to what we are able to learn of their frame of mind?

M. Clemenceau. I will ask M. Cambon to try to inform us about that.

—M. Jules Cambon withdraws.

APRIL 30, 1919

THE QUESTION OF SHANTUNG

—Baron Makino and Viscount Chinda are introduced.*

Baron Makino. We are ready to make the statement that was proposed to us.[4]

Viscount Chinda. But we believe it preferable to make it in the form of an interview, to avoid offending Japanese public opinion.

President Wilson. We will set down in the minutes that the representatives of Japan were invited to inform us of their interpretation of the treaty and the policy their government intends to follow, and that they did so in a way that satisfies us.

Viscount Chinda. However, if the Chinese government, which must ratify the appointments of policemen made by the railway company, doesn't act in good faith and creates difficulties, we will be compelled to invoke our treaty with China.

President Wilson. In that case, you could have recourse to the League of Nations.

Viscount Chinda. Undoubtedly, but the text on which we will be compelled to rely will always be that of our treaty.

President Wilson. As you know, the twenty-one demands presented to China at the beginning of the war produced a very painful impression on the government of the United States. Now, your agreement of 1915 with China derives from the twenty-one demands, and that agreement is mentioned in the convention of 1918. We want that association of ideas and of texts to disappear as much as possible. That is why, in case of conflict, I propose that the League of Nations lend you its good offices to insure the execution of what will be agreed on between us here, and which will be written into a treaty of which the Covenant of the League of Nations constitutes a part.

Viscount Chinda. I don't believe, moreover, that the case will arise; but I wanted to envisage the possibility. We will ask you to use

---

*H., *PPC*, V, 363ff.

[4] At this point he read the following statement:
"The policy of Japan is to hand back the Shantung Peninsula in full sovereignty to China retaining only the economic privileges granted to Germany and the right to establish a settlement under the usual conditions at Tsingtao.

"The owners of the Railway will use special Police only to ensure security for traffic. They will be used for no other purpose.

"The Police Force will be composed of Chinese, and such Japanese instructors as the Directors of the Railway may select will be appointed by the Chinese Government." Printed in *ibid.*, p. 257.

your influence with the Chinese government so that the convention can function in the best possible way.

President Wilson. I would be acting neither in a friendly way nor frankly towards you if I seemed to sanction previous obligations which we don't recognize. But I will always do what I can to avoid difficulties and conflicts.

Do you want your declaration to take the form of an interview?

Baron Makino. It is important for Japanese public opinion to avoid the impression that a declaration of this kind was imposed upon us. That is very important for Japan's foreign relations in the future.

Viscount Chinda. We declare that the commitment taken in this semiofficial form will bind our government.

—President Wilson asks for some information about details, notably about the location of the concession asked by the Japanese in the Bay of Kiaochow. The Japanese delegates assure him that that concession does not include the part of the coast which was fortified by the Germans.

Mr. Lloyd George. Another question which concerns Japan is that of the appointment of a Japanese representative to the Reparation Commission. What was suggested to us is that Japan can take the place of Belgium whenever it examines questions of compensation for losses suffered at sea.

Baron Makino. Couldn't we use a broader formula and say that Japan will be admitted every time a question involving her comes up? We had nationals in Germany; the Germans had property in Japan.

Mr. Lloyd George. The questions that that situation can provoke are outside the province of the Reparation Commission.

Viscount Chinda. Article 13 of the financial clauses gives the Reparation Commission the power to claim enemy properties in China. This concerns us directly.

Mr. Lloyd George. We can indicate that you will have the right to be present every time a question relating to the application of that article will be raised.

President Wilson. I want our Japanese colleagues fully to understand our intention, which is not to increase the number of members of the commission.

Viscount Chinda. We accept the proposal which Mr. Lloyd George just formulated.

I have a last question to raise; it is that of the prisoners of war. We have taken 4,000 prisoners from Germany; the Germans have no Japanese prisoners. Thus, there is no compensation for the

expenses which we have incurred in this regard, and we are asking that they be reimbursed.
Mr. Lloyd George. You are inheriting the rights of the Germans in the Shantung Peninsula; you can apply the costs of the support of prisoners of war against that acquisition.
Baron Makino. We don't accept that point of view; they are two different questions.
Mr. Lloyd George. There would be no great difficulty in giving you satisfaction. But the danger is that the principle will be generalized if we admit a claim like this one. If we ourselves, who had many more German civilian prisoners than the Germans had English civilian prisoners, should ask to be reimbursed, we could arrive at considerable sums.
Baron Makino. If you fear a serious difficulty, we won't insist.

LV

Conversation between President Wilson and MM. Clemenceau and Lloyd George*

APRIL 30, 1919, 4 P.M.

—Mr. Lloyd George reads a memorandum from Mr. Lamont:[1] M. Hymans received a telegram from his government, which states that it cannot accept our proposals without the reimbursement for the marks within a period of two years. Two Belgian ministers are leaving for Paris. Mr. Lamont told M. Hymans that it would be impossible to grant Belgium compensation for the mark at 1.25 francs. Anyway, M. Hymans understands this.

M. Clemenceau. We have news from Italy. It seems there is some prospect of working something out. M. Crespi and Count Bonin Longare are in contact with M. Tardieu. I believe their present

---

*H., *PPC*, V, 368ff.

[1] About the writing of this memorandum, which is missing, by Wilson's chief economic advisers, see the extract from the Diary of V. C. McCormick printed at April 30, 1919, *PWW*, Vol. 58, p. 262. McCormick was disturbed because he thought that Wilson had not "sized the situation up," and because he, McCormick, thought that it was "most important to give the fullest opportunity for Belgium to present its case."

idea would be to accept Fiume as a free city whilst asking that Zara and Sebenico be placed under an Italian mandate.

President Wilson. Such a mandate would only be a camouflage for sovereignty. They want above all to save face.

Mr. Lloyd George. The question of the credentials of the German plenipotentiaries was submitted to our Foreign Ministers, and they are of opinion that the central German government is qualified to sign in the name of all the German states.

M. Clemenceau. I recall again that Bavaria and Saxony were represented at Versailles when the preliminaries of peace were signed in 1871.

President Wilson. The German constitution was not yet made, and since then it has undergone several amendments. I trust the opinion of Mr. Lansing, who has extensive knowledge of international law.

M. Clemenceau. Another question arises: whatever the constitution of the German Empire, Bavaria, at the present time, has few connections with the central government. We must see to it that this state—and perhaps others—cannot repudiate the treaty.

Mr. Lloyd George. This raises a question on which we have to take a stand.

SUMMONING OF THE AUSTRIANS AND THE HUNGARIANS

Mr. Lloyd George. To give us something to do, it has been proposed to study the questions concerning peace with Austria next week. Couldn't we summon the Austrians and the Hungarians here the following week?

M. Clemenceau. I fear we will have much to do in the interval. The Germans are going to ask us questions immediately.

Mr. Lloyd George. The summoning of the Austrians and the Hungarians must be done in such a way that Italy can have no reason to complain. I think it must be done by the General Secretariat.

President Wilson. When it was a matter of summoning the Germans, it was M. Clemenceau, as President of the Conference, who wrote to them.

M. Clemenceau. I am prepared to do the same in the present case, if we agree.

President Wilson. In Austria, there is a regular government; but in Hungary there is only a government of soviets whose authority seems purely local. Have you no objection to opening negotiations now with the allies of Russian Bolshevism?

Mr. Lloyd George. The revolutionaries of Budapest are not guilty of the same atrocities as the Bolsheviks of Russia. They didn't attack our embassy, as was done in Moscow. We have no reason not to talk with them; we can't refuse to make peace with the Hungarians because we don't like their government.

M. Clemenceau. I fear the envoys of Austria and Hungary might stay here for a long time without doing anything.

Mr. Lloyd George. I wouldn't summon them to Paris; couldn't they be sent to Chantilly or Fontainebleau?

President Wilson. I favor the idea of dedicating a week to study of the Austro-Hungarian questions and of summoning the Austrians and Hungarians the week thereafter.

M. Clemenceau. I still believe the Germans will give us enough to do.

President Wilson. What wins me over to Mr. Lloyd George's proposal is the moral effect the summons will have on Austria. The dispatches we receive from Vienna indicate the urgency of supporting the present government.[2] The famine, the feeling that peace is not in sight, are creating a dangerous state of mind. Our representatives in Austria recommend that Austria be brought as soon as possible to defend her cause before the powers.

Mr. Lloyd George. As for the Hungarians, we would gladly have received Tisza if he was still in power. Therefore, we can receive the envoys of the socialist government of Budapest.

—*It is decided that the representatives of Austria and Hungary will be summoned for May 12 to Chantilly.*

THE RUSSIAN QUESTION

—Mr. Lloyd George communicates the latest information received by the British government on the situation in Russia.

Mr. Lloyd George. I propose to hear M. Chaikovskii, head of the government of Archangel, whose views seemed to me very reasonable, and to compare the English, French, and American information about the present state of Russia. What we receive indicates that Kolchak is advancing and can undoubtedly reach Archangel before our troops are withdrawn from there and, on

---

[2] Wilson was here paraphrasing a letter of April 28 from the other American commissioners—Lansing, White, Bliss, and House—which summarized recent dispatches from Austria and Hungary. The commissioners urged Wilson to receive not only representatives of Austria, but also of Hungary, as soon as a representative government existed there. Their letter is printed in *ibid.*, p. 205.

the other hand, that the government of Lenin is still powerful, but leans little by little towards a more moderate policy.

M. Clemenceau. Our information tends to show that the power of the Bolsheviks is declining.

Mr. Lloyd George. Here our information differs.

—*It is decided to ask the French General Staff for a report on the morale and the military situation of Russia.*

President Wilson. You will remember that General Bliss was to study the article of the peace treaty providing for the prolongation of certain provisions of the Armistice. He deems that article dangerous, especially given the very general terms of the draft.[3]

M. Clemenceau. I am inclined to agree with him.

President Wilson. So the article disappears, unless its drafters give us new reasons to keep it.

QUESTIONS CONCERNING ALSACE-LORRAINE*[4]

—MM. Tardieu and Klotz and the financial experts are introduced.

M. Tardieu. Aside from the question of the installations of the port of Kehl, on which I am not ready to give you my report, because I am awaiting the return of the British expert, I have three articles to present to you.

Article 12 provides that the pensions of the inhabitants of Alsace-Lorraine who were civil servants of the German Empire will continue to be paid at Germany's expense. A certain number of those civil servants served elsewhere than in Alsace-Lorraine.

President Wilson. I see that the British delegation makes reservations about this article.

An English expert.[5] If Alsace-Lorraine had remained German, the pensions would have to be paid out of resources provided by that province. In these circumstances, it seems fair to us to leave the cost of the pensions to France, which is recovering Alsace-Lorraine.

Mr. Lloyd George. On this question, I don't want to oppose the French government's views.

—*Article 12 is adopted.*

---

*H., *PPC*, V, 373ff.

[3] T. H. Bliss to WW, April 30, 1919, *ibid.*, pp. 262-63.
[4] The articles relating to Alsace-Lorraine are printed in *PPC*, V, 376-86.
[5] O. T. Falk, of the British Treasury, an expert in the British delegation.

M. Tardieu. Article 24 relates to the use of the balance of the liquidation of German private property in Alsace-Lorraine; it earmarks it for the settlement of local claims. In general, any balance of this kind should be charged to the asset side of the reparation account; we are asking for an exception for Alsace-Lorraine. Our justification is as follows: if there is a great accumulation of German property in Alsace-Lorraine, that is the result of the Germanization of that province. That is why, if there is a credit balance, we are asking that it be set aside for Alsace-Lorraine for the expenditures which will be made in the interest of the inhabitants of that province.

Mr. Lloyd George. I cannot agree to that article; it would have the effect of giving Alsace-Lorraine a priority over the total claims of the Allies. My opinion is that the general principle must be applied here; any balance must go to the total, and no special privilege must be given to any of the participants. If we set aside our principle, the result would be that the Alsatian claims, which normally would have been classed at a low rank, would appear in the first rank.

You speak of the Germanization of Alsace-Lorraine. But if by that you mean the result of German effort, which greatly increased the wealth of that province, I don't believe the argument is valid. If we gave Alsace-Lorraine the special treatment claimed for her, we couldn't refuse it to others.

So I think that our principle of the payment of any surplus into the total must be maintained. Otherwise, pensions to go to former civil servants of the German Empire would have priority over those which are to go to your soldiers and ours.

M. Clemenceau. Mr. Lloyd George is right, and I abandon Article 24.

M. Tardieu. Article 30 relates to the damages suffered by the inhabitants of Alsace-Lorraine. These are hereafter French nationals; they will appeal to the Reparation Commission, like other French citizens. Shall we say that there are two classes of citizens? Here we have a question of equity and a question of sentiment. We are asking that the people of Alsace-Lorraine have the benefit of clauses of the treaty relating to reparation.

Mr. Lloyd George. We have already considered the same question concerning the Poles, the Czechoslovaks, and the Yugoslavs. Poland was devastated as much as any other country; it is nonetheless true that the Poles of Germany—no doubt against their will—fought against us. The people of Alsace-Lorraine also fought under the German flag. We said that Poland would have no right to reparation, although we admitted that the Poles were not free to do what they wanted during the war. What you are asking for the people of Alsace-Lorraine, if we accept it now, we couldn't refuse to the Poles, to the Czechoslovaks, and to the Yugoslavs, and France would have more to lose than she would gain.

Moreover, I will observe that the devastations which might have taken place at certain points in Alsace and Lorraine were caused mainly by French artillery. It was the French army which invaded and bombarded part of Alsace-Lorraine in order to liberate it from German domination; it would be a bit thick to place this devastation in the same category as that caused by the invader in France and Belgium.

I repeat that, if the principle was generalized, the result would be to decrease what should go to France. I ask you not to insist on the insertion of that clause.

M. Tardieu. I recognize the validity of your objections; but it wasn't material repairs we had especially in mind; there are widows, orphans, and invalids in Alsace-Lorraine who have the right to pensions under the heading of reparation.

Mr. Lloyd George. Despite everything, these widows are the widows of German soldiers, and there are victims of our own bombardment amongst these invalids. It is difficult to support that claim.

M. Klotz. We don't want a discrimination to be made between the people of Alsace-Lorraine and other French citizens, which could be considered an injustice.

Mr. Lloyd George. The great danger is that the principle might be generalized. We have declared that it was impossible to apply it to Poland.

President Wilson. The American experts are of the same opinion. Besides, I quite understand the weight of the argument of sentiment, after forty-eight years of protest against the annexation of Alsace-Lorraine to Germany.

M. Clemenceau. We won't insist on Article 30.

—*The question of Kehl will be studied later.*

President Wilson. Another article is still being studied by the experts—Article 7—relating to the compensation for the marks. The question applies in the same way as in Belgium.

Mr. Lloyd George. We are compelled to refuse that compensation to Belgium.

President Wilson. Then Article 7 must disappear.

An English expert. No. In our view, that article must stay as it is; it only provides for a later agreement between France and Germany for the exchange of marks still in the hands of the French government.

President Wilson. A provision of that kind obligates us towards the Belgians.

M. Clemenceau. That is hardly desirable.

Mr. Lloyd George. Doesn't the present text compel the Germans to take back the marks at a fixed rate?

The English expert. Not at all.

President Wilson. We must avoid giving that impression.

Mr. Lloyd George. The best thing is to eliminate the article. Such as it is, it insures no benefit to France.

M. Klotz. This article is only the declaration of a state of fact. It is to the advantage of the Germans themselves to avoid our having in our hands billions of marks which, if they were thrown on the market, could have the most disastrous effect on German exchange. Such as it is, the article provides only for a later agreement between France and Germany. If Belgium can be content with a stipulation of the same kind, it would present no great problem.

Three and a half months ago, at the time of the negotiation of the Armistice, the Germans expressed to M. de Lasteyrie their desire to recover possession of part of their marks remaining in Alsace-Lorraine, precisely because they feared the danger of which I have just spoken. They offered seventy centimes immediately, and the remainder at the time of the signing of the treaty. That proposal was rejected because of the Belgians, who didn't want to hear of it; for my part, I regret it, and I observe that the article as it is drafted would not at all obligate the Germans to accept a fixed rate of exchange.

President Wilson. According to the explanation you have just given, this article gives the French government no power that it doesn't already possess. Why place an article in the treaty to enable you to make an agreement with Germany which you will always have the right to make when you wish? At first glance, that clause will create a wrong impression of your true intentions.

Mr. Lloyd George. Any German who reads this text will believe we want to compel Germany to buy back those marks at a forced rate.

M. Clemenceau. I think we should abandon the article.

M. Klotz. The third paragraph, in any case, must be retained. It forbids the Germans to stamp their banknotes so as to be able in future to make a distinction between marks which are in our hands and those which are now in Germany.

President Wilson. I understand this stipulation perfectly.

Mr. Lloyd George. Understood.

—*The third paragraph of Article 7 is retained.*

M. Klotz.* We still have to consider a question of the first importance, that of financial interdependence. Article 1 of the draft indicates that the Allied and Associated Governments are imposing on Germany an acknowledgment of the sums she owes as reparation. Now we must know whether we must write "Germany" or "the enemy Powers." If the principle of interdependence is accepted, will Italy have the right to claim reparation from Germany for the totality of her damages, in case she could obtain nothing from Austria and Hungary? If the principle of interdependence is accepted without any restriction, the German pledge of payment in our hands is considerably reduced. But an equitable arrangement of partial interdependence can be envisaged. That interdependence would be calculated pro rata according to the military effort by the enemy power on a given front. For example, if it is estimated that Germany occupied one tenth of the Italian front, we will say that she is responsible for one tenth of the damages suffered on this front. Without this qualification, the admission of the principle is very dangerous and contrary to equity.

Mr. Lloyd George. This question has always seemed very embarrassing to me. We want to settle it fairly. As for Italy, the Germans sent only five divisions there, and for a relatively short time. On the other hand, Italy only declared war on Germany thirteen months after her declaration of war on Austria. Can Germany be asked to provide the money for pensions when they go to soldiers killed or wounded at a time when Italy was still at peace with her?

President Wilson. About the number of German divisions employed on the Italian front, Italy gives information which differs from ours: she insists that the Germans had six divisions there.

Mr. Lloyd George. There never were more than five of them. In Serbia, obviously, the Germans played a great part in the devastation of the country; Serbia could present rather considerable claims. It is the same for Rumania. In Italy, the devastations are relatively minor.

*H., *PPC*, V, 387-88.

President Wilson. Losses at sea must be taken into account. German submarines sank a rather large number of Italian ships.

Mr. Lloyd George. No doubt about that. But the principle of interdependence defined according to the formula presented by M. Klotz seems acceptable to me.

M. Klotz. So we will write: "in proportion to the military and naval effort by each of the enemy states on the front being considered."

Mr. Lloyd George. Add that "that proportion will be determined in the last resort by the Reparation Commission."

LVI

Conversation between President Wilson and MM. Clemenceau and Lloyd George*

MAY 1, 1919, 11 A.M.

M. Clemenceau. Is there any news from Belgium?

President Wilson. Not to my knowledge.

Mr. Lloyd George. The Belgian financial experts have asked to see Mr. Keynes.

President Wilson. Yesterday, Mr. McCormick informed me that M. Hymans and M. Cartier, Belgian Minister to Washington, would like to have a meeting with me alone. I answered them that I did not want to appear to be opening separate negotiations with Belgium. Mr. McCormick's impression was that the Beligians believed they had received a promise from your governments for compensation for the exchange of the marks.

M. Clemenceau. I would like to know when and how.

President Wilson. I am not absolutely sure that is what they said: it is the impression that my conversation with Mr. McCormick left me with.

—M. Stéphen Pichon is introduced.

M. Clemenceau. M. Pichon has come to speak to you about Italy.

M. Pichon. There will probably be an incident this afternoon when M. Cambon presents the credentials of the Allied and Associated plenipotentiaries to the Germans. The Germans will ask where the full powers of Italy are; we won't be able to present them.

*H., PPC, V, 389ff.

Italy alone is responsible for this situation; but this responsibility must appear clearly to the Italian public itself. It is essential to have legality on our side. By mutual agreement, we have decided that we would make no separate peace. It must be obvious that it is Italy which separates herself from us, and not we from Italy. If there is an incident today, the Italian government would have to be notified of it by telegram, without any commentary. The Italian government will reply as it pleases. The important thing is to establish clearly that, if Italy doesn't return to take her place at the conference, it is her fault and not ours.

President Wilson. What sort of telegram does M. Pichon propose to write?

M. Pichon. The telegram will only report the event; we'll say that the exchange of full powers has taken place, that the Germans asked for Italy's, and that we had to reply that they were not in our hands.

Mr. Lloyd George. And if the Germans don't ask for anything?

M. Pichon. In that case, there will be nothing to do.

Mr. Lloyd George. I strongly doubt that they will ask anything whatsoever. They will say: "Who are you?" When M. Cambon has answered them, they won't ask why so and so isn't present.

M. Clemenceau. If there is no incident, obviously there will be no reason to telegraph the Italian government.

Mr. Lloyd George. If the Germans say: "Are you prepared to make peace in the absence of Italy?", what will M. Cambon reply?

M. Clemenceau. M. Cambon will reply that that is the business of the heads of governments.

Mr. Lloyd George. But what will the heads of governments do?

M. Clemenceau. They will reply to the Germans that we are prepared to negotiate with them. M. Orlando promised me to telegraph from Rome if he was ready to return; I have received nothing from him.

Mr. Lloyd George. Italy signed the Pact of London[1] and, by withdrawing from the conference, it is she who will have broken it.

President Wilson. And in a very singular way, by demanding that she be given assurances on treaties other than the one we are presently concerned with—the treaties with Austria and Hungary.

I believe that the Italians, at heart, want to return. If we make no show of budging, I am convinced we will see them in ten days.

---

[1] That is, the Pact of London of September 5, 1914.

Mr. Lloyd George. The news I receive from Italy says: Italian public opinion is supported by the French press and by the statement that M. Poincaré made in favor of Italy.

M. Clemenceau. M. Poincaré has written to Italy?

M. Pichon. It was three lines which appeared in the newspaper *France-Italie* on the occasion of the anniversary of the death of Leonardo da Vinci.[2]

M. Clemenceau. The President of the Republic is not to intervene without referring the matter to me.

Mr. Lloyd George. All I can say is that, if the King had sent a message of this kind, even if the message had been perfect, that would create a serious incident in a situation like this one.

M. Clemenceau. In our present situation, the President of the Republic has no right to do that without consulting the government.

President Wilson. It is an affront to the United States.

M. Pichon. The letter of the President of the Republic was submitted to me before its publication. I was asked if I saw a problem in its being published; I said no.

—Reading of the text:

"Italy and France, closely united in the war, will remain united in the peace. The cooling of their friendship would be a catastrophe for Latin civilization and humanity. France, faithful to her commitments, sympathies, and traditions, will keep her hands joined to those of Italy. Nothing will separate them.—Raymond Poincaré"

President Wilson. This text can be understood as a commitment on the part of the French government.

M. Clemenceau. In these circumstances, my opinion is to send no telegram to the Italian government.

M. Pichon. It seemed to me that this letter from the President of the Republic was only a ceremonial message.

Mr. Lloyd George. The Italian press has the impression that French opinion is on Italy's side.

M. Clemenceau. The French press was paid. A few months ago, Count Bonin Longare came constantly to complain about attacks by the Parisian press; if, all of a sudden, it has been seized with enthusiasm for Italy, we know what that means.

---

[2] In the Paris *France-Italie*, May 1, 1919. The text is printed below. For the background, publication, and discussion of this message, see Raymond Poincaré, *Au Service de la France*, 11 vols. (Paris, 1926-74), XI, 387-88, 414-16. Poincaré was a member of a hard-line cabal in the French government, which included Foch and former Prime Minister Aristide Briand. Jean-Baptiste Duroselle, *Clemenceau* (Paris, 1988), *passim*.

Mr. Lloyd George. So we send no communication to the Italian government?

President Wilson. That is my opinion.

SUBMARINE CABLES

President Wilson. The question of the submarine cables is not settled. The difficulty came from us, and here is our point of view.

The article relating to the cables was first inserted into the military clauses. A discussion took place and, after a conversation with me, Mr. Balfour drafted a memorandum[3] in the following sense: where the cables were cut and diverted by the Allies, the Germans have the right to recover the abandoned sections and to reestablish their former communications. Mr. Lansing and I don't find, in the text as it has been drafted, that the right left to the Germans is sufficiently stipulated. Moreover, Germany would have to obtain new permission in order to lay her cables at certain points, for example in the Azores.

This would give Great Britain absolute control over telegraphic communications in the Atlantic, and it would be the same for Japan in the Pacific. We have a serious objection to make against an arrangement which would give the absolute monopoly of the cables to two of the great naval powers.

Mr. Lloyd George. Don't you have cables yourself?

President Wilson. The American government doesn't have control of any, although America participates financially in some of these enterprises. Our concern is that the possession and administration of the world's cables should not be in the hands of one or two powers.

Mr. Lloyd George. Until now, our representatives haven't been able to agree; you are on one side; the representatives of France, Great Britain, and Japan are on the other. I believe we can take no decision without again hearing our specialists.

M. Pichon. It was earlier agreed that I would come this afternoon with Admiral de Bon and Mr. Balfour with his expert.

President Wilson. Let us confirm this meeting for this afternoon, at the Quai d'Orsay.

M. Clemenceau. Then a meeting this afternoon at the Quai d'Orsay, at four o'clock.

M. Pichon. Yesterday you indicated your intention to summon the

---

[3] Wilson meant Balfour's resolution presented to the Council of Ten on March 24, 1919, for the text of which see *PWW*, Vol. 56, p. 219.

representatives of Austria and Hungary for May 12. There is a distinction to be made between the two. In Vienna, there is a government, properly speaking; but the government of Béla Kun is not really genuine, and the information we receive indicates that it is hardly stable. It is better to wait a bit longer. On the other hand, in the meantime we shall see if the Italian situation clears up. We can't make peace with Austria without determining the boundaries of Italy. So there is an advantage in not hurrying too much.

If we want to get started immediately on something other than the treaty with Germany, we can summon the Bulgarians for the fifteenth. I don't think we can be ready to work seriously on the Austrian treaty on the twelfth of this month. We could be ready for the Bulgarians.

President Wilson. M. Pichon doesn't know the reasons why we thought of summoning the Austrians at an early date. Our idea is to support the government in Vienna by showing that we are disposed to negotiate with it; that admits of no delay. Likewise, in Hungary, if the government wavers, it might be better to avoid a series of upheavals by sending our summons now. I insist on an immediate summons.

—M. Pichon withdraws.

PROTECTION OF NATIONAL AND RELIGIOUS MINORITIES

President Wilson. One of the things that troubles the peace of the world is the persecution of the Jews. They have been or are held in very poor esteem in many countries. You know that they are especially badly treated in Poland, and that they are deprived of civic rights in Rumania. In the treaty with Germany, we make stipulations regarding Poland. We must demand guarantees for both national minorities and religious minorities.

I would propose to insert in the treaty, along these lines, two articles which would apply, not only to Poland, but also to Bohemia and to the other new states. It is a matter of saying that "(1) the state of ——— agrees to grant all racial and national minorities the same treatment in law and in fact as to the majority; (2) the state of ——— agrees to place no obstacle in the way of the practice of any religion, if that practice is not contrary to public order or morals."

Mr. Lloyd George. I would propose the extension of this principle to the countries subject to the mandate system.

President Wilson. A detailed text was prepared on the status of the citizens of Poland indicating that in a more explicit fashion.[4] This plan was drafted after consultation with the representatives of the minorities. What I don't like is that a sort of autonomy is required for national minorities.[5]

Mr. Lloyd George. This is a claim of the Jews, who wish to form a kind of state within the state. Nothing could be more dangerous.

President Wilson. The reason why I ask that the general provisions that I just indicated be included in the treaty with Germany is that Poland is incorporating several million German subjects into her territory.

Mr. Lloyd George. In any case, these provisions must be imposed upon the Poles. There is obviously something to be said to justify the hostile feeling of the Poles against the Jews. M. Paderewski told me that, during the war, the Jews of Poland were by turns for the Germans, for the Russians, for the Austrians, and very little for Poland herself.

President Wilson. It is the result of a long persecution. The Jews of the United States are good citizens.

Mr. Lloyd George. It is the same in England.

M. Clemenceau. And in France.

President Wilson. Remember that, when the Jews were outside the law in England, they acted as a people outside the law. Our wish is to bring them back everywhere under the terms of the law of the land.

Mr. Lloyd George. I will recall the benevolence of Cromwell towards them.

President Wilson. I propose to bring together a small committee of

---

[4] "Draft clauses for the protection of Minorities in Poland," April 29, 1919, prepared by David Hunter Miller, printed in ibid., Vol 58, pp. 290-93.

[5] Jewish leaders at Paris had requested that each national minority in Poland should have a right to elect a proportion of all representatives in all elective bodies, based upon the ratio of its numbers in the respective electoral areas to the entire population therein. The only monograph on the minorities question at the Paris Peace Conference is Erwin Viefhaus, Die Minderheitenfrage und die Entstehung der Minderheitenschutzverträge auf der Pariser Friedenskonferenz 1919 (Würzburg, 1960). In addition, see Lundgreen-Nielsen, The Polish Problem at the Paris Peace Conference, pp. 302-307, 341-48, 371-85; Oscar I. Janowsky, The Jews and Minority Rights, 1898-1919 (New York, 1933); Allan Taylor, Prelude to Israel: An Analysis of Zionist Diplomacy, 1897-1947 (New York, 1959); Manley O. Hudson, "The Protection of Minorities and Natives in Transferred Territories," in House and Seymour, What Really Happened at Paris, pp. 204-30; Lloyd George, The Truth about the Treaties, II, 1363-92; Temperley, History of the Peace Conference of Paris, V, 112-49; and the biographies and autobiographies cited in the bibliography of Melvin I. Urofsky, American Zionism from Herzl to the Holocaust (Garden City, N. Y., 1975).

experts to draft the articles which will settle that question in Poland. If this text doesn't find its place in the treaty with Germany, it will be necessary in any case to insert it in the treaty which will determine the status of the Polish state.

Mr. Lloyd George. The best thing is to put it in the German treaty.

President Wilson. We will tell the committee to prepare as short a text as possible.

Mr. Lloyd George. It will be necessary to provide many other clauses for these new states and first to impose upon them the same international obligations as those of other civilized countries.

President Wilson. I don't see how all that could be inserted in the treaty with Germany.

Mr. Lloyd George. Yet we cannot recognize these states without such guarantees.

President Wilson. We have already recognized them; but in reality it remains to create them. How shall we do it?

Mr. Lloyd George. The best thing is to do it by the peace treaties we are going to sign.

I notice a clause anticipating later conventions for the details of the military occupation, which will have the same force as the treaty itself.

M. Clemenceau. That is very well. But why not maintain the present occupation arrangement, which is functioning perfectly?

Sir Maurice Hankey. General Weygand made proposals for these agreements, which will be examined in Versailles by the military experts; then they will come back to you.

Mr. Lloyd George. One of these days, I would like us to study the mandate system, which has been established only in very general terms.

M. Clemenceau. In any case, that question doesn't pertain to the peace treaty; it doesn't concern the Germans.

Mr. Lloyd George. The dominions are very much concerned about it.

M. Clemenceau. There is no urgency. We have much to do, and that is a question that will be settled amongst ourselves.

Mr. Lloyd George. We cannot meet the Germans at Versailles before Monday. My idea is to hold a meeting next Sunday in which we will communicate the text of the preliminaries to the representatives of the Allied and Associated Powers.

President Wilson. That could create difficulties for me with American public opinion.
Mr. Lloyd George. I fall in with you.
M. Clemenceau. So it will have to be held on a Saturday.
Mr. Lloyd George. Are there many articles that aren't ready?
M. Clemenceau. I'll bring them to you this afternoon.
President Wilson. The question of the disposition of German merchant ships is not settled.
Mr. Lloyd George. The treaty will say only that the Germans must hand over the ships. The division we will make of them is our business. What I proposed is that the United States keep those which she has taken and pay for them into a fund to determine the surplus value in relation to her losses in tonnage. Mr. Keynes proposes a different version: the surplus to be paid into a common fund would be calculated in relation to what the United States would receive if the ships she seized were paid into the aggregate. Mr. Keynes also proposes an amendment which provides that instead of serving as compensation to American subjects, the German properties seized in America would go into the aggregate of reparations.
President Wilson. The difficulty arises from American legislation. The enemy properties were seized by a decision of Congress, and it is Congress, in principle, which must dispose of them.

The general principle is that each government compensates its nationals and that the surplus goes into the aggregate; this general rule must obviously be applied to ships.

THE QUESTION OF THE BLOCKADE

President Wilson. I recall that our experts have several times proposed to lift the blockade of Germany.
Mr. Lloyd George. We must wait until the ratification of the treaty.
President Wilson. If we wait, Germany will fall to pieces.
Mr. Lloyd George. In any case, she could buy nothing on credit.

The most useful thing is to make the Germans hope now that they could soon receive raw materials for their industries.
President Wilson. It is necessary to give them assurance about it.
Mr. Lloyd George. An assurance pure and simple would not be enough. They have waited months for the fulfillment of our promises concerning food. If we want them to sign, they must be given certainty, and they must be informed that we don't intend to refuse them the raw materials required to put their population back to work at the conclusion of the peace.

LVII

Conversation between President Wilson and MM. Clemenceau, Lloyd George, Lansing, Balfour, Pichon, and J. Cambon*

MAY 1, 1919, 5:45 P.M.

M. Jules Cambon. I report on the first contact we just had with the Germans at Versailles. We were instructed to receive their credentials and to transmit those of the Allied and Associated plenipotentiaries. This morning, we received a telegram from the German delegation informing us that the credentials of the Germans would be presented to us by three persons whose names were given, but who would not include the head of the delegation. We replied that the presence of Herr von Brockdorff-Rantzau was required.

The meeting took place at three o'clock at the Trianon Palace. Herr von Brockdorff-Rantzau was present. I said a few words about the object of the meeting. Herr von Brockdorff-Rantzau introduced his colleagues. The credentials were exchanged without incident. I said that, if the German delegation had any observation to make, we were ready to listen.

It was my impression that the German plenipotentiaries were deeply moved. Their attitude towards the Allies was what it had to be. Herr von Brockdorff-Rantzau, who knows French very well, spoke German, as did the civil servants who accompanied him. They had brought an interpreter.

This raises a question that I feel compelled to place before you. Since French and English are the two languages used in the conference, should we request the German representatives to speak either French or English?

Mr. Balfour. If we accept the use of German, that means that the speeches will have to be translated twice.

M. Clemenceau. We can't prevent them from speaking their own language.

Do you have any impression about the kind of publicity the Germans will give the treaty when they are acquainted with it?

M. Jules Cambon. My impression is that they will only do it in very general terms. However, they said nothing very definite about it.

President Wilson. It might be useful to obtain from them an answer

*H., PPC, V, 403ff.

to this question: "Would the publication of the treaty in the Allied countries and in America be advantageous or disadvantageous from their point of view?

M. Jules Cambon. I didn't ask that question.

Mr. Lansing. Are the credentials of the Germans in the hands of the Commission on Verification?

M. Jules Cambon. Yes, and they have ours in hand. The Germans will take time to examine these documents; I know their ways. We ourselves need about forty-eight hours.

M. Clemenceau. If there is any difficulty, you will refer it to us.

M. Jules Cambon. The commission will meet tomorrow, and I will report to you on Saturday morning.

President Wilson. We are informed that the treaty cannot be printed before Tuesday. In these circumstances, I can only see advantages in having you examine the credentials very minutely.

Mr. Lloyd George. This morning we discussed the question of whether we had to inform the Italians of the date when the negotiations will open. I think it would be correct on our part to inform the Italian Ambassador[1] that, on account of the difficulties of drafting, the opening of the negotiations with the Germans is delayed until Tuesday. If we say nothing, that would risk unnecessarily increasing the irritation of Italian public opinion.

Mr. Balfour. That communication would have to be made to Marquis Imperiali, to whom the Italians entrusted their affairs when they withdrew.

M. Clemenceau. Should we not rather communicate with their Ambassador in Paris, Count Bonin?

Mr. Balfour. M. Sonnino wrote me, on leaving Paris, that he was leaving his affairs in the hands of Marquis Imperiali.

President Wilson. That meant that, if we had some proposal to make to him, it would be necessary for us to address Marquis Imperiali.

Mr. Lloyd George. In these circumstances, it is better not to make a communication like the one I am suggesting to Marquis Imperiali, but to ask M. Pichon to notify Count Bonin.

President Wilson. That's it, and the best thing is to make a verbal communication to him.

Mr. Lloyd George. We have to make sure the Italians can't say that they were not informed.

M. Clemenceau. M. Pichon will tell the Italians that the treaty will be ready only on Tuesday because of the delay in drafting.

---

[1] That is, Count Bonin Longare.

Mr. Lloyd George. I would go further and tell them that we will meet the Germans on Tuesday.
President Wilson. This communication must be made in the name of the French Foreign Minister and not in the name of the conference.
M. Clemenceau. And we will refuse to discuss anything at all.
Mr. Balfour. Have you no information from Rome?
M. Pichon. Some indications about the criticism of the government, directed especially by M. Luzzatti and M. Tittoni.
President Wilson. I received from Trier a letter from Colonel Conger informing me about an interview he had with Brockdorff-Rantzau, en route to Paris, on April 28.[2] Brockdorff asked his impression about the way in which the negotiations would take place. The Colonel told him that the United States would show much latitude in allowing the Germans to explain themselves, but that the time would come when they would be requested to sign, and to sign without delay. Brockdorff asked if it would be known in advance when the moment would be. The Colonel replied that they would be informed.

Some American agents in Germany have had interviews with several of the most important people in Germany, and it might be interesting to summarize them.[3] Ebert appears to be very pessimistic; he believes it is impossible to sign such a peace as the French press seems to forecast. On the other hand, he believes that, if Germany doesn't sign, the consequence will be chaos for Germany and the world. He hopes he can sign. He has shown no desire to turn the Italian incident to his advantage. He hopes the conference will be a true conference, and that Germany will not be asked to make territorial cessions in contradiction of the Fourteen Points.

Erzberger says that the ruling of March 30—it is, I think, a statement made at the German Assembly—is still valid. Germany will sign the treaty if the Fourteen Points are respected. He appears to be very anxious to obtain commercial credit for Germany

[2] See the memorandum by Arthur Latham Conger, dated April 28, 1919, printed in *PWW*, Vol. 58, p. 307. Conger was an American intelligence officer in Germany. See Fritz T. Epstein, "Zwischen Compiègne und Versailles: Geheime amerikanische Militärdiplomatie in der Periode des Waffenstillstandes 1918/19: Die Rolle des Obersten Arthur L. Conger," *Vierteljahrshefte für Zeitgeschichte*, III (Oct. 1955), 412-24; and Klaus Schwabe, *Woodrow Wilson, Revolutionary Germany, and Peacemaking, 1918-1919: Missionary Diplomacy and the Realities of Power* (Chapel Hill, N. C., 1985), pp. 309-12.

[3] "INTERVIEWS OF A CONFIDENTIAL AGENT WITH MEMBERS OF THE GERMAN GOVERNMENT," dated April 30, 1919, printed in *PWW*, Vol. 58, pp. 308-10.

in America. About Italy, he seems to believe that the warning given by President Wilson to Orlando is addressed indirectly to Clemenceau. Our old friend Count Bernstorff also adheres to the statement of March 30. He wants Germany to have good relations with the United States. (If he has this desire, he will do well not to return to America.) He states that he will help in the signing of the peace with all his power.

Scheidemann declares himself favorable to signing unless it is absolutely impossible. He laments Germany's internal difficulties, speaks of the necessity of having an army in order to deal with them. About the war indemnities, he had a conference with some German bankers, who don't see how the country can ever pay its debts. The revenues of the state have considerably diminished at the same time that the salaries of the civil servants have greatly increased. The postal administration has just been compelled to grant its subordinate personnel salaries which vary from 6,000 to 8,000 marks a year. Scheidemann says that he is prepared to sign any peace which will allow Germany to live. He asks if the German merchant ships will be returned: without them, all Germany's trade is lost. If the present government—he says—can't make peace, no other government can. The only means of saving order in Germany and in Europe is the signing of an acceptable peace.

M. Clemenceau. Altogether, this information is not too bad.

President Wilson. General Bliss saw Marshal Foch, as he had agreed, about keeping certain arrangements of the Armistice in the peace treaty. The Marshal says that, not knowing the text of the treaty, he doesn't know where contradictions between this text and that of the Armistice Agreement occur and what must be done to reconcile the two.

Mr. Balfour. I hope that what is necessary was done to prevent what General Wilson fears: he says that, if certain arrangements of the Armistice are not kept in the treaty, the occupation army will find itself at a moment's notice deprived of the right of requisition, lodging, etc.

President Wilson. I wouldn't willingly run the risk of allowing this article to remain as it is without a definite justification.

M. Clemenceau. We have taken no final decision about the message which is to be sent to the Austrians. I propose to reproduce the text of the one I sent the Germans, with few changes.

"The Supreme Council of the Allied and Associated Powers has decided to invite the delegates of Austria (or Hungary), provided with full powers, to meet at Saint-Germain on the evening of May 12, in order to consider the terms of peace with the Allied and Associated Powers."

The word "consider" is the only difference between this text and that of the message to the Germans.

Mr. Balfour. Are you going to treat the Austrians completely differently from the Germans?

President Wilson. I certainly hope so.

M. Clemenceau. We will send two separate invitations, one to the Austrians, the other to the Hungarians.

President Wilson. We can invite the Austrians for May 12 and the Hungarians for the fifteenth.

Mr. Balfour. Will you be ready?

President Wilson. There are two difficult questions. The first is that of the Adriatic, which doesn't concern Austria as she exists today.

Mr. Lloyd George. All we have to tell the Austrians concerns the territory we are leaving them. I only see one delicate point—the Tyrol.

President Wilson. The second difficult question is the division of debts and reparations.

Mr. Lloyd George. That can only be settled through the work of a commission.

Mr. Balfour. It is very difficult to discuss the question of the Tyrolean frontier without the presence of the Italians.

President Wilson. The Italians know what was decided here and in the commission.

Mr. Lloyd George. Besides, there was no contrary proposal.

M. Clemenceau. The telegram will continue thus:

"The Austrian—or Hungarian—goverment is thus invited to communicate as soon as possible the number, names, and qualifications of the delegates which it proposes to send to Saint-Germain, as well as those of the persons who will accompany them. The delegates will have to be limited strictly to its mission and can only include persons qualified for the part which is assigned to them."

I substituted Saint-Germain for Chantilly, because Saint-Germain will be much easier to reach.

Mr. Balfour. What is the method of discussion you propose to establish with the Austrians and the Hungarians?

President Wilson. I propose that we don't commit ourselves to that in advance.

Mr. Lloyd George. The Italians will have to be informed that this invitation was issued.

M. Clemenceau. We can transmit this dispatch to them.
President Wilson. Better confine ourselves to informing them of it.

LVIII

Conversation between President Wilson and MM. Clemenceau and Lloyd George*

MAY 2, 1919, 11 A.M.

THE ITALIAN QUESTION

M. Clemenceau. The question arises of whether we must not now publish the letter drafted by Mr. Balfour about the Italian question, the original of which was sent to M. Orlando.[1] It would require two lines of preamble to say that we authorize the publication. M. Orlando mentioned that letter in his speech in Rome.

Mr. Lloyd George. M. Orlando didn't read its text; that follows from what Marquis Imperiali told us yesterday. M. Orlando thought that reading it would make a bad impression and would compromise the future of Italy's relations with England and France; he only read a summary which, according to his letter to Marquis Imperiali, produced a disagreeable effect. Marquis Imperiali came to ask me not to publish that document.

President Wilson. I will ask you, on the contrary, to publish it. M. Orlando's tactics are to isolate the United States, or rather to make it be believed that it is isolated, whilst deceiving Italian public opinion about the true position of the French and British governments.

M. Clemenceau. I don't see how we could avoid publishing that letter now.

President Wilson. A sort of Italian communiqué, which appeared in the newspapers this morning, says that Italy is waiting for the proposals we are going to make to her. You see the game.

M. Clemenceau. We don't have to make proposals.

President Wilson. What especially agitates Italian public opinion is the question of Fiume. According to my information, the Dalmatian question ranks second.

*H., PPC, V, 407ff.

[1] That is, the document printed as an appendix to XLV.

Mr. Lloyd George. Baron Sonnino understood very well, at the last moment, the madness of the situation in which they have placed themselves. If they were adroit, they could ask us purely and simply for the execution of the Treaty of London.

M. Clemenceau. M. Fromageot, in the name of the Drafting Committee, asks if the name of Italy should be omitted in the treaty. In that case, the wording of a great many articles has to be modified. In the meantime, I note that Italy continues to participate by correspondence in the work of certain commissions and makes reservations as if she had not withdrawn from the negotiations.

—M. Clemenceau reads a letter from M. Crespi to M. Klotz, containing observations about certain financial clauses.

Mr. Lloyd George. This letter shows that M. Crespi has been kept informed.

President Wilson. In my opinion, we should be content with acknowledging receipt of that letter. Italy has no right to continue to participate in the discussions in this indirect manner.

Mr. Lloyd George. For myself, I would bluntly ask M. Crespi this question: "Are you a member of the conference or not?" We must, however, avoid any form which would not be perfectly polite. If there has to be a rupture, we must rather sin by an excess of politeness.

President Wilson. What we have to do is to avoid writing anything to him that might be considered an invitation.

Mr. Lloyd George. M. Klotz, to whom M. Crespi has written, can answer him in a personal way: "I don't know how to act towards you; do you continue to belong to the commission or not?" He could use this opportunity to inform M. Crespi of the decision we have taken on the subject of the principle of interdependence, a decision which affects the interests of Italy in an unfavorable way.

President Wilson. M. Crespi won't be able to reply to a question asked in that way.

Mr. Lloyd George. I insist on the latter point. The day before yesterday, we took a decision concerning interdependence contrary to Italy's interests, and we took it in the absence of her representatives; I don't much like that. I am not sure we didn't leave in M. Orlando's mind the impression that we were rather leaning towards the contrary solution. The Italians leave Paris, M. Klotz arrives with a proposal, we unanimously take a decision which is to our advantage and which limits Italy's participation in the indemnities. I believe that our decision is justified, and that the principle we have set forth is fair. But I don't much like having done it in the absence of Italy's representatives.

M. Clemenceau. I don't much like it either.

Mr. Lloyd George. Our situation is different from President Wilson's, because America has no direct interest in the problem of reparation. But the restrictive formula we adopted can bring to England seven billion more francs, and to France more than twelve billions, and it will do that by diminishing what Italy believed she could claim, and precisely at the moment when she had just left the conference.

President Wilson. We mustn't forget that Italy's attitude is unjustifiable; she withdrew from the German negotiations because she was not given territories which belonged to Austria-Hungary and which don't have to be mentioned in the treaty with Germany.

Mr. Lloyd George. On the part of France and of England—America is in a completely different situation—our decision takes the appearance of a bad deed, and I must say that I am not very satisfied with it. There is no doubt that to eliminate a portion of the debt which, if another principle was adopted, Germany would owe to Italy, is advantageous to France and England. If there is a rupture with Italy—which could lead to a blockade of Fiume—we have to be able to face the situation with a clear conscience.

I persist in believing that M. Klotz should write personally to M. Crespi and tell him: "I don't know where I stand with you." At the same time, he would inform him of the decision we have taken on the question of reparations.

President Wilson. The Italian government cannot answer you with anything precise.

M. Clemenceau. The Italians will say: "We are ready to return if you make proposals which please us."

Sir Maurice Hankey. We are receiving a telegram which announces the sending of two Italian cruisers and several destroyers to Smyrna.

President Wilson. They are behaving in an unacceptable manner. But we obviously must inform them of a decision which affects their interests.

Mr. Lloyd George. I warned them of the danger to which they would expose themselves by withdrawing. I clearly told M. Orlando of the risk Italy would run from the point of view of her material interests. But they always believe that we people of the North bluff the way they do.

Colonel Hankey is going to tell us, according to the minutes, in what capacity M. Crespi has been left in Paris.

Sir Maurice Hankey. M. Orlando said that M. Crespi would remain in Paris in order to handle technical questions.

President Wilson. M. Klotz will have to say that the decision in question was taken after two meetings to which M. Crespi was summoned and to which he didn't come.

M. Clemenceau. The best thing is to invite M. Klotz to come here to speak to him about it.

Mr. Lloyd George. We can have a letter drafted by Mr. Philip Kerr.

—Mr. Philip Kerr is introduced and receives the necessary instructions.[2]

Mr. Lloyd George. This draft is very important, for we mustn't forget that all these documents will be published if things turn out badly.

M. Clemenceau. In the meantime, what should I reply to M. Fromageot? Must we summon him here in order to ask him what change he suggests in the wording?

President Wilson. The Drafting Committee has much to do at this time, and it is better not to distract it.

M. Clemenceau. We can meet this afternoon at the Quai d'Orsay, and we will see M. Fromageot there, without his having to leave the Drafting Committee for a long time.

Will we not do well to reread the letter from Mr. Balfour to M. Orlando which I propose to publish?

—Mr. Lloyd George reads aloud the letter.

M. Clemenceau. I don't believe we can refrain from publishing this letter now.

President Wilson. I recall that it was at first agreed that this letter would be published the day after mine. The game of the Italians is to make it appear that the United States is isolated, and M. Poincaré's letter contributes to that impression.

Mr. Lloyd George. Let us think carefully about the consequences before publishing the letter drafted by Mr. Balfour. If the Italians

---

[2] The letter, L. L. Klotz to S. R. Crespi, May 2, 1919, is printed in *PWW*, Vol. 58, p. 341. It said that, since the Italians had withdrawn from the deliberations of the Reparation Commission on April 22, the American, British, and French members had been obliged to take "very important decisions" concerning the draft treaty with Germany, in particular concerning the prorating of reparations. The letter then explained the formula to be applied.

don't return, they will try to throw the responsibility for it on to us.

President Wilson. They are dying to return.

Mr. Lloyd George. Perhaps, but not without some initiative on our part, which is impossible for us to take. We must act in such a way that they cannot say later: "It was the letter signed by Messrs. Clemenceau and Lloyd George which prevented us from returning to Paris."

President Wilson. We must do what is right, no more and no less.

Mr. Lloyd George. We must try to get out of this situation honorably. We must try to bring Italy back to us and, if that is not possible, to establish that it is not our doing. I fear that the publication of the letter might prevent both. If they had a mind to return, they will no longer be able to do it. At the same time, the publication will excite public opinion against us. It is very well known that this letter has been written. The longer it stays in M. Orlando's hands without being published, the greater its effect will be. The British public is not with Italy, but it wants the matter to be worked out.

President Wilson. American public opinion has a lively interest in this dispute and doesn't understand why the United States appears to be isolated. It seems to me that, for the entire world, the support of American public opinion is more important than that of Italian public opinion.

Mr. Lloyd George. Much more, I acknowledge.

President Wilson. I have spoken with many people who know Italy better than I myself know her. They think the only way of arriving at a satisfactory result is to show Italy that she can count on no outside support. If you leave her the hope of a compromise on the question of Fiume, she will continue to maneuver and carry on press campaigns which will have the effect of separating American public opinion more and more from European public opinion. The letter prepared by Mr. Balfour, bearing the signatures of M. Clemenceau and Mr. Lloyd George, will show Italy that she is in an impossible situation, and that she is risking complete isolation.

In the meantime, we have to continue our work, with the danger of taking, in Italy's absence, decisions contrary to her interests. This is an embarrassment for us, and it raises constant questions of conscience for us as long as the situation isn't clarified.

Mr. Lloyd George. The decision to publish this statement is a grave decision. I don't believe Italian public opinion can imagine that the United States is isolated, because I know there is a very strong sentiment in Italy against British public opinion. That is due principally to the attitude of *The Times*, which is always considered in Italy as a semiofficial organ, although it has completely ceased to be one.

I am informed that English soldiers have been insulted in the streets in several cities of Italy. Italy believes we are in agreement with the United States. If there is a contrary impression in America, that comes from Hearst and the press he controls; that is the game he has always played in order to divide us in the interest of the Germans. I believe rather that England is considered as being more favorable towards the Yugoslavs than she is; the bulk of public opinion in England knows very little about them and is not much interested in them.

If I believed this publication would force Italy to take a decision, I would favor doing it immediately; I fear, on the contrary, that it would only prolong the crisis. Italy must return, and return voluntarily. On the contrary, publication could cause a crisis which will bring Giolitti or Tittoni here, who would play the part of Germany's spies amongst us; that is the role Tittoni played during the war. We were compelled to receive him in our councils; but we whispered amongst ourselves "Shh—Tittoni is here.—"

Remember that Marquis Imperiali has just informed us that he telegraphed M. Orlando about this publication, and that M. Orlando said his greatest desire was that it shouldn't take place.

President Wilson. The dominant impression in America is that the United States is not supported in this affair, or at least that it is not openly so. I believe you will prolong the present situation more by your silence than by your action. By throwing a crystal into a liquid, one sometimes crystallizes it entirely.

Mr. Lloyd George. Sometimes, one also provokes an explosion.

President Wilson. The explosion has already occurred. The fear of seeing us negotiate with the Germans without Italy will act on the minds of the Italians. On the other hand, I see that they are sending ships to Fiume and to Smyrna. I can send our largest battleship, the *George Washington*,[3] which is now in Brest, either to Fiume or to Smyrna. If I do it, that can produce a result—and far from me is the desire that that result should be war. But Italy's attitude is undoubtedly aggressive; she is creating a threat to the

---

[3] This, according also to Hankey's minutes, was what Wilson actually said. U.S.S. *George Washington* was of course then a troop transport, not, as Hankey records Wilson as saying, "one of the latest United States battleships waiting to take him home." PPC, V, 412.

peace in the very middle of the peace conference in which she once participated and from which she has withdrawn.

Mr. Lloyd George. A dispatch received by M. Vénisélos, who acquainted us with it, indicates that there is an agreement in Asia Minor between the Italians and the Turks, who are resuming their policy of terrorism against the Greeks. M. Vénisélos asks us to send a warship to Smyrna and proposes to send a Greek ship there himself.

President Wilson. The Italians say they are sending their ships to Asia Minor to protect their nationals.

Mr. Lloyd George. My opinion is that all three of us should send ships to Smyrna.

M. Clemenceau. What a beginning for the League of Nations!

Mr. Lloyd George. There is a lesson to be learned here. The other day, the Italians landed at Adalia, they said, in order to protect an Italian convent. We have to show them that we won't allow them to do it.

M. Clemenceau. But there remains an immediate question: what are we to do with regard to the Germans?

Mr. Lloyd George. We shall see M. Fromageot this afternoon about this.

M. Clemenceau. The game of the Italians is to separate us from the United States by invoking the Treaty of London. In order to avoid that, they must be clearly told that, if they stay away, our alliance with them and, consequently, our treaty are broken. If we don't take precautions, they will hold us by the throat.

President Wilson. How do you interpret the mutual engagement not to make a separate peace? Italy was party to the Armistice Agreement, to our decision to negotiate with Germany; she participated in the preparation of the treaty. Now she is withdrawing; it is she who is breaking the commitment.

M. Clemenceau. We'll tell them: "If you break the Pact of London, the treaty of April 1915 falls, and you will suffer the consequences."

President Wilson. We have to tell them that it is they who are abandoning us; they are doing it by the fact of their absence from the conference.

M. Clemenceau. They must be given that warning before Tuesday.

Mr. Lloyd George. I agree with M. Clemenceau.

M. Clemenceau. M. Orlando has already refused to sign the invitation we addressed to the Germans to come to Versailles. You remember that he made his reservations and finally refused his signature.

President Wilson. Almost all the articles of the treaty were drawn up with their agreement, and it is after that that they withdrew. It is obviously an act of rupture.

M. Clemenceau. I put the question to M. Orlando; I asked him: "Will you be there when the Germans come to Versailles?" He told me he would send his answer from Rome; he hasn't done it.

President Wilson. It is enough to notify them Monday that they have broken the treaty.

Mr. Lloyd George. Mustn't we tell them now that we are omitting their name in the text of the treaty?

President Wilson. You have already told them that.

M. Clemenceau. All the more reason to repeat it to them at the time they find themselves excluded. Every time the Treaty of London was mentioned, Mr. Lloyd George and I have said that we were prepared to respect it; all the more reason to notify them of our position on this question of a rupture, which would free us from an obligation we have never denied.

President Wilson. If you notify them, won't they answer that it is you who are violating the pact?

M. Clemenceau. All the more reason to indicate our position clearly.

President Wilson. It is fair to say that they have been warned and that their absence is a violation of their commitments. M. Clemenceau, would you like to draft something along these lines?

M. Clemenceau. I promise you to do it.

—Reading of a memorandum from the General Secretariat of the Conference about the admission to the session for the delivery of the treaty to the German plenipotentiaries of the representatives of the powers which broke diplomatic relations with Germany without declaring war on her. The Secretariat asks if the credentials of the delegates of these powers have to be presented to the Germans, and if these delegates will be admitted to the preliminary reading of the clauses of the treaty.

These questions are settled in the affirmative.

LIX

Conversation between President Wilson and MM. Clemenceau and Lloyd George*

MAY 2, 1919, 4 P.M.

—M. Loucheur is introduced.

M. Loucheur. We have continued to study amongst the experts the question of the reparation due to Belgium. Mr. Keynes proposes that we decline to substitute, as the Belgians request, Germany for Beligum for the payment of the debt contracted towards the Allies, but that we declare that the payments of Belgium shall be dependent upon those of Germany.

Mr. Lloyd George. I am not much disposed to accept this text.

President Wilson. We must treat Belgium like a sick country and, moreover, we must remember that it is a matter of rather small sums.

M. Loucheur. Belgium asks, moreover, that she be assured a proportion of 15 per cent out of a total of the payments made by Germany over ten years. We could make her accept 11 per cent or 12 per cent.

Mr. Lloyd George. I don't want to enter into these arrangements; the Belgians must accept being treated as we ourselves are. Scotland has a population less than that of Belgium, and she had more men killed than Belgium in order to liberate Belgian soil; tomorrow she will have a debt of 180 pounds per inhabitant, whilst Belgium will have none.

M. Loucheur. Belgium will remain encumbered with the sum representing the marks we have refused to redeem.

Mr. Lloyd George. It is the Belgians' fault if they reimbursed them at 1.25 francs.

M. Loucheur. We have granted them an advance of two and a half billion; they are asking us not to deduct from that sum the reimbursement of their debt contracted since the Armistice. France makes that concession. We telegraphed the American Treasury, whose consent is hoped for, and Mr. Keynes seems to believe that the British Treasury will also consent.

Mr. Lloyd George. I will make no trouble about that.

—This last proposal is accepted.

*H., PPC, V, 418ff.

President Wilson. We can finish quickly with the article on Kehl which M. Loucheur presents to us. I believe no one is opposed.

—*The article relating to the port of Kehl is adopted.*

—Reading of a letter from M. Hymans about colonial territories conquered by Belgian troops and which Belgium wants to keep.

President Wilson. We must answer that this is the business of the Council of the League of Nations, of which Belgium will be part, and which will distribute the mandates for the colonies taken from Germany.

—M. Loucheur withdraws.
—The members of the Drafting Committee are introduced.

M. Clemenceau. We still don't know if Italy will or will not be present at the time of the signing of the peace treaty. Can you draft a text which would serve in both cases?

M. Fromageot. That is rather difficult. Up to now, we have distinguished between two groups, what we call "the five powers" and, on the other hand, "the Allied and Associated Powers," which includes a great number of other states. The only solution would be to say "the great powers"; but it seemed to us that we could not use that expression without your express order.

Mr. Lloyd George. Is there any objection to the use of the expression "the great powers"? It is very customary.

M. Fromageot. It has always raised very vehement objections on the part of the small powers.

The omission of the name of Italy is a serious measure which your Drafting Committee can take only on your express order.

Mr. Lloyd George. If we use "the great powers," in that case there is only a single page to be changed in the text. At the head of the treaty, the list of the great powers will be inserted in order to define that expression.

M. Fromageot. If Italy isn't there, will she then find herself excluded from the "great powers"?

Mr. Lloyd George. You have to write "the great powers indicated below" and refer to the list.

President Wilson. It is very customary, in legal documents, to use succinct formulas which are defined at the beginning of the instrument.

Instead of "the great powers," would it not be possible to say "the principal powers"?

M. Fromageot. We can only do it on your formal instruction.

Mr. Lloyd George. We could say "the principal powers concerned."

M. Clemenceau. Is there anything else to do other than change the first page?

M. Fromageot. There are many places where the change has to be made; this revision will take a day or two.

Moreover, our work is advancing rather slowly; we are running into obscurities, we often have to send the text to the experts. In addition, we have adopted the policy of refusing any amendment, unless it comes directly from the council of the heads of governments.

President Wilson. Surely a good proofreader is sufficient to put the words "principal powers" everywhere there was "five powers."

Mr. Lloyd George. That is the kind of job one has a little clerk do in a solicitor's study.

M. Fromageot. We are working furiously; but one should have no illusions about the result. We can't be ready before Tuesday, and it will take twenty-four hours more to finish the printing.

Mr. Lloyd George. You only have to name Italy on the first page. Then, whether or not Italy is present, that changes nothing in the text if you put "the principal powers" everywhere. If it is later necessary to add a page, you would only have to put the number 2b, or 4b, as the case may be.

M. Clemenceau. The best thing is to say "the great powers"; that is the usual term.

Mr. Hurst. The small powers will prefer the expression "principal powers."

Mr. James Brown Scott. It is better yet to say "the principal Allied and Associated Powers."

Mr. Lloyd George. When is the earliest you will be ready?

Mr. James Brown Scott. I hope we will be able, with a great effort, to finish on Sunday evening.

—The members of the Drafting Committee withdraw.

M. Clemenceau. I would propose to deal finally with the question of the cables. Whilst awaiting the arrival of the experts, we can get through with two other questions: the relations of Germany with Austria and the relations of Germany with Russia. For Austria, according to the text I propose, Germany recognizes "the inalienable independence" of this country.

President Wilson. What does "inalienable" mean? That Austria can never be united with Germany?

M. Clemenceau. I know very well that we cannot prevent that union indefinitely if the people want it. But that formula will greatly assist the Austrian party which wants Austria to remain an independent state.

President Wilson. Like you, I think it desirable to prevent the immediate union of Austria to Germany; but I would omit the word "inalienable."

M. Clemenceau. If we omit it, the use that Austria can make of her independence tomorrow is to proclaim her union with Germany.

The goal of the article about Russia is principally to prevent the Germans from colonizing Russia. I will then ask them to acknowledge the "inalienable" independence of all the countries which were part of the former Russian Empire, to acknowledge definitively the abrogation of the Treaty of Brest-Litovsk, and to agree that Russia's rights to restitution and reparation are reserved.

President Wilson. I can immediately accept the middle paragraph, the one that relates to the abrogation of the Treaty of Brest-Litovsk.

Mr. Lloyd George. I accept the first two; but I don't quite understand the meaning of the last.

President Wilson. Do we have the right to stipulate thus for Russia?

M. Clemenceau. We cannot allow the Germans to make themselves the masters of Russia and thereby to become again the most formidable power in Europe.

Mr. Lloyd George. After having looked at the last clause more closely, I understand its meaning; it can be very useful when Russia, as we hope, will be again in the hands of a government moved by friendly intentions.

M. Clemenceau. We will then be able to turn to the Russians and say: "Here is what we have done for you."

Mr. Lloyd George. That can only have good effects.

President Wilson. I accept your draft for Russia. Concerning Austria, I fear committing an offense against the right of self-determination. It isn't Germany which concerns me in that matter, but Austria. We can forbid an annexation; but we can't refuse a country the right to unite with another if it wants to. We can't forbid Luxembourg to unite with Belgium or France.

Mr. Lloyd George. Suppose there was an independent Rhineland and we judged its permanent separation from Germany absolutely essential to the security of Europe; why not impose it?

President Wilson. I cannot accept this principle. I insist on maintaining the right of self-determination.

M. Clemenceau. Even if it isn't a matter of joining with our allies and associates of the League of Nations?

President Wilson. I insist on taking a favorable attitude towards the Austrians.

M. Clemenceau. So do I.

Mr. Lloyd George. What would most risk throwing Austria into the arms of the Germans would be, rather, the annexation of part of the German Tyrol by Italy.

President Wilson. That is a question to be re-examined if Italy parts company with us.

I don't want to impose a permanent obligation on Austria; but, on the other hand, to fix a time limit would be the equivalent of inviting Austria to join Germany at the end of the determined period.

Mr. Lloyd George. A text presented by our experts compels the government of Germany to refrain from schemes aimed at the union of Austria to the German state.

M. Clemenceau. Germany will sign an article of this kind, do the opposite the next day, and deny the fact.

Mr. Lloyd George. I acknowledge that this text is not worth much.

President Wilson. Can't we write that Germany acknowledges and will respect the independence of Austria, which will remain inalienable, except by a decision approved by the League of Nations?

M. Clemenceau. Very well.

Mr. Lloyd George. I gladly accept this text.

M. Clemenceau. I am going to read the entire text relating to Russia:

"Germany acknowledges and will fully respect the inalienable independence of all the territories which were part of the former Russian Empire.

"Germany definitively accepts the annulment of the Treaty of Brest-Litovsk and of all treaties or agreements whatever they might have been which Germany concluded since the Maximalist [Bolshevik] revolution of November 1917 with any government or political groups formed on the territory of the former Russian Empire.

"The Allied and Associated Governments formally reserve all rights for Russia to obtain from Germany the restitutions and the satisfactions based on the principles of the present treaty."

—*This text is adopted.*

—Mr. Balfour is introduced.

Mr. Lloyd George. Here is a question asked by the Drafting Committee: will Italy's name continue to figure in the Covenant of the League of Nations? You will notice that Italy is inscribed in the list of members, although she is not yet a signatory of the Covenant.

President Wilson. That embarrasses me. But if Italy eventually fails to sign the Covenant, she can't be a member of the League.

Mr. Lloyd George. M. Orlando said she couldn't sign because her signature would prejudice the solution of territorial questions.

President Wilson. Precisely.

Mr. Lloyd George. Is there no formula which permits us to get out of this?

President Wilson. We can use the same expression everywhere in the treaty with Germany: "the principal powers" instead of "the five powers." The difficulty is that, if there remain only four great powers in the Council of the League of Nations, they will be on equal footing with the small powers, whose number we cannot reduce, since those which are to sit on the Council are already designated.

Mr. Lloyd George. It would be rather serious if the mandates were distributed by a Council on which we had only half the votes.

President Wilson. The influence of the great powers couldn't fail to operate.

Mr. Lloyd George. That seems rather dangerous to me. I already see Mr. Hughes' objections.

President Wilson. I don't see any other way to proceed: I think we must leave Italy off the list; we still have plenty of time to make the necessary changes until the signing of the treaty.

—*The proposed change is adopted.*

Mr. Lloyd George. The danger remains of there being four against four in the Council.

President Wilson. It is a question we can raise in the Plenary Session.

Mr. Lloyd George. I fear Belgium will make difficulties and will try to blackmail us, and that Spain, whose role was questionable during the war, will be a dangerous element. Then we would be rather badly off.

President Wilson. Concerning mandates, we will make the distribution by an agreement amongst ourselves, before the signing of the treaty. All we have to say for the moment to the Drafting Committee is to substitute everywhere the expression "the principal powers" for the words "the five powers."

THE QUESTION OF THE SUBMARINE CABLES

—Viscount Chinda and the experts on the question of the submarine cables are introduced.[1]

President Wilson. The decision being contemplated aims, above all, at reducing the charges for transoceanic telegraphic communications to reasonable rates. What our experts ask for is the establishment of a world system of communications, which is impossible without an international convention.

Mr. Balfour. I have found out about the present situation of the cables. I have found that Great Britain has, at the present time, control of none of the cables which cross the Atlantic. The cables which unite Great Britain and America, not including the one we took from Germany, are thirteen in number: seven belong to American companies; six to British companies, but these were leased to American companies by a lease which has still ninety years to run.

Here is what happened. A cable from England to America is without value if there is not some arrangement between those who possess that line and those who direct the telegraphic service on the American continent. In Europe, the telegraphs are state property; in the United States, they belong to private companies. The latter manipulated their rates and put at their mercy the English companies owning the cables, which were compelled, in the end, to put their cables at the disposal of the American companies by a lease.

The system as it is functions well; the rates are more or less high, but the service is good. All I want to call to your attention is that control is entirely in the hands of Americans.

President Wilson. If a cable can't function without an arrangement with the land lines, that is true in England as well as in America, and in England, telegraphic service is in the hands of the government.

Mr. Balfour. I have nothing to say against an arrangement that the British government has up to now completely approved of.

Mr. Lloyd George. The only use we have made of our control of land lines was to compel the cable companies, some years ago, to reduce their rates.

Mr. Balfour. The conclusion is that it is pointless to regulate the transoceanic telegraphic system by an international agreement if

[1] The council at this point began to discuss the draft articles relating to submarine cables, printed in PWW, Vol. 58, pp. 345-46. Hankey mistakenly labeled this meeting as one of the Council of Ten.

we don't have the means to prevent the companies which own the telegraphic land lines from imposing their terms.

In time of war, we will never be able to deny any state its full right to use, according to its needs, telegraphic installations existing on its own territory. No international agreement will be able to prevent a state from acting as it must for its security during war. To be sure, I hope these circumstances won't arise. But in any case, in the first place, it is an illusion to think that any international agreement whatever about cables will be enough in and of itself if it isn't completed by an agreement relating to land communications, and, in the second place, to think that it will be possible to prohibit any state, in time of war, from using installations on its territory. Besides, it seems to me impossible to prevent a state from having communication with a territory which belongs to it by a cable placed under its sovereignty. I agree with President Wilson that the solution of this question can only be determined by an international conference.

Mr. Lloyd George. If, at the beginning of the war, the German cables had been international cables, we wouldn't have been able to cut them?

Mr. Balfour. No.

Mr. Lloyd George. That could have been dangerous.

President Wilson. We are now debating questions which were not raised. All I asked is that the problem of the transoceanic cables be settled by an international decision. As Baron Makino remarked the other day, we have taken rather remarkable liberties with international law. For myself, the right to seize cables resting on the bottom of the sea remains very debatable.

The question arises in the following manner. It is proposed that the cables seized from the enemy be assigned in a final way to two or three powers which took part in this great war. What I propose is to entrust their disposition to trustees, who would be none other than the members of the Council of the League of Nations. We can have confidence in them, that is to say in ourselves, to take a fair decision.

It might be thought desirable by the great nations to lay new lines, either to establish communications which are lacking, or to lower rates. We won't succeed in that if, instead of treating that question from the international point of view, we admit that these cables are becoming the property, pure and simple, of some of us.

Mr. Lloyd George. I don't see the question in that light. The truth is that there is at the present time an American monopoly of the cables. The American trust preferred to make London its center, but for reasons of its own.

Mr. Rogers (*American expert*). London is the natural center of telegraphic dispatching for Europe, because of the way the principal currents of business run, either across the Atlantic or on the Mediterranean side. But this only applies to the relations between Europe and America; in other directions, the monopoly belongs to Great Britain.

Mr. Lloyd George. There are thirteen lines between Great Britain and the United States, all controlled by the Americans. We took a German line, and we diverted it towards Canada. The Canadian government wants to be able to continue to use it and to lay a new cable. Would these two cables be placed under international control? I don't believe that could work in a satisfactory manner.

If what the government of the United States wants is to break the monopoly of the American trust, the question boils down to laying new cables, and they can be laid for 700,000 or 800,000 pounds sterling. In these circumstances, why deprive ourselves of a capture which, in our eyes, is as legitimate as that of a telegraphic land line or of a shipping line whose boats would have been seized? I don't really see the reason why Canada should be deprived, by a sort of international control, of something which is essential to her life. The diversion of the cable cost the British Empire more than 200,000 pounds sterling.

President Wilson. Our intention is not to deprive Canada of a means of communication necessary to her, nor to establish, eventually, an international administration of the cables. What we want is an international agreement on the use of all cables. If the one of which you speak is from today on declared to belong purely and simply to Canada, we no longer have a right to intervene, and what I am asking is an international inquiry to see what arrangement we could agree upon.

Mr. Lloyd George. I would have preferred the proposal of Admiral de Bon, according to which the treaty would only contain Germany's renunciation of the cables; afterwards, we would have an international conference which would study the whole problem of telegraphic communications in the entire world.

President Wilson. The difference between this proposal and mine is that I propose the immediate establishment of trustees in whose hands the cables would be placed provisionally; the goal is the same.

Mr. Balfour. I propose to omit, in the first paragraph of the article submitted to us, the word "jointly" and to replace the second paragraph by a provision worded as follows:

"Those cables should continue to be worked as at present, without prejudice of the decision to take by the principal powers."

The third paragraph would remain as you propose it.

President Wilson. I would accept that. The best thing is to revise the draft and send a copy to our Japanese colleagues; we could take our decision tomorrow morning.

Has Viscount Chinda an observation to present at this time?

Viscount Chinda. We think that the cables of Tsingtao must be removed from the list; they are part of what was conceded to us along with the economic rights of the Germans in Kiaochow.

Mr. Lloyd George. In our conversation the other day, we had in fact acknowledged the rights of Japan to these cables.

Admiral de Bon. I think we can agree on the proposed text; it is only a question of wording now.

LX

Conversation between President Wilson and MM. Clemenceau and Lloyd George*

MAY 3, 1919, 10 A.M.

Mr. Lloyd George. Shouldn't we ask the Foreign Ministers to join us when we discuss the decisions to be taken regarding Italy?

President Wilson. Strictly speaking, we could do it without them; it is a matter which concerns the general management of the conference.

Mr. Lloyd George. It would be very helpful to us to profit from their experience.

M. Clemenceau. I am quite ready to summon them. As for myself, my decision is very firm. But I see no reason to refuse to hear what our Foreign Ministers might have to say.

Mr. Lloyd George. I must say that there is still some uncertainty in my mind between two courses. I would feel more at ease if I had Mr. Balfour at my side.

*H., PPC, V, 426ff.

—Mr. Balfour is introduced.

President Wilson. I have some dispatches from our Ambassador in Italy, Mr. Nelson Page;[1] his feelings are sympathetic towards the Italians, but he understands my policy very well. He says that the irritation against the United States has diminished—undoubtedly because the sense of danger is increasing. It was thought pointless to continue to guard the embassy. There is obviously a desire for agreement. But the Italians believe that agreement can only be obtained by new proposals on our part, and that these new proposals must take into account their claims to Fiume, without which any solution would leave a dangerous bitterness in Italy. The sense of this telegram is that Fiume is the essential point for the Italians: they have only themselves to blame for that, for it is the result of a systematic campaign.

Mr. Lloyd George. Our Chargé d'Affaires, Mr. Erskine, saw Baron Sonnino, who told him that he was doing his best to quiet the agitation. Baron Sonnino added that, in his opinion, the next initiative must come from Paris, but that the Italian government could no longer be content with what it would have accepted before leaving Rome.

President Wilson. Baron Sonnino no doubt realizes that popular sentiment concentrates on questions which are not the most essential for him. In that, he is in a situation different from M. Orlando's, who has taken the position of a popular leader, speaking neither of obligations nor of treaties, but of the intangible claims of the nation.

M. Clemenceau. I myself have just received a telegram that M. Barrère sent me last night at midnight. Baron Sonnino stated to him that he was formally protesting against the summoning of the Austrian and Hungarian delegates without the Italian government having been consulted.

Mr. Lloyd George. How could we have consulted it?

M. Clemenceau. We informed it; we can't consult absent people. It was notified twenty-four hours in advance.

Mr. Lloyd George. I have just received a message from Marquis Imperiali. He says that he received a coded telegram from Rome and will come here as soon as the decoding is finished.

Mr. Balfour. The contents will undoubtedly be the same as those of the communication made by Baron Sonnino to M. Barrère.

Mr. Lloyd George. Our legal advisers have prepared an outline for

---

[1] T. N. Page to WW, May 2, 1919 (three telegrams of that date), printed in *PWW*, Vol. 58, pp. 357-59.

the text on the rupture of the Pact of London due to the refusal of the Italians to participate in the peace negotiations.[2]

Mr. Balfour. It would be a disaster for the world if Italy didn't sign the treaty with us. The ditch which has just been dug would become impassable. The five powers would be divided, and one of them would become a threat to peace. A document like the one Mr. Lloyd George has just spoken of would aim at showing Italy the danger of breaking with the four great powers which guarantee the peace of the world.

Mr. Lloyd George. The best thing would undoubtedly be to transmit it in a friendly and unofficial way through our Ambassador in Rome, Sir Rennell Rodd, along with a letter warning the Italians of the magnitude of the peril.

—Mr. Lloyd George reads the text of that letter.[3]

Mr. Lloyd George. We could also send this message on behalf of the three governments; but that would perhaps take too solemn and too final a form.

President Wilson. The document prepared by your legal advisers doesn't sufficiently recall the circumstances which prove that Italy alone bears responsibility for the rupture. Italy participated in the Armistice, she associated herself with the statements of principle which are the bases of the peace, she participated in all the work of the preparation of the treaty—until the time when her plenipotentiaries withdrew because of a question which had nothing to do with the treaty between ourselves and Germany.

M. Clemenceau. I have also had a document of this kind prepared.[4]

—M. Clemenceau reads aloud this text:

(*Summary*) M. Orlando has not replied to the letter signed by Messrs. Lloyd George and Clemenceau. Since then, the Germans have arrived in Versailles; it becomes necessary for the situation to be clarified and for the Germans to know if Italy will sign the treaty. The pact of September 5, 1914, has been carried out by France and England. The peace has been prepared in common and with the cooperation of Italy. As for the

---

[2] Printed in *ibid.*, p. 376. It said that the Italians would break the Pact of London if they did not return to the conference and would make impossible the fulfillment of promises made by the British and French governments to Italy.

[3] Printed in *ibid.*, pp. 376-77. This was another warning that Italy, if she refused to sign the preliminary treaty with Germany, would violate the Pact of London and "render future unity of action [on the Austrian treaty] a matter of the extremest difficulty." The letter concluded: "To us such a result seems little short of disaster to civilization."

[4] Printed in *ibid.*, pp. 377-78.

treaty of April 1915, it gave Fiume to the Croats, and the Italian claim on Fiume makes it impossible for Italy's allies to execute the obligations which rested on the condition that Fiume would not be Italian. If Italy withdraws from the negotiations with Germany, the Pact of London is broken, and a great danger results for all of us from it. M. Orlando is invited to reply to the appeal which has been made to him by his allies.

This letter would be signed by the French and English governments.

President Wilson. Any initiative of this kind would seem to highlight the isolation of the United States. The document you have just read to us seems to indicate that, if Italy wants to insist on the execution of the Treaty of London, a deal can be made. Now, the entire world knows that the United States cannot consent to the execution of the Treaty of London. If the Italians should accept, the United States could only refuse its participation; this is a rather serious possibility, at least as serious as the isolation of Italy.

Mr. Lloyd George. I put the question to my colleagues. I told them: "We are risking a dispute either with Italy or with the United States. We know well enough which of the two would be more serious for the peace of the world. We also know the importance that the Germans attach to the action of the United States in comparison to that of Italy. This is why I am almost more alarmed at the idea of seeing M. Orlando return than at that of seeing him remain in Rome."

On the other hand, there is no doubt that part of our public opinion hardly likes our present situation.

(*Speaking to M. Clemenceau:*)

You wouldn't like to be at M. Orlando's mercy, if he asked you for the execution of the Treaty of London. In fact, at the same time, he is asking for something else, which is not compatible with the treaty. But I want President Wilson to understand well that, if we don't still say today: "We are and will remain faithful to our commitments," we could be accused of being responsible for the rupture.

President Wilson. In America, the present impression is that the United States doesn't have the sympathy of France and England. I am not reproaching my French and English colleagues, whose true feeling I know and whose difficulties I appreciate. But that was the reason I wanted publication of the letter drafted by Mr. Balfour. That publication will dissipate the impression that I am abandoned by the governments of Great Britain and France. In Rome, it was said that M. Clemenceau had inspired my statement, and the French embassy issued a denial, adding—unfortunately—that M. Clemenceau had not even known about that statement before it was published!

All that is creating in Italy and elsewhere the impression that I acted arbitrarily, apart from you. If you don't pay close attention, the effect in America will be such that the public will only have one idea—that of taking no further interest in European affairs.

Mr. Lloyd George. We also have to take into account another dangerous feeling which could develop in the public opinion of our countries: it is that Europe is submitting to the bullying of America. I know that this sentiment exists in London. If Europe and America should fall apart on this Italian question, nothing could be more deplorable.

M. Clemenceau tells me that the Paris press doesn't represent the true sentiment of French public opinion: I am glad of it. What I can say is that there exists in England a certain feeling which still shows itself very little, but which is real and is spreading. Everything must be done to avoid what we consider to be a catastrophe.

President Wilson. If you give the impression in Italy that we are divided, nothing would do more harm. On the contrary, we must show that we are united.

Mr. Lloyd George. Unfortunately, it must be acknowledged, we are not. We are united on the question of Fiume; but the great difficulty comes from the fact that we are not in your situation; we are bound by the Treaty of London.

President Wilson. We are united not by our situation, but by our judgment.

Mr. Lloyd George. That is not sufficient when we are compelled to take a decision. France and England are compelled to say to Italy: "If there is some change to be made in the provisions of the Treaty of London, it is up to you to propose it." But if Italy comes to say to us: "The only thing left is to execute the Treaty of London, purely and simply," there is nothing more to be done, and we are headed for catastrophe.

President Wilson. I am convinced that you are not bound to that extent.

Mr. Lloyd George. We must honor our signature. If M. Orlando returns and forces the execution of the Treaty of London upon us, I don't know what we can do.

President Wilson. I don't accept that. So you would force the action of your associate because of a treaty concluded prior to his collaboration?

Mr. Lloyd George. We don't have the right to denounce a treaty which has been carried out by Italy; she lost 500,000 men in the course of its execution. I think unceasingly of the danger which could result from this situation, and I have a downright terror of seeing the Italians come back.

President Wilson. In that case, it is not necessary to invite them here or to force them here. If we explain the facts from now on in a very clear manner, we are establishing indubitably that they have broken the Pact of London.

Mr. Lloyd George. I fear they will return, because I fear being placed before the alternative.

Mr. Balfour. If we were free of any commitment, we could act as America can; but we are bound by our treaty, and we don't have the right to say that we are withdrawing our consent because the circumstances have changed. We must establish clearly the fact that it was Italy which broke the pact.

President Wilson. She broke it in two ways, by asking for more than her treaty granted her and by withdrawing from the conference.

Mr. Lloyd George. The argument of the security necessary for Italy in the Adriatic is not, in my opinion, without weight. If we say: "We consider that you have broken the treaty," everything is over; do we have the right to do it? If we warn them, nothing is more dangerous.

President Wilson. In that case, they can return and demand the execution of the Treaty of London.

Mr. Lloyd George. To break with Italy would be very serious; but to break with the United States would be a disaster for the peace of the world.

President Wilson. Why mention the Treaty of London in the letter which you are preparing? You have been very frank with M. Orlando, and you need not give him new assurances about your fidelity to the treaty. Say simply that the Italians are now breaking the mutual agreement not to make a separate peace.

Mr. Balfour. The opinion of our legal experts is that Italy has now broken the pact.

Mr. Lloyd George. A word must be added to say that Fiume was promised to the Croats and that the interest of the Croats is identical today with that of our allies, the Serbs.

M. Clemenceau. The first thing to do is to publish the letter drafted by Mr. Balfour and signed by Mr. Lloyd George and myself. That can have some drawbacks; but I believe that it will make our position understood. I agreed with the general sense of President

Wilson's pronouncement, I don't want to give the impression of disapproving it before the world. We are on the eve of a grave decision; it is important to show that the United States and we have always marched together. Between two serious drawbacks, we must choose the lesser.

Mr. Lloyd George. I can't say that I approved everything in President Wilson's statement; that is the very reason why we are compelled to make a separate statement.

M. Clemenceau. Yes, but our statement will show that our attitude towards Italy is not contrary to President Wilson's.

President Wilson. The letter shows your position as it is.

As for myself, I am obliged to reply, to the questions asked of me by my secretary back in Washington,[5] that we are not in disagreement; that shows you sufficiently the impression which exists in the United States.

Mr. Balfour. I must say that I was compelled to reply to a question which was asked of me on this subject by Lord Reading before a public speech he was to give in the United States.

President Wilson. My secretary is a regular barometer of public opinion. Now he telegraphs me: "Is it true that you are not in agreement with the French and English governments on the Italian question?"

Mr. Lloyd George. We must anticipate what will follow. The Italians are installed in Fiume. If there is a rupture, it will be necessary to make them leave either voluntarily or by force. If the League of Nations allows itself to be defied with impunity, it will disappear. Moreover, if we didn't intervene, there would be a war between the Italians and Yugoslavs.

M. Clemenceau. We haven't reached that point yet.

Mr. Lloyd George. The decision we are going to take will bring us to it.

President Wilson. You have said that you didn't want to publish Mr. Balfour's letter because it would prevent the Italians from returning. But today it is precisely their return that you fear.

Mr. Lloyd George. Then I hoped the Italians would accept the compromise I suggested, which gives them possession of the islands to which the Yugoslavs do not seem to be much attached. But if they return to demand impossible things, I prefer not to see them again.

President Wilson. If the Yugoslavs accepted your solution, I would have no objection to make; but I doubt they will.

[5] Joseph Patrick Tumulty.

—Messrs. Berthelot, Headlam-Morley, and David Hunter Miller are introduced.*

—Mr. D. H. Miller presents the text proposed for the recognition of Poland.[6]

—The discussion involves the question of whether the status of Poland will be written into the treaty with Germany or if it is preferable to place only a brief provision in the treaty, which would be followed by a convention between the Allies and the Polish state.

—*It is decided that Annex A will be inserted into the treaty.*

Mr. Headlam-Morley. Since the question of the rights of minorities involves the very constitution of the state, it is preferable to have the time to study it closely and to come to agreement with the parties involved; it is better to make it the object of a special treaty.

Mr. Lloyd George. I read in your text that no distinction must be made amongst the "inhabitants"of Poland by reason of their race, nationality, language, or religion. Is not the word "inhabitants" too vague and broad?

Mr. D. H. Miller. We are compelled to use it, because the treaty says nothing about citizenship in Poland. It is specified that the inhabitants of Prussian Poland must become Polish citizens. But nothing is indicated about the other inhabitants of Poland.

Mr. Lloyd George. It is better indeed to reserve this entire question for the treaty between ourselves and Poland. We don't have the time to do what is necessary in the very short period remaining to us.

President Wilson. Anti-Semitism in Poland is very sharp; on this subject I remind you of the personal attitude of M. Dmowski. On the other hand, the Jews form a considerable element of the population. In these circumstances, will we be able to negotiate by mutual agreement with the Poles about this question of religious equality? What does Mr. Miller think?

Mr. D. H. Miller. You will make Poland sign what you want, on the condition that you ask her for it before the signing of the treaty which grants to her her borders and international status.

*H., *PPC*, V, 439ff.

[6] Actually Miller, on behalf of the Committee on New States, presented two drafts of treaties between the Principal Allied Powers and Poland. The first, called Annex A, provided simply that Poland would sign treaties with these powers to protect ethnic and religious minorities in that country, the freedom of transit, and open commerce with all nations. The second, Annex B, provided for the formal recognition of the Republic of Poland by the Principal Powers and then went on to spell out the provisions that would go into the treaties mentioned above. These drafts are printed in *PWW*, Vol. 58, pp. 388-90.

Mr. Lloyd George. So long as we have not told them that we are resolved to hold out against the protests of the Germans concerning Danzig and Silesia, the Poles are in our hands.

The text of Annex A mentions only a question of the freedom of the religious communites. Why not say "the inhabitants"?

Mr. Miller. That is better, because a strict interpretation of the word "community" would allow the exclusion, not only of isolated individuals, but of communities which could form later.

As for the word "inhabitants," I repeat that it was preferred to the word "citizens," because the latter would allow the exclusion of the Jews.

Mr. Headlam-Morley. What took place in Rumania must be avoided.[7] The Rumanians evaded their international obligations, which imposed the equality of all the citizens of their state upon them, by declaring that the Jews were not "citizens."

President Wilson. The best thing is to prepare the text of a treaty between ourselves and Poland.

Mr. Lloyd George. I repeat that we have a hold on the Poles as long as the treaty with Germany is not signed.

[7] Rumania, after promising in the Treaty of Berlin of July 13, 1878 (which treaty established Rumania as an independent state), to refrain from discrimination of any kind against religious minorities and to grant full civic and political rights of all inhabitants, had completely disregarded these provisions in spite of repeated protests by the major European powers. See W. N. Medlicott, *The Congress of Berlin and After: A Diplomatic History of Near Eastern Settlement, 1878-1880*, 2d edn. (London, 1963), pp. 140-41, 358, and Cyrus Adler and Aaron M. Margalith, *With Firmness in the Right: American Diplomatic Action Affecting Jews, 1840-1945* (New York, 1946), pp. 99-139.

LXI

Conversation between President Wilson and MM. Clemenceau, Lloyd George, and Balfour*

MAY 3, 1919, 4 P.M.

Mr. Lloyd George. Since we met, I received the visit from Marquis Imperiali. He said to me: "Have you received a communication from my government?" I answered no; he seemed surprised and made a rather long statement to me, referring to a memorandum

*H., PPC, V, 451ff.

of which he did not want to give me a copy. One of the things he told me is that there is no agreement between France and England, on the one hand, and President Wilson, on the other.

M. Clemenceau. Count Bonin told me the same thing. I replied to him that this is a matter between ourselves and the President of the United States.

Mr. Lloyd George. Marquis Imperiali told me: "You assure us that you will be faithful to the Treaty of London; but that doesn't bring us closer to a solution, because we know very well that the United States doesn't want to hear about this treaty. What guarantee can you offer us?"

I answered him: "What do you mean by 'guarantee'? Do you want us to promise to make war on the United States?" He protested that he did not, but without proposing anything and without explaining the word "guarantee."

The conversation continued in the following manner:

"Marquis Imperiali.—In carrying on negotiations with Germany, you are making a separate peace.

"L.G.—That is a bit thick! It is you who have withdrawn from the conference. If you are not here on Tuesday, we are no longer bound by the Treaty of London.

"I.—That is very serious.

"L.G.—I warned you, and I warned M. Orlando in the conversation which took place at my residence before his departure; M. Orlando didn't want to believe me.

"I.—Is no offer possible?

"L.G.—Who will make the offer? Who will transmit it?

"I.—I could transmit to my government what you might propose.

"L.G.—To send an offer 1,500 kilometers away, to men who could routinely send it right back to me? * * * Warn the Italian government that, if it isn't present here next Tuesday, it won't hear a word from us.

"I.—But if the Italian delegates return without any solution being in sight, a most serious situation can result.

"L.G.—It won't be more serious than now: you don't realize your situation. You are in Fiume, and you can remain there only against the provisions of the Treaty of London."

Marquis Imperiali showed great uneasiness.

I resumed:

"Beyond doubt, if the Italian government believes it can be confident of Fiume in any circumstances whatsoever, it will do best to remain in Italy.

"I.—The delegates cannot return if no hope is left them on Fiume.

"L.G.—That is a point on which there is unanimity amongst us. Fiume was promised to the Croats by the Treaty of London. All we can grant you is the establishment of Fiume as a free city in exchange for a concession on the Dalmatian coast."

Marquis Imperiali asked me if I wanted to confirm for him in writing what I had just told him. I answered—as he himself had done in refusing his memorandum—that what had just taken place between us was only a conversation.

M. Clemenceau. I have, for my part, received the visit from Count Bonin, and I told him straightforwardly what I thought:

"You made a contract with us; you have not kept it, because you declared war on Germany one year after the time when you should have done it. Today you are claiming Fiume, which the Treaty of London promised to the Croats, and, at the same time, you want to compel us to execute the Treaty of London. Be assured that on Fiume, we are absolutely in agreement with President Wilson. By withdrawing from the conference, you have broken the treaty of alliance."

He answered me: "Oh, that would be difficult for you to prove."

I replied: "I have in this drawer the formula which was prepared by our legal experts and which proves our right to declare the Pact of London broken, and by your transgression. I have delayed sending it; but it is ready. Believe me: you would do better to present us with some reasonable proposal."

It was then that Count Bonin spoke of the difference between us and President Wilson, and that I replied to him: "Leave us to arrange our business with President Wilson as we intend to do."

He then told me: "If we make you a proposal, will you help us?" and I answered him: "I will do everything I can if you take a reasonable attitude."

He observed that it would be difficult for M. Orlando to return, but that he was going to see what it was possible to do. He insisted once again on Fiume, and I told him that the question should not even be raised, because that could lead to nothing.

My impression is that we will have a proposal within twenty-four hours.

President Wilson. The Italian Ambassador in Washington[1] is in Paris. He sent me several messages asking to see me. But this is a

---

[1] That is, Count Macchi di Cellere.

man easily moved when I tell him about things as they are; he is very distressed, and nothing happens.

Mr. Lloyd George. I also told Marquis Imperiali: "We are going to make peace with Germany and Austria." He answered: "But you have summoned the Austrians without consulting us." To that I said: "Whom could we consult? Your delegation wasn't here. We notified you; but we can't delay the conclusion of the peace because it suited your delegates to withdraw."

President Wilson. The only question about which you have to take a decision now is how to inform the Italians of your views on the Pact of London.

Mr. Lloyd George. I wonder if the conversation I had with Marquis Imperiali and if M. Clemenceau's with Count Bonin aren't enough to inform the Italian government of our intentions.

President Wilson. The visit of the Italian Ambassador in Paris can be considered as official.

Mr. Lloyd George. The visit of Marquis Imperiali didn't have that character.

Mr. Balfour. On his part, no. But a statement made by the Prime Minister of Great Britain can be considered as official.

Mr. Lloyd George. I told him I could give him nothing in writing since he himself was not disposed to give me a copy of the memorandum he had prepared. But I must say that Marquis Imperiali asked for permission to telegraph to Rome what I had just said to him.

M. Clemenceau. Count Bonin asked me the same.

President Wilson. Then the Italian government is notified.

Mr. Lloyd George. I added that I wasn't sure that President Wilson would now be disposed to accept the compromise to which he probably would have agreed last week.

Marquis Imperiali recalled the proposal to grant a mandate to Italy for the two cities of Zara and Sebenico. I told him that President Wilson had never consented to it and that, if I had spoken of it myself, I was going a bit further that I had a right to do.

President Wilson. Were they sufficiently made to understand that their position is a violation of the Pact of London?

Mr. Balfour. On this point, Mr. Lloyd George can write a note to Marquis Imperiali, reminding him of a part of their conversation. He could tell him that Italy's refusal to participate in our meeting with the German plenipotentiaries next Tuesday would be a violation of the Pact of London.

President Wilson. From the point of view of form, isn't it preferable that a warning of this kind come from the President of the Conference?

M. Clemenceau. I think we must prepare a memorandum to explain the situation clearly.

Mr. Lloyd George. To put an end to an alliance which has lasted four and a half years in the midst of the most tragic events is a very serious thing. That memorandum must be drafted with the greatest care.

President Wilson. If we write: "If you aren't present on Tuesday, this and this will happen," it is a sort of invitation to return. I would prefer that you simply write: "Your absence will constitute a rupture of the pact."

Mr. Lloyd George. That wording is possible. But it would be a bit too much to seem to be telling them that the treaty is already broken. What they must be made to understand is that they have nothing to hope for regarding Fiume.

M. Clemenceau. Count Bonin said that what especially concerns the Italians is that Fiume not be in the hands of the Slavs.

President Wilson. If Fiume is established as a free city by a compromise contrary to the provisions of the Treaty of London, that makes the entire treaty fall.

Mr. Lloyd George. Nevertheless, the Treaty of London didn't commit us directly towards the Croats.

Mr. Balfour. We are bound to the Slavs. At the time of the signing of the treaty, Italy had already shown much covetousness. Then it was Russia which defended the cause of the Slavs. Mr. Asquith forced the hand of the representatives of Russia, because he was convinced at that time of the vital importance of the Italian alliance.

Mr. Lloyd George. We also tried to induce the Serbs to accept a deal with the Bulgarians concerning Macedonia, and it was then that we sought compensation for them in the North. The Serbs refused, though, to consent to that arrangement, so that the offer we had made fell through.

I lunched today with one of my colleagues of the Asquith cabinet, Mr. Herbert Samuel, who recalls very well the negotiation with Italy in the month of April 1915; he is of opinion that Italy blackmailed us.

President Wilson. Would a private individual consider himself bound by blackmail?

Mr. Lloyd George. Since that time, Italy has made war, and we cannot repudiate our signature.

M. Clemenceau. I have some information about Brockdorff-Rantzau's state of mind. It seems that he is highly disappointed to discover that we are in agreement; he is disappointed not to have been able to get in touch with the Americans and would like to have a "completely frank" conversation with a French statesman!

President Wilson. The impression given by Brockdorff-Rantzau to those who saw him present his credentials is that of a man who is preparing himself for the supreme humiliation; if his legs didn't tremble under him, he was close to it. There is obviously a contrast between what the Germans hoped to find here and what they are indeed finding before them.

Mr. Lloyd George. According to Mr. Keynes, Herr Melchior seems to be a bit more optimistic than he was earlier. That seems to indicate that he believes the German delegation will be able to sign, for that is what he himself wants.

President Wilson. Isn't the letter drafted by Mr. Balfour on the Italian question a bit long and dialectical for publication?

M. Clemenceau. We need to explain ourselves to the public. The text of the treaty won't be ready before Tuesday, and I would like to give the Italians twenty-four hours to make up their minds. Each of us can attempt a draft. If you authorize me to do it, I will tell Count Bonin that we are taking a decision on Monday.

President Wilson. That would be a sort of invitation to come. I fear seeing them here at least as much as you do.

Mr. Lloyd George. But I told them it wasn't worth the trouble to come if they didn't resign themselves to the loss of Fiume.

President Wilson. What you said was not in the form of a document; it will only be the equivalent of these reports of conversations with M. Orlando that our Ambassador sends me.

Mr. Lloyd George. They can only come here to yield.

President Wilson. They can yield by demanding the execution of the Treaty of London.

Mr. Lloyd George. What Marquis Imperiali said shows that they see the danger in it; they know the opposition of America.

President Wilson. We can't be sure that Marquis Imperiali transmitted your conversation without changing a word of it.

Mr. Lloyd George. I can write a memorandum as Mr. Balfour proposes. But I didn't leave them in any doubt, either about our understanding with the United States or on the question of Fiume.

President Wilson. When Marquis Imperiali spoke of a guarantee, you told him that you couldn't give any. However, if the Italians yield Fiume and claim the execution of the Treaty of London—since you have declared yourselves bound by that treaty—that is the guarantee you will give the Italians.

Mr. Lloyd George. I recall that I said: "We will not even debate the question of the execution of the treaty before your troops have evacuated Fiume."

President Wilson. But if they evacuated Fiume, you would have to execute the Treaty of London.

Mr. Lloyd George. I don't believe they will resign themselves to the idea that Fiume belongs to the Croats.

President Wilson. If the Treaty of London is carried out, the United States won't be able to sign.

Mr. Lloyd George. Then there will be no peace with Austria.

President Wilson. There will be, but the United States will not participate in the signing.

Mr. Lloyd George. That would be a true catastrophe.

President Wilson. I can't interpret the word "guarantee" used by Marquis Imperiali otherwise.

Mr. Balfour (*to Mr. Lloyd George*). The President of the United States thinks you are speculating on the impossibility that the Italians will abandon Fiume purely and simply. But if they did, it must be acknowledged that the difficulty would become insoluble.

Mr. Lloyd George. I agree with that; that is what I fear above all.

President Wilson. A compromise proposed to our Ambassador in Rome by a person of eminent position envisages the establishment of Fiume as a free city.

M. Clemenceau. We have to reply to the letter from M. Hymans, who asks for assurances about the fate of the territories conquered by the Belgians in German East Africa.

President Wilson. We have settled the question concerning all the German colonies; they will be administered by mandate of the League of Nations, and the assignment of the mandates, for the first time, will be made by the great powers.

Mr. Lloyd George. I think it necessary to settle the mandate system as soon as possible. Lord Robert Cecil fears difficulties if we delay making this settlement. It is a matter of clearly determining the terms of the mandates and perhaps of adding new clauses to them, notably one which would prevent religious missions from persecuting one another.

President Wilson. Isn't the most urgent thing to name the mandatories?

Mr. Lloyd George. I don't know why Lord Robert Cecil is in such a hurry to see the form of the mandates defined. That is not without difficulties, notably for Asia Minor, where there will obviously be different kinds of mandates. I believe, moreover, that we will be able to agree without difficulty, and that the choice of the mandatories is, as you think, what must concern us first.

President Wilson. We have the time; the League of Nations won't begin its operations before the ratifications of the treaty have been exchanged. In my opinion, the place where the problem arises in the most difficult way is Palestine. Our governments, at least the British and American governments, have undertaken a commitment to the Jews to establish something which resembles a Jewish state in Palestine,[2] and the Arabs are very much opposed to it.

Mr. Balfour. I recall that this terrible Treaty of London is still mixed into the question because of our agreements with Italy about Asia Minor.[3]

President Wilson. The mandate in Palestine will have to include a system of guarantees for the different populations vis-à-vis the Jews, and vice versa.

Mr. Lloyd George. I have a small observation to make on a point of wording. I see that, concerning the compensation to be paid by the United States for the German ships it will retain, it is said that that compensation will be provided "subject to the decision of Congress." I don't object to that stipulation in itself; but I fear the British Parliament will ask why, in a similar case, its name and right are not mentioned in the treaty.

President Wilson. You are aware of the conditions that the Constitution of the United States imposes upon us, and especially the role of the Senate in the ratification of treaties.

Mr. Lloyd George. Concerning the cables, the question arises for Great Britain in the same manner as that of the ships of the mer-

[2] That is, the so-called Balfour Declaration, issued in the form of a letter from Balfour to Lord Rothschild, a British Zionist, on November 2, 1917. It said that the following declaration had been approved by the British cabinet:

"His Majesty's Government view with favour the establishment in Palestine of a national home for the Jewish people, and will use their best endeavours to facilitate the achievement of this object, it being clearly understood that nothing shall be done which may prejudice the civil and religious rights of existing non-Jewish communities in Palestine, or the right and political status enjoyed by Jews in any other country."

The United States formally adhered to this declaration in a letter from Wilson to Stephen S. Wise of August 31, 1918. For the declaration, Wilson's letter, and the major works on this subject, see *PWW*, Vol. 45, p. 149, and Vol. 49, p. 403.

[3] Under the Treaty of London of April 26, 1915, Italy was to acquire the Dodecanese Islands and to have the Turkish province of Adalia in the event of the partition of Turkey. Also, the Agreement of St.-Jean de Maurienne, concluded April 19-21, 1917, between Great Britain, France, and Italy, and subject to the assent of Russia (which was never given), stipulated that, in the event of the dismemberment of the Ottoman Empire, France would obtain Adana (Seyhan) province, while Italy would receive the remainder of southwestern Anatolia, including Smyrna.

chant fleet for America. However, I don't deem it necessary to mention Parliament's right of ratification, because it is a thing that goes without saying. I think any mention of this kind in the treaty is pointless, and that it would be better to settle the question amongst ourselves by an exchange of notes.

President Wilson. All right, I accept.

LXII

Conversation between President Wilson and MM. Clemenceau and Lloyd George*

MAY 5, 1919, 11 A.M.

—Colonel Henry is introduced.

M. Clemenceau. I must acquaint you with an incident that took place yesterday between the German delegates and Colonel Henry, who is our representative to them. They have complained about the lengthy delays in the opening of the negotiations and have spoken of returning to Germany. It seems there has been, since then, another incident, which Colonel Henry will tell you about.

Colonel Henry. Yesterday evening they said to me: "It is too late to leave now." But this morning they warned me that fourteen people are going to leave this afternoon. I asked the names, which is necessary in order to know how the persons being transported to the station should be treated and what means of transportation should be provided. Such is the state of the matter. It was a very junior employee who gave me this message. This afternoon, I must see Baron von Lersner about this matter.

M. Clemenceau. You will give him our schedule. M. Fromageot tells me that the text will be distributed to us this evening or tomorrow morning. On the other hand, the Italians are announcing their return; does not that compel us to make some changes in the text?

Mr. Lloyd George. I favor placing the name of Italy in the treaty by hand. The Italians will see by that that we were ready to treat with the Germans without waiting for the return of the Italian delegation.

*H., PPC, V, 463ff.

M. Clemenceau (*to Colonel Henry*). Tell the Germans that a certain amount of time was necessary to examine the credentials, that the treaty is being printed, and that they will be summoned to the Trianon Palace on Wednesday at three o'clock.

—Colonel Henry withdraws.
—M. Pichon is introduced.
—M. Pichon reads a message from Count Bonin Longare:

M. Orlando and Baron Sonnino will leave Rome Monday evening and will be in Paris on Wednesday morning, where they hope to be present at the handing of the preliminaries of peace to the German delegates.

Mr. Lloyd George. According to our information, Italy's game is to demand the execution of the Treaty of London and then to negotiate with the Croats in order to obtain Fiume in exchange for the cession of Dalmatia.

President Wilson. The Italians are sending troops to Sebenico. An appeal from the people of Rhodes and the Dodecanese informs me that the inhabitants have been brutalized and massacred by the Italians for having proclaimed their union with Greece. The Vicar General of the Archbishop of Rhodes was killed in his church.[1]

Mr. Lloyd George. We have this news also; it is ghastly, we cannot tolerate that. It is something more than the murder of a priest. Believe me: the Italians have a grandiose plan of action in the eastern Mediterranean.

—General Sir Henry Wilson is introduced and shows on the map the position of the occupation troops in Austria, Hungary, and the Balkans.

Mr. Lloyd George. The Italians have occupied Bulgaria and sent 30,000 men there, instead of the one division which should have been stationed there, which gives them an overwhelming superiority in the Balkans. In Asia Minor, they have just occupied the port of Marmaris; they say they intend to create a coaling station there. They are sending troops from Adalia towards Buldur. We have news showing that they are landing or preparing to land at three other points.

At the time of the Tripoli expedition,[2] they hid their game so cleverly that, despite our vigilance, they landed before anyone

---

[1] Skevos Zervos and Paris Roussos to WW, May 2, 1919, printed in *PWW*, Vol. 58, pp. 355-56.

[2] That is, during the Turco-Italian war of 1911-1912, at the end of which Italy annexed what is now Libya.

knew anything about it. We'll discover one of these days that they have occupied half of Anatolia.

On the other hand, they are inciting the Bulgarians to attack the Greeks and the Serbs—especially the Serbs. They are, mark it well, the only ones in Europe who are not demobilizing at present. I believe that we ourselves have contributed to the situation in the Near East: the Bulgarians are not disarmed.

M. Clemenceau. Yes, they are: all the breech blocks of the guns have been removed and concentrated in Sofia, under our guard.

Mr. Lloyd George. This information wasn't communicated to us. But since there are only Italian occupation troops in Bulgaria, if the breech blocks of the guns are in Sofia in their hands, that is not a guarantee.

I wish that you had sent General Henrys there. You still believe that I am prejudiced against General Franchet d'Esperey. But he isn't a very wise man.

M. Clemenceau. I have full confidence in General Henrys. I can send General Franchet d'Esperey the order to have the breech blocks seized immediately.

Mr. Lloyd George. The Italians won't act themselves; they'll make the Bulgarians act. If we could withdraw the English occupation troops from the Caucasus, we could send them to Bulgaria. That is one of the questions I wanted to raise this morning. We are going to find ourselves in the presence of a *fait accompli*: the Italians will be in Anatolia. The only means to guard against it is to settle the question of the mandates as soon as possible and to settle the question of the occupation immediately. That will allow us to leave the Caucasus and to send troops to Bulgaria; the Americans will occupy Constantinople and the French, Syria. We must allow the Greeks to occupy Smyrna. There are massacres beginning there and no one to protect the Greek population.

M. Clemenceau. Do you know how many ships Italy now has at Smyrna? She has seven there.

Mr. Lloyd George. It is better to decide all that amongst ourselves before the return of the Italians. Otherwise, I am convinced they will beat us to it.

M. Clemenceau. I am entirely ready for it. In fact, they must find our decisions taken.

Mr. Lloyd George (*to Sir Henry Wilson*). Don't you think it would also be necessary to occupy Armenia without delay?

Sir Henry Wilson. That is difficult.

Mr. Lloyd George. Even from Trebizond?

M. Clemenceau. There is no difficulty at present in Armenia.

Sir Henry Wilson. It mustn't be forgotten that, at the present time, there is an agreement between ourselves and Italy to confer the occupation of the Caucasus on them.[3]

President Wilson. I would hardly like to see them there at present.

Mr. Lloyd George. That is in a written document which was to serve as the basis for settling the zones of occupation.

President Wilson. This is a document prepared by the military experts, which hasn't been signed by us.

Sir Henry Wilson. In any case, someone must be in the Caucasus if we leave it; otherwise, there will be war between the different populations and general massacre.

Mr. Lloyd George. Without forgetting the Bolsheviks, and even Denikin, who at this moment seems to be trying to seize Georgia.

President Wilson. What would be the effect of the presence of the Italians?

Mr. Lloyd George. As bad as possible. It is important to fix the occupation zones; this is urgent.

M. Clemenceau. We can settle the question of the disarmament of the Bulgarians and the occupation of Bulgaria today.

Mr. Lloyd George. I wish you would send General Henrys there.

M. Clemenceau. That is possible.

Mr. Lloyd George. I will ask the Americans to occupy the Caucasus, otherwise the Italians will do it. As for us, we already have too many burdens. We are always being accused of wanting new territories. The Caucasus has immense resources; but it is a burden on our shoulders.

President Wilson. By taking from the Italians something which seems to have been promised to them, you are increasing the danger of conflict.

Mr. Lloyd George. The Italians have 30,000 men in Bulgaria; they want to put pressure on us. We are demobilizing, you are returning to America, and Italy remains armed. She can, in a few months, present us with a *fait accompli*, having occupied the greater part of Asia Minor, and she can even take an aggressive position in the Balkans. I favor forestalling them and presenting them with a *fait accompli*. In order to do that, an immediate decision is necessary. Let's call for a meeting of our military and

---

[3] Actually, there was no such formal agreement. The Supreme War Council, in February, had proposed a plan for the distribution of occupation troops in Turkey and its former provinces. This plan provided for the occupation of the Caucasus by Italian troops, but the plan was never approved by the Council of Ten or the Council of Four. See *PWW*, Vol. 55, pp. 61-62, and Vol. 56, p. 108.

naval experts, who will review this question of the occupation zones in Turkey.

M. Clemenceau. We'll gladly have our experts attend.

Mr. Lloyd George. Admiral de Bon is one of your best advisers; I have much respect for his judgment.

M. Clemenceau. M. Pichon asks if there is any objection to publishing the memorandum which was sent to him by Count Bonin. If you agree with me, we will have it announced only that the Italians are returning to Paris.

Sir Henry Wilson. Then I'll call for a meeting of the military and naval experts, according to your instructions.

Mr. Lloyd George. A few days ago, I saw one of my fellow countrymen, a great lawyer, who was leaving for Rome; he asked me if any settlement was in sight. I explained the situation to him. Since then, he has seen M. Orlando; he telegraphs me that the Italians are asking for the execution of the Treaty of London. They will tell the Croats: "Give us Fiume, we will hand over Dalmatia to you." I propose to tell them now that the occupation of Fiume is contrary to the treaty.

President Wilson. They'll say that they occupied Fiume by virtue of the armistice, which provides for the occupation of different points to maintain order. Besides, we ourselves have sent troops there.

Mr. Lloyd George. The Italians must be compelled to evacuate Fiume.

M. Clemenceau. We'll have to evacuate it, too. Will you place the Serbs there?

President Wilson. It is better not to leave any Allied troops there. I will observe that the Italians are at this moment occupying Sebenico, which is outside the armistice zone.

Mr. Lloyd George. We must compel them to hold strictly to the provisions of the armistice and to carry out themselves the Treaty of London, whose execution they wish to ask of us. They won't do it, because they don't want to evacuate Fiume.

President Wilson. You are playing a game of chance. They will be here Wednesday morning, and you'll only have a few hours to see them before the conference.

Mr. Lloyd George. I won't debate with them before the conference, because we will still have other business.

President Wilson. They write: "We hope to be present at your meeting with the Germans." That indicates an intention to lay down terms before deciding if they will be present or not.

Mr. Lloyd George. Look at the game they are playing: they think the Croats are capable of yielding Fiume in order to regain Dalmatia.

THE PUBLICATION OF THE TREATY

Mr. Lloyd George. There is a question to which I must return—the publication of the treaty.

M. Clemenceau. The Germans have said they would issue a communiqué to the press.

Mr. Lloyd George. M. Cambon had promised to inform us about their intentions.

M. Clemenceau. It was he who must have told me that.

Mr. Lloyd George. General Smuts writes me that we would make a very serious error in publishing the text of the treaty. There could be things to be inserted in it; we don't have time to reread everything now. Contradictions between articles, difficulties raised by one draft or another, will undoubtedly appear, which always happens when one debates, for example, a piece of legislation. If you publish the text now, any change you might introduce afterwards will seem to public opinion a deplorable victory for the Germans.

M. Clemenceau. We can't leave the public in the dark. I remind you that we have decided to publish a summary.

Mr. Lloyd George. Is this summary prepared?

M. Clemenceau. M. Tardieu sent it to you. It was prepared expressly for the press.

President Wilson. Isn't that what he is to read to the plenipotentiaries?

M. Clemenceau. I believe it is better to give an oral explanation to the plenipotentiaries. That succeeded very well for me before our Council of Ministers.

Mr. Lloyd George. I have just seen M. Tardieu's summary; it would fill three pages of *The Times*, it is far too much. We have a slightly shorter English summary, but it will fill fully two pages.

President Wilson. That is true, but don't forget that the treaty fills a whole book.

M. Clemenceau. Should we call M. Tardieu, Mr. Mair, and your American drafter for tomorrow morning?

—(*Adopted.*)

Mr. Lloyd George. I have a word to say on the question of responsibilities. General Botha called to my attention the fact that the Germans would never accept an article which compels them to deliver men without naming them expressly. He himself refused to do it at the time of his negotiations with Kitchener. He told Kitchener: "What would you do if you were presented with a similar request?" Kitchener answered him: "I would fight to the last man." However, Lord Milner, who is a very obstinate man, refused to yield, and the result was to prolong the war by seventeen months. At the end, the list of names was given to the Boers, as they had asked: it concerned three rebels of the Cape, two of whom had been killed in the meantime.

—An exchange of views takes place about the persons who should be present at the session where the text of the terms of peace will be handed to the Germans.

President Wilson. Have you thought about the representation of the press?

Mr. Lloyd George. Without having too much sympathy for the Germans, I don't like to give the appearance of exhibiting a vanquished enemy.

President Wilson. The Germans have also brought journalists.

Mr. Lloyd George. Think about flash photography and movie film!

President Wilson. That is out of the question. But I believe it is necessary to admit the press, subject to available space.

M. Clemenceau. I propose to call M. Dutasta here this afternoon and to give him instructions.

Mr. Lloyd George. It was decided that the occupation costs would be deducted from the sum of reparations. At present, these costs amount to 300 million pounds sterling a year, and there is no limit in the treaty to the occupation forces.

M. Clemenceau. We'll settle that amongst ourselves; I'll be as reasonable as possible.

President Wilson. Didn't M. Clemenceau say that he only wanted to have a nominal force there, with our flag?

Mr. Lloyd George. Yes, but it isn't only a matter of the reduction of American and English forces, but of the army of occupation as a whole.

M. Clemenceau. I am quite ready to attend to this question.

Mr. Lloyd George. We must think now of preparing the organization of the administrative set up of the League of Nations. It is impossible to begin this preparation in Geneva now; operational funds would be necessary, which we will have only after the exchange of ratifications. Sir Eric Drummond* proposes doing it in London, which would involve practically no costs.

President Wilson. No objection.

M. Clemenceau. As you wish.

—M. Clemenceau communicates a memorandum from the Secretary General of the Conference, making it known that the Germans, because of the promise made to them about freedom of movement according to the needs of their mission, are asking for authorization to have persons other than couriers circulate between Versailles and Berlin.

Couriers ought to be enough for them.

President Wilson. There is no great problem being liberal here.

Mr. Lloyd George. What do we have to fear from these people?

M. Clemenceau. All right. That's settled.

*Already named as Secretary General of the League of Nations.

LXIII

Conversation between President Wilson and MM. Clemenceau and Lloyd George*

MAY 6, 1919, 11 A.M.

Mr. Lloyd George. M. Paderewski told me that the formula we have adopted for reparations would have for Poland the result of making her pay for state forests and old Polish buildings which the Germans seized at the time of the partition of Poland. If that is so, we must obviously do what is necessary to remedy it.

—(*Assent.*)

M. Clemenceau. It is necessary for today's Plenary Session that M. Tardieu and I, on the one hand, and you, on the other, be agreed on what will be said about the treaties by which Great Britain and the United States will commit themselves to intervene in the case of German aggression against France.

—M. Tardieu is introduced.

M. Clemenceau (*to M. Tardieu*). We must know what you will say

*H., PPC, V, 474ff.

this evening about the commitments taken between France, England, and the United States.

M. Tardieu. I have prepared a statement which will indicate the sense of the commitments, stating clearly that they are outside the treaty.

—M. Tardieu reads aloud this text.[1]

President Wilson. I don't like this draft very much, because it confuses things which are separate. For example, concerning Articles 42 and 43, one might think that any violation of these articles—the construction of a railway line which could be considered strategic, or any other detail of this kind—would be enough to call forth the intervention of the United States. It must be clearly stated that it can be a question of intervention only in a case of plain and unprovoked aggression.

—President Wilson reads aloud from the letter containing the commitment of assistance to be taken towards France by the British government, and adds: a text of this kind needs no commentary.

M. Tardieu. I will only have to omit from my report the paragraph mentioning Articles 42 and 43 of the treaty.

President Wilson. I have another observation to make. We must not give our commitments the appearance of a pact amongst the three powers: the American Senate would object. I propose to indicate clearly that there are two separate commitments taken towards France by Great Britain and by the United States.

Mr. Lloyd George. The best thing is to read the letters sent to the French government by you and by me, for they were drafted with care.

M. Clemenceau. In order to explain the situation, I need to publish a few lines which could be worded as follows:

[1] This was a statement embodying pledges undertaken by Wilson and Lansing on behalf of the United States and Lloyd George and Balfour on behalf of the British government. It declared that the American and British leaders had promised to conclude treaties with France under which the United States and Great Britain would come immediately to France's assistance in the event of any move of unprovoked aggression by Germany against France by any violation by Germany of Articles 42 and 43 of the treaty relating to the left bank of the Rhine and the neutralized zone on the right bank. This agreement was to be submitted to the Council of the League of Nations for approval by majority vote and would remain in force until the signatories considered that the League itself constituted a sufficient guarantee of the security of France. Printed in *PWW*, Vol. 58, pp. 479-80. The British and American letters referred to below are printed in *ibid.*, pp. 480, 487-88.

"Concerning the question of the French frontier on the Rhine, the American government and the British government have agreed to submit to their respective parliaments the text of a treaty by the terms of which the Republic of the Untied States and the Kingdom of Great Britain would come immediately to the aid of France in the case of unprovoked German aggression."

President Wilson. After "the text of a treaty," we must add: "subject to the approval of the League of Nations."

M. Clemenceau. So be it.

President Wilson. If you wish, I am going to draft this formula in a way that will clearly distinguish the commitment which Great Britain will take from that which the United States will take.

—President Wilson drafts the formula, which is worded as follows:

"In addition to the securities afforded in the Treaty of Peace, the President of the United States of America has pledged himself to propose to the Senate of the United States, and the Prime Minister of Great Britain pledged himself to propose to the Parliament of Great Britain an engagement, subject to the approval of the Council of the League of Nations, to come immediately to the assistance of France in case of unprovoked attack by Germany."

—The members of the Drafting Committee are introduced.
—Mr. James Brown Scott reads the text relating to Russia. One change was made in the original text in order to avoid a contradiction with other articles of the treaty. This change was approved by the Council of Four. The Drafting Committee today received a note asking it to return to the previous text, and it wishes instructions on this subject. Its impression is that there is a misunderstanding.

—*After a short exchange of observations, the modified text is maintained.*

Mr. James Brown Scott. The question of the border between Germany and Austria isn't mentioned in the treaty. It is necessary at the very least to indicate that this, as well as the questions concerning the other borders of Austria, will be settled in another treaty.

Mr. Lloyd George. Isn't it necessary to say that the boundary between Germany and Austria must remain what it was in 1914?

—*This proposal is adopted.*

Mr. Lloyd George. Sir Robert Borden, in the name of the Canadian government, asks for Canada the right to be represented in the labor organization of the League of Nations. I recall the important part Sir Robert Borden has played in the Commission for Labor Legislation, and Canada wouldn't understand if a place was not reserved for her in the League of Nations, given her importance in comparison with other American states which, not being attached to a great empire like ours, cut a figure as independent states. In fact, the influence of the United States on these states is much greater than ours is on Canada, and I have no need to recall the considerable part that Canada played during the war.

President Wilson. I have no objection to make; but your ideas about the relations between the small American powers and the United States are not entirely correct.

—*The proposal is adopted.*

M. Clemenceau. I have to ask for a change of the article which contains the general provisions on reparation.[2] After having mentioned the reparation due to the civilian population, the article ends thus: "* * * as they are defined in Appendix I."

It has been called to my attention that Appendix I does mention the pensions which have to be given to disabled soldiers or to the families of soldiers killed by the enemy, but that, according to a strict interpretation, the Germans could claim that it concern only direct damages to the civilian population, such as they are defined in this appendix. In order to avoid any discussion on this point, I propose to insert: "* * * and generally all damages defined by Appendix I."

President Wilson. I don't see the point of that change. We ourselves have declared in the note published at the time of the Armistice that by "reparation" we meant reparation of damages suffered by the civilian population and, in addition, we all agreed to acknowledge that pensions had to be included in the list, which we indicated in the clearest fashion in Appendix I. What more do you want?

M. Clemenceau. I want to prevent any interpretation that could cause debates. I want to prevent certain recriminations which have arisen amongst my own colleagues. I am asking you urgently to consent to the change which I present to you.

—*The proposed amendment is adopted.*

—M. Loucheur is introduced.

---

[2] Printed as an appendix to XXIII. Clemenceau explains the problem clearly. For the revised text, see *PWW*, Vol. 58, p. 481.

M. Loucheur. It seems essential to insert in three places clauses to prolong the procedure for restitution provided by the Armistice and the annexed agreements until the system established by the treaty functions, failing which the restitutions begun will stop and will remain suspended for some time.

Mr. Lloyd George. There would indeed be a serious difficulty there.

President Wilson. I have no objection to that change.

—*M. Loucheur's proposal is adopted.*

Mr. Lloyd George. The case of the property of the Polish state remains. I remember what M. Paderewski said. In order to avoid that Poland might possibly have to pay for the restitution of her state forests and old buildings, mustn't some stipulation be provided which might be studied by our experts?

—*This proposal is adopted.*

M. Loucheur. M. Crespi came to tell me that the he had to protest against your decision concerning the interdependence of the enemy powers in the matter of reparations, which was taken in the absence of the representatives of Italy.[3] He is invoking the Treaty of London. By Article 11 of that treaty, we promised Italy that she would have a part of the indemnities to be received, should the occasion arise, corresponding to her efforts and sacrifices.

Mr. Lloyd George. That Article 11 places us in a very embarrassing situation.

M. Loucheur. It seems to me very dangerous not to accede to that request.

M. Clemenceau. It would suffice to return to the old text, which provides for the reparation of damages only in general terms, according to justice and the right of each.

—(*Adopted.*)

—M. Loucheur withdraws.

—M. Dutasta, Secretary-General of the Conference, is introduced.

President Wilson. A certain number of states have not been invited to the session tomorrow, where the text of the preliminary treaty will be communicated to the Germans; I mean the states which declared war on Germany without taking part in the hostilities.

Mr. Lloyd George. We have indeed decided to admit only the fighting nations.

[3] For which, see LVIII, n. 2.

President Wilson. Aren't you going to admit China, at least?

M. Clemenceau. I believe sympathy must be shown towards her, and it is difficult to exclude a state which represents 400 million inhabitants.

Mr. Lloyd George. Besides, 200,000 Chinese worked behind our lines, and some even fought at Amiens.

M. Dutasta. There is also a claim from Siam.

M. Clemenceau. Siam sent us some aviators.

—*The admission of China and Siam is decided.*

—M. Dutasta reads aloud from a note and a proposed article about the arrangement of the neutral zone and the free zone in Savoy and the region of Gex. The treaties of 1815 and 1816 obligated the Kingdom of Sardinia to disarm the northern part of Savoy and to agree not to maintain troops there. That same region was placed under a special customs arrangement, opening it towards Switzerland. These provisions were retained when Savoy became French in 1860.

Now it would be a matter of freeing the French state from the obligation which was imposed upon its predecessor, the Sardinian state, in 1815 and 1816, by the great powers which signed the Treaty of Vienna, and, in that way, of allowing her to settle this question with the Helvetic Confederation. An agreement has already taken place between France and Switzerland, the latter having no objection to the proposed abrogation.

Mr. Lloyd George. I must say that I know nothing about that question and that I would prefer that it be sent to the Foreign Ministers, to whom we should give full power to take an immediate decision.

M. Clemenceau. I favor that proposal.

—M. Dutasta withdraws.

Mr. Lloyd George. M. Orlando and M. Sonnino will be here tomorrow morning. What are we going to do with them if they appear at our meeting? I think we will have enough to do tomorrow morning before meeting the Germans without recommencing the discussion of the Italian questions. If our Italian colleagues tell us they want to go into the question of Fiume immediately, I propose to answer them that we can't do it, that we don't have the time.

Sir Maurice Hankey. Should I inform them of the time of the meeting, as I have always done?

Mr. Lloyd George. Undoubtedly. *Le Matin*, which I read to inform myself about what the Italians want, indicates that they will ask for sovereignty over Fiume, under an arrangement to be established by the League of Nations.

President Wilson. How long will it take them to learn that they cannot have Fiume under any condition? The only reason that would cause me to give them Fiume is that, by doing so, we would be destroying the Treaty of London. I noticed that this treaty also gives them the Dodecanese.

M. Clemenceau. It is true, and it is a shame.

President Wilson. The United States cannot sanction such a treaty. In the Dodecanese islands, the Italians, as we saw the other day, are oppressing the people because they declare themselves to be Greek, and are killing priests in their churches. They are behaving like tyrants in every respect.

Concerning the present movements of the Italians in Asia Minor and your desire to see American troops participate in the occupation of different Asiatic regions, I am sorry to tell you that the participation won't be possible, because I am bound by the Constitution of the United States: I don't have the right to send American troops into a country with which the United States is not at war. All I can do is ask Congress, as I will do anyway, to pass a law which will authorize the execution of the peace treaty and, in particular, the operation of the mandate system under the authority of the League of Nations. But Congress can't take a decision immediately.

Mr. Lloyd George. In the meantime, if we let them, the Italians will have occupied all of Anatolia. We haven't even yet discussed amongst ourselves the question of mandates for that part of Asia.

President Wilson. I am told that the Turks want the areas inhabited by their race not to be divided, and also that there is a movement amongst them in favor of an American administration.

Mr. Lloyd George. That wouldn't surprise me; of all Westerners, the Americans are those against whom they have the fewest grievances.

President Wilson. I have no hope that American public opinion will consent to it. Hatred of the Turk is unbelievable in America. What American public opinion will approve is the protection of the Armenians or of any people whatever against the Turks. It will also approve the occupation of Constantinople, if it is entrusted to us, because, in that way, Constantinople will be taken from the Turks. But I confess that to place as turbulent a power as Italy in Anatolia seems dangerous to me, as much because of the Turks and their possible reactions as because of the relations which will be established between the Italians and the neighboring mandatories. As for the Italians, I don't know whether they will be altogether satisfied to have great mandates in Asia when they see what costs that will impose on their budget.

Mr. Lloyd George. It is a bit like the dreadnoughts that one proposes to keep instead of destroying them: those who keep them will see what it will cost just to maintain them.

President Wilson. It is like the official yacht of the President of the United States, the *Mayflower*: I use it scarcely four times a year, and its maintenance, along with the pay for the crew, costs something like one hundred thousand dollars a year.

I have also received news from Albania: the inhabitants are protesting against the idea of being subjected to a permanent Italian protectorate.[4]

Mr. Lloyd George. The history of the Italian protectorate in Albania is rather curious. The Italians acted surreptitiously and unexpectedly. Afterwards, they denied having established a protectorate over Albania.

President Wilson. The Albanians are horrified at the idea of being subjected to Italy. I think they must be allowed their independence.

Mr. Lloyd George. I don't really know what they would do with it, except cut each other's throats. Their independence will resemble that of the Highlands of Scotland during the fifteenth century.

President Wilson. Don't speak ill of the mountains of Scotland; it is my family's place of origin.

Mr. Lloyd George. I indeed seem to recognize the old Celtic blood in you now and then.

I insist again that we mustn't allow Italy to present us with a *fait accompli* in Asia. We must allow the Greeks to land troops at Smyrna.

President Wilson. The best weapon to stop Italian ventures is the financial weapon. The moment might come when we will tell them that, if they don't evacuate such and such a territory, they must not expect us to provide them with the money required to remain there.

Mr. Lloyd George. Have we ever prevented the Turks and the Balkan powers from making war, even though they have always suffered from lack of money? My opinion is that M. Vénisélos must be told to send troops to Smyrna. We will give our admirals in-

---

[4] The Delegates of the Albanian Colony of Turkey, the Albanian Political Party of America, the Albanian Colony of Rumania, and the National Albanian League of America to WW, May 5, 1919, cited in *PWW*, Vol. 58, p. 477, n. 14.

structions to allow the Greeks to land everywhere there is a threat of disturbances or massacres.

President Wilson. Why not tell them to land now? Do you have any objection?

Mr. Lloyd George. None.

M. Clemenceau. I don't have any either. But must we notify the Italians?

Mr. Lloyd George. Not in my opinion.

I have just received a note from Mr. Balfour: the Italian government asks that tomorrow's session be delayed by twenty-four hours and that Italy's name be reinserted into the printed text of the treaty. As far as I am concerned, I think that we don't have to delay our date with the German plenipotentiaries. If the Italians aren't there, it is not our fault.

M. Clemenceau. We warned them sufficiently before their departure for Rome.

President Wilson. Is there time to put their name back in the treaty?

Mr. Lloyd George. I believe we should leave the treaty as it is and, when the Italian plenipotentiaries are here, add Italy's name everywhere it is necessary by pen. Until now, they have informed us only that they "hoped" to be able to attend tomorrow's session. We don't know whether they will lay down terms before returning here. In this situation, it seems to me that we don't have the time to reinsert Italy's name in the text of the treaty.

—(Assent.)

LXIV

Conversation between President Wilson and MM. Clemenceau and Lloyd George*

MAY 6, 1919, 5 P.M.

Mr. Lloyd George. I have already drawn your attention to the necessity of deciding on the distribution of the mandates without delay. In Africa, French and British troops together conquered Togoland and the Cameroons. Is there an agreement between ourselves and France for the future administration of these territories? I don't know.

*H., PPC, V, 491ff.

M. Clemenceau. We can hear M. Simon, Colonial Minister; he tells me that he agrees with Lord Milner on this question.

Mr. Lloyd George. Whilst awaiting his arrival, I will say a word to you about the islands of the Pacific. It is already agreed that, for some, a mandate will be granted to Australia, and for others, to New Zealand. There is only one of them about which there has been a difficulty, and that is the island of Nauru, which is claimed by both the Australians and the New Zealanders. Wouldn't it be best to give the mandate to the British Empire, with a view towards a later solution?

President Wilson. I see no objection to that. But it is clearly understood that the transfer, either to New Zealand or to Australia, could only be made by a decision of the League of Nations.

Mr. Lloyd George. That is no problem.

What is causing the rivalry between New Zealand and Australia over the island of Nauru is that there are phosphates located there which are used in both countries.

President Wilson. Like all other territories under mandate, that island would be placed under the regime of the open door.

Mr. Lloyd George. In any case. Besides, it is the system followed by all British colonies, if not by the dominions, which make their own laws.

President Wilson. The text of the Covenant of the League of Nations provides that territories administered by a mandatory of the League will have to offer the same facilities to all nations.

Mr. Lloyd George. I hope that won't prevent New Zealand and Australia from extending their customs systems to the islands which they will occupy?

President Wilson. That won't work without difficulty in the Samoan Islands, divided, as you know, between the British Empire, the United States, and Germany. The German islands, which the United States might have claimed, are going to pass under a New Zealand mandate; they'll have trouble if New Zealand duties are applied there.

Mr. Lloyd George. The point is that New Zealand and Australia would be very much hampered in making a budget for these islands if the revenues from the customs were refused them.

President Wilson. In the former German colonies, the dominions will have mandatory, not sovereign rights.

Mr. Lloyd George. Undoubtedly; but it has been agreed that, in certain cases, for example, South-west Africa, the territory subjected to a mandate of the League of Nations constitutes an actual extension of the territory of the mandatory state and must be treated accordingly.

President Wilson. We have indeed anticipated that case. But although South Africa can make a preferential tariff in favor of Great Britain on her own territory, she won't have the right to do so in South-west Africa, where she will only act in the capacity of mandatory. In short, what is introduced by the Covenant of the League of Nations is equality in the application of the tariff, not the tariff itself.

Mr. Lloyd George. This satisfies me.

President Wilson. Have you received replies from Vienna and Budapest?

M. Clemenceau. Our message to Vienna has been transmitted; we have no direct reply yet. We have no news from Budapest.

—M. Henry Simon, Colonial Minister, is introduced.

M. Clemenceau. We would like to know what agreement has been made between you and the British Colonial Secretary concerning Togoland.

M. Simon. There is nothing in writing. The situation is settled in practice by the occupation. But the occupation divides the country longitudinally, which doesn't appear to provide a suitable basis for a final agreement. Since my hearing before the Council of Ten, I have been authorized by you to engage in a discussion with Lord Milner, in order to prepare a convention which will also take account of the advantages which Dahomey might obtain, on one side, and Nigeria, on the other. That arrangement will have the effect of giving us a greater part of the neighboring coastal territory, in order to complete the insufficient coast of Dahomey, whilst Great Britain will take a greater part of the interior, which is linked economically to her colony of the Gold Coast. We stopped there concerning Togoland. We are also trying to create boundaries conforming to the interests of the tribes, which must not be cut up arbitrarily. We are very close to an agreement with Lord Milner and the Colonial Office.

President Wilson. And what about the Cameroons?

M. Simon. Concerning the Cameroons, there is an agreement signed in London. There is a chain of mountains there which defines the boundary. As far as possible, we also took account of ethnographic divisions and tribal travel grounds.

Mr. Lloyd George. Couldn't we give France the mandate over the Cameroons, whilst adding that the border between the Cameroons and Nigeria will be fixed in agreement with the League of Nations?

President Wilson. Yes, but England would also be a mandatory for the part of the Cameroons which would be granted to her.

Mr. Lloyd George. That would be very inconvenient, for it involves a relatively narrow strip of territory.

President Wilson. The peace treaty places all the German colonies at our disposal in order to establish the mandate system over them.

Mr. Lloyd George. That provision in the peace treaty doesn't have such precision; the German colonies are simply handed over to the great powers, which must decide their fate. It would really be very difficult to administer that strip of territory on the edge of Nigeria as a mandate.

M. Simon. We especially need the coast of Togoland, and the English colony of the Gold Coast needs the interior region.

Mr. Lloyd George. Can't we settle the question now by a Franco-British agreement?

President Wilson. Concerning the fate of Togoland, I propose that France and England make a recommendation to the League of Nations.

Mr. Lloyd George. I accept that procedure.

M. Clemenceau. I also accept it.

Mr. Lloyd George. France will have the mandate over the Cameroons, with the reservation that I made. Concerning the drawing of the boundary on the bank of the Niger, since it can only be done with the approval of the League of Nations, I will ask M. Simon to draft a plan which should be submitted to us tomorrow morning at eleven o'clock.

M. Simon. I will ask you to make a distinction in the Cameroons between the territory which originally made up this colony and what was taken from France in 1911[1] and must return to us without conditions.

Mr. Lloyd George. That is entirely fair; it is impossible not to restore purely and simply to France what Germany tore away from her by threat in 1911.

President Wilson. You will only have to mention it in the recommendation that you present to the League of Nations.

---

[1] Following the so-called Second Moroccan Crisis of 1911, the French and Germans signed a convention on November 4, 1911, under which Germany in effect accepted French absorption of Morocco, and France, in return, ceded to Germany part of the French Congo with two strips of land connecting the German Cameroons with the Congo and Ubangi rivers.

LXV

Conversation between President Wilson and MM. Clemenceau, Lloyd George, and Orlando*

MAY 7, 1919, 11 A.M.

—M. Dutasta, Secretary-General of the Conference, is introduced.

M. Clemenceau. We still have to settle some details about this afternoon's session. A copy of the treaty will be given to each delegation.

Mr. Lloyd George. That almost amounts to the same thing as publishing the treaty.

M. Clemenceau. We will send each delegation a letter indicating that this communication is being made confidentially.

Mr. Lloyd George. Very well.

I read in the French newspapers that the French press will be accompanied by a photographer; we agreed amongst ourselves that photographers would be excluded.

M. Clemenceau. M. Dutasta asks if this exclusion extends to sketch artists.

Mr. Lloyd George. The objection is not the same, and besides, I don't see how we can prevent a journalist or any other person from sketching.

M. Clemenceau. Then, no photographers.

—M. Dutasta withdraws.

Mr. Lloyd George. I want to explain my situation regarding the Irish Americans, who are asking to be heard by the conference.[1] They came to see me at the time of their arrival in Europe, and I advised them to go to Ireland—not forgetting Ulster—and to see the situation for themselves. They soon jumped into the arms of

―――――――――
*H., *PPC*, V, 496ff.

[1] The third Irish Race Convention, which had met in Philadelphia on February 22-23, 1919, had chosen an American Commission for Irish Independence, composed of Francis Patrick Walsh, Edward Fitzsimons Dunne, and Michael J. Ryan. The commission was instructed to go to Paris to present to the peace conference the case for Irish independence. See Charles Callan Tansill, *America and the Fight for Irish Freedom, 1866-1922* (New York, 1967), pp. 296-302, 312-22, and Alan J. Ward, *Ireland and Anglo-American Relations, 1899-1921* (London, 1969), pp. 166-88.

the Sinn Feiners, took part in a great number of separatist and republican demonstrations, and worked with instigators of sedition to such an extent that Field Marshal French wanted to arrest them. At present, to my great regret, it is impossible for me to receive them.

Sir Maurice Hankey. The commission entrusted with Polish and Ukrainian affairs is asking for the right to send telegrams in the name of the Allied and Associated Governments to the Poles and Ukrainians in order to stop the continuing hostilities. Without this power, the commission says it cannot control the situation.

M. Clemenceau. I don't much like telegrams being sent in my name that I haven't signed myself.

President Wilson. It is certainly necessary to act with urgency. M. Paderewski told Mr. Lansing that he would not send General Haller's army to Lemberg, and you see that he announces the presence of parts of that army opposite the Ukrainians.

—*The request of the commission is granted, on the condition that the heads of governments be informed of every telegram referring to anything other than the execution of decisions already taken.*

Mr. Lloyd George. I would like to talk to you about Russia. The situation there is changing in the most remarkable fashion: we are witnessing a true collapse of Bolshevism, to such a degree that the British cabinet is asking for an immediate decision about our policy in Russia. According to our information, Kolchak is on the verge of joining his forces with those from Archangel; it is also possible that he will soon arrive in Moscow and establish a new government there. Perhaps he will only succeed in making an incursion there; but we can't know what the consequences will be. M. Paderewski, whom I saw very recently, expresses alarm at Kolchak's tendencies, and even more at those of Denikin, whom he accuses of being a Germanophile, surrounded by men who are suspect from this point of view; his chief of staff, in particular, is even more certainly a friend of Germany than he is. M. Chaikovskii, the head of the government of Archangel, expresses himself somewhat in the same way.

If both are correct, we must take the decision to impose our terms on Kolchak and Denikin without delay, if they want us to go on helping them. For the moment, they give us very few guarantees. Their program, supposedly liberal, is nonexistent. It is the kind of program reactionaries always sign when they want to give themselves the appearance of liberalism. For example, they say: "Agrarian reform is necessary," without specifying further.

M. Paderewski fears the triumph of Russian militarism, which would then seek a rapprochement with Germany.

M. Clemenceau. The Poles mustn't be trusted too much when judging Russian affairs. Their judgment is impaired by hatred.

President Wilson. We can say to a new Russian government, whatever it is, that the execution of our plan for victualing will depend upon the guarantees that it gives for civil liberties.

Mr. Lloyd George. I propose to hear M. Chaikovskii. This man makes the best impression on me, and he wants the Allies to help him protect Russia against a reaction. He believes that, if the military and reactionary element of old Russia regains the ascendancy, the danger of a rapprochement between Germany and Russia will be great.

Kolchak is a soldier pure and simple; but Denikin is something more; he is surrounded by Germanophile influences. It seems to me urgent to hear M. Chaikovskii, for we may learn any day that Kolchak has arrived in Moscow.

President Wilson. What would you give to Kolchak and Denikin?

Mr. Lloyd George. Arms and munitions.

M. Clemenceau. I recall that we must have a discussion about the question of colonial mandates. M. Simon is here.

—M. Henry Simon is introduced.

M. Simon. The texts you asked me to draft are not completely ready, and I would prefer, if there is no objection, to present them to you this afternoon.

Mr. Lloyd George. For my part, I wired to Lord Milner; I hope to have his reply this afternoon. In the meantime, I will invite M. Simon to get in touch directly with Lord Milner's secretary, who is in Paris.

M. Simon. I will do that, and I'll report at once to the President of the Council.

—M. Henry Simon withdraws.

President Wilson. I received a letter from the Montenegrins, signed by M. Plamenatz, who calls himself "President of the Council";[2] they ask for a place at the conference as an allied and belligerent power.

Mr. Lloyd George. It is true that they fought with us; but they certainly betrayed the Serbs.

[2] Jovan S. Plamenatz (Plamenac) to WW, May 6, 1919, *PWW*, Vol. 58, p. 507.

President Wilson. In any case, the question of the presence of the Montenegrins doesn't arise for today's session; it will come up when it is a matter of negotiating with the Austrians.

Mr. Lloyd George. We have never taken a decision about the position of Montenegro; we have, I believe, declared that she had the right to be represented at the conference, but we have added that we didn't know by whom she could be represented at the present time.

President Wilson. My impression is that the Montenegrins have, for some time, been treated rather brutally by the Serbs. I commented about this to M. Vesnić; he replied with accusations against the King of Montenegro,[3] which might be perfectly justified, but which are beside the point. What must be known is what decision we will take on the subject of the participation of the Montenegrins in the negotiation of the Austrian treaty.

Here is still another communication. I received a letter from an American lady married to an important person from Persia, who reminds me that that country has asked to be heard by us.

Mr. Lloyd George. The time will come; but we can't attend to Persia before having grappled with the Turkish problem. I can say as much about the subject of the request of the Mohammedans of India, who wish to be heard on the question of Constantinople.

President Wilson. What will we do after our meeting with the German plenipotentiaries?

Mr. Lloyd George. In my opinion, we must begin the study of the Austrian peace immediately.

President Wilson. The Austrians will be here in a few days. But what do you know about the Hungarians?

M. Clemenceau. I have no news of them. Their government no longer exists.[4]

Here are two telegrams[5] I just received from M. Allizé, our representative in Vienna. The first tells us that the Austrian delega-

---

[3] Nicholas I.

[4] In the wake of the advance of Rumanian armed forces to the east bank of the Tisza River less than eighty miles from Budapest, similar incursions into Hungary by Czech armies, and mounting internal economic and political problems, rumors of the imminent demise of the Hungarian Soviet Republic were common at this time. Actually, Béla Kun and the new People's Commissar for Defense, Vilmos Böhm, were just undertaking a *levée en masse* in order to rejuvenate the Hungarian Red Army, which would soon begin a successful offensive against the Czech invaders. See Mayer, *Politics and Diplomacy of Peacemaking*, pp. 734-49.

[5] See *PWW*, Vol. 58, pp. 508-509.

tion isn't ready to come here on the twelfth; the objection comes especially from the Christian Socialists, who complain that Dr. Klein, champion of union with Germany, has been chosen as President, and they hope that decision will be revoked.

The second telegram relates to the Hungarians; according to the British delegation in Vienna, the British government expressed the desire to change the date of the summons.

Mr. Lloyd George. I know absolutely nothing about that, and I am going to ask what that means. As for the Austrians, I believe it is preferable to keep the date of the summons we set.

M. Clemenceau. I propose to reply that the date of the twelfth will be retained for the arrival of the Austrians, unless they should ask for a delay for good reasons.

Mr. Lloyd George. Besides, I believe that the discussion with the representatives of Austria has to be confined to a limited field. There is no reason, for instance, for them to participate in the discussion that will take place about the boundary between Italy and the Yugoslavs. The border between Austria proper and Italy is already fixed.

M. Orlando. It is impossible to make peace with Austria-Hungary today, since the Austro-Hungarian state has disappeared. What represents the equivalent of peace with Austria-Hungary is the determination of all the boundaries of the states which were born out of the dissolution of the monarchy. Concerning Austria in the present sense of the word, it seems to me that her boundary is already determined on all sides, for a decision was taken about our boundary, and the commissions have reported on those which will separate the Yugoslavs and the Czechoslovaks from Austria.

Mr. Lloyd George. In any case, if we proceed separately for each state, Austria, as presently defined, doesn't have to be consulted about the frontier between Italy and the Yugoslavs.

President Wilson. I believe the question is more complicated than that. Although separated from one another, these different states still represent diverse parts of an enemy state, and the problem is complicated by this fact—that in a nation like the Yugoslav state, some populations fought on our side, whilst others fought against us.

Mr. Lloyd George. I believe the peace with Austria must be treated as a single problem.

President Wilson. Moreover, Croatia was attached to the Kingdom of Hungary. It is possible that you can't settle the Yugoslav questions without connecting them to the Hungarian questions.

Mr. Lloyd George. I believe it is perfectly possible to separate the problems. What we want to do is to make peace: let us do it everywhere possible, without looking for complications.

M. Orlando. Negotiations with the different states born out of the Austro-Hungarian monarchy can be conducted simultaneously.

Mr. Lloyd George. Certainly. But there is no reason to wait, in order to conclude one of these negotiations, for the conclusion of the other.

President Wilson. Moreover, we must avoid making a peace that lacks guarantees because the problems were treated too separately.

LXVI

Conversation between President Wilson and MM. Clemenceau, Lloyd George, Vénisélos, Admiral George P. Hope, and General Sir Henry Wilson*

MAY 7, 1919, NOON.

M. Clemenceau (*to M. Vénisélos*). We are contemplating the landing of Greek troops at Smyrna to prevent massacres and preempt an Italian landing. General Franchet d'Esperey tells us that you have no troops ready for a landing.

M. Vénisélos. We have a division in Macedonia which had been made ready to be sent to Russia.

Mr. Lloyd George. Is that all you can send to Smyrna?

M. Vénisélos. We can take two divisions from Macedonia without any difficulty. But in that case, we would be able to act eventually in Thrace only by withdrawing the troops we have in Bessarabia.

M. Clemenceau. There is no question of acting in Thrace; we don't want that, for it would create an immediate conflict with the Bulgarians.

Mr. Lloyd George (*to Admiral Hope*). Can you tell us how long it would take us to find transport for two Greek divisions which might be sent from Macedonia to Smyrna?

*H., *PPC*, V, 501ff.

Admiral Hope. I don't have the necessary information, but I can get it for you this very day.

President Wilson. In any case, it is necessary to get the Greek divisions ready.

M. Vénisélos. One of them is completely ready to embark at Kavalla.

Mr. Lloyd George. Can they embark there?

Admiral Hope. Yes, because that division has only mountain artillery. Embarking would be impossible with heavy artillery.

President Wilson. What is the strength of your Greek divisions.

M. Vénisélos. Sixteen thousand men, of which nine thousand are infantry. The Turkish divisions, at the end of the war, were—and they still are—very much reduced.

Mr. Lloyd George. Can't you find out what forces the Turks have, either at Smyrna or in the area?

President Wilson. Under the terms of the armistice, the Turks must not resist, for the armistice gives us the right to send troops everywhere we judge there is danger for the Allies. Greece is an Allied state.

M. Vénisélos. Besides, there are thirty thousand subjects of the Kingdom of Greece in the city of Smyrna.

General Sir Henry Wilson. I will observe that, since the armistice reserves the right of occupation to the Allies, the Italians can, if they see the Greeks land, also land troops.

President Wilson. If the Greeks land with our mandate, the Italians can't make a landing without making an agreement with us or without provoking a serious incident.

General Sir Henry Wilson. I daresay the Greek troops sent to Smyrna will remain under the command of the head of the Army of the East,[1] and not of General Allenby?

Mr. Lloyd George. It is better not to get Allenby mixed up in this affair.

M. Vénisélos. It is important to act so that the Turks are warned at the last minute only. If the Turkish officers, whom I know well, don't receive the order to resist, they will make no resistance. As for the inhabitants of Smyrna, their attitude will be very friendly.

Mr. Lloyd George. Isn't there always the danger that the Turkish coastal forts will fire on the Greek troops?

M. Vénisélos. That danger doesn't exist if our troops enter the roadstead on ships flying the flags of the Allies.

M. Clemenceau. Isn't it better to warn the Turks?

---

[1] That is, General Franchet d'Esperey.

President Wilson. That is more correct; but that presents risks for the landing.

Mr. Lloyd George (*to M. Vénisélos*). Can you make your preparations secretly?

M. Vénisélos. Certainly. When we were asked to send troops to Odessa, we were able on our own to find enough tonnage to transport ten thousand men. It is true that they were tightly packed; but the Greek soldier is not very demanding in this respect.

M. Clemenceu. What shall we do?

Mr. Lloyd George. Admiral Hope is returning to England to see what can be done about the transport and, whilst informing us about it, he will prepare the operational plans. For his part, M. Vénisélos will assemble the available Greek ships, without saying what they are intended for, and give orders to get the divisions ready.

M. Vénisélos. I repeat that there is one division completely ready. Without your help, we cannot transport two divisions at once.

M. Clemenceau. For the moment, we are saying nothing to the Italians?

Mr. Lloyd George. No. Does General Franchet d'Esperey know that we have this project in mind?

M. Clemenceau. I haven't told him anything about it; but I am sure he knows, because of the preparatory measures which have begun.

President Wilson. It is important to keep this whole business as secret as possible.

LXVII

Conversation between President Wilson and MM. Clemenceau, Lloyd George, Orlando, Balfour, Baron Sonnino, and Henry Simon*

MAY 7, 1919 (VERSAILLES)—4:20 P.M.

Mr. Lloyd George. We made an appointment with M. Simon for

*H., *PPC*, V, 506ff.

this afternoon in order to agree about the question of mandates in Africa and the Pacific.

M. Simon. I would accept the memorandum provided by the British government, with a reservation about the Cameroons. This text provides indeed that a French mandate will be established in the Cameroons, except for the part neighboring Nigeria, which would give rise to a rectification of the border in favor of the British Empire. I believe this division would not be without difficulty for the mandatory.

President Wilson. We are not settling the question at this time; it is only a matter of bringing a proposal before the League of Nations.

M. Simon. That is true; but if we agree to make common recommendations to the League of Nations, we are thus prejudging the solution. I must also observe that the formula adopted would have the effect of giving France a mandate from the League of Nations over the territories taken from her, under German threat, by the treaty of 1911: France has the right to demand their restitution, pure and simple.

President Wilson. If it is a matter of restitution, it should have been provided for in the peace treaty.

M. Simon. The peace treaty provides for the abrogation of treaties signed between France and Germany and, consequently, of the treaty of 1911. But that must be specified; it would be unacceptable for France to administer as a mandatory territories which were taken from her so recently, whilst part of the Cameroons might be added purely and simply to British Nigeria.

Mr. Lloyd George. The best way to guard against this is to use here the same formula for Togoland and the Cameroons, that is, to declare, without going into details, that a recommendation will be made to the Council of the League of Nations by France and England. It will be easy for us to agree.

—*This proposal is adopted.*

M. Orlando. I must observe that Italy is not mentioned in this distribution of mandates over the colonies taken from Germany. I said earlier that, whether the mandate be a burden for the nation to which it was entrusted, or whether it be an advantage for it, Italy had the same right to participate. The treaty which binds France and Great Britain to Italy provides colonial compensation for the latter in Africa, in case the war insured a territorial increase in that part of the world to either one of these powers.

M. Simon. It is true that the Treaty of London provides compensation for Italy, in the event the peace treaty grants France and

Great Britain benefits in the colonial field. This is a matter of boundary rectifications, notably in Libya; they are stipulated in Article 13 of the treaty.

Mr. Lloyd George. I acknowledge the validity of the article. Like the French government, the British government is prepared to discuss its application with the Italian government.

M/